Supported by the National Science Foundation and Microsoft Rese

ASSETS 2011

—— 24-26 October 2011 ——

Dundee, Scotland

ASSETS'11: Proceedings of the 13th International ACM SIGACCESS Conference on Computers and Accessibility

Association for Computing Machinery

Advancing Computing as a Science & Profession

Sponsored by:

**Association for
Computing Machinery**

Advancing Computing as a Science & Profession

The Association for Computing Machinery
2 Penn Plaza, Suite 701
New York, New York 10121-0701

Notice to Past Authors of ACM-Published Articles
ACM intends to create a complete electronic archive of all articles and/or other material previously published by ACM. If you have written a work that has been previously published by ACM in any journal or conference proceedings prior to 1978, or any SIG Newsletter at any time, and you do NOT want this work to appear in the ACM Digital Library, please inform permissions@acm.org, stating the title of the work, the author(s), and where and when published.

ISBN: 978-1-4503-0919-6

Additional copies may be ordered prepaid from:

ACM Order Department
PO Box 30777
New York, NY 10087-0777, USA

Phone: 1-800-342-6626 (USA and Canada)
+1-212-626-0500 (Global)
Fax: +1-212-944-1318
E-mail: acmhelp@acm.org
Hours of Operation: 8:30 am – 4:30 pm ET

ACM Order No: 444110

Printed in the USA

ASSETS 2011 Chairs' Welcome

Welcome to Dundee, Scotland – The City of Discoveries – for ASSETS 2011, the Thirteenth International ACM SIGACCESS Conference on Computers and Accessibility. We come to the city that is said to be built on Jute, Jam, and Journalism to try to make some discoveries of our own. We are fortunate to be close to the University of Dundee whose school of computing has such a rich history of accessibility work. It is an ideal location for the international ASSETS community to come together to collaborate and share innovative research on the design and use of both mainstream and specialized assistive technologies.

We are delighted to welcome Professor Alan Dix, who specializes in Human Computer Interaction at Lancaster University, as our keynote speaker for 2011. He will discuss the changing face of our world brought about by the data-centric web and what it means to interactions and accessibility.

The technical program of 27 podium presentations and 45 posters & demonstrations has been selected through peer-review by a distinguished international program committee. This committee had the very difficult job of assembling a conference program from the diverse set of very high-quality submissions. We received submissions from more than 20 different countries. The podium presentations were selected from 90 full-length submissions (a 30% acceptance rate), and have been organized into 9 themes including design issues for assistive technologies, comprehension studies, interfaces for mobile & ubiquitous systems, and web accessibility. The accepted papers address a variety of assistive technology users including older adults, people who use sign language, and people with visual, intellectual, mobility, and severe speech impairments. The program committee was also involved in the poster and demonstration program which was chaired by Leo Ferres. These 45 presentations were selected from 79 submissions (a 57% acceptance rate). The posters and demonstrations provide an opportunity to showcase late-breaking results as well as work in progress and practical implementations.

Posters & demonstrations and selected ACM Student Research Competition entries, chaired by Krzysztof Gajos, are represented by abstracts in these proceedings and in two poster sessions during the conference. The winners of the ACM Student Research Competition (sponsored by Microsoft) will go on to compete in the ACM-wide grand finals, where ASSETS entrants have established a strong track record including last year's third place winner in the undergraduate category.

The poster sessions will also showcase participants in the Doctoral Consortium. This one-day workshop preceding the main conference was chaired by Professors Clayton Lewis and Faustina Hwang, and generously sponsored by the U.S. National Science Foundation. It brought together 11 emerging researchers working on accessibility to discuss their ideas with a panel of established experts. A special edition of the SIGACCESS newsletter will feature extended abstracts from these doctoral students.

We are pleased that this year's conference also hosted the 2nd International Workshop on Sign Language Translation and Avatar Technology (SLTAT), which featured a variety of presentations focused on symbolic translation of sign language, animation of sign language using avatars, and usability evaluation of practical translation and animation systems.

We come to the City of Discoveries for an exciting and diverse program centered on accessibility for all. We thank the many members of the research community who have contributed to this conference and hope that it will result in some discoveries of our own leading to new perspectives in assistive technologies and making a positive difference in peoples' lives.

Kathleen F. McCoy
ASSETS 2011 General Chair
University of Delaware, USA

Yeliz Yesilada
ASSETS 2011 Program Chair
Middle East Technical University
Northern Cyprus Campus

Table of Contents

Keynote Address
Session Chair: Kathleen F. McCoy *(University of Delaware, USA)*

Session 1: Assistive Technology Design Paradigms
Session Chair: Vicki Hanson *(University of Dundee)*

Session 2: Navigation and Wayfinding
Session Chair: Julio Abascal *(University of Basque Country, Spain)*

Session 3: Understanding Users
Session Chair: Clayton Lewis *(University of Colorado, USA)*

Session 4: User-centric Design
Session Chair: Matt Huenerfauth *(The City University of New York, USA)*

Session 5: Sign Language Comprehension
Session Chair: Shari Trewin *(IBM T.J. Watson Research Center, USA)*

Session 6: Multimedia and TV
Session Chair: Enrico Pontelli *(New Mexico State University, USA)*

Session 7: Web Accessibility
Session Chair: Jeffrey P. Bigham *(University of Rochester, USA)*

Session 8: Mobile and Ubiquitous UI
Session Chair: Simon Harper *(University of Manchester, United Kingdom)*

Session 9: Supporting Visual Interaction
Session Chair: Andrew Sears *(Rochester Institute of Technology, USA)*

Session 10: Posters and Demonstrations
Session Chair: Leo Ferres *(University of Concepcion, Chile & Carleton University, Canada)*

Session 11: Student Research Competition
Session Chair: Krzysztof Gajos *(Harvard University, USA)*

ASSETS 2011 Conference Organization

General Chair: Kathleen F. McCoy *(University of Delaware, USA)*

Program Chair: Yeliz Yesilada *(Middle East Technical University Northern Cyprus Campus, Cyprus)*

Treasurer & Registration Chair: Jinjuan (Heidi) Feng *(Towson University, USA)*

Posters & Demonstrations Chair: Leo Ferres *(University of Concepcion, Chile & Carleton University, Canada)*

Doctoral Consortium Chairs: Clayton Lewis *(University of Colorado, USA)*
Faustina Hwang *(University of Reading, UK)*

Student Research Competition Chair: Krzysztof Gajos *(Harvard University, USA)*

Local Arrangements Chairs: Lorna Gibson *(University of Dundee, Scotland)*
Kyle Montague *((University of Dundee, Scotland)*

Accessibility Chair: Anna Cavender *(Google, USA)*

Mentor Chair: Torsten Felzer *(Darmstadt University of Technology, Germany)*

Web Chair: Tiago Guerreiro *(Instituto Superior Técnico, Portugal)*

Publicity Chair: Amy Hurst *(UMBC, USA)*

Graphic Design Chair: Joshua Hailpern *(University of Illinois at Urbana-Champaign, USA)*

Program Committee: Julio Abascal *(University of Basque Country, Spain)*
Ray Adams *(University of Middlesex, UK)*
Chieko Asakawa *(IBM Research Japan, Japan)*
Melanie Baljko *(York University, Canada)*
Armando Barreto *(Florida International University, USA)*
Jeffrey P. Bigham *(University of Rochester, USA)*
Yevgen Borodin *(Stony Brook University, USA)*
Giorgio Brajnik *(University of Udine, Italy)*
Andy Brown *(University of Manchester, UK)*
Anna Cavender *(Google, USA)*
David Duce *(Oxford Brookes University, UK)*
Alistair D.N. Edwards *(University of York, UK)*
Simon Edwards *(Newcastle University, UK)*
Michael Evans *(BBC Research and Development, UK)*
Torsten Felzer *(Darmstadt University of Technology, Germany)*
Harriet Fell *(Northeastern University, USA)*
Jinjuan Heidi Feng *(Towson University, USA)*
Leo Ferres *(University of Concepcion, Chile)*
Kelly Ford *(Microsoft, USA)*

ASSETS 2011 Sponsor & Supporters

Sponsor:

Doctoral Consortium Supporter:

Student Research
Competition Supporter: Microsoft Research

Living in a World of Data

Alan Dix

Talis
43 Temple Row
Birmingham, XXXX, UK

InfoLab21
Lancaster University
Lancaster, LA1 4AW, UK

alan@hcibook.com

http://www.hcibook.com/alan/papers/assets2011-world-of-data/

ABSTRACT

The web is an integral part of our daily lives, and has had profound impacts on us all, not least both positive and negative impacts on accessibility, inclusivity and social justice. However, the web is constantly changing. Web2.0 has brought the web into the heart of social life, and has had mixed impact on accessibility. More recently the rise in API access to web services and various forms of open, linked or semantic data is creating a more data/content face to the media web. As with all technology, this new data web poses fresh challenges and offers new opportunities.

Categories and Subject Descriptors

H.5.4 [**Information Systems**]: Hypertext/Hypermedia – *user issues*; I.2.0 [**Artificial Intelligence**]: General – *philosophical foundations*; K.4.1 [**Computers And Society**]: Public Policy Issues; K.4.2 [**Computers And Society**]: Social Issues – *assistive technologies for persons with disabilities*;

General Terms: Design, Economics, Human Factors

Keywords: web2.0, API, open data, physicality, embodiment, empowerment, long-tail, inclusiveness

1. THE RISE OF DATA

For most of us it is hard to imagine the pre-web world, even though the web is a mere 15 years old. However, the web is itself changing, five years ago many of us had never heard of Facebook or Twitter, yet now social media are supplanting the browser as being 'the Internet' for many users. Another move, that some have called web3.0 (or web4.0 depending on counting), is the move to a more data-centric web.

Many web sites (including Facebook, Twitter and Google) offer APIs so that third party developers can add functionality, or alternative interfaces. The Google Maps API was perhaps the first to capture the imagination of users beyond the highly technical developers, however the success of APIs is widespread. Arguably one of the reasons for Facebook's ongoing success is the proliferation of third-party apps enabled by its early API and more recent Open Graph Protocol [9]. Similarly, one of the drivers of Twitter's growth has been mobile access, and yet it has only recently launched its own iPhone App, relying before on third party apps using its API. Many of the next generation start-ups are taking this to the extreme with API-only web services.

There is also a growing move to make data more available on the web. Tim Berners Lee has long been an advocate of the Semantic

Web, making the human readable web available to computer interpretation [3]. While this dream has been long in coming and may turn out differently, there are clear signs of a more data-rich web. Web pages themselves are becoming more richly annotated, some with 'proper' semantic web markup such as RDFa [1], but perhaps more commonly with semi-semantic markup such as microformats or the recently agreed schema.org vocabulary, where the major search providers (Yahoo!, Google, Bing) agreed a common standard for semantic mark up.

As well as marking up web pages, raw data is increasingly available. Many governments, including the UK (data.gov.uk) and USA (data.gov) are making open data a key aspect of public policy, and some media organisations, notably the BBC [2] and the Guardian [11] have strong data-focused initiatives. Sometimes this data is in traditional formats, such as Excel or CSV spreadsheets, some is in more web formats such as RSS feeds, and some in Semantic Web RDF. Critically, many of these semantic data resources are linked through common identifiers leading to what is called the Linking Open Data (LOD) Cloud [4].

The web has had an impact on accessibility and inclusivity: opening up the world to some, and closing it off from others.[1] This new data web similarly both poses challenges and offers opportunities for a more inclusive world.

2. EMBODIMENT AND PHYSICALITY

Computers, and more critically the Internet, have enabled us to live in a parallel world of the virtual, where Negroponte's bits rather than atoms are most critical. Like the faerie lands in folk tales, this is not dissociated from the real world, in particular, the people of the virtual world are (usually) those of the real world; however, it does offer the potential to break some of the physical and, to a lesser, but still real, extent, the social and material constraints of day-to-day life. This is evident in chat rooms, multiplayer games, and second life, and epitomised in the character of Zona Rosa in Gibson's Idoru [10].

I have been interested for many years in the nature of human physicality. By understanding how our cognition is attuned to the physical world we are in a better position to design for digital environments, both in physical digital devices [8] and on the web [7]. Philosophical theories of embodiment focus on the way we interact with the world directly and often emphasise that we do not need internal representations in our heads as the "world is its own best representation" [6]. However, there is also strong

---

[1] E.g. vast download sizes of software updates and Apple's decision to make Lion available principally through App Store, excludes or penalises those not in urban areas of developed countries, with fast broadband connections.

evidence that we do use internal representations, for remembering, planning and similar activities, but that these representations are strongly influenced by our physical being [5, 14]. This is important from an inclusivity perspective as not only the cultural aspects of the data structures we encounter, but potentially also their implicit cognitive structure may be biased by normative perceptual, social and motor assumptions.

As well as being virtually present in the web, increasingly our physical-world activities are sensed, tracked and distributed. Some of this, such as CCTV or credit card transactions, happens completely outside our control, some we are aware of peripherally, such as GPS and accelerometer data gathered on smart phones, and some is deliberately gathered, such as medical or fitness data. This personal sensed data offers medical and assistive opportunities both for individuals, and also, through visual analytics, to enable trends to be established, for example, between exercise and illness, or as in a recent Lancaster study, between children's school routes and pollution levels [13]. However, this same data may be used by insurance companies to limit benefits, or increase premiums.

3. ECONOMICS AND THE LONG TAIL
A few years ago Web2.0 became the sexy buzzword capturing various technical and social changes in the web. At a technical level AJAX-based interfaces offer rich user experiences, yet often at the expense of accessibility. There are techniques to ameliorate this, or even make potentially more accessible web pages (e.g. 'plain' downloaded HTML that is later rewritten and reformatted using CSS and Javascript). An API, data driven world could improve this, by making the raw data available to accessibility software, but more often makes things worse as Javascript directly accesses data APIs. Underlying the vast majority of web sites today is some form of database or content management system; indeed over 20% of new domains are now being powered by WordPress alone. This has the potential to unlock the data to be re-presented in new forms, but this is by no means guaranteed.

Web 2.0 also created a focus on 'the long tail', rather than focusing on a few large market segments, instead finding ways to serve the very many, very small interests (e.g. Facebook Pages, Google AdSense). This offers hope for the more marginal in society for whom virtual connectivity can create groups large enough to be significant in a market-driven economy. A data-focus can help this, for example, allowing third-party interfaces both on multiple devices (important for the 'next billion' users in the developing economies) and potentially also for different perceptual and physical abilities. However, there is a corresponding danger that providing data APIs could be used as a 'get out' rather than providing truly accessible interfaces.

4. EMPOWERMENT AND OPEN ACCESS
The social and data web can be radical and empowering. Social media was at the heart of the Arab Spring, but also of course the recent London riots. The increasing availability of government open data is allowing community and activist groups to create mash-ups reflecting unique concerns. At its best open data means those who would otherwise have been information poor are able to access similar resources to large corporations or government. Furthermore, the web allows alternative data to be made available alongside the official versions, for example iraqbodycount.org, which has produced independently verified figures on civilian deaths since the invasion in 2003. Just as blogging sites, such as

wordpress.com and blogger.com, and YouTube allowed anyone to contribute to the social media of web2.0, a growing number of data publishing sites are available allowing anyone to easily publish data both in more traditional table formats (e.g. Google Fusion Tables) or Semantic Web linked data (e.g. Talis' Kasabi.com). However, potential and opportunity do not mean inevitability. Statistics from the Indian open data initiative suggest that the majority of users are older, more highly educated and male – perhaps simply reinforcing existing power structures [12].

5. SUMMARY, POTENTIAL OR THREAT
In each of these areas, we have seen both threats and also potential for a more inclusive society. However, potential must always be actively realised. Standing at a cusp point in the development of the web, we can make the difference to the future.

6. REFERENCES
[1] Adida, B. and Birbeck, M. 2008. *RDFa Primer*. W3C. http://www.w3.org/TR/xhtml-rdfa-primer/

[2] BBC. 2011. Backstage: Open Data and Resources from the BBC. http://backstage.bbc.co.uk/

[3] Berners-Lee, T., Hendler, J. and Lassila, O., 2001, *The Semantic Web*, *Scientific American*, (17th May 2001), 35-43. http://www.scientificamerican.com/article.cfm?id=the-semantic-web

[4] Bizer, C., Heath, T. and Berners-Lee, T. 2009. Linked data - the story so far. *Int. J. Semantic Web Inf. Syst.*, 5, 3, 1–22.

[5] Chatterjee, A. Disembodying Cognition. *Language and Cognition*. 2-1 (2010), 79-116

[6] Clark, A. 1998. Being There: Putting Brain, Body and the World Together Again. MIT Press.

[7] Dix, A. 2011. A Shifting Boundary: the dynamics of internal cognition and the web as external representation. In: *Proceedings of the ACM WebSci'11*, (Koblenz, Germany , June 14-17 2011). http://journal.webscience.org/436/

[8] Dix, A., Gill, S., Ramduny•Ellis, D. and Hare, J. 2011. *Touch IT: exploring the physicality of the world and the design of digital products*. http://physicality.org/TouchIT/

[9] Facebook. 2011. *Open Graph protocol*. http://developers.facebook.com/docs/opengraph/

[10] Gibson, W. 1996. *Idoru*. Viking.

[11] Guardian. 2011. *Data Store: Facts are Sacred*. http://www.guardian.co.uk/data

[12] Gurstein, M. 2011. *Are the Open Data Warriors Fighting for Robin Hood or the Sheriff?*: http://gurstein.wordpress.com/2011/07/03/are-the-open-data-warriors-fighting-for-robin-hood-or-the-sheriff-some-reflections-on-okcon-2011-and-the-emerging-data-divide/

[13] Pooley, C., Whyatt, J., Walker, M. Davies, G., Coulton, P. and Bamford, W. 2010. Understanding the school journey: integrating data on travel and environment. *Environment and Planning* A, 42, 4, 948-965: http://dx.doi.org/10.1068/a41405

[14] Wilson M. 2002. Six views of embodied cognition. *Psychonomic Bulletin & Review*, 9(4):625-36

The Design of Human-Powered Access Technology

Jeffrey P. Bigham
ROC HCI, Computer Science
University of Rochester
Rochester, NY 14618
jbigham@cs.rochester.edu

Richard E. Ladner
Computer Science and Engineering
University of Washington
Seattle, WA 98195
ladner@cs.washington.edu

Yevgen Borodin
Computer Science
Stony Brook University
Stony Brook, NY 11709
borodin@cs.stonybrook.edu

ABSTRACT

People with disabilities have always overcome accessibility problems by enlisting people in their community to help. The Internet has broadened the available community and made it easier to get on-demand assistance remotely. In particular, the past few years have seen the development of technology in both research and industry that uses human power to overcome technical problems too difficult to solve automatically. In this paper, we frame recent developments in *human computation* in the historical context of accessibility, and outline a framework for discussing new advances in human-powered access technology. Specifically, we present a set of 13 design principles for human-powered access technology motivated both by historical context and current technological developments. We then demonstrate the utility of these principles by using them to compare several existing human-powered access technologies. The power of identifying the 13 principles is that they will inspire new ways of thinking about human-powered access technologies.

Categories and Subject Descriptors:
H5.2. Information interfaces and presentation: User Interfaces

General Terms: Design, Human Factors

Keywords
Crowdsourcing, Human Computation, Access Technology

1. INTRODUCTION

People with disabilities have always overcome accessibility problems by enlisting people in their community to help. Far from being passive recipients of this assistance, disabled people have a rich history of managing these interactions, and have formed organizing structures around assistance that serve to increase independence and ensure that their expectations are met. Initially, disabled people relied mostly on people near them for assistance, but the increasing connectedness enabled by the Internet has dramatically expanded the pool of people who could help. As disabled people have become more connected via networked devices, their ability to ask for assistance has increased.

The tendency in technical fields is to concentrate on fully automated solutions, but it is clear that, despite tremendous advances over the past few decades, technology alone is still far from being capable of solving many real accessibility problems that people with disabilities face in their everyday lives. For example, OCR seems like a solved problem until it fails to decipher the text on a road sign

captured by a cell phone camera [33], object recognition works reasonably well until the camera is held by a blind person [15, 28, 38], and the laudable 99% accuracy reported by commercial automatic speech recognition systems [4] falls off precipitously on casual conversation or any time it has not been trained for the speaker [45]. Even the automatic techniques used by the screen-reading software to convey the contents of the computer screen to blind people are error-prone, unreliable, and, therefore, confusing [16, 17, 30]. As a result, many access technologies are used only by people who are technically-savvy [41]. When access technology is unreliable, it is abandoned altogether [22, 24, 35].

Instead of relying on technological solutions, people with disabilities constantly rely on a loose network of friends, family, volunteers, and strangers. For instance, a volunteer may sign up to offer a few minutes of her time to read a blind person's mail aloud, or a fellow traveler may answer a quick question at the bus stop, e.g., "Is that the 45 coming?" Professional workers, such as sign language interpreters and audio descriptionists [39], interpret and convert sensory information into alternative forms, enabling a deaf student to participate in a traditional lecture and a blind person to enjoy (or learn from) a movie. Human support is drawn from a large group of people when needed and contributes to the larger goal of making the world more accessible for people with disabilities. We loosely define *human-powered access technology* as technology that facilitates and, ideally, improves interactions between disabled people and human assistants.

Examples of human-powered access technology abound, including video relay services that facilitate communication between deaf and hearing people; services that let blind people ask a network of volunteers to improve the accessibility of the web sites they visit; and web sites that collect electronic forms of printed material so that it can be presented in a better way for someone with a print disability. It is clear that people with disabilities have led the way in overcoming technological limitations with human assistance.

Including humans in the loop has been a popular direction in access technology over the past few years [23]. In particular, many projects have looked to the crowd as a source of human power that can be harnessed to improve accessibility (see examples in Section 4), where the *crowd* is loosely defined as a large group of people recruited through an open call [26]. In this paper, we choose to focus more broadly on human-powered access technology, which may range from a single employee paired with single disabled user [40] to groups of disabled users helping one another [11].

Despite the long history of human-powered access technology, a unifying framework with which to evaluate, compare and classify technology in this space is missing. As a result, it is difficult to (i) identify the broader contributions of new work in this space, (ii) make connections between existing work that may target different groups but share underlying traits, and (iii) reveal gaps in existing work that may be important areas for future research.

Our contributions in this paper are the following:

1. We present a motivating historical account of human-powered access technology that includes examples of how people with disabilities have structured services for human assistance to meet their needs and expectations.
2. We identify and describe 15 diverse examples of human-powered access technology that vary across a number of important dimensions.
3. We isolate 13 design dimensions from our examples that help to characterize human-powered access technology and form a framework by which human-powered access technologies can be compared.
4. We use the framework to evaluate and compare several existing human-powered access technologies, and propose several future research directions motivated by gaps that we have identified through this process.

2. HISTORY OF HUMAN-POWERED ACCESS TECHNOLOGY

People with disabilities have always enlisted the assistance of people in their immediate community, including friends, family and volunteers, to help them make accessible what their own senses miss or help them act on the world in ways they could not by themselves. Blind people found readers to relay written correspondence, deaf people found volunteer interpreters, and physically-impaired people would ask for assistance moving about or getting items that they needed. These volunteers were often just members of their local community—for example, members of a religious congregation who knew some sign language would often provide interpretation of religious services.

As accessibility-related services matured, they evolved from informal community assistance to formal organizations. For example, a number of agencies now provide services such as sign language interpretation and real-time captioning for people who are deaf or hard of hearing, personal assistance for those who have severe mobility disabilities, reading support for those who are blind, and support services for those who are deaf-blind. This evolution came about due to the demand for services, and because, in many cases, trained volunteers and professionals (experts) can do better than non-expert friends, family, and others.

Historically, many services for people with disabilities have adopted strict codes of confidentiality. As an example, sign language interpreters have a code, laid out by their professional organization, the Registry of Interpreters for the Deaf, that prevents them from interjecting their own comments into the conversation and from repeating information they have interpreted. In fact, all the major professional organizations that provide services to people with disabilities have developed codes of ethics that require that their employees or volunteers adhere to strict confidentiality, respect the customer, and take on only the jobs for which they are qualified.

Technology for people with disabilities has made it possible to access human assistants anywhere. A particularly interesting case is sign language interpreting. In just the past 10 years, remote sign language interpreting has become ubiquitous in the United States [36]. There are at least two forms of remote sign language interpreting: Video Relay Service (VRS) and Video Remote Interpreting (VRI). In VRS, a skilled sign language interpreter translates a phone call between a sign language user and a hearing person, while in VRI the interpreter translates a face-to-face interaction between a sign language user and a hearing person. In both cases, the interpreter is at a site remote from the two people trying to communicate. With the more mature VRS, when a phone call is requested, an interpreter from a pool of interpreters is assigned to the call, usually within a few seconds, and the call is set up with minimal delay. No prior scheduling of a call is needed. One VRS company, Sorenson VRS, employs thousands of sign language interpreters.

Going back to the 1970s, before VRS, the deaf community used TTY Relay Services in the same way, except there was no video, just texting over telephone lines [40]. TTY Relay Service operators translated text from the deaf customer to speech and speech from the hearing customer to text. Generally, TTY Relay Service operators need far less training than VRS interpreters, who must be fluent in two very different languages.

For those with sensory impairments, a key to improving access is converting information from one form to another. For example, inaccessible visual text may be made accessible to a blind person by converting it to aural speech, and, conversely, aural speech may be made accessible to a deaf person by converting it to text. The past few decades have seen remarkable improvements in finding ways to automatically convert one form of information into another, especially, with the help of artificial intelligence. In particular, converting text to speech is nearly a solved problem, converting speech to text works in some settings and, optical character recognition (OCR) can also work very well [33].

Nonetheless, there are even more conversion problems that seem to defy automation and, to date, seem to require human intelligence and, sometimes, specialized expertise. Far from idling while waiting for artificial intelligence to catch up to human intelligence and expertise, people with disabilities have successfully been getting answers to questions about their environments all throughout history—by *crowdsourcing* them. Notoriously hard problems, like speech to sign language translation, visual graphic to tactile graphic translation, video description, and many more seem to require humans, and, in some cases, the humans are recruited and utilized by automated means.

To address cases in which available automatic technology is not enough, models were proposed in the realm of access technology that combined artificial and human intelligence. For instance, in Zimmerman *et al.'s* Rainbow Model, automatic approaches are tried first but a staff of experts provides support when automatic approaches fail [1, 31]. In the past few years, the confluence of two technical trends has changed this landscape again, making it possible to recruit assistance remotely, on-demand, for only as long as needed. First, network connectivity has expanded dramatically in terms of bandwidth, latency, and availability. As a result, it is now practical to request and provide assistance remotely, greatly expanding the community of assistants and the number of people who could potentially ask for assistance. Second, the expansion of connectivity meant that there were new pools of assistants available. Microtask marketplaces for small jobs like Mechanical Turk [9] and social networks like Facebook [5] and Twitter [9] have grown in popularity [6] providing large pools of potential workers already connected and available in nearly real-time.

The history of how people with disabilities have employed crowd work and the more recent trends mentioned above, it is no surprise that people working with those with disabilities were quick to capitalize on the latest crowdsourcing technologies. Whether through remote readers for a blind person or video relay services employed by a deaf person, people with disabilities are already accustomed to using and relying on remote, near real-time human assistance in their everyday lives — something that is less common in current mainstream crowdsourcing applications. Consequently, mainstream applications may learn from the lessons learned in the disabled community.

Crowdsourcing and, in particular, human computation have been embraced by many fields in computer science and beyond over the past few years (see [29] for a survey). Human computation includes people as part of computational processes. Although human computation has been developed largely outside of the accessible computing community, one of the original motivations for human computation was an accessibility problem – labeling images [20]. People with disabilities have become leaders in human computation by virtue of their rich history using human assistance, although this leadership has gone somewhat unnoticed.

3. EXAMPLES

In this section we describe 15 examples of human-powered access technology. These examples were chosen for the breadth of human support they represent, and will be referenced in the rest of the paper. The examples are roughly ordered from services that operate asynchronously to those that are synchronous.

1) **ASL-STEM Forum:** The ASL-STEM Forum is a community-driven portal for building up sign language in technical fields from the bottom-up [19]. Users can contribute signs for terms, and comment/rate the signs contributed by others. It works much like Wikipedia [44], in that people on the web choose what and when to contribute.

2) **Tactile Graphics Project:** The Tactile Graphics Project [32] uses a workflow with multiple automatic tools in order to help improve the throughput of a human worker in converting figures in textbooks to a tactile form (Figure 1-b).

3) **GoBraille:** GoBraille is a smart phone application that tethers the phone to a refreshable Braille device and supports travel by blind and deaf-blind people on public transportation. One feature of the application is its GoBraille Repository where users can contribute information about bus stops that are relevant to other blind and deaf-blind travelers [11]. This is similar to open street map [8], which is a community-driven site that includes accessible routes.

4) **ESP Game:** The ESP Game is an online game in which two remote players are asked to enter labels for images that are shown to them [20]. The players receive points for agreeing on the labels. Because the players do not know one another and cannot otherwise communicate, the best strategy is to enter accurate labels.

5) **Bookshare:** Bookshare is a web site that collects and makes available accessible versions of print materials (mostly books) [2]. Members are a primary source of scans, contributing books that they have scanned themselves.

6) **Respeaking:** Despite tremendous progress over the past few decades, automatic speech recognition (ASR) does not yet work well enough to accurately transcribe arbitrary speech. A common practice is to have human speakers "re-speak" what they hear [34]. ASR is applied to this audio instead, which works much better than on the original because the the ASR is trained on the speaker and the speaker re-speaks in a controlled environment (quiet room, headset microphone, etc).

7) **Social Accessibility:** The Social Accessibility project [21] lets blind web users ask for assistance in improving the accessibility of the Web from sighted volunteers (Figure 1-c). Improvements generally take on the order of a few hours. This project also highlighted one of the difficulties with user-initiated accessibility improvement – disabled users may often not

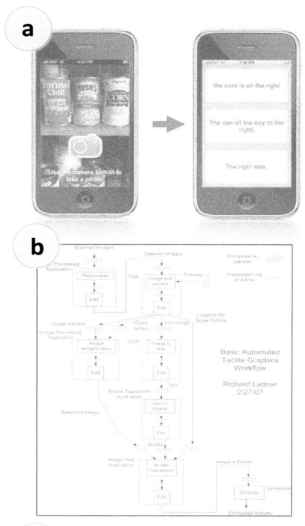

Figure 1: Examples of human-powered access technology. (i) VizWiz is a mobile phone applications that allows blind people to take a picture, speak a question, and receive answers quickly from the crowd; (ii) Tactile Graphics Project supports a workflow in which figures in textbooks are converted to tactile form by a close partnership between a human worker and automated tools; and (iii) Social Accessibility engages a network of volunteers to fix accessibility problems on the web.

realize that there is an accessibility problem and never request that it be fixed [37].

8) **Remote Reading Service:** The Remote Reading Service was pioneered by the Smith-Kettlewell Eye Institute in the mid-1990s [13, 42]. This service enabled a blind person to send a fax to an expert who would read the contents of the faxed image to a blind user over the phone. This service used existing technology in an interesting new way.

9) **Video Relay Services:** Video relay services are companies that have a pool of sign language interpreters who are available to translate a video phone call from a deaf person to a voice phone user. Video relay services began in Sweden in 1997 [36] and are now found in most of the developed countries of the world.

10) **Remote Real-Time Captioning:** In remote real-time captioning, a remote captionist converts speech of one person or a group of people into text for someone with a hearing disability. Television captions for live shows and some captioned meetings are done this way. Captioned telephone calls also use pools of captionist to serve phone calls. A common form of remote real-time captioning is called computer-assisted real-time transcription (CART). CART captionists are highly trained to work as court reporters where accuracy is paramount [40].

11) **Scribe4Me:** Scribe4Me is a prototype mobile application that lets deaf and hard of hearing people quickly receive transcriptions of the audio events around them [43]. The application runs on existing mobile phones and keeps a buffer of the last 30 seconds of audio heard on the device. When a user wants to do so, they can send the audio off to a remote worker who transcribes the audio and sends it back to the phone. In its original formulation, the transcription was done by a person involved in the study, i.e. an expert.

12) **MAP-Lifeline:** MAP-Lifeline enables the distributed support of people with cognitive disabilities as they go about their daily routine [18]. Caregivers are able at their discretion to inject prompts to a number of people under their care.

13) **Solona:** Solona is a service that originally let a blind person submit a picture of a web page containing a CAPTCHA and receive the answer to that CAPTCHA [12]. A small number of expert volunteers handle requests, and generally respond in less than 30 minutes.

14) **VizWiz:** VizWiz is an accessible iPhone application that lets blind people take a picture, speak any question about it, and receive answers in under 30s from people on Amazon's Mechanical Turk [25] (Figure 1-a). A primary contribution of the system was *quikTurkit*, a programming library designed to solicit answers quickly. LookTel is similar, but connects users to remote operators or family members [27].

15) **IQ Engines / oMoby:** IQ Engines provides an API that will provide a label for photos that are sent to it in nearly real-time [7]. This has been put into an accessible iPhone application called oMoby that many blind iPhone users use.

4. DESIGN OF HUMAN-POWERED AT

The experiences of people with disabilities can inform the design of current crowdsourcing systems. The following are some of dimensions that people with disabilities have addressed in the past and that future systems will need to consider. These dimensions are drawn from the examples presented in the previous section.

4.1 Initiative

Initiative refers to who instigates assistance: the end user, to the workers themselves, to organizations, to technology working on behalf of any of these parties. Inviduals may be both users and workers, such as in Bookshare and GoBraille.

End User – The end user often decides when to solicit help from human supporters. Examples include services like remote real-time captioning and relay services, and crowdsourcing systems like Social Accessibility and VizWiz.

Workers – Systems like the ASL-STEM Forum and GoBraille allow workers to decide when and what information they will provide. For instance, what terms they will sign in the Forum or what landmarks they will label in Go Braille.

Organizations – Groups of people will sometimes decide to solicit the help of human workers or to guide their efforts. For instance, workers are recruited to work on specific topic areas in the ASL-STEM Forum.

4.2 Source of Human Workers

A number of sources of human workers now exist, from professional organizations and microtask marketplaces to friends and family on social networks. This is a challenge that is relatively new for the disabled community—too many sources of help! Along with the source of workers is associated a number of relevant characteristics, such as the business model that is employed and the sustainability of the service.

Professionals/Experts – Professionals are hired to provide assistance and generally receive wages or fees for their participation. A number of business models may support these workers.

Crowd Workers – Crowd workers are recruited anonymously through an open call, are generally composed of non-experts, and cannot be assumed to stay around for a significant amount of time.

Volunteers – Volunteers work for free, are generally not anonymous, and generally participate for a longer amount of time than crowd workers.

Organized Volunteers – Volunteers are recruited through an organization that may help ensure that people are available when needed, may vet workers, or provide structured training.

4.3 Motivation

As in everything we do in our lives, human workers have a variety of reasons for helping others. These reasons range from altruistic intrinsic motivation to the desire to make money.

Intrinsic – People are often willing to contribute their time for causes they deem valuable. They may be motivated by the fact that their relatives and/or friends have disabilities, or just want to help without expecting anything in return.

Status – Others are better motivated when their contributions are made public through announcement, awards, and banquets. These people can often be instigated by their public status and completion. For instance, ESP game is an example when scoring competitors motivates people to contribute more captions.

Financial – Some people are best motivated by money, either in small amounts for fulfilling tasks at microtask marketplaces or as adequate compensation for their professional services.

Enjoyment – Some systems make it fun to provide assistance, for example the ESP Game turns image labeling into a game.

Self – Users may provide assistance because it helps them. For instance, users may contribute books that they scanned for themselves to Bookshare for shared use.

4.4 Financing

Depending on the source of human workers and their expertise, different financing mechanisms can be utilized.

Public – Many human-powered access technologies are publicly funded. For instance, video relay services are usually publicly funded, subsidized by fees that everyone pays on their phone bill,

Personal/Private – Sometimes human assistance is funded by the user, either personally or through the user's workplace, educational institution, or insurance. Private funds and trusts fall in the same category.

Unpaid – Some assistance is provided for free. For instance, the ESP Game attracts workers through a game. Solona is operated by volunteers and so it is free to use.

4.5 Worker Competence

Different sources of human work may provide workers with different competencies. Even within a particular source, worker competence may vary dramatically.

Expert / Skilled – Many services will require skilled workers. For instance, a video relay service requires proficient sign language speakers.

Amateurs – Some services may be supported by amateurs. For instance, the ASL-STEM Forum invites anyone to contribute, under the assumption that the rest of the community will filter out the good contributions from the bad.

Non-Expert – Some assistance can be provided by non-experts. For instance, VizWiz uses workers recruited from Mechanical Turk. In this case, the ability to see is the only qualification.

4.6 Latency

Different sources of human assistance may have different expected latencies. It might be acceptable to wait a few hours (or even days) for a volunteer to read your mail, but sign language interpreting may need to happen right away.

Interactive – Some human-powered access technologies are interactive. For instance, video relay services work in real-time.

Short Delay – Many services operate under the assumption of a short delay. For instance, VizWiz returns answers in less than 30 seconds. Social Accessibility takes on the order of a few hours to resolve an accessibility problem on average.

Undetermined – Some services have an undetermined delay. For instance, workers may never choose to add a video for a particular term on the ASL-STEM Forum, or they may add it immediately.

4.7 Accuracy Guarantees

Humans can provide services that are still too difficult to provide solely automatically, but may provide poor quality assistance for a number of reasons, including workers' misunderstanding of what they are asked to do, lazy or even malicious workers, or underspecified questions. Human-powered access technology uses a number of methods for quality control.

Vetted Workers – Many human-powered access technologies improve accuracy by using only workers who have been vetted. Workers may be vetted by their employer, by volunteer organizations, or via reputations gained over time. This is how the Video Relay Service and Remote Reading Services work (among others). These services can be costly and may need to be arranged in advance.

Abstractions – Some technologies use abstractions to help guarantee accuracy. For instance, the abstraction introduced by the

ESP Game makes it unlikely for the two game players to agree on a label if the label does not accurately describe the image.

Redundancy – One way to help ensure accuracy is by requiring multiple assistants to make the same suggestions. For instance, the ESP Game requires that multiple players submit the same label.

User Mediated – In some cases, users are presented with alternatives provided by human assistants and asked to decide whether they are correct. For instance, VizWiz provides users with answers from multiple workers.

Worker Mediated – Humans sometimes serve not only as assistants but also as mediators. In the ASL-STEM Forum, contributors help to decide which signs work best by contributing new signs and rating the ones that are already there.

4.8 Reliability

Many sources of human assistance are not always available; for instance, a simple approach to engage a human worker would be to simply send a text message to a friend or family member. This method is unreliable because the friend or family member may not always be available. Many of the methods of recruiting human assistance assume a network connection, which may not always be available (e.g., in a basement conference room or on a plane during takeoff). Traditional approaches, like hiring a sign language interpreter, do not face these reliability concerns.

Always Available – Few sources of human assistance are always available as networking connectivity is a requirement, if nothing else. Nevertheless, services like VRS employ workers who are available at all times, increasing reliability.

Assumed Available – Services built on microtask marketplaces (like VizWiz) are assumed to be reliably available, but there are not guarantees that this will always be the case.

Undetermined – Services like the ASL-STEM Forum have undetermined reliability. While people may come to contribute and rate signs, they also may not.

4.9 Assistance Provenance

Providing feedback to users about the human computation that is occurring on their behalf is critical for them to make informed decisions. In particular, it can be useful to know who or what has provided assistance.

Transparent – Users are informed regarding who or what will be assisting them beforehand. Most VRS operate in this way, where users are first connected to the person that will be assisting them.

Opaque – Users are not informed who or what assisted them. The service operates like a "black box."

Obfuscated – Users are told the general source or sources of assistance, but they have no way of knowing who or what actually assisted them for a particular request. IQ Engines / oMoby works this way – pictures are described by either computer vision or human workers, but are not labeled as to the source of assistance.

4.10 Confidentiality, Privacy, and Anonymity

When humans are included in the loop, new issues arise in terms of confidentiality, privacy, and anonymity. This dimension concerns how a human-powered access technology seeks to provide such guarantees.

Trusted Worker Pools – Remote interpreting services require workers to agree to strict confidentiality rules; oversight helps to ensure that workers comply.

User Feedback – Some tools may provide feedback to users to help them realize the implications of recruiting assistance. For instance, a tool might detect that a face is included in a photograph before sending to an untrusted sources.

No Guarantees – Many tools provide no guarantees regarding confidentiality, privacy or anonymity. By making no guarantees, these tools may have some benefits, e.g. operating more cheaply.

4.11 Consideration of Broader Context

To the extent that privacy, anonymity and confidentiality are considered in human-powered access technology, the focus is generally exclusive on the end user. For instance, technology may go to great lengths to help protect their identity. Often, the effects on others in the broader context in which the technology is used are ignored. For instance, bystanders may unwittingly find themselves in the lens of a blind user using VizWiz. Workers may be asked to answer a question with consequences (e.g. what is the dosage listed on this medication bottle?).

User Consideration – For the user to be considered, mechanisms should be in place to match the user's expectations. Video Relay Services do this well.

Worker Consideration – Workers may be protected from providing assistance in situations in which they feel uncomfortable. Workers may be told the consequences of their assistance and allowed not to assist without penalty.

Community Consideration – Mechanisms may be in place to protect people who are not directly involved in the use of the technology from accidentally becoming part of an interaction.

4.12 Broader Applicability of Human Work

The work that humans perform in the context of access technology can be more broadly applicable to other people.

Individual Reuse – In some cases, individuals may be able to reuse the work done on their behalf.

Group Reuse – Many services allow broad groups to reuse the work that was done on the behalf of others. For instance, accessibility improvements made in Social Accessibility can be used by other people who visit the same web page. The annotations made in Go Braille can be used by other travelers.

No Reuse – In many cases, it does not make sense to reuse work (or the application doesn't support it). For instance, in VRS it does not make sense for others to reuse the sign language interpretation of a conversation.

4.13 Targeted Disability

Technologies vary based on what disability is targeted. Sensory disabilities are widely regarded as the most popular targets of automatic technology and this seems to be true for human-powered access technology as well. Some examples of application for other types of disabilities exist, such as the MAP-Lifeline tool to support people with cognitive disabilities. We do not attempt to provide a breakdown of different types of disabilities – many such classifications exist (e.g. [18]).

5. DISCUSSION

Increasing connectedness represents great opportunities to engage human power in access technology. Development of this new technology need not start from a blank slate, but can rather build from the rich history of people helping people with disabilities.

In this paper, we have motivated a set of 13 design considerations for human-powered access technology. These dimension do not prescribe a set of requirements on access technology, but instead present a framework on which new technologies can be compared and evaluated. For instance, consider a video system installed in the home of an older adult that allows remote workers to check up on them. It is tempting to dismiss such a product outright because of the obvious privacy concerns; however, it has been documented that older people are willing to trade such incursions into their privacy if it means that they can live in their homes longer [10]. In such a situation, it may be appropriate to make sure that confidentiality has been ensured in lieu of privacy, perhaps by only employing fulltime workers who are subject to confidentiality agreements, or create technology that only provides minimal views (for instance, restricted to a foot off of the ground or less, in order to detect falls).

5.1 Application to Existing Technologies

Our design principles allow for meaningful and standardized comparison of the technology in this space. Figure 2 presents a comparison of the 15 technologies described in Section 3.

For instance, in some ways the Social Accessibility Project and Solona are similar – they both will describe images on the web for blind people. However, we can see in Figure 2 where these tools differ and the trade-offs in their design. Namely, whereas Solona uses a few expert describers, Social Accessibility uses a broader network of volunteers. Solona is able to achieve lower latency and may afford greater guarantees of confidentiality. Social Accessibility's broader pool of workers may make it more reliable. Importantly, these dimensions do not make one service inherently better or worse, but our design principles give us terminology useful in discusses their relative advantages.

As another example, VizWiz and Scribe4Me target different groups – one answers visual questions for blind people and the other describes audio events – but they are similar in other ways. For instance, both rely on the user to initiate the human assistance piece and both target low-latency responses. They differ in the source of the human assistance – VizWiz uses Amazon's Mechanical Turk whereas Scribe4Me relied on trained experts – but are similar in their goal of enabling user-initiated real-time answers to sensory questions.

5.2 Implications for Crowdsourcing

Most efforts in mainstream crowdsourcing have thus far concentrated on achieving acceptable results from crowd labor (high quality, low cost, high speed, etc.), but it is becoming evident that we also need to think about the broader crowdsourcing ecosystem. Because people with disabilities have come upon these issues for some time, it makes sense to look to their experiences for guidance. As one example, the expectations of workers are usually considered only to the point at which they are helpful for receiving better work. How can we give appropriate feedback to workers to let them know the implications of their work? If a VizWiz worker is asked to decipher dosage information on a pill bottle, they might reasonably choose to skip the task if they feel that they cannot do it well. Perhaps, our technology can even learn to give feedback to users when many workers decide to skip a particular question.

Our interest is primarily in the domain of access technology, in which it is particularly important to meet user expectations and ensure their control. Nevertheless, we believe these principles could be more broadly applied to mainstream human-powered technology. The design dimensions explored here are relevant to mainstream technology, but only a few have been explored in the broader context mainstream technology. In particular, the extensive experience of disabled people with human-powered technology suggests that we are likely to see additional structure, guarantees, and consideration for workers in the future.

Design Dimensions for Example Applications	Initiative (end User, Workers, Organizations)	Source (Experts, Crowd, Volunteers, Organized Volunteers, Artificial Intelligence)	Mtoviation (Intrinsic, Status, Financial, Enjoyment, Personal)	Financing (Public, peRsonal, Unpaid)	Competence (Expert, Amatuers, Non-Expert)	Latency (Interactive, Short Delay, Undetermined)	Accuracy (Vetted workers, Abstractions, Redundancy, User mediated, Worker mediated)	Reliability (Always, aSsumed, Undetermined)	Provenance (Transparent, Opaque, oBfuscated)	Confientiality, Privacy, Anonymity (Trusted workers, User feedback,)	Broader Context (User, Worker, Community, None)	Broader Applicability (Individual, Group, None)	Target Disability
1. ASL-STEM	W	C, V, O	I, S	U	E, A	U	U, W	U	T	N	U	G	Deaf
2. TGP	W, O	P, V	I, E	P, U	E, A	U	V	U	B	N	N	G	Blind
3. GoBraille	U, W	C, V	I, P	U	A, N	U	U	U	B	N	U, W, C	G	Blind
4. ESP Game	W, O	C	S, E	U	N	U	R	S	B	N	N	G	Blind
5. BookShare	U, W	E, V, O	I, F, P	P, R, U	E, A	U	V, U, W	S	B	N	U, W, C	G	Print
6. Respeaking	U, O	E, V, O	I, F	P, R, U	E, A	U	V, W	U	T	T	U, W	N	Deaf
7. SA	U	C	I, S	U	A, N	S	U	S	B	N	U	G	Blind, Other
8. Remote Read	U	E, O	F	P, R, U	E	I	V	A	T	T	U, W	N	Blind
9. VRS	U	E	F	P, R	E	I	V	A	T	T	U, W	N	Deaf
10. RRTC	U	E	F	P, R	E	I	V	A	T	T	U, W	N	Deaf
11. Scribe4Me	U	E	I	U	A, U	S	V	A	B	T	U	U	Deaf
12. MAP-LL	W	E	F	P, R	E	S	V	A	B	T	U, W	N	Cognitive
13. Solona	U	E, O	I	U	A	S	V	S	B	T	U	N	Blind
14. VizWiz	U	C	I, F	R	N	S	R, U	S	B	T	U	N	Blind
15. IQ Engines	U	C, AI	F	R, U	N	S	V	A	O	N	N	G	Blind

Figure 2: An analysis of the 15 example applications on the 13 design dimensions for human-powered access technology. Reported values are simplifications but support analysis of design trade-offs and comparison. For instance, VizWiz and Solona are both human-powered systems for describing images, but they use different sources of human labor. Solona's expert workers increase confidentiality, competence and accuracy, but at the cost of latency and reliability. Values reported are abbreviations drawn from the set in the top row.

5.3 Sustainability

An important question for human-powered access technologies is how they will be organized and sustained. Some mature services like VRS have established business models. The Universal Access Tax on telephone services finances VRS in the United States. VRS companies are paid by the minute for each VRS call that is made. VRS workers are highly trained at interpreter training programs and at the companies themselves. Other services mentioned, like GoBraille and VizWiz, are experimental with their development financed by research grants. Should VizWiz move to be commercial then the money for paying the photograph readers could either come from users themselves or from a government funded agency. In some cases like Bookshare, where volunteer workers are used, there may be a need for a paid coordinator to recruit and train volunteers. It is clear that for any successful human-powered access technology there must be a mechanism to sustain it over time. No single model fits all these technologies, and a given technology may be successful under several different models.

6. FUTURE WORK

The design dimensions discussed in this paper highlight a number of important areas for future work in access technology that enables people to help one another.

Although there is progress to be made on all of the dimensions outlined in this paper, Figure 2 shows a specific gap in the *Consideration of Broader Context* and *Latency* dimensions. Although the user should remain of primary concern, human-powered access technology should consider workers and others in the community, as such concerns are paramount for adoption [14]. Technology that is low latency requires experts to be recruited in advance. For instance, a technology that uses human assistance to help a blind user read a menu in a restaurant or a deaf student interact with her hearing peers is not useful if it cannot do so in nearly real-time. Future work may look to extend the benefits of pairing users with a specific expert to cheaper sources of non-expert assistance, without losing the advantages of asking experts.

Our coverage of human-powered access technology has highlighted some gaps in existing work. For instance, to our knowledge, most human-powered systems have targeted sensory disabilities, but future work might try to further extend this idea to technology aiding people with cognitive or motor disabilities [18], which will present new challenges to overcome. Few projects have explicitly considered the broader context in which human-powered access technology exists; therefore, an interesting area for future research is to consider how design methodologies that explicitly consider broader contexts, such as value-sensitive design [3], may be applied in this space.

7. CONCLUSION

Advances in human-powered access technology have the potential to make the world more accessible to people with disabilities. Far from starting from a blank slate, people with disabilities have a long history to draw on as they help to form the structure of new technologies that facilitate human assistance. We hope that our design principles will serve as a common framework in this area to catalyze discussion and highlight fruitful new areas of research.

8. ACKNOWLEDGMENTS

This work has been supported by NSF Awards #IIS-1049080, #IIS-0808678, and #CNS-0751083.

9. REFERENCES

1. *Amazon's Mechanical Turk*. http://mturk.com.
2. *Bookshare*. http://bookshare.org.
3. *ChaCha*. http://www.chacha.com.
4. *Dragon Naturally Speaking*. http://www.nuance.com/talk/.
5. *Facebook*. http://www.facebook.com.
6. *Facebook Stats*. http:// facebook.com/press/info.php?statistics.
7. *IQ Engines*. http://iqengines.com.
8. *Open Street Map*. http://www.openstreetmap.org.
9. *Twitter*. http://www.twitter.com.
10. Adlam, T., Carey-Smith, B., Evans, N., Orpwood, R., Boger, J., & Mihailidis, A., *Implementing Monitoring and Technological Interventions in Smart Homes for People with Dementia: Case Studies*, in *Behaviour Monitoring and Interpretation - BMI: Smart Environments*. 2009, IOS Press.
11. Azenkot, S., Prasain, S., Borning, A., Fortuna, E., Ladner, R.E., Wobbrock, J.O, *Enhancing Independence and Safety for Blind and Deaf-Blind Public Transit Riders*, in *CHI* 2011: Vancouver, BC.
12. Baillie, M. and J.M. Jose, *An Audio-Based Sports Video Segmentation and Event Detection Algorithm*, in *CVAVI 2004*.
13. Bernstein, M., Miller, R.C., Little, G., Ackerman, M., Hartmann, B., Karger, D.R., and Panovich, K., *Soylent: A Word Processor with a Crowd Inside.*, in *UIST 2010*.
14. Beyer, H. and K. Holtzblatt, *Contextual design: defining customer-centered systems*. 1998, San Francisco: Morgan Kaufmann.
15. Bigham, J.P., et al., *VizWiz::LocateIt - Enabling Blind People to Locate Objects in their Environment*, in *CVAVI 2010*.
16. Borodin, Y., et al., *More than meets the eye: a survey of screen-reader browsing strategies*, in *W4A 2010*. p. 1-10.
17. Borodin, Y., et al., *What's new?: making web page updates accessible*, in *ASSETS*. 2008, p. 145-152.
18. Carmien, S., et al., *Increasing workplace independence for people with cognitive disabilities by leveraging distributed cognition among caregivers and clients*, in *GROUP* 2003, p. 95-104.
19. Cavender, A.C., et al., *ASL-STEM Forum: enabling sign language to grow through online collaboration*, in *CHI* 2010, p. 2075-2078.
20. Chu, W.-T., W.-H. Cheng, and J.-L. Wu, *Semantic context detection using audio event fusion: camera-ready version*. EURASIP J. Appl. Signal Process. **2006**: p. 181-181.
21. Cowling, M. and R. Sitte, *Comparison of techniques for environmental sound recognition*. Pattern Recogn. Lett., 2003. **24**(15): p. 2895-2907.
22. Dawe, M., *Desperately seeking simplicity: how young adults with cognitive disabilities and their families adopt assistive technologies*, in *CHI 2006*, p. 1143-1152.
23. Ferres, L., *Proc. of the International Cross-Disciplinary Conf. on Web Accessibility*. 2011.
24. Goette, T., *Factors leading to the successful use of voice recognition technology*, in *ASSETS 1998*, p. 189-196.
25. Horowitz, D. and S.D. Kamvar, *The anatomy of a large-scale social search engine*, in *W4A 2010*, p. 431-440.
26. Howe, J., *Why the Power of the Crowd Is Driving the Future of Business*. 2009: Crown Business.
27. J. Sudol, O.D., C. Blanchard and T. Dorcey, *LookTel — A Comprehensive Platform for Computer-Aided Visual Assistance*, in *CVAVI 2010*.
28. Jeffrey P. Bigham, C.J., Hanjie Ji, Greg Little, Andrew Miller, Robert C. Miller, Robin Miller, Aubrey Tatarowicz, Brandyn White, Samuel White, and Tom Yeh, *Vizwiz: Nearly Real-time Answers to Visual Questions*, in *UIST 2010*.
29. Kassirer JP, G.G., *Clinical problem solving: A behavioral analysis*. Ann Internal Medicine, 1978. **89**: p. 245-255.
30. Kawanaka, S., et al., *Accessibility commons: a metadata infrastructure for web accessibility*, in *ASSETS 2008*, p. 153-160.
31. Kittur, A., E.H. Chi, and B. Suh, *Crowdsourcing user studies with Mechanical Turk*, in *CHI 2008*, p. 453-456.
32. Ladner, R.E., et al., *Automating tactile graphics translation*, in *ASSETS 2005*, p. 150-157.
33. Manduchi, R., J. Coughlan, and V. Ivanchenko, *Search Strategies of Visually Impaired Persons Using a Camera Phone Wayfinding System*, in *ICCHP 2008*, p. 1135-1140.
34. Miyoshi, S., et al., *Support Technique for Real-Time Captionist to Use Speech Recognition Software*, in *Computers Helping People with Special Needs*, K. Miesenberger, et al., p. 647-650.
35. Phillips, B. and H. Zhao, *Predictors of Assistive Technology Abandonment*. Assistive Technology, 1993. **5.1**: p. 36-45.
36. Porrero, P., *Improving the Quality of Life for the European Citizen: Technology for Inclusive Design and Equality*. 1998, IOS Press.
37. Richard, O.G.a.G., *Automatic transcription of drum sequences using audiovisual fea- tures*, in *ICASSP 2005*, p. 205-208.
38. Samuel White, H.J., and Jeffrey P. Bigham, *EasySnap: Enabling Blind People to Take Photographs*, in *UIST 2010 - Demos*.
39. Snyder, J., *Audio description: The visual made verbal*. International Congress Series, 2005. **1282**: p. 935-939.
40. Stinson, M., Eisenberg, S., Horn, C., Larson, J., Levitt, H., Stuckless, R. . *Real-Time Speech-to-Text Services: A report of the National Task Force on Quality of Services in the Postsecondary Education of Deaf and Hard of Hearing Students*. 1999; Available from: http://netac.rit.edu/publication/taskforce/realtime.
41. Takagi, H., et al., *Collaborative web accessibility improvement: challenges and possibilities*, in *ASSETS 2009*, p. 195-202.
42. Tara Matthews, S.C., Carol Pai, Janette Fong, and Jennifer Mankoff, *Scribe4me: Evaluating a mobile sound translation tool for the deaf*, in *Ubicomp 2006*, p. 159-176.
43. Union, I.T., *Trends in Telecommunication Reform 2007: The Road to NGN*. 2007.
44. Viegas, F.B., et al., *Talk Before You Type: Coordination in Wikipedia*, in *Proc. of the 40th Annual Hawaii International Conf. on System Sciences*. 2007, IEEE Computer Society. p. 78.
45. Wald, M., et al., *Correcting automatic speech recognition captioning errors in real time*. International Journal of Speech Technology, 2007. **10**(1): p. 1-15.

Empowering Individuals with Do-It-Yourself Assistive Technology

Amy Hurst   Jasmine Tobias

University of Maryland, Baltimore County (UMBC)

1000 Hilltop Circle, Baltimore, MD 21250

{amyhurst, jtobias1}@umbc.edu

ABSTRACT

Assistive Technologies empower individuals to accomplish tasks they might not be able to do otherwise. Unfortunately, a large percentage of Assistive Technology devices that are purchased (35% or more) end up unused or abandoned [7,10], leaving many people with Assistive Technology that is inappropriate for their needs. Low acceptance rates of Assistive Technology occur for many reasons, but common factors include 1) lack of considering user opinion in selection, 2) ease in obtaining devices, 3) poor device performance, and 4) changes in user needs and priorities [7]. We are working to help more people gain access to the Assistive Technology they need by empowering non-engineers to "Do-It-Yourself" (DIY) and create, modify, or build. This paper illustrates that it is possible to custom-build Assistive Technology, and argues why empowering users to make their own Assistive Technology can improve the adoption process (and subsequently adoption rates). We discuss DIY experiences and impressions from individuals who have either built Assistive Technology before, or rely on it. We found that increased control over design elements, passion, and cost motivated individuals to make their own Assistive Technology instead of buying it. We discuss how a new generation of rapid prototyping tools and online communities can empower more individuals. We synthesize our findings into design recommendations to help promote future DIY-AT success.

Categories and Subject Descriptors

K4.2 **[Computers and Society]**: Social Issues – Assistive technologies for persons with disabilities

General Terms
Design

Keywords

Assistive Technology, Do-It-Yourself, Empowerment, Human-Centered Computing, Online Communities, Personal-scale Manufacturing, Rapid Prototyping

1. INTRODUCTION

Many people in the US rely on Assistive Technologies to maintain, increase, or improve their functional capabilities. Assistive Technology has been defined to broadly include any product, device or equipment that is acquired commercially, modified, or customized to accomplish something that was not otherwise possible [1]. Assistive Technology covers a wide range of equipment from simple low-tech devices such as handrails and grips, to high-tech equipment that includes power wheelchairs and robots. The US Census has reported that at least 54 million individuals (or 19% of the non-institutionalized US population) have a disability, approximately 13 million people use a mobility aid (wheelchair, cane, or walker), and 11 million people need personal assistance with everyday activities [12].

While there is a large market for both medical and non-medical devices that are used as Assistive Technology, many studies have shown that the overall abandonment rate of Assistive Technology is high: 29.3% overall [7], 8% for life-saving devices [10], 36% for dressing aids [7], 61% for crutches [7] and up to 75% for hearing aids [10]. High abandonment rates leave many individuals without the technology they need and waste time, money, and energy developing and purchasing technology that isn't used.

In a survey of 227 adults with disabilities who use Assistive Technology Phillips found that almost 1/3 of all devices were completely abandoned [7]. She identifies four factors related to abandonment 1) *User involvement in device selection*. She found that user opinions matter, and quotes one participant saying, "Listen to me! I know what works for me." 2) *Ease of procuring the device*. Surprisingly, devices that are easy to obtain (purchased at drugstores, mail-order catalogs, etc) were not always the most appropriate device for the user's needs. 3) *Device performance*. Participants cared about reliability, comfort, ease of use, safety, and durability. 4) *Change in ability (both improvement and decline) and preferences*. User needs, lifestyles, and priorities change over time, resulting in previously used Assistive Technology devices becoming irrelevant to one's current needs.

Phillips concluded that one of the best ways to fight abandonment is to develop policies and services that emphasize consumer involvement and consider long-term needs [7]. We believe that adoption rates can be improved by empowering individuals to create and modify their own Assistive Technology rather than being forced to rely on "off-the-shelf" products.

We are studying how existing DIY culture and tools can be applied to create, modify, or enhance Assistive Technology. A new generation of affordable rapid prototyping tools make it possible for individuals to build and customize physical devices such as wheelchair accessories, prosthetics, and tools to support activities of daily living such as eating, dressing, and accessing a computer.

The success of online communities enables users to share designs, modifications, experiences and inspiration. By empowering individuals with the means and knowledge to create their own Assistive Technologies (and iterate on these designs as their needs change), they will have full control over most of the factors that are problematic in adoption (user opinion, speed of delivery, performance, and understanding user needs).

In this paper we investigate the potential for Do-It-Yourself Assistive Technology. We first present case studies and interviews that investigate opinions and experiences creating customized Assistive Technology. Then, we survey recent cultural trends and tools that we believe can make DIY-AT possible. Next, we discuss how these technologies can improve the Assistive Technology adoption process. We conclude with future DIY-AT challenges: teaching novices and encouraging participation in online communities.

2. Case Studies of Experiences and Interests

This section presents three case studies about experiences and interests in Do-It-Yourself Assistive Technology, where people found their own designs to be better and less expensive than the available off-the-shelf solutions. The first case study is about instructors in an adaptive art class working to help individuals paint without using their hands. The second describes someone who makes a wide variety of Assistive Technologies and has created his own online community to share designs. The third, summarizes findings from interviews with individuals who rely on Assistive Technology about their impressions of DIY-AT.

2.1 Case Study 1: Iterative Design of a Head Pointer for Painting

Motivated by the problem of how to teach art to individuals who couldn't use their hands, instructors at UCP Pittsburgh tried several off-the-shelf and custom-built head pointers that let people paint by moving their head. They spent a year and about $600 searching for a solution that was affordable, lightweight, sturdy, and adjustable. We interviewed one of these instructors to learn more about what they built and their design process. This case study illustrates the drawbacks of off-the-shelf solutions, and how custom-built Assistive Technology can be less expensive; yet work better, than those solutions.

2.1.1 Exploring Off-The-Shelf Solutions

The instructors did not expect that they would develop their own solution, and originally believed that they would be able to find a pre-existing solution and buy it "off the shelf". They began by getting a small grant and started looking at head pointers in catalogs. In general, they found solutions to be expensive (ranging from $100-$300) and found it difficult to tell how well these designs would work in advance.

> "There was no way to make sure the stuff [we saw in the catalogs] worked. We didn't want to waste the money and then find out this stuff didn't work."

Ultimately, they bought several pre-made head pointers (Figure 1, top left), but found they didn't meet their requirements. The biggest problem was that the head pointers weren't steady while in use, and would slide around on the user's head while painting.

2.1.2 Building a Better Solution

After exploring the commercial options available and not being satisfied with the available options, the instructors decided to make their own head pointers that would be more stable and comfortable while in use.

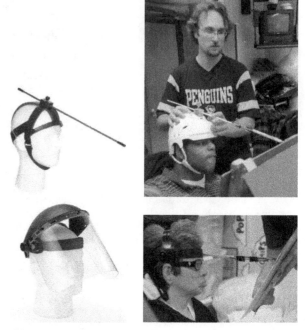

Figure 1. Exploration of head pointers for painting. Off-the-shelf head pointer that was unstable during use, cost $100-300 (top left). Early custom design with a $40 helmet, that was also unstable (note: instructor holding it in place) (top right). A $15 adjustable face shield (bottom left) made the final design (bottom right) less expensive, lighter, and more sturdy than the off-the-shelf solutions.

They did this on their own, and didn't seek ou the help of any Mechanical Engineering or Assistive Technology experts, and didn't look for ideas online.

They combined parts from the products they bought online, and tried attaching them to different kinds of helmets, but found this design also moved too much during use (Figure 1, top right). It wasn't until an instructor brought in a face shield (Figure 1, bottom left) to protect himself from accidentally getting paint in his eye, that they found the perfect base for their head pointer. They used an adjustable face shield that can be commonly bought at any hardware store and costs between $15-$20. They found this solution ideal because it was adjustable, could fit snugly on the head, and stayed still while in use. They removed the screen from the shield, and attached a wooden dowel rod and paintbrush to it on the side (Figure 1, bottom left).

The instructors tested different head pointer designs during weekly art classes, and their participants were very involved in the process and had strong preferences between the different designs. Overall, the participants were very patient throughout the process and even though some designs were uncomfortable and difficult to use, participants were excited to be painting. The instructors don't remember the participants having ideas about how to improve the designs, but they were always willing to try out different designs and were happy with the final design that was comfortable and worked well. These head pointer designs have now been in use for several years, and have empowered many individuals to paint without using their hands. The instructors have made local demonstrations of their design, but have not shared their work with any online communities because they do not know where to share it, and don't know how much time it would take to do this.

2.1.3 Lessons Learned

This case study demonstrates that custom-built Assistive Technology can be less expensive, yet work better than the off-the-shelf solutions. In this example, the instructors first purchased the pre-made solutions, but found they didn't meet their requirements. They were able to identify the limitations of the off-the-shelf solutions, and created their own designs to overcome them. In the end, they spent less on the entire iterative design process than they did on a single off-the-shelf head pointer.

Even though, the instructors were willing to spend money on expensive pre-made solutions they found it frustrating that they couldn't predict had no idea how well they would work. This problem is not unique to Assistive Technology, as many products we buy online include customer reviews and ratings. If the instructors had found online reviews or communities discussing these products, they would have saved a lot of money. It is unfortunate that so much research and experimentation went in to developing these head pointers, but their knowledge and design has not been shared online for others facing this same problem.

2.2 Case Study 2: Building DIY-AT and an Online Community as a Hobby

Our second case study investigates the DIY-AT experiences of Jeary[1], an able-bodied retired finance professional who has an engineering degree and has been designing and building adaptive technology for 40 years as a hobby. He has created many designs for a wide range of applications and physical disabilities and posts them to his own website (workshopsolutions.com) that features over 170 Assistive Technology designs (a mix of his own designs, and designs that have been submitted by others). The primary goal of the website is to share Assistive Technology designs with others, with the aim that they can make the designs themselves.

Figure 2. Homemade miniature wheelchairs – the "founding project, 1972".

2.2.1 Inspiration and Design Work

Nearly 40 years ago, Jeary walked into a room full of paraplegic children sitting on floor mats or adult sized wheel chairs that were too big. This inspired him to create his first adaptive device: miniature wheelchairs in the shape of go-karts. The miniature wheelchairs swiveled, had brakes, and were made of ½" plywood with upholstered seats, back cushions, and a swinging utility tray for getting in and out easily. On delivery of the carts, the children were instantly mobile. Not long after, a lightweight stick was added to each miniature wheelchair to allow the children to push

---

[1] Our participant asked that we use his real name in this paper, and include the real name of his website.

---

elevator buttons and move between floors. These miniature wheelchairs fit the children well, and were functional, popular, and used for several years (Figure 2).

Since then, Jeary has worked out of his home workshop to create hundreds of devices for people with disabilities. Located in a 12'x14' room in his basement, he uses standard hand tools plus a bandsaw, table saw sander, drill press, router table, welding and soldering equipment, and plastic bending and forming tools. In an adjacent furnace room, he stores a large supply of wood, metal, foam, leather, and Velcro. He has helped people with motor impairments do things that would normally be very difficult, such as eating with one hand, operating a TV remote control without fingers, and skiing without lower limbs.

Jeary's homemade adaptive devices are much more economical to build than similar products that may be commercially available. For instance, a homemade wheelchair cup holder posted on his site costs less than $2 to make but similar products from medical supply companies have a suggested retail of $110 (Figure 3, left and right). In his experience, Jeary believe that consumers tend to think that because products are from medical supply companies they're better but, he asserts "It's just more expensive because it's 'medical'. You can buy something and just modify it for less."

"THE PROBLEM: To provide a multipurpose drink holder allowing both hands to be free to control wheelchair movement.

THE SOLUTION: A wide variety of holders can be built quickly and cheaply using 4" cut off lengths of 3" diameter PVC pipe. Lightly sand and varnish for a finished look. Drill cross holes of appropriate diameter at the bottom to glue in lengths of black fiberglass rod from a discarded umbrella. Appropriate brackets can be made from scraps of PVC and bonded strongly with PVC glue or attached with nuts and bolts depending on where on the wheelchair/scooter they are going to be used."

Figure 3. Jeary's homemade wheelchair cup holder (left), and a cup holder with u-bolt wheelchair Rail Mount by RAM for suggested retail of $110 (from1800wheelchair.com, right). Text from Jeary's webpage describing the solution (bottom).

2.2.2 Creating an Online Community to Share Designs with Others

Jeary has not patented any of his ideas and freely shares them on a website he and his son created, funded, and currently maintain. Originally launched in 1998, the website was created to serve persons with disabilities, family members, or caregivers who are looking for an adaptive device that they can build. Jerry claims that his designs aren't high tech, and anyone who is somewhat handy should be able to build them. The site has not changed much from its original inception and is simple by design.

As of this writing, 47% of the adaptive devices posted on Jeary's website were added by site visitors, many of whom have contributed more than once. Most of the contributions are made by individuals, but some are made by small teams of designers and builders. Some contributors are handy people wanting to help and may have been inspired by Jeary's work or personal experiences with the disabled community. Others are caring for loved ones and want to share solutions that have worked for them. It's a small online community in which visitors contribute content via email. For ease of use and consistency, contributors follow a standard format (Figure 3, bottom) of submitting one paragraph describing the problem, one paragraph for the solution, and up to six photos. The submissions are revised to follow the standard format, often resizing images and revising the copy to fit within the "Problem" and "Solution" framework but, within a few days, the contribution is manually posted to the website for all to browse and freely use or share.

According to a visitor counter on the website, it has received almost 70,000 visitors. Jeary receives email inquiries pertaining to 1) how the devices can be purchased, 2) details about how to build an idea, and 3) requests to have something built for them. For those inquiring about purchases, Jeary clarifies the concept of the site and explains that nothing is for sale. Although many people ask Jeary why he doesn't try to make a profit, he exclaims, "This has nothing to do with money." With a few exceptions, anything that Jeary builds for others is at no cost. He buys all materials at his own expense and perceives it to be just like any other hobby related cost. "I bet I don't spend more in a year than a golf enthusiast does," he says. Instead of selling online to those who inquire, he often provides very detailed information and drawings as to how they can create possible solutions for themselves. As for those requesting something to be built, Jeary explains:

> "I can't help all of these people because they're in Peru or somewhere and I'm over here… I need to really be in front of the disabled person to see their unique situation and come up with a good solution."

2.2.3 Summary and Implications for Future DIY-AT

Jeary's work and the number of contributors posting to his website illustrate that there are people who are dedicated to helping others make their own Assistive Technology, and are willing to donate their ideas online in an effort to freely help people with disabilities. The inquiries received from people looking for solutions online, trying to pay for a custom build, and asking for more detailed instructions are evidence that there is consumer demand for homemade adaptive devices and people are building things from the ideas shared. Further, users of his site have found cost benefits when comparing a homemade device to a commercial one. Jeary's humble site, absent of automation and newer technology, has mostly a local Canadian audience. Perhaps a more robust site, could grow a larger online community, and gain broader outreach.

2.3 Exploring the Potential of DIY-AT

We gauged potential interest in DIY-AT from motor-impaired individuals who hadn't made their own Assistive Technology through face-to-face interviews. We interviewed four individuals (1 female) at United Cerebral Palsy Pittsburgh about their experiences with Assistive Technology, and talked about what modifications they would want to make to their current Assistive Technology (assuming there were no limitations). All participants had concrete ideas for modifications they felt would increase their comfort, safety, or quality of life. Surprisingly, almost all of these modifications would be extremely simple and affordable to implement.

We conducted two interviews in pairs, and all participants were power wheelchair users for over 8 years. In Group A, P1 (33, male) and P2 (21, male) controlled their power wheelchairs with their hand using a joystick. In Group B, P3 (30, female) had an Augmentative and Alternative Communication (AAC) device mounted on her chair. P4 (54, male) had an upper extremity impairment and controlled his power wheelchair using a joystick mounted near his chin. A preset list of questions was used in both groups, and participants in Group B were asked about modifications group A were interested in.

2.3.1 Modification Desires

None of our participants had experience modifying their Assistive Technology beyond simple customizations such as decorating their wheelchair with stickers or keychains, or hanging bags from the chair's frame. All of the modification interests our participants mentioned were related to their power wheelchairs (likely since this is such a crucial piece of Assistive Technology in their lives). All of our participants had modifications ideas if money, difficulty, and ability were not a factor. The majority of these modifications were relatively minor and easily do-able. We summarize the modifications our participants identified below.

Modification Interest in Group A

Group A (P1 and P2) had a lot of ideas to modify their wheelchair, and they felt strongly that their wheelchairs should have more car-like features (since their power wheelchairs were as expensive as a car). The two most difficult modifications were a bigger motor (so they could go faster), and hydraulic shocks (for a smoother ride). However, they were equally interested in adding safety lights (turn signals, head, and tail lights) to their chair and having their chair play music (while waiting or travelling). They wanted the chair to have speakers and be the source of the music itself, rather than have a personal device (such as a cell phone or mp3 player) do this.

Both participants had an acrylic tray over their lap that was always attached to their wheelchair. They expressed in interest in modifying these with customizable edges (adjustable color and height) to prevent things from falling off the tray. They also wanted a place to securely hold objects they used frequently (cups, cell phone, remote controls), and easily reach drink straws without having to contort their face, or risk poking their eye.

Modifications Interests in Group B

Group B (P3 and P4) also had many ideas how to modify their chair, but they tended to be more interested in the comfort than the function of their chairs. Both participants expressed interest in having the seat of their chair be heated and be able to vibrate (for a massage).

P3 was interested in having safety lights on her chair, but P4 was not.

When we asked about being able to play music from her chair, she demonstrated that she was able to play MP3 files through her AAC device. She frequently used this feature while volunteering at a local children's hospital to entertain children. She usually plays seasonal songs for the holidays and the local football team. P4 liked the idea of having access to music, and said he would want to have it come out of his headrest.

P4 had the simplest modification requests: access to the time and water. He wished he had access to a clock on his wheelchair so he wouldn't always have to ask someone else for the time. He wanted to mount the clock under his wheelchair's display (Figure 4, right), but didn't know how to do this. He was interested to learn that P3 had a small clock mounted to a bar on her chair (Figure 4, left).

Figure 4. P3 has a small clock to the left of her AAC Device (left). P4 wished he had a clock under his power wheelchair's controller (right).

P4 drives his wheelchair using a joystick with his chin, and switches modes using a push button mounted on the opposite side of his head as the joystick. Unfortunately, the switch is on the same side as his Drink-Aide (an adjustable straw that is too short for him and hard to reach without accidentally hitting the switch). He wanted to have the Drink-Aide mounted somewhere where it would be more comfortable and not interfere with his wheelchair's controls.

2.3.2 Reactions to DIY-AT

After discussing modification interests, we asked our participants their opinion about creating their own Assistive Technology, and explained personal-scale manufacturing to them (Section 3.1).

Participants P1 and P2 immediately saw the potential for DIY-AT and these new technologies, and thought it was the way of the future, and something they should learn more about. However, they were concerned about making changes to the chair that would risk breaking the equipment, or violate the warranty. They felt uncomfortable letting a 3rd party make customizations, but would be more comfortable if they were involved in the process.

P3 saw building her own Assistive Technology as a way to control the aesthetics of her devices. She expressed disappointment that the color of her wheelchair chair and AAC device did not match (and were not her favorite color).

P4 had no interest in the aesthetics of his devices, only in their function. Unlike P1 and P2, he was not concerned about using custom-built parts on his wheelchair if it meant he didn't have to rely on someone else to fix them. He stated, "When things break, I stay in bed", referring to the two months he had to stay in bed when the controls on his wheelchair broke.

2.3.3 Summary of Interview Findings

Overall, our participants were interested in customizing their Assistive Technology, and had many achievable ideas for modifications they would want to make. Participants who were concerned about these solutions impacting the chairs' performance (or their warranty) were willing to modify their equipment so long as they were involved in the process. Another participant saw being more involved in making his own modifications a way to gain independence. Unsurprisingly, aesthetics were found to be an important consideration for some. We feel that these findings are very promising for the potential and success of DIY-AT.

3. Relevant Tools and Online Communities for the Do-It-Yourself Revolution

The popularity and increasing growth organizations such as Make Magazine (http://www.makezine.com) and Martha Stewart (http://www.marthastewart.com) illustrate the DIY revolution happening now. A renewed interest in making things is due to peoples' desire to save money, customize goods to fit their interests and needs, feel less dependent on corporations [5]. Today, this interest spans a wide range of activities from gourmet cooking, fashion, home improvement, and electronics. This culture highlights a set of values where sharing, learning, and creativity are valued over profit and social capital [4]. A culture where people are interested in modifying or creating is not new, and has appeared throughout history notably through amateur radio enthusiasts in the late 1920s, and model railroad enthusiasts in the 1950s [6]. According to Von Hippel, 10-40% of users engage in developing or modifying products [13].

> "Users that innovate can develop exactly what they want, rather than relying on manufacturers to act as their (often imperfect) agents. Moreover, individual users do not have to develop everything they need on their own: they can benefit from innovations develop and freely shared by others" [13].

This section surveys recent innovations and trends in personal-scale manufacturing and online communities, and past work building customized Assistive Technology.

3.1 Rapid Prototyping Tools for Personal-Scale Manufacturing

Over the past decade a new generation of *rapid prototyping tools* (machines that manufacture objects quickly so they can be used in the iterative design process; the quality and durability of their output varies) have emerged that have the potential to make *personal-scale manufacturing* possible. "Personal-scale manufacturing tools enable people that have no special training in woodworking, metalsmithing, or embroidery to manufacture their own complex, one-of-a-kind artisan-style objects [3]. This technology provides new opportunities for individuals with disabilities to build their own physical objects, using tools such as Computer Numeric Controlled (CNC) tools that can precisely cut or build a variety of materials. Such tools include 3D printers that can build solid objects out of plastic, laser cutters that can precisely cut (or etch) flat materials (such as cardboard, acrylic, wood, and metal), and multi-axis milling machines that can transform metal into almost any 3D shape.

3.1.1 Tools that Make Building Accessible

Traditional manufacturing machines (band saws, lathes, and drill presses) frequently require many physical requirements of their users. These include the ability to stand, precise manual dexterity, and accurate vision, all of which limit whom can operate these machines. Furthermore, operating these machines requires special training and knowledge, and can be extremely dangerous when misused. CNC machines remove many of these barriers since they are computer-controlled, and the main task of the user is to create the design, and to supervise the machine during the build process. This development provides an exciting opportunity for individuals without Mechanical Engineering or manufacturing backgrounds to build things. To create something for one of these machines, a user only needs to be able to access a computer and create (or download) a file in the correct format.

Over the past decade, these machines have become more affordable and ubiquitous. In the past, access to these machines was predominantly limited to large manufacturing companies and research labs because the machines were prohibitively expensive for other organizations. However, there are now CNC machines that are affordable enough for people to have in their own homes or their local community. For example, the MakerBot (http://www.makerbot.com) is a 3D printer that connects to a desktop computer via USB and builds 3D objects by layering plastic. Costing under $1300, the MakerBot is stark contrast to professional 3D printers that cost tens of thousands of dollars and use expensive materials. For example, a hand splint could be easily printed on a MakerBot using less than $1 of plastic filament. The MakerBot is currently sold as a kit that the end-user must assemble (much like the Apple I from 1976), so it may not be an appropriate choice for someone with limited mobility now, but it is likely that more accessible options will become available in the near future. In the meantime, community-oriented ownership, such as libraries or disability centers, will enable individuals with disabilities to take advantage of the opportunities offered by such devices to create DIY-AT.

With the cultural movement of people interested in DIY activities, there are a growing number of people buying (or building) CNC machines for their homes. Additionally, shared and public workshops such as Hackerspaces (http://www.hackerspaces.org) and Fabrication Labs (http://fab.cba.mit.edu) are becoming more common, and give individuals the option to rent time on shared machines. Those who do not have access to nearby CNC machines can manufacture almost any part using online services such as Ponoko (http://www.ponoko.com), and Shapeways (http://www.shapeways.com), and eMachineShop (http://www.emachineshop.com). These companies tend to offer high quality manufacturing for a variety of services including 2D and 3D manufacturing of metal, wood, glass, and plastic. They offer reasonable turnarounds, competitive pricing, and support small order volumes.

As manufacturing become more accessible, it is possible for almost anyone to become a machine operator, but an important question is how novices will create designs. Following in the footsteps of software designed to help non-programmers build and customize software such as Alice (a 3D animation programming environment, http://www.alice.org), there has been an influx of software projects to help non-engineers build 3D models. Examples include Google's Sketchup (http://sketchup.google.com), 3DTin, (http://www.3dtin.com), and Tinkercad (http://www.tinkercad.com). These applications are WYSIWYG (What You See Is What You Get) and output a standard format.

3.2 Sharing Ideas and Online Communities

The origins of open-source software, or freely sharing source code, can be traced back to the 50s when researchers started sharing software in user forums. Since then, open-source software has become tremendously successful and provides a reasonable alternative to mass-marketed software, at a fraction of the cost (or no cost). Open-source hardware is a recent parallel to the open-source software movement: the same values and ideas are present where designs, materials, discussions, and source code are all publicly available.

One of the most successful open-source hardware projects is the Arduino (http://www.arduino.cc), a microcontroller that is relatively easy to interface with, yet extremely powerful and versatile. The Arduino platform has been used by engineers,

hobbyists, and children for a variety of projects including home automation, robots, and art projects. The Arduino platform was originally created to make it easier for non-engineers to build electronics projects. Since its creation, thousands of people have created projects using the Arduino by building their own Arduino board (or one of the dozens of Arduino-compatible boards), or buying kits that interface with an Arduino and include all the parts required to complete a project.

3.2.1 Relevant Online Communities

There are many successful online communities that help individuals share designs, inspiration, and experiences to fuel the open-source movement. Example sites include the Make Magazine Blog (http://blog.makezine.com), Instructables (http://www.instructables.com), and Thingiverse (http://www.thingiverse.com).

The Make Magazine Blog posts interesting projects and news from both professionals and amateurs in the DIY community. Posts are made by members of an editorial staff and who post anything from interesting research innovations, interviews with professional makers, and first time projects. While the blog is curated, it also engages novices through in-post discussions, active forum discussions, and promoting an inclusive community.

Instructables is an online community whose members can easily share how to make anything. This site supports sharing by allowing photo and video uploads and posting step-by-step instructions. Contributors learn from other members who rate their projects or ideas and leave comments that often lead to improvements. Forums and Groups also allow members to engage in specific categories with like-minded people.

Thingiverse is an online community for sharing completed designs and works-in-progress. This website encourages its members to upload all of the digital files required to build anything. For example, Thingiverse hosts all the digital files and information you would need to print a robot on a 3D printer. Thingiverse supports the needs of both expert designers who want to disseminate their work, and novice makers who don't know how to create 3D models, but have access to rapid prototyping tools.

3.3 Prior DIY-AT Projects

3.3.1 Low-Tech Custom-Built Assistive Technology

While we believe that rapid prototyping tools and online communities have the potential to transform custom-built Assistive Technology, there have been successful DIY-AT projects that do not use these modern tools. For individuals living in Third World countries, building their own Assistive Technology may be the only option, since they may not have access to pre-made Assistive Technology or insurance. Werner has developed a guide for community health workers, rehabilitation workers, and families to make Assistive Technology for disabled village children [14]. This guide is sold as a printed book, and is also available freely available online (http://www.hesperian.org). This guide summarizes how to build a wide range of Assistive Technology such as splints and braces out of found materials such as sticks, branches, or cups.

Therese Willkomm is known as "The McGyver" of Assistive Technology, and has written books and given workshops on how to help people solve their own needs. Her solutions are designed to be affordable and use inexpensive and readily available materials such as tapes, adhesives, fasteners, and recycled materials. Her work includes mounting and modifying switches, and creative fastener and padding solutions [15].

Werner and Willkomm's work is tremendously innovative, and has solved important Assistive Technology needs. However, their manufacturing techniques are limited by what can be made without electricity and using found objects. We feel this impacts the items durability, generalizability (i.e. Werner's work is mostly for small children), and aesthetics. These limitations may impact the adoption rate and potential for long-term use solutions. While their work is currently online, we did not find online communities discussing or extending their work.

3.3.2 High-Tech Custom Built-Assistive Technology

Inspired to help a Graffiti artist with Amyotrophic Lateral Sclerosis (ALS) a small team of professional artists and programmers spent two weeks to create an open-source eye-tracking apparatus that lets people draw with only their eyes. This team developed the EyeWriter (http://www.eyewriter.org) a $50 eye tracker that uses a webcam and open-source software. Since its initial development, this project has grown and people all over the world have built their own EyeWriter as both an art tool, and as an inexpensive eye tracker.

The Open Prosthetics Project (http://www.openprosthetics.org) is an open-source collaboration between users, designers, and funders to develop and share prosthetic innovations. This initiative includes several ongoing projects, where all of the design work is openly published online. They encourage end users to provide design ideas and evaluate designs, and mail them products to test. One of their projects is the Trautman Hook Project, to revive a design from 1925, which is no longer commercially produced. This group analyzed the original patents of this device and created 3D models of this hook, and printed them in metal using different rapid prototyping machines. (http://openprosthetics.wikispot.org/Trautman_Hook)

These high-tech projects are lead by professionals, but illustrate the potential for rapid prototyping tools and online communities to create and promote custom-built Assistive Technology.

4. How DIY-AT can Improve the Assistive Technology Adoption Process

In this section, we analyze Rogers' five stages of adoption, and discuss how each stage relates to Assistive Technology adoption, and how online communities or rapid prototyping can help in each stage. We then discuss how the stakeholders involved in the adoption process and the length of this process can impact the adoption of the Assistive Technology.

4.1 Rogers' Five Stages of Adoption

Rogers [9] identified a five-stage adoption process that an individual or group makes for new innovations. The first three stages build up to the individual choosing the innovation, and the last two focus on what happens after it has been adopted. We present each stage and discuss how rapid prototyping and online communities can help individuals adopt the most appropriate Assistive Technology.

1) *Knowledge* (or awareness) of the technology, including basic knowledge of how it functions, and how to operate it. Online communities have made it easier for individuals to learn about new technologies, and websites such as YouTube (http://www.youtube.com) have made it easier to understand how technologies work. In a study of how people search for craft knowledge (a very popular DIY activity) on the Internet, Torrey found that individuals frequented blogs, forums and mailing lists, or relied on their social networks to stay informed [11].

2) *Persuasion* (internal or external) to adopt the technology. Common questions adopters have in the second stage are "What are the technologies' consequences?" and "What will be the advantages/disadvantages for my situation?" Individuals considering new Assistive Technology could greatly benefit from online communities to better understand the technologies and the experiences of others. "When someone who is like us tells us of their positive evaluation of a new idea, we are more often motivated to accept it" [9].

3) *Decision* to adopt, or reject the technology based on information gathered in the previous stages. In this stage, individuals commonly test the technology before making an adoption decision. Some individuals are able to test out Assistive Technology through government-supported lending libraries (such as Pennsylvania's Assistive Technology Lending Library: http://disabilities.temple.edu/programs/assistive/atlend), but these resources do not always have the technology the individual is looking for. Rapid prototyping offers an alternative solution: fast and affordable manufacturing of prototypes a user can interact with to test the technology. For example, an individual could quickly and inexpensively test a hand brace by downloading a design from Thingiverse, print it out of plastic (an inexpensive material) to see if the size and shape are comfortable. If they like it, they could make it out of a more durable material (metal).

Rogers states that the trial of a new technology by a peer or opinion leader can substitute for the adopter using the device him/herself in this stage. Online communities can serve a useful role here because individuals can share stories (and videos) about their experiences. A relatively common practice on YouTube currently involves users making videos while unboxing (unpacking) new technology, or posting short videos (or screenshots) of themselves interacting with it.

4) *Implement* (or test) technology by incorporating it into one's life and putting it to use. While interacting with this technology, the user may find modifications that they want to make to it (a term Rogers calls "re-invention"). He points out that research and development agencies frequently see re-invention as negative (because they know best). However, re-invention is often beneficial for the adopter:

> "Flexibility in the process of adopting an innovation may reduce mistakes and encourage customization of the innovation to fit it more appropriately to local situations or changing conditions. As a result of re-invention, an innovation may be more appropriate in matching an adopter's preexisting problems and more responsive to new problems that arise..." [9]

We see rapid prototyping and online communities playing a large role in this stage by helping individuals identify solutions to problems they have with a technology, learn how to fix them, and engage in re-invention.

5) *Confirmation* that the technology is appropriate (or not), after it has been in use for a significant period of time. During this stage, the individual seeks reinforcement of their decision, and may choose to do so through research or talking with others who have also adopted the technology. The same online communities that apply to the knowledge and persuasion stage can play a positive role here to help individuals decide if a technology is appropriate.

4.2 Stakeholders

Dawe found that many parties (parents, teachers, clinicians, friends, caregivers, and Assistive Technology specialists) can be involved in the different stages of Assistive Technology adoption

[1]. Her work found that having multiple parties involved could lead to tension that creates unintended challenges. We believe that empowering individuals to research and create their own Assistive Technologies may alleviate the challenges caused by having multiple opinionated stakeholders. Furthermore, affordable and rapid production enables individuals to try out more technologies (reducing the burden of having to make only one choice). Additionally, having access to online communities of others who have used, modified, or designed their own technology can provide valuable decision making information.

4.3 Duration of Adoption Process

Currently the time between the decision stage and implementation stage for Assistive Technology can be very long. Our interview participants reported that it took at least a year to get their power wheelchair. This delay can be due to a number of factors, but frequently is due to having to negotiate with insurance companies and other agencies. Dawe cites this delay as a major problem in the adoption process because an individual's needs may have changed (and they may not even need the device) by the time it arrives [1]. DIY-AT can remove these barriers, helping people gain access to the technology they need faster in both the decision and implementation stages of adoption.

5. Future Challenges and Conclusion

5.1 Empowering Novices

A key element to DIY-AT being a success is empowering individuals to share and create Assistive Technology designs. Social websites that let users download open-source designs (such as Thingiverse) enable individuals to share, iterate upon, and discuss designs. While these sites offer a unique way to build a community and distribute designs, they currently do not provide support to help novices customize the designs.

We believe that tools that let novices easily customize pre-existing designs will play a crucial role in the future of DIY-AT. These tools should let users easily make minor changes such as adjusting the dimensions of the design, and also help them make more major changes (such as changing how it interfaces with other technology). In addition to teaching how to use this new technology, we must teach end users how to assess their needs and identify appropriate solutions that match their needs.

5.2 Contributing to Online Communities

In our case studies, we told the story of individuals who had created their own Assistive Technology, but haven't shared their designs with any mainstream communities. Some of the reasons they haven't shared their designs is because they don't know what high-traffic sites to post their work, and feel that they do not have the time to find this community. In order for online communities that support DIY-AT to succeed, they must be easy to contribute to, easily discovered by online search, and be well known within the community.

5.3 Conclusion

This paper has explored the potential of DIY-AT and illustrated how it can increase the adoption rate of Assistive Technology. Our case studies have illustrated that it is possible to custom-build Assistive Technology that is less expensive, and preferred over off-the-shelf solutions. Our interviews with individuals who rely on Assistive Technology show that they have concrete modification ideas that are easily achievable. Additionally, they have an interest in learning how to make modifications on their own and to be involved in the process. We believe that the combination of personal-scale manufacturing and online communities provide a unique opportunity to empower individuals to create their own Assistive Technology that is more likely to be adopted than off-the-shelf solutions.

6. ACKNOWLEDGMENTS

We thank the following people and organizations for their help with this research: UCP Pittsburgh, the students in the Spring 2011 IS698 AT class at UMBC, MakerBot Industries, Adaptive Design Associates, Maryland Technology Assistance Program, Scott Hudson, Jennifer Mankoff, Robert McGuire, Andrew Sears, Heather Markham, Dan Sieworick, and Lisa Anthony.

7. REFERENCES

[1] Assistive Tech Act of 1998, Section 3, http://www.section508.gov/508Awareness/html/at1998.html, accessed: 5/3/2011

[2] Dawe, M. 2006. Desperately seeking simplicity: how young adults with cognitive disabilities and their families adopt assistive technologies. In Proceedings of the SIGCHI conference on Human Factors in computing systems (CHI '06), ACM. 1143--1152.

[3] Hod Lipson, M. K. 2010. Factory @ Home: The Emerging Economy of Personal Manufacturing. Report Commissioned by the Whitehouse Office of Science & Technology Policy.

[4] Kuznetsov, S. and Paulos, E. 2010. Rise of the expert amateur: DIY projects, communities, and cultures. In Proceedings of the Nordic Conference on Human-Computer Interaction (NordiCHI '10), ACM. 295--304.

[5] Lupton, E. 2006. DIY: Design it yourself. Princeton Architectural Press.

[6] Obrist, M. 2008. DIY HCI: Do-It-Yourself Human-Computer Interaction. VDM Verlag Dr. Mueller.

[7] Phillips, B. and Zhao, H. 1993. Predictors of assistive technology abandonment. In Assistive Technology. Taylor & Francis. 5(1): 36--45.

[8] Riemer-Reiss, M. L. and Wacker, R. R. 2000. Factors associated with assistive technology discontinuance among individuals with disabilities. In Journal of Rehabilitation. National Rehabilitation Association. 66(3):44--50.

[9] Rogers, E. M. 1995. Diffusion of Innovations. Free Press.

[10] Scherer, M. J. 1996. Outcomes of assistive technology use on quality of life. In Disability & Rehabilitation. Informa Healthcare. 18(9): 439--448.

[11] Torrey, C., Churchill, E. F., and McDonald, D. W. 2009. Learning how: the search for craft knowledge on the Internet. In Proceedings of the SIGCHI conference on Human Factors in computing systems (CHI '09), ACM. 1371--1380.

[12] US Census Bureau Newsroom: Facts for Features & Special Editions: Facts for Features: 20th Anniversary of Americans with Disabilities Act: July 26, http://www.census.gov/, accessed: 5/3/2011

[13] Von Hippel, E. 2005. Democratizing innovation. The MIT Press.

[14] Werner, D. 1988. Disabled village children. Hesperian Foundation Palo Alto, CA.

[15] Willkomm, T. 2005. Make a Difference Today! Assistive Technology Solutions in Minutes. ATECH Services.

Towards a Framework to Situate Assistive Technology Design in the Context of Culture

Fatima A. Boujarwah, Nazneen, Hwajung Hong, Gregory D. Abowd, Rosa I. Arriaga

School of Interactive Computing, Georgia Institute of Technology

85 5th St NW, Atlanta, GA 30332, USA

{fatima, nazneen, hwajung, abowd, arriaga}@gatech.edu

ABSTRACT

We present the findings from a cross-cultural study of the expectations and perceptions of individuals with autism and other intellectual disabilities (AOID) in Kuwait, Pakistan, South Korea, and the United States. Our findings exposed cultural nuances that have implications for the design of assistive technologies. We develop a framework, based on three themes; 1) lifestyle; 2) socio-technical infrastructure; and 3) monetary and informational resources within which the cultural implications and opportunities for assistive technology were explored. The three key contributions of this work are: 1) the development of a framework that outlines how culture impacts perceptions and expectations of individuals with social and intellectual disabilities; 2) a mapping of how this framework leads to implications and opportunities for assistive technology design; 3) the presentation of concrete examples of how these implications impact the design of three emerging assistive technologies.

Categories and Subject Descriptors

H.1.2 [**User/Machine Systems**]: *Human Factors*

General Terms

Human Factors

Keywords

Assistive Technology, Culture, Autism Spectrum Disorders

1. INTRODUCTION

Our cultures influence the way we perceive the social world. How does culture impact the design of assistive technologies for individuals with social and intellectual disabilities? In particular, what should technology designers understand about culture, and what factors must they take into consideration in their designs? These are questions that we seek to explore in our research.

Our goal is to develop adaptive technologies for individuals with autism. Autism is understood as a spectrum of social and communication disabilities characterized by a triad of differences: difficulties in communication; difficulties in social interaction, and overly focused or repetitive thoughts and behaviors [9]. In our research, we have developed numerous technologies to support a variety of stakeholders linked to autism, but we focus on three particular examples here. The first is a communication system designed to assist young adults in living independently and integrating socially.

The second is an authoring system that uses crowdsourcing to assist in designing interactive social problem-solving scenarios. The third technology is designed to support caregivers in the capture of events of interest in natural settings. We propose that the design of such assistive technologies must be informed by data on the culture of the individual using or being impacted by the technology, since what constitutes appropriate behavior is largely a social construct. In addition, we hypothesize that culture mediates the expectations society has for these individuals. For instance, while living independently is desirable in some cultures, it is not expected, or even acceptable, in others. This is especially important because increases in autism awareness have not occurred uniformly across cultures and societies, and thus these cultural perceptions and expectations will affect the way technologies are adopted.

In this paper, we present the findings of a qualitative study exploring the societal expectations for social and adaptive behaviors for individuals with autism and other intellectual disabilities (referred to as AOID in this document) in four countries: Kuwait, Pakistan, South Korea, and the United States. This study was motivated by the fact that the authors are nationals of these countries. This allowed us the unique opportunity to have the data in each country collected by a native to that culture, and for the data analysis to be done by the multicultural team. This arrangement ensured cultural sensitivity in data collection and data analysis.

Our study indicates that the lifestyle, socio-cultural infrastructure, and monetary and informational resources of each of the four societies were important factors impacting the perceptions and expectations of individuals with AOID in each country. These factors provide a framework within which to frame the design of technologies to support individuals with AOID. There are three key contributions of this work: 1) the development of a framework that outlines how culture impacts perceptions and expectations of individuals with intellectual disabilities; 2) a mapping of how this framework leads to implications and opportunities for assistive technology design; 3) the presentation of concrete examples of how these implications impact the design of three emerging assistive technologies.

This paper is organized as follows: (1) related work from the areas of anthropology, and psychology related to the implications of culture on perceptions of disability, (2) description of our study methodology and data analysis approach, (3) presentation of findings and the resulting framework, (4) implications of these findings on the development of three technologies to support individuals with autism.

2. RELATED WORK

Autism is a phenomenon that has touched the lives of many families around the world, and encompasses individuals with a wide range of needs and abilities [3]. It is considered prevalent in all cultures, races, and social classes [2] and is recognized as being present in at least 80 countries [7]. Researchers have identified a great need for studying autism in the context of culture [7,11]. A significant exploration of autism across cultures is presented in Grinker's *Unstrange Minds* [11], which describes his experiences raising his daughter who has autism in the US and the experiences of families living with autism in South Korea, South Africa and India. He notes that autism may not be a "culture" in and of itself, as some suggest, but instead that the way in which people with autism are understood and integrated into a community can differ radically. This is in line with research that has shown that differences in practices and values across societies, cultures, and the socio-economic strata, lead to variations in the experience of autism [25]. In short, it is important to understand both intra-cultural and inter-cultural factors that impact this experience. We seek to explore these factors in our work.

2.1 Diagnosis and Assessment

Culture influences the ways we understand, classify and address autism [11]. Studies have been conducted that compare two or more cultures along one dimension of autism. For instance, a cross-cultural comparison of sensory behaviors in children with autism and typically developing children in United States and Israel revealed that there were significant differences both between the typically developing children and the children with autism in each country [20]. The authors indicate that it is important that cultural differences are taken into consideration and that culturally sensitive assessments and interventions to address difficulties in sensory modulation in the autism population be developed. The cultural influences on the behavioral symptoms of autism in Kenya and the US have also been investigated [27]. This work shows that significant differences exist between individuals with autism in these two countries in the three core areas of impairment associated with autism; social interactions, communication, and stereotypical behaviors. Similarly, Daley has studied the trajectory from parental recognition of symptoms to receipt of an official diagnosis, and the way different types of specialists understand and deploy diagnostic criteria of autism in India [8]. Her studies provide effective justification for approaches that look at a range of clinical practices both within and across cultures.

Others have found that screening tools designed for one culture's behavior norms, like eye contact, may not be transferable to cultures where it is not appropriate for a child to gaze directly into an adult's face [25]. It is apparent that autism diagnosis is largely dependent on social measures, which in turn are framed by cultural factors. Further, these findings have implications beyond diagnosis and impact the expectations that societies have for individuals with autism throughout their lives. Exploring these expectations is one of the goals of our cross-cultural study.

2.2 Perceptions

Research has also shown that the meaning parents attach to their child's symptoms and their associated beliefs about the causes of symptoms, prognosis, and most appropriate course of care can be described within the context of culture [18]. For instance, researchers found that parents in Japan do not notice social concerns in their children's behavior as readily as parents in western cultures, because social behavior in Japan lends itself more to those behaviors going unnoticed [17]. Perception also impact diagnosis. In South Korea, for example, children with autism are frequently diagnosed with a condition called Reactive Attachment Disorder — often associated with child neglect — and among the Efe pygmies in Central Africa, a child who begins exhibiting autistic behavior is understood to be under attack by the family's ancestors and is sent to another village far away where he will not have contact with blood relatives [11].

Several studies exist exploring how religious practices influence perceptions of autism. Researchers in Kuwait indicate that it is not uncommon for mothers to resort to Allah (God) as a strategy for coping with the stress of caring for a child with a disability [22,1]. This finding is echoed in a study that explores the role of religion in coping in Christian families [23], and in a review of literature on coping strategies used by families of children with autism [18]. Other researchers suggest that in some cultures high levels of functioning are not desired, as people with autism are believed to be closer to the spiritual world [7]. Analogously, the way people view, or appraise, disability is often a function of their cultural values. For example, some Latino mothers view having a child with a severe disability as a way for the mother to sacrifice part of her life and to receive opportunities and blessings or less frequently, as a punishment from God [4]. Similar viewpoints may be common among other cultural, ethnic, or religious groups [17]. In this paper we present findings from Kuwait, South Korea, Pakistan and the US related to perceptions of autism and the influence of religion on these perceptions.

2.3 Education and Services

In a study of educators in selected inclusive education classrooms at sites in the United States and South Korea [14], researchers have examined how educators view the meaning of autism, and how they construct communication and interpret unconventional or undesirable behaviors through interactions with students with autism. It was found that the social requirements and interpretation of communication and behaviors differ between the individualist-oriented culture of the U.S. and a more collectivist-oriented culture of South Korea. In addition to studying individual cultures, researchers have explored multicultural issues in autism and argue that students with autism with multicultural backgrounds are challenged on at least four dimensions: communication, social skills, behavioral repertoires, and culture [10]. This work explored multicultural perspectives on teaching students with autism and present culture-specific strategies for meeting the educational needs of students with autism. Finally, research has shown that eco-cultural approaches that incorporate the components of a family's social and cultural environment create 'best fit' interventions and services that have higher efficacy and that families are more likely to comply with [19,5]. Understanding the educational approaches used, and the availability and appropriateness of services, was an important motivating factor for the work presented in this paper

3. STUDY DESIGN

Based on this literature review, and our personal experiences, we propose that the design of assistive technologies for individuals with AOID must be informed by data on the culture of the individual using or being impacted by the technology. Furthermore, we hypothesize that culture mediates the expectations society has for these individuals. Following is a description of the study we conducted to explore these notions.

3.1 Data Collection

The first phase of data collection began in 2009. To date, data has been collected from 107 participants at four sites: Atlanta, GA, Kuwait, Lahore, Pakistan, and Seoul, South Korea. The majority of the participants were parents and teachers, but others included administrators, speech language pathologists, psychologists, counselors, and therapists who interact regularly with individuals with AOID (table 1). We recruited participants by word-of-mouth, and chose to expand recruitment beyond only those who work with children with autism because autism diagnoses are not given consistently across these four societies. We have also begun to interview individuals with AOID, but we believe that data merits separate analysis. Also, we realize that there is an imbalance in the distribution of participants across cultures; however, we were able to interact with at least one participant from each category in each country. In the future we intend to equalize this data.

Table 1. Participant Information

	Kuwait	Pakistan	South Korea	U.S
Parents	6	4	3	14
Teachers	10	7	3	17
Therapists	4	2	1	8
Administrators	8	7	3	10
Total (99)	28	20	10	49

The research was conducted at special needs schools, activity and vocational centers, group homes, autism centers, and adult social skills and special interest groups in each country. A researcher who is native to the culture visited each of the research locations and collected the data via direct participatory observation and contextual inquiry. Researchers began by observing educational sessions, social skills practice, and other activities that make up the daily routines of the participants. Each observation session lasted at least two hours, and each site was observed on at least two separate occasions. Throughout these observations detailed field notes were taken that included photographs.

Semi-structured interviews were also conducted with participants in all four countries. Each interview was audio recoded and varied in length from 40 to 70 minutes. Two classes of questions were asked; 1) individual level, and 2) society level. Individual level questions included questions about the child's life in general, as well as information about their verbal abilities and level of functioning. Specific questions were asked about the social skills that are required to be successful in each culture. We also asked participants to describe their current instructional practices for social skills, life skills, and vocational skills. Throughout the interviews we focused on understanding the participants' motivations and practices in their cultural context, in an attempt to identify the impact of their culture on their perception and expectation of socially adaptive behaviors. Society level questions included inquiries related to information gathering practices, technology use, services available, and funding sources. We concluded the interviews by asking the participant what their long-term goal was for their child or students. Most of the research was conducted in-person, but six of the interviews were conducted over the phone. To compensate for this difference, participants who were interviewed over the phone were asked additional questions and provided pictures and other media to enable us to better understand their practices.

3.2 Data Analysis

A researcher who is a native and fluent in the local language collected the data at each of the sites. This allowed for the flexibility of interacting with the participants in the language they felt most comfortable in. This led for data to be collected in English in the US, Korean in South Korea, Arabic and English in Kuwait, and Urdu and English in Pakistan. This data was then translated, and all analysis was done in English.

We used an inductive thematic approach to identify and develop emergent themes. These themes create a framework that outlines the cultural aspects that define the expectations of individuals with AOID and the environments that they must navigate in order to be successful. We drew on analysis techniques described in the *Grounded Theory* approach [21] as it provides a helpful structure for coding the raw transcripts, and a means by which the categories formulated during *open coding* could be developed into richer explanations of the cultural influences on individuals with AOID.

Using an *open coding* approach, three researchers worked together to label instances that were deemed relevant to the lives of individuals with AOID. This inductive process led to seven categories - family structures, linguistic environment, religion, technology and civic infrastructure, programs and services, monetary concerns, and informational resources. Affinity diagrams were also created to help us better understand the relationship between the categories.

Axial and selective coding was then used to develop the explanations of each category further. The categories were connected to other concepts following the methods describing causal, contextual and intervening relationships. This process elicited a variety of patterns; each of which we returned to the original transcript and field notes, to find evidence that confirmed or rejected it. This enabled us to identify three central phenomena that encompass all seven categories: **lifestyle**, **socio-technical infrastructure**, and **monetary and informational resources**. This hierarchy of concepts creates a framework within which the cultural implications and opportunities for technology can be explored. Following is a detailed description of our findings.

4. FINDINGS

The process described above lead to the development of a framework that allows us to provide a cultural lens onto the AOID communities in the four countries that were studied. This framework may help members of society understand ways they can support these individuals in a greater context, and in particular, with respect to technology design and development.

4.1 Lifestyle

Lifestyle has been defined as *"the distinctive pattern of personal or social behavior characteristic of an individual or a group"*[24]. Through our data analysis, three categories emerged that fall under the umbrella of lifestyle. These are family structure, linguistic environment, and religion.

4.1.1 Family Structure

Family structure, size, and expected family member roles significantly influence the daily routines of individuals with AOID. We found that family size impacts the distribution of care giving responsibilities, in that it is shared across the family members. In Kuwait and Pakistan the tendency towards large cohabiting families makes it such that care giving and decision-making responsibilities are shared. For example, several parents mentioned that grandparents often had the final say in what treatments and services the child received.

The perception of the desirability of living independently also varied drastically across the four cultures. While participants in the United States reported that independent living is seen as a mandatory part of growing up and living a successful life, this was not the case in the data from Kuwait and Pakistan. In these two cultures it is common practice for all children to remain in the family home even after they are married. Indeed, moving out is sometimes perceived as unacceptable. Participants from South Korea appeared to have a more flexible attitude towards the importance of independent living. They reported that the individual situation of the person was the deciding factor, such as whether they are they financially stable or whether they just had a child and need help.

In Pakistan and Kuwait, hired help, such as nannies and drivers, often also support the care of children. This simplifies the coordination that parents are required to orchestrate. We found that in South Korea and the United States parents sometimes struggle to coordinate their daily schedule. Korean mothers indicated that they take on most of these; arranging for things like school and therapy drop-off and pick-up. A Korean teacher reported that at least two mothers she knew were not able to keep their jobs as a result of how demanding both their schedule coordination and housework responsibilities were. American mothers also stressed the difficulties they faced in organizing and providing care for their child.

4.1.2 Linguistic environment

In general, children spend most of their time with their families at home or with teachers at school. We found that the use of language greatly influences not only casual social interactions but also education. Each of the countries studied had at least one official language. In addition, we found that in many instances, other languages are informally introduced into an individual's everyday life. Participants in South Korea and the United States reported that, for the most part, their children were exposed to monolingual environments. This was not the case in Pakistan and Kuwait, however. Most Kuwaitis and Pakistanis speak the local language at home and in the community (Arabic and Urdu respectively), but most special needs schools in these countries use English language curriculums. In addition, in Kuwait teachers who teach the English curriculums are not always native speakers of English. One parent indicated, for instance, that they believe that their child had not progressed as much this year at school because his teacher's English was difficult for him to understand.

In Kuwait, the language demands on the individual are further compounded by the fact that many nannies in Kuwait are neither native Arabic nor fluent English speakers, and instead speak a third language. Similarly, in Pakistan, despite using educational materials that are in English, informal interactions at school are mostly conducted in Urdu because many teachers are not fluent speakers of English. Both parents and teachers reported that this inconsistency of language use compounds the communication difficulties many individuals with AOID already struggle with. These findings are similar to those reported for children with AOID with a multicultural backgrounds [10].

4.1.3 Religion

In Kuwait and Pakistan religion plays an important role in defining lifestyle. For instance, many schools cater to religious restrictions arising from a perceived Islamic way of life. Participants from a school in Kuwait reported that they segregated male and female students to classrooms on different floors in the school building, to encourage parents to allow their children to attend the school. Several teachers, in both Pakistan and Kuwait, also reported that they tried to use religion as a means to teach (despite some teachers not being Muslim), in order to relate to the child, and bridge the gap between what they were learning at school and at home. For example, in Kuwait, a Canadian teacher at a special needs school indicated that he was reading and studying the Quran in order to draw lessons from it to use with his students. In addition, religion appeared to play a role in even the simplest activities, like artwork done at school, and music classes.

Participants from both societies also indicated that in many cases, adherence to religious norms was enforced with the individual with AOID (e.g. girls made to wear a head scarf, children expected pray five times daily), and these religious practices were taught as life skills, even though the individual did not always understand the motivation behind them. Lastly, our interactions with the parent participants lead us to conclude that sometimes faith leads to complacency. When asked about their goals for their child, our findings were similar to those of researchers studying Indian culture [7], as several of the parents indicated, "it is in God's hands." Many Muslims believe that individuals with special needs are blessed (guaranteed entrance to heaven) and that the goal should be to keep them happy and healthy. This is in sharp contrast to the US where it is expected that individuals with AOID should be encouraged to achieve their potential.

The role of religion that emerged in the United States and South Korea was drastically different. Despite the fact that in both societies faith-based schools are not uncommon, participants reported that religion played a minimal role in the educational and clinical services for individuals with AOID. In both societies, public schools and most therapeutic centers strive to remain secular. In the US, the population is very diverse, and several participants indicated the importance of respecting parents' and children's personal beliefs while not making them a central part of the educational or clinical services being delivered. For instance, a psychologist at an autism center in the US who's specialty is sexual health and education, indicated the importance of customizing interventions such that they adhere to the child's religious and moral values.

4.1.4 Summary

Family structure, linguistic environment, and religion emerged as important cultural factors influencing the perceptions and expectations of individuals with AOID. We found that the level of support provided to individuals with AOID and their caregivers varies based on family structure. The data also suggested that language demands on individuals with AOID may compound communication difficulties. Lastly, it was seen that the impact of religion varies across the four countries, from marginal to dominating most aspects of everyday life. For these reasons, we believe there are opportunities for technology to help balance support across cultures for individuals with AOID and their caregivers, including such tasks as facilitating coordination. There are also opportunities for technology to be used to promote linguistic consistency in the child's interactions. Finally, it is important for technology to adapt appropriately to reflect the role of religion in the life of the individual. This includes respecting boundaries of appropriate behavior, and understanding how religious morals and values are incorporated into practices, and in turn how they should be considered into the design of technology.

4.2 Socio-Technical Infrastructure

As a member of a community, activities an individual engages in are socially situated. In other words, activities cannot be isolated from the context in which they are occurring. Artifacts, including available tools and large-scale systems such as technologies and civic infrastructure, construct this context. In addition, the milieu, which refers to the individual, caregivers, friends, neighbors and other community members and the home, school and other social settings all frame the social environment of the individual. In our study, we found that an individuals' level of functioning was measured by their ability to perform adaptive activities by making use of technological and social infrastructure. Our data indicated that each country had varying levels of infrastructure development, which affected the individual's activities and goals.

4.2.1 Technology and Civic infrastructure

The importance of knowing how to use the Internet in order to live independently and obtain employment was a notable example of how technology adaptation could influence the individual's goals. It was apparent that having computer skills and other relevant simple technology competency is important across all four cultures. The need for these skills was largely dependent on the existence of advanced technology infrastructure and the level of access the average person had to the technology. The development of this infrastructure in Pakistan has not occurred as quickly as in the other three countries, therefore the importance of these skills was less emphasized.

In addition, in the United States and South Korea a great deal of educational material has been transferred to an interactive medium. Thus, to access the material, individuals need to understand how to use a computer. In these two countries, many modern jobs require proficient computer skills. To aid in the acquisition of these skills, participants in South Korea indicated that training courses were offered to recent graduates seeking employment to aid in learning to use the Internet, mobile phones, and other ubiquitous technologies. In all four countries job opportunities are directly proportional to level of technical competency. For this reason, our findings lead to the conclusion that the level of independence of the individual is closely related to his or her ability to understand and use technologies, though how much so is dependent on the level of technological development of the country.

We found that besides technology civic infrastructure also impacts the skills an individual needs to be successful. Public transportation systems are an example of complex large-scale civic infrastructures found in modern society [6]. Due to higher centralization of resources to the city, South Korean families tend to move to the capital for better education. This has caused high traffic in the city area that makes the use of public transportation essential. All South Korean parents and teachers indicated that they wanted their children and students to learn to navigate the public transportation system, in order to develop the ability live more independently. The teachers explained that a special curriculum exists to address these skills. It includes practice scenarios to teach students a variety of skills associated with transportation. These range from getting a ticket from a kiosk, to planning their route, and getting off the bus when they get to their destination. The curriculum also addresses relevant social skills, such as how to ask for helps if you get lost.

Despite parents and teachers in South Korea emphasizing the importance of understanding the public transportation system to an individuals' independence, participants we interacted with in the United States did not mention these skills. We believe that this is due to the fact that the transportation system in the metropolitan city in which our participants reside is not convenient. Instead, participants in the United States stated that learning to drive was important, but very difficult, and often not feasible for certain individuals. This lead to difficulties in scheduling for parents, as it becomes necessary for them to provide all transportation. In Pakistan and Kuwait issues of transportation did not arise as concerns for teachers or parents. This was because in both of these countries it is easy and affordable to obtain hired help (i.e. a driver

or a taxi) and there are often other family members around that can provide the individual with transportation.

4.2.2 Programs and services

Community-based activities and services, which arise from grass-root efforts by community members, are an important part of the lives of individuals with AOID. For example, South Korean teachers organized practice sessions where individuals could go through the steps of taking a bus to come to school. Community members like the bus driver, ticket salesperson, and bookstore clerk near the bus stop where the individual was supposed get off were notified about the rehearsal in advance and asked to help if the individual had any trouble. In this way, individuals were able to acquire a set of contextualized skills.

Participants from other countries also reported similar activities. For example, in the United States, we attended weekly social group meetings for adults with autism in which individuals on the spectrum and neurotypical volunteers meet to engage in fun social activities like bowling. This affords the individual with autism the opportunity to socialize in a real, but low stress environment. In Kuwait, one of our participants (a therapist) explained that she hosted teatime for girls with AOID every week. During these meetings the girls would practice the social skills necessary to interact with other women in a culturally appropriate manner, and share their experiences. Many of our participants explained that they believe that the existence of supportive community members is a key factor in the design social and life skills curriculums.

Examples of many additional services arose. In South Korea and the United States participants acknowledged the importance of the family that lives with the individual, and the challenges associated with the care of an individual with AOID. For this reason, in both societies family counseling services are available. In Kuwait and Pakistan, parents often receive this support from family members, rather than counseling services. In addition, a variety of extracurricular activities exist for individuals with AOID in all four countries. These range from Special Olympics (all four), and Challenger Little League Baseball Leagues (United States and Kuwait) to sensory friendly movie screenings (United States) and Rock Climbing (South Korea).

Lastly, curriculum development for academic programs arose as an important differing point between countries. In Kuwait, we found that most special need schools use American, Canadian or British curriculums. This fact makes it such that often, the content of the curriculums is foreign to the students, as they cannot relate to it. This is not the case in Pakistan, Korea and United States, where curriculums are developed locally. Furthermore, in Korea and the United States our data showed that multiple curriculums are often available, and attempts are made to customize them according to the student's abilities.

4.2.3 Summary

As hypothesized, we found that the expectations and goals for individuals with AOID varied depending on the socio-technological system in their immediate environment, as some societies may require individuals to acquire more complex skills in order to be successful and independent. The data in this section also suggests that in all four countries efforts are being made at the community level to support individuals with AOID. There is a need, however, to facilitate collaboration among community members, and to aid in the process of customizing curriculums for particular individuals and cultures. We believe that there are ways that technology can help promote collaboration among interested stakeholders, and facilitate the customization of curriculums adopted from other cultures. There are also opportunities for technology to facilitate the acquisition of complex skills and to help individuals with AOID to live more independently.

4.3 Monetary and Informational Resources

4.3.1 Monetary Concerns

In our work, monetary concerns refer to socio-economic status and the availability of funding sources. In Kuwait the majority of the population is financially stable. Many of our participants indicated having paid out of pocket to travel to the United States or Europe to seek assessment and diagnostic services, and treatments. In addition, we learned that the government funds special education for all nationals. However, non-nationals, which make up half of the population, often struggle to fund education and services. We found that there is great variation in financial status of the population in the other three countries. This leads to the polarization of educational opportunities. Participants indicated that many special needs schools and services in Pakistan, South Korea, and the Unites States are very expensive and only the wealthy can afford to pay for them.

In Pakistan, teachers indicated that schools are often in need of funding for supplies due to limited government monetary resources. For this reason, donations from affluent locals are a key source of funding. In one of the schools we observed that the fee structure varied from child to child, in that the parents were charged a fee equivalent to what the child's siblings who attended mainstream schools had to pay.

In Korea teachers indicated putting a great deal of effort towards working on proposals to raise funding. Providing high quality services was very important to them, and this tended to increase the overall cost of education. Participants in the United States also indicated that they are often in need of funding to purchase materials. This money is generally obtained from parents and fundraising in the community.

4.3.2 Informational Resources

In this section we discuss data related to both global and local information gathering of informational resources. Each culture has their own unique way of gathering and sharing the resources used to support individuals with AOID. In Kuwait schools adopt programs from abroad, and Google, Yahoo! Groups and other sites are commonly used for information gathering. This information is then adapted for use locally. In Pakistan Internet accessibility is not as ubiquitous, instead alternative media (e.g. TV programming) and information sessions given by experts are important sources of information. Our data from the United States and South Korea showed that numerous local organizations exist where interested parties meet to share ideas; these include universities and autism centers. In addition, in all four countries local workshops are conducted to keep caregivers informed. These venues provide stakeholders in the community with opportunities to meet and share information. In the United States, in particular, various specialized conferences provide a good source of information.

4.3.3 Summary

We found that socio-economic status and levels of government support leads to polarization in access to services. We also learned that there is great interest in sharing information across the cultures and efforts are made in each country towards the localization and customization of resources. These findings imply that there is a need to provide inexpensive technology that can make use of existing infrastructure to provide services in a more affordable and equitable way. Further, there are ways for technology to ease knowledge sharing and support activism.

5. Implications for Technology Design

Work has been done in identify ways in which the disability studies influence the field of assistive technologies [16]. These researchers indicate that there is a need for work that can connect culture to the use of technology. Our work begins to address this need. In particular, our findings provide a framework within which technology developed for individuals with AOID can be connected with culture.

Great cultural differences exist across the four societies that were studied. The three themes discussed in the previous section provided a framework within which it was possible to understand the nuances present in each of these cultures. In addition to helping members of society understand ways in which they can support these individuals in a greater context, these nuances have implications for the design of technologies and services for individuals with AOID in these societies. Following is a discussion in which we provide a cultural lens onto three technologies developed for individuals with autism. These technologies are impacted by these implications because they address such culturally dependent factors as; life skills and independent living goals, social skills, and data collection in the home environment.

5.1 Supporting Independent Living and Social Integration

As children with autism mature into adults concerns arise as to how this individuals will become integrated into society whether through going to college or getting a job. Regardless of culture, participants addressed the need for services that help them achieve these milestones.

We are developing a prototype that is connected to an online social network service (SNS) to help adolescents practice daily living skills. When an individual feels the need to ask for advice relevant to what he or she is doing at home, the system provides an opportunity to send questions to a trusted set of family, friends, and professionals and receive advice from them via the SNS. This solution may support parents who have been overwhelmed by the responsibility of supervising and supporting their children and facilitate intensive coordination. Thus, the online system will enable the distribution of labor related to caregiving across a set of people who already exists in the individual's real social environment (e.g. grandparents and other relatives in Pakistan and Kuwait or neighbors in South Korea). The individual with autism will also have access to support at any time from anywhere.

Facilitating the process of making life skills related inquiries in a semi-closed online community benefits not only caregivers in terms of distributing responsibility, but also the individuals with autism, by enabling them to get quick feedback. Inevitably such a system may raise concerns about trust and privacy. Knowledge of regulations that are specific to this population is required to answer the following questions. Who has the authority to control membership in the trusted network? Who do individuals with AOID feel comfortable asking for help? What if questions or advice related to matters that are inappropriately personal are disclosed? The relationship and trust level between the individuals and people in their social environment cannot be generalized. As our data showed, relationships with family members and individuals in the community vary greatly across cultures. For this reason, policies related to privacy must be culturally sensitive.

The expected level of independence also varied across cultures. The prevalence of hired help in Pakistan and Kuwait alleviates many concerns regarding the acquisition of basic life skills such as those related to household chores and transportation. However, performing daily living tasks is necessary for young adults who move away from home. Money and time management are significantly important as well. Further, more sophisticated life skills—understanding social norms (*e.g. etiquette, taboos*)—are crucial in enabling the individual to integrate into the social world smoothly. The data we collected implied a number of those social norms are closely related to spirituality in Islamic cultures, but are veiled as hidden rules. To ensure the individual receives culturally contextualized feedback, we carefully design a verification system into the registration process that selectively allows for enrolling trusted people who understand the individual's culture. For those whom want to give advice, but are unfamiliar with the social norms (e.g. a foreign teacher or relatives living in another country), the SNS can function as a repository of social rules that collects feedback from verified members and categorizes them, providing guidelines to ensure the appropriateness of the advice.

To support the contextualization of advice for an individual, one approach is to share a picture of the problematic moments and the day's calendar of events that shows what the individual has on their schedule. This disclosure may conflict with perceptions of appropriate behavior in some cultures. For example, sharing pictures with anyone besides immediate relatives is not encouraged in Islamic culture, especially for women. Our work, and that of others [29] indicates, that out of respect for cultural conventions and spirituality, the design of technology should be framed by the religious and cultural values of the proposed user.

5.2 Supporting the Acquisition of Social Problem-Solving Skills

We are developing software to help non-expert authors (i.e. individuals who have little or no experience teaching social skills) to create customized social problem-solving skills instructional modules. These modules are designed to help an individual with autism prepare for a particular social context by presenting them with a social situation in which an unexpected obstacle arises, and guiding them through the process of overcoming the obstacle. It is obvious that, in the real world, many complex social situations exist in which a vast number of obstacles can arise, and each of these obstacles can be overcome in a variety of different ways. Each of these is culturally dependent; the situations, the obstacles, and the appropriate solutions. For this reason, it is crucial that the authoring tool be flexible enough to allow for the incorporation of cultural variations.

When designing software to support the acquisition of social problem-solving skills, it is imperative to understand the social context that the individual must navigate. Our data confirmed that what is seen as appropriate behavior is largely a social construct. The study also provided insight into the different cultural factors that must be considered—such as linguistic environment, religious values, and the social environment in which the individual must succeed to name a few. For instance, who you are expected to ask for help differs across cultures (e.g. mother, aunt, cousin, etc), and learning how to ask for help and what to ask is an important social problem-solving skill.

Our approach enables the author to customize the modules for their child, thereby allowing them to incorporate culture appropriately. However, the technology also uses crowdsourcing techniques to support and guide the author as they create the modules. Crowdsourcing is defined as *"the act of outsourcing a task to an undefined (and generally large) network of people in the form of an open call."* [13] As such it is important that several measures be taken to insure that the data that is collected addresses the important cultural factors. For example, it is necessary to determine the cultural perspective of the laborers responding to the open call. One way to do this would be to explicitly ask culturally related questions as part of the task (e.g. what language do you speak at home?). In addition, language is not the only determining factor of cultural variations. It may be necessary to include means by which to determine the cultural biases of the respondent. This may be done by asking additional culturally sensitive questions that will enable us to understand the respondent's cultural background without explicitly asking for it. Measures such as these will be very important in ensuring the cultural sensitivity of such a crowd-based system.

The tool could enable individuals to receive social skills instruction even if it may not otherwise have access to it because they cannot afford it or it is not available. As such, it addresses one of the other needs that emerged in our findings; the need for inexpensive technology that makes use of existing infrastructure to provide services in a more affordable and equitable way.

5.3 Facilitating the Capture of Problem Behaviors

Children with autism sometimes engage in problem behaviors such as tantrums, biting, and other potentially self-injurious or aggressive behaviors. Behavior assessments used to begin to address these behaviors generally have a long turnaround time. A single limiting factor is the enormous manpower that is required to observe the child in his or her natural environment. As a result, many times treatments must be determined based on parent report, instead of direct observation. Smart video recording technology can significantly reduce this turnaround time. Researchers have developed a new approach to recording called Selective Archiving [12], which, instead of continuously recording, only captures the event of interest when implicitly or explicitly triggered.

In large cohabitating families like those found in Kuwait and Pakistan this technology can be put to use very effectively. There is a wider care giving circle that can make use of the technology to capture videos of the individual with autism exhibiting problematic behaviors. These videos can then be used by a behavior analyst to make an assessment more quickly. In smaller nuclear families like those found in Korea and the United States, with both parents working, extensive use of this technology is limited. Making this technology "smarter" via automatic recognition of problem behaviors, taking the human out of the loop, can alleviate this problem.

As with any video recording, privacy is a major concern. There is no environment in which culture plays a more critical role than the home. People in all cultures have reservations towards the idea of recordings of them being captured in their home, which is generally a private environment. Some cultures, however, are more sensitive to the issue. In Kuwait and Pakistan, some religiously conservative families may not allow video recording at all and others may allow it subject to the condition that no female member of the family can be seen on the video. Civil law may also effect the adoption of technology. For instance, parents in the US are hyperaware of being perceived as being abusive to their children. Further, if a researcher in the US witnesses behavior that could be considered as child abuse then they are obligated by the law to report the abuse without the need to inform the parents. Though all 4 countries have strict child abuse laws, US society tends to be more vigilant than the other three countries. Therefore, having their activities recorded at home would have different implications in the US. In addition to limiting the capture of data, attitudes towards sharing recorded videos also differs across cultures. For these reasons, it is imperative that the design of such captures systems is informed by information about the privacy practices, and general cultural values of the particular family by which it will be used.

6. CONCLUSION

Our research in technology and autism, and our personal experiences motivated us to study the expectations and perceptions of individuals with autism and other intellectual disabilities (AOID) in Kuwait, Pakistan, South Korea, and the United States. As hypothesized, this study exposed cultural nuances that have implications for technology development. Our findings allowed us to develop a framework, within which the cultural implications and opportunities for technology were explored. We believe this work can be expanded into a broader framework for developers of assistive technologies to use to situate their technologies in the cultural context.

7. ACKNOWLEDGMENTS

Blank for blind review.

8. REFERENCES

[1] Al-Kandari, H. and Al-Qashan, H. Maternal Self-Efficacy of Mothers of Children with Intellectual Developmental Disabilities, Down Syndrome, and Autism in Kuwait Child and Adolescent Social Work Journal, 27(1), 21-39. 2009.

[2] Autism Society of America. What is autism? Advocate: The newsletter of the Autism Society of America, 33, 3. 2000.

[3] Baron-Cohen, S. Autism and Asperger's Syndrome. Oxford University Press, 160. September 2008.

[4] Blacher, J. and McIntyre, L.L. Syndrome Specificity and Behavioral Disorders in Young Adults with Intellectual Disability: Cultural Differences in Family Impact. Journal of Intellectual Disability Research, 50(3), 184-198. 1999.

[5] Brookman-Franzee, L. Using Parent/Clinician Partnerships in Parent Education Programs for Children with Autism. Journal of Positive Behaviour Interventions, 6(4), 195-231. 2004.

[6] Carmien, S., DePaula, R., Gorman, A., & Kintsch, A. Increasing Workplace Independence for People with Cognitive Disabilities by Leveraging Distributed Cognition Among Caregivers and Clients. Proceedings of GROUP 2003.

[7] Daley, T. C. The Need for Cross-cultural Research on Pervasive Developmental Disorders, Transcultural Psychiatry 39(4): 531-550. 2002.

[8] Daley, T.C. and Sigman, M.D, Diagnostic Conceptualization of Autism Among Indian Psychiatrists, Psychologists, and Pediatricians. Journal of Autism and Developmental Disorders, 32(1). 2002.

[9] Diagnostic and Statistical Manual of Mental Disorders DSM-IV-TR Fourth Edition, American Psychiatric. Assoc. 2000.

[10] Dyches, T. T., Wilder, L. K., Sudweeks, R. R., Obiakor, F. E., and Algozzine, B. Multicultural Issues in Autism. Journal of Autism and Developmental Disorders, 34, 211-222. 2004.

[11] Grinker, R.R. Unstrange Minds: Remapping the World of Autism. New York: Basic Books. 2007.

[12] Hayes, G.R., Gardere, L.M., Abowd, G.D., Truong, K. CareLog: A Selective Archiving Tool for Behavior Management in Schools, Proceedings of CHI 2008.

[13] Howe, J. The Rise of Crowdsourcing. WIRED Magazine, (14.06), 2006, last accessed 12/29/2010.

[14] Kim, K. Constructions and Reconstructions of Autism: Teachers' Perspectives at Selected American and South Korean Inclusive Education Sites. Syracuse University. 2008.

[15] Mandell, D.S. and Novak, M. The Role of Culture in Families' Treatment Decisions for Children with Autism Spectrum Disorders. Mental Retardation and Developmental Disabilities Research Reviews, 11, 110-115. 2005.

[16] Mankoff, J., Hayes, G., & Kasnitz, D. Disability Studies as a Source of Critical Inquiry for the Field of Assistive Technology. In Proceedings of ASSETS '10. 1-8. 2010.

[17] Marshall, E.S, Olsen, S.F, Mandleco, B.L, Dyches, T.T, Allred, K.W, Sansom, N. "This is a Spiritual Experience": perspectives of Latter-Day Saint families living with a child with disabilities. Qual Health Res. 2003.

[18] Meadan, H. Halle, J.W., Ebata, and Aaron, T. Families with Children who have Autism Spectrum Disorders: Stress and Support. Exceptional Children, 77(1). 2010.

[19] Moes, D. and Frea, W. Contextualized Behavioral Support in Early Intervention for Children with Autism and Their Families. Journal of Autism & Developmental Disorders, 32(6), 519. 2002.

[20] Schaaf, R., Caron, K., Gal, E., and Benevides, T. Cross-Cultural Comparison of Sensory Responses in Children With and Without Autism Spectrum Disorder. World Fedaration of Occupational Therapists Conference, 2010.

[21] Strauss, A. and Juliet, C. Basics of Qualitative Research: Techniques and Procedures for Developing Grounded Theory. Sage Publications, Inc, Thousand Oaks, CA, 1998.

[22] Taleb, M. and Al Khandari, M. Parenting an Autistic Child in Kuwait: Kuwaiti mothers' Voice and Experiences with Children Labeled Autistic. Syracuse University. 2006.

[23] Tarekeshwar, N. and Pargament, K. Religious Coping in Families of Children with Autism. Focus on Autism and Other Developmental Disabilities. 16(4). 2001.

[24] Veal, A. J. The concept of lifestyle: A review. Leisure Studies, 12 (4), 233-252. 1993.

[25] Wallis, K. and Pinto-Martin, J, The Challenge of Screening for Autism Spectrum Disorder in a Culturally Diverse Society. Acta Pediatrica, 97, 539-540. 2008.

[26] Wakabayashi A, Baron-Cohen S, Uchiyama T, Yoshida Y, Tojo Y, Kuroda M, and Wheelwright S. The Autism-Spectrum Quotient (AQ) Children's Version in Japan: A Cross-cultural Comparison. Journal of Autism and Developmental Disorders, 37, 491-500. 1995.

[27] Weru, J. W. Cultural Influences on the Behavioral Symptoms of Autism in Kenya and the United States of America, University of Texas. 2005.

[28] Wyche, S. P., Caine, K. E., Davison, B. K., Patel, S. N., Arteaga, M., & Grinter, R. E. (2009). Sacred Imagery in Techno-Spiritual Design. Proceedings of CHI 2009.

Supporting Spatial Awareness and Independent Wayfinding for Pedestrians with Visual Impairments

Rayoung Yang, Sangmi Park, Sonali R. Mishra, Zhenan Hong,
Clint Newsom, Hyeon Joo, Erik Hofer, Mark W. Newman
School of Information, University of Michigan
Ann Arbor, MI 48109, USA
{rayang, sangmipa, srmishra, guoerhzn, newsomc, thejoo, ehofer, mwnewman} @ umich.edu

ABSTRACT

Much of the information designed to help people navigate the built environment is conveyed through visual channels, which means it is not accessible to people with visual impairments. Due to this limitation, travelers with visual impairments often have difficulty navigating and discovering locations in unfamiliar environments, which reduces their sense of independence with respect to traveling by foot. In this paper, we examine how mobile location-based computing systems can be used to increase the feeling of independence in travelers with visual impairments. A set of formative interviews with people with visual impairments showed that increasing one's general spatial awareness is the key to greater independence. This insight guided the design of Talking Points 3 (TP3), a mobile location-aware system for people with visual impairments that seeks to increase the legibility of the environment for its users in order to facilitate navigating to desired locations, exploration, serendipitous discovery, and improvisation. We conducted studies with eight legally blind participants in three campus buildings in order to explore how and to what extent TP3 helps promote spatial awareness for its users. The results shed light on how TP3 helped users find destinations in unfamiliar environments, but also allowed them to discover new points of interest, improvise solutions to problems encountered, develop personalized strategies for navigating, and, in general, enjoy a greater sense of independence.

Categories and Subject Descriptors

H.5.2 [**Information Interfaces and Presentation**]: User Interfaces – *User-centered design*; K.4.2 [**Computers and Society**]: Social Issues – Assistive technologies for persons with disabilities

General Terms

Design, Human Factors

Keywords

Accessibility, Spatial Awareness, Wayfinding, Mobile Computing

1. INTRODUCTION

Pedestrians with visual impairments miss out on a great deal of information about their immediate environment that sighted individuals may take for granted. While many are adept at compensating for missed information through increased awareness of other environmental cues [14] and the use of navigational aids, both low-tech (e.g., white canes or guide dogs) and high-tech (e.g., GPS devices or electronic obstacle avoidance systems), there are still many situations in which individuals with visual impairments are not able to travel as independently as they would like. For individuals with visual impairments, traveling to a new environment can be a particularly challenging experience. As a result, when travelers with visual impairments seek out unfamiliar destinations, they often need to plan ahead extensively in order to obtain and memorize directions, and many seek assistance from others—including friends, family members, and professional mobility trainers—in order to familiarize themselves with an unknown place. Even when traveling somewhat familiar routes, it can be challenging to handle unforeseen needs that arise during a journey, such as finding food, drink, or a toilet. In essence, each new need can require the mastery of an additional route, and it can be difficult to anticipate all the routes one might need to know in advance. Additionally, travelers may miss the chance to serendipitously discover new information about their environments, such as new points of interest, and special events.

Based on the insights derived from formative interviews [19], we designed a system that would provide greater independence for travelers with visual impairments by increasing their awareness of aspects of their immediate environment. In particular, we sought to leverage the potential of location-based mobile computing technology in order to add a layer of "legibility" to the environment that would help foster greater spatial awareness, which would in turn help with wayfinding activities, including both task-oriented and exploratory traveling. By focusing on spatial awareness rather than efficiently directing users to their destinations, our approach differs from the bulk of prior work in this area. Our view is that placing the user in control of the information accessed and encouraging them to explore information about locations not directly linked to a particular navigational goal will help foster a greater sense of spatial awareness while also allowing users to find specific destinations. These specific goals are in the service of the larger goal of increasing individuals' sense of independence and confidence in exploring new destinations, regardless of their level of sight.

The result of our design is Talking Points 3 (TP3). As the name suggests, TP3 is the third in a series of systems that have been developed to leverage positioning technology to assist people with visual impairments. Talking Points 1 [5] used a mobile RFID reader to detect tags in the environment, which would result in descriptions of the tagged objects or locations being communicated to the participant. Since travelers with visual impairments cannot be assumed to know where the tags are placed, the RFID reader required a great deal of power to be able to detect tags at a sufficient distance. The power demands were deemed too great for a truly mobile system, and so Talking Points 2 [21] was designed to use commodity Bluetooth hardware for detecting Bluetooth beacons in the environment. This second generation of the system also included support for richer data about points of interest and a shared database supporting community generated content contributions, but lacked a workable strategy for deciding which points of interest would be the most valuable to include and what information would be most useful to our target users. TP3, then, was redesigned from the ground up, starting with formative interviews, followed by design, prototype development, and a user study. As described in this paper, TP3's design includes a comprehensive framework for deciding which points of interest to present to users, an indoor/outdoor coordinate-based positioning system that provides users with a greater range of options for exploring their environment, and a combination of push- and pull-based information retrieval that allows users to exert more or less initiative in the interaction with the system, depending on the task and personal preference. TP3 is implemented as a smartphone application that uses GPS, WiFi, and a compass to determine the user's location and orientation and communicates with a web-based database to retrieve information about nearby locations.

In this paper, we describe the design of the TP3 system and the results of a user study with eight legally blind participants who used TP3 to navigate through three large buildings on a university campus. Through this, we aim to make two main contributions:

1. An approach to supporting generalized spatial awareness consisting of
   a. making the environment legible for travelers with visual impairments by representing *paths*, *areas*, *landmarks*, *decision points*, *functional elements*, and *physical characteristics of the environment*, and
   b. supporting user control by providing a set of mechanisms for interactively browsing spatial information rather than providing turn-by-turn directions.
2. An evaluation of our approach, demonstrating that the above features
   a. help users navigate unfamiliar environments that they would otherwise find intimidating, and
   b. support important aspects of spatial awareness beyond procedural wayfinding, potentially giving travelers with visual impairments a greater sense of independence.

2. RELATED WORK

The idea of providing location-based orientation and navigation assistance to pedestrians with visual impairments is not new. The seminal work of Loomis, et al. [11] described the essential components of such a system as comprising a positioning system, a geographical information system (GIS), and a user interface. Subsequent work has focused on providing solutions in one or more aspects of this basic framework. For example, while most systems in this class have used GPS-based positioning, other solutions have been proposed to support indoor navigation (e.g., [7]) and fine-grained object finding (e.g., [12]). Regarding the GIS component, systems have been proposed that provide more detailed location data (e.g., [7]) more sophisticated route calculations (e.g., [18]), and the ability of end-users to update the GIS database directly (e.g., [24]). Perhaps the largest number of projects have focused on exploring alternatives for the user interface, proposing approaches ranging from verbal instructions (e.g., [16]), to non-verbal auditory cues (e.g., [24]), to tactile feedback (e.g., [17]). In addition to the research systems sampled

above, commercial/open-source systems based on GPS and widely available GIS data have been marketed for a number of years. Notable examples in this category include the Trekker Breeze[1], which includes GPS positioning, a button-based input device, and voice-based output for spatialized information and route instructions; and the feely available Loadstone GPS[2] which allows users to create and update information about points of interest with each other through a shared database.

While these systems cover a wide range, there are a few generalizations that can be made. First, with a few exceptions (e.g., [20] and Loadstone GPS), the emphasis of much of the work in this area has been on providing route-based instructions to specific, pre-selected locations. While this is surely an important goal, it fails to address other important goals, such as exploration, serendipitous location discovery, and general spatial awareness. Indeed, several authors have suggested that systems that focus on providing turn-by-turn navigation instructions can cause users to disengage from their surroundings [9] and may impact their ability to master the spatial organization of the environment [8]. Second, due in part to the emphasis on providing route instructions, little work has been done to describe the structure of the *content* that should be represented in a system to support general spatial awareness, rather than primarily procedural route finding. A notable exception is [6], which determined a broad set of preferences governing what individuals with visual impairments would want from a navigation system, though this study did not distinguish between needs related to navigational efficiency and general spatial awareness.

3. THE TALKING POINTS SYSTEM

Talking Points 3 is a location- and orientation-aware smartphone-based system that provides information to users about nearby points of interest in the environment. It supports a set of interactive mechanisms for accessing information about the local environment, with all information being conveyed to the user via text-to-speech through the smartphone's audio output. Information is stored in a central database that can be accessed freely and updated by users, community members, and stakeholders associated with the locations represented in the database. The key distinguishing features of TP3 are the structure provided for determining which location data to include and the interactive controls for accessing that data.

The design of TP3 is based on a formative study that explored how people with visual impairments orient themselves and navigate when traveling [19]. That study highlighted that while navigating familiar routes is generally not problematic for travelers, unfamiliar routes can pose a daunting challenge. Familiar routes can pose problems as well, especially when changes to the routes occur due to the appearance of physical barriers (e.g., construction or temporary blockages) or changes to environmental cues (e.g., a change in restaurant ownership causing a change in the ambient scent). Moreover, the study found that existing GPS-based navigation solutions can be unsatisfactory for certain needs such as error recovery, exploration, or dealing with route alteration due to unexpected needs. These systems provide information primarily in the form of turn-by-turn instructions, which were seen as particularly fragile in the face of

---

[1] http://www.humanware.com/en-usa/products/blindness/talking_gps/trekker_breeze/_details/id_1 01/trekker_breeze_handheld_talking_gps.html

[2] http://www.loadstone-gps.com/

dynamic environments. Based on the findings, as well as the limitations of prior work noted above, we decided to focus the design of TP3 around increasing the "legibility" of the environment rather than simply helping people find specific destinations.

Lynch [13] describes the *legibility* of an environment as the ease with which people can draw a mental image of the environment and use it to orient themselves and navigate to its different parts. Passini offers a more specialized definition of legibility as the clues embedded in a built environment that enable users to navigate through it [15]. Arthur and Passini [1] describe legibility as crucial to wayfinding, characterizing wayfinding as a constant decision-making process in which decisions are usually made at key areas, called decision points. By focusing on enhancing legibility, we seek to go beyond simply directing pedestrians with visual impairments to specific locations. With a focus on enhancing legibility in order to foster greater spatial awareness, we designed TP3 to meet three high level goals:

1. TP3 should support generalized environmental legibility by providing spatially-anchored information along with interactive controls for allowing users to explore the space dynamically and according to their own navigational and/or exploratory preferences.

2. TP3 should provide information about spatial features and points of interest specifically relevant to the needs of travelers with visual impairments in addition to information of interest to a wider audience.

3. To accommodate the increased information demands suggested by (2), TP3 should allow community-generated content to be attached to spatial anchors, allowing the most relevant content to be generated by the community members who value it most.

3.1 Content Structure

The basic unit of information in TP3, as in many location-based information systems, is the Point of Interest (POI). At base, a POI is a record that maps information to a specific geographical point and consists, at a minimum, of the point's latitude, longitude, altitude, name, and type. The POI data structure is extensible, allowing specific POI types to include additional information such as hours of operation, detailed description, and user comments.

In a study comparing blind and sighted pedestrian navigation, Passini and Proulx [1] reported that "[t]he blind participants made significantly more wayfinding decisions and used more units of information (e.g., landmarks) than did the sighted group," highlighting the fact that travelers with visual impairments would require detailed information about the environment that differs in key ways from the information that would be desired by sighted users. In order to support the acquisition of sufficiently detailed information, we follow [24] in supporting community-generated content. Moreover, we suggest that information for each site (e.g., building, campus, neighborhood) be "seeded" manually by working with the site's stakeholders to identify key POIs of each type and collect crucial information like physical description, layout, and type-specific information. The seeded information should ideally be enough to provide basic utility to the travelers, subsequently allowing the information to be supplemented by community members [22].

3.1.1 POI Types

Lynch [13] identifies key elements of space that aid in orientation and navigation through cities: landmarks, nodes, paths, edges and districts. Arthur and Passini state that making informed decisions at decision points is crucial for successful wayfinding [1]. Our interviewees [19] identified additional specific location types that pedestrians with visual impairments find useful in navigation, including entrances, doorways, staircases, and restrooms. These findings, along with Lynch's more general framework, suggest that an effective wayfinding solution for people with visual impairments must take into consideration a variety of different types of spatial information. We base contextual information provided by TP3 on the following types of locations and features, here adapted to the indoor environment:

· Paths are channels through which people travel, such as corridors, pathways, hallways (derived from Lynch's *paths*)

· Areas are spaces with recognizable characteristics, such as food courts, lobbies, atriums (derived from Lynch's *districts*)

· Landmarks are particular places which can be used as a reference point, such as stores, restaurants, classrooms (derived from Lynch's *landmarks*)

· Decision Points are focal point—the intersections of Paths (derived from Arthur and Passini's *decision points*)

· Functional elements are locations that support navigation and other needs, such as restrooms, stairs, entrances, elevators (derived from our formative study)

3.1.2 POI Metadata

Völkel et al. [23] note that people with visual impairments require geographic annotations as well as specific kinds of POIs to support orientation and navigation. Specifically, information regarding obstacles, layout of streets and paths, and environmental cues such as ground surface are necessary to complement missing information on existing map data. To address this need, each POI in TP3 has a mandatory "physical characteristics" field to go along with the aforementioned latitude, longitude, altitude, name, type, and arbitrary type-specific annotation fields. The physical characteristics field is meant to capture descriptive information about each POI, such as the physical layout, salient characteristics like railings or columns, and a description of the entryway.

3.2 Interacting with the Content

An additional challenge in providing contextual information is to determine how the system will provide that information to the user. Cheverst et al. [2], note that both "pushed" and "pulled" information have a role to play in location-based systems, where information which is immediately relevant should be "pushed" to users, whereas the system should allow users to "pull" more detailed information at their discretion. We designed TP3 to push selected information about the immediate surroundings to the user, while making available more detailed information about immediate and distant surroundings for the user to retrieve at will.

3.2.1 POI Retrieval Mechanisms

As illustrated in Figure 1, TP3 supports three mechanisms to allow users to access information about points of interest:

· Automatic Notification: TP3 automatically notifies users of POIs within 10 feet of their current position. The notification consists of a sound alert, the name of the POI, and the user's distance to the POI in feet.

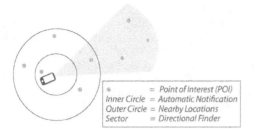

Figure 1. Talking Points 3 provides three mechanisms to allow users to access information about points of interest.

- Nearby Locations: Users can request a list of locations within 30 feet of their current position. When scrolling down the list, a user is given the name of the POI and the distance to it.

- Directional Finder: Users can point the phone and click a button to pull a list of POIs up to 100 feet away within a 45 degree angle of that direction. For example, if a user points the phone northwest, TP3 might say, "You are facing northwest, there are three locations in this direction." Direction is determined using an Android compass function.

3.2.2   User Interface

TP3 was designed with two main modes representing the Nearby Locations and Directional Finder features. By default, TP3's user interface provides the list of Nearby Locations, allowing users to access information about nearby POIs. To access information about more distant POIs, users can press a button to switch to the Directional Finder mode. Automatic Notifications are pushed to users in either mode.

Users interact with the TP3 client using a set of five simple touch screen gestures (up, down, left, right, and double-tap), a single button press, and a shake gesture. These seven input operations can be implemented in different ways for different hardware. Roughly speaking, the directional gestures are used for navigating through the TP3 menu hierarchy to retrieve detailed POI information, a double tap is used for selecting a menu item of interest, and button clicking and phone shaking are used for switching between the Nearby Locations and Directional Finder modes. All of these gestures were designed to be simple, learnable, and one-handed, so that they could be made by users who were also holding a cane or a guide dog.

3.3   Implementation

As shown in Figure 2, the current implementation of TP3 employs a client-server architecture with a Java-based Android client running on a Nexus One smartphone. The client communicates with a Ruby on Rails-based server via HTTP. The server maintains the database of POIs, and supplies the client with a continually refreshed set of nearby POIs based on the currently detected location and compass heading. The POI database is updatable via a web interface, which is also served by Ruby on Rails. On the client side, all information about points of interest are communicated to the user via text-to-speech, as are most system menu and feedback messages, though audio and haptic cues are also used to support low-level interaction such as the successful completion of a command.

TP3 depends on receiving continuous updates about the user's current position and orientation. The Nexus One features GPS-based positioning and a built-in compass, and our prototype makes use of both in outdoor environments. Additionally, we are in the process of implementing an indoor positioning system (IPS)

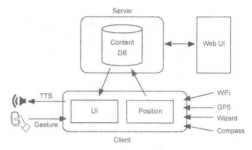

Figure 2. Talking Points System Architecture

for Android based on WiFi trilateration [3]. Our IPS performs well in the lab, achieving an average positioning error of less than 5 meters under controlled conditions (i.e., the mobile client receiving a strong signal from at least three access points, which are all less than 20 meters away). However, achieving such results is much more difficult in a naturalistic, uncontrolled setting, where WiFi access points may be spaced unevenly throughout the environment and, indeed, we found that there were large regions of the buildings we selected for our target deployment where determining an accurate position via trilateration was impossible because the client could not see at least three access points. We also learned that the Nexus One compass does not work well in some indoor environments due to magnetic interference, and we are investigating ways to overcome this limitation for indoor operation. Thus, to test the *user experience* of TP3 while working to improve the IPS and orientation system to an acceptable level, we developed a "Wizard of Oz" (WOz) positioning tool that allows us to simulate the detection of users' locations and orientations by clicking on a web-based building map. As we will describe in the next section, the wizard tool proved to be essential for our user testing efforts.

4.   USER STUDY DESIGN

The goal of our study was to determine whether TP3 increased the legibility of the environment for its users in order to assist in their wayfinding. We wanted to explore whether and how TP3 enhances spatial awareness; whether it gives users a greater sense of independence in traveling; and what the strengths, weaknesses, and usability problems of the prototype were. Because indoor navigation is not yet well supported for pedestrians with visual impairments, we decided to test our system's strength in an indoor setting. We elected not to execute an experimental study design due to the difficulty of creating an appropriate control condition. Two control alternatives were considered: a no-assistance condition, in which the only aid given would consist of verbal instructions given in advance; and an orientation condition, in which participants would be given an orientation to the building by a sighted guide, resembling a standard orientation given by mobility trainers. However, a set of pilot studies showed us that the no-assistance condition rendered the tasks nearly impossible for participants to complete and the orientation condition was too easy because the typical interaction with an orientation specialist includes highly personalized instructions that would be infeasible to replicate in an automated system. Choosing instead to conduct an exploratory study of the user experience of interacting with TP3, we designed the study to simulate a pedestrian with a visual impairment visiting an unfamiliar location. In addition to seeing whether participants could find a set of target locations, we were interested in learning whether TP3 would allow users to learn about additional locations of interest (i.e., ones not associated with any of the tasks) and observing specific ways that TP3 helped or hindered participants' ability to navigate in the new environment.

4.1 The Talking Points 3 Testbed

We selected three campus buildings for our testbed deployment based on their proximity to each other and the variety of environments they contained. They were a student union, an academic building containing classrooms and offices, and a mixed-use building containing a library and a number of specialized spaces for technical and creative work.

To prepare our system for the study, we analyzed each of the testing locations to identify the paths, areas, landmarks, decision points, and functional elements they contained. For each POI, we used the web-based editor to create a database entry including the name of the POI, its location, its type, a description of its physical characteristics, and any relevant information like hours of operation. Across all three buildings, we ended up "seeding" 68 POIs, though only a subset of these were actually used for the study tasks. No community-generated content was used in our study testbed—all content was created by the study team.

As mentioned in the previous section, our indoor positioning and orientation systems were not performing adequately, driving us to employ a Wizard of Oz (WOz) testing approach [4]. While choosing a WOz approach does not allow us to claim that the system we tested is currently deployable, we are confident that rapid improvement in the quality and cost-effectiveness of indoor positioning systems in recent years (e.g., [10], as well as commercial systems such as Ekahau[3] and Cisco MSE[4]) indicates that robust and accurate indoor positioning systems will be more and more common in the years to come.

Our WOz positioning tool was slightly more accurate than is currently achievable with existing approaches to WiFi positioning. While average estimation errors of around 2 meters have been achieved by several WiFi-based techniques (e.g., [10]), we determined that the average estimation error of our WOz tool was slightly less than 1 meter[5]. In retrospect it would have been a good idea to "fuzz" the output of the WOz tool to increase the error to a more realistic level, though as we will report later, our test participants experienced the WOz positioning system as being quite a bit less accurate than our 1 meter average error would suggest. This is most likely due to a 2-5 second lag between the WOz tool and the TP3 client, which resulted in a magnification of the inaccuracy of the position reports when the user was moving.

4.2 Task Selection and Design

When preparing for a visit to an unfamiliar building, people with visual impairments typically get directions either from the information desk or other people working at the destination, or from passers-by they encounter when arriving. Based on this information, we designed scenarios in which participants were given "natural" instructions for reaching their destination. These instructions included directions for where to turn at certain

intersections along the route and select details about the destination.

We assumed that TP3 would have different levels of usefulness in fostering spatial awareness in different types of indoor environments, so we designed our tasks to include three different styles of floor layout. Specifically, participants had to travel through "regular" environments, which were characterized by rectilinear floor plans consisting of straight passageways intersecting at more or less right angles; "complex" areas consisting of passageways that intersect at odd angles or include multiple floors; and "open space" areas which lack features that might otherwise aid navigation such as sidewalks or walls to follow. Given the set of environments available in the selected buildings, we designed tasks that would expose participants to various layouts, while unifying the tasks with a coherent scenario:

(1) Your friend dropped you off at the information desk of the building where you're attending a meeting today. You arrived a little early, and wonder if you can get a drink before you go to the meeting. You ask the person at the information desk where you can get a drink and receive directions to a small shop in the first building. (2) After you get your drink, you want to go to the meeting. You remember the room number, so you ask the clerk at the store for directions. You receive directions to the meeting, which turns out to be in an adjacent building connected by a corridor. (3) During the meeting, you learn about a new design lab in the next building over. There's a project to compose music with electronic sound, and you'd like to hear one of the works. You have time to visit there before your friend is picking you up. One of the people at the meeting was heading in that direction, so he guides you to the information desk of the third building. There you ask where the design lab is and receive directions.

4.2.1 Directions

We asked two different information desk workers (at different times) for directions to our task destinations, to make sure that the directions we gave participants mirrored directions they might be given in reality. We were told which direction to go at each intersection along the route and details that would help identify critical points along the way. The directions we provided in each task prescribed routes with 1-4 decision points. As an example, the directions for task 1 were as follows:

Walk down the hallway until you reach the connector to D---. Before you enter the connector, turn left and walk straight. At the end of the hallway, there's a U---, convenience store, on your left.

4.3 Participants

We had eight legally blind participants (4 female, 4 male), meaning they had visual acuity of less than 20/400. Two participants traveled with guide dogs, five were cane travelers, and one traveled with her vision, which was sufficient for avoiding obstacles. All participants were very familiar with computing technology in general and were regular users of screen readers on personal computers. Three participants had experience using handheld touch screen devices.

4.4 Procedure and Data Analysis

Participants were asked to answer a short questionnaire about their visual impairment, navigation skills, and familiarity with assistive and touch screen technology. They were given a tutorial on the TP3 prototype, followed by a training session to allow participants to become familiar with the application. Training was conducted in a different part of the first building from the testing

---

[3] http://www.ekahau.com/products/real-time-location-system/overview.html

[4] http://www.cisco.com/en/US/products/ps9742/index.html

[5] This was determined by having one team member secretly select 60 locations on the map and position himself at those locations to establish "ground truth" while the team member who acted as "wizard" during the test followed him and attempted to select each position using the WOz tool. The difference between the two measurements for each point was used to calculate the average error.

locations, and participants practiced using TP3 while walking through a hallway with several locations around them.

After the training session, participants were presented with the scenario and asked to perform the three tasks described above. We asked participants to try their best to complete the tasks. There was no time limit. To begin each task, the test moderator guided the participant to a specific starting point and provided the directions to the destination following a written script. Participants were allowed to have the directions repeated until they understood the route. At any time during the task, participants could ask for the name of the destination or for the scripted directions to be repeated.

During the test, participants were asked by the moderator to think out loud as they did the tasks and two additional study members observed silently, recorded video, and took notes. If participants had trouble figuring out where they were and which way to go, the moderator encouraged them to try the appropriate functions of TP3 to reorient themselves. If the participant got lost or had much difficulty trying to orient themselves, the moderator gave clues by reminding them of TP3's functions or repeating the task instructions.

After each task, a study member asked brief questions about whether the task was easy or difficult and clarification questions for some of the actions participants took during the tasks. After participants had completed the tasks, we conducted a semi-structured interview to learn about their experience with TP3.

All sessions were audio and video taped for later analysis. While observing, team members also made notes of task completions and failures, moderator-provided help, critical incidents, bugs, observations, and user comments. Three to four team members were present for every user study session. After the conclusion of the sessions, two team members reviewed the observation notes and video and audio recordings to understand how the features of TP3 were used during task execution and how it did or did not help participants to accomplish their goals. They also examined comments and navigation patterns that related to other aspects of participants' experience of using TP3, including evidence of serendipitous discovery, route improvisation, and error recovery.

5. FINDINGS

All three tasks were completed successfully by all participants except for two failures in task 2 and two failures in task 3. P08 accounted for half of these, as he had great difficulty using TP3 and was unable to complete tasks 2 and 3. P03 believed she had completed task 3, but had actually found a neighboring location. P02 abandoned task 2 after struggling with it for some time as she had a time constraint and she did not attempt task 3.

Most users were able to complete the assigned tasks, despite usability issues we discovered with the touchscreen-based interface. While some of our participants were fluent with touchscreens, others were uncomfortable with them and struggled with making the correct gestures. Our sessions were also occasionally hampered by technical limitations, including issues with the WOz positioning tool, prototype malfunctions, and dropped internet connections. Because of these interruptions, we did not find completion time to be a useful metric; however, our perception is that participants completed the tasks within a reasonable amount of time. In addition to assessing task completion, we were interested in how TP3 was used during the tests. For much of each session, the Automatic Notifications were sufficient for participants to stay on the correct route. However,

for open or complex areas, where there were fewer in-built cues like walls to guide participants along their route, the Automatic Notification was not always adequate. In these cases, participants found the Directional Finder useful for reorienting themselves. Consequently, the Directional Finder was used nearly twice as much in tasks 2 and 3, which featured more open and complex environments, than for task 1, which took place in a more regular environment.

In the remainder of this section, we will describe our specific observations that illustrate the benefits and weaknesses of TP3 and to demonstrate how TP3 helped participants navigate the environment, gave them a greater sense of spatial awareness, and increased their sense of independence.

5.1 Wayfinding
Throughout most of the test sessions, TP3 helped users orient themselves and make accurate wayfinding decisions. Although TP3 is not a turn-by-turn direction system, participants still reported that the system was useful for helping them find their destination. In general, participants found Automatic Notifications useful for determining if they were going in the right direction, and the Directional Finder helpful for deciding which direction to go. At the same time, there were differences in how people incorporated TP3 into their wayfinding strategies, indicating that TP3 can support different styles of navigation.

5.1.1 Staying on track
Most participants made use of the distance information included in each location report to determine whether they were going in the right direction. Three participants compared this process with the children's game "Hot or Cold" in which players find a hidden object by means of clues like "you're getting warmer" or "you're getting colder." Participants made heavy use of distance reports to determine if they were getting closer to or further away from target POIs and to determine whether to maintain their current course or go back. Some participants used the distance reports to decide when to switch to another mode of navigation entirely. In particular, as these participants came closer to their targets, they engaged other travelling skills to determine if they had reached their destination, such as feeling the wall for a door or a Braille sign, listening for sounds, or relying on their guide dogs.

5.1.2 Finding the way back: Recovery from errors
TP3 also helped users recover from errors. Two participants became disoriented at the start of the second task, which required participants to retrace their steps to get to a classroom in another building. One participant made a wrong turn and started walking in the opposite direction. When she realized she wasn't getting notified of any of the POIs she had passed before, she realized that she had taken a wrong turn and quickly went back. A second participant began in the right direction, but believed he was going the wrong way and headed back the way he had come. When he heard the Automatic Notification for his previous location at a convenience store, he remembered that he was supposed to turn left at that POI, and ultimately succeeded in finding his way. By providing environmental cues, TP3 allowed this participant to recognize his instructions rather than recall them with ease.

5.1.3 Navigating complex environment
Not surprisingly, participants in general found regular environments easier to navigate than open or complex spaces. Indeed, Some participants found the regular layout featured in task 1 simple enough to navigate that they felt they would have been able to find their destination without the aid of TP3, working

only on the directions provided at the beginning of the task. Even these participants, however, found open and complex spaces much more challenging. In these environments, the Directional Finder helped participants determine which direction to go in by telling them what POIs lay ahead of them. As P02 noted, "[TP3] can make that open space a little less daunting because you can actually know [where to go]." Another participant commented that the Directional Finder was especially useful for him because his guide dog tended to lead him straight through open spaces. Without TP3, he might have missed a crucial turn and had more difficulty reaching his destination.

5.1.4 Developing individual strategies

Two interesting but distinct strategies emerged among participants for using TP3 to move them towards their destinations. The few participants who were comfortable navigating using cardinal directions would use the Directional Finder to try to find the direction of the next destination and then repeatedly check their heading (also using the Directional Finder) to determine if they were still on course. Other participants used the Directional Finder far less frequently, and would strike out in the direction in which they believed the next destination lay, waiting for an Automatic Notification to tell them when they had reached it. As some of these participants felt they were getting closer to the destination, they started using Nearby Locations to actively check if the destination was near, only occasionally using the Directional Finder to make sure they were still on track.

5.2 Spatial Awareness

5.2.1 Serendipitous discovery

TP3 allowed participants to gain serendipitous information about their surroundings to which people with visual impairments are not usually privy. While users may still follow directions from starting point to destination, they can use TP3 to learn about what they pass along the way. P01 exclaimed that TP3 "[made him] realize how much [he] really was missing before," commenting that, "It's always good to know what's around you. It expands the things that you can do." This information, including notices of new services and upcoming events, open hours, and the location of unsought objects like computer stations or bathrooms, can be of use in meeting future or unforeseen needs. Obtaining location information while en route, even when it is not specifically related to any predefined destination, may help users make informed decisions and spontaneously improvise new routes to various locations when necessary. On hearing a notification for the 'Piano Lounge,' P02 cited this serendipity as her favorite aspect of TP3: "Even if you didn't want to go to those particular places, it's kind of fun to know..., I could go and practice my piano." Additionally, several participants specifically noted that just knowing where the restrooms were was extremely valuable.

5.2.2 Supporting exploration

Although our study design did not explicitly encourage exploration *all* participants observed that TP3 would be useful for exploring new areas and discovering new locations around them. P07 pointed out that people with visual impairments often have difficulty exploring unfamiliar areas because they do not know what type of locations to expect. Moreover, they often find it unhelpful to ask sighted people for help in exploration: sighted consultants usually ask travelers where they want to go instead of explaining generally what lies in a certain direction. Nor are their directions always useful. P07 said, "I could go exploring, [I] could

go into a non-familiar area and know what was there without the vagueness that you get from asking sighted people."

5.2.3 Description and physical characteristics

Participants found it useful hearing about the characteristics of specific POIs. For example, P01 was impressed that TP3 told him about a railing that guided the line at a Panda Express. P03 and P06 thought it was useful to know about the menu, hours, and products offered at various locations. They noted that user comments would be useful as well, once available. The physical descriptions which TP3 provided could also be useful in avoiding dangerous obstacles. P05 commented that it was great to hear that the store had an L-shaped counter, noting that, "If you didn't know that [it was an L-shaped counter] and you're at the register, you could potentially hurt yourself."

5.3 Independence

As noted in our formative study [19], when people with visual impairments learn about a new environment, they often need sighted people to assist them by describing main landmarks within the environment and helping them memorize routes by walking with them more than once. Thus travelers with visual impairments typically bring a sighted friend or guide with them when visiting a new building. However, this arrangement is not always convenient and can impose a significant time burden on both the traveler and their companion(s). This burden can constrain the extent to which travelers can explore new environments—travelers with visual impairments may be unwilling to travel or explore as much as they would like in order to minimize the demands upon their companion(s).

Six out of eight participants stated their belief that TP3 would increase their level of traveling skill, while one was neutral and one felt it would have a negative impact. Five out of eight participants stated that they believed they would feel a greater sense of independence with a system like TP3. Participants' specific statements highlight the reasons that TP3 fosters a greater sense of independence. One reason for increased confidence was that participants felt less anxious about getting lost. P05 described, "[With TP3] I honestly would feel like I can get where I need to be and if I get lost, I can find my way out." In addition to having increased confidence in finding specific destinations, participants felt that TP3 gave them more control by giving them more knowledge about the space around them. P01 commented that "Sighted guide[s]... couldn't possibly tell you all the stuff... [with] Talking Points, I feel like it's in my control."

6. DISCUSSION

The results of our user study indicate that a system aimed at fostering spatial awareness through increasing the legibility of the environment can enable pedestrians with visual impairments to visit unfamiliar locations with a greater sense of independence, and can further enrich their navigational experience. In particular, the spatial awareness provided by TP3 enables pedestrians with visual impairments to explore their environments and grants them access to information about resources in the environment that they may not otherwise have received. Indeed, it may well be the case that a system designed to provide turn-by-turn directions would have allowed our participants to complete their wayfinding tasks more effectively and more efficiently than they were able to do with TP3. However, we argue that the additional benefits that accrue from allowing users to have greater control over their navigational strategy and from being exposed to spatial information not directly related to a particular task outweigh any reduction in user performance. A promising direction for future work is to seek ways to integrate the best of both approaches—indeed several participants found it hard to keep the task directions in mind while navigating with TP3, indicating that at least a recording mechanism for directions would be helpful, if not a full-blown turn-by-turn directions feature.

6.1 Limitations

As noted earlier, our prototype suffered from usability shortcomings and was not entirely robust, which may have impacted the efficacy of TP3 in this study. It is possible that a more stable prototype would have further improved the experience of participants in our study, and the efficacy of TP3 in both spatial awareness support and wayfinding.

A potential concern remains surrounding the amount of data required to make TP3 useful. Currently, there do not exist extensive lists of POI data for indoor environments, and even outdoor environments are lacking much of the data required for supporting travelers with visual impairments. TP3 addresses this lack by supporting community-generated content and suggesting strategies for seeding the data for particular sites. However, it remains in an area for future work to understand how much the value of TP3 would be affected by the quantity of location data available to the users and where the threshholds lie for impacts on the user experience.

7. CONCLUSION

Our observations from the TP3 user study indicate that providing users with specific types of information about the environment along with tools for accessing it is helpful for supporting general spatial awareness among individuals with visual impairments. This increased spatial awareness is, in turn, helpful for supporting wayfinding in a broad sense for travelers with visual impairments. Further, our participants' experiences with TP3 indicate that, through fostering an increased awareness of the environment, mobile location-based technology can increase the sense of independence for users of such tools and enable them to embark on journeys that they might otherwise avoid.

8. ACKNOWLEDGMENTS

We are grateful to Jim Knox, Royster Harper and Ann Arbor Center for Independent Living for their support. We would also like to thank our participants and all previous members of the Talking Points team (http://talking-points.org/team).

9. REFERENCES

1. Arthur, P. and Passini, R. 1992. *Wayfinding: People, Signs, and Architecture*. McGraw-Hill Ryerson, Toronto.
2. Cheverst, K., Mitchell, K. and Davies, N. 2001. Investigating Context-aware Information Push vs. Information Pull to Tourists. In *Proc. MobileHCI 2001*. ACM, New York, NY, 1-6.
3. Cook B, Buckberry G, Scowcroft I, Mitchell J, Allen T. 2005. Indoor Location Using Trilateration Characteristics, In *Proc. London Communications Symposium*. 147-150.
4. Dahlbäck, N., Jönsson, A., and Ahrenberg, L. 1993. Wizard of Oz studies: why and how. In *Proc. IUI '93*, ACM, New York, NY, 193-200.
5. Gifford, S., Knox, J., James, J., and Prakash, A. 2006. Introduction to the talking points project. In *Proc. ASSETS '06*, ACM, New York, NY, 271-272.
6. Golledge, R.G., Marston, J.R., Loomis, J.M., & Klatzky, R.L. 2004. Stated preferences for components of a personal guidance system for non-visual navigation. *Journal of Vision Impairment and Blindness, 98*, 135-147.
7. Helal, A., Moore, S.E., and Ramachandran, B. 2001. Drishti: An Integrated Navigation System for Visually Impaired and Disabled. In *Proc. ISWC '01*, 149-156.
8. Ishikawa, T., Fujiwara, H., Imai, O., and Okabe, 2008. A. Wayfinding with a GPS-based mobile navigation system: A comparison with maps and direct experience. *Journal of Environmental Psychology 28*, 1, 74–82.
9. Leshed, G., Velden, T., Rieger, O., Kot, B., and Sengers, P. 2008. In-car GPS navigation: engagement with and disengagement from the environment. In *Proc. CHI '08*, ACM, New York, NY, 1675-1684.
10. Lim, H., Kung, L.-C., Hou, J.C., and Luo, H. 2010. Zero-configuration indoor localization over IEEE 802.11 wireless infrastructure. *Wireless Networks 16*, 2, 405–420.
11. Loomis, J.M., Golledge, R.G., Klatzky, R.L., Speigle, J.M., and Tietz, J. 1994. Personal guidance system for the visually impaired. In *Proc. ASSETS '94*, ACM, New York, NY, 85-91.
12. Loomis, J.M., Marston, J.R., Golledge, R.G., and Klatzky, R.L. 2005. Personal guidance system for people with visual impairment: A comparison of spatial displays for route guidance. *Journal of Visual Impairment & Blindness 99*, 4, 219-232.
13. Lynch, K. 1960. *The Image of the City*. The MIT Press, Cambridge.
14. Passini, R. and Proulx, G. 1988. Wayfinding without vision: an experiment with congenitally totally blind people. *Environment and Behavior 20*, 2, 227-252.
15. Passini, R. *Wayfinding in Architecture*. 1984. New York: Van Nostrand Reinhold.
16. Petrie, H., Johnson, V., Strothotte, T., Raab, A., Fritz, S., and Michel, R. 1996. MoBIC: Designing a travel aid for blind and elderly people. *Journal of Navigation 49*, 45-52.
17. Pielot, M. and Boll, S. 2010. Tactile Wayfinder: comparison of tactile waypoint navigation with commercial pedestrian navigation systems. In *Proc. Pervasive 2010*, Springer-Verlag, Berlin, Heidelberg. 76-93.
18. Pressl, B. and Wieser, M. 2006. A computer-based navigation system tailored to the needs of blind people. In *Proc. ICCHP 2006*, Springer-Verlag, Berlin, Heidelberg, 1280-1286.
19. Quiñones, P., Greene, T.C., Yang, R., and Newman, M.W. 2011. Supporting Visually Impaired Navigation: A Needs-finding Study. In *Ext. Abstracts of CHI '11*, ACM, New York, NY, 1645-1650.
20. Sanchez, J.H., Aguayo, F.A., and Hassler, T.M. 2007. Independent Outdoor Mobility for the Blind. *Virtual Rehabilitation*, 114-120.
21. Stewart, J., Bauman, S., Escobar, M., Hilden, J., Bihani, K., and Newman, M.W. 2008. Accessible contextual information for urban orientation. In *Proc. Ubicomp '08*, ACM, New York, NY, 332-335.
22. Viégas, F.B., Wattenberg, M., and McKeon, M.M. 2007. The hidden order of Wikipedia. In *Proc. OCSC '07*, Springer-Verlag, Berlin, Heidelberg, 445-454.
23. Völkel, T., Kühn, R., and Weber, G. Mobility Impaired Pedestrians Are Not Cars: Requirements for the Annotation of Geographical Data. In *Proc. ICCHP '08*, Springer-Verlag, Berlin, Heidelberg, 1085-1092.
24. Walker, B.N. and Lindsay, J. 2006. Navigation performance with a virtual auditory display: Effects of beacon sound, capture radius, and practice. *Human Factors, 48*, 2, 265-278.

Situation-based Indoor Wayfinding System for the Visually Impaired

Eunjeong Ko, Jin Sun Ju and Eun Yi Kim
Dept. of Advanced Technology Fusion Engineering
Konkuk University
Seoul, Korea
+82-2-450-4135

{rritty33, vocaljs, eykim}@konkuk.ac.kr

ABSTRACT

This paper presents an indoor wayfinding system to help the visually impaired finding their way to a given destination in an unfamiliar environment. The main novelty is the use of the user's situation as the basis for designing color codes to explain the environmental information and for developing the wayfinding system to detect and recognize such color codes. Actually, people would require different information according to their situations. Therefore, situation-based color codes are designed, including location-specific codes and guide codes. These color codes are affixed in certain locations to provide information to the visually impaired, and their location and meaning are then recognized using the proposed wayfinding system. Consisting of three steps, the proposed wayfinding system first recognizes the current situation using a vocabulary tree that is built on the shape properties of images taken of various situations. Next, it detects and recognizes the necessary codes according to the current situation, based on color and edge information. Finally, it provides the user with environmental information and their path through an auditory interface. To assess the validity of the proposed wayfinding system, we have conducted field test with four visually impaired, then the results showed that they can find the optimal path in real-time with an accuracy of 95%.

Categories and Subject Descriptors

K.4.2 [**Computers and Society**]: Social Issues – *Assistive technologies for person with disabilities;* I.5.4 [**Pattern Recognition**]: Applications – *Computer vision.*

General Terms

Algorithms, Measurement, Performance, Design, Experimentation, Human Factor.

Keywords

Wayfinding system, 2D Color code, Situation awareness, Visually impaired people, Speeded-Up Robust Feature (SURF), Vocabulary tree.

1. INTRODUCTION

1.1 Background

The number of blind people in the world is close to 39 million,

with another 246 million that have significant visual impairments. One of the major challenges faced by this population is 'wayfinding'-the ability to find one's way to a destination [1].

Over the past few decades, a wide range of technologies have been developed to help the visually impaired find a specific location or object, with most recent work focusing on GPS (Global Positioning Systems) [2]. However, while systems using GPS sensors work well as wayfinding aids in an outdoor environment, they are unable to provide accurate spatial positions within ten meters, making them inadequate to keep a walker on an intended path in an indoor environment.

Accordingly, the goal of the present study is to develop a wayfinding system that can be effective in indoor environments, such as shopping malls, hospitals, and schools.

1.2 Related Work

In previous studies, RFID [3] and WIFI [4] have been commonly used to estimate the current position. Although these approaches work well indoors, they also have certain limitations: for example, RFIDs can only be read within a short distance, so that their location should be roughly estimated, thereby making it difficult for visually impaired people.

As an alternative, vision-based wayfinding has been intensively investigated, where computer vision techniques are used to sense the surrounding environments through scene texts, signs, and meaningful objects [5, 6]. In [5], a body mounted single camera is used for wayfinding indoors and outdoors. When an input image is given, environmental landmarks are made at the current position, and then compared with pre-established landmarks. However, this requires a preliminary process to build a set of landmarks, making it useless in unknown environments. In addition, methods using a stereo camera and bionic eyeglass were developed in [6]. In the off-line stages, key objects are learned using a neural network (NN) and genetic algorithm (GA). Then, in the on-line stage, salient features are extracted from an input image and classified as learned objects. Their main advantage is that no infrastructure or modification of the environment is required, as objects are directly recognized as associated with certain environments, however, the disadvantages are insufficient reliability and a prohibitive computational complexity.

Most recently, color code-based wayfinding systems for the visually or cognitively impaired have been developed using mobile phone cameras, where a barcode or QR code [7] is used to describe environmental information and key objects, as shown in Fig. 1. Such codes, especially a QR code, can hold a large amount of information, including numeric, alphabetic characters, symbols, and control codes.

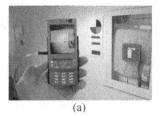

(a)   (b)

Figure 1. Indoor wayfinding system using color codes:
(a) wayfinding using 1-D barcode and color target [9]
and (b) using QR codes [7]

Such systems using color codes are also effective indoors and have already proven to be practical for indoor wayfinding and grocery store shopping [8]. However, the major drawback is a limited detection range: 1) the codes can only be detected within a short distance to enable the dense spatial patterns of the color codes to be decoded; 2) the codes can only be detected when they are in the direct line of the camera, thereby limiting the application in certain situations, such as a corridor.

To enhance these limitations, Coughlan et al. [9] placed as a distinctive color target that quickly guides the system to an adjacent barcode (See the Fig. 1(a)). Although this can improve the detection distance to a maximum of 1.5m (when the diameter of color target is 6cm and the resolution of the captured image is 320 X 240), it is unable to deal with oblique viewing angles.

1.3 Proposed Method

This study presents a new situation-based wayfinding system for visually impaired and blind people. Unlike existing methods that use complex color codes, the proposed method uses new situation-based color codes that play different roles according to the position/environment of the user, allowing color codes for more simple shapes to represent lots of environmental information. The main assumption is that people require different information according to their situations. Thus, location-specific codes and guide codes are designed to represent the position where the user is standing and the direction to a specific location, respectively.

The overall system is composed of three main modules: the situation awareness, hierarchical color code detection and recognition, and user interface. This situation awareness, as the core of the proposed system, classifies the user's current situation as either requiring just location information or requiring both location and directional information. Second, according to the situation, the necessary color code is localized and recognized using color and edge information. Finally, the recognized results, such as the position and direction to a given destination, are verbally notified to the user through an auditory interface.

Experiments were conducted in various indoor environments, and the results showed that the proposed system can detect the color codes with an accuracy of almost 100% at a distance of 2.5m and viewing angle of (+20º, -20º), and recognized their meaning with an accuracy of above 99%. In addition, to demonstrate its feasibility as a real-time wayfinding aid for the visually impaired, field tests were performed with four subjects, all of whom were able to find the optimal path in real-time with an accuracy of 95%.

2. 2-D COLOR CODE DESIGN

For indoor wayfinding to help the visually impaired, a color code is first designed. For this, real environments were observed to provide visual clues to guide the walker. Although various differences exist according to the type of building, visual clues can mainly be divided into two groups: location–specific information and directional information to a given destination. In addition, visual clues with positioning information are mostly observed in front of doors, while clues with directional information tend to be observed in halls or corridors.

Accordingly, a situation-based color code is presented, where the color code is separated into a *location-specific code* and *guide code*. The former is used to represent the position where the user is standing, while the latter is used to provide directions to a specific location. In addition, to avoid modifying the environment, the codes are designed based on mimicking real visual clues.

2.1 Location-specific Code

In real environments, since location information is represented by numbers or pictograms, corresponding color-barcodes and pictograms are designed.

A *color-barcode* describes the number of a place, such as an office or class room, using colors and their order. The number of color patches in the color-barcode should be chosen carefully. And another important design issue is selecting the colors. The colors used in the color-barcode should be 1) distinctive to be easily recognized and 2) robust to various illuminations and cluttered backgrounds. This study used 8 color patches to represent the place numbers of common buildings, and selected colors from the following RGB representations: {Black(0,0,0), White(255,255,255), Red(255,0,0), Green(0,128,0), Blue(0,0,255), and Yellow(255,255,0)}. Black and white colors have different brightness characteristics. Meanwhile, for red, green, and blue, the difference between the RGB color channels is clear. In a real environment, since regular green (0,255,0) appears similar to fluorescent green with a diffuse reflection, this study uses a darker green. Among six colors, green is used to denote the quiet zone[1] and others are mapped to one number between 0 and 4. Thus, quinary encoding is used to identify a specific number. As a result 10^4 numbers can be represented using a decimal code.

Pictograms are affixed to the walls in many buildings to label locations, such as toilet, exits, and elevators. However, there are some differences in form according to the building. Therefore, this study uses pictograms defined by official institutions [10]. Among 34 pictograms, 10 pictograms were selected that are commonly used in many buildings.

Figure 2. Pictograms

Fig. 2 shows the pictograms used in our system: from top-left to right-bottom, direction (left, right), toilets (unisex, men, and women), impaired access, information, exit, no entry, and elevator.

2.2 Guide Code

The guide code is used to provide directions to a specific location, which includes both location and directional information. Thus, it is represented by a combination of location-specific codes and arrow pictograms.

---

[1] The quiet zone helps the scanner find the leading edge of the barcode so reading can begin.

Fig. 3 shows some examples of guide codes, where the guide code on the left tells the user to turn right to arrive room 02 to room 27, while one on the right tells user to turn right to take an elevator.

Figure 3. Examples of guide codes

Table 1. Specifications of color codes (cm)

Types	Color-barcode	Pictogram	Guide code
Width×Height (ratio)	12×8 (1.3:1)	20×20 (1:1)	40×20 (2:1)
Height from the floor	135	155	155

Table 1 shows the specifications of the respective color codes, including size and ratio differences for the respective color codes to facilitate a quicker and more accurate wayfinding system. In the proposed system, the first stage is to recognize the current situation, and then find the necessary color codes according to the situation. Then, the different appearance of the three color codes enables more accurate discrimination between them.

The designed color codes are placed in positions that will help the user to find a destination, for example, adjacent to a door, elevator, and information desk, as shown in Fig. 4. This alignment is similar to real environments.

Figure 4. General locations of color codes

2.3 Design Verification

When designing a color code, there are two important requirements: 1) it should be detectable at distances of up to 1~2m in a cluttered environment and 2) robust to various illumination and cluttered backgrounds.

Thus, a verification process was performed based on several experiments that considered the following three environmental factors: 1) Distance from user (camera) to color codes, 2) Viewing angle between user and color codes, and 3) Illumination.

Around 800 images were collected when changing the distance from 25cm to 2.5m, the viewing angle from -40° to 40° and the illumination from direct sun-light to fluorescent light. As such, for each type of illumination, the distance was fixed at a specific value and the color code detection then tested when changing the viewing angle.

Table 2 summarizes the results, where the performance was analyzed in terms of the maximum detection distance (MDD) and maximum detection viewing angle (MDW). For example, when the color-barcodes were at a distance of 1m, they were perfectly detected within a viewing angle of [-30°, +30°], whereas they could not be detected at a viewing angle of [-40°, +40°]. As shown in Table 2, the proposed color codes were perfectly detected within a distance of 2.5m when the codes were placed in a direct line with the user or maximally within a viewing angle of ±20°. However, some performance differences were observed among the three color codes. 1) The pictograms were perfectly detected

in all the experiments, as the height at which they were affixed was higher than that for the other codes, allowing them to be easily found. 2) The detection of the guide codes was lowest: some guide codes were not detected at a close distance (within 1m), as they were not covered by the camera's focal length. In the experiments, the illumination did not affect on the color code detection. However, it did affect the recognition accuracy, which will be discussed in Section 4.1.

Table 2. Detection results according to distance between camera and color codes and viewing angle

Distance range	View point	Direct Sunlight			Fluorescent		
		CB*	P*	GC*	CB	P	GC
50cm~1m	±40°	○	○	-	○	○	-
	±30°	○	○	-	○	○	-
	0~±20°	○	○	○	○	○	○
1m~1.5m	±40°	-	○	-	-	○	-
	±30°	○	○	○	○	○	○
	0~±20°	○	○	○	○	○	○
1.5cm~2m	±40°	-	○	-	-	○	-
	±30°	○	○	○	○	○	○
	0~±20°	○	○	○	○	○	○
2m~2.5m	±40°	-	○	-	-	○	-
	±30°	-	○	○	-	○	○
	0~±20°	○	○	○	○	○	○

* CB, P, GC means Color-barcode, Pictogram and Guide code respectively.

3. WAYFINDING SYSTEM

Our system is implemented using iPhone 4G. Due to the limited computational power of a smart phone and real-time requirement of the wayfinding system, the algorithm must involve as few operations per pixel as possible. Thus, a situation-based wayfinding system is developed.

In this work, *situation means the type of place the user is located*, which is categorized into four types: {door, corridor, hall, and junction}. While the first three situations (door, corridor, and hall) are self-contained, the last situation (junction) transposes one situation to another, making it a combination of two or more situations. Thus, the first three situations are called primitive types, while the last situation is a complex type.

Our main assumption was that humans require different information according to their situation; when in front of a door, only the location is required to determine if the current place is the destination; however, in the case of a complex situation, like a junction, directional information is necessary. Meanwhile, when the situation is a hall or corridor, both location and direction are required. In this case, the directional information to proceed is considered more important than the location, followed by such pictograms as 'exit', 'info', and 'toilet', and finally the color-barcodes. Accordingly, the color codes are hierarchically searched and recognized based on the current situation.

Fig. 5 shows the outline of the proposed system that is composed of three main modules: situation awareness, hierarchical color code detection and recognition, and the user interface.

First, the current situation is categorized as a 'door', 'corridor', 'hall' or 'junction'. The first situation (door) only requires the location information at the current position, however, the others primarily involve directional information, followed by pictograms and color-barcodes. Once the current situation is recognized, the necessary color codes are hierarchically searched and recognized, as shown in Fig. 5. Finally, the recognized results, such as the orientation and way to a given destination, are notified to the user through an audio or visual interface. These stages are repeated until the user reaches their destination.

3.1 Situation Awareness

For situation awareness, specific characteristics need to be identified to distinguish the four situation types, that is, visual patterns associated with each type of situation.

However, the same type of situation can appear quite differently in images due to a cluttered background or different viewpoint, orientation, scale, and lighting conditions. Thus, to handle these variations, a speeded-up robust feature (SURF) is used. SURF is known as a scale- and rotation- invariant feature detector [11]. To establish a link between the four situation types and SURFs, 200 images representing the four situation types were collected in various environments and used to extract SURF local descriptors.

Fig. 6 shows the characteristics of the detected SURF descriptors corresponding to the four situation types. Figs. 6(a) and (b) show the SURFs overlapping the original images, while Figs. 6(c), (d) and (e) show the accumulated SURF descriptors over 5, 10, and 20 images, for each situation type. Interestingly, in Figs. 6(c) to (e): 1) the accumulated SURFs for the 'corridor' images revealed an 'X'-shaped pattern, as shown in the top images: 2) a rectangular-shaped pattern was observed for the 'door' images (second images from the top); 3) the SURFs for the 'hall' images were crowded around the upper boundaries with a horizontal and thick line-shaped pattern in the center; 4) no specific patterns were related to the 'junction' image SURFs, which were complexly and sparsely distributed across the images. Thus, common patterns were revealed among the images that belonged to the same situation type, except for the complex 'junction' situation.

Therefore, SURF descriptors are used to index the collected sample images and to match the input image with the indexed image to recognize the current situation. For indexing, a vocabulary tree is used, which is a very popular algorithm in object recognition [11, 12].

Fig. 7 provides an overview of the situation awareness, which is performed in two stages: the off-line phase to build the vocabulary tree and on-line phase to recognize the current situation.

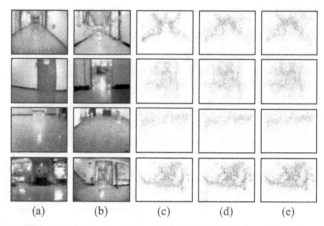

Figure 6. Characteristics of SURF distributions: (a) and (b) SURFs extracted from 'corridor', 'door', 'hall' and 'junction' images, (c), (d) and (e) SURF distribution accumulated with 5, 10 and 20 images, respectively

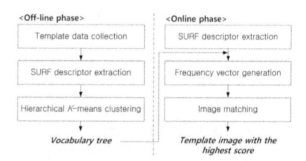

Figure 7. Outline of proposed situation awareness

3.1.1 Off-line phase

First, 200 template data were collected to represent the four situation types in various environments, and 20,289 SURF descriptors were then extracted from local regions in these images. Thereafter, the extracted descriptors were quantized into visual words, defined by the hierarchical K-means [12] of the SURFs. Here, K defines the branch factor (number of children of each internal node), not the number of clusters, which was set at 10.

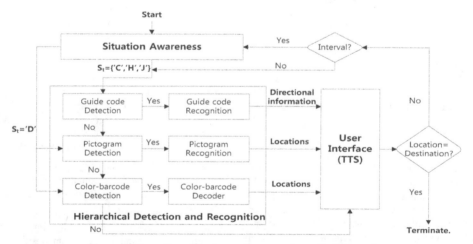

Figure 5. Overall architecture of proposed wayfinding system

The process of hierarchical *K*-means quantization is as follows: first, an initial clustering is performed on normally 20,289 initial descriptors, thereby defining the *K* groups, where each group consists of the descriptor vectors closest to a particular cluster center. This process is then recursively performed, and finally a vocabulary tree is built. Each node in the vocabulary tree is an associated inverted file with reference to the images containing a descriptor corresponding to that node.

Once the quantization is defined, a weight, w_i based on entropy is assigned to each node *i* as follows:

$$w_i = \ln \frac{N}{N_i} \qquad (1)$$

, where *N* is the number of images in the template database and N_i is the number of images in the DB with at least one descriptor vector path through node *i*. Inspired by the TF-IDF scheme [12], this is used to ignore effects of the most frequent and infrequent features (noise) in the template database.

3.1.2 On-line phase

The on-line phase determines the most relevant image in the template DB in relation to the current image, which is calculated based on the similarity of the paths down the vocabulary tree of the descriptors from the DB image and those from the input image.

According to the weights assigned to each node in the vocabulary tree, the template *t* and input image *q* are represented as follows:

$$t = \{t_i = m_i w_i\}, \qquad (2)$$

$$q = \{q_i = n_i w_i\}, \qquad (3)$$

, where m_i and n_i are the number of descriptor vectors with a path through node *i* in the template and input image, respectively.

To compute the difference, both vectors are firstly normalized, then the similarity is calculated using the following dot product:

$$s(q,t) = \|q - t\|_2^2 - 2 - 2 \sum_{\{\text{for all } i | q_i \neq 0, t_i \neq 0\}} q_i t_i \qquad (4)$$

The template image with the best matching score is selected and its situation type is assigned to label the current situation.

3.2 Hierarchical Color Code Detection and Recognition

In our system, color codes used the green color (0, 128, 0) to represent the quiet zone and they have rectangular shape, thus the color codes are detected by finding a green-rectangle in a scene.

The process for detecting the color codes is as following:

1) Preprocessing: As time-varying illumination requires a contrast adjustment, a histogram specification is employed.

2) Binarization: Each pixel in the input image is classified as green or non-green. Then the color green is defined as follows:
$$(C_r < 1.7 \ \& \ C_g > 1.5 \ \& C_b > 1.7) \&\&(H > 90 \& H < 160) \qquad (5)$$

3) Labeling: On the binary image, row-by-row labeling is performed, thereafter the area and circularity are calculated from all components. These properties are used to remove noise: if the circularity of a region is larger than a predefined threshold or its area is too small, it is considered as noise. So, only components corresponding to color codes are filtered through this stage.

4) Post processing: After the noise filtering, adjacent components are merged to prevent the color codes from being split.

Fig. 8 shows the process used to localize the color-barcodes, where Figs. 8(a) to 8(d) show the input image and results of the binarization, labeling, and post-processing. As shown in Fig. 8(b), the binary image includes a lot of noise, which is removed using the geometric characteristics (see Fig. 8 (c)). However, the color code is split into two components, which is merged by the post processing, as shown in Fig. 8 (d).

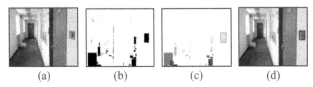

(a) (b) (c) (d)

Figure 8. Process of color code localization: (a) input image, (b) binarization result, (c) labeling result and (d) detected color code

The proposed system only localizes and recognizes the necessary color codes according to the current situation, and this is determined by comparing with predefined width-height ratios of three color codes (refer to Table 1).

3.2.1 Color-barcode decoder

The color-barcode is composed of 8 color patches, so the color-barcode is first segmented into color patches. For fast computation, all operations are only applied to the median lines.

The boundaries between color patches are retained by applying a Gaussian filter and Prewitt edge operator in turn. Once a color patch is separated, a cascade filter is applied to the pixels within the color patch, as shown in Fig. 9.

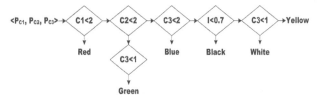

Figure 9. Color mapping cascade

This cascade filter is determined based on the color range of each pixel, where the thresholds and sequence of the cascade were chosen by experiments. Pixel P is converted to the $<C_1, C_2, C_3>$ color model, then P $=<P_{c1}, P_{c2}, P_{c3}>$ is compared according to the sequence of the color mapping cascade. After mapping each pixel to one color out of {red, green, blue, black, white, yellow}, the majority color within the patch is assigned to that patch. Finally, a quinary number is obtained based on the colors of the respective patches, and this number is then translated to a decimal code.

3.2.2 Pictogram recognizer

Pictograms are recognized based on matching with templates. For each pictogram, one template is predetermined.

The operation to recognize a pictogram is only applied to the median lines on the vertical and horizontal axes. From these median lines, color histograms are then calculated for the red, green, blue and white channels. Thus, all eight histograms are used to identify the closest match. The respective histograms are first normalized and compared with the corresponding histograms in the templates. The results of comparing the templates with the extracted pictogram are represented by a matching score. The matching score between a pictogram template and the pictogram is calculated using the hamming distance. The pictogram template with the best matching scores is then selected.

3.2.3 Guide code recognizer

A guide code is a combination of a location-specific code and arrow, thereby requiring partition. However, this is straightforward, as there is a green-colored interval between the location-specific code and the arrow.

To recognize the direction of the arrow, the occupancy of the color white is used, where the higher occupancy rate determines the direction. Therefore, the location specific code is recognized using the color-barcode decoder or pictogram recognizer described above, and the combined results notified to the user.

3.3 User Interface

When starting the system, the user first enters their intended destination using speech recognition or keypad for users with low vision. After entering the destination, the system continues to work and to give users instructions until reaching the final destination, all the while notifying its result to the user by TTS (Text to Speech). Additionally, the detection of color code is notified to users by beeping produced on iPhone. If the color code is within the distance for the system to recognize, the short beeps are repeated.

Table 3. Action table

Situation	Type of detected code	Action Before code recognition	Action After code recognition
Start	Pictogram 'i'	Approach to the detected code until reaching to recognizable range (direction is notified by a hour system [13])	Ask where target place is
Start/Hall/ Corridor	Guide code		Change the path according to guided direction (left or right)
	Location-specific code		If destination, "success" and off; otherwise "go back to your path"
Junction	Guide code		Change the path according to guided direction
Door	Location-specific code		If destination, "success" and off; otherwise "go back to your path"
All types of situation	Not found	Go straight to his/her own path	

Table 3 illustrates the instructions to be guided to users. The goal of this study is to allow people to easily navigate to specific locations within a building. In many buildings, the information center is placed on the first floor or ground. Thus, our wayfinding system makes the users first find the 'information pictogram' when starting, to get the information for a destination, such as the floor and room number. Thereafter, it finds and recognizes the color codes, and gives some instructions to users according to current situation and meaning of color codes, as shown in Table 3.

4. EXPERIMENTAL RESULTS

This study developed a new situation-based wayfinding system for the visually impaired. To prove its validity, two experiments were performed. The first one was designed to evaluate the efficiency of the proposed wayfinding system based on measuring the accuracy of each module. Plus, a field test was designed to prove the feasibility of the proposed system in real environments.

4.1 Efficiency Test

For a quantitative performance evaluation of the proposed system, the color codes were first affixed to the walls of buildings, then test images of these locations were collected at different times of the day and under different lighting conditions. In addition, for certain of the affixed color codes, the distance from a camera and viewing angles were also changed. As a result total of 2,000 images were collected.

4.1.1 Results for situation awareness

In the proposed wayfinding system, the performance of the situation awareness is crucial, as it forms the basis for the next stages (see Fig. 5). Some examples of the situation awareness results are shown in Fig. 10. The images on the first row show the SURF features overlapping the original input images. These input images are then compared with the template data to be indexed using the vocabulary tree, and the most relevant images are selected. The images on the second row show the most relevant images selected from the template data.

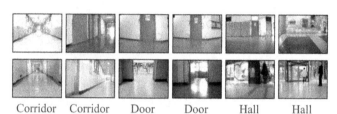

Corridor   Corridor   Door   Door   Hall   Hall

Figure 10. Situation awareness results

Table 4. Confusion matrix of situation awareness (%)

	Door	Corridor	Hall
Door	100	0	0
Corridor	0	93	7
Hall	0	12	88

Table 4 summarizes the performance of the situation awareness under various indoor environments. The 'junction' situation is a combination situation of three other primitive types and has no distinctive features. Thus, the accuracy of the situation awareness was only measured for the situation of 'door', 'corridor', and 'hall'. As shown in Table 4, the average accuracy was above 90%.

4.1.2 Color code detection and recognition results

For a quantitative performance evaluation of the color code detection, two measures were used: the FPR (False Positive Rate) and the FNR (False Negative Rate), where the former represented the rate of mistaking non-codes as color codes, while the latter represented the rate of missing color codes. These measures have also been used to evaluate other wayfinding system [9].

The overall detection performance is summarized in Table 5. For a distance range of 25cm to 2.5m, the FPR was 0, whereas the FNR gradually increased when increasing the distance.

Table 5. Performance of color code detection (%)

	FPR	FNR
100cm	0	0
150cm	0	0.013
200cm	0	0.013
250cm	0	0.083

Table 6. Color code recognition accuracy (%)

View point	Direct sunlight			fluorescent		
	CB	P	GC	CB	P	GC
0°~ ±20°	98	100	100	100	100	100
±20°~ ±30°	92	100	90	100	100	90

Table 6 shows the color code recognition accuracy according to the viewing angle and illumination, where 'CB,' 'P' and 'GC' are the abbreviations of color-barcode, pictogram and guide code, respectively. The performance of our system is affected by the illumination as well as viewing angle: the result on under fluorescent lightening is better than one of under direct sunlight, however the difference is not significant. In summary, the proposed method was able to detect codes with an accuracy of almost 100% at a viewing angle ranging within ±20°.

4.1.3 Processing time
For practical use by the visually impaired, a wayfinding system should be portable and effective in real-time.

Table 7. Processing time (.ms)

Stage	Time
Situation awareness	143
Sign localization	60
Sign recognition	5
Total	227

Table 7 shows that the average time taken to process a frame through all the stages was about 227ms. The situation awareness was performed at 2 second intervals, followed by an average processing of up to 10 frames/second, providing that the proposed system can be used as an effective wayfinding aid in real-time.

4.1.4 Comparisons with QR code-based wayfinding
As further proof of the effectiveness of the proposed system, its performance was compared with that of another method. Here, a wayfinding system using QR codes was adapted [7], as QR codes are widely used in various applications due to their high capacity and reliability. QR codes sized at 12×12 were affixed at the same places as the proposed color codes, and the affixed height optimized to the performance of the QR code reader. To evaluate the robustness to MDD and MDW, the two methods were tested when changing the distances and viewing angles.

Table 8. Performance comparison with QR-based system (°)

	QR code	CB	P	GC
50cm	45	40	40	20
1m	0	40	40	30
1.5m	-	30	40	30
2m	-	20	40	30
2.5m	-	0	40	30

Table 8 summarized the performance of the QR code based system and the proposed system, and some significant differences were observed: 1) the QR codes were only detectable within 1m, whereas the proposed color codes were detectable up to a distance of 2.5m; 2) within a short distance of 50cm, the QR codes were localized with a larger viewing angle than the proposed color codes, however, beyond 1m, the proposed color codes were accurately detected within an average viewing angle of 30°. In

terms of the process time, the QR code-based method was faster than the proposed method, however, the proposed system was also effective in real-time. The overall performance of the proposed method was superior to that the QR code-based method.

4.2 Field Test
To prove its feasibility for indoor wayfinding, the proposed system was tested with four visually impaired people. For the experiment, test map was constructed, as shown in Figs. 11, which included the various situation types, color codes, and three destinations. For the maps, it was assumed that the users started at a predefined point and were navigating an unknown environment to a known destination. When starting, the system first finds 'information' pictogram to get the information for the destination, then it finds 'elevator' to allow the user to arrive the target floor (Fig. 11(a)). Goal 2 and 3 were to find the toilet and a specific office (Fig. 11(b)). Then, the space contained textured and cluttered background and reflective lighting with shadow.

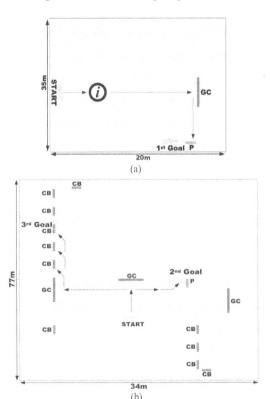

Figure 11. Test maps. (a) and (b) have three goals

Each user was given a basic introduction on how to operate the proposed system. And we asked them to make their path from the start point to the destination using the instructions provided by our wayfinding system. We walked behind the user and measured the complete time and decision error rate elapse from the start point on the run till the goal. In addition, the paths used to reach the destinations were also compared with the optimal route (taken by people with normal vision).

Fig. 12 shows the tracks made by the test subjects, where Figs 12(a) and (b) correspond to the three goals and each color line represents the trajectory of one test subject. When using the proposed system, all the test subjects took a near optimal route in the unfamiliar indoor environment without any point of reference. Plus, the average lateral space relative to the optimal path was around 0.5m. Thus, even through some errors occurred, field test results showed that the proposed system produced an error decision rate (hit rate) of less than 5% on average.

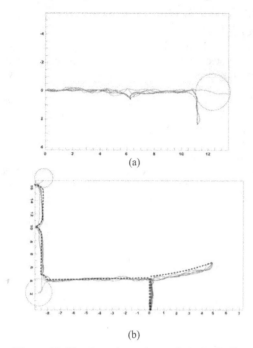

(a)

(b)

Figure 12. User's trajectories: red circles indicate positions of mistaken decisions, black line shows optimal route, and 4 color lines are mapped four test subjects

Fig. 13 shows the average travel time taken for respective users to accomplish the three goals. In the case of goal 1, test subject 4 took a long time to reach the destination, as some recognition errors occurred. However, the differences between the completion times for each of the subjects were small, which tells that the proposed system can be easily used regardless of users' experience and prior knowledge for the systems.

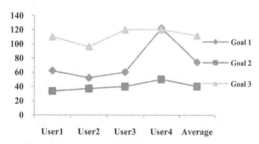

Figure 13. Average time taken to accomplish the respective goal for each user (.s)

Overall, the results confirmed the feasibility of the proposed system as a wayfinding aid for the visually impaired.

5. CONCLUSION

This study developed a new situation-based wayfinding system to help those who are visually impaired or blind recognize their location and find their way to a given destination. Thus, new color codes are designed to represent environment information and a wayfinding system developed to detect and recognize the meaning of these color codes. To assess the validity of the proposed wayfinding system, we have conducted field test with four

visually impaired, then the results showed that they can find the optimal path in real-time with an accuracy of 95%.

The main advantage of the proposed system is that it significantly improves the detection range than other state-of-the-art approaches. Furthermore, the color codes are simple and inexpensive to install with less modification of the environment. Notwithstanding, the color code recognition of the current system is still not perfect. Thus, to improve the accuracy, check digits need to be added to the current color codes, as with QR codes, and this is currently being investigated.

6. ACKNOWLEDGMENTS

This research was supported by the MKE(Ministry of Knowledge Economy), Korea, under the ITRC(Information Technology Research Center) support program supervised by the NIPA(National IT Industry Promotion Agency)(NIPA-2011-C1090-1101-0008), and Basic Science Research Program through the National Research Foundation of Korea(NRF) funded by the Ministry of Education, Science and Technology(No. 20110002565).

7. REFERENCES

[1] World Health Organization (2011) http://www.who.int/blindness/en/.

[2] Cecelja, F. Garaj, V. Hunaiti, Z. and Balachandran, W. A Navigation System for Visually Impaired. IEEE IMTC, pp. 25-27, 2006.

[3] Ando, B. Baglio, S. Marletta, V. and Pitrone, N. A Mixed Inertial & RF-ID Orientation Tool for the Visually Impaired, IEEE SSD, pp.1-6, 2009.

[4] Beydoun, K. Felea, V. and Guyennet, H. Wireless sensor network system helping navigation of the visually impaired. IEEE ICTTA, pp.1-5, 2008.

[5] Treuillet, S. Royer, E. Chateau, T. and Dhome, M. Body Mounted Vision System for Visually Impaired Outdoor and Indoor Wayfinding Assistance. CVHI, pp.1-6, 2007.

[6] Anderson, J.D. Lee, D.J. and Archibald, J.K. Embedded Stereo Vision System Providing Visual Guidance to the Visually Impaired. IEEE LiSSA, pp. 229-232, 2008.

[7] Smart Camera project (2009) http://www.davidsweeneydesign.com/project/wayfinding/.

[8] Kulyukin, V.A. and Kutiyanawala, A. Demo: ShopMobile II: Eyes-Free Supermarket Grocery Shopping for Visually Impaired Mobile Phone Users. IEEE CVPRW, pp.31-32, 2010.

[9] Coughlan, J. and Manduchi, R. Color targets: Fiducials to Help Visually Impaired People Find Their Way by Camera Phone. *EURASIP J. Im. Vis. Pr.*, Vol. 2007, pp.1-13, 2007.

[10] Korean Standards Service Network (2010) http://www.kssn.net/.

[11] Bay, H. Tuytelaars, T. and L.V. Gool, SURF: Speeded-up robust features. ECCV, pp.1-14, 2006.

[12] Stewenius, H. and Nister, D. Scalable recognition with a vocabulary tree, CVPR, pp.2161-2168, 2006.

[13] Sanchez, J. and de la Torre, N. Autonomous navigation through the city for the blind, ACM ASSETS, pp.195-202, 2010.

Navigation and Obstacle Avoidance Help (NOAH) for Older Adults with Cognitive Impairment: A Pilot Study

Pooja Viswanathan[1], James J. Little[1], Alan K. Mackworth[1], Alex Mihailidis[2]

[1]Computer Science
University of British Columbia
2366 Main Mall, Vancouver
British Columbia, Canada V6T1Z4

{poojav, little, mack}@cs.ubc.ca

[2]Occupational Sciences and Occupational Therapy
University of Toronto
500 University Avenue, Toronto
Ontario, Canada M5G 1V7

alex.mihailidis@utoronto.ca

ABSTRACT

Many older adults with cognitive impairment are excluded from powered wheelchair use because of safety concerns. This leads to reduced mobility, and in turn, higher dependence on caregivers. In this paper, we describe an intelligent wheelchair that uses computer vision and machine learning methods to provide adaptive navigation assistance to users with cognitive impairment. We demonstrate the performance of the system in a user study with the target population. We show that the collision avoidance module of the system successfully decreases the number of collisions for all participants. We also show that the wayfinding module assists users with memory and vision impairments. We share feedback from the users on various aspects of the intelligent wheelchair system. In addition, we provide our own observations and insights on the target population and their use of intelligent wheelchairs. Finally, we suggest directions for future work.

Categories and Subject Descriptors

K.4.2 [Computers and Society]: Social Issues–Assistive technologies for persons with disabilities

General Terms

Design, Human Factors.

Keywords

Intelligent wheelchair, dementia, collision avoidance, navigation assistance.

Permission to make digital or hard copies of all or part of this work for personal or classroom use is granted without fee provided that copies are not made or distributed for profit or commercial advantage and that copies bear this notice and the full citation on the first page. To copy otherwise, or republish, to post on servers or to redistribute to lists, requires prior specific permission and/or a fee.
ASSETS'11, October 24–26, 2011, Dundee, Scotland, UK.
Copyright 2011 ACM 978-1-4503-0919-6/11/10...$10.00.

1. INTRODUCTION

It is estimated that 60-80% of the residents in long-term care facilities have dementia [1]. These residents often experience limited mobility due to the lack of strength to walk and/or propel themselves in a manual wheelchair. Use of powered wheelchairs would help restore their mobility and independence, however safe operation of these wheelchairs requires significant cognitive capacity, thus excluding drivers with cognitive impairments and making them highly dependent on caregivers to porter them around. In order to address this issue, we propose an intelligent powered wheelchair that can ensure safe and effective navigation, thus increasing independence in older adults with cognitive impairment and reducing caregiver burden.

This paper describes quantitative and qualitative results obtained from a user study of a novel vision-based collision avoidance and wayfinding system for powered wheelchair users with cognitive impairment. We target older adults who have limited mobility due to lack of strength to operate manual wheelchairs, and face difficulties in safe and independent navigation due to cognitive impairment. The results from this study highlight the benefits that intelligent wheelchairs can provide to the target population. It also provides valuable insights gained from the users and suggests areas for future development and testing.

2. RELATED WORK

Although several intelligent wheelchairs have been developed recently [2-5], these wheelchairs navigate autonomously, thus taking control away from the user. On the other hand, wheelchairs that leave planning and navigation to the user and only provide collision avoidance support are not appropriate for users with cognitive impairment since they often lack planning abilities. We suggest a control strategy that provides supportive, passive navigation assistance that increases independence, while ensuring safety. In addition, we seek to build a system that is portable, cost-effective, and performs reliably in real-world settings. Existing intelligent wheelchairs have used various active sensors (acoustic, sonar, infrared, laser, etc.) that are often large, expensive, power-hungry, unsafe, and prone to cross-talk issues [6]. In this paper, we describe a system that relies on a stereo-vision camera due to its low power consumption, ability to perform in natural environments, and relatively low cost. In addition, cameras capture and provide a richer dataset than can be used for high-level scene understanding to build maps and determine what type of room the wheelchair is in (e.g., kitchen).

Other assistive technologies for older adults include Nursebot [7], a robot that guides the elderly in assisted living homes and

Figure 1. NOAH wheelchair system (commercially available wheelchair equipped with stereo-vision camera and laptop)

the Assisted Cognition project [8], which focuses on learning user models in order to predict when the user needs help. The prototype in [9] is a system that demonstrates the use of machine learning methods to assist users with cognitive impairment in outdoor wayfinding. Most outdoor wayfinding systems rely on GPS, which is unreliable in indoor settings, while indoor wayfinding systems typically use beacon and RFID technology, which require modifications to the environment. By using vision-based methods we achieve accurate localization, while reducing or eliminating the need for environment modifications. COACH [10] is an example of a vision-based adaptive prompting system that assists users with dementia in the task of handwashing. We apply similar techniques to the problem of navigation by combining adaptive prompts with collision avoidance to allow wheelchair users to reach their destination in a safe and timely manner. The study reported in this paper advances other studies with older adults with dementia driving anti-collision wheelchairs [11] [12] by adding a wayfinding component.

3. SYSTEM OVERVIEW

The intelligent wheelchair system consists of a Pride Mobility wheelchair, a 4mm Bumblebee® 3D stereo-vision camera mounted on the front of the wheelchair, and a laptop computer placed at the bottom of the wheelchair (see Figure 1). The wheelchair includes a Quantum Logic Controller, which sends signals from the laptop to the wheelchair, enabling/disabling motion of the wheelchair in specific directions. The main modules in this system are the Collision Detector, the Route Planner, and the Prompter (see Figure 2). We discuss each module in subsequent sections.

The modules are integrated using the Robot Operating System (ROS) framework (www.ros.org), which allows us to run multiple processes in a distributed fashion. The images collected by the camera are grabbed at 640 X 480 resolution. In order for the system to determine the wheelchair's position at any time, a map is first created of the test environment. This only needs to be done once for every new environment that the wheelchair has to navigate in. For this study, we constructed the map using a Pioneer robot equipped with a SICK laser using methods in [13] as seen in Figure 3. This allowed us to create an accurate and dense map that can be used by the Route Planner module. The map is loaded into a graphic interface in a visualization module provided by ROS called Rviz, where start and goal locations can be specified by clicking on appropriate regions.

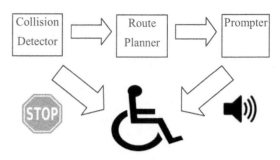

Figure 2. System Diagram of NOAH containing three main modules that aid in collision avoidance and wayfinding.

3.1 Collision Detector

In order to detect collisions with obstacles, we generate *depth maps* from stereo images that contain the distances from the wheelchair to visible objects in the environment. When an obstacle is detected within a pre-specified distance threshold, the wheelchair is stopped to avoid a collision. In addition, movement of the wheelchair towards the object is prevented to encourage the user to navigate around the obstacle. An earlier prototype also provided audio prompts suggesting an immediate direction for the user to drive in to avoid the obstacle, however these prompts were disabled in this study (only long-term navigation audio prompts were provided). Further details on this module can be found in [14]. While the Route Planner module only observes the position of the wheelchair at a pre-specified time interval, the Collision Detector module is on at all times to ensure safety.

3.2 Route Planner

After specifying the starting and goal locations on the map of the test environment, we use existing localization [15] and path planning techniques [16] to determine the position and orientation of the wheelchair at any specified time, as well as the optimal route to the goal. We compute whether the user is on-route, off-route, or stopped using the wheelchair's position and orientation. We also analyze the route for upcoming turns. This module is tested in [17] and is extended by incorporating information from the Collision Detector in order to ensure that the user is not guided towards an obstacle. The Prompter module is then used to issue an audio prompt.

3.3 Prompter

We use a decision-theoretic method called a Partially Observable Markov Decision Process (POMDP) to model the user's behavior and cognitive state (similar to [10]), as well as the wheelchair's status along the route, using noisy visual observations received from the Route Planner. The Prompter tries to estimate whether the user needs help, and then issues an appropriate prompt. For example, if the user is not *aware*, he/she is likely to perform an incorrect behavior (e.g. make a detour or stop before reaching the goal). If the user is *responsive*, he/she is likely to perform the correct behavior when an audio prompt is issued. Probabilities for the different user behaviors are specified using domain knowledge. Possible system actions are *do nothing*, *prompt*, or *call caregiver*. Possible prompts are "off route – turn right/left/around" if the user is off route, "move slightly to the left/right" if a minor correction is required or an upcoming turn is detected, and "move forward" if the user is stopped or moving backwards. Since we wanted to encourage the users to follow

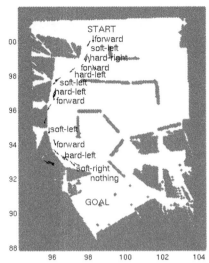

Figure 3. Laser map of the facility with examples of system prompts for participant 5 in a run during phase B.

Figure 4. Scene view of the maze. Participants were required to navigate around wall and maneuverability foam obstacles.

directional prompts in this study, the cost of the *call caregiver* action was set to be very high to assign this action low preference. In a realistic setting, this action could alert caregivers in the event that the user is wandering and unresponsive to prompts. Refer to Figure 3 for an example of system prompts issued to participant 5 during a run of phase B.

4. EVALUATION
4.1 Study Design
The study consisted of two phases A and B. In phase A, the automated collision avoidance and wayfinding system was deactivated (baseline), while phase B was conducted with the system in use (intervention). We used a within-subjects, counterbalanced study design where we randomly chose half of the participants for A-B phase ordering, and assigned the other half B-A ordering. Each phase consisted of one training session and eight driving sessions (runs). All participants (n=6) completed a total of sixteen runs.

The study was conducted in a dedicated research room (approximately 50 metres x 50 metres in size) of the long-term care facility. A video camera was mounted above the wheelchair to capture joystick motion while the user was driving, and an additional camera was used by the research assistant to capture the scene view. All participants provided consent to videotape their sessions and to log any verbal feedback or observations during the period of the study. During the trials, the researcher followed each participant closely in order to provide assistance in case the participant was confused or anxious, or to stop the wheelchair in the case of an emergency.

4.2 Task
Prior to each phase, a training session was conducted for each participant, where he/she was taught how to operate the powered wheelchair (with or without the anti-collision and wayfinding system depending on the phase being conducted) in an open area. They were taught how to navigate around sample obstacles. In phase B, the researcher explained the stopping mechanism of the collision avoidance and taught the participant to use enabled joystick motions as well as to move backwards (to create more free space) and then move around the obstacle. Additionally, the

various audio prompts delivered by the system were played to the participant in phase B training to ensure that they were able to follow the prompts. The training session in both phases was concluded by escorting the participants in their manual wheelchair along the optimal route to a specified goal (a stop sign) at the end of the maze.

The maze was assembled out of Styrofoam boards (see Figure 5). The use of Styrofoam for obstacles ensured that collisions did not harm the participants. The course included 5 types of movements: 90° right turn, 90° left turn, entering a narrow straight line path, weaving motion (around maneuverability obstacles along the route) and stopping. These movements were based on existing tests used to assess powered wheelchair mobility [18] [19]. The maximum speed of the wheelchair was set to 0.25 m/s to ensure safety. In order to reduce learning effects, we alternated between two different layouts of maneuverability obstacles, so that subsequent runs contained slightly different positions of obstacles. In addition, we constructed a random ordering of five different starting orientations, such that the participant started every run facing in a different direction than the previous run. This ordering was repeated in both phases.

At the beginning of each run, the user was asked to report on whether they were confident in navigating along the specified route using learning transference acquired from the training period and/or previous runs. The participant was then asked to find the stop sign by following the route specified during the training session and performing the movement tasks described above. During each run, the researcher recorded the number of collision events that occurred, the time taken to reach the goal, as well as the length of the route navigated by the participant (measured with a distance measuring wheel). At the end of each run, the participant answered questions for perceived ease of use of the powered wheelchair, using the standardized NASA-TLX questionnaire [20]. At the end of each phase, the researcher administered a QUEST 2.0 (Quebec User Evaluation of Satisfaction with Assistive Technology) questionnaire [21] regarding the participant's perceived satisfaction, as well as a custom questionnaire to solicit general feedback from the user regarding the device and their mobility needs.

4.3 Outcome Measures
The primary outcome measures in the study were:
1. The number of frontal collisions encountered with obstacles by the participant;

2. The amount of time taken to reach the goal;
3. The length of the route navigated by the participant.

The secondary outcome measures for the study were:
1. Quebec User Evaluation of Satisfaction with Assistive Technology (QUEST 2.0);
2. NASA-TLX (Task Load Index) scores;
3. User's rating of self-confidence in following the route specified during training;
4. General feedback regarding the device obtained using the custom questionnaire;
5. Verbal comments and visual observations relating to user interactions with the device.

4.4 Participants

A purposive sampling method was used. Six participants from the long-term care facility were recruited for this study. Since it was a pilot study, a larger sample size was not needed. Also, a minimum of four single subjects is suggested to give preliminary evidence that the initial findings did not occur by chance [22].

To be included in the study, participants had to:
- be over the age of 65;
- have a mild-to-moderate cognitive impairment (assessed by the Mini Mental State Exam (MMSE) or equivalent);
- provide written consent from his/her substitute decision maker;
- be able to sit in a powered wheelchair for an hour per day;
- be able to follow prompts and have basic communication skills;
- be able to operate a joystick and identify directions.

Preference was given to individuals who met the criteria above and had difficulties with staying oriented and/or experienced short-term memory loss (as determined by MMSE or equivalent test results) and/or had visual impairments. Participants were excluded if they had a history of aggression or significant prior experience with a powered wheelchair due to potential historical effects on the validity of the outcome measures.

Table 1. Participant Information

ID	Age	Gender	Impairment Level (MMSE Score)
1	97	Female	Moderate (15)
2	71	Male	Mild (19)
3	66	Male	Moderate (15)
4	86	Female	Moderate (15)
5	91	Female	Mild/Intact (25)
6	80	Female	Mild (19)

Three of the selected participants had short-term memory deficits (participants 1, 3 and 5), and participant 1 also had a severe visual impairment (according to their quarterly assessments). Participant 1 could not understand some of the audio prompts, so the recordings were slightly simplified and modified to include one of her native languages. She had severe mood swings, as indicated in her assessment, and thus her participation in the trials was highly inconsistent. She was able to propel herself in her manual wheelchair. None of the participants had significant experience driving powered wheelchairs, however participants 2 and 3 had

used a similar wheelchair in a few previous studies, and used manual wheelchairs on a regular basis, with participant 2 mainly propelling himself backwards. Participant 4 was unable to propel herself in her manual wheelchair and required total assistance to complete activities of daily living according to her assessment. Participant 5 used a walker and was highly mobile, but tended to wander because of the memory deficits and high disorientation found in her cognitive assessment. She completed all sixteen runs with the same starting orientation (facing the entrance of the maze), since any other orientation was found to increase her anxiety. Participant 6 used a walker and was able to navigate around the facility independently. She had left-right confusion, and was thus provided with markers on her hands to help her in identifying directions. Refer to Table 1 for information on each participant's age, gender and level of cognitive impairment.

5. RESULTS

In this paper, we report on the primary outcomes: number of frontal collisions and length of the route traveled. Although we do not report on the time taken here, we summarize related observations in the discussion.

5.1 Collision Avoidance

Figure 5 shows the number of collisions for all participants. Regardless of ordering, we can see that the total number of collisions for all participants is lower with the system (phase B). Participants 1 and 6 benefited the most from the collision avoidance system. While most participants did not show any learning trends, participant 2 demonstrated learning effects, as seen in Figure 5. The overall performance of each participant per phase can be summarized by the mean number of collisions as shown in Table 2. The mean number of collisions is lower with the system for all participants.

Table 2. Collision Avoidance Performance

ID	Mean Number of Collisions	
	Phase A (8 runs)	Phase B (8 runs)
1	8	1.38
2	1.13	0
3	0.13	0
4	0.25	0.13
5	0.5	0.13
6	3.13	0.25

Table 3. Wayfinding Performance

ID	Mean Length of Route Taken (in metres)	
	Phase A (8 runs)	Phase B (8 runs)
1	18.21	11.31
2	11.31	11.31
3	13.92	11.31
4	11.68	11.31
5	18.91	11.94
6	11.31	11.31

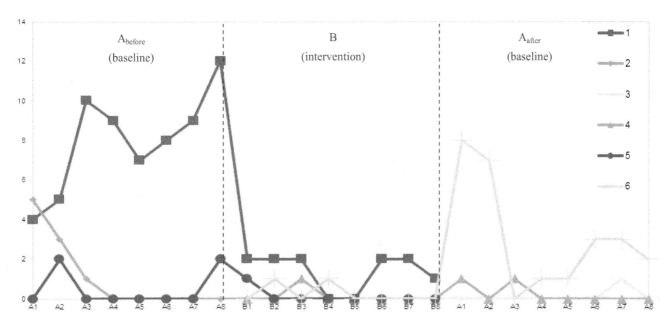

Figure 5. Number of collisions for each participant. Note that participants 1, 2 and 5 have A-B (A_{before} and B) phase ordering, while participants 3, 4 and 6 have B-A (B and A_{after}) ordering, where A is the baseline phase and B is with the system activated.

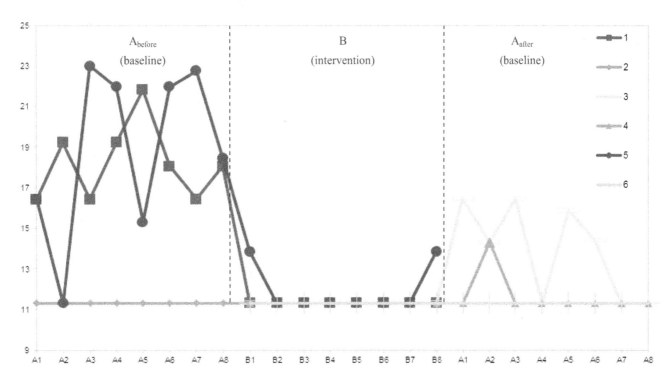

Figure 6. Length of route taken (in metres) for each participant. Note that participants 1, 2 and 5 have A-B (A_{before} and B) phase ordering, while participants 3, 4 and 6 have B-A (B and A_{after}) ordering, where A is the baseline phase and B is with the system activated (intervention phase).

5.2 Wayfinding Assistance

Figure 6 shows the length of the route traveled by all participants. Participants 1 and 3 traveled along the optimal route when the system was engaged, but often traveled longer distances without the system since they had short-term memory impairments that prevented them from learning the shortest route. Participant 5 also traveled along the optimal route more often in the intervention phase, however she traveled slightly longer distances in her first and last run during the intervention phases due to a delayed prompt, which resulted in a missed turn. The system was able to redirect her to the destination subsequently. While the other participants did not benefit greatly from this module, the system did not hurt their performance either. Participants 2 and 6 followed the optimal route in every run in both phases. Participant 4 deviated from the optimal route in one of her baseline runs due to temporary disorientation, thus traveling a longer distance. Table 3 shows the mean distances of the routes traveled by all participants.

5.3 User Surveys

We collected qualitative feedback using the NASA-TLX, the QUEST 2.0, and a custom questionnaire regarding the device and task loads. These surveys included simple Likert-scale questions, which have been used successfully with older adults with cognitive impairments in order to provide useful and valid self-reported information, such as level of pain [23] and quality of life [24-27]. Because of space constraints, we focus here on four main areas: collision avoidance, concerns with powered wheelchair use, overall satisfaction with the system, and attitudes towards autonomy.

5.3.1 Collision Avoidance

Participants 3, 4 and 5 did not feel that they required a collision avoidance system. This could be due to the fact that they had high baseline driving abilities. In addition, the test environment was static and was free of safety hazards (such as sharp and hard objects), thus possibly reducing anxiety and fear of collisions. Participant 2, on the other hand, felt that he really needed a collision avoidance system and did not trust himself to drive without colliding into obstacles. Due to his tendency to push himself backwards in his manual wheelchair, he often had minor collisions in the long-term care facility, thus possibly making him more concerned about safety. Participant 6 also shared a high level of anxiety regarding collisions, and wanted a collision avoidance system. Although participant 1 could not answer any of the custom survey questions, she expressed a fear of collisions. She slowly overcame this fear during the baseline phase through repeated trials, however, she reported lower levels of anxiety and higher levels of performance in the NASA-TLX survey when the system was in use.

5.3.2 Concerns with Powered Wheelchair Use

When asked about what the participants liked least about the wheelchair system, most responses were found to be hardware-related (relating to the commercial wheelchair) rather than software-related. Some participants expressed that they did not like the need to charge batteries. While participants 2 and 3 wanted to be able to drive faster, participants 1, 4 and 5 were satisfied with the speed, and participant 6 wanted the chair to be slowed down. Participants 2 and 4 found the chair to be bulky and preferred a smaller and lower chair, while participant 3 preferred a bigger chair.

5.3.3 Overall Satisfaction

When asked about the effectiveness of the collision avoidance and wayfinding system, most participants were quite satisfied, with participants 2 and 4 stating, "it seems to be doing what it's supposed to be doing". Participant 3 liked the just-in-time method of prompting, and said that he was happy to receive directions and assistance as long as it was not excessive and distracting. When asked whether they would use the wheelchair if it was available to them, participants 2 and 4 said they

definitely would. Participant 4 was the most interested in the wheelchair since she felt "[she] would go to all the places [she] couldn't currently go to" on her own. Participants 3 and 5 felt that they did not need a powered wheelchair since they felt they were able to fulfill their mobility needs with their own mobility devices. Participant 3 did, however, mention that he would be interested in a powered wheelchair if it gave him the ability to navigate significantly faster. Although participant 6 was found to be quite mobile with her walker, she said she would like to be able to use the wheelchair when she was too tired to walk. Participant 1 could not communicate her responses, however we noticed high levels of enthusiasm (due to increased performance and shorter driving times leading to lower fatigue) when the system was activated. Without the system, the participant traveled longer distances for greater amounts of time, and often needed to be motivated to complete the task. With the system, she was able to independently follow prompts, and often asked for "more!" when she reached her destination, suggesting greater satisfaction.

5.3.4 Autonomy

We solicited feedback to gain insight on participants' reactions to a completely autonomous wheelchair that would take them to their desired locations. Participant 5 emphatically stated, "I want to be in control!". Due to her high levels of anxiety, it is highly likely that an autonomous system would frustrate her. However, her willingness to follow instructions suggests that a prompting system that allows her to make her own decisions (such as the system described in this paper) is well-suited to her needs and cognitive abilities. Participants 2, 4 and 6 said they would like to use an autonomous chair as long as it functioned correctly, thus suggesting that high system reliability is a crucial requirement of an autonomous wheelchair. Participant 3 was open to using an autonomous wheelchair, but preferred to be in control, only receiving assistance when required. We could not gain any feedback from participant 1 on this topic. It is interesting to note that participants with higher levels of confusion due to memory impairment (3 and 5) expressed a higher need to be in control, while participants who were not confused were more willing to give up control. Further studies with the target population would help us determine whether these observations generalize to other older adults with cognitive impairment.

6. DISCUSSION

The results in this study indicate that users with dementia have varying functional abilities. Users with short-term memory deficits but high (observed) visuo-spatial awareness often possessed sufficient planning abilities to be able to maneuver around obstacles; however they could not remember the optimal route to the goal. Participant 3 learnt, over time, what he was looking for (the stop sign) and was able to reach the destination on his own by exploring the maze, although the system helped him navigate along the shortest path more often. Participants 1 and 5, on the other hand, needed constant reminders about the purpose of the task and often retraced their paths in the same run. Interestingly, when the system was not used, participant 5 viewed the task as simply a driving task with no time constraint. She often asked questions such as "Where am I going?". However, interview responses indicated that when the system was in use, she viewed the task as "trying to get from one room to another". She did not seem to benefit from the collision avoidance module since her baseline driving ability was quite high. Participant 1 also did not show any signs of learning the optimal route because of her memory and visual impairments. Since she could not see obstacles clearly, she benefited from both the collision avoidance and wayfinding modules. Participant 4 usually had excellent memory and high maneuverability skills. However, on rare occasions, she was found to experience temporary disorientation and deviate from the optimal route.

Participants 2 and 6 were found to have excellent memory, but had more collisions than most of the other participants. It is unclear whether this was due to low visuo-spatial awareness, delayed reaction times, or impatience. It is important to consider that the foam obstacles might not have been perceived as dangerous by the participants, possibly making the participants more likely to drive through them. However, it is difficult to conduct a study with real obstacles because of safety concerns.

The above discussion indicates that the abilities of collision avoidance and wayfinding might be independent. Main predictors of success in these two tasks might be short-term memory and visuo-spatial awareness. The POMDP could be extended to include these predictors as different variables that lead to distinct user behaviors. For example, the model could specify that users with low visuo-spatial awareness are more likely to collide with obstacles, thus needing additional prompts that identify free space and obstacles. Users with poor short-term memory are more likely to deviate from the optimal route and need directions, while those who are able to learn the route might simply require task reminders (e.g., "Find the stop sign").

In addition, some participants required justification for the stopping action of the wheelchair and were frustrated by the blocked wheelchair motions. Participant 3 commented during a trial "it's not going where I'm telling it to go". Participant 4 said the wheelchair was more "regulated" when the system was activated, and that, in contrast, the wheelchair was more "responsive" when the system was deactivated. Although she did not feel that the collision avoidance module harmed her, she did not perceive it as a necessity and appreciated being told why the wheelchair was being stopped. The stopping action was, in general, found to be confusing for some participants and was found to increase the time taken to complete the course in some cases.

We also found differing levels of responsiveness to prompts. Participant 5 constantly relied on instructions from caregivers to perform day-to-day tasks, and her compliance with the prompting system was found to be quite high. Participant 1 was mostly compliant with the system, and often responded "yeah" when she heard a prompt, as she tried to follow it. However, when the system seemed to guide her towards an obstacle hidden from the camera's view, she said "no sense!", showing that she did not agree with the system, and correctly disobeyed. Participant 3 seemed to wait for and comply with the prompts when he was unsure of which direction to navigate in, but was found to correctly ignore incorrect prompts when he was confident of which direction the destination was in. Most errors in prompting occurred towards the end of the run, due to accumulated localization errors, thus suggesting the need for re-initialization of position estimates based on pre-registered landmarks. Alternatively, wheel encoders or inertial measurement units could be added to provide additional

information on distance traveled and to increase localization accuracy. Although the isolated prompting errors did not seem to frustrate users during the study, we anticipate that reducing these errors will help increase user satisfaction.

Although we showed that the distances traveled were longer for some participants when the system was not used, it is important to note that the longer distances reported were specific to the maze constructed for this study in a limited amount of space. One can see that in a more realistic environment, even a single deviation from the optimal route can lead to arbitrarily longer routes depending on the floor layout. Thus, the effectiveness of the system in guiding the participants along the optimal route can lead to increased timeliness, and, more importantly, decreased fatigue, which is a major factor in wheelchair use.

7. FUTURE WORK

In the future, we hope to test alternative methods of collision avoidance such as automatic correction of wheelchair heading, moving the user away from the obstacle. This could help reduce stop times and thus ensure faster navigation to the goal. Another possible area of future work is haptic and/or visual feedback to provide more useful information on what the correct user behavior should be in a collision event. We will also investigate increasing computational speed of the collision avoidance and wayfinding modules in order to allow participants to navigate faster, while maintaining high system accuracy.

We plan on modifying/expanding the user model to incorporate the results found in this study. For example, the likelihood that a driver needs detailed collision avoidance prompts is higher if he/she has low visuo-spatial awareness. However, someone with poor memory and high visuo-spatial awareness might only require wayfinding assistance. Also, users with left-right confusion might require added visual prompts.

Finally, we would like to improve localization accuracy and test the system in a more realistic environment to help users navigate to real locations in the long-term care facility. Through this study, we hope to evaluate the effects of the system on their day-to-day mobility and social well-being.

8. CONCLUSIONS

Very few intelligent wheelchair studies have been conducted with older adults with cognitive impairment. We hope that this study provides key insights on the benefits of intelligent wheelchairs to the target population. We have shown quantitative evidence that such a wheelchair could allow safe and independent mobility for cognitively-impaired older adults. Our system is able to lower the total number of frontal collisions and help users in navigating along the shortest route to the specified goal. We found that users with short-term memory and/or vision impairments benefited most from the system. We hope that continued development and testing of the system will help refine user needs and allow us to create an intelligent wheelchair that truly improves quality of life of older adults with cognitive impairment.

9. ACKNOWLEDGMENTS

We would like to thank CIHR and NSERC for funding this research. We would also like to thank all the participants in the study for their continued enthusiasm and insightful feedback. In addition, we would like to thank Amanda Calvin, Tammy Craig, Tuck Voon-How, and Rosalie Wang for their assistance in conducting the trials and helpful suggestions.

10. REFERENCES

[1] Payne, J. L., Sheppard, J. E., Steinberg, M., Warren, A., Baker, A., Steele, C., Brandt, J., and Lyketsos, C. G. (2002). Incidence, prevalence, and outcomes of depression in residents of a long-term care facility with dementia," International Journal of Geriatric Psychiatry; vol. 17, pp. 247-253.

[2] Simpson, R.C., Poirot, D., and Baxter, F. (2002). The Hephaestus Smart Wheelchair System. IEEE Transactions on Neural Systems and Rehabilitation Engineering, 10,(2): 118-122.

[3] Odor, J.P., Watson, M., Nisbet, P., and Craig, I. (2000). The CALL Centre smart wheelchair handbook 1.5. CALL Centre.

[4] McGarry, S., Moir, L., Girdler, S., and Taylor, L. (2009). The smart wheelchair: is it an effective mobility training tool for children with cerebral palsy? The Centre for Cerebral Palsy, Coolbinia, WA, UK.

[5] Honore, W. et al. (2010). Human-Oriented Design and Initial Validation of an Intelligent Powered Wheelchair. RESNA Annual Conference.

[6] Simpson, R.C. (2005) Smart wheelchairs: A literature review. J Rehabil Res Dev. Jul-Aug;42(4):423-36.

[7] Pollack, M.E. et. al. (2002). Pearl: Mobile robotic assistant for the elderly. In AAAI Workshop on Automation as Eldercare, pages 85–92.

[8] Liao, L., Fox, D., and Kautz, H. (2004). Learning and inferring transportation routines. In Proc of the 19th Natl Conf on AI.

[9] Liu A., et al. (2009). Informing the Design of an Automated Wayfinding System for Individuals with Cognitive Impairments, Proc. 3rd Int'l Conf. Pervasive Computing Technologies for Healthcare, IEEE CS Press.

[10] Hoey, J., Von Bertoldi, A., Craig, T., Poupart, P. and Mihailidis, A. (2010). Handwashing Assistance For Persons With Dementia Using Video and A Partially Observable Markov Decision Process. Computer Vision and Image Understanding, 114(5), 503-519.

[11] How, T.V., Wang, R.H., and Mihailidis, A. (2011). Clinical Evaluation of the Intelligent Wheelchair System. Rehabilitation Engineering and Assistive Technology Society of North America (RESNA), Toronto, ON, Canada, June 5-8, 2011.

[12] Wang, R. H., Mihailidis, A., Dutta, T., & Fernie, G. R. (accepted). Usability testing of a multimodal feedback interface on a simulated collision avoidance power wheelchair for long-term care home residents with cognitive impairments. Journal of Rehabilitation Research and Development.

[13] Grisetti, G., Stachniss, C., and Burgard, W. (2007). Improved Techniques for Grid Mapping With Rao-Blackwellized Particle Filters, in IEEE Transactions on Robotics, pp.34-46.

[14] Viswanathan, P., Hoey, J., Boger, J., and Mihailidis, A. (2007). A comparison of stereovision and infrared as sensors for an anti-collision powered wheelchair for older adults with cognitive impairments. 2nd International Conference on Technology and Aging, Toronto.

[15] Konolige, K., Grisetti, G., Kümmerle, R., Burgard, W., Limketkai, B., and Vincent, R. (2010). Sparse Pose Adjustment for 2D Mapping. In Proc. of the IEEE/RSJ Int. Conf. on Intelligent Robots and Systems (IROS). Taipei, Taiwan.

[16] Alton, K., and Mitchell, I. M. (2008). Fast Marching Methods for Stationary Hamilton-Jacobi Equations with Axis-Aligned Anisotropy. SIAM Journal on Numerical Analysis, 47(1) pp. 363-385.

[17] Viswanathan, P., Alimi, P., Little, J. J., Mackworth, A. K., and Mihailidis, A. (2011). Navigation Assistance for Intelligent Wheelchairs. 3rd International Conference on Technology and Aging/ RESNA, Toronto.

[18] Dawson, D., Kaiserman-Goldenstein, E., Chan, R., and Gleason, J. (2006). Power-Mobility Indoor driving assessment manual.

[19] Kirby, R.L. (2008). Wheelchair Skills Program Manual v4.1. [Online]. http://www.wheelchairskillsprogram.ca/eng/4.1/WST_Manual_Version4.1.51.pdf

[20] Hart, S. G., and Staveland, L. E. (1988). Development of the NASA-TLX (Task Load Index): Results of empirical and theoretical research, N. Meshkati, Ed. Amsterdam: North Holland Press, pp. 239-250.

[21] Demers, L., Weiss-Lambrou, R., and Ska, B. (2002). The Quebec User Evaluation of Satisfaction with Assistive Technology (QUEST 2.0): An overview and recent progress. Technology and Disability, no. 14, pp. 101-105.

[22] Barlow, D.H. and Hersen, M. (1984). Single care experimental designs: Strategies for studying behavior change, Second edition. New York: Allyn & Bacon.

[23] Fisher, S. E., et al. (2006). Obtaining Self-Report Data From Cognitively Impaired Elders: Methodological Issues and Clinical Implications for Nursing Home Pain Assessment. The Gerontologist, vol. 46, pp. 81-88.

[24] James, B.D., et al. (2005). How Do Patients With Alzheimer Disease Rate Their Overall Quality of Life? American Journal of Geriatric Psychiatry, vol. 13, pp. 484-490.

[25] Cahill, S., et al. (2004). I Know Where this is Going and I Know it won't Go Back' Hearing the Individual's Voice in Dementia Quality of Life Assessments. Dementia, vol. 3, pp. 313-330.

[26] Brod, M. et al. (1999). Conceptualization and Measurement of Quality of Life in Dementia: The Dementia Quality of Life Instrument (DQoL). The Gerontologist, vol. 39, pp. 25-35.

Understanding the Computer Skills of Adult Expert Users with Down Syndrome: An Exploratory Study

Jonathan Lazar[1], Libby Kumin [2], and Jinjuan Heidi Feng[1]

[1] Towson University
8000 York Road
Towson, MD, USA 21252

[2] Loyola University Maryland
4501 North Charles Street
Baltimore, MD 21210

jlazar@towson.edu, lkumin@loyola.edu, jfeng@towson.edu

ABSTRACT

Recent survey research suggests that individuals with Down syndrome use computers for a variety of educational, communication, and entertainment activities. However, there has been no analysis of the actual computer knowledge and skills of employment-aged computer users with Down syndrome. We conducted an ethnographic observation that aims at examining the workplace-related computer skills of expert users with Down syndrome. The results show that expert users with Down syndrome have the ability to use computers for basic workplace tasks such as word processing, data entry, and communication.

Author Keywords

Down syndrome, cognitive impairment, workplace technology, employment, assistive technology, human-computer interaction

ACM Classification Keywords

K.4.2 [Computers and Society]: Social Issues – Assistive technologies for persons with disabilities.

General Terms

Design, Human Factors, Legal Aspects

INTRODUCTION

Over the last 3 decades, the model of developmental and educational growth for people with Down syndrome in the United States has changed. In the 1970s, many people with Down syndrome were locked in institutions, away from society. They had inadequate cognitive and language-based stimulation and adequate education was rarely provided [16]. Starting in the late 1970s and the 1980s, individuals with Down syndrome were offered the benefits of early intervention programs in speech and language, occupational and physical therapy, and mainstreamed education, where they could learn the academic and social skills necessary to interact with others in society. Change has occurred as a result of legislation, home rearing, and advocacy. However, as individuals with Down syndrome transition into adulthood, career options are limited. Very often, adults with Down syndrome are employed working in fast food cleaning tables, as a janitor, or in landscaping. The employment rate for people with cognitive disabilities in the US is estimated at 17-27%, depending on how

you define a cognitive disability such as Down syndrome [23]. Computer skills potentially are useful as increasing numbers of individuals with Down syndrome lead longer lives and attempt to enter the workforce. In our previous research [8, 9], we examined how children and young adults with Down syndrome (age 4-21) learn how to use computers, and what challenges they face. In this study, we observed older, more experienced computer users with Down syndrome, to learn how they interact with computers, and to understand how they potentially could use computers in employment.

BACKGROUND LITERATURE

There is very little research in the human-computer interaction literature related to people with Down syndrome. The first case study involving people with Down syndrome in computer interface design was published in 2007 [14]. The goal of that project was to build a web site, to help teach computer skills to people with Down syndrome. The project was run by the National Down Syndrome Society, and 6 young adults with Down syndrome (age 16-23) participated in the design. The only other work in the HCI literature that is exclusively about people with Down syndrome, is a survey that examined how children and young adults interact with interfaces [8]. There were 561 responses to the survey, which provides a baseline of information about human-computer interaction for younger users with Down syndrome. Results of the survey document that the majority of children and young adults with Down syndrome can use the mouse to interact with computers, which was previously believed to be challenging for individuals with Down syndrome, due to the spatial, cognitive, and fine motor skills needed. Of the survey respondents, they tended to start computer use very young, with 72% of the children having started using computers by the age of five and more than 80% having started by the age of six. However, text entry on keyboards appeared to be a problem. Only 10.8% of the respondents type using multiple fingers on both hands, and a majority type using only one index finger, or one index finger on both hands [8].

Further analysis took place on the open-ended responses to questions in the survey with 561 responses [9]. Cluttered screen designs, with many animations, seem to be overwhelming for children with DS. Time limits on application responses are often too short, since children with Down syndrome, who may be slow typists, need more time to complete a response. There is often a gap between the skills that children with DS need to learn in an application, and the style used to present the content. For instance, a ten-year old child with DS might need to learn simple mathematical skills that are typical for a six-year old. Most of the programs or games available for him for learning skills are designed with features that have appeal for typically developing, six-year old children (e.g., childish cartoon characteristics with exaggerated tones and gestures). For a 10-year old child with DS, they will need to learn the skills in an application designed for a typical six-year old, but they still have the stylistic tastes and expectations of their chronological age, and therefore often view educational programs as "uncool." This creates a paradox: children with DS normally outgrow the programs or games that teach them the skills that they need to learn.

According to survey results, due to the typing and memory skills needed, passwords are often problematic for people with DS, especially when security policies require strong passwords (such as a combination of symbols, numbers, and upper and lower case). While there have generally not been attempts to design applications specifically for people with Down syndrome, if there were attempts, they might be challenging, as DS affects multiple channels of cognitive, motor, and perceptual abilities. Furthermore, DS impacts on each of these multiple channels at different levels of severity for each individual, so to make assumptions that everyone with Down syndrome can perform a certain skill is misleading. Even within the Trisomy 21 genotype (the most common form of Down syndrome, with over 95% [19]), there is diversity in cognition, communication, skills, and capability, for reasons that are still not understood [1] ; [4].

While the causes of such diversity within the group of people who have the same genotype is unknown, from the human-computer interaction point of view, the goal is to understand the diversity within the user group as it relates to interaction with computers. Another goal is to understand any potential factors influencing computer skills, which are not related to the genotype, and are instead caused by early exposure to technology, formal computer training, experience, education, personal encouragement, or public policies.

In addition, the skills of individuals with Down syndrome change greatly over time, and the previous survey data was reported by parents of children and young adults, but may not relate to individuals over age 21. Other studies in the HCI literature have included people with Down syndrome in the broader category of "people with cognitive impairments," without noting their specific strengths and challenges. For instance, Hoque (2008) examined computers for measuring speech challenges of people with Autism and Down Syndrome (which only included 1 participant with DS). [12]. Dawe interviewed families of people with cognitive impairment, to learn how and why they adopt assistive technology. This included a combination of 4 people with Autism, 5 people with Down syndrome, and 12 people with unspecified cognitive impairment. [6]. Other research has combined people with Down syndrome and people with other genetic syndromes [4,7]. The broad category of "users with cognitive challenges" or "users with disabilities" is not specific enough for research study, since each group of users with a specific disability has their own set of strengths and weaknesses. In addition, there is generally great diversity of computer skill within users with a certain disability, and of course this doesn't take into account the fact that many individuals have multiple challenges. Therefore, there is a need to consider the challenges faced by a group of people with the same disability label, as well as the need to identify the specific strengths and challenges for an individual with the condition.

Although there is little research literature on HCI issues for people with Down syndrome, there is a large body of literature on people with Down syndrome, as it relates to communication, cognition, fine motor, short-term memory and motor planning skills. While we know little about the computer skills of individuals with Down syndrome in childhood or adulthood, there has been research on the physical and behavioral characteristics of children with Down syndrome, that highlights factors that potentially could impact on computer skills. Research has documented difficulties in the sensory areas of hearing [21] and vision [22]. There are sensory and motor issues related to finger and hand movements including both hyper and hyposensitivity to touch (tactile) and difficulty with fine motor movements [2]. Low muscle tone and weak muscles are often a problem in the arms and fingers, which could impact on keyboarding skills. There also is a wide range of functional abilities in individuals with DS related to the extent of impairment in the various sensory and motor channels [2], memory [5], cognition [27], and communication skills [7]. Auditory memory and sequential recall are also difficult areas for children with Down syndrome [20]. There is evidence for a specific verbal auditory memory deficit, i.e., that it is harder to remember information that is heard rather than read [13].

The characteristics that might affect computer skills in a specific child are also related to coexisting conditions which may be present in that child, such as autism spectrum disorders [3], depression and obsessive-compulsive disorder [18]. These sensory, motor, and mental health issues would need to be taken into consideration when investigating computer usage needs in individuals with DS. The impact on perceptual channels could cause potential problems when the individual needs to use computers or computer-related output devices, such as text or menu items on a screen. The impact on fine motor skills and muscle tone may play a role when the individual uses a variety of input devices such as a mouse, keyboard, touch screen or a trackball. But, research has documented visual memory strength in people with Down syndrome and since computer usage is often still a primarily visual medium, it can be a good match for the strengths and challenges experienced by individuals with Down syndrome [17].

RESEARCH METHODS

Our research plan was to recruit 10 expert computer users with Down syndrome, and do ethnographic observations of their computer skills and usage, in their respective homes or workplaces.

Unlike previous research, which was based on data collected from a survey filled out by parents, this research was based on ethnographic observation of adults with Down syndrome, using computers in their natural settings. We had heard many reports of "expert" computer users with Down syndrome, and had informally observed some of these experienced users. This is a typical progression of research, where exploratory surveys and ethnographic observations take place to gain an understanding of a previously unexplored area of interest, and more structured research, such as experimental design, will take place at a later time once there is a foundation of understanding [15]. Our goal was to observe expert users, and we do not claim that these users are typical individuals with Down syndrome. Rather, we were interested in observing the scope, given the best circumstances, of what was possible for adults with Down syndrome as it related to computer usage.

To start with, we needed to define what qualifies an individual 18 years or older with Down syndrome as an "expert computer user." We used the following qualifications in this study:

1. Has used computers for at least 5 years

2. Uses computers at least 5 days each week

3. Uses the computer at least 10 hours per week

4. Is familiar with email or a social networking site such as Facebook. Uses those approaches to communicate with relatives or friends at least 3 days a week.

5. Is familiar with word processing software.

6. Is familiar with the internet. Uses the web for information retrieval and entertainment purpose on a daily basis.

Note that three categories of applications are included: communication (such as e-mail and facebook), information retrieval (web browsing and searching), and office automation (word processing, spreadsheeting, and presentation software). We believe that these are the core computer skills required for office work.

To recruit participants, we sent out recruitment e-mails to Down syndrome community listservers in Maryland and Virginia. We noted the basic requirements, but asked anyone who was interested to fill out a survey documenting their habits and usage skills. Using the survey, we determined that a number of them would not meet the requirements for this phase of the research, because they did not have the minimum amount of computer experience. For those who did qualify for the research, we observed them using computers, for a minimum of two hours, in their respective homes or workplaces. Many of the observations lasted longer than 3 hours. The study received approval from the Institutional Review Board, and all participants signed an informed consent form before they began participation in the study.

These observations were not strictly passive. We specifically asked participants to show us their skills for web searching, communication (e-mail and social networking), and office productivity applications. We observed skill level with keyboard and mouse, as well as usage of any portable electronic devices. We also interviewed the participants beforehand, about their formal and informal training and education related to technology, as well as their usage of technology in any paid or volunteer employment situations. We did not present specific task lists of steps. We just gave a general category of software application, and asked them if they could show us how they typically used it.

The demographic information of the participants is listed in table 1. The hours per week using a computer listed are inclusive of home, workplace, and public places such as libraries. Of the 10 participants, 7 are female. All 10 participants have outside paid or voluntary employment and use computers everyday. All participants were observed at home except P2, who was observed at her workplace. In all 10 observations, we only took written notes, to be analyzed after the session.

All 10 participants have previously taken formal computer training classes, in either keyboarding, internet searching, e-mail, PowerPoint presentations, MS-Word and Excel, web design, video editing, or a combination of these skills. Some of these training classes began as early as elementary school, and many of these participants took training classes in high school and community college. For example, P6 took keyboarding and MS-Office classes in middle school, and has taken advanced MS-Office application training in college. P9 took keyboarding courses in elementary school, e-mail, keyboarding, and MS-Office in high school, and took additional keyboarding classes at the community college. P10 took keyboarding classes in middle school, PowerPoint classes in

high school, and is currently taking college classes to learn how to do video editing.

	Gender	Age	Number of years using computer	Hours/week using computer
P1	F	28	9-10	30
P2	F	38	> 10	30
P3	M	20	> 10	35
P4	F	28	6-8	14
P5	F	28	> 10	35
P6	F	25	> 10	10
P7	F	27	6-8	15
P8	F	23	> 10	25
P9	M	27	> 10	30
P10	M	22	> 10	12

Table 1. Background demographic information for the 10 participants

RESULTS

The participants' everyday usage of computer applications is summarized in table 2. We grouped the applications into three categories: specialized applications (including word processing, Excel, PowerPoint, Database, and calendar); communication tools (including email, instant messaging, Facebook), and security applications (including password and CAPTCHAs). We observed that many of the participants not only are able to use multiple systems, but they jump back and forth between multiple operating systems, computers, and/or devices. For instance, P3 uses three different PCs in the same room (a laptop, and two desktops). P4 uses a Mac, a PC, and a cell phone to text message, and P6 uses both a laptop running Windows 7, and a desktop computer using Windows XP. P9 uses both a Mac laptop and Windows XP desktop at home, and a Windows (unknown version) at work.

Specialized applications

	Word processing	Excel	Power-Point	Data-base	Calendar
P1	√	√	√		√
P2	√			√	
P3	√	√			√
P4	√				√
P5	√		√	√	√
P6	√	√		√	√
P7	√		√		
P8	√	√	√	√	
P9	√				
P10	√	√	√		

Table 2. Use of specialized applications by participants

Word processing

All participants use word processing software very often. All of our participants use multiple fingers on both hands, however, there is great variability in the speed of typing. All of our participants are familiar with the formatting functions such as bold, italic, and underline. They could insert images and tables into the word document. They understand the 'spell check' function and use it to track spelling errors. For instance, P8 is a very accurate typist. According to an assessment she completed in August, 2010, she types at 29 words per minute with 98% accuracy. P8 commented that the Mavis Beacon typing application helped her improve her typing skills, as did two additional participants. She spent a lot of time on computers in high school and wrote class reports on the computer in middle school. Interestingly enough, both P2 and P9 are very detailed-oriented, and type out entire book and movie manuscripts using word processing. None of the participants were observed using the "track changes" feature in word processing, and in the follow-up interviews, no one indicated using it.

Excel

Five participants use Excel spreadsheets for making check lists, tracking prices, etc. These participants essentially use Excel for the layout features. None of the participants have learned or used any of the mathematical, sorting, or other comparatively advanced functions in Excel. Interestingly, many participants and their parents commented that they haven't used Excel because there has not been a need for it, but they do want to learn it. They believe they can pick up the mathematical or other advanced functions if they need them for work-related purposes.

PowerPoint

Five participants have used PowerPoint for presentations. They understood the basic functions of PowerPoint, such as insert a slide, apply a design template, insert a picture to a slide, create a transition, edit text, etc. P7 is a very frequent user of PowerPoint. She and her friends give PowerPoint presentations to groups about their experiences as young adults with DS. In order to improve her skills, P7 took courses on PowerPoint at a local community college. P10 learned how to make PowerPoint presentations in a high school class.

Database

Four participants have used databases as a part of work. Their interaction with databases is generally limited to searching for, adding, editing, and removing records. For instance, P2 adds and deletes and updates records in the work databases that are used for customer mailing. Their interaction with Database applications only involves data entry or simple search and sorting. P5 will receive piles of papers from her supervisor, with individuals to find in the database. She needs to find a certain e-mail address, then either remove it, or transfer it to another database file. None of them has ever received any formal training in database applications. Their existing skills related to database were acquired through hands-on demonstrations from their family and work colleagues.

Calendar

Five participants use an electronic calendar on their computer to schedule and track their activities. Some participants use a shared calendar with their family, the others keep a calendar of their own. Some forwarded email messages for events that needed to be on the calendar to their parents to coordinate schedules.

Communication tools

Table 3 summarizes the communication and security tools used by participants. All participants state that computers are an important tool for them to communicate with their employers, relatives, and friends. All participants use one or more applications or websites for communication purposes.

Emails

All participants use email as an important communication tool and have multiple email accounts, often on different providers, using different interfaces. For instance, P10 has a Yahoo Mail account, as well as a university e-mail account using iPlanet messenger express. P9 has an AOL e-mail account, as well as an Outlook e-mail account at work. P8 has 3 different e-mail accounts; one is at the university (using iPlanet messenger express), and P8 has two different Gmail accounts (one Gmail account is for work, and one is for friends). P6 uses both a Windows Live e-mail account, as well as a Comcast e-mail account.

They check and answer their emails on a daily basis. Interestingly, the majority of the participants prefer to delete their emails as soon as they read and answer them. Therefore, unlike the inbox of a typical computer user that usually contains hundreds of emails, they only have a dozen emails in their inbox, and some have no e-mails in the inbox. P2 deletes e-mails so quickly, that there's a sign next to her desk at work, reminding her to "read e-mail, but DO NOT delete it." We asked why the participants prefer to delete messages from their inbox. There isn't a unanimous explanation. P9 said that he thought hardcopies are safer than electronic messages. So he prints useful emails and then deletes the emails from the inbox. P6 writes down the content of important emails before deleting them. Some participants delete mail from both their inbox and their sent mail box. P6 immediately goes to the sent-mail folder, and deletes those copies of e-mails, as does P2.

	Communication			Security	
	Email	IM	Facebook	Password	CAPTCHA
P1	√		√	Easy	100%
P2	√	√	√	Easy	100%
P3	√			Hard	100%
P4	√	√	√	Easy	100%
P5	√			Easy	100%
P6	√		√	Easy	66%
P7	√			Easy	100%
P8	√	√	√	Hard	100%
P9	√	√		Easy	66%
P10	√		√	Easy	100%

Table 3. Use of communication and security applications

P7 is another example of a frequent email remover. As soon as she responds to an e-mail, she deletes it, as she doesn't want to have a lot of messages in her inbox. She says she doesn't need to keep old e-mails, because she remembers who she e-mailed. All participants take their e-mail responsibilities seriously, as P7 noted, "When at the ARC, I spend a few hours checking my e-mail, because the more e-mail I can do at the ARC, the less I need to do when I get home."

Usage of mail folders by participants varies. For instance, P8 has 30 different mail folders, but P10 has no mail folders. Some participants created different folders in their email account, but there are very few messages in those folders. It seems that the participants have not taken advantage of the message organization functions.

It was also mentioned that some of the participants use the telephone more than email because most of their friends prefer using the phone. Many of their friends do not have email access at home. P10 began using email more last summer because he was enrolled in a post-secondary school program at a local university, and most of his friends there used email to communicate with each other when they were not at school.

Instant messaging

Four participants use instant messaging (IM) to communicate with friends and relatives. All of them have a camera so that they can see their friends when using IM. Some participants also use Skype. While we observed, P9 opened Skype, checked who was available to talk with him (an uncle from Brazil was available), and was able to connect, use Skype and converse with his uncle in Portuguese.

Facebook

Six participants have Facebook accounts. Some of them are active Facebook users. They keep in touch with relatives and friends via Facebook. They also like to use the video IM function on Facebook. For example, P1 has 233 friends on Facebook. She sends e-mail, posts status updates, uses the chat facility, uploads photos, and uses games such as Farmville and yoville. She also uses Facebook mobile on her iPhone. Her parents are also on Facebook, and while they read her status updates, they do not know all of her friends and are unaware of the games that she plays. The parents tend to tag and label the pictures posted on Facebook, and P1 then provides comments on them. P4 has two Facebook accounts, one for old friends, the other for newly developed friends, and she spends several hours a night on Facebook. It is a part of her daily social life, and for communicating with family members and friends who are living at a distance, it replaces face-to-face communication. P6 makes sure to login to Facebook every day. P8 is on Facebook, but her mother must personally approve all of her Facebook friends. The mother of P10 indicated that he used to not be interested in Facebook, but this summer, he was more interested because friends in his college program were on Facebook a lot.

The reason for not using Facebook varies, but the primary reason is security and privacy concerns. Multiple parents stated that they don't think Facebook is a good idea for the participant and have instructed them not to use it. For instance, P2 used to use Facebook, but stopped, because her family did not want her to use it anymore. One participant does not use Facebook because of the privacy requirements of her job.

Security-related applications

Passwords

Eight out of ten participants commented that user authentication using user name and passwords is an easy task. All of them have more than one user name and password. To our surprise, unlike many neurotypical users who write down their passwords or save their passwords in an electronic file, the participants we observed typically just remember the passwords without writing them down. For example, P4 used all different user name and passwords for her five accounts (2 email accounts, 1 IM account, 2 Facebook accounts). One of her user names is 14 digits, including both letters and numbers. Two of her passwords are 12 and 14 digits

long, respectively. Four of the participants, (P2, P5, P7, and P9) have passwords that they use to access workplace servers and databases at their respective workplaces, in addition to their personal accounts. Two participants commented that they have substantial problems remembering the password. For example, both P3 and P8 save the user name and passwords on their computers so that they do not need to enter them when they log in.

CAPTCHAs

The observation for CAPTCHAs is encouraging. While we were primarily asking participants to show us what they typically do (what tasks, web sites, and e-mail programs), for CAPTCHAs, we specifically asked them to complete a task of the researchers' choosing. We asked participants to answer three visual CAPTCHA tests (available at http://www.google.com/recaptcha/learnmore), although due to the various tasks that the users were showing us at the time, not all of the participants attempted three CAPTCHA tests. We therefore reported in percentage of success in CAPTCHA tests attempted. In order to solve this specific type of visual CAPTCHA test, the user needs to recognize and enter two separate words. Eight participants had a 100% CAPTCHA test success rate. Two participants did have one failed attempt each, when they first tried to figure out how the CAPTCHA works (the participants were not offered the opportunity to train or play around with a CAPTCHA first). For example, P6 had a spelling error on the first CAPTCHA test, but answered the next two correctly. P9 hit enter accidently after only typing one word (two words are needed). On the next attempts, both P6 and P9 were able to successfully complete the CAPTCHA tests.

Use of input techniques

	Key-board	Mouse	Phone keypad	Touch screen	Touch pad	Speech input
P1	√	√	√	√		
P2	√	√	√			
P3	√	√	√	√		√
P4	√	√	√	√		
P5	√	√	√			
P6	√	√			√	
P7	√	√				
P8	√	√				
P9	√	√				
P10	√	√	√	√		

Table 4. Use of input techniques

Keyboard and mouse is the primary input solution for all participants (See table 4 for more data on the use of input techniques). Six participants use a phone keypad for text messaging. Five participants use touchscreen or touchpad. P4 demonstrated how she uses the touch screen of iPhone to text message. She texted using both thumbs quite fast and accurately. One participant has tried speech-based input at some point but is not using it currently. It is very interesting to note that none of the participants are currently using any form of assistive or adaptive technology, such as those often used by people with disabilities.

Use of mobile devices

We also interviewed the participants as to their usage of mobile devices such as cell phones (see table 5 for more data on usage of mobile devices). Three participants access emails via their cellphone. Seven participants communicate with their relatives and friends through text messaging. Four participants use iTunes to download and listen to music.

	Communication		Entertainment	
	Email	Text messaging	iTunes	iTouch
P1	√	√	√	
P2		√		
P3		√		
P4	√			√
P5		√		
P6	√			
P7			√	
P8		√	√	
P9				
P10		√	√	

Table 5. Use of mobile devices

Information Searching

All 10 of the participants were frequent users of Google and were comfortable doing keyword searches (see table 6). For most participants, using Google was preferred to typing in a URL or using bookmarks (although P1 indicated her preference for bookmarks, and P6 indicated her preference for typing in the URL). We asked the participants to show us some web sites that they typically visit.

	Google	Facebook	weather/map	youTube
P1	√	√	√	√
P2	√	√	√	
P3	√		√	√
P4	√		√	
P5	√	√	√	√
P6	√	√		√
P7	√			√
P8	√	√	√	√
P9	√			
P10	√	√		√

Table 6. Websites frequently used for information searching

The participants liked video web sites (such as YouTube and Disney Channel), sports web sites (such as the Baltimore Ravens and Washington Redskins), weather web sites (such as weather.com), movie web sites (such as Netflix and local movie times) music web sites (such as iTunes and American Idol) and shopping web sites for pricing comparisons (such as Best Buy, Barnes and Noble, Amazon, Walmart, and Target). A number of the participants also described web sites that they visit in the context of their employment (such as office supply stores and package shipping). The participants adopt various searching strategies when searching within a web site. For example, when searching books in a library catalog, P4 demonstrated four different strategies: search by authors, search by book titles, search by topics, and search by subjects.

DISCUSSION

The results of the current study document the successful use of a variety of applications, communication tools and security applications by adults with Down syndrome. Our findings support that the physical, sensory and behavioral characteristics of adults with Down syndrome can be identified in their patterns of computer usage, e.g. research has shown that individuals with Down syndrome are stronger in visual processing than they are in auditory processing [20]. Although security features such as CAPTCHAs are cognitively abstract, they presented no problems for the participants, who were all able to successfully complete a visual CAPTCHA input task. Research also suggests the obsessive compulsive tendencies of some individuals with Down syndrome [18] and our findings related to deleting emails from the inbox support that characteristic. There is a clear relationship between the characteristics of people with Down syndrome and their specific patterns of usage.

Common Themes Observed

During the study, we observed some common themes among the participants that helped us understand the potential computer related skills that people with DS could achieve, the factors that may contribute to the acquisition of those skills, and how those computer skills could be used in a workplace setting. Obviously, the overall skill level was higher than the average computer users with DS, since we specifically recruited people with a high level of computer skills to explore the potential employment opportunities. Some of the common themes that emerged from the participants included:

- Of the 10 expert users with Down syndrome, all of them used multiple fingers on both hands for keyboard entry, as well as the mouse, with no modifications needed.

- None of the 10 users had any forms of assistive technology or modifications, which is very different from the common expectations that people with cognitive impairments need it.

-Related to security, the 10 users were highly successful when attempting visual CAPTCHAs, which was not expected. The users tended to manage multiple accounts, as well as multiple passwords. However, the strength of password, such as requiring CAPS, numbers, and symbols, may increase the complexity.

- The participants we observed were themselves very observant of the various visual cues in their screen layout, immediately noticing when the laptop battery icon was showing low strength, or when the wi-fi icon was showing a weak Internet connection. Often, the users pointed things out to the observers that we ourselves did not notice.

- Most of the 10 users deleted e-mails very quickly, and kept empty inboxes in their e-mail accounts. Some went as far as to immediately delete e-mail messages as soon as they read them, as well as delete messages in sent-mail right after they were sent. We have been investigating the research literature on behavioral issues in people with Down syndrome, and the findings from others point to people with DS having a high occurrence of obsessive-compulsive disorder and related conditions.

- Most of the 10 users utilized computer skills in employment settings, although it was sometimes in unpaid employment rather than paid employment.

- All 10 participants had taken formal computer classes, at some point in their lives, and most participants had taken multiple computer classes at various stages of their education. Even when formal education was complete, many participants continued to sign up for computer skills classes at a local community college.

Implications

Implications for computer users with Down Syndrome: One of the mantras that we heard from these expert users with Down syndrome was that formal training and practice were important. All of these expert users had taken formal computer training classes in their lives, and most continue to take computer classes on an ongoing basis. Social support may also be important. For instance, some of the expert users had other friends with Down syndrome who were online, and that encouraged them to improve their computer skills. There was one example where a participant wasn't using email and facebook, but once the participant made friends who were online more often, it encouraged them to spend more time online.

Implications for policymakers: Implications for policymakers can generally be separated into implications for design policy and implications for education and employment policy. For design policy, the topic of users with Down syndrome needs to become a part of discussions on accessibility design. The general category of cognitive impairment in design is a tricky one. While the new 2.0 version of the Web Content Accessibility Guidelines does briefly mention cognitive impairment, there aren't many descriptions of how to design for it, and certainly, there are no mentions of Down syndrome [26]. While the advisory board (TEITAC) that provided suggestions for how to redesign the United States Section 508 guidelines actively discussed cognitive impairment in development of the draft version of the new Section 508 design guidelines, there was concern about whether design rules for cognitive impairment should be included at all, since they were "too broad, not measurable, and thus impossible to achieve" and therefore, suggestions for design for cognitive impairment did not make their way into the draft version of the new section 508 [24].

In terms of education and employment policy, there need to be policy changes that encourage formal computer skills education for individuals with Down syndrome, as well as evaluation of and job training for employment that utilizes computer skills. There are often unwritten or not well-publicized policies that limit participation of people with cognitive impairment in information technology employment. For example, some state rehabilitation agencies have policies stating that people who do not have a documented IQ of 90 or above cannot participate in computer skills training, regardless of their existing computer skill level. And in the K-12 environment, students with cognitive impairments are often not given the opportunity to take computer classes which they would benefit from [10].

Implications for researchers: More research needs to be done to understand the diversity within user groups who have the same disability label. "Cognitive impairment" itself is a very broad label, but even within people who have the same genetic syndrome (e.g. Down syndrome or Fragile X syndrome) there may be great diversity in computer skill. The story told from this research on computer usage by adults with Down syndrome is very different from the 2008 survey of children with Down syndrome [8]. Challenges that were prevalent in the 2008 survey (such as problems with typing and security features) were not an issue with these expert users. More research needs to continue, on understanding how people with Down syndrome interact with computers and web sites, and how their patterns of usage (and specific strengths and weaknesses) change as they age. Furthermore, between the large survey and the ethnographic observations, there may now be enough existing research to create experimental design research involving people with Down syndrome.

Implications for designers: For expert users with Down syndrome, it does not appear that there need to be any modifications of interface features, for most of the software applications observed in the study. These expert users were generally fine using the same design as users without any impairments. However, this finding should be interpreted with caution for two reasons. First, the participants had to go with the current design because there was no 'cognitive impairment friendly version' of any of the applications that we investigated. If an application with accommodation were available, it is possible that the participants might be able to spend less time learning the application or might achieve even higher performance. Second, we did observe tasks and applications that some participants did not accomplish or master, such as formulas in spreadsheets, and many functions in database applications. With potential training in these areas, and the opportunities to use these skills in employment, it is very possible that the expert users with DS would be able to learn these skills [10].

Although all of the expert users were generally effective typists, the typing speed might be slower than expert users without any impairments, therefore, existing design rules (such as paragraph p of section 508 web design rules—"When a timed response is required, the user shall be alerted and given sufficient time to indicate more time is required") [25] for accessibility, while not specifically addressing Down syndrome, might also be helpful for expert users with Down syndrome.

Designing for accessibility generally means designing for flexibility, but that doesn't necessarily mean design that provides specific features for a specific disability. For instance, while a number of authors had postulated that blind users, since they use primarily audio output instead of visual output, would prefer narrow, deep menu hierarchies to broad, shallow menu hierarchies, data collection found that blind users, like most users, prefer broad, shallow hierarchies [11]. While the younger users with Down syndrome in our previous survey had trouble with passwords and the gap between the cognitive skill level and the presentation style, neither one of those seemed to be a problem with our older expert users.

CONCLUSIONS

This study shows that some individuals with Down syndrome are capable of acquiring the basic computer knowledge and skills that would be appropriate for office work. This finding is important in that it substantially broadens the potential career opportunities for individuals with DS. Designers, researchers, policymakers, and people with Down syndrome should investigate the impact of this research on their work. For instance, users with Down syndrome should attempt to get more formal training with computers, and policymakers should support this. Researchers must investigate the diversity of computer users with Down syndrome, and in the future, experimental empirical data would be helpful. Rehabilitation specialists should consider and assess computer skills when assisting individuals with DS in searching for jobs. Future research will need to move towards a more detailed understanding of the diversity of computer skills among people with Down syndrome, examine the workplaces, and how workplace tasks can match the specific skills and strengths of people with Down syndrome.

Acknowledgements

This material is based upon work supported by the U.S. National Science Foundation under Grant IIS-0949963. Any opinions, findings, and conclusions or recommendations expressed in this material are those of the authors and do not necessarily reflect the views of the NSF.

References

[1] Abbeduto, L., Pavetto, M., Kesin, E., et al. 2001. The linguistic and cognitive profile of DS: Evidence from a comparison with fragile X syndrome. Down Syndrome Research and Practice, 7. 9-15.

[2] Bruni, M. 2006. *Fine motor skills for children with Down syndrome*. Woodbine House, Bethesda, MD.

[3] Capone, G., Goyal, P., Ares, W., et al. 2006. Neurobehavioral disorders in children, adolescents, and young adults with Down syndrome. American Journal of Medical Genetics Part C-Seminars in Medical Genetics 142C,3. 127-158.

[4] Chapman, R. and Hesketh, L. 2000. Behavioral phenotype of individuals with Down syndrome. Mental Retardation and Developmental Disabilities Research Reviews, 6. 84-95.

[5] Conners, F., Rosenquist, C. and Taylor, L. 2001. Memory training for children with Down syndrome. Down Syndrome Research and Practice, 7,1. 25-33.

[6] Dawe, M. 2006. Desperately Seeking Simplicity: How Young Adults with Cognitive Disabilities and Their Families Adopt Assistive Technologies. *Proceedings of 2006 ACM Conference on Human Factors in Computing Systems (CHI)*, 1143-1152.

[7] Dykens, E., Hodapp, R. and Evans, D. 2006. Profiles and development of adaptive behavior in children with Down syndrome. Down Syndrome Research and Practice, 9. 45-50.

[8] Feng, J., Lazar, J., Kumin, L., et al. 2008. Computer Usage and Computer-Related Behavior of Young Individuals with Down Syndrome. *Proceedings of ACM Conference on Assistive Technology (ASSETS)*, 35-42.

[9] Feng, J., Lazar, J., Kumin, L., et al. 2010. Computer Usage by Children with Down Syndrome: Challenges and Solutions. ACM Transactions on Accessible Computing, 2,3. 1-44.

[10] Hart, M. 2005. Autism/Excel Study. *Proceedings of ACM 2005 Conference on Accessible Technology (ASSETS)*, 136-141.

[11] Hochheiser, H. and Lazar, J. 2010. Revisiting Breadth vs. Depth in Menu Structures for Blind Users of Screen Readers. Interacting with Computers, 22,5. 389-398.

[12] Hoque, M. 2008. Analysis of Speech Properties of Neurotypicals and Individuals Diagnosed with Autism and Down Syndrome. *Proceedings of ACM ASSETS 2008 Conference*, 311-312.

[13] Jarrold, C., Baddeley, A. and Phillips, C. 2002. Verbal short-term memory in Down syndrome. Journal of Speech, Language and Hearing Research, 45. 531-544.

[14] Kirijian, A., Myers, M. and Charland, S. 2007. Web fun central: online learning tools for individuals with Down syndrome. In Lazar, J. ed. *Universal Usability: Designing Computer Interfaces for Diverse User Populations*, John Wiley & Sons, Chichester, UK, 195-230.

[15] Lazar, J., Feng, J. and Hochheiser, H. 2010. *Research Methods in Human Computer Interaction*. John Wiley and Sons, Chichester, UK.

[16] Lee, S. 2002. A vision for the twenty-first century: a blueprint for change. In Cohen, W., Nadel, L. and Madnick, M. eds. *Down syndrome: Visions for the 21st Century*, Wiley-Liss, New York, 119-133.

[17] Lloyd, J., Moni, K. and Jobling, A. 2006. Breaking the hype cycle: using the computer effectively with learners with intellectual disabilities. Down Syndrome Research and Practice, 9,3. 68-74.

[18] McGuire, D. and Chicoine, B. 2006. *Mental wellness in adults with Down syndrome*. Woodbine House, Bethesda, MD.

[19] Patterson, D. and Lott, I. 2008. Etiology, Diagnosis, and Development in Down Syndrome. In Roberts, J., Chapman, R. and Warren, S. eds. *Speech and language development & intervention in Down syndrome & Fragile X syndrome*, Brookes Publishing, Baltimore, 3-26.

[20] Pueschel, S., Gallagher, P., Zastler, A., et al. 1987. Cognitive and learning processes in children with Downs syndrome. Research and Developmental Disabilities, 8. 21-37.

[21] Roizen, N. 1997. Hearing loss in children with Down syndrome: A review. Down Syndrome Quarterly, 2. 1-4.

[22] Roizen, N., Mets, M. and Blondis, T. 1994. Ophthalmic disorders in children with Down syndrome. Developmental Medicine and Child Neurology, 36. 594-600.

[23] RRTC on Disability Statistics and Demographics. Annual Disability Statistics Compendium: 2009 Hunter College, New York, 2009, available at: http://disabilitycompendium.org/.

[24] U.S. Access Board. Draft Information and Communication Technology (ICT) Standards and Guidelines Washington, DC, 2010, Available at: http://www.access-board.gov/sec508/refresh/draft-rule.htm.

[25] U.S. Access Board. Section 508--Subsection 1194.22--Guidelines for Web-based intranet and internet information and applications., 2001, Available at: http://www.section508.gov/index.cfm?fuseAction=stdsdoc# Web.

[26] Web Accessibility Initiative. Web Content Accessibility Guidelines 2.0, 2008, Available at: http://www.w3.org/TR/WCAG20/.

[27] Wishart, J. 1998. Cognitive Development in Young Children with Down Syndrome: Developmental Strengths, Developmental Weaknesses. *Proceedings of Down Syndrome in the 21st Century: 1st Biennial Scientific Conference on Down Syndrome*.

The Vlogging Phenomena: A Deaf Perspective

Ellen S. Hibbard
Ryerson University
350 Victoria St
Toronto, CANADA
ehibbard@ryerson.ca

Deborah I. Fels
Ryerson University
350 Victoria St
Toronto, CANADA(1)-416-979-5000
dfels@ryerson.ca

ABSTRACT

Highly textual websites present barriers to Deaf people, primarily using American Sign Language for communication. Deaf people have been posting ASL content in form of vlogs to YouTube and specialized websites such as Deafvideo.TV. This paper presents some of the first insights into the use of vlogging technology and techniques among the Deaf community. The findings suggest that there are differences between YouTube and Deafvideo.TV due to differences between mainstream and specialized sites. Vlogging technology seems to influence use of styles that are not found or are used differently in face-to-face communications. Examples include the alteration of vloggers' signing space to convey different meanings on screen.

Categories and Subject Descriptors

D.4.2 [**Social Issues**]: *Assistive technologies for persons with disabilities*

General Terms

Documentation, Human Factors

Keywords

vlog, sign language, Deaf, website, access, technology, video

1. INTRODUCTION

Recently, the proliferation of high-speed computer graphics technology and increased network bandwidth has led to the development and widespread availability of online video content and applications. Deaf people have taken this opportunity to begin contributing sign language content to online video sites and this is termed *vlogging* [13]. Websites such as YouTube typically contain video content with text and graphics. One of the issues with highly textual websites is that they present a barrier for Deaf people since a majority whom read and write at about a 4th grade level [3]. A Deaf user would be required use two languages, a signed language and text English while hearing people typically do not require knowledge of a second language to browse websites. There are many distinct sign languages used by different Deaf communities globally, e.g. American Sign Language (ASL). Sign languages are visual-spatial with no written representation whereas spoken English has a text. The use of website text as content or interactive functions therefore forces users to alternate between first and second language languages (e.g., ASL and English text) and preventing equivalent access for people with

disabilities [4]. As a result, the presence of Deaf cultural materials and Deaf users has been limited. The word Deaf is used to describe people who are deaf or hard of hearing, identify themselves as culturally Deaf and primarily communicate through sign language.

The strong cultural value of using ASL at face-to-face gatherings [16] is a defining characteristic of the Deaf community. Skilled ASL storytellers are valued in the Deaf community and are often called on to narrate stories at the gatherings. Now, it is possible for Deaf people to create, record, store and share the signed content as online videos. New specialized websites such as Deafvideo.TV, (DVTV) are tailored to the specific needs of Deaf vloggers because they include posting and replying in video. As a result of these opportunities, many questions arise regarding how Deaf people are using this new found technology to contribute to the online community and culture, and whether there is an impact on the evolution of Deaf culture itself.

In this paper we will examine some of challenges and issues arising from vlogging on mainstream vlogging sites such as YouTube and on DVTV targeted specifically at the Deaf community. In addition, we examine the impact video-based, online technology is having on the presentation and communication of ideas in sign language vlogs.

2. BACKGROUND

Conventionally, ASL content is only conveyed during face-to-face interactions between Deaf people [16]. ASL narratives such as ASL storytelling and ASL jokes have played a central role in developing and fostering Deaf cultural identity [1, 16]. Deaf events are venues in which ASL stories are told and classical ASL literature such as legends about Deaf leaders from 19th century [6] are re-told. A typical Deaf person has to depend on attending events in person in order to obtain accessible discourse that would be limited outside of these events. Veditz [18] argued that Deaf people have struggled to share and pass on signed information. During a national address in 1910 he suggested that the only effective method of passing on this information is through 'moving picture films,' explaining that "Deaf people are people of the eye" [18] and film is the media through which Deaf people can communicate across time and distance. In 1913 few Deaf people had access to film technology to communicate signed content, but now video technology is more accessible and enables more people to communicate signed content.

Veditz's 'people of the eye' concept did not consider issues arising when communication shifts from traditional face-to-face narration to video narration, as is the case for online vlogs. One of these issues might involve how the change from face-to-face to online affects Deaf culture/communication. Ong [15] suggests that when oral-based storytelling moves from a face-to-face method of transmission to a print/text method, the result is increased vocabulary, formalized structures, and new storytelling elements.

Media and communication scholars such as [12] argues that visual media such as websites, to communicate through the visual mode, but visual media do not communicate through the visual modality alone. Mitchell argues that visual media do not truly exist because current visual media (e.g., modern films at theatres, DVDs, or television) are usually presented along with sound. However, for Deaf people, film is essentially a visual-only medium.

In vlogging, visual media usually integrates text, sound and visual images. Websites have text-based content and interactive functions that cannot be decoupled from the other media (e.g., YouTube comments are not only expressed using text but also linked to video pages through text). Deaf people often experience text as a second language but understanding the impact of online video-mediated communication on Deaf culture and communication practices must be mediated by the imposition of textual interface and content structures.

A mainstream, text-centric form of Web-based communication is blogging. Blogs are webpages containing text posts as well as contain photos or other multimedia content [14]. Nardi, et al. [14] suggest that blogs are more than on-line journals; they are considered a social activity in which people express emotional tensions, think out loud by writing, seek feedback, articulate opinions to influence other people and post activity updates. People typically use blogging as a way to interact with others despite its limitations on use (limited access to responses and lack of comments are received on individual posts) [7].

There has been considerably less research on vlogging as a form of interactive communication, although it is recognized as a different form of user-generated content [13]. Lange [9] examined vlogging on a mainstream site, YouTube to determine whether users use it to maintain social relationships through video. He suggests that vlogging is a form of social communication which performs the function of maintaining connections between physically distanced friends and family. After examining issues of public versus private communication, this study found that vloggers attempted to maintain privacy by hiding their faces behind masks, limiting video tagging and/or not socializing with other vloggers in real time (off-line). It is not possible for Deaf people to hide their faces in videos without disrupting comprehension of American Sign Language since ASL uses facial grammar elements. It is possible that sharing videos is a form of social networking for both the Deaf community and hearing people.

Keating and Mirus [8] described video as a new technology that creates a new relationship in how Deaf people narrate their content with their digital selves. They argued the Internet is shaping language practices in the Deaf community because Deaf people are able to communicate across distances and time, not just face-to-face. Further, this communication becomes a permanent record that can be consumed by others at some future time in the absence of a face-to-face conversation. The impact of this ability to communicate anytime and anyplace has yet to be investigated.

They also examined the use of web-cams and web-cam video relay service. A web-cam is a video camera designed for web interfaces and requires participants to adjust their body positions to see and be seen. A web-cam video relay service is an interpreting service for Deaf people, allowing them to communicate with hearing people who do not know sign language. Keating and Mirus [8] reported that members of the Deaf community expressed privacy concerns about using web-cams, generally related to being visually available and they needed to be properly dressed and groomed before using the technology. Their research was focused on real-time communication across distances mediated by web-cam technology and did not consider asynchronous communication situations such as blogs or vlogs.

Keating and Mirus's [8] main findings revealed the production of video sign language and its use of video space altered the spatial dimension of sign language, from four-dimensions (4D) of face-to-face communication to two-dimensions of the on-screen. Deaf people changed their body positions to accommodate the narrow signing window, due to the web-cam's field-of-view constraints, compared with the space available in face-to-face communication. Signers changed to optimize the display of their bodies, face, and hands. Participants worked together to establish optimal viewing for communication by collaborating on what they saw of each other through the web-cam. A new narrative framework was thereby developed in which the relationship between hands and the signer's body and the relationship between signers and the camera became important. Keating and Mirus [8] used one example in which a participant changed how a sign was produced visually; the participant's sign for 'three' was misunderstood as 'two,' so the participant then changed how the sign for 'three' was produced. This exemplifies how spatial-movements were modified to be clearly seen in two-dimensional space.

Web-cam technology changed the relationship between the signer's body and hands and also created a new visual relationship between the signer and the camera. Keating and Mirus [8] observed that feedback from web-cam was more limited than face-to-face interactions, and that participants tended to depend on direct feedback from the signer rather than from looking at their 'virtual' self.

Meaning in ASL comes not only from the use of the hands to produce signs, but also from head movements (e.g. head tilts), facial expressions and use of space around the body [2]. Signs are produced in a very specific body region defined from the waist, with reach of slightly bent elbows to the top of head. Bellugi [2] describes one key element of ASL: meaning of signs is not just inferred from the making the handshape or movement but also the location of the sign in space. The possible implications from Keating and Mirus [8] research in addition to the 4D requirements of ASL may be seen in vlogs in form of non-typical use of space.

While vlogging is a more common experience for hearing people and the impact on mainstream culture is perhaps incremental, the impact on Deaf culture may be a breakthrough, similar, in fact, to that which printing press technology had on hearing cultures. A study of vlogging techniques and behaviours employed by Deaf people may provide some insight into the evolution of Deaf culture as a result of vlogging technology.

3. METHOD

3.1 Research questions

The purpose of this study is to examine how Deaf people are using vlogging technology to express their ideas and communicate in sign language and to observe differences from typical face-to-face communication. In this study existing vlogs from two public websites, DVTV, and YouTube, are examined and analyzed for use by Deaf users. YouTube is a popular mainstream website, while DVTV is a more recent website specifically targeted at the Deaf community.

In this study we then address the following questions:

1. Does vlogging technology afford new or altered communication strategies or uses?
2. Are there differences between the use of mainstream and specialized websites in vlogging content, topics, or vlogging behaviour?

3.2 Participants

Eight vloggers per website and five vlogs per vlogger over a five month posting period were selected for evaluation. In order to be considered for analysis, the vlogger had to be a Deaf adult, use ASL, have experience (created more than 60 posts during their vlogging lifetime), and be active at the time of the study. Within this specified group of vloggers, the eight were randomly selected.

To determine whether the vlogger was Deaf, a vlog statement stating that the individual was Deaf or had attended a Deaf residential school was required. This was most often found in the Deafvideo.TV profile or one of the YouTube vlogs. If text was included in the original vlog, it was excluded from the study to ensure that all content was ASL only.

Deafvideo.TV reports that there are total of 9,050 registered members however, not all members are Deaf or are active vloggers who post original sign language content. Identifying vloggers or vlogs on DVTV is relatively straightforward as vlogs are readily available on the home page of the site. All vlogs posted for that day are found in the "Recent" section of the site. The vlog history of all of the vloggers posting could be easily tracked on this site.

Identifying Deaf vloggers on YouTube was more complex as YouTube contains a very large range of audio/video content with only some ASL content. ASL videos were found on YouTube by using the keyword, 'ASL' as there was no American Sign Language/Deaf community established on YouTube. This search returned a result of 111,000 videos. This first search showed videos created by sign language interpreters or music adapted into sign language. The search was better defined by searching for 'ASL vlogs' which resulted in 5,020 results. Most of these vlogs were dated one to three years ago and only six percent met the study criteria. Vlogs that met the study criteria were selected from the first 125 vlogs found from the search results.

In addition to the formal selection criteria, attempts were made to ensure equal representation of gender and age ranges. Four adult males and four adult females were selected from YouTube and DVTV. Age was categorized into three ranges; young adult, middle age and older adult (see Figure 1a, b, c for examples). A young adult was someone who has the appearance of recently finishing high school, and/or had disclosed recently graduating from high school and/or college. A middle age adult was judged to be someone with the appearance of being about 30-45 years old. An older adult appeared as someone older than 45 but younger than 65 often describing themselves as having adult children. Adults considered as senior citizens (more than 65 years old) were not included in this study.

Figure 1a: Young adult (self identified) **Figure 1b**: Middle age adult **Figure 1c**: Older adult

From YouTube, six middle age vloggers and two older adults were selected. From DVTV, one young adult, five middle age adults and two older adults were selected.

3.3 Selection of vlogs

Vlogs were collected from recent posts on YouTube and DVTV in an attempt to collect the most up-to-date vlogs. Vloggers often posted non-ASL content vlogs between ASL vlogs. For the study, five sequential posts occurring between September 2010 and February 2001, containing ASL were selected. The time period was used to include frequent and infrequent vloggers (posting only every few weeks). Vlogs showing only non-ASL content such as photographs or other video material such as children playing or cars driving on a road were excluded. Vlogs that were posted as a reply to another vlog were also excluded as we focused on analysing new/original topics rather than responses.

3.4 Data collection and analysis

The selected vlogs were assessed for quantitative and qualitative factors, addressing the research questions. The following quantitative factors were measured:

1. *Signing rate*. Signing rate was determined by counting signs in 30 second samples of a vlog and then normalizing the count per second. If the vlog was more than 30 seconds long, 20% of the vlog was sampled randomly and the signs counted (as recommended by Mayberry [10]). The criteria for determining a countable "sign" consisted of: 1) a sign had to be made on visible hands; 2) nouns were counted once (nouns can have repeated sign movements); 3) a word that was finger-spelled was counted one sign e.g., a proper name or website that was finger-spelled was counted as one sign; 4) a head nod or facial expression was counted as one sign; 5) hand shapes such as thumbs-up, or the okay sign were included since those contain content and meaning; 6) if a non-noun sign was repeated, it was counted as a new sign each time it was repeated; 7) the 30 second sample begun when there was no signing (similar to [10]). Signs made off screen and nonsensical hand movements that contained no content or meaning were not included in the sign count.
2. *Average length* (and standard deviation) of posts in seconds.
3. The *number of replies* to each original post (original replies and total). This count included replies in text or ASL. Original replies did not include those made by the vlogger herself, while total included all replies regardless of source.

Qualitative factors that were compared between YouTube and DVTV and face-to-face consisted of:

1. Topic type
2. Technical elements related to video quality: background, lighting, colour, and vlog sign frame used in video posts. The vlog sign frame is defined as the video frame containing the head, body and signs of the vlogger and is categorized as small, medium and large. A small frame shows the elbows, hands, and torso of the vlogger cropped (see Figure 2). A medium frame is when there is more of the torso but the elbows are cropped. A large frame shows the entire head, elbows and hands.
3. Narrative elements (deliberate use of video to create or present new content in a style differing from traditional face to face narration). An example is use of "I love you to conclude the vlog where this sign is normally reserved for close friends in a face-to-face setting.

Figure 2: Image of a vlogger in a small sign frame.

4. Elements occurring that do not typically appear in face-to-face communication. An example of this is moving hand out of typical location in space along Z-axis (see Figure 3).

Figure 3: Image of moving hand out of typical location.

4. RESULTS AND DISCUSSION

A repeated measures ANOVA was conducted with sign rate, replies and length of post as within-subjects factors and Vlog site type (YouTube or DVTV). Mauchly's W showed no significance indicating that the data met the sphericity assumption. There was a within subjects main effect between the five different vlogs [F (4,11) = 3.75, $p < 0.05$, partial eta^2 = 0.21] and for the interaction between rate and Vlog site type [$F(4,11)=3.46$, $p < 0.05$, partial eta^2 = 0.20] indicating an order effect. Overtime for the videos sampled, the signing rate became slower. Further the signing rate slowed more for DVTV than for YouTube videos.

There was also a significant between-subjects effect for vlog site type [$F(1,14)=14.02$, $p < 0.05$, partial eta^2 = 0.5]. The mean sign rate for the YouTube vlogs was 1.1 signs /sec (SD = 0.17), while the mean sign rate for DVTV was 0.87 signs/sec (SD = 0.23). This indicates that vloggers signed slower on DVTV compared with those using YouTube.

The sign rate used in DVTV is similar to that reported for native signers in face-to-face found by Mayberry [10] (mean sign rate of 0.74, SD = 0.10). Bellugi in a comparison study between speaking rate and signing rate, reported mean signs per second for three individuals as 2.3, 2.3, 2.5 signs per second [2]. This compares better with the mean rate found for YouTube. The YouTube vloggers may sign faster than DVTV vloggers because they may be self-conscious or self-aware of the mainstream nature of YouTube or they may be newer signers. Deaf people may think that since hearing people are not fluent in ASL there is no need to take the time to produce well-formed and clear signs. Deaf people vlogging in DVTV may assume that the only people participating in this service are Deaf and may be more comfortable with this audience and slow down to their more normal rate as a result.

There is a significant within-subjects main effect for video [$F(4,11)$ = 3.289, $p < 0.05$, partial eta = 0.19] for the total number of replies but there is no significant within-subjects effect for number of unique replies nor between-subjects effects for either unique or total number of replies. This may mean that there is no difference in people's interest or ability to reply to sign language posts between the two websites or that more data is required.

The DVTV vlog had the most number of different people commenting on a single post with 43 out of total 47 comments. All of the replies were in ASL. The original post suggested, in a playful manner, that people reading the vlog were "troublemakers." The vlogger also included photos of Halloween masks that did not seem to correspond to the signed content topic. Other vloggers who replied to the "troublemaker" topic vlog were largely in agreement or expressed enjoyment at viewing the vlog e.g., "your vlog is so funny, I laugh so hard".

The highest number of total replies for DVTV vlog was 62 with 19 original replies by different people (the remainder were replies made by the same people or from the original vlogger). The vlog was about a young child becoming deaf and the dangers of hearing aid batteries. The vlogger said "I made this vlog to warn you Deaf parents". Most of the replies by other vloggers contained similar stories, e.g., "my daughter became hard of hearing, maybe from medicine for bad ear infection … maybe like your daughter". Some of the replies were not directed to the vlogger's original post but to other replies by other vloggers. Three of the vlogs from DVTV had no replies and contained announcements for an upcoming event or a song.

On YouTube, the greatest number of replies from different individuals for one original post was 20 out of 24 replies. The topic in the original vlog post was about the benefit of Apple's iPhone for Deaf people. All replies were text and most of the replies were on topic. Three vloggers had their replies either flagged as spam **or** deleted for being inappropriate (e.g., one said "I find many hot & sexy deaf girls on Deaf dating site").

The greatest number of total replies on YouTube occurred for a post about a fairly controversial topic within the Deaf community, deaf babies, cochlear implants (CI) and Oralism (movement to prohibit use of ASL) that was posted by a teacher. There were a total of 32 text replies from nine different people. The original vlogger posted replies to each comment and that generated further discussion among the nine others. As this topic is controversial, some of the replies disagreed with the statements made while some were requests for clarifications (e.g., "I'm not deaf and don't understand"). A well-known Deaf vlogger commented "If CIs are the result of the schools returning to Oralism (the neo-Oralism is worse with the incentives of stock market of CIs)." This vlogger did not disagree or agreement, but added a third view which took the discussion on a new tangent.

Six YouTube vlogs had no replies. Topics included a book review, Deaf news, wishing someone congratulations and community announcements. One of these was the longest with 899 seconds. Three of the replies were posted by same vlogger.

A repeated measures ANOVA was carried out for the average length of videos and there was no significant effect between different vlogs or between YouTube and DVTV. The mean length of the vlogs for each of the five videos on YouTube ranged from 275 seconds (SD = 136) to a high of 362 seconds (SD = 309). For DVTV the mean length of the vlogs sampled ranged from a low of 180 seconds (SD = 208) to a high of 303 seconds (SD = 243). It would seem that vloggers typically produced vlogs as low as 180 to as high as 362 overall. It is possible a longer vlog was created but was not posted due to technical limitations. Vloggers either did not have the desire to produce a longer vlog or may not want to bore other vloggers with too long of a post more than 363 seconds. Examining the qualitative factors provides insight and perhaps more understanding of differences than the quantitative factors alone. First, all replies in DVTV were in sign language while all replies on YouTube used English text. The very nature of differences between the two languages and cultures likely produced some of the qualitative differences found. However, other variations including the topics and uses of the technologies such as use of the video frame, space, lighting (visibility), and comfort level with the technology as well as new narrative and sign uses had a unique impact on the differences found.

4.1 Topics

YouTube and DVTV vlog content was observed to be very diverse, as expected. Topics included philosophy, fishing, sports, drinking, marriage, baby signs, iPhones, Deaf educational policy, vlogging, website rules, discrimination, independent, traveling, baking, eating, cyberbullying, American Thanksgiving, borrowing money, football, sex, FaceBook, police, ASL, friends, love, hate, addiction, Christians, abuse, and relationships. The YouTube vlogs contained some references to mainstream politics such as WikiLeaks and US government policy while the vlogs on DVTV had no references to mainstream politics but both mentioned Deaf politics. DVTV had four vlogs that discussed sports while YouTube had none. Overall the types of content in YouTube and DVTV were similar except for mainstream politics and sports.

4.2 Unique elements of technology or practice:

Some of the unexpected results were observed in the new and innovative uses of the technology and video medium for elements such as background, lighting, dress, and sign frame. This included noticeable differences between YouTube and DVTV as well as what is typically found in face-to-face communication and behaviour. Overall vloggers in YouTube and DVTV tended to be dressed casually, e.g. in a t-shirt and hat or even pyjamas but some were dressed more formally in a button-shirt or blouse (Figure 4). Guidelines have been established for people who use video to produce ASL content, e.g. use good lighting, make sure space is visible around head and torso, and wear contrasting clothing without lettering, or stripes [5]. In addition there are conventions for Deaf people who give formal presentations to dress in a specific way. Molyneax reports that hearing people are casually dressed in YouTube vlogs [13]. It is possible that vloggers wanted to appear relaxed and informal to be more like their hearing counterparts or because of the more informal setting.

Figure 4: Image of vlogger in more formal dress

4.2.1 Technical elements:

Most vloggers created vlogs that appeared to be produced at home such as in a bedroom (e.g., suggested by a bed in background), office (e.g., identified by bookshelves) or living room/dining room (e.g., indicated by a table, couch, or television that could be seen in the background as seen in Figure 5). There was only one vlogger each from YouTube and DVTV that used a curtain backdrop. Vlogging in the bedroom has been considered as creating intimacy between viewer and vlogger [13].

Overall lighting was found to range from good to very poor where good lighting made details of the person's hands and face easy to see and poor lighting produced vlogs containing very dim and

Figure 5a: office   **Figure 5b**: bedroom   **Figure5c**: backdrop

difficult to see images (see Figures 6a and b). Being unable to see the ASL contents of a vlog meant that its message could be lost. This is comparable poor audio quality for hearing videos where poor sound quality results in lost information and is generally undesirable by users of vlogs [11].

Figure 6a: Fair lighting   **Figure 6b**: Poor lighting

Past guidelines have been published on which clothing, lighting, and backdrop to use in ASL videos [5]. It appears that these guidelines are not followed by a majority of vloggers in this study. This could be because people want to post sign content quickly and will skip additional technical steps/guidelines that they consider as unnecessary, or vloggers may consider their vlogs as personal and not want to appear too formal or rehearsed.

We suggest that similar phenomena appear in vlogs from hearing contributors. General guidelines are available for producing good quality videos for hearing people (e.g., including lighting, background noise, posture, etc. [17] that are generally not followed by YouTube vloggers. We suggest that vlogging is considered as a more casual, informal and perhaps an even more personal process than other video creation activities.

4.2.2 Use of space

The sign frame used in the vlogs varied considerably among vloggers. How the vlogging space was used presented some innovative and new vlogging techniques that seem to be unique to the medium. We will discuss some general observations that were found among vloggers followed by specific differences between YouTube and DVTV vlogs.

In ASL, the combination of hands, body, and face are considered to be the most important elements in conveying meaning [2]. However, the fidelity of webcam/screen display is highly variable and capturing the movement and nuances of these elements as they are used to express meaning can be difficult and may require adaptation by users.

Keating [8] reported some signs that are replaced with other signs that were easier to view in 2-D because of the limitations of the technology. The vloggers in this study were considered experienced vloggers and there were many examples of where the vlogging space was used in unique ways potentially avoiding problematic signs or body. As a result of the technical limitations, vloggers experimented with different uses of space. Furthermore, these vloggers seemed to introduce innovations in their signing style and delivery to affect meaning.

In addition, vloggers were observed use space or movement of signs that differed from typical use in face-to-face settings. An example was one YouTube vlogger who posted a vlog with only one of her hands, her lips and chin, and the upper part of her torso appearing (see Figure 7). This seems to be intentional and content was about waiting for replies to vlogs and seemed to create a sense of distance. The importance of removing the eyes from the vlog is noteworthy here because the eyes are used in ASL for turn taking cues, grammar, emphasis and meaning. As a result, this vlogger is required to repeat signs to replace the elements conveyed through the eyes. By covering her eyes, this vlogger seems to be saying that her hands are most important in this vlog and that she may want to remain anonymous.

With the exception of one other vlogger who created two vlogs (two out of five observed in this study) by standing up over the video capture device, most other vloggers in the sample taken had their eyes parallel within the video frame.

Figure 7: Image of vlogger showing only hands and face.

Most vloggers in the study had small or medium frames around their body and face. However, this reduction of space in vlogs is very different from typical face-to face. The reduced use of space or limited frame size in vlogs could be due to technical limitations of the camera (limited field of view, angle and focus length) used for creating vlogs; vloggers may need to be closer to the webcam to show their hands and face. DVTV vloggers tended to use a smaller signing space compared with YouTube vloggers. The vloggers in this study were considered experienced vloggers and they may already have developed habits avoiding specific movements in order to optimize their vlog.

A second innovation is greater use of the z-axis to intentionally produce a unique three-dimensional (3D) effect (see Figure 8). Typically, signs used in face-to-face communication are produced in 3D space around the vlogger's body and face but a majority of the signs are moved in x and y directions centred on the signer's torso. Face-to-face signs do not usually move far into the z-axis (away or behind the signer's body). If a signer was to move a hand close to another person's face along the z-axis, this would be considered as rude and inappropriate communication. This innovation seemed to be unique to DVTV vloggers only.

In 12.5% (5 out of 40) DVTV and 2.5% (one out of 40) of YouTube vlogs analyzed, the vloggers moved their hands towards the webcam along the z-axis. It seems that vloggers used this approach to emphasise specific words despite limitations imposed by the lower fidelity camera technology or the 2D effect from the computer screen interface. (e.g., some fine details in sign such as finger position would not be easily visible or blocked by other parts of body).

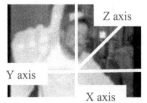

Figure 8: 3D coordinates centred in upper middle chest area.

Another possibility is that vloggers may be targeting their signs to be closer to the webcam because they lack instant feedback from another signer. They may be over-compensating for lack of feedback. However, the observed movement towards the webcam seems to be a very deliberate way to emphasize their signs. Keating and Mirus [8] report that sign language users change their signs for optimal transmission by webcam during real-time conversations. However, [8] were referring specifically to a real-time application instead of vlogging. The deliberate movement of hands closer to the video camera device used to produce vlog does not seem to be for the purpose of optimal transmission but to

create additional emphasis on a sign as a hearing person says a word louder or stronger.

More details of signs were visible in YouTube than in DVTV because more YouTube vlogs were created using larger sign frame and light quality was slightly better. One vlogger on DVTV, however, who typically posted poor quality of lighting and very small frame vlogs yet, had one of the highest numbers of replies. Another vlogger used a large frame and poor light quality but had the largest number of replies in the study. There did not seem to be much relationship between the quality of the lighting, video frame size and number of replies (where number of replies might be an interest of engagement or interest of the vlog to others). It is possible that people who reply are 'fans', personal friends or related to content.

4.2.3 Narrative elements:

Observations were made for intentional narrative elements such as use of formal or informal greetings, and closing by vloggers.

Several vloggers in YouTube and DVTV typically ended their posts with hand-shape representing 'I love you', 'a-okay' or a thumbs-up to close their vlog. Two out of eight YouTube vloggers used this closure method whereas seven out of eight DVTV vloggers used it. Those hand-shapes are typically used in face-to-face at Deaf events among friends as they are considered informal and inappropriate for use with strangers. The use of the informal signing suggests vloggers may be considering their posts to be informal, for friends or those they consider as anonymous viewers of their posts as friends even though they may or may not be.

DVTV vlogs have several qualitative characteristics that differed from YouTube vlogs. The communication style of DVTV vlogs can be described as more informal; several vloggers identified other Deaf people by real name or vlogger name e.g. "this vlog is for you, DeafM". Vloggers' narrative included personal details and anecdotes that are typically shared between known people whereas YouTube vloggers tended to be more formal. The discourse in YouTube was typical of what is found in face-to-face conversations between Deaf strangers. Topics represented in YouTube tended to be of more general interest such how to bake a cake or new Deaf education policy.

There was a greater expression of emotions in DVTV, ranging from anger to love. For example, one DVTV vlogger posted an apology, 'I am so embarrassed, I apologize." This style of vlog was not present in YouTube vlogs at all. Personal opinion or details were not typically provided except for general comments such as "It is rainy today, so I thought I would stay home and make vlogs". Few YouTube vloggers used the greeting "*Hello Everyone*" at the start of their vlogs while in DVTV most vloggers said "*hello friends*". "*Hello Everyone*" greeting that tends to be used at the beginning of a formal speech at a Deaf event.

Another uncommon element observed was the use of 'blunt', straightforward conventions in DVTV. The English word 'blunt' is used in Deaf community to describe the tactic in addressing another familiar person in a very straightforward manner. For example, vloggers were explicit by saying "I 'blunt' to you...Jane Doe" (an English translation of a signed saying). Different vloggers made comments about activities that were explicit and upfront in nature, e.g. a vlogger wearing nothing except for a towel said "Please come shower with me....pleasure". In YouTube vlogs, this type of signed content did not appear at all but discourse of a more general nature such as policies on banning sign language for Deaf babies; a call for website rules needed for

Deaf vloggers; health or exercise e.g. how to do a Yoga activity was found. DVTV vlogs have more content about 'back-stabbing' behavior, e.g. claims of breaking trust or spreading lies in vlogs. DVTV vlogs that contain elements of bluntness or back-stabbing content were some of the more popular vlogs.

The observed discourse in DVTV vlogs suggests a feeling of intimacy, informalness and passion whereas YouTube vlogs seemed to be more formal, addressing safe or commonplace topics and of general interest or news such as announcements about IPhone that has video features of interest to Deaf community.

Use of space, body position and clothing seems to differ between DVTV and YouTube where DVTV vlogs tended to experiment more with different camera angles and use of the z-axis. One DVTV vlogger created vlogs by angling the webcam up at an angle while he stood over the video capture device. A view of the ceiling fan could be seen over his head. YouTube vloggers overall typically produced vlogs in which eyes were parallel with the video frame. None of the vloggers stood up over the webcam in the observed YouTube vlogs in this study.

DVTV vloggers appeared to be more casual that YouTube vloggers in clothing worn, e.g., one DVTV vlogger appeared in a vlog wearing a chemise. In YouTube the most casual clothing was a yoga sports top which was the same vlogger who posted about yoga exercise. It seems DVTV vloggers have a sense of intimacy and closeness by the casual appearance.

Communication was observed to be more like (hearing) English in YouTube than in DVTV. For example, in typical face-to-face ASL communication, Deaf people are very informal, use personal details and identify the object of the conversation at first. This signing style was typically found in DVTV vlogs. In English or when hearing person's conversation is interpreted directly into ASL, the object of the conversation is not identified at first; this style is observed more commonly in YouTube vlogs.

The use of general topics, formal greetings, and larger sign space in YouTube suggests that the vloggers are more distant and formal than in DVTV vloggers. The impression of distance may be that YouTube is a mainstream website in which Deaf people are the minority. It is possible that Deaf people are reserved in creating and sharing vlogs on YouTube because they are trying to "fit in" to the mainstream nature of YouTube website.

Finally, there are some technical or interface differences between YouTube and DVTV that could have influenced some of the differences observed between the two systems. YouTube lacks language selection for ASL although it does have a language categorization for other languages such Filipino or Magyar. YouTube vlogs can be searched by text tags that have been added by the vlogger or in replies while DVTV search does not use tags but the vlogger name or title. Vloggers have more options to search for topics that are not included in title in YouTube while the search function is more limited in DVTV.

YouTube is two years older than DVTV; YouTube was established in February 2005 by three hearing people while DVTV was established in May 2007 by a Deaf man. DVTV was created with WordPress, a mainstream website application. DVTV has some text interfaces such as a text menu and text titles of vlogs. YouTube has the option of text and video replies while DVTV has only video replies. Only two vlogs out of 40 vlogs examined in YouTube had video replies. This could be due to the mainstream nature of YouTube or that most text replies were created by hearing people.

As one of the researchers for this study and as a member of the Deaf community, I was surprised to find that none of the vlogs in this study contained typical folklore that is re-told at Deaf gatherings. I was also very surprised by how many vlogs were posted with a small sign area and poor lighting, which made it difficult to understand the vloggers. Only one vlogger on DVTV produced a vlog that showed classical narrative style of hand-shape stories that can be found in face-to-face gatherings. DVTV, overall, seemed to be more concerned with personal details or some current events while YouTube seemed to be more abstract and general in nature with current news. It is possible that the technology was being used by the Deaf community to express current concerns as opposed to sharing re-telling of classical Deaf folklore. Vloggers may view vlogging as a mechanism for expressing personal ideas and may consider vlogging to be an inappropriate venue for formally re-telling ASL folklore or sharing historical information normally seen face to face. It may also be possible that the technology creates a sense of distance that prevents the desire to share culturally meaningful folklore.

5. Limitations

There were a number of limitations to our preliminary examination of Deaf vlogs including that only a limited number of vloggers were sampled. The range of differences between YouTube and DVTV may not be saturated as a result of this limited sample so further samples are required. In addition, we only analyzed existing vlogs and did not interview vloggers to understand the reasoning behind some of the innovative behaviors and approaches they used. Our next study will be to interview vloggers on why they make specific choices on presentation style, use of sign frame and the webcam technology, vocabulary and expectations for replies.

Another limitation of this research is that the samples were taken over a narrow time frame so we were unable to examine the evolution of vlogging and its impact on Deaf culture over time. Longitudinal studies that track change in the various variables identified in this study (e.g., position, frame size, and narrative innovation, etc.) over time may provide insights into this question.

We also only considered vlogs by experienced users. Examining the process of novice users may also add new data in how vloggers become proficient and what decisions they make along the way. However, this study does provide some evidence that there are differences in different vlogging sites/technologies that are used by Deaf users and that there are innovative expressions behaviors that arise from this technology.

6. Future Work

Future studies will involve interviewing vloggers to analyze their reasoning for using specific vlogging technologies, choosing topics and innovative techniques that they use to address their audience. We also plan to analyze vlogging behaviour and attitudes of a wider range of users from novice to expert and over a longer period of time. Finally, we want to examine the topics and signing styles further using additional vloggers and vlogs. All of this data should provide evidence for understanding the impact of vlogging and vlogging technology on Deaf culture.

7. Conclusion

The quantitative and qualitative observations provide some initial indications that sign language users use YouTube and DVTV differently. Sign rate, narrative style, use of space, clothing and body position show differences. YouTube tends to house more formal, mainstream-oriented vlogs that are potentially influenced by hearing vloggers or content on YouTube. DVTV seems to be more Deaf-centric and informal. There is more variety of replies and number of replies on DVTV even through the technical qualities of the DVTV vlogs is lower. It is problematic to identify vlogs containing ASL content in YouTube while it is simple to find them on DVTV. Vlogging technology also seems to influence the development and use of techniques and styles that are not found or are used differently in face-to-face situations. Examples include the use of space, specifically the z-axis for emphasis or the alteration of the vloggers appearance in the signing space (moving closer to the webcam) to convey meaning. New narrative elements have also appeared that are unique to vlogging. Examples include standing over the webcam or cropping the eyes from the signing space.

This study provides some of the first insights into the use of vlogging technology and techniques among the Deaf community. More time and study is required to better understand the impact of this technology on the evolution of Deaf culture and how to minimize some of the barriers of the text-centric web design.

8. ACKNOWLEDGEMENTS

Funding for this research was generously provided by NSERC grant #184220 and a SSHRC CURA grant. We thank all of the vloggers posting sign language content in YouTube and DVTV.

9. REFERENCES

[1] Bauman, H. ed. *Open Your Eyes: Deaf Studies Talking.* University of Minnesota Press, Minneapolis, 2008.

[2] Bellugi, U. and Klima, E. *The Signs of Language.* Harvard University Press, Cambridge, Massachusetts, 1979.

[3] Davenport, S. Improving communication with the deaf patient. *The Journal of Family Practice*, 4, 6, 1977, 1065.

[4] Fels, D., Gerdzhev, M., Hibbard, E., Goodrum, A., Richards, J., Hardman, J. and Thompson, N. Sign language online with Signlink Studio 2.0. In *UAHCI '09 Proceedings of the 5th International Conference on Universal Access in Human-Computer Interaction. Part III: Applications and Services.* 2009, 492-501.

[5] Fels, D., Konstantinidis, B., Hardman, J., Carey, C. and Porch, W. Providing inclusive video-mediated communication. *Annu. Rev. Commun.*, 57, 2004, 593-601.

[6] Gaillard, H. The Universal Magic of Sign Language. In Buchanan, B. ed. *Gaillard in Deaf America, a portrait of the Deaf community, 1917,* Gallaudet Press, Washington, D.C., 2002, 19-51.

[7] Herring, S., Scheidt, L., Bonus, S. and Wright, E. Bridging the gap: A genre analysis of weblogs. In *Proceedings 37th Annual HICSS Conference.* 2004, 40101b-40112.

[8] Keating, E. and Mirus, G. American sign language in virtual space: Interactions between deaf users of computer-mediated video communication and the impact of technology on language practices. *Lang Soc*, 32, 5 2003, 693-714.

[9] Lange, P. Publicly Private and Privately Public: Social Networking on YouTube. *J. Computer-Mediat. Comm.*, 13, 1 2008, 361-380.

[10] Mayberry, R. I. First-language acquisition after childhood differs from second-language acquisition: The case of American Sign Language. *J. Speech Hear. Res.*, 36, 6 1993, 1258-1270.

[11] McKeague, M. T. *The 21st Century Addiction: User Generated Content Dependency and Media Aesthetic Expectations as Experienced Through YouTube.* Doctorate in Philosophy Thesis, Indiana University of Pennsylvania 2011.

[12] Mitchell, W. J. T. There are no visual media. *J. Vis.Cult.*, 4, 2 2005, 257-266.

[13] Molyneax, H., O'Donnell, S. and Gibson, K. Exploring the gender divide on YouTube: An analysis of the creation and reception of vlogs. *American Commun. J.*, 10, 1 2008.

[14] Nardi, B. A., Schiano, D. J. and Gumbrecht, M. Blogging as social activity, or, would you let 900 million people read your diary? In *CSCW '04 Proceedings of the 2004 ACM conference on Computer supported cooperative work.* 2004, 222-231.

[15] Ong, W. *Orality and Literacy: the Technologizing of the Word.* Routledge Press, New York, 2004.

[16] Padden, C. and Humphries, T. *Deaf in America: Voices from a culture.* Harvard University Press, Massachusetts, 1998.

[17] Schwier, R. A. and Misanchuk, E. R. Technical Quality and Perceived Quality in Multimedia Materials–Are They the Same or Different Things? In *Annual Convention of the Association for Media and Technology in Education in Canada.* Saskatoon, 1997.

[18] Veditz, G. *Preservation of the sign language.* Film. 1913.

Leveraging Large Data Sets for User Requirements Analysis

Maria K. Wolters
School of Informatics
University of Edinburgh
Edinburgh, UK
maria.wolters@ed.ac.uk

Vicki L. Hanson
School of Computing
University of Dundee
Dundee, UK
vlh@acm.org

Johanna D. Moore
School of Informatics
University of Edinburgh
Edinburgh, UK
j.moore@ed.ac.uk

ABSTRACT

In this paper, we show how a large demographic data set that includes only high-level information about health and disability can be used to specify user requirements for people with specific needs and impairments. As a case study, we consider adapting spoken dialogue systems (SDS) to the needs of older adults. Such interfaces are becoming increasingly prevalent in telecare and home care, where they will often be used by older adults.

As our data set, we chose the English Longitudinal Survey of Ageing (ELSA), a large representative survey of the health, wellbeing, and socioeconomic status of English older adults. In an inclusion audit, we show that one in four older people surveyed by ELSA might benefit from SDS due to problems with dexterity, mobility, vision, or literacy. Next, we examine the technology that is available to our target users (technology audit) and estimate factors that might prevent older people from using SDS (exclusion audit). We conclude that while SDS are ideal for solutions that are delivered on the near ubiquitous landlines, they need to be accessible for people with mild to moderate hearing problems, and thus multimodal solutions should be based on the television, a technology even more widespread than landlines.

Categories and Subject Descriptors

H.5.1 [**User/machine systems**]: Human factors; H.5.2 [**User Interfaces**]: Interaction Styles; Natural Language

General Terms

Human Factors

Keywords

requirements capture; spoken dialogue systems; hearing; inclusive design; telecare

1. INTRODUCTION

Older people are a core user group of home care and telecare applications. When creating applications for this user group, designers often use findings from cognitive psychology to motivate the parts of the design space that are explored [12, 28] or to motivate design patterns [36].

Another approach is to use large-scale demographic data to determine how many of the intended users have the physical and cognitive abilities required to use an application successfully. This is the kind of analysis that underpins the i-design toolkit for estimating design exclusion [27, 32]. This toolkit contains an extensive set of assessment procedures, including estimates of the percentage of people excluded from using an application which are based on the 1996/97 Disability Follow-Up Survey (DFS, [6]). The DFS estimates the incidence of a wide range of sensory, motor, and cognitive disabilities and impairments in the UK population.

Analyses of large-scale, general demographic surveys like ELSA complement tools like i-design that are based on more specialised surveys like the DFS. While such surveys collect far less detailed data about respondents' abilities than the DFS, they provide a wealth of contextual data that allows us to examine the socioeconomic situation of people who have specific ability limitations.

In this paper, we propose a three-step approach to using large-scale demographic data sets for scoping out initial design requirements. In a first step, we estimate inclusion, i.e., we determine which user groups would benefit from access to a specific technology (*inclusion audit*). Next, we look at the kinds of platforms that should reasonably be targeted since they will be familiar to the target group (*technology audit*). Finally, we estimate typical problems the target group might have with using the technology (*exclusion audit*). Since large-scale surveys are designed as general-purpose data sets, a lot of this information is bound to be fragmentary, but it enables us to identify areas where more specialised surveys should be consulted.

Specifically, we use this approach to collect information about user requirements for spoken dialogue systems (SDS) that can be easily used by older people. In traditional touch-tone interactive voice response (IVR) systems, users respond to spoken menus or questions by pressing one or more buttons on their phone. SDS, on the other hand, allow users to respond verbally. Touch-tone IVR systems are well-established in telecare and home care [29]; they have been used to deliver appointment reminders, administer standardised questionnaires [17], and even deliver behavioural interventions [10]. As SDS become more robust and reliable, they are increasingly used in situations where developers would previously resort to touch-tone IVR technology [2, 18] or even in situations such as home alarms where users might find it difficult to reach or operate a phone or a GUI-based solution [19].

We would like to stress that an analysis like the one we undertake here is neither comprehensive nor prescriptive. Rather, it is about identifying opportunities and making sure that people who might benefit from particular user interface options, such as SDS, can access and use them. In particular, we do not advocate that all people who have vision problems should be using SDS, nor, vice versa, that all people with hearing problems should use GUIs. There are many reasons why people might want to use SDS (or, more generally, phone-based solutions), and our role as designers and developers of SDS is to ensure that this option is open to them, if they choose to do so.

1.1 Designing for Different Abilities: The Role of Surveys

National and global statistics provide information about population incidences of a number of disabilities of interest to us such as poor vision, limited hand use, mobility difficulties and literacy [11, 9]. From the most recent World Health Organization (WHO) published survey[1] , a reported 37 million people were blind and an additional 124 million had some degree of low vision. Often also included in such surveys is information about abilities in relation to activities of daily living (ADLs) and incidental activities of daily living (IADLs).

Often these surveys provide information about disability broken down into age cohorts. Such information highlights the increasing incidence of disability as we age. In the same WHO study, it was determined, for example, that 82% of all people who are blind are 50 years or older. Would these blind users benefit from SDS? The answer depends on a number of co-occurring factors that are not discernable from such demographic reporting. Do these individuals also have a hearing loss that makes understanding speech difficult? Do they have a neurological disorder such as Parkinson's disease or stroke that might make making speaking (and being understood) difficult? Do they have a cognitive problem, such as a short-term recall deficit, that might make interacting with such systems difficult?

While health surveys provide information about disability, surveys of media use and media literacy yield detailed information about availability and use of various technology devices in the home (e.g., [25]). Such surveys help address questions about appropriate technology to support SDS for older adults, but rarely address the question of whether the users of such devices might have physical or cognitive ability limitations that would affect their ability to use a SDS on these devices.

The English Longitudinal Survey of Ageing (ELSA) is a large multi-purpose survey that includes information not only about general health and well-being, but also about many aspects of people's economic and social lives, including technology available in their home. While ELSA is by necessity not as detailed as the specialist surveys discussed earlier, it allows us to look not just at the incidence of disability, but also at key indicators that could affect whether a specific type of technology is suitable for a user and how this technology should be implemented. By considering these indicators in combination, we are able to get a more accurate picture of numbers of people who would benefit from SDS than we would be able to get from isolated population estimates of individual ability, disability, and technology use based on specialised surveys.

1.2 Research Questions

In this paper, we apply the methodology outlined above to a specific technology, SDS, and a specific user group, people aged 65 and older. Our research questions are:

Why might older people benefit from SDS? Here we look beyond vision (which is an obvious reason) to explore other factors including dexterity, mobility, and literacy. Dexterity affects users' ability to control input devices for graphical user interfaces such as mice or touch screens, mobility affects whether people might want to access certain services remotely because they are difficult to access physically, and literacy affects whether people can understand the written text used in graphical interfaces.

In what familiar technology should SDS be embedded? Much work on telecare and telemedicine focuses on the web and internet-based solutions. While internet, computer, and mobile phone use is becoming more widespread among older people, adoption still lags behind that of younger people [37, 38]. Here, we are interested in the kinds of technology that today's 65-year-olds use, because they will be the ones who will need to access home and telecare services in 5–10 years' time.

What problems might exclude older people from using SDS? Relevant potential limitations include cognition, in particular memory and language comprehension, speech and articulation, and hearing.

2. DATA

2.1 English Longitudinal Survey of Ageing

The English Longitudinal Survey of Ageing [20] is a biannual representative survey of older people in England and Wales that collects information about health, well-being, cognitive function, and financial circumstances of older people. One of its main aims "is to discover what people aged 50 years and above do, and are able to do, in areas that are of great interest to all of us [...]." ([20], p.1)

ELSA contains rich information about a range of activities of daily living, the social networks and families of older people, and the extent to which older people participate in the community, as active volunteers, contributors to organisations, and carers. The sample was designed to reflect the age and gender distribution of the population. So far, four waves of data collection have been completed, beginning with Wave 1 starting in 2002-2003, where the main cohort of core members was recruited into the survey.

Since ELSA covers many aspects of physical, financial, and social status and wellbeing, coverage of very specific areas may be patchy. For example, reading level is an important measure in assessing the accessibility of texts. Unfortunately, reading level itself was not directly assessed. However, we have information on two variables that are linked to reading level, namely level of education and performance on a literacy test. The literacy test also provides indirect information about language comprehension, because people

---

[1]http://www.who.int/whosis/whostat/en/index.html

Table 1: Demographic Data

Variable	Age Group			Signif.
	65-74	75-84	85+	
N	2068	1132	208	
% Male		$\chi^2(2)=7.41$, $p<0.0246$		
	47.58%	43.55%	40.38%	
Education		$\chi^2(8)=60.35$, $p<0.0001$		
Degree	10.59%	9.19 %	6.73 %	
A-Level	17.79%	14.22 %	13.46 %	
GCSE	17.12%	10.87 %	9.13 %	
Other	15.23%	17.93 %	13.94 %	
Not Compl.	39.26%	47.79 %	56.73 %	

who find it difficult to understand spoken language may also find it difficult to interpret the text used in the literacy text. However, since the ELSA respondents were not formally assessed for reading level or dyslexia, it is difficult to separate general comprehension difficulties from problems that are caused specifically by processing written text.

2.2 Sample

For the purpose of this analysis, we used the Wave 2 data set, which was collected in 2004/05, because this is the latest data set for which derived variables characterising cognitive ability have been officially released.[2] First, we identified all core members of the survey who had been interviewed in person and in full, both with or without a proxy, and whose household had been adequately covered according to the sampling criteria (n=8380). Core members are people aged 52 and older who had been recruited into Wave 1 of the survey and are followed up in Wave 2.

From this data set, we excluded 397 participants for whom full information about cognitive function was not available and an additional 1247 who had not provided a response to all items used in our inclusion audit analysis. We then limited the data set to participants aged 65 and older. Since ELSA sampling follows population demographics, this reduces the sample by almost half or 3328 respondents.

The final data set consisted of 3408 participants. Following conventions used in previous ELSA reports, we divided the resulting sample into three age groups, 65–74, 75–85, and 85+. Since centenarians are collapsed into a single 99+ age category in ELSA, it is not possible to establish reliable mean ages.

Table 1 summarises the demographics of the participants whose responses we used for analysis. The overall percentage of male respondents was 45.80%, declining significantly in the older age groups. There are also significant differences in education levels between age groups.

2.3 Statistical Analysis

Most of the statistics in this paper are descriptive, identifying the percentage of our sample that meets specific criteria. We assessed whether differences between age groups were significant using χ^2 tests for categorical variables and oneway non-parametric ANOVA [13] for interval-scaled variables. Differences between proportions are described using

---

[2] At the time of writing, the equivalent derived variables for Wave 3 (2006/7) are only available as a pre-release at the moment.

log odds ratios as implemented in the R package vcd [22]; 95% confidence intervals are given, as well.

When comparing the potential target group for SDS and other respondents in the survey, we used full factorial logistic regression models for binary outcome variables, such as presence of hearing problems, and linear regression for normally distributed variables such as the cognitive measures used in ELSA. The regressions included terms for target group, age group, and sex as well as all possible two-way and the three-way interactions between the three terms. Significance levels are reported based on the analysis of variance (linear regression, F-test for significance) and the analysis of deviance (logistic regression, χ^2 significance test).

All analyses were conducted using the statistics package R version 2.10.1 [30]; the source code is available on request.

3. INCLUSION AUDIT: OPPORTUNITIES

As mentioned in section 1.2, there are four groups of older people who might benefit from SDS, people with limited *vision*, people with *dexterity* issues, people who have *mobility* problems, and people whose low *literacy* makes reading difficult for them.

Traditionally, work on assistive SDS has focussed on people who find it hard to interact with a graphical user interface because of limited vision and/or dexterity [8]. We decided to consider mobility limitations, because people who find it difficult to get to shops, banks, and medical care providers are obvious candidates for services such as telephone banking, telecare, and online shopping, which could potentially be delivered through SDS. Literacy is an important aspect because people with low literacy may find verbal information easier to understand when hearing it instead of reading it.

In the following inclusion audit, we discuss information contained in ELSA that might enable us to identify older people who fall within one of these four target groups, and calculate the proportion of older people that might benefit from SDS.

3.1 Dexterity

Within ELSA, there is only high-level information about dexterity. A major source of information is the prevalence of health conditions that might affect dexterity, such as Parkinson's Disease, stroke, or arthritis. Unfortunately, the type of arthritis and the affected joints were not specified in the survey. This makes it difficult to use arthritis as a proxy for dexterity problems.

Instead, we based our classification on whether people had problems with iADL activities that involved dexterity. The three relevant activities covered by the survey are picking up a five pence coin (the smallest coin circulating in the UK), dressing, including putting on shoes and socks, and eating, including cutting food.

For the purpose of this audit, we assume that older people have substantial dexterity problems if they find it difficult to pick up a five pence coin or if they have problems with both eating and dressing.

3.2 Vision

Although ELSA contains detailed information about medical conditions that affect vision, such as cataracts or macular degeneration, there is relatively little data on their impact on visual function. Therefore, we used data from two self-report items, overall self-reported eyesight and the ability to read newspaper print. Both were rated on a five-point scale labelled excellent, very good, good, fair, poor. These three categories do not necessarily overlap—partially because any eye conditions may have been successfully treated, and partially because self-reported function may not accurately reflect actual function. While 34.10% of the 65+ sample have a relevant medical history, only 13.73% of the total sample would describe their vision as fair or poor, and 11.24% of the sample are limited in their ability to read newspaper print.

For the inclusion audit, we assumed that older people might benefit from spoken dialogue interaction if their vision makes it difficult for them to read the paper and their self-reported eyesight is only fair or poor.

3.3 Mobility

Mobility was assessed extensively in ELSA. In order to determine whether people might find it difficult to walk to local shops, we analysed the self-reported ability to walk a quarter of a mile (400 metres) unaided.

Respondents were also asked about access to relevant facilities such as shops, supermarkets, banks, or the post office. Access could be by car and public transport as well as by walking. Overall, 81.25% of the sample reported no problems with access. When we only consider people who find walking a quarter of a mile very difficult, however, only a third report no problems with accessing facilities.

For this audit, we considered people to have mobility problems that might require them to use speech-based services at home if they had at least some difficulty walking a quarter of a mile and found it difficult to access at least one of facilities mentioned above.

3.4 Literacy

Literacy was assessed using a test that had been used in previous international studies of adult literacy [26]. Participants read a text that described a fictitious medication, Medco Aspirin. They were then asked for four pieces of important information, such as the maximum number of days the medication should be taken or one out of six conditions for which the medication was indicated. For the purpose of the inclusion audit, older people were regarded to have potential literacy problems if they answered less than three questions on the literacy test correctly.

Literacy skills are crucially affected by level of education. 83.98% of those who had been educated to degree level obtained a perfect score, but only 55.06% of those who did not finish formal education scored perfectly. This is an important confounder of any potential age effects, since more than half of the 85+ cohort did not complete any formal education, as opposed to two in five of the 65–74-year-olds.

3.5 Summary

We have identified four groups of people who might benefit from speech interfaces: people with literacy, vision, mobility, and dexterity problems. The older people get, the more likely they are to have at least one problem that means they might benefit from using SDS. By far the biggest relevant problems are literacy and mobility. Literacy scores may be skewed by differences in vision, cognition, and education. Mobility issues are a real hurdle for many older people—their incidence roughly doubles between subsequent

Table 2: Inclusion: Older People Who Might Benefit from SDS

| Limitation | Age Group | | | Sig. |
	65–74	75–84	85+	
Type				
Dexterity	4.98%	8.13%	12.98%	$p < 0.0001$
Vision	5.17%	10.87%	15.38%	$p < 0.0001$
Mob.	7.21%	15.02%	39.42%	$p < 0.0001$
Literacy	11.70%	18.73%	31.25%	$p < 0.0001$
Number				$p < 0.0001$
1 Problem	18.42%	27.12%	37.02%	
2–4 Problems	4.69%	11.22%	26.44%	

age groups. Vision scores are surprisingly good, with many people claiming that they can still read newspaper print. This is not unaided vision, however, so these numbers include people using vision aids such as glasses.

The prevalence of the four problem types in each age group is summarised in Table 2. Overall, 69.37% (n=1044) of the older people interviewed have none of these problems, 22.45% have one, and 8.19% have two or more. People with at least one relevant limitation are more likely to be female (57.66% versus 52.66%, odds ratio OR=-0.20, 95% CI=[-0.35,-0.06], $p < 0.0035$). In the remainder of this paper, we will consider as the 'target group' of potential users those people who have at least one problem that might mean they would benefit from SDS.

4. TECHNOLOGY AUDIT: PLATFORMS

Table 3: What Technology do People Own?

| Variable | Target Group | | P-Value |
	No	Yes	
Telephone			
Landline	98.69%	97.22%	$p < 0.0020$
Mobile	64.93%	43.97%	$p < 0.0001$
Household Technology			
Appliances	98.86%	95.79%	$p < 0.0001$
TV	99.45%	98.95%	$p < 0.2048$
Cable	36.89%	26.44%	$p < 0.0003$
CD Player	81.73%	65.04%	$p < 0.0001$
Video/DVD	92.68%	81.23%	$p < 0.0001$
Information Technology			
Computer	46.02%	25.19%	$p < 0.0001$
Internet	29.95%	14.18%	$p < 0.0001$

In our technology audit, we examined how likely people in our target group were to have technology in their home that could be used as a platform for either SDS or voice-based messages. We identified all such devices and appliances that were covered in the ELSA survey and grouped them into three categories: telephony; household technology such as kitchen appliances (dishwasher, microwave oven, washing machine, dryer), TV, Video/DVD players, and CD players; and information technology proper, such as computers and internet access.[3] For each type of technology, we determined whether the target group was significantly

---

[3]Smartphones were not included as a separate category in the survey.

less likely to own it than the control group using a regression analysis as outlined in Section 2.3. Respondents were only asked whether they owned a particular item, not how often they used it, for what purposes they used it, or how confident they felt using it. We categorised respondents as owning kitchen appliances if they had at least one of the four appliances mentioned. For reasons of space, we only report the results for Target Group as a main factor.

Table 3 shows that the key piece of technology owned by almost everybody, without distinction, is a basic television. People in the target user group for SDS have fewer video or DVD players, and are less likely to have cable or satellite television. In particular, people from the target group are half as likely to own a computer or have access to the internet. Perhaps surprisingly, they are also somewhat less likely to have a landline in their home, and are less likely to own at least one kitchen appliance. Only two out of five people in the target group own a mobile phone; in the other group, that proportion rises to three out of five.

5. EXCLUSION AUDIT: CHALLENGES

Since people in the target user group for SDS are more likely to be older, they are also more likely to be affected by other age-related problems that might make it more difficult for them to use SDS (or indeed any computer interface). We identified three relevant categories of problems: overall cognitive function, neurological conditions that affect speech and cognition, and hearing.

5.1 Cognition

From the set of five cognitive function tests used in ELSA, we report on two that may affect interaction with SDS, memory and fluency [14]. While memory affects people's ability to remember the current state of the dialogue and information that has already been received, fluency can be linked to the relative ease with which people can recall and name concepts that might be relevant to the interaction. The memory measure is a composite index that largely reflects performance on immediate and delayed recall of a word list. Fluency was tested by asking people to name as many different animals as possible in one minute.

As Table 4 shows, both the memory index and fluency are significantly lower in the target population for SDS than in the remainder of the sample. However, most of this is due to the difference in age groups. The absolute differences between means are relatively small and should not be taken to mean that the target group has impaired function.

5.2 Neurological Conditions

ELSA contains information about the prevalence of two broad classes of neurological conditions that can affect speech, stroke and Parkinson's Disease. Although neither condition invariably leads to language impairment, stroke is the most common cause of aphasia, and Parkinson's Disease is frequently associated with hypokinetic dysarthria. Participants were also asked whether they had Alzheimer's Disease or another form of dementia, which affects cognition and in some cases also speech. Unfortunately, the effect of any these conditions on people's ability to communicate was not assessed.

As Table 4 shows, people in the target group are significantly more likely to be affected by one of these three conditions. In at least some of these cases, the neurological condition may be the reason a person is a candidate for SDS. For example, mobility impairments may be the result of a stroke.

5.3 Hearing

In any consideration of SDS for older users, the age-related decline in hearing is the major obstacle. Perhaps not surprisingly, almost half the potential target user group for SDS reported a hearing problem and/or had been fitted with a hearing aid, compared to one in three of the non-target group. However, less than half the people who reported fair or poor hearing (as opposed to excellent, very good, or good hearing) had been fitted with a hearing aid.

Not all of the people in our target group who have hearing problems can easily move to graphical user interfaces instead. For example, people who find it difficult to understand speech in noise are more likely to have a vision problem that puts them into the target user group for spoken dialogue interfaces (OR=-0.77, 95% CI=[-1.03,-0.52], $p <0.0001$).

Table 4: Exclusion: Potential Problems with SDS. (M=Mean Score; SD=Standard Deviation)

Variable	Target Group		P-Value
	No	Yes	
Cognitive Function			
Memory	15.4	13.1	$p < 0.0001$
	(SD: 3.9)	(SD: 4.3)	
Fluency	19.8	17.1	$p < 0.0001$
	(SD: 5.8)	(SD: 5.7)	
Hearing Problems			
Any	39.72%	54.69%	$p < 0.0001$
Hearing Fair/Poor	21.53%	35.25%	$p < 0.0001$
Speech In Noise	35.83%	48.37%	$p < 0.0001$
Phone Calls	0.85%	4.02%	$p < 0.0001$
Hearing Aid	10.28%	18.68%	$p < 0.0001$
Relevant Neurological Conditions			
Stroke	3.89%	12.36%	$p < 0.0001$
Dementia	0.34%	1.53%	$p < 0.0016$
Parkinson's Disease	0.38%	1.44%	$p < 0.0011$

5.4 Summary

We have identified three main reasons why people in our target user group for SDS might have problems with using such a system, cognitive function, neurological conditions, and hearing problems. It is not surprising that the incidence of problems is higher in the target group, since this group is also significantly likely to be older. By far the most significant exclusion factor is hearing. Taken together, around half of the target sample reports problems with their hearing (c.f. also Table 4). Neurological conditions are far less relevant, because they are comparatively rare in the community-dwelling sample recruited for ELSA.

6. DISCUSSION

In this paper, we showed that the kinds of people who would benefit from SDS can be characterised based on surveys that were originally designed for very different purposes, such as the English Longitudinal Survey of Ageing. Surveys such as ELSA, which have been designed to be representative, complement approaches that start from an overview of relevant impairments, because they provide valuable socioeconomic context. ELSA in particular is a good starting point for such investigations, because its design has been replicated in the US [23] and Europe [3] and thus allows cross-cultural comparisons.

In this paper, we focused on the availability of common technology that could be used as a platform for SDS. Other analyses might focus on existing social support networks, or aspects of people's housing that affects which assistive solutions can be used.

6.1 Main Findings

Our inclusion audit showed that just under a third of the people aged 65+ that were surveyed in ELSA are candidate users for SDS because of problems with literacy, vision, dexterity, or mobility.

Half of this candidate user group for SDS, however, may be potentially excluded from using such services because they report hearing problems. These problems range from difficulty understanding speech in noise, an early sign of auditory ageing, to hearing loss that is so substantial that the person was prescribed a hearing aid.

Self-reports can be a useful indicator of hearing loss, but they are not completely accurate—the sensitivity and specificity of these self-reports rarely exceeds 70% [35]. Here, the ELSA data needs to be supplemented with more specialised audiological surveys. However, despite the high prevalence of hearing problems, people can still use devices like phones that allow volume adjustment—while 48.37% people in our target group had problems understanding speech in noise, only 4.02% had problems using a telephone.

Almost all SDS use computer-generated (synthetic) speech output, because relying entirely on pre-recorded utterances makes systems too inflexible. Older people may find older speech synthesis approaches such as formant synthesis [1, 7] or diphone synthesis [31] difficult to understand; more natural and intelligible approaches like unit selection speech synthesis might be a step towards solving this problem [33]. In order to avoid excluding a large number of users from SDS, we need to focus on developing speech synthesis systems that are easy to understand for people with mild to moderate hearing loss. In particular, we need to support digital hearing aids adequately.

Although it is tempting to suggest that people with hearing problems should rely on GUIs, and people with sight problems should use SDS, such a strategy is short-sighted. Vision and hearing impairment frequently co-occur in our sample, and older people are highly likely to have both problems seeing and difficulty hearing as they age. Moreover, perceptual limitations do not necessarily predict the modality in which people would like to receive information such as reminders. McGee-Lennon et al. report that people who reported hearing problems were just as likely to favour auditory reminders as those who did not [21]. What we need is a multimodal strategy, where the same functionality is available both in GUI and in SDS form, and where both modes of delivery are accessible to people with mild to moderate vision and hearing impairment.

6.2 Adapting Dialogue Management

Although users in the target group perform worse on the memory and fluency tasks, the relative decline in performance is small. Instead of drastically simplifying dialogue

design to accommodate their requirements, it might be better to make SDS more flexible. Parameters such as the degree to which the user can take initiative could be varied dynamically (see e.g., [4]). Dialogue systems may not need to start out by presenting fewer options [34], but they may need to be able to reduce the number of options presented if the user appears to be struggling. Systems should automatically adjust relevant parameters based on indicators such as response times, expressions of anger and frustration, or fluency.

6.3 Platforms Matter

Our findings suggest that television-based interactive solutions, in particular those that do not require expensive cable or satellite service subscriptions, would be the most inclusive way of delivering speech-based services. While landlines are slightly less ubiquitous than television sets, they are also very wide spread, in particular among the target user group.

Most of the target group for SDS neither own a computer nor have access to the Internet, which means that there is a place for SDS in delivering access to services via the telephone. Although the Internet will likely continue to become more widely used in the coming decades, a significant proportion of today's 65–75-year-olds may still not be online in five to fifteen years' time, when declining mobility forces them to access more services from home. Web-based solutions, and in particular health information solutions that focus mainly on web sites, may not be appropriate for this user group.

While TV, the most widespread technology, is a promising potential platform for multimodal solutions, this is tempered by the low uptake of cable and satellite services—in the target group, around two thirds of the people who own a TV have a basic service that is linked to standard analogue services.[4]

Phone-based interactive systems can fill this gap, providing automated, interactive services for people who either do not own a computer or are not comfortable with using one, but who are comfortable with using a telephone, a technology they have used all of their lives. Phone-based solutions can also be easily adapted to people with hearing problems by increasing the volume, and hearing aids can easily be connected to both landline and mobile telephones. This would address the key limitation found in our exclusion audit, poor (actual or self-reported) hearing.

6.4 Limitations

Since surveys such as ELSA are general-purpose, they are almost guaranteed to exclude relevant information or gloss over important distinctions. For example, ELSA does not contain detailed information about types of hearing problems, problems with speech production, or prevalence of dyslexia. In addition, the design of the questions used to assess ADLs and IADLs significantly affects the extent to which self-reported dexterity and mobility problems can be detected [15].

Another limitation concerns the data regarding mobile phones. The high percentages found for mobile phones in ELSA may well have been due to the wording of the question—people were asked whether they owned a mobile phone, not

---

[4]In the UK, this will change over the next few years as the roll out of digital television is completed and the remaining analogue transmitters are switched off.

whether they used it. We know that many older adults have mobile phones that are rarely, if ever, used [5, 37].

Finally, the sampling is biased towards people who still live in the community. In addition, since the sample mirrors UK demographics, it includes relatively few people over 80, who are more likely to develop dementia as they age [16].

Fortunately, such biases can be partly corrected by consulting more specialised surveys. In a recent Media Literacy Audit [24], OfCom, the UK telecommunication regulator, identified five types of users; engaged, pragmatist, economist, hesitant, and resistor. Nine out of ten older adults were hesitants or resistors when it comes to technology. Hesitant users owned a mobile phone, but not much else, and found technology difficult to use. Resistors thought that technology was just not for them. Despite this reluctance, many still had a digital television.

Some of the information about communication skills that is missing from ELSA is covered by the Disability Follow-Up Survey (DFS, [6]). In the DFS, locomotion, reach-and-stretch, dexterity, vision, hearing, thinking and communication were assessed in great detail for a representative subset of the UK population using a series of self-report questions. However, Waller *et al.* [32] argue that this data set also has significant limitations when assessing whether users may find it difficult to interact with a given product or service. A large-scale survey is currently underway to provide more detailed information (c.f. www-edc.eng.cam.ac.uk/idesign3) about ability levels relevant to technology use, but it is not clear to what extent this data set will cover the wealth of economic and social data contained in ELSA.

With the results presented in this paper, we have barely begun to scratch the surface of potential analyses. The regressions reported in Section 4 should be extended by taking socioeconomic factors into account, such as income and home ownership. The mobility assessment could be refined by examining whether people have good access to public transport or can still drive a car, and the target group could be divided into people who live on their own versus people who live with family, and people who have strong social networks versus people who live in relative isolation.

7. CONCLUSION

In this paper, we have shown that large-scale demographic data sets such as ELSA contain valuable information for the design and scoping of assistive technology solutions, such as SDS for older users. A key advantage of our analysis is that it is completely open and easy to replicate and extend. ELSA is freely available for research purposes, and updated biennially. Similar surveys are available for the EU and the US. All our analyses were conducted using the open-source statistics package R, which makes them easy to replicate for other research groups.

In our analyses, we found that there is a sizable group of older people who might benefit from using SDS. Among the potential reasons for deploying SDS, literacy, i.e., the ability to read and understand written text, proved to be surprisingly important, even more salient than vision. Literacy is affected by many factors, not just vision and cognition, but also education. In the cohort we studied, which has been designed to be representative of the community-dwelling UK population, well over a third left school without any formal qualifications.

The optimal platform for SDS appears to be the land-line phone, at least for the next 5–10 years. TV, which is more widespread than landlines, is a promising platform for multi-modal solutions. We also identified hearing as the key accessibility challenge for SDS—almost half of the potential target group reported problems with their hearing. Our analyses clearly pointed to three areas where more in-depth surveys need to be consulted—older people's use of technology, in particular mobile phones; the effect of literacy on older people's use of services; and the effect of hearing problems on the usability of SDS that use modern, highly intelligible speech synthesis systems.

8. ACKNOWLEDGMENTS

This research was partially funded by the EPSRC grant EP/G060614/1 MultiMemoHome and the RCUK Digital Economy Research Hub EP/G066019/1 "SiDE: Social Inclusion through the Digital Economy" and a Royal Society Wolfson Merit Award to the second author.

9. REFERENCES

[1] J. Al-Awar Smither. The processing of synthetic speech by older and younger adults. In *Proc. Human Factors Society 36th Annual Meeting. Innovations for Interactions, 12-16 Oct. 1992*, pages 190–192, 1992.

[2] T. Bickmore and D. Mauer. Modalities for building relationships with handheld computer agents. In *CHI '06 Extended abstracts*, page 544, New York, New York, USA, Apr. 2006. ACM Press.

[3] A. Börsch-Supan and H. Jürges, editors. *The Survey of Health, Aging, and Retirement in Europe—Methodology*. 2005.

[4] S.-W. Chu, I. O'Neill, and P. Hanna. Using Multiple Strategies to Manage Spoken Dialogue. In *Proc. Interspeech, Antwerp, Belgium*, 2007.

[5] G. W. Coleman, L. Gibson, V. L. Hanson, A. Bobrowicz, and A. McKay. Engaging the disengaged. In *Proc. 8th ACM Conf Designing Interactive Systems*, page 175, New York, NY, USA, 2010. ACM Press.

[6] Department of Social Security. Social Research Branch. Follow-up to the 1996/97 Family Resources Survey [computer file], 2000.

[7] K. D. R. Drager and J. E. Reichle. Effects of discourse context on the intelligibility of synthesized speech for young adult and older adult listeners: applications for AAC. *J Speech Lang Hear Res*, 44:1052–1057, 2001.

[8] J. Feng and A. Sears. Speech Input to Support Universal Access. In *The Universal Access Handbook*, pages 30-1 – 30-16, Boca Raton, FL, 2009. CRC Press.

[9] S. Fox. Americans living with disability and their technology profile. Technical report, Pew Research Centre, Washington, DC, USA, 2011.

[10] J. H. Greist, I. M. Marks, L. Baer, K. A. Kobak, K. W. Wenzel, M. J. Hirsch, J. M. Mantle, and C. M. Clary. Behavior therapy for obsessive-compulsive disorder guided by a computer or by a clinician compared with relaxation as a control. *J Clin Psychiatr*, 63:138–145, 2002.

[11] E. Grundy, D. Ahlburg, M. Ali, E. Breeze, and A. Sloggett. Disability in Great Britain: Results from

the 1996/97 disability follow-up to the family resources survey. Technical report, Department of Social Security, London, UK, 1999.

[12] D. Hawthorn. Possible implications of aging for interface designers. *Interact Computers*, 12:507–528, 2000.

[13] T. Hothorn, K. Hornik, M. van de Wiel, and A. Zeileis. Implementing a class of permutation tests: The coin package. *J Statistical Software*, 28(8):1–23, 2008.

[14] F. A. Huppert, E. Gardener, and B. McWilliams. Cognitive Function. In J. Banks, E. Breeze, C. Lessof, and J. Nazroo, editors, *Retirement, health and relationships of the older population in England: The 2004 English Longitudinal Study of Ageing (Wave 2)*, pages 217–242, London, UK, 2006. Institute for Fiscal Studies.

[15] C. Jagger, R. Matthews, D. King, A. Comas-Herrera, E. Grundy, R. Stuchbury, M. Morciano, and R. Hancock. Calibrating disability measures across British national surveys. Technical report, Department of Work and Pensions, London, UK, 2009.

[16] M. Knapp and M. Prince. Dementia UK. Technical report, Alzheimer's Society, London, UK, 2007.

[17] K. A. Kobak, J. H. Greist, J. W. Jefferson, J. C. Mundt, and D. J. Katzelnick. Computerized assessment of depression and anxiety over the telephone using interactive voice response. *M D Computing*, 16:64–68, 1999.

[18] E. Levin and A. Levin. Evaluation of spoken dialogue technology for real-time health data collection. *J Med Internet Res*, 8(4):e30, 2006.

[19] L. Lines and K. S. Hone. Eliciting user requirements with older adults: lessons from the design of an interactive domestic alarm system. *Univ Acc Inform Soc*, 3:141–148, 2004.

[20] M. Marmot. Introduction. In J. Banks, E. Breeze, C. Lessof, and J. Nazroo, editors, *Retirement, health and relationships of the older population in England: The 2004 English Longitudinal Study of Ageing (Wave 2)*, pages 1–10, London, UK, 2006. Institute for Fiscal Studies.

[21] M. R. McGee-Lennon, M. K. Wolters, and S. Brewster. User-Centred Multimodal Reminders for Assistive Living. In *Proc. CHI*, 2011.

[22] D. Meyer, A. Zeileis, and K. Hornik. vcd: Visualising Categorical Data. R package version 1.2-9, 2010.

[23] National Institutes of Health—National Institute of Ageing. *Growing Older in America: The Health and Retirement Study*. 2007.

[24] Ofcom. Media Literacy Audit—Report on UK Adults' Media Literacy. Technical report, Office of Communications, London, UK, 2008.

[25] Ofcom. Digital Lifestyles - Adults Aged 60 and Over. Technical report, Office of Communications, London, UK, 2009.

[26] Organisation for Economic Cooperation and Development (OECD) and Statistics Canada. Literacy in the Information Age: Final Report of the International Adult Literacy Survey. Technical report, OECD and Statistics Canada, Paris, France, 2000.

[27] U. Persad, P. Langdon, and J. Clarkson. Characterising user capabilities to support inclusive design evaluation. *Univ Acc Inform Soc*, 6(2):119–153, 2007.

[28] H. Petrie. Accessibility and Usability Requirements for ICTs for Disabled and Elderly People: a Functional Classification Approach. In C. Nicolle and J. Abascal, editors, *Inclusive Design Guidelines for HCI*, pages 29–60. Taylor and Francis, London, UK, 2001.

[29] J. D. Piette. Interactive voice response systems in the diagnosis and management of chronic disease. *Am J Manag Care*, 6:817–827, 2000.

[30] R Development Core Team. *R: A Language and Environment for Statistical Computing*. R Foundation for Statistical Computing, Vienna, Austria, 2009.

[31] R. W. Roring, F. G. Hines, and N. Charness. Age differences in identifying words in synthetic speech. *Human Factors*, 49:25–31, 2007.

[32] S. Waller, P. Langdon, and P. Clarkson. Using disability data to estimate design exclusion. *Univ Acc Inform Soc*, 9(3):195–207, 2010.

[33] M. K. Wolters, P. Campbell, C. DePlacido, A. Liddell, and D. Owens. Making Synthetic Speech Accessible to Older People. In *Proc. 6th ISCA Speech Synthesis Workshop*, pages 288–293, Aug. 2007.

[34] M. K. Wolters, K. Georgila, R. Logie, S. MacPherson, J. Moore, and M. Watson. Reducing Working Memory Load in Spoken Dialogue Systems. *Interact Computers*, 21(4):276–287, 2009.

[35] M. K. Wolters, C. Johnson, and K. B. Isaac. Can the Hearing Handicap Inventory for Adults be Used as a Screen for Perception Experiments? In *Proceedings of ICPhS*, 2011.

[36] M. Zajicek. Aspects of HCI research for older people. *Univ Acc Inform Soc*, 5(3):279–286, 2006.

[37] K. Zickuhr. Generations 2010. Technical report, Pew Research Centre, Washington, DC, USA, 2010.

[38] K. Zickuhr. Generations and their Gadgets. Technical report, Pew Research Centre, Washington, DC, USA, 2011.

Humsher: A Predictive Keyboard Operated by Humming

Ondřej Poláček   Zdeněk Míkovec   Adam J. Sporka   Pavel Slavík

Faculty of Electrical Engineering, Czech Technical University in Prague,

Karlovo nám. 13, 12135 Praha 2, Czech Republic

{polacond, xmikovec, sporkaa, slavik}@fel.cvut.cz

ABSTRACT

This paper presents Humsher – a novel text entry method operated by the non-verbal vocal input, specifically the sound of humming. The method utilizes an adaptive language model for text prediction. Four different user interfaces are presented and compared. Three of them use dynamic layout in which n-grams of characters are presented to the user to choose from according to their probability in given context. The last interface utilizes static layout, in which the characters are displayed alphabetically and a modified binary search algorithm is used for an efficient selection of a character. All interfaces were compared and evaluated in a user study involving 17 able-bodied subjects. Case studies with four disabled people were also performed in order to validate the potential of the method for motor-impaired users. The average speed of the fastest interface was 14 characters per minute, while the fastest user reached 30 characters per minute. Disabled participants were able to type at 14 – 22 characters per minute after seven sessions.

Categories and Subject Descriptors

H.5.2 Information interfaces and presentation: User Interfaces – Input devices and strategies; Keyboard.

General Terms

Measurement, Performance, Design, Experimentation, Human Factors.

Keywords

Non-verbal Vocal Interface, Assistive Technology, Text Input, Predictive Keyboard, Adaptive Language Model

1. INTRODUCTION

Research in the field of text entry methods has been widely documented for some time. In static desktop environments we can observe the dominance of QWERTY keyboard which is caused by its extreme popularity rather than its optimal performance. Learning a new layout is a tedious process that can take more than 100 hours [1]. However, in special circumstances (e.g., impaired users, mobile environment) no dominant text entry method can be identified. This has consequently led to the development of many non-traditional approaches, where users accept longer learning time.

The maximum realistic text entry speed can be defined as a speed of an experienced typist using ten fingers on QWERTY keyboard. The speed will be approximately 250-400 characters per minute (CPM) for a professional typist [2]. With this speed achieved there is a little space for any enhancements like predictive completion, dynamic layouts, etc. as this will effectively slow down the type rate.

Physically disabled people usually cannot achieve such high speed due to their constraints. Their communication with computers is rather limited to only several distinctive stimuli – small number of physical buttons, joystick, eye-tracking, features of the electroencephalographic (EEG) signal etc. This limitation can be compared to a situation when we are typing with one finger only on virtual keyboard displayed on a touch screen. There is a research available [3], showing that typing with one finger on a touch screen with virtual QWERTY keyboard results in a speed 160 CPM for expert users after 30 minutes training. If we reduce the size of the virtual keyboard to 7 cm then the speed will drop to 105 CPM. The speed reached by physically disabled people will be certainly lower. This situation opens a space for research of new entry methods which will take into account various limitations of motor impaired users and increase the entry speed.

There is currently a range of assistive tools available to help users with motor impairments. However, each user may have significantly different capabilities and preferences according to the range and degree of their impairment. In case of severe physical impairment, people usually have to use other interaction methods to emulate the keyboard. One of the methods that has been successfully used by people with special needs is the non-verbal vocal interaction (NVVI) [4]. It can be described as an interaction modality, in which sounds other than speech are produced, for example humming [27] or vowels [28].

Our virtual keyboard, *Humsher*, described in this paper utilizes vocal gestures, i.e. short melodic and/or rhythmic patterns. The user can operate the keyboard by humming. Each key is assigned a pattern. It has been designed for those people with upper-limb motor impairments such as quadriplegia induced from stroke, cerebral palsy, brain injury etc. Additionally, users are required to have healthy vocal folds enough to be able to produce humming. The main advantages of such interaction are its language independence and fast and accurate recognition as opposed to speech [4]. Speech recognition software usually works relatively well for native speakers; however, the accuracy is much lower for accented speakers or for people with speech impairment.

1.1 Definitions of Terms

Probably the most common measures of performance of text entry methods are *words per minute* (WPM) or *characters per minute* (CPM) [29]. Both rates indicate speed of a text entry method. Relation between them is defined by Equation 1. ISO 9241-4 standardizes WPM rate for keyboards at CPM divided by five, i.e. one "word" is considered as five characters including spaces. CPM is defined by equation 2, where |T| is length of written text in characters and S is time in seconds.

$$WPM = \frac{1}{5} \times CPM. \qquad (1)$$

$$CPM = \frac{|T| - 1}{S} \times 60. \qquad (2)$$

A *gestures per character* (GPC) rate [29] is also used in this paper for evaluating purposes. Gesture is regarded as an atomic operation. In the case of the humming input, vocal gestures are treated as atomic operations. Text entry methods with low GPC rate are considered as better than those with high rate; however, other parameters must be taken into account, such as length or complexity of the vocal gesture. The GPC rate is defined by Equation 3, where $|IS_\emptyset|$ is an input stream which contains all vocal gestures produced by the user and |T| is length of written text in characters.

$$GPC = \frac{|IS_\emptyset|}{|T|}. \qquad (3)$$

A sequence of *n* characters is referred to as *n-gram*. The n-grams with length equal to one, two and three character are being called unigrams, bigrams and trigrams respectively. In the paper the term *n-gram* is used for strings of characters of an unspecified length *n*.

2. RELATED WORK

There is a wide range of text entry methods targeting the motor-impaired users. We can notice that the methods described in this section often differ significantly in physical interaction used, which is determined by specific motor impairment. Each method is often unique for concrete impairment conditions and thus it typically makes no sense to compare various methods as they are not in concurrent position. Several principles can be identified in the literature – *predictive completion*, *ambiguous keyboards* and *scanning*.

A text entry method can be accelerated by prediction, when a list of possible completions is updated with each entered character. This reduces number of keystrokes per character. The Reactive Keyboard [5] predicted possible words according to context that had been already written. An adaptive dictionary-based language model was used. Predicted candidates could be selected by the mouse cursor. Expert users of a QWERTY keyboard would be slowed down, however, such prediction is useful for poor typist or people with limited movement of upper limbs. Another predictive keyboard GazeTalk [6] predicted six most probable letters and six words according to current context. If no prediction was correct, there was full keyboard available. This virtual keyboard was controlled by the eye gaze. The keys were activated by dwell-time selection system [7]. The average typing rate achieved by novice users was 16 CPM.

Probably the most prevalent ambiguous keyboard is the commercial T9 system by Tegic Communications [8] that is widely adopted on mobile phones. The idea behind is simple – the alphabet is divided into nine groups of characters and then each group is assigned to one key. The user selects desired characters by selecting the keys and after a sequence of keys is entered the word is disambiguated using a dictionary. For its efficiency, similar ambiguous keyboards were designed for physically impaired people. Kushler [9] describes an ambiguous keyboard in which the alphabet was assigned to seven keys and the eighth key was used as a space key that initiated the disambiguation process. Tanaka-Ishii [10] published similar system, in which only four physical keys were used. Besides disambiguation, the text entry method was capable of predicting words. The average speed of this method was 70 CPM, achieved after ten sessions by able-bodied participants. Harbusch [11] presented similar method in which the whole alphabet was assigned to only three keys and one key was used for executing special command in a menu.

When the number of stimuli, which can be issued by the user, is limited to only one or two, using scanning technique is inevitable. For example in the case of two buttons, the first button can be pressed repetitively (scanning) to select a key and second button is used to confirm the selection. When only one button is available, the keys are selected automatically for a certain amount of time. After the time expires, next key is selected. The button is used to confirm the selection again. Keys can be spatially organized in a matrix and the desired key is then selected by row-column scanning [12]. Combining linear scanning with an ambiguous keyboard is a common technique. For example, Kühn [13] used four-key scanning ambiguous keyboard and achieved 35 CPM without out-of-vocabulary words. Miro [14] limited the number of keys to only two (keys 'a-m' and 'n-z') and estimated its entry rate to 50 CPM for an expert user. Beltar [15] used three keys and developed a virtual mobile keyboard. In QANTI [16] three keys are mapped to the alphabet. The keyboard is operated by one switch that is triggered by intentional muscle contractions. The typing rate ranges from 12.5 to 33 CPM.

An efficient system is Dasher [17], which is based on a dynamically modified display and adaptive language model [18]. The characters are selected by moving the mouse cursor around the screen. Continuous "one finger" gestures are used as the input method. This is a very suitable input method for motor impaired users, who can operate a pointing device. The writing speed achieved is approximately 100 CPM with experienced users reaching up to 170 CPM. For users who have no hand function, a modification of the Dasher system can be made to allow input via eye tracking. A longitudinal study [19] found that an average writing speed of 87 CPM after ten 15-minutes sessions could be achieved. This speed was a large increase from the initial speed of just 12.5 CPM. Speech Dasher [20] is another interesting modification of Dasher. It combines speech input with the zooming input of Dasher. The system must first recognize a user's utterance. Errors are then corrected via the zooming input. Expert users reached a writing speed of approximately 200 CPM.

Sporka et al. [21] describe the NVVI-based method of keyboard emulation. Each vocal gesture is assigned a specific key on the keyboard, when a gesture is produced a corresponding key is emulated. The average reported typing rates varied between 12 and 16 CPM, which was measured in a study with able-bodied participants. Different assignments of NVVI gestures to keys were investigated, namely the pitch-to-address, pattern-to-key and Morse code mappings. In the pitch-to-address mapping, the keyboard was mapped onto a 4×4×4 matrix, while a sequence of three tones of specific pitches determined an address in the matrix. In the pattern-to-key mapping each key was assigned a specific gesture.

Another keyboard operated by NVVI is CHANTI [25]. It is an ambiguous keyboard, where the alphabet is split into only three groups. The keyboard combines philosophy of the ambiguous keyboard QANTI [16] and humming input. Scanning technique is replaced by direct selection of a key by vocal gestures. The keyboard was tested with five severely motor-impaired people, the speeds ranged from 10 to 15 CPM after 7 sessions.

Additionally, the P300 speller [22] is a method that utilizes the electroencephalographic (EEG) signal in the human brain to control a virtual keyboard. The keyboard is a 6x6 matrix containing alphanumeric characters. The user focuses on a character and as the character flashes, the brain produces a stimulus. At least two flashes are needed to input a character. According to Wang et al. [22], the writing speed achieved is approximately 7.5 CPM.

3. HUMSHER DESIGN

Our virtual keyboard, *Humsher*, has been designed for severely motor-impaired people, who can control it by vocal gestures. It utilizes the same language model as Dasher [17] (prediction by partial match; PPM [18]). The model provides n-grams and their probability, which have been predetermined by a given context. The model is initialized from a small corpus of English text, but it adapts as the user types.

3.1 Dynamic Layouts

The interfaces described in this section employ dynamic layout. The n-grams, which are extracted from the PPM model, are offered sorted according to their probability. The probability is predetermined by already written text. Practically it means that after typing an n-gram, the context is updated, probabilities of following n-grams are recounted and the layout is displayed accordingly.

We designed and implemented three different user interfaces (Direct, Matrix and List) with dynamic layout of characters. Each interface differs in either vocal gesture set or in mapping of gestures to actions. The Direct and Matrix interfaces utilize six vocal gestures as depicted in Fig. 1, whilst the List interface utilizes only three simple vocal gestures as depicted in Fig. 2. The vocal gestures are explicitly identified by its length (short/long) or by its pitch (low/high). In order to distinguish low and high tones a threshold pitch needs to be adjusted for each user – e.g. the difference between male and female voice is as much as one or two octaves. Only two different pitches were chosen as with increasing number of pitches, more precise intonation is required and the interaction becomes more error prone.

All three interfaces offer n-grams, containing the characters how the text might continue, sorted according to the probability. The n-grams can be unigrams (individual characters) as well as bigrams, trigrams, etc. The length of n-grams is not limited, only probability matters. N-grams to display are chosen according to the following steps:

1. Add all unigrams to the list L that will be displayed.

2. For each n-gram in the list L compute probability of all (n+1)-grams and add them to the list L if their probability is higher than a threshold.

3. Repeat step 2 until no n-gram can be added.

4. Sort the list L according to probability of each n-gram.

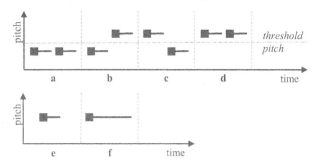

Figure 1. Vocal gestures used in Direct and Matrix interfaces

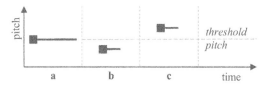

Figure 2. Vocal gestures used in List and Binary interfaces

3.1.1 Direct interface

The *Direct* interface (see Fig. 3) allows users to directly choose from four cells (labeled cell 1 to 4) in the Active column (part A). These cells contain n-grams that have been determined as the most probable following characters of the written text. Cells can be selected by vocal gestures depicted in Fig. 1a-d:

a. two consequent low tones (cell 1),

b. a low tone followed by a high tone (cell 2),

c. a high tone followed by a low tone (cell 3),

d. two consequent high tones (cell 4).

If there is no cell in the Active column that contains the desired character, the user has to move the leftmost column in the Look ahead (part B) to the Active column by producing a single short tone (see Fig. 1e) and keep repeating it until the desired n-gram appears in one of the cells in Active column. Text, which has been already written, can be erased by producing a long tone (see Fig. 1f). The longer the user keeps producing the tone the faster are the characters erased.

3.1.2 Matrix interface

The *Matrix* interface (see Fig. 4) utilizes the same vocal gestures as the Direct interface, however, the user interaction is different. Users are presented with a 4×4 matrix of the most probable n-grams. Cells in the left column of the matrix contain the highest probable n-grams, whilst the rightmost cells contain the lowest probable n-grams.

Selection of the correct cell is accomplished in two steps by specifying a column and a row. First, the user must select a column by producing a corresponding vocal gesture (Fig. 1a-d). The column is then highlighted and the same vocal gestures can be used to select the desired cell by selecting a row. If a character does not appear in the matrix, the user has to produce a short tone (see Fig. 1e) in order to display less probable n-grams. Written text can be erased by producing a long tone (see Fig. 1f), in the same manner as in the Direct interface.

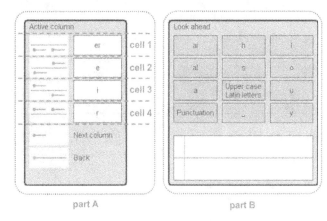

Figure 3. Direct interface. A– active column, C B – look ahead matrix

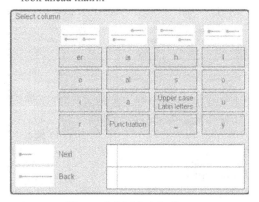

Figure 4. Matrix interface

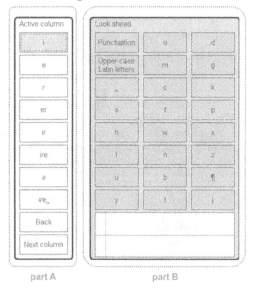

Figure 5. List interface. A – active column, B – look ahead matrix

3.1.3 List interface

The *List* interface (see Fig. 5) is controlled by just three simple and easy-to-learn gestures (see Fig. 2). The Active column (part A) presents the user a list of cells containing the eight most probable n-grams. The topmost cell is selected. Users can move the selection up and down by producing a short high or low tone (see Fig. 2b,c). A long tone (see Fig. 2a) is used to confirm the desired selection. This interface does not utilize special vocal gestures to select the next column or erase written text. Instead, these two functions are always made available by introducing two special cells Back and Next column at the bottom of the Active column list.

3.2 Static Layout

Static layout was designed in order to simplify the process of visual location of desired character. In dynamic layouts users have to locate a character visually by linear scanning and they cannot rely on the visual memory. The process of locating correct character can be tedious for low-probable characters. Moreover, users sometimes do not notice a correct character and they have to rotate through the whole list of characters and n-grams once again. This consequently can lead to users' frustration. Therefore we decided to implement a static interface, called Binary interface, that keeps position of characters and the characters are sorted alphabetically. Time needed to locate a character is then modeled by Hick-Hyman law [24] and it is logarithmically dependent on the length of the alphabet. Locating characters visually in the static layout is obviously faster than the same task in dynamic layouts as logarithmic scanning is used instead of linear.

3.2.1 Binary interface

In the *Binary* interface (see Fig. 6) the characters are always displayed in an alphabetic order. Such order gives us an opportunity to select desired character by binary search algorithm adopted from basic programming techniques. The algorithm locates position of a character in the alphabet by splitting it into two halves and deciding which half is used in the next step. Then the half is split again and again until the correct character is found. Each character is located in following number of steps:

$$steps = \lceil \log_2 N \rceil \qquad (4)$$

N is size of the alphabet. In our case the algorithm would require $\lceil \log_2 36 \rceil = 6$ selections as our alphabet contains 36 symbols. The user would have to produce six vocal gestures to enter a character. Therefore the best theoretical GPC rate achieved by the binary search is equal to six, which is quite high. But what happens if the alphabet is split according to the probability of characters rather than into two exact halves? Then a character with high probability could be located in fewer steps, however, character with low probability might be located in even more than six steps. The actual GPC rate measured empirically in a user study presented later is much lower than six.

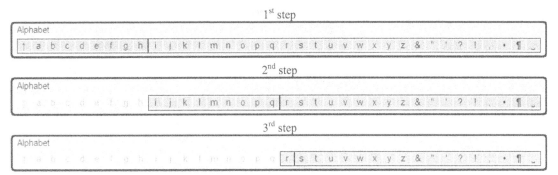

1st step

2nd step

3rd step

Figure 6. Binary interface, typing "*r*" after "*Text ent*"

The Binary interface is based on modified binary search algorithm. In each step the alphabet is split into two groups with balanced probability, i.e. the sum of probabilities of characters in each group is as close to 0.5 as possible. The boundary between groups is then computed according to the Equation 5, where k is the index of boundary character, p_i is a probability of character i and N is a size of the alphabet.

$$\min_{1<k<N} \left(\left(\frac{1}{2} - \sum_{i=1}^{k-1} p_i \right)^2 + \left(\frac{1}{2} - \sum_{i=k}^{N} p_i \right)^2 \right). \quad (5)$$

The Binary interface utilizes only three vocal gestures (see Fig. 2) as well as the List. Short low tone (Fig. 2b) and short high tone (Fig. 2c) are used for entering text, while the long tone (Fig 2a) is used for corrections.

An example of user interaction with the Binary interface is depicted in Fig. 6. Let us assume that the user has already entered the text "Text ent" and wants to continue by entering character "r". In the first step the alphabet is split into two groups "shift -h" and "i-space". The user chooses the second group by producing a high short tone. In the second step the rest of the alphabet is split into groups "i-q" and "r-space". Again the second group is chosen by the same high short tone. In the last step "r" is the only character in the first group because of its high probability. Remaining characters are in the second group. The character "r" is now entered by low short tone. In this case the character was selected only in three steps by three short tones.

When comparing Binary interface to the other three interfaces, several features can be observed:

- User can easily locate desired character as letters are sorted alphabetically and characters do not change their positions while entering text.
- Simple vocal gestures are employed (similar to List interface). Only two gestures are used for entering text and one for deleting text.
- The Binary interface offers only single characters unlike the interfaces with dynamic layout. It is not possible to enter more characters at once.

4. EVALUATION

In order to evaluate the interfaces we conducted two user studies. The goal of the first one was to compare all four interfaces, measure their speed and find out user's opinions on them. In the second study four disabled participants were recruited to validate potential of Humsher for motor-impaired users.

4.1 Comparison of interfaces

The aim of the user study was to measure the writing speed of each interface and subsequently determine which interface was the most efficient. In the study 17 able-bodied participants (10 men, 7 women, mean age=26, SD=2.1) took part. Each participant completed four sessions. According to Mahmud et al. [23], four sessions are needed to minimize the error rate of the NVVI. The schedules of each session are outlined below:

- **Session 1:** Participants were trained in producing the required vocal gestures. After reaching an accuracy of 90%, they were presented with all interfaces and asked to enter short phrases with each of them. This session lasted approximately 30-60 minutes depending on the user's abilities.

- **Sessions 2 and 3:** Participants were asked to enter two simple phrases using all interfaces. The sessions were conducted remotely and they lasted roughly 20 minutes.

- **Session 4:** Participants were asked to enter three phrases using all interfaces. The session was conducted remotely and it lasted roughly 30 minutes. Objective data from this session were collected.

After the last session each participant performed a subjective evaluation of each interface by means of remote interview. The participants received approximately 24 hours rest between the sessions. In order to minimize the learning effect, the sequence of interfaces was counterbalanced. Objective results (CPM, GPC rate and number of corrections) are shown in Table 1.

Table 1. Means and standard deviations (SD) of the typing rate (CPM), vocal gesture per character (GPC) rate and total number of corrections.

Interface	CPM		GPC		Corrections	
	Mean	SD	Mean	SD	Mean	SD
Direct	14.4	2.8	1.8	0.23	13.0	11.0
Matrix	11.8	2.1	1.9	0.32	16.1	14.6
List	13.0	3.2	3.5	0.58	6.4	6.6
Binary	11.7	1.8	3.4	0.18	14.5	8.5

The ANOVA test and Scheffé's method [26] were used to find statistically significant differences in mean quantities among interfaces. When comparing mean CPM rates, the Direct interface was significantly faster ($F(3,67) = 4.20$, $p < .01$) than the Matrix interface and it was also significantly faster than the Binary interface. Other differences in speed were not significant.

In the case of List and Binary interfaces, the users had to produce significantly more ($F(3,67)= 107.7$, $p < .01$) vocal gestures per character than Direct and Matrix interfaces. This corresponds to number of vocal gestures used in the interfaces. Direct and Matrix interfaces utilize six complex gestures (see Fig. 1), while the other interfaces only three simple gestures (see Fig. 2). As mentioned in section 3.2.1, theoretical GPC rate for standard binary search is 6, when the alphabet contains 36 symbols. By modifying the binary search, we succeeded to reduce the GPC rate to 3.4 empirically measured in the user study.

After the last session, participants were asked to comment on the interfaces. The Direct interface was mostly perceived as accurate and fast. The Matrix interface was in many cases perceived as fastest among all interfaces, although it was slower than Direct and List interfaces. Additionally, the List interface, which is not the slowest, was reported as the slowest. The List interface was also reported as cumbersome – some participants complained that it was not transparent enough and the navigation was tedious. This is probably due to the high number of cells in columns, which makes the visual searching more difficult. The Binary interface was found easy and fast by most participants, although it was the slowest one. The participants appreciated static layout of the interface, however, eight participants complained about the fact that only one character can be entered at one time and the method does not offer n-grams as the dynamic layout interfaces. The participants also made positive comments on simplicity of vocal gestures used to control the interface. Although there were no significant differences in objective data between List and Binary interfaces, participants strongly preferred the Binary one.

We identified two main searching strategies employed by participants when using Direct and List interfaces. Some of them visually scanned only the first column (Active column, see Fig. 3 and 4). When searched character was not found in this column, they moved forward and scanned the first column again. Some of them also reported that the Look ahead matrix is redundant and confusing. The other participants visually scanned all cells in Active column and Look ahead matrix. When searched character was not found, they moved forward and scanned the last column. They reported that this strategy allows them to plan vocal gestures in advance, which they found faster.

Ten participants reported fatigue of vocal folds during the experiment, which they mostly compensated for by lowering their pitch and dropping their voice.

Table 2. Performance of expert users

Interface	Expert 1			Expert 2			Expert 3		
	CPM	GPC	corr	CPM	GPC	corr	CPM	GPC	corr
Direct	29	1.5	1	24	1.7	8	30	1.5	2
Matrix	23	1.6	3	20	1.9	15	23	1.5	2
List	25	2.8	0	17	3.4	4	26	2.9	1
Binary	23	3.6	1	16	3.6	23	20	3.2	10

4.1.1 Typing rate of expert users

Learning a new text entry method is always a long-term process. The study presented results of novice users, who were given only necessary amount of training. In order to determine possible upper limit of performance of all Humsher interfaces, three experienced NVVI users were given 4-6 hours of training. The typing rate was recorded after their performance did not improve significantly. Table 2 summarizes CPM, GPC rates and number of corrections for each interface. The speed varied between 16 and 30 CPM. Expert 1 and 3 preferred the Direct, while expert 2 preferred Matrix interface.

4.2 Case studies with disabled people

The goal of the study was to find out whether Humsher can serve as an assistive tool for motor-impaired people. Four people were recruited in cooperation with local non-profit associations. The study was longitudinal, it was organized in seven sessions and each session lasted 30-60 minutes. First, the participants were asked to use the Binary interface because of its simple vocal gestures. Then they were asked to learn more complicated gestures and use the Direct interface, because it was the fastest one. The rough schedules of each session are outlined below:

- **Session 1:** The participants were asked to describe how they use ICT and how they enter text. Then they were trained in producing vocal gestures starting with the easiest ones (see Fig. 2). Binary interface was presented and the participants were asked to enter a phrase.

- **Session 2:** Participants trained more complicated vocal gestures (see Fig.1) until required accuracy was achieved. Then the Direct interface was presented to them and they were asked to enter a few phrases.

- **Session 3 – 7:** Participants were asked to enter phrases using the Direct interface. On the last day the participant were asked to describe experience using the interfaces.

While training the vocal gestures, the thresholds for low/high and short/long tones were personalized for each user. Two users with speech impairments were not able to consciously alter pitch of their tone, therefore a new gestures were designed especially for them.

4.2.1 Participant 1

The participant was 30 year old IT specialist in a small company, quadriplegic since birth. Due to privacy protection, he only participated in the study remotely. We conducted interviews with him via telephone and e-mail.

He uses a mouth stick to operate his PC (keyboard and mouse). Apart from the Sticky Keys tool available in Microsoft Windows he uses no other assistive technology. He uses various system administration tools, word processors, graphic and sound editors and he feels no disadvantage in comparison with other users.

He found the Direct interface precise and pleasant to use. Overall, he said he felt in control when using the tool. "The system allowed me to write whatever I wanted. I was not forced into any options." He used the word "intelligent" to describe the suggested options provided by the tool when typing text. He achieved a mean type rate of 22 CPM. He reported, however, that his current text entry rate achieved by the mouth stick is higher.

4.2.2 Participant 2

Another disabled participant was 19 years old, quadriplegic since an accident about 3 years ago. He is a high-school student who uses computer to access study materials, talk with his friends over text media (especially e-mails), make telephone calls and watch movies. He spends typically 2 to 4 hours using his laptop equipped with NaturalPoint SmartNav4 head motion tracker and Click-N-Type keyboard emulation software. However, he is able to use the head motion tracking system only for 2-4 hours and then he gets too tired. He had a previous experience with another NVVI based interface for entering text.

When working with Binary interface, his mean type rate was 12 CPM. After switching to Direct interface, the type rate increased to 21 CPM. Although he was almost two times faster with the

Direct interface, he reported that the Binary interface was quicker and more responsive ("I like that it is fast. I can see it all in front of me and I know exactly what to do next."). He felt more in control than when using the Direct interface ("I am a bit lost when using the Direct interface as I sometimes do not notice the right option."). The participant considered our method similar in speed to his current assistive technology and he would use it as an alternative solution when his head gets too tired.

4.2.3 Participant 3

The participant was a 58 year old woman with cerebral palsy. All her limbs are affected by the disease. She can sit on a chair, but she needs a wheelchair for movement. She has a lot of unintentional movements in her arms. Her voice is also affected. She speaks slowly and she does not articulate properly. Her health state is slowly but steadily declining.

She used to work as an office staff in a non-profit organization, but she is unemployed for one year now. She used to type on a typewriter and a computer keyboard. However, now her performance decreases and she types very slowly on a keyboard. The only assistive technology that she uses is a trackball to control the mouse pointer. She also tried speech recognition, but it did not work for her at all.

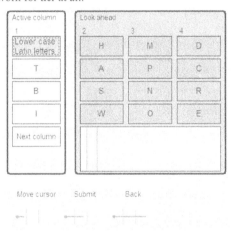

Figure 7. Modified List interface

She spent first and second sessions trying to learn voice gestures for the Binary interface. However, after two sessions she could hardly write a phrase. She was not able to effectively alter pitch of her tone, which led to many corrections. Therefore the vocal gestures were changed to short, medium long and long tone. Then she was asked to use it for another two sessions and she reached 8 CPM.

As the participant was unable to produce more complicated gestures, we modified the List interface (see Fig. 7) for use with the new gesture set. Short tone was used to move cursor in the Active column down, medium tone to submit selected n-gram and long tone for correction. She used this interface for remaining three sessions and reached 15 CPM.

The participant reported that the speed of the modified List interface is similar to her current typing rate and she was interested in purchasing it as a product. She also made comments on speech recognition ("This is much better than speech for me"). She reported that after one hour of humming her vocal chords were not tired at all.

4.2.4 Participant 4

The participant was 51 years old, quadriplegic since an accident about 22 years ago. His legs and right arm are paralyzed. He can use his left arm to operate wheelchair, however, fine motoric of his left hand is reduced. His vocal chords and neck muscles are also slightly affected.

Before the accident he used to work as a machine engineer. Since that he is unemployed. He has never worked with computers, but he regularly uses cell phone for couple of years, mainly for calling and writing short text messages. However, composing message is a tedious process for him.

The participant started with Binary interface and used it for two sessions. He experienced similar problems to participant 3. As he was not able to produce low and high tone properly, his performance was about 1 CPM with a lot of corrections. In the third session he switched to the modified List interface (see Fig. 7) as participant 3 and his performance increased rapidly with minimum mistakes. Using this interface and the vocal gestures based on length he reached type rate of 14 CPM.

He stated that typing text with Humsher is faster and better than typing on his cell phone. Generally he was pleased with the modified List interface. However, his vocal chords got tired after 40 minutes of humming.

5. CONCLUSION

This paper has presented and evaluated four interfaces of Humsher – an adaptive virtual keyboard operated by humming. Three of them (Direct, Matrix and List) used dynamic layout, in which characters were sorted according to its probability. The layout was updated after entering a character. The last interface (Binary) used a static layout, in which characters were displayed alphabetically and did not change their position. A character was selected by modified binary search algorithm that took into account probability of each character.

Most novice users preferred the Binary interface, even though it was not the fastest one. They appreciated mostly the static layout of characters and simple vocal gestures used to control the interface. On the other hand expert users preferred interfaces with dynamic layouts. Interfaces with dynamic layout were perceived worse, however, users appreciated that sometimes several characters could be entered together. The Direct interface was the fastest one with average speed 14.4 CPM achieved by novice and 28 CPM by expert users.

Acceptance of our tool for the target group was verified by the inclusion of four motor-impaired participants. Two of them could not use speech recognition software as their speech was also impaired. Cases of all disabled participants are described separately in a longitudinal and qualitative study. Their speed achieved after seven sessions varied between 14 and 22 CPM.

While some techniques, such as Dasher [19], offer their users type rates up to 100 CPM, they may not be used by people with severe motor impairments without expensive hardware, such as eye trackers. Our method requires no additional hardware to a standard PC and performs better than the NVVI Keyboard [21] and CHANTI [25] methods which have the identical hardware requirements and for which a similar performance is reported: 16 CPM for NVVI Keyboard, 15 CPM for CHANTI, and 22 CPM for Humsher.

6. ACKNOWLEDGMENTS

This research has been supported by the MSMT research program MSM 6840770014 and the Veritas project (IST-247765).

7. REFERENCES

[1] Silfverberg, M. 2007. Historical Overview of Consumer Text Entry Technologies. In Text Entry Systems: Mobility, Accessibility, Universality, I. S. MacKenzie and K.Tanaka-Ishii (eds.). Morgan Kaufmann, 3-26.

[2] West, L. J. 1998. The Standard and Dvorak Keyboards Revisited: Direct Measures of Speed. http://samoa.santafe.edu/media/workingpapers/98-05-041.pdf, Technical report, Santa Fe Institute.

[3] Sears, A., Revis D., Swatski, J., Crittenden, R., Shneiderman, B. 1993. Investigating touchscreen typing: the effect of keyboard size on typing speed. In J. Behaviour and Information Technology, vol. 12, 17-22.

[4] Igarashi, T., Hughes, J F. 2001. Voice as sound: using non-verbal voice input for interactive control. In Proceedings of UIST '01, ACM Press, 155-156.

[5] Darragh, J. J., Witten, I. H., James, M. L. 1990. The Reactive Keyboard: A Predictive Typing Aid. Computer Journal, vol. 23, IEEE Press, 41-49.

[6] Hansen, J., Johansen, A., Hansen, D., Itoh, K., Mashino, S. 2003. Language technology in a predictive, restricted on-screen keyboard with ambiguous layout for severely disabled people. In Proceedings of EACL Workshop on Language Modeling for Text Entry Methods.

[7] Jacob, R. J. K. 1990. What you look at is what you get: eye movement-based interaction techniques. In Proceedings of CHI'90, ACM Press, 11-18.

[8] Grover, D. L., King, M. T., Kushler, C. A. 1998. Reduced keyboard disambiguating computer, Technical report, US Patent Publication.

[9] Kushler, C. 1998. AAC: Using a Reduced Keyboard.

[10] Tanaka-Ishii, K., Inutsuka, Y., Takeichi, M. 2002. Entering text with a four-button device. In Proceedings of the 19th International Conference on Computational Linguistics, Association for Computational Linguistics, 1-7.

[11] Harbusch, K., Kühn, M. 2003. Towards an adaptive communication aid with text input from ambiguous keyboards. In: Proceedings of EACL'03, Association for Computational Linguistics, 207-210.

[12] Simpson, R., Koester, H. 1999. Adaptive one-switch row-column scanning. In IEEE Transactions on Rehabilitation Engineering, vol. 7, no. 4, IEEE Press, 464-473.

[13] Kühn, M., Garbe, J. 2001. Predictive and highly ambiguous typing for a severely speech and motion impaired user. In Proceedings of 1st International Universal Access in Human-Computer Interaction Conference, UAHCI '01.

[14] Miro, J., Bernabeu, P. 2008. Text entry system based on a minimal scan matrix for severely physically handicapped people. In Computers Helping People with Special Needs, LNCS 5105, Springer, Heidelberg, 1216-1219.

[15] Belatar, M., Poirier, F. 2008. Text entry for mobile devices and users with severe motor impairments: handiglyph, a primitive shapes based onscreen keyboard. In Proceedings of ASSETS '08, ACM Press, 209-216.

[16] Felzer, T., MacKenzie, I., Beckerle, P., Rinderknecht, S. 2010. Qanti: A software tool for quick ambiguous non-standard text input. In Computers Helping People with Special Needs, LNCS 6180, Springer, 128-135.

[17] Ward, D. J., Blackwell, A. F., MacKay, D. J. C. 2000. Dasher – a data entry interface using continuous gestures and language models. In Proc. of UIST '00, ACM, 129-137.

[18] Teahan, W. 1995. Probability estimation for PPM. In: Proceedings of the New Zealand Computer Science Research Students' Conference.

[19] Tuisku, O., Majaranta, P., Isokoski, P., Räihä, K. J. 2008. Now Dasher! dash away!: Longitudinal study of fast text entry by eye gaze. In Proceedings of the 2008 symposium on Eye tracking research and applications, ETRA '08, ACM Press, 19-26.

[20] Vertanen, K., MacKay, D. J. 2010. Speech dasher: fast writing using speech and gaze. In Proceedings of CHI '10, ACM Press, 595-598.

[21] Sporka, A. J., Kurniawan, S. H., Slavík, P. 2006. Non-speech operated emulation of keyboard. In: Clarkson, J., Langdon, P., and Robinson, P. (eds.) Designing Accessible Technology, Springer, London, 145-154.

[22] Wang, C., Guan, C., Zhang, H. 2005. P300 brain-computer interface design for communication and control applications. In: Proceedings of the 27th Annual International Conference of the Engineering in Medicine and Biology Society, IEEE-EMBS'05, 5400-5403.

[23] Mahmud, M., Sporka, A. J., Kurniawan, S. H., Slavik, P. 2007. A Comparative Longitudinal Study of Non-verbal Mouse Pointer, In Proceedings of INTERACT 2007, Springer, Heidelberg, 489-502.

[24] Hyman, R. 1953. Stimulus Information as a Determinant of Reaction Time. Journal of Experimental Psychology, vol. 45, 188-196.

[25] Sporka, A. J., Felzer, T., Kurniawan, S.H., Polacek, O., Haiduk, P., MacKenzie, I.S. 2011. CHANTI: Predictive Text Entry Using Non-verbal Vocal Input. In proceedings of CHI'11, ACM Press., 2463-2472.

[26] Maxwell, S.E., Delaney, H.D. 2004. Designing Experiments and Analyzing Data: A Model Comparison, ISBN 0805837183, Lawrence Erlbaum Associates, 217–218.

[27] Sporka, A.J., Kurniawan, S. H., Slavik, P. 2004. Whistling user interface (u3i) In 8th ERCIM International Workshop "User Interfaces For All", LCNS 3196, Springer, 472-478.

[28] Harada, S., Landay, J.A., Malkin, J., Li, X. and Bilmes, J.A. 2006. The Vocal Joystick: Evaluation of voice-based cursor control techniques. Proceedings of ASSETS '06,ACM Press, 197-204.

[29] Wobbrock, J.O. 2007. Measures of text entry performance. In Text Entry Systems: Mobility, Accessibility, Universality, I. S. MacKenzie and K.Tanaka-Ishii (eds.). Morgan Kaufmann, 47-74.

ACES: Aphasia Emulation, Realism, and the Turing Test

Joshua Hailpern
Department of Computer Science
University of Illinois
201 N Goodwin Ave
Urbana, IL 61801
jhailpe2@cs.uiuc.edu

Marina Danilevsky
Department of Computer Science
University of Illinois
201 N Goodwin Ave
Urbana, IL 61801
danilev1@illinois.edu

Karrie Karahalios
Department of Computer Science
University of Illinois
201 N Goodwin Ave
Urbana, IL 61801
kkarahal@cs.uiuc.edu

ABSTRACT

To an outsider it may appear as though an individual with aphasia has poor cognitive function. However, the problem resides in the individual's receptive and expressive language, and not in their ability to think. This misperception, paired with a lack of empathy, can have a direct impact on quality of life and medical care. Hailpern's 2011 paper on ACES demonstrated a novel system that enabled users (e.g., caregivers, therapists, family) to experience first hand the communication-distorting effects of aphasia. While their paper illustrated the impact of ACES on empathy, it did not validate the underlying distortion emulation. This paper provides a validation of ACES' distortions through a Turing Test experiment with participants from the Speech and Hearing Science community. It illustrates that text samples generated with ACES distortions are generally not distinguishable from text samples originating from individuals with aphasia. This paper explores ACES distortions through a 'How Human' is it test, in which participants explicitly rate how human- or computer-like distortions appear to be.

Categories and Subject Descriptors

H.5.0 [**General**]; K.4.2 [**Social Issues**]: Assistive technologies for persons with disabilities

General Terms

Experimentation, Human Factors

Keywords

Aphasia, Assistive Technology, Disabilities, Empathy, Emulation Software, Language, Speech, Turing Test

1. INTRODUCTION

If a traveler visits a foreign country whose language is not her own, there is no social expectation that she can speak the local tongue. Travelers often get the benefit of the doubt, because their conversation partners have been in a similar situation, and can empathize with the challenges of being

in a foreign country. However for more than one million individuals with Aphasia [15], the "foreign language" is their native tongue. Aphasia is an acquired language disorder caused by damage to the left or dominant hemisphere of the brain (often associated with strokes). The disorder impairs an individual's ability to produce and understand language in both written and spoken forms [1]. To an outsider it may appear that an aphasic individual has poor cognitive function. However, the problem resides in the individual's receptive and expressive language, and not in their ability to think. Unfortunately, many friends and family avoid interacting with individuals with aphasia because they do not understand the disorder, lack empathy, and simply find interacting to be difficult. This lack of empathy can "erode the social bonds that give life meaning," and greatly diminish quality of care in a professional setting (e.g. by doctors and nurses) [11].

In 2011, we published ACES (**A**phasia **C**haracteristics **E**mulation **S**oftware), a novel system that enables users to experience the speech-distorting effects of aphasia [9]. ACES uses a probabilistic model (based on literature in Cognitive Psychology and Speech and Hearing Science) that can distort a user's Instant Messages (IMs), transforming the original message into text that appears as though it had originated from an individual with aphasia. Results from an evaluation of 64 participants indicated that ACES strongly increased understanding and empathy for aphasia, and individuals with aphasia.

While our original ACES paper presented the first language disorder emulation system and its impact on empathy, it did not validate the quality or realism of the distortions ACES applied. This paper seeks to demonstrate how discernible ACES distortions are from actual statements generated by individuals with aphasia. If we demonstrate that distortions users experienced were realistic, we will increase the impact and validity of our original study. Further, if ACES appears to be nearly indistinguishable from realistic distortions, it will indicate that ACES may prove a valuable and realistic aid for increasing empathy for family members, friends, clinicians in training and other caregivers.

This paper illustrates the "realism" of ACES distortions in two ways. First, we perform a Turing Test study in which participants must distinguish samples of distorted text generated by a human from samples of text distorted by a computer. Much like the original Turing Test proposed by Alan Turing [22], if participants cannot reliably tell the origin of distortions (whether computer or human generated), the computer could be said to have passed the test. Second, we ask participants to explicitly rate the realism of distortions in text samples on a Likert scale. If participants rate both computer and human generated text samples as being equally realistic, it adds further quantitative support to the realism of ACES distortions. The foremost contribution of this paper is the demonstration that ACES generates realistic aphasic distortions, thus validating the applicability of ACES as aphasic emulation software and supporting the feasibility of other language emulation software research.

2. RELATED WORK

We describe aphasia, the theory of linguistic changes in conversation and how our work builds upon, and extends, the existing literature.

2.1 Aphasia

Aphasia is an acquired language disorder that results from by damage to the left or dominant hemisphere of the brain. It impairs an individual's ability to produce and understand language in both written and spoken forms [1]. Because the severity and pattern of aphasic symptoms vary, classification systems were developed to identify different sub-types of aphasia. For example, diagnostic batteries [8, 19] based on the Boston classification system are designed to categorize an individual's aphasia symptoms as either a type of nonfluent aphasia (Broca's, Transcortical Motor, Global) or fluent aphasia (Wernicke, Transcortical Sensory, Conduction, Anomic). Across all sub-types, aphasia impairs the ability to generate written text (though the degree of impairment varies). It should be noted that the linguistic deficits in writing will generally be consistent with those of the person's spoken language [2].

2.2 Empathy and Aphasia

Empathy is one of the fundamental underpinnings of interpersonal communication. It is an emotional response to the experiences of others, through which an empathetic person can understand and predict the feelings, emotions, and thoughts of others [6, 21].

If individuals relating to those with aphasia lack empathy and understanding, it may greatly reduce quality of life for aphasic individuals [11]. Often, family members deny or underestimate the severity and presence of aphasic errors [4]. Further, in speech therapy, empathy is necessary to motivate the aphasic client, with motivation being one of the three key aspects of effective treatment [20]. To date, research has shown that family members' ability to relate and empathize is based on how well they understand the distortions that their family member makes [7].

3. ACES

Motivated by the need to maintain social bonds for those with aphasia, we built a system called **A**phasia **C**haracteristics **E**mulation **S**oftware (**ACES**), that enabled a user to experience the speech-distorting effects of aphasia first hand [9]. ACES introduced a novel system and model that enabled users (e.g., caregivers, speech therapists and family) to experience, firsthand, the communication-distorting effects of aphasia. The ACES system was designed to distort a user's Instant Messages (IMs) from the original message to one that appeared like a message spoken/written by an individual with aphasia (see Figure 1). Thus, the conversation that

developed between the user and their IM partner has similar difficulties and hurdles to those experienced by an individual with aphasia. Similar to spending a day in a wheelchair so as to heighten awareness of the challenges confronting a paraplegic [5], ACES allows a neurologically typical individual to "walk in the shoes" of an individual with aphasia. The goal of ACES was to increase empathy, awareness and understanding of individuals with aphasia. The design and motivation of ACES was grounded in speech and hearing science and psychology literature, and informed by an initial pilot study. Results from a study of 64 participants indicated that ACES provided a rich experience that increased understanding and empathy for aphasia.

While full details of ACES, and the original experiment can be found in the original paper [9], we briefly highlight the key aspects of ACES and our original study that tests ACES' impact on empathy.

Figure 1: ACES Instant Message Window.
The current (red) user's partner (blue) has their text distorted. This is a log from [9]'s experiment.

3.1 System Design

ACES is a configurable probabilistic model of the linguistic distortions associated with aphasia situated in an IM client. To emulate the distortions generated (and probability of occurance), we leveraged the vast literature in psychology and speech and hearing science (e.g. Schwartz et. al.[18] and Sarno's *Acquired aphasia* [17]). An initial pilot study in 2009 with 10 faculty and practitioners in Psychology and Speech and Hearing Science further informed the system design. Using these as the basis of our models and manifestations of the distortions, we created a system that could emulate a wide variety of distortions across five conceptual categories of distortions. We also allow a user to change the severity and type of aphasia they wished to emulate, thus giving ACES increased flexibility and a broader set of applications.

To a user, ACES appears as an IM client. However, a user's original text is changed to appear like a message written/spoken by an individual with aphasia (see Figure 1). Thus, the conversation that develops between the user and their IM partner has similar challenges to those experienced by an individual with aphasia. In effect, users can "walk in the shoes" of an individual with aphasia. We envisioned ACES to have a multitude of applications; from teaching empathy and awareness to therapists, to helping family and friends understand what their loved ones are experiencing.

ACES was implemented using Java 1.6, allowing the software to execute on nearly any machine. The IM protocol was facilitated by the JBuddy Library [24].

3.2 Empathy User Studies

Upon completion of the ACES system in 2010, a detailed study was conducted. The focus of this in-depth user study was to observe the effects of ACES on awareness and empathy. Sixty-four participants were recruited (both experts on aphasia and individuals from the general population), and tasked to have two IM conversations using ACES in which one participant played the "role" of an individual with aphasia (having their text distorted by ACES so that it appeared generated by an individual with aphasia) while the other participant played the role of a "neurologically typical" individual (non-distorted text). Participants switched role after the first conversation. One half of the participants were assigned to the placebo or **control group** (no distortions applied) and one half were in a **treatment group** (ACES distorted messages sent), in a between subject design.

Participants in the treatment group, who experienced the distortions of aphasia, had a stronger response than those in the control group. Across the metrics used, there was a highly significant effect of ACES on empathy, awareness and how "useful" ACES would be for building empathy. While participants in the treatment group reported "strong" effects from the experiment, those in the control group reported little or no change in their empathy towards aphasia[1][9].

4. RESEARCH QUESTION & MOTIVATION

The initial ACES user study examined the impact of ACES on empathy and awareness of aphasia. However, there was no examination of the distortions themselves, their perceived quality, or their realism. While ACES' distortions were deeply grounded in literature (providing both the probabilistic underpinnings and the manner in which text is distorted), creating a novel and unique form of language emulation has the potential to produce distortions at varying degrees of realism. Therefore this paper seeks to answer the following:

> **Can users differentiate computer-generated distortions from distortions generated by individuals with aphasia?**

> **How realistic are the distortions of aphasia generated by ACES?**

We answer these questions with a two-step experimental design, detailed in the following section. We then describe our target population, outline the methods for analysis, and present results for each of our two experiments. Discussion of our results follow, along with implications for future work.

5. EXPERIMENTAL DESIGN

To answer our research questions, we recruited 24 participants to examine distortions generated by ACES, utilizing an online questionnaire. Each questionnaire presented users with a set of demographic questions, in addition to 48 data generating questions. Each page of the online questionnaire contained only one data generating question. A data generating question consisted of a text sample and a question

about the sample. One half of the text samples were generated by ACES, while the other half were taken from transcripts generated by individuals with aphasia. These two halves will be referred to as the **Computer Group** and the **Human Group**, respectively. In an experimental context, these can be thought of as a treatment group and a control group. If ACES distortions are indistinguishable from human generated distortions, which is the goal of this project, *the desired outcome is to see a lack of statical significance ($p \geq 0.05$)* when comparing the Computer Group to the Human Group.

To control for order effects, we presented the questions in one of two sequences. The question order within each sequence was created randomly. Users were randomly assigned to one of the two presentation sequences. No text sample was presented to a user more than once (to control for learning effects). At the end of the study, participants received a $7 Amazon.com gift certificate.

The next section describes the types of aphasia targeted in this study. We then detail the two sets of questions asked of participants, and discuss the origin of all text samples presented to users.

5.1 Types of Aphasia

Based on the Boston classification system, there are numerous types of aphasia that can be broadly categorized as non-fluent aphasia (Agrammatic, Broca's, Transcortical Motor, Global) or fluent aphasia (Wernicke, Transcortical Sensory, Conduction, Anomic). Individuals within each subtype of aphasia have distinctive characteristics to their speech, and the errors that are made. We therefore wished to control for aphasia type in this experiment. Rather than tackling all known subtypes, we focused on two of the more common **Types of Aphasia**: Agrammatic and Anomic aphasia. Individuals with Agrammatic aphasia generally have difficulty with sentence structure and proper grammar, while having no difficulty with word selection. Common errors include difficulties in verb tense, dropping function words, inconsistency with the length or fluidity of sentences, and incorporating many breaks and pauses. Individuals with Anomic aphasia have difficulty with selecting and producing correct content words, though their grammar is generally correct. For example, words may be replaced by other words that are semantically related ('birthday' with 'anniversary' or 'cake'), that have no semantic relationship (cat with airplane), that have similar phonetic sounds ('population' with 'pollution'), or non-words ('castle' with 'kaksel'). The availability of Anomic and Agrammatic aphasia transcripts, in addition to their general prevalence of individuals with these types of aphasia, influenced our selection.

5.2 Test Questions

The 48 data generating questions were evenly divided into two distinct **Tests**: *The Aphasia Turing Test* and the *"How Human" Test*. Each user first answered the 24 *Turing Test* questions, followed by 24 *"How Human"* questions. Each question was presented on a separate page. This limited participants ability to make judgments based on the other questions' distortions. Further, participants were unable to return to prior questions, thus preventing them from changing their answers. The questions and the presentation of each Test are detailed in the following sub-sections. At the

---

[1]There were no statistical differences in the effect of ACES between experts in aphasia and individuals from the general population.

end of each test, we asked users to describe their approach for answering the Tests' questions.

5.2.1 Aphasia Turing Test

For the *Aphasia Turing Test*, participants were presented with 24 text samples. For each text sample participants were instructed, *"for each sentence, please mark if it is 'Human' or 'Computer' in origin."* The following example is an actual text sample used in this test, with the distortion generated by ACES emulating an anomic individual with aphasia:

> *Well she was a kaur girl and she qobred in a house where she was mopping the under foot. Then there was something about a shoe and when she wore it she would be Cinderella. uh... She was told that a mumpkur would be her stagecoach... um... and little rats would be a horse. And so she went up to the castle. Her new shoes um... uh... fit uh... um...her like a... grove.*

Participants *were* told that some text was generated by an actual individual with aphasia (Human Group text samples), and some text was distorted by ACES (Computer Group text samples). Participants were not told it was a 50/50 split of text samples from the Human Group and Computer Group. Section 5.3 details how text samples were generated/collected.

In this regard, this experiment was designed as a variation of the Turing Test as proposed by Alan Turing in 1950 [22]. The goal of this Test was to determine if our subjects could reliably differentiate machine from human. To "pass" the Turing Test, we would expect to see approximately a 50% accuracy at labeling text as computer or human (with no statistical difference in the accuracy between groups). Since modern computers cannot reliably pass the Turing Test, we did not hypothesize a priori that ACES would completely pass our Turing Test either. Even without passing the Turing Test, results can illuminate the believability of ACES' distortions, and if there is one type of aphasia (see Section 5.1) which ACES emulates more successfully.

5.2.2 "How Human" Test

For the *"How Human" Test*, participants were presented with 24 pairs of text samples (one pair per page). For each pair of text samples, the first was labeled as "Original Text" and the second as "Distorted Text." The "Original Text" was undistorted, while the "Distorted Text" had aphasic distortions applied to it. The following example is an actual text sample used in this test, with the distortion generated by ACES emulating an agrammatic individual with aphasia:

> **Original Text:** *Well the man is trying to wake up because of the alarm clock. And then he goes back to sleep. His wife is angry. Then the man eats breakfast, while his wife is showing him the time on the clock; the wife is saying "hurry up." And the man running out onto the street to get to work. The man was so tired, he goes to sleep at the office.*

> **Distorted Text:** *uh... the er... uh... is tri... wake up because the alarm clock uh... And... he goes back uh... His wife is angry, Then the man eat uh... breakfast, his wife is ah... eh... showing him the time... the wife is saying "um... up." uh... er... And the man running ah... onto the street to get to work. The uh... was so tired he goes to sleep at the office.*

Participants were asked to help researchers "improve" the distortion algorithms by rating how "human" the distortions appear on a Likert scale from 1-5 (where 1 is indistinguishable from a human who has aphasia, and 5 is unquestionably a computer). Like the *Aphasia Turing Test*, one half of the "Distorted Text" samples were generated by an individual with aphasia (Human Group text samples), and the other half of the text samples were distorted by ACES (Computer Group text samples). Section 5.3 details how both the original text and distorted text were generated/collected.

By design, this task forces users to make an implicit judgment call about the origin of each distorted text sample: "was this text distortion generated by a human or by a computer?" To allow participants to focus on the realism of the distortions/errors in the text samples rather than puzzling over their source, participants were told that all text was distorted by ACES. This deception allows us to objectively measure the realism of ACES distortions (Computer Group). It also provides an objective and comparable benchmark of human distortions (Human Group).

5.3 Text Samples

All text samples used in this experiment were extracted from published transcripts of individuals with aphasia [3, 13] or from the unpublished data files used in [12, 14], which were provided to the researchers by Lise Menn, University of Colorado. Some transcripts were from picture describing tasks from the Wechsler Bellevue Intelligence Scale [23]. Other text samples were from transcripts of individuals with aphasia reading children's stories[2]. The remainder of the text samples were from individuals with aphasia narrating children's stories from memory.

For each text sample, an original or intended version of the text was generated. If the transcript was from an individual reading a story, the read text was used as the original version. For transcripts that were not of an individual reading text, researchers attempted to fix the errors and create a non-distorted version of the same text (following similar sentence structure, word choice, and phrasing). For the *"How Human" Test*, these original versions of the text samples were used. The original versions of each text sample were also used as the basis for the ACES distortions. Each non-distorted, or error-free text sample would be sent through ACES, thus applying the ACES distortions to the text. Section 5.3.1 details the procedure for choosing and applying ACES distortions so as to ensure the distorted texts used were not "cherry picked." There were therefore three versions of each text sample, the aphasic version, the 'original' version, and the ACES version. Selection of text samples to be included in the experiment was random, thus not giving any preference to 'more believable' ACES text.

Our text samples came from six individuals. We ensured that there were an equal number of text samples from each

---

[2]Reading does produce errors in speech production [13].

individual within both Tests (e.g. aphasiac individual Alice contributed four text samples to the Turing Test, and four text samples to the "How Human" Test). Further, the text samples taken from each participant were split evenly across the Human Group and Computer Group (e.g. if aphasiac individual Bob contributed eight text samples, four were used directly from his transcript and four were used to construct an undistorted text sample, which was then distorted by ACES). No text sample was repeated across Tests or within a Test, and only one version (the true aphasic version or the computer version) of each text sample was used.

5.3.1 Generating ACES Distortions

For each set of transcripts generated by one individual, researchers constructed an ACES model that attempted to emulate his or her manifestation of aphasia. This was done by taking text [3], running it through ACES, and adjusting the software's distortion parameters until the distorted text appeared 'similar' to the transcripts that were be generated by said individual. Only the sliders on the ACES interface were adjusted (no code was edited).

Once a model was set, every 'original' version of text sample generated by that individual was then run through ACES once. No text sample was repeated. This ensured that our study used whatever distortions ACES applied, without preference to more 'successful' distortions. These distorted sentences were then cleaned, fixing spacing or punctuation issues that may be a byproduct of removing or adding words. No word spellings, phrasing or other changes were made to the ACES text, further ensuring that the distortions shown to participants were precisely the ones generated by ACES.

5.4 Population

We recruited 24 participants (3 male, 21 female) for inclusion in this study. Participants were students or faculty in Speech and Hearing Science Departments, as well as professionals in the Speech and Hearing Science community. We chose Speech and Hearing Science students, faculty and professionals as our target population because their training is specifically targeted towards the identification and treatment of speech disorders. Part of this training includes analyzing transcripts of conversations, diagnosing disorders based on language production (thereby distinguishing one from another), and treating the speech disorders themselves. We felt that this population was uniquely qualified to perform the discrimination tasks in this experiment.

We actively recruited from multiple institutions to cultivate a wide perspective on aphasia. Of our participants, all had taken at least one class that covered aphasia, and 67% of participants had personal experience with aphasia, or had taken a class that only covered aphasia. The population contained four current BS/BA students, 13 current MS/MA students, five participants with an MS/MA degree, and two participants with a PhD. The mean age of our participants was 26.4 (range 19 to 60 years).

5.5 Analytical Methods

To examine the quality of the ACES distortions, we compared the participants' responses to the 24 *Aphasia Turing Test* questions separately from the 24 responses to the "How

	Text Sample Group	Participants' Label	
		Correctly	Incorrectly
Overall	Human	146 (50.69)	142 (49.31)
	Computer	155 (53.82)	133 (46.18)
	Total	301 (52.26)	275 (47.74)
Anomic	Human	87 (60.42)	57 (39.58)
	Computer	78 (54.17)	66 (43.83)
	Total	165 (57.29)	123 (42.71)
Agrammatic	Human	59 (40.93)	85 (59.03)
	Computer	77 (53.47)	67 (46.53)
	Total	136 (47.22)	152 (52.78)

Table 1: Aphasia Turing Test Results
Occurrence count with row percentages (accuracy) in parentheses

Human" Test questions. For each Test, we treated all responses to that Test's questions as one uniform data set. Since a participant contributes more than one data point within a test, the responses are correlated. Therefore, statistical tests must take into account the correlated nature of the data. For statistical comparison, we compared responses to text samples in the Human Group with responses to text samples in the Computer Group.This compares participants accuracy in distinguishing human distortions from distortions generated by ACES.

It is important to note that in this experiment, lack of statistical significance is the desired outcome. Statistically significant tests results generally, by definition, look for differences. If ACES distortions are indistinguishable from human generated distortions, we would see a lack of statistical significance ($p \geq 0.05$) between the Computer Group data set and the Human Group data set.

Responses to the *Aphasia Turing Test* were binary (users marked each text sample as Human or Computer in origin). This would suggest using a Pearson's Chi-Squared, Fisher Exact or Binomial test. However, these tests do not account for the correlated nature of the data (each participant answered multiple questions that were analyzed collectively). Generalized estimating equations (GEE) [10] with a logistic regression [4] were used to account for these correlations. To augment our analysis, we also examined the percentage of data points that were labeled correctly, and the percentage labeled incorrectly. Lastly, we separated out the Anomic and Agrammatic text samples to determine if aphasia type impacted participants' ability to discriminate.

Responses to the *"How Human" Test* were categorical. This would suggest using a Two-Sample Wilcoxon Rank-Sum (Mann-Whitney) test, a more conservative metric than the Student's T-Test as it makes no assumptions about the data distribution. However, Rank-Sum tests do not account for the correlated nature of the data (each participant answered multiple questions that were analyzed collectively). Generalized estimating equations (GEE) [10] with a linear regression [5] were used to account for correlation.

To further inform our analysis of the *"How Human" Test*, we also examined the distribution of data points. As an explicit measure of similarity of our two data sets, we utilized

---

[3]To remove bias, text used to calibrate distortions was unrelated to the aphasic transcripts used in this study.

[4]Logistic regressions were used to test associations with binary outcomes (correct/incorrect labeling by participants).
[5]Linear regressions were used to test associations with scale responses (Likert scale 1-5) as outcomes.

Rita and Ekholm's measure of similarity[6][16]. This similarity metric utilizes a θ, or tolerance in the means between two data sets. We set a conservative θ to be one fifth of a Likert interval (0.2). This represents 5% of the possible answer range, and just over one eighth (13%) of the overall variance (1.50) in subject responses to the "How Human" Test Likert questions.

6. RESULTS

Our data set consisted of 1152 observations (data points), from 24 participants. Of these, 576 observations were from the *Aphasia Turing Test*, and 576 were from the *"How Human" Test*. The following sections detail the quantitative results from our analysis.

6.1 Results for Aphasia Turing Test

As shown in Table 1, overall participants correctly discriminated Human vs. Computer slightly better than chance (52.26%). Similarly, within the two text sample Groups, participants correctly categorized slightly over 50% of the text samples. GEE tests indicated no statistical difference between subjects' ability to discriminate text samples from the Human group with text samples from the Computer Group ($z= -0.75$, $p=0.46$).

Further analysis of Anomic text samples (Table 1) shows similar results to that of the overall dataset. A comparison of the accuracy of rating the Human Group versus the Computer Group indicated no statistical difference between the two groups ($z=1.06$, $p=0.29$). Analysis of the Agrammatic text samples (Table 1) produced different results. Specifically, participant performance dropped considerably in their ability to correctly label text samples from the Human Group: 60% with Anomic text samples, 40% with the Agrammatic text samples ($z= -2.08$, $p=0.04$).

We performed a post hoc analysis (GEE test), comparing participants' performance between Anomic distortions and Agrammatic distortions within each text sample group (e.g., Anomic Human Group vs. Agrammatic Human Group) to determine if the participants could differentiate Anomic or Agrammatic better. Results showed no statistical difference between Anomic and Agramatic text samples from the Computer Group ($z=0.12$, $p=0.91$). However a highly significant difference was seen between Anomic text samples from the Human Group and Agrammatic text samples from the Human Group ($z=3.28$, $p=0.001$). This may indicate that the ability of participants to differentiate Agrammatic text samples that were from the Human Group (41%) was significantly poorer than when examining Anomic text samples from the Human Group (60%).

6.2 Results for the "How Human" Test

Table 2 shows summary statistics and sparklines for the distribution of participant responses to the "How Human" test, ranging from 1 (Definitely Human) to 5 (Definitely Computer). Overall, participants rated ACES generated distortions as 3.05, showing a slight favor towards being

---

[6]Rita and Ekholm measure uses a similarity limit, θ such that the difference in the averages of the two data sets is smaller than θ in absolute value. This can be determined by examining the 95% confidence interval for the difference between the two data sets. If the θ is greater than the right 95% confidence interval *and* $-\theta$ is less than the left 95% confidence interval, 'there is a difference' with $p<0.05$.

computer in origin. Likewise, participants rated text samples from the Human Group as 2.94 overall, showing a slight favor towards being human in origin. However these slight shifts in preference showed no statistical significance ($z=-1.17$, $p=0.24$). Using the Rita and Ekholm's similarity measure [16], the two data sets were found to be statistically similar ($p<0.05$).

When we stratify our data by Aphasia Type, our results diverge. For text samples that had Anomic distortions, we observed a statistically significant difference ($z=-4.10$, $p<0.001$). Participants rated text samples from the Human Group as being more human (2.73) than text samples from the Computer Group (3.26). While these differences are about 1/4 of a Likert point away from a neutral score of 3.0, this result indicates that Anomic distortions were slightly less believable. This is confirmed with Rita and Ekholms' similarity measure ($p \geq 0.05$).

Results of the Agrammatic text samples, however, ran contrary to ground truth. While there was a statistically significant difference between the Human Group and Computer Group ($z=2.32$, $p=0.02$), the mean responses were opposite to the origin of the text. Participants rated text samples from the Human Group as being more computer (3.15) than text samples from the Computer Group which were rated more human (2.84). These responses were biased in the wrong direction. It is also true that these results were statistically not-similar using Rita and Ekholms' similarity measure ($p \geq 0.05$).

7. DISCUSSION

In general, our results indicate that ACES provides a realistic set of distortions of aphasia. Our participants overall had difficulty differentiating between the origins of our text samples, and generally rated distortions as being right between definitely computer in origin, and definitely human in origin. Unlike most experimental setups, lack of significance is a positive outcome, validating the realism of ACES distortions. The remainder of this section discusses the specific results from each Test.

7.1 Aphasia Turing Test

Participants were unable to discriminate between distortions generated by humans with aphasia and distortions generated by ACES. In this regard, ACES distortions passed our variation of the Turing Test. With overall accuracies for both the Human and Computer Group hovering around 50% (nearly equivalent to random chance), and no statistical significance found between the two groups, we can conclude that ACES distortions are indistinguishable from those generated by humans with aphasia.

While the accuracy for identifying Anomic text samples from the Human Group rose slightly, the ability to correctly label Anomic text samples from the Computer group remained constant, and we saw no statistically significant difference between the Control and Human Group.

However, the results from Agrammatic text samples demonstrate an inability of participants to correctly identify text samples that originate from humans (41% accuracy). This probability is worse than chance, and is a statistically significant drop-off as compared to the accuracy for Anomic text samples. Further, the ability to correctly identify Agrammatic text samples from the Computer Group remained constant when compared to Anomic text samples(not sta-

	Text Sample Group	Mean (St. Dev.)	95% Conf. Int.	Histogram
Overall	Human	2.94 (1.22)	[2.80, 3.08]	
	Computer	3.05 (1.22)	[2.91, 3.19]	
	Total	3.00 (1.22)	[2.90, 3.10]	
Anomic	Human	2.73 (1.16)	[2.54, 2.92]	
	Computer	3.26 (1.21)	[3.06, 3.46]	
	Total	3.00 (1.21)	[2.86, 3.14]	
Agrammatic	Human	3.15 (1.25)	[2.95, 3.36]	
	Computer	2.84 (1.20)	[2.64, 3.04]	
	Total	3.00 (1.24)	[2.85, 3.14]	

Table 2: Summary Statistics and Histogram Sparkline for "How Human" Test
Response Range from 1(Distortions Definitely Human in Origin) to 5 (Distortions Definitely Computer in Origin).
Histogram shows frequency of each Likert scale rating with 1 on the left, and 5 on the right.

tistically significant). Therefore we attribute the only statistically significant difference in the Aphasia Turing Test to participants' inability to correctly identify text samples from the Human Group, rather than an increase in their ability to identify text from the Computer Group. Taking this into consideration, we continue to see that participants had approximately a 50/50 chance of correctly labeling text samples from the Computer Group, still indicating that participants were unable to distinguish text samples from the Human and Computer Groups.

We can therefore conclude that, across the board, participants are generally unable to distinguish human distortions from ACES distortions, thus passing our variation on the Turing Test. This adds support to the claim that ACES creates realistic distortions of aphasia.

7.2 "How Human" Test

The overall results from the "How Human" Test paralleled those of the Aphasia Turing Test. Participants' ratings between Human and Computer Group showed no statistical difference. However, differences emerge when data is stratified by Aphasia Type. In general, Anomic distortions in the Computer Group tend to be labeled as more computer-like, while actual distortions in the Human group are correctly marked as being more human. Analysis confirms that this is a statically significant difference.

However, analysis of the text samples with Agrammatic distortions showed that participants generally believed that the ACES distortions were more human (2.84 on Likert scale 1-5), and the real text samples were more likely to come from a computer (3.15 on Likert scale 1-5). This difference was statistically significant. We therefore speculate on the possible causes of this surprising finding. First, our participants may have had difficulty in identifying Agrammatic aphasia. Second, transcripts (ours, or in general) may not have fully captured the nuances of Agrammatic aphasia. Third, the models and distortions ACES used were based on the same literature that is used to teach speech and hearing science students. It is possible that the literature does not fully describe the nature of Agrammatic aphasia. Therefore ACES may more closely match our participants' expectations of Agrammatic aphasia as compared to actual transcripts.

It is worth noting that mean scores (across Aphasia Type and Text Sample Group) are relatively close to the center of the 5 point Likert scale (equally human and computer).

Examination of the distributions (last column of Table 2), reveals a single or double hump bell curve around a value of 3 on the scale. Thus indicating that participants generally were unable to categorize a text samples' errors as 'definitely' human or computer in origin.

Upon further examination, we determined that no one user performed notably better or worse when answering the "How Human" Test, suggesting that the results were consistent across participants. We also examined participants' qualitative responses, at the end of the "How Human" Test, commenting on how they made their decisions. Surprisingly, participant responses were not consistent. One participant mentioned placement of pauses in sentences, whereas another participant relied upon how 'obvious' a semantic replacement was. However, no two participants mentioned the exact same aspect of speech as being a key informative factor. Moreover, many participants' responses contained a phrase similar to that of participant 23, *"I was really surprised by how realistic the distortions were to me."*

7.3 Future Work & Limitations

This work represents an important step forward in validating ACES, and it's impact. As there are many distinctive subtypes of aphasia, the Aphasia Turing Test should be repeated with each of them, to explore the ability of ACES to emulate each specific type of aphasia. This vein of research would also help guide future development of ACES distortions, and improve the quality of the requisite distortions.

In addition, results from the "How Human" Test highlight that participants find Anomic distortions generated by ACES to be slightly more computer than human. However the specific reasons are unclear given the variety of user responses to the general question "How did you make your decisions?" We therefore propose a future investigation into ACES distortions, focusing only on Anomic errors. This study would ask participants to justify their decision on each question, rather than prompt for one reflective statement at the end of the study. This may provide specific insight into why ACES distortions fail and/or succeed.

Lastly, given the surprising Agrammatic text sample results in the "How Human" Test, future investigations need to be conducted as to why ACES distortions appear more human, and real transcripts appear more computer-like. In addition, this test should be repeated to ensure that this result was not in error.

8. CONCLUSION

Empathy and understanding from family members, friends, professionals and caregivers directly impacts the quality of life and quality of care of individuals with aphasia. To this end, Hailpern et. al. developed ACES, a system which allows users (e.g., caregivers, speech therapists and family) to "walk in the shoes" of an individual with aphasia by experiencing linguistic distortions firsthand. ACES' distortion model was directly based on the literature in Cognitive Psychology and Speech and Hearing Science. While results from an initial experiment illustrate that ACES increases empathy and understanding of aphasia, the original paper did not explicitly validate the distortion model. Our work has made several contributions to address this limitation.

First, this paper shows that participants from the Speech and Hearing Science community, whose training is specifically targeted towards the identification and treatment of speech disorders, cannot consistently differentiate computer and human generated distortions. Second, from our investigation of the realism of ACES distortions, we discover that overall, both human and computer generated distortions appear equally "realistic." However, when stratified by type of aphasia, we can see that ACES' emulation of Anomic aphasia is slightly less realistic than ACES' emulation of Agrammatic aphasia. Third, by validating the distortions used in Hailpern's original experiment, this paper strengthens the original paper's findings, showing that the distortions experienced were believable approximations of aphasia. Lastly, by coupling the results of this paper and those of the original study, we add support to the feasibility of other language emulation research targeting other language deficits.

9. ACKNOWLEDGMENTS

We would like to thank our reviewers, participants, family and friends. We would like to acknowledge the help and support of Yonatan Bisk and Wai-Tat Fu. We would like to thank Julie Hengst for her time and discussions at the beginning of the original ACES project. We would like to thank Gary Dell for his many hours of assistance on all of the ACES research and publications. Lastly, a special thanks to Lise Menn who provided many text samples which were critical to this work being completed.

10. REFERENCES

[1] D. Benson. *Aphasia, Alexia and Agraphia: Clinical Neurology and Neurosurgery Monographs*. Churchill Livingstone, New York, 1979.

[2] D. Benson. *The neurology of thinking*. Oxford University Press, USA, 1994.

[3] F. Boller and J. Grafman. *Handbook of Neuropsychology, 2nd Edition : Language and Aphasia*. Elsevier Science Health Science div, 2001.

[4] P. Czvik. Assessment of family attitudes toward aphasic patients with severe auditory processing disorders. *Clinical Aphasiology Conference*, 1977.

[5] S. Doerksen. Recreation for persons with disabilities (rpm 277). *Pennsylvania State University Department of Recreation, Park and Tourism Management*, Fall, 2009.

[6] R. Dymond. A scale for the measurement of empathic ability. *Journal of Consulting Psychology*, 13(2):127–133, 1949.

[7] E. A. Furbacher and R. T. Wertz. Simulation of aphasia by wives of aphasic patients. *Clinical Aphasiology*, page 227, 1983.

[8] H. Goodglass, Goodglass, and Kaplan. *Boston Diagnostic Aphasia Examination: Stimulus Cards–Short Form*. Lippincott Williams & Wilkins, 2001.

[9] J. Hailpern, M. Danilevsky, A. Harris, K. Karahalios, G. Dell, and J. Hengst. Aces: Promoting empathy towards aphasia through language distortion emulation software. In *Proceedings of the ACM's SIG CHI Conference 2011 Conference.*, CHI 2011, Vancouver, BC Canada, 2011. ACM.

[10] J. Hardin and J. Hilbe. *Generalized estimating equations*. Chapman and Hall/CRC, New York, 2003.

[11] J. Liechty and J. Heinzekehr. Caring for those without words: A perspective on aphasia. *The Journal of Neuroscience Nursing*, 39(5):316, 2007.

[12] L. Menn, A. Kamio, M. Hayashi, I. Fujita, S. Sasanuma, and L. Boles. The role of empathy in sentence production: A functional analysis of aphasic and normal elicited narratives in Japanese and English. *Function and Structure*, pages 317–356, 1998.

[13] L. Menn and L. Obler. *Agrammatic aphasia: A cross-language narrative sourcebook*. John Benjamins, 1990.

[14] L. Menn, K. Reilly, M. Hayashi, A. Kamio, I. Fujita, and S. Sasanuma. The interaction of preserved pragmatics and impaired syntax in Japanese and English aphasic speech. *Brain and language*, 61(2):183–225, 1998.

[15] National Institute on Deafness and Other Communication Disorders. Aphasia. http://www.nidcd.nih.gov/health/voice/aphasia.htm, 2010.

[16] H. Rita and P. Ekholm. Showing similarity of results given by two methods: A commentary. *Environmental Pollution*, 145(2):383–386, 2007.

[17] M. T. Sarno. *Acquired aphasia (Third Edition)*. Academic Press, San Diego, CA, 1998.

[18] M. Schwartz, G. Dell, N. Martin, S. Gahl, and P. Sobel. A case-series test of the interactive two-step model of lexical access: Evidence from picture naming. *Journal of Memory and Language*, 54(2):228–264, 2006.

[19] C. Shewan and A. Kertesz. Reliability and validity characteristics of the western aphasia battery (wab). *Journal of Speech and Hearing Disorders*, 45(3):308, 1980.

[20] M. Shill. Motivational factors in aphasia therapy: Research suggestions. *Journal of Communication Disorders*, 12(6):503–517, 1979.

[21] E. Stotland. Exploratory investigations of empathy. *Advances in experimental social psychology*, 4:271–314, 1969.

[22] A. Turing. Computing machinery and intelligence. *Mind*, 59(236):433–460, 1950.

[23] D. Wechsler. Manual for the Wechsler Adult Intelligence Scale. 1955.

[24] Zion Software. Jbuddy messenger.

We Need to Communicate! Helping Hearing Parents of Deaf Children Learn American Sign Language

Kimberly A. Weaver and Thad Starner
School of Interactive Computing
Georgia Institute of Technology
Atlanta, GA, USA 30332-0760
kimberly.weaver@gatech.edu, thad@cc.gatech.edu

ABSTRACT

Language immersion from birth is crucial to a child's language development. However, language immersion can be particularly challenging for hearing parents of deaf children to provide as they may have to overcome many difficulties while learning American Sign Language (ASL). We are in the process of creating a mobile application to help hearing parents learn ASL. To this end, we have interviewed members of our target population to gain understanding of their motivations and needs when learning sign language. We found that the most common motivation for parents learning ASL is better communication with their children. Parents are most interested in acquiring more fluent sign language skills through learning to read stories to their children.

Categories and Subject Descriptors

K.3.1 [**Computers and Education**]: Computer Uses in Education—*Computer-assisted instruction*

General Terms

Human factors

Keywords

American Sign Language, mobile devices, computer assisted language learning

1. INTRODUCTION

In the United States, 90 to 95 percent of deaf children are born to hearing parents [7]. Typically, these parents have had no exposure to American Sign Language (ASL), the most accessible language to deaf Americans, before the birth of their deaf child. Parental involvement plays a large role in a deaf child's language development. Maternal communication in particular, is a significant indicator of language development, early reading skills, and social-emotional development [2]. The better the language skills of the parents, the higher chance deaf children will have of succeeding in school and beyond. The language skills of deaf children with hearing parents lag far behind those of hearing children of hearing parents and deaf children of deaf parents [12, 8]. The slower development of deaf children of hearing parents has been attributed both to incomplete language models and less parent-child interaction [9, 3].

In order to improve parental language ability in ASL, we have been developing SMARTSign. The goal of SMART-Sign is to provide parents with ASL practice via a mobile phone. Prior research has been focused on validating the mobile phone as the content delivery system for learning ASL [4, 11]. Henderson-Summet demonstrated that novice sign language learners can learn to recognize more vocabulary when using a mobile phone as the content delivery system as opposed to a computer. However, participants had difficulty across both platforms in producing the signs they learned [4]. Weaver et al. demonstrated that a modern mobile phone display possesses a sufficiently large screen area to enable novices to reproduce signs from example videos with high accuracy [11].

To ensure that SMARTSign is providing appropriate types of assistance to hearing parents attempting to learn ASL for their young deaf children, we conducted interviews with members of our target population. These interviews were focused on understanding parents' motivation for learning ASL, existing methods and support for learning, reactions to a prototype system, and current mobile technology usage.

2. RELATED WORK

Two similar interview studies have been performed with parents of deaf children on a number of relevant topics [5, 6]. Little info has been reported on parents' learning habits to understand difficulties when learning sign language.

Jackson et al. interviewed nine parents of eight children [5]. Their children's ages ranged from one to to nineteen. The goal of the interview was to make recommendations to service providers on how best to serve families with deaf children in early interventions. Parents' reliance on oral methods and their child's hearing ability had the most impact on parental willingness to learn ASL as a communication method. One key finding from the interviews was that parents said the time demand from caring for their deaf child was "equivalent to caring for two to three children." We had already assumed that demand on parent time was one reason why it was difficult for parents to learn ASL. Managing the doctor and therapist meetings for their deaf child can also put a significant limit on parental free time.

Meadow-Orlans et al.'s data came from a mixed methods approach including surveys, individual interviews and focus group interviews [6]. The purpose of their study was to gain basic understanding of the experiences of parents of young deaf children. They focused on reactions to their child's identification, communication method decisions, and reactions to care providers. Parents sometimes had no choice over what communication methods they used. Instead they were limited by the opportunities available to them based on their place of residence. Two reasons for parents deciding to sign included giving their children any chance they could to communicate and leaving as much choice in the hands of their children for when they were older. Mothers rated their skills in sign language better than the fathers 95 percent of the time. An interesting area for investigation could be exploring opportunities for supporting fathers learning ASL using SMARTSign.

Vaccari and Marshark wrote a summary paper on the impact of parental communication ability on a deaf child's development [10]. They found that the deaf children who are most competent in social and linguistic development are those whose parents engaged them actively in linguistic interaction from a young age. Linguistic interaction is difficult for hearing parents with deaf children who have so little formal sign training that they cannot use it for daily needs, feel uncomfortable signing, and only sign when directly addressing their child. The goal of my interview study is to determine how to address these three problems.

3. METHOD

The study took the form of a semi-structured interview with hearing parents of deaf children. The interview topics followed four categories: family, ASL learning, prototype reactions, and phone ownership. The goal of the family topic was to understand basic background information about the parents and their deaf children to determine the level of support parent and child had for learning ASL. Conversation about ASL learning was directed towards uncovering current difficulties parents experience while learning ASL in order to determine if SMARTSign can be designed to alleviate those difficulties. Parents were shown the prototype SMARTSign system to gauge reactions and determine utility and desirabilty of the existing functions. Because the ultimate goal of this research project is to deploy a working system long-term to parents, phone ownership was important for understanding what devices were favored by parents if data plans were used.

3.1 Parental Recruitment

Parents were recruited through a number of methods. E-mails were sent both to the SKI-HI (Sensory [Kids] Impaired Home Intervention) coordinator at Georgia PINES, the state-wide early intervention program for Georgia and to the social worker at the Atlanta Area School for the Deaf. Parents were also recruited from the 10th Annual Early Hearing Detection and Intervention Conference (EHDI 2011) in Atlanta, Georgia. EHDI is a national conference with tracks for both practitioners and parents. Only one parent was already acquainted with the SMARTSign project before participating in the interview. She is a regular user of an early web-based iteration of the project.

3.2 Participant Demographics

Eleven parents were recruited for the interview study, nine mothers and two fathers, representing ten different families. One of the participants is currently a single parent, and one of the other participants was a single parent when her child was born but is now married. The other eight families represented two-parent households. Due to recruitment at a national conference, participants represented eight different states from three geographic regions of the United States, the Southeast, Northeast, and Midwest. A summary of participant demographics is shown in Table 1.

The parents interviewed had between one and seven children ($\mu = 2.5$, $\sigma = 1.84$). All of the participants were the parents of at least one deaf or hard of hearing child. One mother had two children who were hard of hearing. Three of the parents only had one child.

The ten families included eleven deaf or hard of hearing children. Their ages varied between 10 months and 16 years ($\mu = 5.26$ years, $\sigma = 4.04$ years). The age of their child's hearing loss identification also varied between birth and 3 years ($\mu = 11.18$ months, $\sigma = 12.65$ months). Four of the children were identified at birth. Many of the parents reported that their children had initially failed their neonatal hearing tests but passed on follow up tests, leading to delayed diagnosis. Despite the late identification of deafness for some of the children, only one child's deafness was not congenital or acquired shortly after birth. This child became deaf after suffering from meningitis at 13 months. Three of the eleven children had other serious medical conditions. This ratio is consistent with the findings of Meadow-Orlans et al. [6]. The two deaf siblings have cystic leukoencephalopathy which is a progressive degeneration of white matter in the brain. Another child is autistic. One child is adopted, and the birth mother abused drugs: high levels of bilirubin (extreme jaundice) caused the deafness which was not diagnosed until the child was 3 years old.

All of the children possessed some form of sensory device: hearing aid or cochlear implant. Five of the children had at least one ear with a cochlear implant although two parents reported that their children did not like to wear their implants. Five of the children wore hearing aids. One of the children wore a cochlear implant and a hearing aid.

4. MOTIVATION FOR LEARNING ASL

Discussions with educators and social workers early in the SMARTSign development process led to the impression that parents might not be interested in learning ASL. In our interviews, we learned parents had a number of reasons for deciding to learn ASL. The primary reason was communication with their child, which is consistent with previous parent interview studies. Some parents expressed an interest in providing their children with a bilingual education and access to the deaf community. Parents also related some negatives that made their decision more difficult.

4.1 Communication

Eight of the ten families said that a desire for communication with their child was a reason for their decision to learn ASL. One mother said that when her parent mentor came to her home and told her all of the potential options, her decision was based on how her son could learn language the fastest. Other parents felt like they had no choice. For others it was less of a conscious decision and more the only

Table 1: Summary of participating family demographics

Family	Interviewed	Region	Children (Hearing:Deaf)	Child Age	Identified	Sensory Device	Medical Issues	Learning Duration
1	mother	Southeast	(0:1)	8 yrs	2 yrs	cochlear implant		6 yrs
2	mother	Northeast	(2:1)	3.5 yrs	3 mos	hearing aid		2.5 yrs
3	mother	Southeast	(1:1)	16 yrs	13 mos	cochlear implant (does not use)	meningitis	13 yrs
4	mother	Southeast	(2:2)	3.5 yrs & 2 yrs	18 mos & birth	hearing aids	cystic leukoen-cephalopathy	1.5 yrs
5	mother	Northeast	(6:1)	6 yrs	2 yrs	cochlear implant (does not like)		4 yrs
6	mother	Northeast	(1:1)	4 yrs	birth	cochlear implant		3 yrs
7	mother	Southeast	(1:1)	5 yrs	birth	cochlear implant & hearing aid	autistic	5 yrs
8	mother	Midwest	(0:1)	10 mos	5 mos	hearing aid		4 yrs
9	father	Midwest	(1:1)	5 yrs	birth	hearing aid		3 mos
10	mother & father	Southeast	(0:1)	4 yrs	3 yrs	cochlear implant	maternal drug usage, adopted	2 yrs

option they had. Communication was not happening by any other method, and they "had to do something."

One mother realized that she had to work harder to learn ASL after an experience at an amusement park. Her son was four and playing in the pool and therefore was not wearing his cochlear implant. The lifeguard was whistling at him to tell him not to climb over the edge. Without his implant, the son couldn't hear the whistle. The mother had no idea how to attract her son's attention, and she felt embarrassed when all the other families turned to stare at her. When she tried to take her son away, he could not understand her.

The Baby Sign movement is having a positive effect on parents' willingness to learn sign language. Two mothers stated that they had already planned on using sign language with their child before their child's diagnosis. One mother had already used Baby Sign successfully with her two older children. She said it did not feel as "scary" as she feels it might be for others because of her prior exposure. Another mother said that she had always wanted to teach her children sign language, and her husband pointed that desire out when they learned their child was deaf. Her reaction was to say "that's not the point" – there is a difference between learning a handful of vocabulary by choice as a temporary measure while a child is young and learning a new language as a primary means of communication.

Some parents treat sign language as a temporary measure until their child gets an implant, hearing aids allow their child to learn language, or their child's hearing gets better. In some cases a transition to oral communication might be possible. One mother related how, as her son masters a spoken word, he will drop the use of the relevant sign. This viewpoint can also backfire. One mother said they had started learning ASL, and they stopped when he was implanted. At age three, their son had behavioral problems due to lack of communication. They then decided to start signing again and have been doing so for 13 years.

In two other cases, this lack of communication became so apparent that their child became very frustrated. One family said that they and their son were frustrated because they didn't know what he wanted, and they didn't know how to respond to him. Another mother said that knowing single words wasn't enough to ease the communication barrier.

If parents wait too long to learn ASL, then they find they have work harder to be able to match their child's higher language abilities. One mother reported experiencing this situation. The child became the language model for the parent. This situation becomes frustrating not just for the child but for the parent as well.

4.2 Linguistic and Cultural Benefits

Parents also made the decision to learn ASL for more than just communication. Three parents expressed interest in ASL as a way to provide their children with a bilingual education. One mother said "we always considered it an option because if nothing else, we figured he'd be bilingual." This sentiment is evidence that old ideas of learning one language impairing the ability to learn a second language are becoming less prevalent. Bilingualism is now thought of as an advantage rather than a disadvantage. Another parent said a bilingual education would help her child "learn as much as possible." One father took his son to Gallaudet (the university for the Deaf) in Washington DC shortly after his child was identified as deaf. Despite pressure from those in his community who wanted him to focus on one communication method, either oral or signing, the father said that they wanted to "empower him [their son] with choices." The father said that their son would then have the opportunity to choose his desired communication method later.

Two families mentioned the role of the Deaf Community in their decision process. One parent said that he wanted to learn ASL because it was the language of choice for the Deaf Community. Another parent said the experiences of a Deaf friend who learned sign first and then started learning spoken English convinced them to learn sign language. In the first example the father is learning ASL to help his child gain access to the Deaf Community. In the second example, the Deaf adult served as proof that sign language did not hurt a child's chances to eventually learn to speak.

ASL has one other benefit for parents as expressed by one of the fathers. In this father's state, the dominant language promoted by early education providers is Signed Exact English (SEE). SEE is another visual language but is based on English grammar. SEE goes farther than just sign language in English word order and also includes signs for word endings such as "-ed" and "-ing." The father said that SEE was unnatural, too difficult to learn, and his son had given up using it. The feeling of dislike for SEE's difficulty and appreciation for ASL was shared by another mother.

Two of the parents made a point to emphasize how their children were normal, though deaf. These parents focused not just on communication with their child but inclusion in family life. One mother, after listening to stories by a deaf individuals who spent childhoods sitting at the dinner table not being engaged by their family and not knowing the names of their aunts and uncles, resolved that her child's experience would not be the same. Another father went to visit Gallaudet to make sure he explored all of the opportunities his son could have and to ensure that all possible avenues were open for his child to choose. Both of these parents are working to make sure to find ways to make their children's childhood "the best possible experience," as one mother expressed.

4.3 Disincentives

There are a number of disincentives which make the decision to learn ASL difficult. One mother related her annoyance of going out and having people stare at them. Children would ask what was wrong with her son. Using a visual language automatically identifies one as being different which can be uncomfortable for parents.

Lack of prior experience with deafness can make it difficult to embrace a new language and culture. Only one parent had prior experience with Deaf individuals before their own child's identification. One mother was a special education teacher even before her child was identified. She said that all she was taught about deafness in school was "deaf is bad."

ASL is not an easy language to learn. Even parents who have been learning ASL for many years are hesitant to say they know or use ASL. A mother claimed that the sign they used in the house was more of a pidgin of ASL. One mother, who works in her son's school, says that she is uncomfortable when she is asked to read "aloud" at school because she is constantly worrying about whether she is signing correctly. She also said that when she first started signing she was afraid to sign in the grocery store for fear that people might see her doing it incorrectly. One father stopped signing because his child said his signing was bad and was embarrassing. Now the father does not have the confidence to use ASL with his Deaf friends.

Treating sign language as if it is a temporary language before oral English is acquired can be another disincentive to learning ASL fully. As technology for hearing aids and cochlear implants advances, there are some children who are able to gain enough ability to interact in society without the need for sign language. Religion can also play a role in the belief that ASL knowledge is only a temporary necessity. None of the parents expressed this belief personally but one father related an experience he had with his father. The grandfather quoted how Jesus healed the deaf, the blind, and the mute, implying that faith could heal his grandson as well. The father's reply was "My son is not broken. He is whole. He just happens to be whole and not hearing." This attitude is more likely to help his child develop the skills necessary to succeed in a hearing society.

Another barrier to learning sign language is lack of opportunities to practice. Two mothers talked about their lack of opportunity. One mother has experienced frustration because her son is autistic. She feels that the response from her son is not enough for her so she will seek out other forms of communication. Later, she did state that he does surprise her sometimes when he uses a sign that she was unaware he knew. The mother whose child is still an infant disscussed her difficulties because she cannot use her sign language every day. Her child does not yet have the capacity to learn more complex language, so she has to work and focus on learning so she is ready to teach when her child is ready.

5. LEARNING TOOLS

Participants were asked about the tools they used to learn and practice their sign language skills. While most parents agreed that classes were the most beneficial, they reported using a wide range of tools including books, DVDs, and websites. Some parents even described tools they used while they were mobile. Many states provide services for parents where an educator will come into the home to help parents and family members. Table 2 shows a summary of participant use of, and reaction to, a number of different tools for learning ASL. We will start by investigating characteristics of the tools which had the most positive reactions (Early Intervention Services) and the most negative reactions (books).

5.1 Interventions

Early Intervention Services received the most positive comments of any of the other learning tools. Of the ten families, six had access to early intervention services. These services are typically provided for the family while the child is between the ages of zero and three and can provide many different forms of assistance. One parent was matched with a deaf mentor. The mentor played a significant role in helping the mother with her confidence in learning sign language and with helping her feel comfortable interacting with the Deaf community. Other home providers help parents by teaching them ASL in their homes. One home provider taught the extended family as well as the parents in their home once a week. Home providers can also help parents learn event-specific vocabulary. One mother whose home provider visits twice a month talked about looking ahead at the calendar and asking her to help with vocabulary related to visiting the dentist office so that her son would not be nervous. Another service can be helping parents keep pace with vocabulary related to the topics their child is learning in school. A third way home providers can assist parents is by helping them with the transition to communicating in a more visual language. One parent talked about how his early childhood educator did a good job of teaching about communication and turn-taking to help them understand how to convey the significance of the signs to their child. Inter-

Table 2: Summary of Learning Tools

Learning Tool	Positive	Neutral	Negative	Total
Early Intervention Services	4	1	1	6
DVDs	4	2	2	8
Websites	2	6	1	9
Classes	3	1	3	7
Mobile Phone	0	2	0	2
Books	1	2	4	7

ventions are largely positive experiences for parents because they are largely customized to the family, providing relevant and timely information.

Not all reactions to the home providers were positive. One parent commented about the wide range of potential personalities and styles. She commented that one home provider will argue with parents about the proper way to perform signs. Given that parents are already experiencing low confidence with their sign language skills, this confrontational style could discourage them further. Parents may also feel overwhelmed by the amount of information provided by their home providers at once. Despite these problems, the parent admitted that she knew the home providers meant well and that it was better than not having any support like those who lived in more rural regions of her state. The disadvantage of Early Intervention Services then lies in the variability of the home providers.

5.2 Books

Parents reacted to books the most negatively. Seven of the ten families reported using books to help them learn sign language. Of those seven families, four of the parents were not happy with the books they had. Parents found them difficult to understand. Because motion plays a large role in the meaning of a sign, it can be difficult to convey a complete sign through static images. One mother said it was difficult to look at a single picture with lots of arrows pointing in "seemingly random" directions and determining what to do. One father said that he does not know the sign for FOREVER because of the two dimensional representation. He knows how the sign ends but cannot figure out how to start the sign.

Parents reported owning big ASL dictionaries, pocket dictionaries for quick reference while mobile, text books, and other reference books. All of these books are focused on vocabulary acquisition. One parent who reported not owning any books lamented the lack of real books in ASL to enable her to tell stories to her child.

5.3 DVDs

DVDs, while still focusing primarily on vocabulary, have an advantage over books in their ability to present signs in a more understandable format. DVDs were employed by eight of the ten families. The Signing Time^{TM} series was the most popular with five of the families reporting its use. Signing Time^{TM} is targeted at helping children learn signs, but many of the parents felt they learned a lot from them as well. One mother said that the fact that the videos had sound with them helped because she could put the DVD on and then, when the DVD said a word she was interested in learning, she could pay attention. With DVDs without an auditory component it was easy to start playing one, get distracted, and realize an hour later they were supposed to be learning. Parents liked DVDs because, unlike in books, they were able to see the whole sign and how it was performed.

Parents sometimes became frustrated with the DVDs because they were mostly focused on vocabulary. The songs provided a little bit of flow, but for the most part the signs were not being presented together to create full phrases. One parent said there was too much extra in the DVDs, and they just wished they could get to the vocabulary. Another disadvantage with the DVDs is that there was no assistance when experiencing difficulty learning a sign. The only choice was

to watch the section of the DVD over and over again until understood. DVDs are meant to be played and watched for a duration; they are not as useful for quick referencing.

One parent reported having an ASL story DVD and said he could follow the signs generally word for word. However, he would become confused when the video showed a classifier. Classifiers are signs that represent a general category of objects. Classifiers in ASL are similar to pronouns in English in that the referent depends on their context of use. They can be used to represent an object, how it moves, or how it relates to other objects. This ambiguity is understandable for parents who have had a largely vocabulary-based ASL education.

5.4 Websites

Websites are becoming more popular with parents. Only one family reported not using websites to help them learn sign language. Most families use dedicated sites for ASL such as ASL Pro, lifeprint.com or SigningOnline. All of the websites provide a dictionary. Some are not browsable without acquiring a login which may cost money. Lifeprint.com provides different workbooks and practice tools. Signing-Online provides access to course material for a fee. Two families reported using generic search strategies for finding sign videos online. One family uses YouTube. Another family searches for signs using Yahoo! and the search terms "sign language for" to find vocabulary. The problem with the Yahoo! strategy is that sometimes she gets videos that are not what she is looking for. It can be a very slow process to weed out the inappropriate videos.

The advantages and disadvantages of the websites are similar to those of the DVDs. Parents like seeing the videos of the actual signs instead of the illustrations they find in books. They also feel like they want to see more than just vocabulary. Support for more connected sign is limited. Websites have one advantage over DVDs in that they can immediately find the sign for which they are looking. Some parents felt that it was difficult to spend much time online.

5.5 Classes

Classes received the most divided responses of all of the tools discussed. Seven of the families have attended formal classes at some point in their attempts to learn ASL. Classes were offered through three different sources: higher education institutions, schools for the deaf, and churches. Two families attended classes at higher education institutions. One mother took ASL 1 at the University of Georgia while she was a student. ASL was not considered a language by the university so it did not fulfill her language requirement. Another family took ASL 1 at the local community college. This mother discussed expense of taking the class when they were not interested in the course credit. Three families attended classes at their local school for the deaf. Reactions to these classes were largely positive. Parents talked about the fun games they played, the camaraderie they gained from learning with other parents in similar situations. One mother said she took ASL 1 and 2 multiple times each because every time she experienced learning from different deaf adults. One family attended classes at their church. They felt that there was too much information at once. They were more interested in learning the basics.

Another mother who did not specify the location of her classes said she registered for ASL classes twice but dropped them. She felt that the class took too much time. The teacher spent most of the time talking and the mother felt that she was not learning enough to justify the amount of time spent. Overall it appears that the classes at the school were the most accessible to the parents. More general classes were frustrating to parents who were most interested in immediate communication needs with their children.

5.6 Mobile Learning

Five of the parents talked about using some form of language learning tool while outside of their homes or classroom. Two mothers had small dictionaries they would carry with them to look up unknown signs. Another mother reported that every time they were in the car, she would play one of the SigningTime DVDs. Two families reported using a mobile phone for looking up new signs. One mother used the SMARTSign website on her smart phone to look up vocabulary. Another mother would search for words on the ASL Pro website. No parents mentioned using any of the applications available for the Android or iOS operating systems. All of the parents were very interested in an all-in-one application for learning ASL such as SMARTSign.

5.7 Other Sources

Other people also provide support for parents attempting to learn sign language: their deaf children, church community, deaf adults, and other professionals. Three parents talked about adult acquaintances. The advantage of being around deaf adults is that parents are able to gain experience with full conversations. As one mother said, talking with a deaf adult is much different than a conversation with their child. Two of the parents mentioned the importance of immersion in acquiring their language skills. Both of these mothers have become involved with their child's school in order to improve their language.

One mother who has struggled with learning ASL says that now the family is mostly learning from their child. They are now trying to "catch up" with his language skills. However, the family is not always sure the signs he is teaching them are correct.

Parents will frequently ask others around them if they are unsure of a word. Two mothers talk about asking deaf adults they know. One mother said she will talk to the speech pathologist at the school if she is unsure of a sign. The church community can also be helpful for parents learning sign language. One father said that three people from his church immediately started learning ASL when his son was identified. Two of them are training to become interpreters. He is now learning ASL from one of those individuals.

6. SYSTEM PROTOTYPE RESPONSE

During the interview, parents were presented with a prototype of the SMARTSign system. They were asked for reactions to the current components as well as suggestions for improvement. Possible expansions of the system were described, and parents reflected on the impact or importance of the proposed additions to their own learning.

The vocabulary for SMARTSign is based on the MacArthur Communicative Development Index [1]. The Index consists of common words and phrases that children between the ages of 0 and 3 use or understand and has been validated for a number of languages besides English including ASL. Because our target population is native English speakers, SMART-

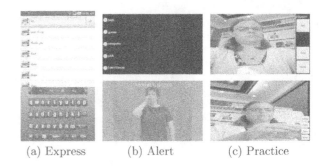

(a) Express   (b) Alert   (c) Practice

Figure 1: The three SMARTSign components

Sign incorporates both the English and ASL indexes. The database contains 728 unique ASL videos which correspond to 831 English words. Words that do no have an ASL equivalent, such as animal sounds, were omitted.

6.1 Current Components

The prototype of SMARTSign has three components focused on ASL vocabulary acquisition. These components are shown in Figure 1. The system is designed to function without the need for an active Internet connection as much as possible. The first component, *Express*, allows parents to search for and watch ASL videos by typing or saying the associated English word. The second component, *Alert*, gives parents the chance to learn new vocabulary through a quiz-based interface. The final component, *Practice*, takes advantage of a device's front-facing camera to provide parents with the ability to record themselves signing and compare with the source video.

Parents reacted positively to all three components and to the system as a whole. Parents saw the system not just as a tool for them to learn sign language, but something their whole family including siblings and extended family could use to learn. Two parents talked about how the interface was easy for them to use and understand. Two parents commented on the quality of the videos and how easy it was to see the motion in them. One mother said it was a good system for people without access to classes. Two parents expressed the sentiment that it would have been good for them when they started learning "and now too."

Although nothing negative was said about the *Express* component, the search functionality had the least amount of positive reactions (six of the ten families). This lack of reaction may be due to the fact that basic search functionality is something that parents are familiar with on the Internet and with books. One mother mentioned the desire to incorporate English phrases. She noted that sometimes only "one sign is needed to convey four English words" as in English idioms and some negated signs like DON'T-LIKE. The mother who used Yahoo! as her primary source for new sign information liked *Express* because it was a lot faster than using the Internet and because you could just type in a few letters to get the sign instead of the whole word.

The first participant made suggestions that led to the positive reception of the *Alert* component by the rest of the participants. Her impression was that *Alert* was useful for practicing vocabulary that had been learned elsewhere but did not have value in discovering new vocabulary. She suggested that when parents selected an incorrect English word they should be shown the video of the sign they selected.

This modification to the original system was appreciated by two of the later participants. One of the participants said that guessing the signs would help them learn. One of the parents appreciated the *Alert* component because reception of signs was the hardest thing for him to master.

Parents seemed the most impressed with the *Practice* component of SMARTSign. One mother said that in her class they were asked to record themselves signing so it was really useful to incorporate the recording mode to help people perfect what they are doing. Another parent was impressed with the opportunity to compare his signs with the example sign. He did stipulate that he tended towards being over-exacting. One mother thought that the *Practice* component might be useful for her child as well who liked to act out movies. A number of interesting applications were discussed. Because it is possible to record anything, other suggestions that arose from the interviews included recording stories for their children in sign and leaving messages. One parent asked if the system could evaluate the signs. Although a desirable addition, sign recognition is beyond the current capabilities of the system.

6.2 Proposed Additions

Four potential extensions were described to the parents to obtain feedback. These extensions are aimed at helping parents advance past simple vocabulary acquisition and help them to learn grammar and fluency.

The extension that seemed most exciting to parents involved teaching vocabulary and grammar with the goal of learning how to read a story to their children. All ten parents expressed interest in this capability. Two parents also suggested nursery rhymes. One mother talked about wanting to read Bible stories to her child but not having access to anything at the appropriate level. Another mother said that a dialogue with someone talking and asking you to answer a question which you could record might be useful as well. Parents were very interested in a system that would help them with their production skills and improve fluency.

Small grammar lessons were less interesting to the parents. One mother said that they are important, but she did not feel parents would use them because it might make it feel too much like school. Others said it would be great to know or be useful information.

Deaf Culture lessons received even more mixed reactions. Two parents stated explicitly that they were not interested in Deaf culture tips. One said it would be more useful for Deaf families. A third person was unsure of their usefulness. She was not interested in general Deaf culture, but she was interested in information about politeness when interacting with Deaf adults. She wondered whether it was rude to approach two signing adults you did not know and whether it was rude to watch people signing in the same way it would be rude to listen in on someone else's conversation.

Five parents were in favor of Deaf culture lessons. Three of them said that they did not know anything so any information was good. One parent said as long what was being shown was understandable, the Deaf culture lessons would be interesting. The comment about understandability led to a discussion of how to present information. Parents liked the idea of signed video lessons with subtitles, but wanted to see more than just a direct English translation in the subtitles. Parents liked the idea of subtitles with a literal transcription from the sign glosses so they could understand

the grammar and vocabulary in the videos. One mother provided suggestions for these lessons. She thought it would be interesting to give information about technology for the Deaf such as lights that flash when the doorbell rings. She emphasized that for these tips to be useful they needed to be really "parent friendly."

Parents were also asked about their interest in lessons aimed at helping them interact with their child. Half of the parents were interested in these lessons. Two parents said that they've known for many years about their child's hearing status, and they still did not know anything. Another parent said that these lessons would especially be useful for parents whose children had recently been diagnosed. One parent said that he was not interested in interaction lessons because early intervention had done a good job telling him the information he needed. Two parents suggested potential lessons. One mother talked about getting her child's attention, and another talked about reminding herself to sign.

7. PHONE OWNERSHIP

The next phase of the SMARTSign project will involve deploying software for parents to use in their daily life; therefore, the last portion of the interview was intended to learn about current technology ownership. Four of the parents already owned smart phones. Five parents also paid for monthly data plans. All of the parents were willing to switch phones in order to be able to use the SMARTSign system.

Parents provided valuable information about what was important to them in a phone. Two mothers were really interested in the devices with front-facing cameras. One mother said that since her son is getting older, he will start going out alone to play with friends. If she wants to be able to communicate with him, sign language would be the most convenient. Phones also serve an added bonus as entertainment for their children while waiting. Doctors' offices don't usually activate captioning on their TV, so mothers can give their phones to their children to play games as entertainment. Parents are also excited about potential educational opportunities for their child that can be provided by smart phones. Parents noted the convenience of having access to SMARTSign on a mobile phone. As one mother said she would be able to use the software anywhere: "public, home, library, shopping." She said she would probably be on the phone all of the time.

8. DISCUSSION

We interviewed hearing parents from ten different families who had deaf children to better understand their needs when learning ASL. Based on what we learned about parental motivation, the main aim of our tool should be providing assistance to increase parent-child communication.

8.1 Situation SMARTSign as a Learning Tool

Looking at the reactions to the various learning tools discussed in the interviews, we can gain an impression of the characteristics that make a successful or unsuccessful learning tool. Classes and Early Interventions share the traits of being regularly scheduled and interactive, but Early Interventions received more positive reactions. One reason for the positive comments is the fact that Early Interventions are more individualized than classes and very specific to the needs of an individual parent and child. A successful intervention should focus on the specific needs of hearing parents and should not focus on general sign language learning. This aim is also reflected in comments parents made about classes not focusing on what was important for them to learn to satisfy their immediate needs. Learning material needs to be as relevant as possible to reducing the communication gap.

Another characteristic of learning tools that lead to more positive reactions is dynamic presentation of signs in the form of videos instead of static images. DVDs, websites, and mobile phones all shared this trait. Websites and mobile phone users had similar response patterns which is consistent with the fact that parents used their mobile phones to access the websites and not standalone applications. DVDs had more positive reactions, perhaps due to the fact that they are usually designed around themes and accessible to whole family. Static images for presenting signs, as represented in books, are not desirable.

A learning tool should not focus merely on vocabulary. The vocabulary focus was a commonly stated negative of many of the learning tools: DVDs, websites, and books. While the current version of SMARTSign does only focus on vocabulary, we hope that with the addition of some of our proposed components we can help parents improve not only their vocabulary ability but also their fluency and understanding of the ASL language as a whole.

8.2 Improving SMARTSign

Parents were generally satisfied with all three of the existing SMARTSign components, so the discussion here will focus mainly on the four suggested additions. The parents we interviewed were unanimously in favor of a tool that focused on providing vocabulary and connected signs associated with reading a story to their children. This desire aligns with a number of characteristics noted in the previous section. One of the biggest advantages is the focus on more than just vocabulary. Story telling would also be, by definition, interactive because it would require the parents to produce the signs in order to tell the story to their child. It also fulfills an immediate need that parents said they had. Many parents talked about their desire to read stories to their children, and the lack of opportunities to do so even before this addition was mentioned.

The remaining three additions: lessons on grammar, Deaf culture, and interaction strategies received equally mixed reactions. The varying responses towards these additions creates an opportunity for parents to customize their experience. Parents will be able to adjust their preferences for receiving these lessons so they can get the information that is most relevant to them.

9. CONCLUSION

Hearing parents' desire to learn ASL is based not on mastery of the language for its own sake, but to fulfill a specific need of improving communication with their child. The parents we interviewed expressed strong motivation to learn and use ASL more, but they still only experience limited success. The focus of SMARTSign will not be on convincing parents of the necessity to learn ASL, but in providing parents with the appropriate tools to help them gain more experience with a difficult language.

Initial reactions to the prototype system aimed at vocabulary acquisition were positive. The next step in this research will be to evaluate a method for presenting vocabulary lessons to parents on their mobile phones through an in-the-wild study. These lessons will be based on aiding parents in learning to read stories in ASL to their children, which was found to be the most compelling motivator for increasing fluency. This study will evaluate both usability and learning outcomes. Through this research we hope to increase hearing parents' ASL language skills and communication ability with their child. With hearing parents better able to communicate with their child in an accessible language, we hope to reduce the linguistic gap between deaf children of hearing parents and other children their age.

10. REFERENCES

[1] D. Anderson and J. Reilly. The MacArthur Communicative Development Inventory: Normative data for ASL. *J. of Deaf Studies and Deaf Education*, 7(2):83–106, 2002.

[2] R. Calderon. Parental involvement in deaf children's education programs as a predictor of child's language, early reading, and social-emotional development. *J. Deaf Stud. Deaf Educ.*, 5(2):140–155, Apr. 2000.

[3] H. Hamilton and D. Lillo-Martin. Imitative production of ASL verbs of movement and location: A comparative study. *Sign Language Studies*, 1986.

[4] V. Henderson-Summet. *Facilitating Communication for Deaf Individuals with Mobile Technologies.* Doctoral thesis, Georgia Institute of Technology, Atlanta, GA, USA, 2010.

[5] C. W. Jackson, R. J. Traub, and A. P. Turnbull. Parents' experiences with childhood deafness. *Communication Disorders Quarterly*, 29(2):82 –98, Feb. 2008.

[6] K. P. Meadow-Orlans, M. Sass-Lehrer, and D. M. Mertens. *Parents and their deaf children: the early years*. Gallaudet University Press, Apr. 2003.

[7] R. E. Mitchell and M. A. Karchmer. Chasing the mythical ten percent: Parental hearing status of deaf and hard of hearing students in the United States. *Sign Language Studies*, 4(2):138–163, 2004.

[8] H. S. Schlesinger and K. P. Meadow-Orlans. *Sound and sign: childhood deafness and mental health.* University of California Press, 1972.

[9] P. Spencer and A. Lederberg. Different modes, different models: Communication and language of young deaf children and their mothers. In L. Adamson and M. Rornski, editors, *Research on communication and language disorders: Contributions to theories of language development*. Brooks, Baltimore, 1997.

[10] C. Vaccari and M. Marschark. Communication between parents and deaf children: Implications for social-emotional development. *J. of Child Psychology and Psychiatry*, 38(7):793–801, 1997.

[11] K. A. Weaver, T. Starner, and H. Hamilton. An evaluation of video intelligibility for novice ASL learners on a mobile device. In *ASSETS 2010*, page 107–114, New York, NY, USA, 2010. ACM.

[12] G. Wells. *Language Development in the Pre-School Years*. Cambridge University Press, June 1985.

Evaluating Importance of Facial Expression in American Sign Language and Pidgin Signed English Animations

Matt Huenerfauth
The City University of New York
Queens College and Graduate Center
Computer Science and Linguistics
365 Fifth Ave, NY, NY 10016
+1-718-997-3264

matt@cs.qc.cuny.edu

Pengfei Lu
The City University of New York
CUNY Graduate Center
Computer Science
365 Fifth Ave, NY, NY 10016
+1-212-817-8190

pengfei.lu@qc.cuny.edu

Andrew Rosenberg
The City University of New York
Queens College and Graduate Center
Computer Science
365 Fifth Ave, NY, NY 10016
+1-718-997-3562

andrew@cs.qc.cuny.edu

ABSTRACT

Animations of American Sign Language (ASL) and Pidgin Signed English (PSE) have accessibility benefits for many signers with lower levels of written language literacy. In prior experimental studies we conducted evaluating animations of ASL, native signers gave informal feedback in which they critiqued the insufficient and inaccurate facial expressions of the virtual human character. While face movements are important for conveying grammatical and prosodic information in human ASL signing, no empirical evaluation of their impact on the understandability and perceived quality of ASL animations had previously been conducted. To quantify the suggestions of deaf participants in our prior studies, we experimentally evaluated ASL and PSE animations with and without various types of facial expressions, and we found that their inclusion does lead to measurable benefits for the understandability and perceived quality of the animations. This finding provides motivation for our future work on facial expressions in ASL and PSE animations, and it lays a novel methodological groundwork for evaluating the quality of facial expressions for conveying prosodic or grammatical information.

Categories and Subject Descriptors

I.2.7 [**Artificial Intelligence**]: Natural Language Processing – *language generation, machine translation*; K.4.2 [**Computers and Society**]: Social Issues – *assistive technologies for persons with disabilities*.

General Terms

Design, Experimentation, Human Factors, Measurement.

Keywords

Accessibility Technology for People who are Deaf, American Sign Language, Pidgin Signed English, Facial Expression.

1. INTRODUCTION

Due to various factors, a majority of deaf high school graduates in the U.S. have a fourth-grade (age 10) English reading level or

below [30]. This means that many deaf adults have difficulty reading English text on websites, captioning, or other media. Over 500,000 people in the U.S. use American Sign Language (ASL), a language with a distinct word order, linguistic structure, and vocabulary than English [23]. Other deaf people in the U.S. use Pidgin Signed English (PSE), a signing system that more closely follows English word order (and can be performed while speaking or mouthing English words simultaneously to hand movements) [21]. Technology for presenting information in the form of computer animations of ASL or PSE can make information and services accessible to deaf people with lower English literacy, as explained in [15]. Animated characters have advantages over video for content that is often modified, is generated or translated automatically, or if the author's anonymity should be preserved. Unfortunately, modern ASL and PSE animation systems require a human to specify when linguistically essential facial expressions should occur and to carefully specify the facial movements to be performed. This is a difficult and time-consuming process.

We have previously conducted studies in which signers evaluate the understandability and naturalness of ASL animations [16, 17]. During these studies focusing on various aspects of ASL (e.g., speed/pauses, use of space around the body, verb movements), there was a trend: in open-ended feedback, participants rarely mentioned the aspect we were studying at the time. The most frequent comments were about the character's facial expressions. Comments included: "face was bland," "too stiff - she needs more facial expression," "eyebrows don't raise enough," "lack of facial expressions affect[ed] some comprehension," "need more head turn and up/down," etc. One participant noted the character attempted a "relationship between the facial movements and the content being said," but felt the timing was off, saying: "Close but no cigar." Another found the overly deadpan facial expression so disturbing that he said: "I'm gonna have nightmares because of that drugged-looking signer." Facial expression seemed to be a key element of ASL animation that signers still feel is incorrect in state-of-the-art systems. Signers were attuned to this aspect of ASL, and it dominated their impression of current technologies. Before investing significant resources in research on facial expression in ASL animation, we wanted to empirically verify and quantify our earlier research participants' comments. So, we conducted studies in which ASL and PSE signers evaluated animations of ASL and PSE with and without various types of facial expressions. Sections 2 and 3 give background on the linguistics of ASL/PSE and the use of facial expression in each. Section 4 surveys current signing animation systems and facial expression. Sections 5, 6, and 7 describe our experimental studies and results, and Section 8 includes conclusions and future work.

2. ASL: USE OF FACIAL EXPRESSION

Mouth shape, eye-brow height, and other face/head movements are a required part of ASL, and identical hand movements may have different meanings depending on the face/head [24]. Facial expressions change the meaning of adjectives (e.g., color *intensity* or distance *magnitude*) or convey adverbial information (e.g., *carelessly* or *with relaxed enjoyment*). The head/face indicates important grammar information about phrases; Fig. 1 shows: YN-question expression occurs during yes/no questions, WH-question expression occurs during interrogative questions ("what, where, how" etc.), negative-expression (and head shaking) negates the meaning of a sentence, and topic-expression indicates that an entity is an important topic for further discussion. A sequence of signs may have different meanings, depending on the head/face; e.g., the ASL sentence "JOHN LOVE MARY" without facial expression means: "John loves Mary." With a yes/no facial expression, it indicates "Does John love Mary?" With a negative expression and headshake added during "LOVE MARY," then the same sequence of signs indicates "John doesn't love Mary." (Facial expressions are timed to co-occur with hand movements for signs during specific parts of a sentence.) Further, ASL signers also use facial expressions to convey emotional subtext. Thus, facial expressions are essential to the meaning of ASL sentences.

Fig. 1. ASL facial expressions: yes/no-question, wh-question, negative face (with left-right headshaking), topicalization.

3. PSE: USE OF FACIAL EXPRESSION

Some people who are deaf or hard-of-hearing use forms of signing communication that more closely resemble English; these include: Manually Coded English (MCE) or Pidgin Signed English (PSE).

- MCE includes a variety of communication systems that follow English word order. Unlike ASL, MCE systems are not natural languages but are artificially invented, formally specified systems for conveying English using the hands. Most MCE systems adopt ASL signs to convey content words; some systems use additional signs to indicate English word endings ("-ed," "-ing") or function words ("the," "of") [21]. MCE can be slower to perform than spoken English or ASL but is used in educational settings to convey English grammar to students.

- Pidgin Signed English (PSE) is less formally specified than the MCE systems. PSE is a hybrid between English and ASL in which signers perform ASL signs for the main content words of an English sentence (in English word order), but they generally do not include extra signs to indicate English word endings or function words [4, 21]. Individual signers vary in how English-like or ASL-like their PSE is, and many ASL signers in the U.S.

can switch into PSE when communicating with someone that has weaker ASL-skills but strong English-skills.

In our prior research [16], we focused on ASL animations. Because PSE uses English word order, knowledge of English is needed to understand PSE; thus, many deaf people with lower English literacy prefer translation to ASL when possible. In this paper, we are studying both PSE and ASL animations – for the following reasons: (1) From a technical perspective, creation of PSE animations from English text is easier than for ASL, because English and PSE are more similar. (2) For low-literacy deaf users, PSE animations may still be somewhat easier to understand than English text, if vocabulary is better understood in the form of signing. (3) Because PSE follows English word order, a character can "mouth" or speak an English sentence simultaneous to PSE performance. Deaf users developing speech-reading (lip-reading) skills may benefit from a system for automatically producing an animated character with accurate lip-movements performing PSE while mouthing/speaking an English sentence provided as input.

While hand movements of PSE convey the content words of an English sentence, this is only part of the message. Spoken English uses prosody (pitch, timing, and volume variations) to convey information in parallel to the words that are spoken. Speech can be divided into *what* is being said (lexical content) and *how* it is said (prosodic content). Prosody can affect the interpretation of a set of words; e.g., rising pitch at the end of a phrase yields a yes/no question ("John and Mary are friends?") and falling intonation yields a statement ("John and Mary are friends."). Prosody is used to indicate topicality and focus, where topic words and foci are often produced with intonational prominence [14]. When new concepts are introduced, they are typically made prominent, and concepts introduced previously are typically de-accented, or made less prominent [5]. Prosody can convey the speaker's state, e.g., anger, frustration [19], or incredulity [32]. Prosody can convey structural information to a listener. Phrases that occur at the start of a segment of discourse are produced with higher pitch, volume, and speed than those at the end of one [18].

PSE can include facial expressions to convey some *prosodic* information. In fact, English speakers (not just PSE signers) tend to perform facial expressions correlated with their vocal prosody:

- The face conveys emotions like anger, frustration, sadness [6] – each of which have characteristic vocal prosody [19].
- Changes in eye-brow height correspond to vocal prominence (emphasizing words or phrases) [7] and changes in pitch [9].
- Head nods can also correspond to vocal prominence [20].
- Use or avoidance of eye-contact during a pause in speaking can differentiate an end of a speaking turn from a temporary pause to think [25] – these correspond to different vocal intonations.
- The face can indicate disbelief/incredulity (e.g., rolling your eyes), and prosody can indicate a speaker's uncertainty [32].
- Visible facial movements can indicate when speakers are asking questions [29] – which also have characteristic prosody.

Speakers don't perform these facial expressions as consistently as ASL signers perform grammatical facial expressions (governed by rules of ASL), but these visible facial movements can suggest prosody. Thus, it could be communicatively useful for the virtual character in a PSE animation system to perform these facial expressions to suggest prosodic information. Due to the influence of ASL on PSE, some systematic ASL facial expressions (e.g., for wh-questions) can also appear during PSE signing.

4. RELATED WORK

Researchers have studied the selection and synthesis of facial expressions for speaking animated characters, e.g.: in "talking heads" with accurate lip movements [22, 29], rule-based selection of facial expressions for English sentences [3], planning facial expressions to give feedback in conversation [13], and planning of eye-movements and facial expressions with discourse impacts [26]. However, this research has not addressed facial expression during animations of PSE or ASL signing.

In an earlier survey [15], we described current systems for producing animations of sign language or other signing; these include: scripting or generation (e.g., [8, 10, 11]). *Scripting* software allows a human to "word process" an ASL/PSE sentence by arranging signs from a dictionary onto a timeline; the software produces an animation of a virtual character based on this timeline (so the human user does not need to manually control all of the joints of the character's body). *Generation* software plans an ASL/PSE sentence based on an English input sentence or other information, without a human manually selecting signs. Despite the importance of facial expressions, current ASL/PSE systems include only a small repertoire of hard-coded facial movements. A generation system automatically planning an ASL/PSE sentence must decide which facial expressions are needed and when they begin/end. Due to the subtle prosodic factors that affect the facial expression, making these decisions automatically is beyond the state of the art, except for simple cases (e.g., add a wh-question expression during a sentence if it starts with "who," "what," etc.).

In a scripting system, the user is typically able to select one facial expression from a list and specify that it occur during a portion of the sentence. For example, in VCom3D Sign Smith Studio [31], a commercially available scripting system for ASL/PSE, the user assembles a sentence on a timeline: with signs on one track and facial expressions on a parallel track. The system's repertoire of linguistic facial expressions is finite: 11 grammatical expressions (and 10 that function as degree adverbials). Like other current ASL/PSE systems, it cannot overlay one facial expression onto another simultaneously, and when two are performed sequentially, the character interpolates the facial pose from one to the next.

Human signers often perform facial expressions simultaneously (e.g., negative headshake + wh-question, sadness + topicalization, etc.). When humans transition from one grammatical facial expression to the next, complex rules govern how these transitions occur, not simple interpolation. Further, the intensity of facial expressions is often based on the timing of the signs performed by the hands: e.g. intensity of a negative headshake may be strongest during the sign "NOT" in a sentence [24]. Handling these complex aspects of facial expression selection, timing, simultaneous performance, and transitions is beyond the state of the art of current ASL/PSE systems. Animating facial expressions accurately is too difficult for generation systems to handle automatically and time-consuming for users of scripting systems. Thus, we want to explore how to better automate facial expression selection and synthesis in our future ASL/PSE animation research.

5. DESIGN OF EVALUATION STUDIES

Before beginning this new line of research, we wanted to know whether improvements in the quality of the facial expression of characters in ASL/PSE animation systems would actually lead to benefits for deaf users. Specifically, would the users' perception of the naturalness or ease-of-understanding of the animations improve if they included more accurate facial expressions?

Section 1 described how we had some informal evidence from study participants' comments, but prior research (section 4) has not included a user-based evaluation of the comprehension impact of facial expression in signing animations. The remainder of this paper describes our efforts to obtain quantitative evidence of the importance of facial expressions for ASL and PSE animations.

While some of the information conveyed by facial expressions is categorical (i.e., whether or not the sentence is negated, whether or not the sentence should be interpreted as a question), other information conveyed by facial expressions is more subtle and a matter of interpretation/degree (i.e., what emotional subtext is being conveyed, how much emphasis is the signer placing on a particular word, is the signer conveying a sense of incredulity or doubt). Especially for these non-categorical (matters of degree) cases, there are natural variations in the way in which some facial expressions are performed and are interpreted by viewers. This presents a challenge when designing evaluation studies designed to measure whether the facial expressions in an ASL or PSE animation are accurate – because we can expect some natural variation in responses to questions about these animations.

Further, sometimes the way in which the prosodic information affects the meaning of a sentence is quite subtle. For instance, a sentence like "I didn't order a pizza" with some vocal prominence on the word "I" could indicate that the speaker believes someone else ordered the pizza. With prominence on the word "pizza," it could indicate that the speaker placed an order, but for something else. In either case, the basic truth value of the statement is unaffected: the speaker did not order a pizza. What is affected by the prosodic variation is the *implication* that can be inferred. Evaluating subtle implications by users in a study can be difficult.

Fortunately, research on human speech suggests successful methods for measuring the impact of prosodic information on how messages are understood and interpreted by human listeners, e.g., [2, 27]. These researchers designed sets of sentences or short stories that – in the absence of prosodic information – contain some degree of ambiguity in how they can be interpreted (similar to the "I didn't order a pizza" example above). When prosodic information is added to the sentences, then it is clear that one interpretation is more correct. Participants in the study who listen to audio performances of these sentences are then asked to answer multiple-choice or Likert-scale questions about the meaning of the sentences. These questions are carefully engineered such that someone would answer the question differently – based on which of the alternative possible interpretations of the spoken sentence they had mentally constructed. For example, someone who heard the sentence "*I* didn't order a pizza" (with prominence on "I") may be more likely to respond affirmatively to a question asking: "Does the speaker think that someone else ordered a pizza?" In designing the studies in sections 6 and 7, we have used similar experimental design, stimuli, and comprehension questions.

6. EVALUATION OF PSE ANIMATIONS

To evaluate whether facial expressions added to a PSE animation could enable viewers of the animation to identify the prosodic content of the English sentences being performed, we designed a study with 28 sets of 1-2 sentence English passages – inspired by those used in previous speech prosody evaluation projects [2, 27]. Without the prosodic aspect of their spoken performance, these passages contained some degree of ambiguity in how they could be interpreted. Fig. 2 contains examples of some of the passages used in the study as English and PSE transcriptions.

Original Spoken English Sentence (transcript of audio):
My brother said he ordered a pizza, but the pizza never arrived.
(Incredulous emphasis tone during the word "said.")

Pidgin Signed English (sequence of signs performed):
MY BROTHER SAY HE ORDER PIZZA HOWEVER PIZZA
NEVER ARRIVE
(Incredulous emphasis facial expression during the word "SAY.")

Four Comprehension Questions (correct answer in parentheses):
Does Sue know why the pizza has not arrived? (yes)
Is Sue upset at the pizza restaurant? (no)
Does Sue believe that her brother ordered a pizza? (no)
Did the pizza arrive? (no)

Original Spoken English Sentence (transcript of audio):
What did you just tell Charlie about me?
(Angry/accusatory tone during the whole sentence.)

Pidgin Signed English (sequence of signs performed):
WHAT DO YOU RECENT TELL #CHARLIE ABOUT ME
(Angry/accusatory facial expression during the whole sentence.)

Four Comprehension Questions (correct answer in parentheses):
Is Sue accusing you of something? (yes)
Is Sue upset about something? (yes)
Does Sue care about Charlie's opinion about her? (yes)
Did you just tell Charlie something? (yes)

**Fig. 2. Examples of stimuli and comprehension questions.
(The '#' symbol indicates a word that was fingerspelled.)**

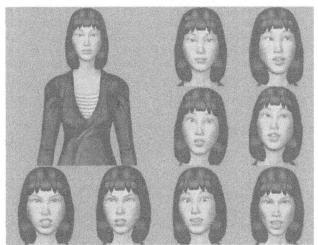

**Fig. 3. Signing character and face images (listed top row first):
neutral face, continuing, contrastive emphasis, incredulous
emphasis, anger, sadness, yes/no question, & wh-question.**

The 28 passages used in the study can be divided into several
categories, based on the type of prosodic information contained:

- QUESTION: Some passages contained a sentence that was a
  question, but in the absence of prosodic cues could instead be
  interpreted as a declarative statement or relative clause: "I went
  to that new restaurant you suggested. It's Chinese?" (Without
  prosody, the second sentence could be a declarative statement.)
  "Last Friday, I saw Metallica. Which is your favorite band?"

- EMPHASIS: Some passages contained a single word or phrase
  that received stronger vocal prominence; this emphasis of the
  word indicated some form of contrast or incredulity: "Bill
  bought some shirts yesterday. The *green* ones were nice." (This
  suggests the others were not.) "My brother *said* he ordered a
  pizza, but the pizza never arrived." (This suggests disbelief.)

- EMOTION: Some passages were performed with a strong
  emotion that affected their meaning: "What did you just tell
  Charlie about me?" (With an angry tone, this suggests that the
  speaker is aware of what was said and disapproves.) "Yesterday
  my sister took me to a concert. It was country music." (A sad
  tone during the second sentence suggests dislike of this music.)

- CONTINUE: Some passages ended with a slightly rising tone
  and lack of deceleration so as to convey that the speaker was not
  yet finished a thought but was only momentarily pausing: "Mary
  is busy: she plays sports, she goes to school…"

To produce the PSE animations, we began by collecting audio
recordings of a native English speaker performing each passage.
In that way, we could determine the timing of the hands and the
facial expressions (corresponding to the vocal prosody) for our
animation based on the timing of the audio. The spoken utterances
were recorded using a Sennheiser Mk3 headset microphone in a
quiet room. The speaker was a female, non-professional speaker
reading from a script with prosodic performance notes.
Productions that contained mispronunciations, disfluencies, or
insufficiently clear prosodic content were re-recorded.

To determine the precise timing of each phoneme (each
consonant/vowel sound), we implemented an automatic speech
recognition system. Our 44.1kHz 16bit mono audio recordings
were forced-aligned to transcripts of each passage using HTK [33]
with tri-phone acoustic models trained on TIMIT [12] and the
CMU pronunciation dictionary. The forced-alignment procedure
generated phoneme and word start- and end-times with a precision
of 10ms. This information can be used to determine the correct
shape of the lips for each moment of time in the animations, based
on the sound being pronounced. This information also gives us
precise timing when each word occurs in the audio so that we can
build an accurate timeline of the hand movements for each sign
during the PSE animation of the English sentence.

We used VCom3D Vcommunicator [31] to create animations of a
character with accurate lip movements speaking each passage;
Vcommunicator allows for hand gestures to be added to an
animation timeline. We inserted PSE signs for each of the words
in the sentence to produce a PSE performance. Although lip
movement was included, the animations contained no audio.
Vcommunicator includes a finite repertoire of facial expressions
that can be added to the timeline, and it allows for head and eye
movement controls. Working within this repertoire (and based on
observation of a native English speaker performing these
passages), we selected a facial expression, head pose, and eye aim
for each of the different types of prosodic performance in our 28
passages. Fig. 3 contains images of the facial poses selected. We
weren't entirely satisfied with the wh-question expression, which
we felt looked a little angry, but it was the closest approximation
we found, working within the face options available in the system.

In prior work, we discussed how to recruit and screen signers for
experiments evaluating animations [16, 17]. Ads for the study
were posted on Deaf community mailing lists and websites in
New York, and participants were asked if they had grown up
using PSE at home or attended a school using PSE as a child. The
6 men and 6 women recruited for the study were ages 22-39
(median age 31). Six had used PSE since birth, five began using
PSE prior to age 6, and one had learned PSE as an adult (with
over 20 years of daily use of PSE in a professional capacity). This
included 2 hearing participants, each of which had over 20 years
of PSE use; one since birth, growing up with deaf family members.

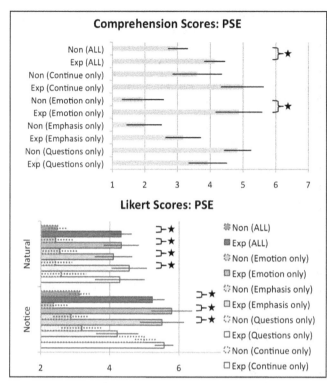

Fig. 4. Results of the PSE study: "Non" animations lacked facial expressions; "Exp" animations included them.

Each animation was produced in 2 versions, with and without facial expressions. Each participant in the study viewed 28 PSE stories in a fully-factorial within-subjects design such that: (1) no participant saw the same story twice, (2) the order of presentation was randomized, and (3) each participant saw 28 animations of each version (facial-expression vs. no-facial-expression). After viewing each story, subjects were asked four comprehension questions (see Fig. 2), answers were recorded on a 7-point Likert scale from "definitely no" to "definitely yes." When tabulating results, the response scale for questions for which the correct answer was "no" was inverted. The top graph in Fig. 4 displays results; the thin line on each bar is the standard error of the mean.

Adding facial expressions led to an increase in comprehension scores. Significant pairwise differences are marked with stars in Fig. 4 (Mann-Whitney test, p<0.05). Overall, comprehension scores are somewhat low; this may be because answering these questions relied on participants drawing subtle inferences based on the prosody. In each set of four comprehension questions for a passage, we only included one question that asked a basic fact (usually the last question); the other three questions relied on the participant making subtle inferences based on the prosodic information – see sample questions in Fig. 2. The EMOTION and CONTINUE categories displayed larger benefits from adding facial expression than the EMPHASIS or QUESTION categories. In fact, adding facial expressions to the QUESTION category *reduced* comprehension scores; this may be due to the "angry" looking facial expression we used for wh-question in this study.

In addition to comprehension questions, we asked participants to respond to a 1-to-10 Likert scale question about how natural the animation appeared. See the "Natural" bars in the lower graph in Fig. 4. There was a significant increase in the scores for the "Exp"

(with facial expression) animations when considering all data and considering data within EMOTION, EMPHASIS, or QUESTION categories only: significant pairwise differences marked with stars in Fig. 4 (Mann Whitney test, p<0.05). This result suggests that adding facial expressions to the animations led participants to report that the animation was more natural in appearance: this quantitative result confirms the qualitative feedback comments of participants in earlier evaluation studies (discussed in section 1).

For each passage, we also asked participants to answer a question in which they reported on a 1-to-10 Likert scale if they believed that signer was: conveying an emotion, asking a question, emphasizing a word, or still speaking at the end of the animation. An appropriate question was included for each passage based on which category it was. See the "Notice" bars in the lower graph in Fig. 4. The "Exp" animations received higher scores for this question; this result suggests that participants overtly noticed the specific prosodic effect that the facial expression was meant to convey in each of these animations. Of course, if the facial expressions had been completely successful at conveying the intended prosodic meanings, we would have expected scores of "10" for this question. The average response score for the "Exp" animations was 5.2; so, there is still room for improvement in the selection and synthesis of facial expression animations for PSE.

Because it was informal feedback comments collected at the end of a study that prompted us to investigate the issue of facial expression, we continued to collect such comments in this study. Six participants mentioned that they felt that the character could benefit from more facial expressions (but it is unclear whether their comments may be in reaction to half of the animations they viewed during the study lacking any facial expression). Five participants mentioned that the speed of the animations was too fast, especially for words that were fingerspelled. We had set our PSE timing based on the audio of the human, who spoke at a slow but natural pace. In future work, we may study how to systematically slow down the timing from an English audio recording when producing a PSE animation so that there is more time for performing complex signs or fingerspelled words. Two participants noticed that the wh-question facial expression used in this study looked incorrect or somewhat angry. For this study, we were using a pre-existing human animation system [31], and we had merely selected the closest facial expression in the repertoire that matched what we wanted. However, in future facial expression research, we may rely on detailed comments and suggestions from participants about ways to modify subtle aspects of a face movement to achieve a clearer facial expression.

7. EVALUATION OF ASL ANIMATIONS

In order to understand whether the addition of facial expressions to ASL animations would also affect deaf users' perceptions of the naturalness and understandability of the animations, we conducted a second study. In order to make the results of this study more directly comparable to that of the prior PSE study, we used the same set of 28 passages and questions. Each of the passages was translated into ASL by a native ASL signer (who works as a professional interpreter). Next, we used VCom3D Sign Smith Studio [31], a commercially available tool for scripting ASL animations, to produce an animation for each of the 28 passages. The new animations used proper ASL word-order and required grammatical facial expressions. Next, the native signer selected facial expressions to add to portions of each animation to convey the prosodic information that had originally been conveyed by the vocal prosody in the original English passages.

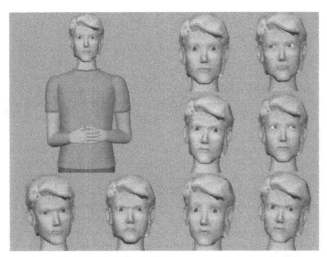

Fig. 5. ASL character and face images (listed top row first): neutral face, continuing, contrastive emphasis, incredulous emphasis, anger, sadness, yes/no question, & wh-question.

See Fig. 5 for illustrations of the facial expressions used in this study. Note that the character used in the study was different because we were using a different animation tool to produce the animations: one that was specially designed for producing sign language animations, not speaking characters. The character for the ASL animations did not move its lips to speak English words. Also, note that the specific facial expressions used in the animations and their exact timing during the ASL-translated version of each sentence differed slightly from the PSE/English examples in the prior study. For this study, a native signer was asked to produce facial expressions that linguistically or naturally conveyed the prosodic information for ASL sentences. Each animation was produced in two versions: with facial expressions conveying prosodic information and one without. However, even "without" versions may have included some facial expression: any linguistically required facial expressions not directly related to the specific prosodic information that was the focus of that passage still remained in the "without facial expression" animations. For example, the ASL passage "YESTERDAY #BILL BUY SHIRTS. GREEN SHIRTS NICE" (Yesterday, Bill bought some shirts; the green shirts were nice), included a special facial expression during the sign YESTERDAY (used during conditional/when phrases) in both versions of the animation. In the "with facial expression" version of the animation, a special contrastive-emphasis facial expression was added during the word "GREEN."

To evaluate whether the addition of facial expressions to these ASL animations would affect native ASL signers' judgments of their naturalness or ability to understand their content, we ran a study similar in design to the PSE study in section 6. We recruited 12 native ASL signers who evaluated ASL computer animations of two types: with facial expressions indicating prosodic information and without such facial expressions. A fully-factorial within-subjects design was used such that: (1) no participant saw the same story twice, (2) the order of presentation was randomized, and (3) each participant saw 28 animations of each version (facial-expression vs. no-facial-expression). In prior studies, we created a set of best-practices to ensure that responses given by participants are as ASL-accurate as possible [16]. The participants should be native ASL signers, and it is important to ask questions to screen for such participants. Further, the study environment should be

ASL-focused with little English influence. All of the instructions and interactions for this study were conducted in ASL by a native signer (a professional interpreter). Advertisements posted on Deaf community websites in New York asked potential participants if they had grown up using ASL at home or attended an ASL-based school as a child. Of the 7 men and 5 women in the study, 8 used ASL since birth, 3 began using ASL prior to age 10 when they began attending a school with instruction in ASL, and 1 learned ASL at age 18. This final participant has used ASL for over 22 years, attended a university with instruction in ASL, and uses ASL daily to communicate with a spouse. Participants were ages 21-46 (median age 32).

In Fig. 6, thin lines indicate standard error of the mean; significant pairwise differences are marked with stars (Mann-Whitney test, $p<0.05$). The addition of prosodically motivated facial expressions led to an increase in the comprehension scores; the result was significant when considering all data and when considering only the passages in the EMOTION sub-category (Likert 1-to-7 scale data). We see similar results for the questions in which signers were asked to rate the naturalness of the animations or respond to a question in which they indicated if they overtly noticed that the sentence: conveyed an emotion, emphasized a word, asked a question, or indicated that the signer had more to say (see the "Natural" or "Notice" bars in Fig. 6, Likert 1-to-10 scale data).

For ASL (Fig. 6) and for PSE (Fig. 4), it is notable how much of a comprehension benefit was provided by the facial expressions conveying EMOTION, as compared to the results for the other three sub-categories: CONTINUE, QUESTION, and EMPHASIS. From this result, it is clear that future research on facial expression in ASL/PSE animations should continue to explore how to overlay emotional information onto sentences.

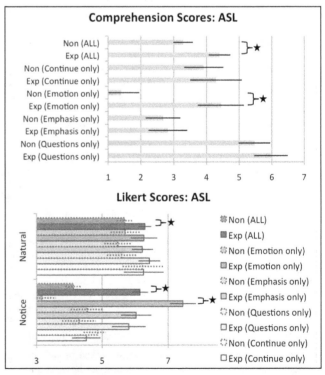

Fig. 6. Results of the ASL study: "Non" animations lacked facial expressions; "Exp" animations included them.

Comparing the results for PSE (Fig. 4) to ASL (Fig. 6), the PSE animations seemed to benefit more from the addition of facial expression in the CONTINUE and EMPHASIS categories. In future work, we want to study further whether human ASL signers do use facial expression to convey this type of information in ASL (and which facial expressions they really use). It is possible that ASL signers instead use other mechanisms to emphasize words or to indicate that they are not yet at the end of a conversational turn, e.g., changes in timing, speed, size of movements, selection of different word-order or phrasing. It is interesting is that signers did appear to *notice* that some emphasis had occurred when facial expressions were added; note the larger (though not significantly so) "Notice" bar for "Exp (EMPHASIS only)" in Fig. 6. Yet, this didn't lead to a change in how they answered the comprehension questions; this may indicate that while signers noticed that some emphasis had been added to a word/sign in the ASL sentence, it did not lead them to draw the same inferences about the meaning. This is an issue we plan to examine further in future work; it will be important for us to distinguish whether we merely had the wrong facial expression in our animations or whether this is not information that is primarily conveyed on the face in ASL.

8. CONCLUSIONS AND FUTURE WORK

The research described in this paper is an example of the benefits of including actual users with disabilities in experimental evaluations of accessibility technology – and encouraging them to offer open-ended feedback and suggestions. This line of research began when looking through quotes from participants in past studies in which they critiqued aspects of our ASL animation technology that we were not explicitly focusing on at the time. We noticed a trend in their comments and decided to conduct formal studies to examine whether the effect they were suggesting could be measured quantitatively. In this case, we did observe that adding facial expressions to animations of ASL and PSE led to significant improvements in users' subjective evaluation of the naturalness of the animations and in scores on comprehension questions about the information conveyed. This is the first study on ASL or PSE animations to measure such an effect, and it provides motivation for future research on automating the insertion of accurate facial expressions to ASL/PSE animations.

Further, this paper has laid a methodological foundation for future research on facial expressions or conveying prosodic information in ASL and PSE animations. By adapting experimental techniques used by speech researchers studying prosody, we have designed sets of stimuli and questions for measuring the impact of facial expressions in ASL and PSE. We can use these methods as we examine detailed aspects of facial expression in future work; e.g., comparative studies of variations in face movements can determine precisely which facial expressions are most successful at conveying particular prosodic information in these animations. The methodologies we have used in this paper could be adapted for use by researchers studying other sign languages used internationally or studying other ways of conveying prosody in ASL/PSE animations (e.g., speed/timing variations).

The ultimate goal of our future research on facial expressions in ASL and PSE is to construct computational models of when to perform facial expressions during ASL/PSE animations and how to articulate the character's face so as to convey these facial expressions most clearly (including under complex conditions when multiple facial expressions are performed sequentially or simultaneously). Determining when to insert facial expressions and how to set all of the parameters of the face correctly is difficult for generation systems to do automatically and is very time-consuming for users of ASL/PSE scripting systems. We want to study how to automate the synthesis of these animations.

A challenge in synthesizing ASL/PSE facial expressions is that users seem sensitive to minor errors in face articulation, leading them to misidentify an expression. In the PSE study, 2 participants commented they were misled in their interpretation of some sentences because they felt the character had an angry face, not a wh-question face. While these facial expressions are similar, there was other evidence in the sentence that it's a question (including "wh" words like "who"). Even still, users thought the character was angry, not questioning, because it didn't have a perfect wh-question face. This is an interesting contrast to the robustness we observed in deaf users in prior studies who tolerated errors in the location or orientation of the character's hands for certain signs; they were often able to use contextual information to guess the correct sign. If there is a difference in the degree to which users are able to tolerate errors in facial expression, then this would add a new layer of challenge to this line of research. There is linguistic precedent: humans listening to speech performed by non-native speakers are more sensitive to errors in the prosody/intonation than to errors in the pronunciation of individual consonant/vowel phonemes [1]. In future work, we will examine if there is analogous sensitivity to prosody errors in ASL/PSE animations.

Another new methodological foundation laid by this current study is that, as the first time our lab studied PSE animations, we had to develop speech recognition software for determining lip/hand timing for PSE animations and to recruit a new type of participant (with PSE experience). Because ASL animations have greater accessibility benefits for many deaf users with low English literacy, we will continue to study ASL animations at our lab. However, English-to-PSE systems may benefit users with less ASL skill or who prefer a character that speaks/mouths an English sentence while it signs. In fact, several participants in our PSE study wrote feedback comments that expressed excitement at having a PSE animation system with lip movements and signing, especially for English instruction applications in educational settings for deaf children. We anticipate interesting challenges in balancing the timing demands of English speech audio with the movements of the hands in PSE animations, and we are excited about examining these issues further in our future work.

Finally, our future work will include collaboration between animation researchers and speech-recognition researchers who study how to automatically detect prosody and intonation in speech. The AuToBI toolkit [28] provides a mechanism to generate hypothesized prosodic phrases and pitch accents; this "automatic prosodic analysis" technology could be used to *automatically* select and set the timing of facial expressions for PSE animation characters. Our future work will investigate robust techniques to convey this acoustic/prosodic information visually.

9. ACKNOWLEDGMENTS

This material is based upon work supported by the National Science Foundation under Grant No. 0746556 and 1065009. This work was supported by the Research Enhancement Committee at Queens College, PSC-CUNY Research Award Program, Siemens A&D UGS PLM Software, and a free academic license for character animation software from Visage Technologies AB. Jonathan Lamberton recruited participants and collected response-data during the user-based evaluation study.

10. REFERENCES

[1] Anderson-Hsieh, J., Johnson, R., Koehler, K. 1992. The relationship between native speaker judgments of non native pronunciation and deviance in segmentals, prosody and syllable structure. *Language Learning,* 42: 529-555.

[2] Allbritton, D.W., Mckoon, G., Ratcliff, R. 1996. Reliability of prosodic cues for resolving syntactic ambiguity. *Journal of Experimental Psychology: Learning, Memory, & Cognition,* 22: 714-735.

[3] Cassell, J., Pelachaud, C., Badler, N., Steedman, M., Achorn, B., Becket, T., Douville, B., Prevost, S., Stone, M. 1994. Animated conversation: Rule based generation of facial expression, gesture and spoken intonation for multiple conversational agents. In *Computer Graphics Annual Conference Series (SIGGRAPH'94),* 413-420.

[4] Cokely, D.R. 1983. When is a Pidgin not a Pidgin? An alternate analysis of the ASL-English contact situation. *Sign Language Studies,* 12(38): 1–24.

[5] Dahan, D., Tanenhaus, M., Chambers, C. 2002. Accent and reference resolution in spoken-language comprehension. *Journal of Memory and Language,* 47: 292-314.

[6] Ekman, P. 1982. *Emotion in the human face.* Cambridge, England: Cambridge University Press.

[7] Grandstrom, B., House, D., Lundeberg, M. 1999. Prosodic cues in multimodal speech perception. In *Proc. Int'l Congress of Phonetic Sciences (ICPhS 99),* 655-658.

[8] Elliott, R., Glauert, J., Kennaway, J., Marshall, I., Safar, E. 2008. Linguistic modeling and language-processing technologies for avatar-based sign language presentation. *Univ Access Inf Soc* 6(4), 375-391. Berlin: Springer.

[9] Flecha-Garcia, M.L. 2009. Eyebrow raises in dialogue and their relation to discourse structure, utterance function and pitch accents in English. *Speech Communication,* 52:542–554.

[10] Filhol, M., Delorme, M., Braffort, A. 2010. Combining constraint-based models for Sign Language synthesis. In *Proc. 4th Workshop on the Representation and Processing of Sign Languages: Corpora and Sign Language Technologies, Language Resources and Evaluation Conference (LREC), Valetta, Malta.*

[11] Fotinea, S.E., E. Efthimiou, G. Caridakis, K. Karpouzis. 2008. A knowledge-based sign synthesis architecture. *Univ Access Inf Soc* 6(4):405-418. Berlin: Springer.

[12] Garofolo, J.S., Lamel, L.F., Fisher, W.M., Fiscus, J.G., Pallett, D.S., Dahlgrena, N,L., Zue, V. 1993. *TIMIT Acoustic-Phonetic Continuous Speech Corpus.* Philadelphia, PA: Linguistic Data Consortium.

[13] Granström, B., House, D., Swerts, M. 2002. Multimodal feedback cues in human-machine interactions. In *Proc. of Speech Prosody (SP-2002),* 347-350.

[14] Hedberg, N., Sosa, J. 2007. The prosody of topic and focus in spontaneous English dialogue. In: *Topic and Focus: Cross-Linguistic Perspectives on Meaning and Intonation.* Berlin: Springer.

[15] Huenerfauth, M., Hanson, V. 2009. Sign language in the interface: access for deaf signers. In C. Stephanidis (ed.), *Universal Access Handbook.* NJ: Erlbaum. 38.1-38.18.

[16] Huenerfauth, M., L. Zhao, E. Gu, J. Allbeck. 2008. Evaluation of American sign language generation by native ASL signers. *ACM Trans Access Comput* 1(1):1-27.

[17] Huenerfauth, M. 2009. A Linguistically Motivated Model for Speed and Pausing in Animations of American Sign Language. *ACM Trans. Access. Comput.* 2, 2, Article 9 (June 2009), 31 pages.

[18] Hirschberg, J., Nakatani, C. 1996. A prosodic analysis of discourse segments in direction-giving monologues. In *Proceedings of the 34th conference on Association for Computational Linguistics,* 286-293.

[19] Juslin, P.N., Laukka, P. 2003. Communication of emotions in vocal expression and music performance: Different channels, same code? *Psychological Bulletin 5.*

[20] Krahmer, E., Swerts, M. 2007. The effect of visual beats on prosodic prominence: Acoustic analyses, auditory perception and visual perception. *Journal of Memory and Language,* 57(3): 396-414.

[21] Lucas, C. 2001. *The Sociolinguistics of Sign Languages.* Washington, DC: Gallaudet University Press.

[22] Massaro, D., Beskow, J. 2002. Multimodal speech perception: A paradigm for speech science. In B. Granstrom, D. House, & I. Karlsson (eds.), *Multilmodality in language and speech systems,* Kluwer Academic Publishers, Dordrecht, The Netherlands, 45-71.

[23] Mitchell, R., Young, T., Bachleda, B., & Karchmer, M. 2006. How many people use ASL in the United States? Why estimates need updating. *Sign Lang Studies,* 6(3):306-335.

[24] Neidle, C., D. Kegl, D. MacLaughlin, B. Bahan, R.G. Lee. 2000. *The syntax of ASL: functional categories and hierarchical structure.* Cambridge: MIT Press.

[25] Novick, D., Hansen, B., & Ward, K. 1996. Coordinating turn-taking with gaze. In *Proceedings of ICSLP-96, Philadelphia, PA,* 3, 1888-91.

[26] Pelachaud, C., Badler, N. I., Steedman, M. 1996. Generating Facial Expressions for Speech. *Cognitive Science,* 20:1–46.

[27] Price, P., Ostendorf, M., Shattuck-Hufnagel, S., Fong, C. 1991. The use of prosody in syntactic disambiguation. *Journal of the Acoustical Society of America.*

[28] Rosenberg, A. 2010. AuToBI - A Tool for Automatic ToBI Annotation. In *Proc. 11th Annual Conference of the International Speech Communication Association INTERSPEECH 2010.*

[29] Srinivasan, R., Massaro, D. 2003. Perceiving prosody from the face and voice: distinguishing statements from echoic questions in English. *Language and Speech,* 46(1): 1-22.

[30] Traxler, C. 2000. The Stanford achievement test, 9th edition: national norming and performance standards for deaf & hard-of-hearing students. *J Deaf Stud & Deaf Educ* 5(4):337-348.

[31] VCom3D. 2011. Homepage. http://www.vcom3d.com/

[32] Ward, G., Hirschberg, J. 1985. Implicating uncertainty: The pragmatics of fall-rise intonation. *Language,* 61: 747-776.

[33] Young, S.J. 1994. The HTK Hidden Markov Model Toolkit: Design and Philosophy. *Entropic Cambridge Research Laboratory, Ltd.* 2: 2-44.

Assessing the Deaf User Perspective on Sign Language Avatars

Michael Kipp, Quan Nguyen, Alexis Heloir
DFKI
Embodied Agents Research Group
Saarbrücken, Germany
firstname.lastname@dfki.de

Silke Matthes
University of Hamburg
Institute of German Sign Language and
Communication of the Deaf
Hamburg, Germany
silke.matthes@sign-lang.uni-hamburg.de

ABSTRACT

Signing avatars have the potential to become a useful and even cost-effective method to make written content more accessible for Deaf people. However, avatar research is characterized by the fact that most researchers are not members of the Deaf community, and that Deaf people as potential users have little or no knowledge about avatars. Therefore, we suggest two well-known methods, focus groups and online studies, as a two-way information exchange between research and the Deaf community. Our aim was to assess signing avatar acceptability, shortcomings of current avatars and potential use cases. We conducted two focus group interviews (N=8) and, to quantify important issues, created an accessible online user study (N=317). This paper deals with both the methodology used and the elicited opinions and criticism. While we found a positive baseline response to the idea of signing avatars, we also show that there is a statistically significant increase in positive opinion caused by participating in the studies. We argue that inclusion of Deaf people on many levels will foster acceptance as well as provide important feedback regarding key aspects of avatar technology that need to be improved.

Categories and Subject Descriptors

I.2.7 [**Artificial Intelligence**]: Natural Language Processing—*language generation, machine translation*; K.4.2 [**Computers and Society**]: Social Issues—*assistive technologies for persons with disabilities*

General Terms

Acceptance, Experimentation, Measurement

Keywords

German Sign Language, Sign Language Synthesis, Accessibility Technology for Deaf People

1. INTRODUCTION

Sign language avatars or *signing avatars* could be a useful tool for the many deaf[1] people who use sign language as their preferred language. For a deaf person, learning to read and write a spoken language, without auditory cues, is an inherently difficult task. Studies have shown that many deaf pupils leave school with significant reading/writing problems [6]. This implies that access to written content, e.g. in the internet, is limited for many deaf individuals. Therefore, an increased use of video-recorded human signers can be observed. However, video recordings imply considerable production cost, their content cannot be modified after production, and they cannot be anonymized with the face being a meaningful component of sign language. In contrast, when using signing avatars, i.e. virtual characters that perform sign language, one can change appearance (gender, clothes, lighting), they are inherently anonymous and the production of new content is potentially easy and cost-effective (no studio setup, no expert performer required, may even be created collaboratively) [8]. Most importantly, avatar animations can be dynamic, i.e. they can be computed and adjusted on-the-fly, allowing for the rendering of dynamic content (e.g. inserting locations, dates, times ...) and interactive behavior (question answering). In this paper, we focus on avatar technology that allows for this flexibility.

However, new technology always faces the question of *acceptability* in the targeted user group. Given a generally small proportion of Deaf people in research positions, signing avatars are almost exclusively developed by hearing researchers [2]. Deaf individuals may be skeptical about any technology invented by the hearing for historical reasons. However, the question of acceptance is essential for the success of a later implementation of such a technology, and therefore also crucial for governmental and other agencies when deciding on funding. While prior work has invested considerable effort in involving Deaf people in animation [7] and evaluation [16], a larger effort to clarify general acceptance is, to the best of our knowledge, still missing. Acceptance implies identifying potential negative sentiments or fears concerning this technology. Exposure to and assessment of current avatar technology is prerequisite for such an assessment, and there is the potential of eliciting new ideas

---

[1]We follow the convention of writing *Deaf* with a capitalized "D" to refer to members of the Deaf community who use sign language as their preferred language, whereas *deaf* refers to the audiological condition of not hearing [15].

for avatar applications. Ultimately, not only the assessment of acceptance but also the question of how to increase acceptance must be addressed. In the study reported here we found that the mere participation in our user studies increased acceptance to a measurable degree.

Signing avatars have been in the focus of research for over two decades [8, 12, 10]. Important goals of this research are methods for translating from spoken languages to sign languages, notation systems to describe sign language and animation methods to automatically create natural and comprehensible sign language movements with avatars. It is important to stress that automated animation is not nearly as natural as hand-animated movies (Toy Story or Avatar) or computer game animations. Therefore, while significant results have been achieved, the sentence-level comprehensibility of avatars remains relatively low, averaging around 60%, with a single result of 71% in a particular scenario [10]. Compared to spoken language processing research, the community is small and lacks the budget to create the same international networks that have fostered spoken language research.

To investigate the potentials of signing avatars for the internet, the German Federal Ministry of Labour and Social Affairs (Bundesministerium für Arbeit und Soziales, BMAS) commissioned us to investigate the technical feasibility of signing avatars for German sign language (DGS[2]) and the acceptance in the German Deaf community. In this paper, we focus on the acceptance aspect of this study. The major goals of this study were to include Deaf people early on to identify key aspects, send out a signal to the Deaf community that we intend a close cooperation and to develop methods for conducting studies with Deaf people.

We see the following contributions for the research community:

- A combination of methods for assessing signing avatar acceptability, identifying shortcomings of current avatars and eliciting ideas for possible applications. Our methods consist of pure sign language dual-moderator focus groups, complemented by an accessible internet questionnaire.

- Identifying problematic aspects of existing avatars from the perspective of German Deaf users. These comprise mostly *nonmanual* aspects, especially facial expression, mouthing and torso movement.

- Showing that, in Germany, Deaf people have a mildly positive "baseline" attitude towards avatars and, more importantly, that this positive attitude can be increased by participating in either focus group or online study.

In this paper, we first outline the background in opinion mining within the Deaf community, then we present our methods, including design and participation, and analysis, before we discuss results and limitations and conclude with a summary and future work.

2. BACKGROUND

In this section, we survey the potential methods for opinion mining and highlight work done in the context of the Deaf community. The research area of signing avatars is

---
[2]Deutsche Gebärdensprache

located on the crossroads of *language technology, linguistics* and *human-computer interaction* (HCI). In contrast to spoken language technology the targeted language community of Deaf people is underrepresented in active research [2]. This makes it especially important to closely include Deaf individuals at all stages of research. When considering methods from HCI, we distinguish methods depending on the phase in development (early stage vs. prototyping) and the qualitative/quantitative dimension (Fig. 1). In this paper, we focus on user studies at an early stage of development.

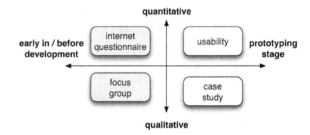

Figure 1: **In the space of possible HCI techniques, focus groups and internet questionnaires combine the virtues of qualitative and quantitative studies.**

Focus groups are a well-known HCI method to elicit empirical data and are applied in marketing, political campaigning and social sciences research. The goal is to elicit people's perceptions and attitudes about any particular product or concept early on in the design process before actual prototypes exist. Focus groups offer a context for comments, interaction, and exchange, thereby giving access to *in-depth* information about what issues participants consider important, what preferences they have and how they prioritize these. A focus group is a guided discussion with 3-10 participants led by a trained moderator where a preset agenda guides the discussion. In contrast, *single case studies* have been shown to be highly useful for eliciting not only usability issues but also socially-situated side conditions, for instance the concern of a blind person to be "marked out" as being blind by a speaking watch [17]. Focus groups with Deaf people were pioneered in 1999 in five groups with an experience hearing moderator and a sign language interpreter/assistant [1]. It was stressed that a shared mode of communication (sign language) in a non-threatening atmosphere needs to be established. Deaf focus groups in a technology context have been conducted for American Sign Language (ASL) in the *MobileASL* project [3] to elicit requirements and scenarios for video cell phone usage for Deaf people. They conducted a one-hour session with four participants where a hearing researcher was present mediated by a sign language interpreter. For the *ClassInFocus* project [4] about visual notifications a two-hour, loosely structured focus group plus prototype testing session was conducted with eight participants. Other researchers used one-on-one interviews with Deaf individuals to elicit user needs [5, 13]. Matthews et al. [13] interviewed 8 Deaf subjects about the design of a sound visualization system. The first part contained structured questions, the second part asked for open feedback on ten design sketches. Tran et al. [18] claim to be the first to design an internet questionnaire (N=148) specifically for Deaf people, testing the usability of MobileASL, and point

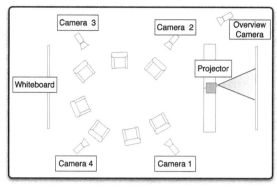

(a) Setup of the second focus group G2.

(b) Screenshot of the video used for the analysis.

Figure 2: Focus group setup and analysis video.

out the importance of offering both ASL and textual explanations, both for understandability and to show respect for Deaf culture.

Usability testing in the area of signing avatars is mostly concerned with the *comprehensibility* of avatar signing. To assess the comprehensibility of the sign language output produced by an avatar is not straightforward and no agreed-on methodology exists. [9] found that there is a low correlation between Deaf participants own judgement on how well s/he understood a sentence and the objective assessment of understanding. A number of in-depth comprehensibility tests have been done in the ViSiCAST/eSIGN projects [10, 16]. These tests usually featured a rather low number of participants. However, more recent evaluation studies use much higher quantities of participants and materials [7]. We present a method for comparing avatar performance directly with video-recorded human signers in [11] to complement the work presented here.

3. METHOD

Our approach is to combine in-depth discussion and the elicitation of ideas that is possible in focus groups with the quantitative strengths of online studies. We suggest the following improvements over prior work on focus groups with Deaf individuals: Ensure a pure sign language environment [9], rely on mostly visual materials (icons, images and video) [14], combine open discussion with structuring and voting, and complement focus groups with accessible internet studies [18] for the quantification of results.

3.1 Focus groups

The overall aim of the focus groups was to elicit opinions, criticism and priorities early in the project and to actively involve the Deaf community. We wanted participants to discuss signing avatars in a non-threatening environment, i.e. without hearing researchers in the room, and in their preferred mode of communication, i.e. sign language [1]. We decided for a *dual-moderator focus group*. The main moderator would guide the discussion, while an assistant would be able to prepare keyword cards for "voting" phases, where participants could indicate their priorities with stickers. The assistant would also act as a communication link with the (hearing) researchers for the case that clarification was needed. As a moderator we hired a well-connected Deaf

community member and sign language instructor, while for the assistant we hired a formerly deaf person, fluent in German Sign Language (DGS), with cochlear implant who could speak.

For technical reasons, participants had to sit in a circle, tables were removed to not obstruct the view. All sessions were videotaped for later analysis (all subjects signed an agreement to grant us scientific usage of the material). The videos were recorded by five cameras which had to be set up so as to minimize occlusion of participants by other participants (see Fig. 2(a)). For later analysis the videos had to be synchronized and cut together in one video (Fig. 2(b)). Synchronization is best done with a clear visual/auditory marking at the beginning (e.g. a person clapping).

We conducted two focus groups, G1 and G2, with 3 and 5 participants each. Each group took about four hours. Participant selection was done by the moderator and assistant according to the following criteria: Participants should be native signers and should consider themselves members of the Deaf community. For G1 we aimed for more computer literate, educated and open-minded members. For G2 we wanted a more representative sample of different education levels. Each of the 8 participants (6m, 2f), of age 25-50, was compensated with 30 Euro plus travel cost. Because of our selection criteria we had to include more remote cities for recruiting (up to 360 km in one case).

During the focus groups we used different media to stimulate discussion: a projector was used to show videos of existing avatars and still images e.g. to illustrate suggested applications, and a whiteboard was used to stick flash cards with keywords on it that could be used for voting (participants could put red dots on those flash cards they found most important). Accept from the keywords, written text was avoided throughout the session.

Each focus group was structured in cycles of information–discussion–voting. This way, we would guarantee sufficient background knowledge, active participation and a synthesis and quantification of results. Each focus group was first welcomed by the moderators and the scientific staff was introduced (outside the actual focus group room) to show that the researchers have genuine interest and respect and to create a pleasant atmosphere. Afterwards, subjects, moderator and assistant entered "their" focus group room. During the focus group, there were five blocks:

1. Introduction and initial questions The project was introduced by a sign language video and two initial questions were asked: "Do you think avatars are useful?" and "Do you think Deaf people would use avatars?" Answers were rated on a 5-point Likert scale from *not at all* to *absolutely* which were visually enhanced with smiley icons and color coding (red/yellow/green).

Figure 3: Three of the presented existing avatars (left to right): The Forest, Max and DeafWorld.

2. Avatar critique Videos of six existing signing avatars were shown (Fig. 3). Those avatars were The Forest[3] (ASL), Max[4] (DGS), DeafWorld[5] (International Sign), Sign4Me[6], the Grandpa Project[7] (BSL) and a Finnish signing boy[8]. This material was intended to give the participants a broad impression of what is possible today. We showed mainly avatars that could be used for automatic animation from a notation; such avatars typically look very robotic. Therefore, to allow participants to think about future possibilities we included the fully hand-animated *DeafWorld* clip. Since the range of existing avatars is quite limited we had to include avatars that used different sign languages (ASL, DGS, International Sign and others) and were communicating in different domains (government, poetry, festival invitation etc.). After each video, participants discussed and criticized the avatar. Keywords were taken and a round of voting on the relative importance of the keywords was conducted. Since this discussion turned out to be time-consuming, we reduced the amount of videos from six to four in group G2 because of the higher number of participants in this group.

3. General applications The participants saw images of several application scenarios, depicted on a photo montage, and discussed these. Our suggestions were: *at the doctor's*, *at the employment agency*, and *accommodation search*. Then, own suggestions were developed. Finally, votes for the most interesting applications were collected.

4. Internet applications This block was similar to the previous block, with the difference that applications specifically for the internet were presented, discussed and voted on. Our suggestions for internet applications were *online shopping*, *Deaf internet portals* and *forums*.

5. Final questions The participants were asked the first two initial questions once again. Additionally, we asked

[3]www.youtube.com/watch?v=80L2XcOK8Jg
[4]www.einfach-teilhaben.de/DE/GBS/Home/Aktuelles/avatar_inhalt.html
[5]www.youtube.com/watch?v=QiY5LU-II6Q
[6]www.youtube.com/watch?v=-NfQGMrqEWY
[7]www.deadcreative.com/deadcreative/projects.asp
[8]www.youtube.com/watch?v=eI9DbYxdmzc

the participants whether they thought that the government should invest money in this technology.

After these blocks, the participants left the room and the official wrap-up was done, including payment and personal discussion with the scientific staff. The analysis of the focus groups was conducted on the basis of the video recordings by a sign language interpreter who prepared an audio translation which was analyzed and summarized by a sign language researcher.

Figure 4: Our accessible online study provided DGS videos and used 5-point answer scales.

3.2 Online Study

To quantify several results from the focus groups we created an accessible internet user study (Fig. 4). It was based on the structure and results from the focus group. The online study was open to the general public but only advertised within the Deaf community via mailing lists, personal contacts, and the popular German Deaf web portal *www.taubenschlag.de*. For accessibility we provided DGS video explanations for all questions. Replies were collected on 5-point scales, visually enhanced by smileys and color-coding.

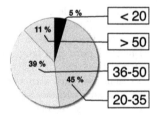

Figure 5: Age structure (online study)

The content of the survey was analogous to the blocks from the focus groups. In the avatar critique block, we only presented the three avatars shown in Fig. 3. Participants were asked how much they liked/disliked the following aspects of the avatars on a 5-point scale: comprehensibility, facial expression, naturalness, charisma, movements, mouthing, appearance, hand-shapes, clothing. In the other blocks we asked open questions, e.g. suggestions for applications after showing the same example applications as in the focus groups. Also, these questions were asked at beginning and end: "Do you think avatars are useful?" and "Do you think Deaf people would use avatars?". Additionally, we asked "Do you think that the government should investigate money in this technology?" at the very end.

In total, 317 people completed the questionnaire. 42% were male, 58% female. There were more deaf (85 %) than hard of hearing (2%) or hearing (13%) participants. The age of the participants was quite balanced between the two largest age groups 20–35 and 36–50 (Fig. 5). On average, the participants had little or no experience with avatars. Fig. 6 shows the distribution of professional backgrounds. It is noteworthy that many people came from technical areas.

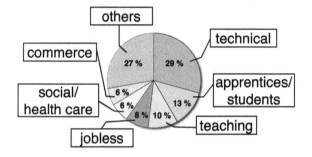

Figure 6: Professional background (online study)

4. ANALYSIS

In this section, we give a topic-oriented account of the results from focus groups and online study.

4.1 Existing Avatars

In focus groups and online study participants were shown 3-6 videos of existing avatars (Fig. 3) and were asked to criticize them. We first discuss our findings from the focus groups organized by topic.

Style and personality Most of the avatars presented were found to have hardly any emotional expression, therefore lacking charisma and naturalness. Their presence was described as stiff and sometimes robot-like. It was found that missing personality can easily be interpreted as cold or unfriendly. While the DeafWorld avatar, as a positive exception, was pointed out to have a very positive and pleasing presence, it was also noted that its cartoonish style may only be suitable for certain contexts.

Upper body movement and manual components No matter whether the language produced by the avatar was DGS or a foreign sign language, the focus of the participants' criticism was usually *not* on the manual component of the signs (i.e. the hands) but rather on the upper body movement as a whole. While the amount of movement varies between the avatars presented, the overall criticism was that it is not sufficient: except for hands and arms also a variety of head, shoulder, and torso movements are needed. For the torso, movements like hunching and twisting were mentioned to improve naturalness, as well as clear sideway rotations (e.g. for marking role shift). It was also found that there was a limited use of the signing space as the hands mainly show horizontal and vertical movements (e.g. pointing straight to the front instead of sidewards). In general, the participants wished for more smooth and relaxed movements of all parts of the upper body.

Facial expressions and mouth patterns While facial expressions are essential for sign languages to deliver

Important avatar aspects
Facial expression (7)
Natural movement (5)
Mouthing (4)
Emotions (4)
Body motion/posture (4)
Appearance (3)
Synchronisation of sign and mouthing (3)
Charisma (2)
Comprehensibility (2)

Table 1: Voting on most important avatar aspects (focus groups)

emotions as well as grammatical information, most of the avatars show very little. This was highly criticized by all participants, and for many avatars the face was described as stiff and emotionless. Specifically mentioned were missing variations in eyebrow, eyelid, as well as ocular movement. Permanent eye contact was regarded as unnatural and causing discomfort. The absence of mouth patterns, especially mouthings (i.e. mouth patterns derived from the spoken language), seemed to be one of the most disturbing factors for the participants since this is an important element of DGS. Besides more movement of cheeks and lips, teeth and tongue were said to be needed as a crucial element for understanding certain mouthings. While more facial and mouth movements seems to be essential, the participants stressed that exaggeration of movements should be avoided.

Movement synchronization The participants' feedback made very clear that the overall image is crucial for understanding the avatar's performance. For those avatars showing mouthing it was found that there was a mismatch between the duration of the signs and their corresponding mouthings. While commonly the signer's face is kept as a focus point, this mismatch provokes an disturbing oscillation of the observer's gaze between hands and face.

Technical remarks Good lighting and a clear contrast between the avatar's skin, clothes and the background is important for the perception of the signing avatar. Additional shadows were noted as favorable as they support a 3D effect. In order to meet individual needs speed and perspective should preferably be under user control.

Avatar appearance Of all avatars presented, the Deaf-World cartoon animation was ranked as the best one. However the participants emphasized the need of having different avatars for different domains: while a cartoonish child would be suitable for children and for entertainment, a more realistic adult avatar is recommended for the use in serious applications (e.g. politics).

Voting on important avatar aspects Table 1 shows what participants deemed most important for an avatar. It is striking is that many *nonmanual* components were mentioned whereas hand/arm movements were not explicitly mentioned. Also, the importance of realism and high-quality rendering should not be underestimated.

Online Study Results In the internet questionnaire we asked for ratings (between -2 to +2) for those aspects that were identified in the focus groups. For readability we merged the online study results for the avatars Forest and Max and compared this with the DeafWorld animation ratings. Fig. 7 clearly shows the large quality gap between a purely hand-

Application (general)	Application (internet)
Simple help/info dialogue (9)	Lexicon (7)
Train/airport (5)	News (4)
Fixed texts (4)	Education (3)
Forms (2)	Insurance (3)
Exam quest. (2)	Consumer protection (3)

Table 2: Voting on possible applications, only top 5 each (focus groups)

made animation like DeafWorld and the quality of automated avatars. We also compared this against the voting in the focus group and found a loose correspondence between aspects deemed important by participants and low values for the Forest/Max avatars. It was also apparent that nonmanual aspects are at least as important as the manual ones.

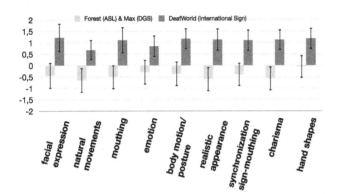

Figure 7: Ratings of aspects of the presented avatars (online study). Ratings for Forest and Max were averaged to juxtapose them against the fully handmade DeafWorld animation.

4.2 Application Scenarios

In the focus groups, possible applications for avatars were mainly seen for one-way communication situations with less complex content. The participants could not envision dialogic interaction with an avatar. Many ideas emerged during discussion such as: (Online) translation services for simple sentences, static announcements (job offers, company newsletter, election campaigns) and static texts (legal texts, manuals), information usually communicated via speakers (train station, airport), daily news and news feeds, lexicons and dictionaries, museum guide.

When voting on the relative importance of applications there were quite concrete and technically realistic scenarios that won (Table 2), while avatars were not considered necessary for very trivial texts such as accommodation ads or restaurant menus.

The online study (Fig. 8) showed a much more diverse picture, probably due to the fact that the individual scenarios were not discussed with other Deaf people in terms of being technically realistic and actually relevant to everyday life. Also, more entertainment and leisure time applications came up. For internet applications the top applications were educational (17%), for social network websites (16%) and (public) administration pages (11%).

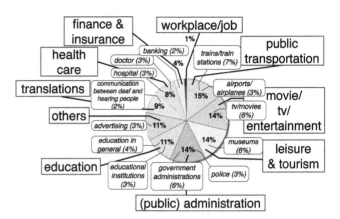

Figure 8: General applications (online study)

4.3 Risks and Potentials

In the focus groups, it was extremely important for all participants that avatars should not be seen as a replacement for human interpreters and that every Deaf person should always have the choice between the two. This is reflected in the online study where 25% of mentioned effects concerned job cuts for interpreters or for Deaf people. Another concern was the danger that using an avatar may lower the motivation for Deaf individuals to properly learn reading/writing. Maybe not surprisingly, the online study participants were much more concerned about technical feasibility (20%) and reliability (22%) of avatars since they had not discussed potential scenarios in depth. See Fig. 9 for the possible risks mentioned in the online study.

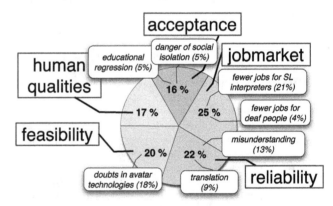

Figure 9: Fears of potential negative impacts in these areas (online study)

However, there were also a number of potentials seen in avatar technology. Focus group participants found it most important that avatars are *available anytime*, while interpreters are often hard to find. *Personalization* is possible, e.g. regarding appearance, speed, or perhaps even language output (sign language vs. sign supported spoken language). Avatars also allow for *anonymity* in the internet (e.g. for the discussion of controversial topics).

4.4 Acceptance

While all three participants of G1 already had a very positive attitude towards the use of avatars prior to the focus group interview, they stated that their opinion was even higher after the discussion. For G2 the rating was initially neutral to slightly negative, but increased throughout the discussion to a slightly positive attitude. The participants regarded avatars as a good opportunity to provide full access to information in some domains. They assumed, however, that the acceptance across the Deaf community may vary depending on age, technological knowledge and sign language competence.

The general acceptance trend of the focus groups was confirmed in the online studies. The average value for the two questions at the beginning and the end ("Are avatars useful?" and "Would Deaf people use avatars?") on a scale of -2 (not at all) to $+2$ (very much so) was only slightly positive in the beginning ($M = 0.46; SD = 1.08$ and $M = 0.46; SD = 1.11$). In the end, the value increased significantly ($M = 0.74; SD = 1.12$ and $M = 0.71; SD = 1.03$). A paired t-test showed the that the increase was highly significant for both questions ($p < 0.001$ and $p < 0.001$). The question whether the government should invest in this technology was positive ($M = 0.77; SD = 0.77$).

5. DISCUSSION

5.1 Deaf User Opinions

The feedback of both the focus groups and the online study clearly shows that much improvement in the performance of sign language avatars is still needed. In the focus groups the criticism was not so much focussed on a single aspect than rather on the general appearance that was mostly described as stiff, emotionless and unnatural. Most of the criticism targeted nonmanual features, mainly facial expression and mouth patterns, but also movements of the head, shoulders and torso. The wish for naturalness and emotions also show that the general appearance should not be underestimated. On the contrary, manual components (i.e. the hands) were not in the participants' focus. This might be due to the fact that in former research comparatively much attention has been paid to improving the animation of the hands. However it also shows that other components are still underestimated in linguistic as well as technological research. The most positive votes in the focus groups as well as the online study were given to a fully handmade animation. This underlines the gap between avatar approaches which can be automated and handmade animations. However, it also shows that in principle animated characters can reach high levels of acceptance.

Application scenarios, as discussed in the focus groups, are mainly situated in the area of one-way communication situations. The participants can neither envision avatars in dialogic settings nor for very complex or emotional content. They also expressed worries regarding a potential replacement of human interpreters by avatars in these contexts. In the online study, an even higher emphasis was put on feared negative effects as job cuts when implementing avatars.

The general attitude towards avatars, as asked for in the beginning and at the end of the focus groups, was overall positive and increased throughout the sessions. In the online studies, this effect even reached high statistical significance. This underlines the potential of involving the Deaf community, not only for general assessments but also for increasing acceptance.

5.2 Method

The focus group interviews turned out to be an excellent method to elicit criticism, constructive suggestions and opinions of Deaf participants. Especially for a topic like avatars, where participants might not have a clear idea of the opportunities associated with this new technology, the focus group interviews allowed them to develop their criticism and suggestions throughout the session. We decided to establish a pure sign language environment. While this adds considerable overhead in terms of preparation (training the moderator) and analysis (video analysis) we believe that it creates an open atmosphere during the session, where new ideas can be discussed and clarification questions can be asked, and respect for the Deaf community is signaled by involving them in key positions of a scientific procedure. In terms of participants, we deem four participants the maximum number in terms of later analysis.

Thinking about the limitations of our approach, our results first of all apply to *German* Deaf users. However, we think that many aspects are valid for avatars of any sign language. In terms of participants, we would have liked to put more focus on specific groups (by age, by education, by gender) to be able to compare focus group results. Also, we would have liked a better male-female ratio. However, depending on the region, there may be very few Deaf people that meet all of the targeted criteria. We had a heterogenous mixture of avatar video material (different languages and domains). While this was positive in terms of conveying the breadth of research, it made comparison between avatars difficult and introduced order effects, e.g. seeing an avatar signing in the familiar DGS may have put more positive emphasis on it. Lastly, the topic of avatars often puts avatars in direct comparison with sign language interpreters. Since this is not a realistic near-future development the moderator should probably guide the participants more toward a comparison between avatars and videos (of signing humans).

In the focus groups, the participants' perception of the shown avatars were sometimes inaccurate or false. While a strength of focus groups lies in the possibility to correct this in the discourse, sometimes the contrary happens and the whole group is "infected" by an erroneous assumption, e.g. that mouthing was particularly good or bad. This is why complementary methods must be combined for an objective picture of Deaf people's opinions. Internet questionnaires can statistically validate the generality of some assumptions, e.g. which aspects are the most problematic with existing avatars. However, to focus more on avatar *performance* one has to measure the *comprehensibility* of an avatar in a test setup where a Deaf participant tries to understand an avatar's signing performance (see [11]).

6. CONCLUSIONS

We presented our approach for assessing the opinion of the German Deaf community about sign language avatars. Focus group interviews were complemented by a large internet study. We conducted the focus groups in a pure sign language environment and elicited valuable feedback on existing avatars and ideas on application scenarios. A significant increase in positive opinion in both focus groups and internet study showed that both methods help increase acceptance in the community. Therefore, including the Deaf community or Deaf individuals in this way works in two directions:

Not only does it benefit research, it also reverberates in the Deaf community through the dense, nationwide networks. We hypothesize that the positive influence on the opinion of a few will quickly spread throughout the community.

We found that nonmanual components were found to be at least as important as manual ones. This indicates that research needs to make a major shift toward new challenges in the nonmanual area. In terms of applications, Deaf people favored non-interactive, simple scenarios where avatars give information (train station, museums) or help in educational contexts (sign language lexicon, exam questions). However, also many other small everyday scenarios which may be made easier with an avatar were identified.

While focus groups and questionnaires give a good general impression of general shortcomings, the actual development of animated avatars needs a much deeper involvement of Deaf individuals. Comprehensibility studies allow to quantify the performance of an avatar by comparing its comprehensibility with that of a human signer on video. This can be measured by asking for a retelling or letting experts judge the participants' understanding. We explore these questions in a separate publication [11].

For the future we hope to conduct further focus group interviews on more specific topics, with better avatar materials or interactive mockup scenarios (like in [16]). An important question is how to combine different media (video, text, avatars) to reach a maximum of comprehensibility and comfort for people with different degrees of reading and signing skills. The ultimate question in the avatar domain is, however, how nonmanual components can be automatically integrated into existing systems and how that improves comprehensibility which will in turn affect overall acceptance.

7. ACKNOWLEDGMENTS

This study was commissioned by the German Federal Ministry of Labour and Social Affairs (eGovernment Strategie Teilhabe). Thanks to our excellent Deaf moderators Iris König and Peter Schaar, to Thomas Hanke (Univ. Hamburg) and Horst Ebbinghaus (HU Berlin) for preparatory discussion. Parts of this research have been carried out within the framework of the Excellence Cluster Multimodal Computing and Interaction (MMCI), sponsored by the German Research Foundation (DFG).

8. REFERENCES

[1] G. I. Balch and D. M. Mertens. Focus group design and group dynamics: Lessons from deaf and hard of hearing participants. *The American Journal of Evaluation*, 20(2):265 – 277, 1999.

[2] A. Braffort. Research on computer science and sign language: Ethical aspects. In *Gesture and Sign Language in Human-Computer Interaction*, LNAI 2298, pages 3–12. Springer, 2002.

[3] A. Cavender, R. E. Ladner, and E. A. Riskin. MobileASL: Intelligibility of sign language video as constrained by mobile phone technology. In *Proc. 8th intl. ACM SIGACCESS conf. on computers and accessibility (ASSETS)*, pages 71–78. ACM, 2006.

[4] A. C. Cavender, J. P. Bigham, and R. E. Ladner. ClassInFocus: Enabling improved visual attention strategies for deaf and hard of hearing students. In *Proc. 11th intl. ACM SIGACCESS conf. on computers and accessibility (ASSETS)*, pages 67–74. ACM, 2009.

[5] F. W.-l. Ho-Ching, J. Mankoff, and J. A. Landay. Can you see what i hear? the design and evaluation of a peripheral sound display for the deaf. In *Proceedings of the SIGCHI conference on Human factors in computing systems (CHI)*, pages 161–168. ACM, 2003.

[6] J. A. Holt. Demographic, Stanford achievement test - 8th edition for deaf and hard of hearing students: Reading comprehension subgroup results. *Amer. Annals Deaf*, 138:172–175, 1993.

[7] M. Huenerfauth. A linguistically motivated model for speed and pausing in animations of american sign language. *ACM Trans. Access. Comp.*, 2(2):1–31, 2009.

[8] M. Huenerfauth and V. L. Hanson. Sign language in the interface: Access for deaf signers. In C. Stephanidis, editor, *The Universal Access Handbook*, chapter 38, pages 1–18. CRC Press, 2009.

[9] M. Huenerfauth, L. Zhao, E. Gu, and J. Allbeck. Evaluating american sign language generation by native ASL signers. *ACM Trans. Access. Comp.*, 1(1):1–27, 2008.

[10] J. R. Kennaway, J. R. W. Glauert, and I. Zwitserlood. Providing signed content on the internet by synthesized animation. *ACM Trans. Computer-Human Interaction*, 14(3):15–29, 2007.

[11] M. Kipp, A. Heloir, and Q. Nguyen. Sign language avatars: Animation and comprehensibility. In *Proc. 11th Intl. Conf. on Intelligent Virtual Agents (IVA)*. Springer, 2011.

[12] V. Lombardo, F. Nunnari, and R. Damiano. A virtual interpreter for the Italian sign language. In *Proc. 10th Intl. Conf. on Intelligent Virtual Agents (IVA)*, pages 201–207. Springer, 2010.

[13] T. Matthews, J. Fong, and J. Mankoff. Visualizing non-speech sounds for the deaf. In *Proc. 7th intl. ACM SIGACCESS conf. on computers and accessibility (ASSETS)*, pages 52–59. ACM, 2005.

[14] R. Nishio, S.-E. Hong, S. König, R. Konrad, G. Langer, T. Hanke, and C. Rathmann. Elicitation methods in the DGS (German Sign Language) corpus project. In *Proc. of the 4th Workshop on the Representation and Processing of Sign Languages: Corpora and Sign Language Technologies*, 2010.

[15] C. Padden and T. Humphries. *Deaf in America: Voices from a Culture*. Harvard University Press, 1988.

[16] M. Sheard, S. Schoot, I. Zwitserlood, M. Verlinden, and I. Weber. Evaluation reports 1 and 2 of the EU project essential sign language information on government networks, Deliverable D6.2, March 2004.

[17] K. Shinohara and J. Tenenberg. Observing Sara: A case study of a blind person's interactions with technology. In *Proc. 9th intl. ACM SIGACCESS conf. on computers and accessibility (ASSETS)*, pages 171–178. ACM, 2007.

[18] J. J. Tran, T. W. Johnson, J. Kim, R. Rodriguez, S. Yin, E. A. Riskin, R. E. Ladner, and J. O. Wobbrock. A web-based user survey for evaluating power saving strategies for deaf users of mobileASL. In *Proc. 12th intl. ACM SIGACCESS conf. on computers and accessibility (ASSETS)*, pages 115–122. ACM, 2010.

Evaluating Quality and Comprehension of Real-Time Sign Language Video on Mobile Phones

Jessica J. Tran[1], Joy Kim[2], Jaehong Chon[1],
Eve A. Riskin[1], Richard E. Ladner[2], Jacob O. Wobbrock[3]

[1]Electrical Engineering
University of Washington
Seattle, WA 98195 USA
{jjtran, jaehong,
riskin}@ee.washington.edu

[2]Computer Science & Engineering
University of Washington
Seattle, WA 98195 USA
{jojo0808, ladner}@cs.washington.edu

[3]The Information School
DUB Group
University of Washington
Seattle, WA 98195 USA
wobbrock@uw.edu

ABSTRACT

Video and image quality are often objectively measured using peak signal-to-noise ratio (PSNR), but for sign language video, human comprehension is most important. Yet the relationship of human comprehension to PSNR has not been studied. In this survey, we determine how well PSNR matches human comprehension of sign language video. We use very low bitrates (10-60 kbps) and two low spatial resolutions (192×144 and 320×240 pixels) which may be typical of video transmission on mobile phones using 3G networks. In a national online video-based user survey of 103 respondents, we found that respondents preferred the 320×240 spatial resolution transmitted at 20 kbps and higher; this does not match what PSNR results would predict. However, when comparing perceived ease/difficulty of comprehension, we found that responses did correlate well with measured PSNR. This suggests that PSNR may not be suitable for representing subjective video quality, but can be reliable as a measure for comprehensibility of American Sign Language (ASL) video. These findings are applied to our experimental mobile phone application, *MobileASL*, which enables real-time sign language communication for Deaf users at low bandwidths over the U.S. 3G cellular network.

Categories and Subject Descriptors

K.4.2. [**Social Issues**]: Assistive technologies for persons with disabilities; H.5.1 [**Information Interfaces and Presentation**]: Multimedia Information Systems – Video.

General Terms

Performance, Experimentation, Human Factors.

Keywords

PSNR, video compression, bitrate, spatial resolution, online survey, mobile phones, American Sign Language, Deaf community.

1. INTRODUCTION

Real-time mobile video chat is becoming popular for communication. This enables deaf people to communicate in a language accessible to many of them, American Sign Language (ASL). However, some mobile video chat programs like iPhone's FaceTime [1] only work over Wi-Fi, and other mobile video chat

Figure 1: One frame of a paired-comparison of 192×144 (left) and 320×240 (right) spatial resolutions transmitted at 10 kbps and displayed at 320×240 pixels.

programs like Qik, Fring, Purple, and ZVRS [10,20,21,36] require access to expensive and not widely available 4G cellular networks and smartphones. Also, many cellular networks (AT&T and Verizon) no longer provide unlimited data plans, further limiting access to mobile video calls. To address these limitations, we created an experimental mobile phone application called *MobileASL* [2], which enables Deaf people to communicate in real-time via sign language at low bitrates over the U.S. cellular network. What distinguishes MobileASL is that it is able to transmit over 3G in addition to 4G and Wi-Fi and uses region of interest identification [5] to enable transmission of intelligible sign language video at very low bitrates, making sign language video available to many more devices and people.

Research on audiovisual quality [15,34,35] has indicated that when hearing people are shown video with visually detailed scenes at low bitrates, sound becomes increasingly important to compensate. We investigate whether video quality is perceived differently among deaf and non-deaf users since sound cannot be used to compensate for low video quality for deaf[1] people. Since comprehension of video is a subjective measure, objective metrics like peak-signal-to-noise ratio (PSNR), a widely used measure of objective video quality [32], do not necessarily reflect comprehension and subjective quality as perceived by viewers [11,13]. Researchers have tried to create algorithms [17,28,31] to mimic the human visual system to measure subjective quality, but the success at which algorithms reflect users' perceptions varies with users, video content, and data transmission rates. Therefore, we turn to the user to investigate *perception* (between ASL and non-ASL speakers) and *comprehension* (ASL speakers only) of video quality at varying low bitrates and spatial resolutions.

We created and deployed a national video-based online survey to investigate user preferences and comprehension when varying the

---

[1] Using capital "Deaf" is accepted practice when referring to members of Deaf Culture, while lower case "deaf" is used when referring to an individual with hearing loss.

bitrates (10-60 kbps in increments of 10 kbps) and spatial resolutions (192×144 and 320×240) of ASL video that would be transmitted for mobile video phone communication. We seek to answer four questions:

1) When users are shown ASL video encoded at different spatial resolutions and bitrates, which combinations do they prefer?

2) How does the objective video quality measure (PSNR) compare to the subjective video quality preferences for varying bitrates and spatial resolutions?

3) For respondents who are fluent in ASL, does video quality preference influence comprehension of video content with varied spatial resolutions and bitrates?

4) For respondents who are fluent in ASL, how do varied spatial resolutions and bitrates affect their perceived ease/difficulty of comprehension?

In our survey, both ASL and non-ASL speaking respondents overwhelmingly preferred the video quality of the larger spatial resolution at bitrates of 20 kbps ($\chi^2_{1,N=95}$=68.4, p<.0001) and higher. However, the objective PSNR measurements showed a crossover point at 50 kbps and higher, where transmitting the larger spatial resolution (320×240 instead of 192×144) had higher objective video quality than the smaller spatial resolution transmitted at the same bitrates. Despite PSNR not accurately reflecting subjective quality, it did accurately correlate *with comprehension of ASL video*. We found that comprehension was made easier when the larger spatial resolution was transmitted at 50 kbps (Z=100.0, p<.001) and higher, the same crossover point as for the PSNR. These findings and others are presented in detail in our results section.

The main contributions of this paper are identifying that subjective video quality preferences do not differ among ASL and non-ASL speakers; that the perceived ease/difficulty of ASL video comprehension is affected by bitrate and spatial resolution at which video is transmitted; and that PSNR may correlate with perceived ease/difficulty of comprehending ASL video. These results can be used to understand how video comprehension relates to PSNR, which may enable designers of video telephony systems to optimize their choices; for example, to save battery life on mobile devices whose power resources are highly constrained.

2. RELATED WORK

Numerous metrics and algorithms have been created in an attempt to bridge the gap between PSNR and subjective video quality. However, the PSNR has not been shown to accurately represent subjective video quality [8,18,22,30] and a standard subjective metric has not yet been adopted.

Feghali *et al.* [8] created a subjective quality model that takes into account encoding parameters (quantization error and frame rate) and motion speed of video during calculation of their new subjective quality metric. They used the Pearson's correlation, *r*, which is a measure of how well their subjective model matches subjective video quality, where values closer to 1 indicate a perfect positive linear relation. They were able to achieve, on average (across five videos with different motion levels) an *r* = .93 when comparing the assessed subjective quality to their new subjective quality metric. For high motion video, such as a football game, the assessed subjective quality compared to the PSNR resulted in *r* = .57, while the new quality metric resulted in *r* = .95; however, a smaller difference in *r* was found for slow motion video. Nemethova *et al.* [18] created a different rule-based

algorithm that adapts the PSNR curve to the mean opinion scores (MOS) by scaling, clipping, and smoothing the PSNR results. The new MOS adapted from the PSNR curve was compared to the assessed subjective MOS whose results demonstrated an average *r* = .89. Both algorithms demonstrated success in increasing the accuracy of measuring subjective video quality; however, both researchers recognize that their algorithms are content-dependent and have higher performance with fast motion video, of which sign language video would be considered one.

Related research by Ciaramello and Hemami [7] developed an objective measure of ASL intelligibility which relies on region-of-interest (ROI) encoding of different areas of video. They encoded ASL video at three different bitrates (20, 45, and 80 kbps) and five ROI settings that vary the allocation of bits to the background and the signer in the foreground during video encoding. This resulted in video with the background appearing blurrier than the ASL signer depending on the bitrate and ROI combinations. In a paired comparison experiment with 12-respondents, they found that at higher bitrates, respondents preferred the background and signer in the foreground to be equal in blurriness; however, at lower encoding bitrates respondents preferred the signer to be less blurry than the background. Our experiment is different than theirs since we are evaluating both subjective video quality *and* comprehension while they only evaluated subjective video quality. We are interested to learn how preferences and comprehension may change with varying spatial resolutions and bitrates since a person may not like a video quality, but still may be able to understand its content.

A related research topic is investigating tolerance of image artifacts when lowering bitrates and image resolutions. Bae *et al.* [4] conducted a 7-respondent experiment that assessed absolute perceived quality and relative perceived quality of compressed images at different bitrates. In the absolute perceived quality assessment, respondents were shown uncompressed images and asked to score the image on a 5-point Likert scale. Next, compressed sets of images were presented to the participant, who selected the one image that they preferred the most. Bae *et al.* discovered that as bitrates decrease, respondents preferred to maintain image quality by selecting a lower image resolution. Respondents were willing to accept an increase in image distortion (compression noise) introduced by the coding algorithms when shown an image at smaller spatial resolutions.

A similar research topic has been conducted to understand how varying frame rate and display size of ASL video affects comprehension when shown on a computer. Hooper *et al.* [12] conducted a subjective study to determine if varying frame rate and display size of ASL video would impact learning comprehension. Their study investigated three frame rates (6, 12, and 18 fps) and three video display sizes (240×180, 320×240, and 480×360) with the bitrate for each video held constant at 700 kbps. They found that the display size of video did not affect comprehension, but varying the frame rates did. Our study is different than Hooper *et al.*'s because we are interested in comprehension of video at bitrates ten times less than what they used in their study and transmitting smaller spatial resolutions at a constant frame rate. Our previous research on MobileASL [5] has investigated varying frame rates [6,26] for data transmission and will not be elaborated on. We expand by varying spatial resolutions and bitrates to investigate subjective video quality preferences and comprehension all while comparing these results to PSNR measurements.

3. PSNR CURVES

Selecting a specific spatial resolution and bitrate combination to transmit video on MobileASL is important because there are tradeoffs with computational complexity, video quality, and resource availability on a cell phone such as battery life and data rate consumption. Larger video resolutions and higher bitrates result in higher video quality at the expense of increased computational power to transmit the data in real time. Before we can investigate how resource allocation is affected by video transmission, we need to determine at which bitrates and spatial resolutions we can get high enough video quality for intelligible conversations.

Despite the fact that PSNR may not be suitable for measuring subjective video quality, it still is a reasonable measurement of video quality when used across the same content [25]. We calculated PSNR of two different spatial resolutions (192×140 and 320×240 pixels) and 15 bitrates (10-150 kbps in increments of 10 kbps) of the same ASL video. The smaller spatial resolution was transmitted at 192×140 pixels and then enlarged and displayed at 320×240 pixels using bilinear interpolation [27] before PSNR was calculated.

The same 12-second video clip of a local deaf woman signing at her natural signing pace with a stationary background was used in the calculation of PSNR. The video was recorded at 320×240 pixels at 15 fps. Duplicate videos were created at the smaller spatial resolution before calculating the PSNR. The x264 codec, an open source version of H.264 codec, was used to compress the videos at each spatial resolution and bitrate combination [3,24]. As Figure 2 demonstrates, the PSNR values for each spatial resolution increase monotonically with increasing bitrate.

We found that the PSNR curves demonstrated a crossover point where, at lower bitrates (40 kbps and below), the smaller spatial resolutions had higher PSNR values than the larger spatial resolution. Visual inspection of the same ASL video (displayed at the same size) transmitted at lower bitrates (10-40 kbps) showed more blocky artifacts in videos sent at 320×240 pixels than at 192×144. The crossover in the PSNR plots occurred because at very low bitrates, the higher resolution video is quantized more heavily and thus has very poor visual quality (such as blockiness and loss of fine details). The same videos at lower spatial resolutions are not quantized as heavily which results in higher measured video quality. As bitrates increase, the higher resolution has higher measured video quality than the smaller spatial resolutions. This is due to blurriness from enlarging the video. The crossover of PSNR curves has been found in other video compression techniques [16,19,29], but the results, to our knowledge, have not been used to evaluate human comprehension, which, along with subjective quality measures, is the focus of our online survey.

4. ONLINE SURVEY METHOD

From a technological perspective, transmitting video at the smaller spatial resolution and at the lowest bitrates takes the least amount of computational power and resources; however, without feedback from users, we cannot confirm that sign language communication with this video is intelligible.

We created and deployed a national three-part online survey to investigate user preferences and comprehension when varying the bitrates (10-60 kbps in increments of 10 kbps) and spatial resolutions (192×144 and 320×240) of ASL video. We did not consider bitrates higher than 60 kbps since the larger spatial

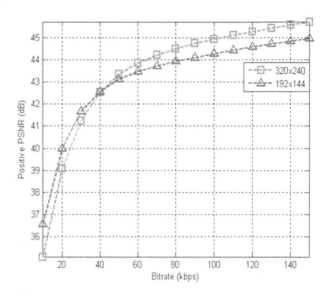

Figure 2: PSNR(dB) *vs.* Bitrate (kbps) for spatial resolutions displayed at 320×240 pixels. Higher PSNR means higher objective video quality. Whether it means higher subjective perception of quality is a topic of this research.

resolution always had higher video quality than the smaller spatial resolution.

The online survey began by asking participants to self-report their fluency in ASL. The survey asked different questions depending on the response to this question. Part 1 was a paired-comparison experiment which investigated the subjective video quality preferences of ASL speakers and non-ASL speakers (see Figure 3). Part 2 was a single-stimulus experiment which examined comprehension of ASL video of varying bitrates and spatial resolutions (ASL speakers only) (see Figures 4 and 5). Finally, part 3 asked demographic questions.

To determine how subjective video quality preference differs between ASL speakers and non-ASL speakers, it was important to get an equal number of ASL and non-ASL speaking respondents. We selected an online survey over a laboratory study because an online survey is accessible to most people with Internet access, so more respondents could be included from across the nation.

4.1 Videos Used in Online Survey
4.1.1 Videos in Part 1
The same 12-second video clips used to measure PSNR (see section 3, above) of ASL video were used in part 1 of the survey. A 12-second video duration was used because it was long enough for respondents to make a video preference selection while keeping the overall survey manageable to complete in 4-7 minutes. Recall that all videos were transmitted at their respective spatial resolution (192×144 and 320×240) at varied bitrates, and then displayed at 320×240 pixels (with the smaller spatial resolution enlarged using bilinear interpolation).

4.1.2 Videos in Part 2
Twelve different video clips of the same local deaf woman signing different short stories at her natural signing pace were used.

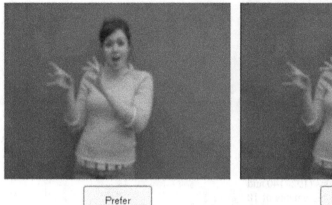

Prefer   Prefer

Figure 3: Screenshot of one 12-second video pair from the paired-comparison experiment. Respondents selected which video they preferred to watch.

All videos were recorded with the same parameters listed in section 3. Each video was again truncated to the first 12-seconds of the story to keep the overall duration of the survey manageable and to test respondents with comprehension question about that segment. A duplicate set of the twelve videos were created and downsampled to a spatial resolution of 192×144 pixels. Next, the *x*264 codec was used to compress the videos at the six different bitrates [3,24].

4.2 Paired-Comparison Experiment
As Figure 3 demonstrates, part 1 of the survey used a paired-comparison method with simultaneous presentation as described in prior work [14]. For each of the six bitrates, a pair of videos

Q1) I found the video <u>easy</u> to comprehend.

Strongly Agree	○
Agree	○
Somewhat Agree	○
Neutral	○
Somewhat Disagree	○
Disagree	○
Strongly Disagree	○

Next >>

Figure 4: Q1 was a 7-point Likert scale for the ease of comprehension. Q1 was shown after the video was removed from the screen.

Q2) What was the happiest day in her life?

Camping	○
Graduation	○
Seeing a movie	○
Going on vacation	○

Next >>

Figure 5: Q2 asked a simple comprehension question pertaining to the video shown. Q2 was shown after Q1 was removed from the screen.

(each at the two different spatial resolutions) was shown. This yields six pair-wise combinations, one at each bitrate. The videos were shown side-by-side on the same screen with synchronous playback. Respondents could watch the video pairs repeatedly until a selection was made. Each of the six pairs was presented twice, switching the left/right display order to counterbalance and prevent bias from video placement. None of the test pairs contain videos at different bitrates, since previous research [5] confirmed that higher bitrates were always selected when given the option. This study design resulted in twelve trials per participant. Randomization was done with an algorithm that randomly selected the next video after eliminating the previous selection. During each trial, respondents were asked to select the video whose quality they preferred. To make sure respondents watched the video pairs, they could not select a preferred video until four seconds after a video pair began playing. In addition to recording which video the participant preferred, we also recorded the amount of time it took for a participant to select his or her choice.

4.3 Single Stimulus Experiment
A single stimulus experiment, as described in prior work [14], was used to evaluate comprehension of ASL video transmitted and encoded at each combination of spatial resolution and bitrate. These combinations yield twelve videos in the single stimulus experiment. Before beginning part 2, they were shown a practice video to familiarize themselves with the layout.

Each video was shown once (without the option to repeat the video), then removed from the screen and replaced by two questions shown one at a time. Figure 4 is an example of question 1 which asked the participant to rate their agreement/disagreement on a 7-point Likert scale with the statement, "I found the video easy to comprehend." The 7-point Likert scale was shown in descending vertical order from *strongly agree* to *strongly disagree*. The word 'difficult' replaced the word 'easy' for every other respondent, but always remained the same within a respondent. This approach prevented bias from respondents' interpretations of "easy" or "difficult." Figure 5 is an example of question 2 which asked a trivial comprehension question pertaining to the video shown. Since the ease/difficulty of comprehension varied with each 12-second video segment, the comprehension questions were only used as a way to confirm that the participant had been paying attention to the video.

4.4 Demographic Questions

After respondents completed parts 1 and 2, they were asked background questions which included: "What is your age?"; "What is your gender?"; "Do you own a cell phone or Blackberry?"; "Do you text message on the cell phone or Blackberry?"; "If applicable, what operating system is on your cell phone?"; "Do you video chat?"; "If applicable, which video chat program do you use?"

ASL speaking respondents were also asked: "If applicable, how many years have you spoken ASL?"; "If applicable, from whom did you learn ASL?"; "What language do you prefer to communicate with family?"; "What language do you prefer to communicate with friends?"; "Are you Deaf?"; "Do you use a video phone?"; "Do you use video relay services?"

5. RESULTS

Recall, at the start of the survey, respondents self-declared their fluency in ASL. In part 1 of the survey, we investigated (1) the preferences of both ASL speakers and non-ASL speakers for spatial resolution as bitrates varied, and (2) how subjective video quality preferences compared to measured PSNR values. In part 2 of our survey, we were interested in whether comprehension of ASL video content by respondents fluent in ASL was affected by transmission bitrate and spatial resolution.

A total of 103 respondents completed the survey; however, in part 1, we eliminated results from those who used internet browsers incompatible with our survey. We kept results from respondents who completed part 1 but failed to finish the entire survey (part 2 and demographics sections). In part 1, we analyzed data from 95 respondents: 56 ASL speakers (30 men, 15 women, and 11 who did not specify) and 39 non-ASL speakers (13 men, 25 women, and 1 who did not specify). Their age ranged from 18-71 years old (mean: 37 years). Of the respondents who self-reported fluency in ASL, 41 were deaf, 35 self-declared using ASL as their daily language, and the number of years they have spoken ASL ranged from 3-58 years (mean: 26 years). Seventy-eight respondents (43

ASL, 35 non-ASL) owned a cell phone, and 72 of those cell phone owners (43 ASL, 29 non-ASL) used it to text message.

For part 2 of the survey, we analyzed data from 53 respondents (33 men, 18 women, and 2 who did not specify). Their age ranged from 18-71 years old (mean: 27 years) and all but five respondents were deaf. The self-reported number of years they have spoken ASL ranged from 3-58 years (mean: 27 years). Forty-one respondents indicated they use ASL as their daily language. Finally, 48 respondents indicated they own a cell phone, with all of them using text messaging, and all but three respondents said they use video phones and/or video relay services.

5.1 Subjective Video Quality Preferences

Respondents were asked to select which video they preferred when presented with two videos playing simultaneously side-by-side at the same bitrates. Figure 6 shows the percentage of people *vs.* bitrate who selected the 320×240 spatial resolution over the 192×144 spatial resolution by ASL and non-ASL speaking respondents.

A one-sample Chi-Square test was performed to test whether the proportion of subjects who picked the 320×240 spatial resolution *vs.* the 192×144 spatial resolution was significantly different than chance at each bitrate (10-60 kbps in increments of 10 kbps). Recall that both videos were *displayed* at the same spatial resolution (320×240).

At 10 kbps, both subject groups overwhelmingly preferred the video quality of the lower 192×144 spatial resolution over the 320×240 spatial resolution ($\chi^2_{1,N=95}$=97.347, $p<.0001$). At transmission bitrates of 20 kbps and higher, both subject groups preferred the video quality of the 320×240 spatial resolution ($\chi^2_{1,N=95}$=68.40, $p<.0001$).

5.2 Video Comprehension

Respondents were asked to rate their perceived ease/difficulty of comprehending each of the twelve videos on a 7-point Likert scale. Recall that the wording of this question alternated *between* respondents, but remained the same *within* each participant.

Nonparametric analyses were used to analyze our 7-point Likert scale responses for rating the perceived ease/difficulty of comprehension. Since we gathered ordinal and dichotomous response data, a Friedman test [9] was used to analyze the main effect of bitrate and spatial resolution on comprehension. Separate Wilcoxon tests [33] were performed to investigate the effect of spatial resolution *within* each bitrate.

The Friedman test indicated a significant main effect of spatial resolution on video comprehension ($\chi^2_{1,N=53}$=8.33, $p<.01$). The Friedman test also indicated a significant main effect of bitrate on video comprehension ($\chi^2_{5,N=53}$=146.15, $p<.0001$).

Wilcoxon tests with Bonferroni correction were performed *within* each bitrate to identify the effect of spatial resolution on comprehension. Of the 53 respondents, 24 were asked to rate the difficulty of comprehension and 29 were asked to rate the ease of comprehension. The results of the Wilcoxon test for the perceived ease/difficulty of comprehension are presented separately, below.

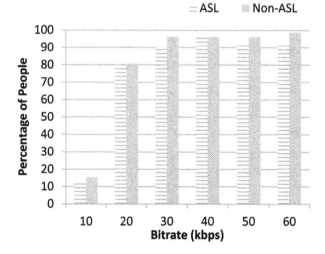

Figure 6: Percentage of People *vs.* Bitrate (kbps) who selected 320×240 instead of 192×144 spatial resolution in the paired-comparison experiment. Data is from 56 ASL speakers and 39 Non-ASL speakers.

Table 1: Mean Likert Scale responses (1-7) for difficulty of comprehending video quality. Note *lower* Likert scores correspond to *less* perceived difficulty.

| | Spatial Resolution | | | |
| | 320×240 | | 192×144 | |
Bitrate	Mean	Std. Error	Mean	Std. Error
10	6.00	0.28	**5.71**	0.24
20	**4.38**	0.35	4.54	0.29
30	3.83	0.33	**3.54**	0.32
40	**2.75**	0.33	3.79	0.33
50	**2.75**	0.33	3.42	0.31
60	**2.67**	0.30	3.41	0.35

Table 2: Mean Likert Scale responses (1-7) for ease of comprehending video quality. Note *higher* Likert scores correspond to *easier* perceived comprehension.

| | Spatial Resolution | | | |
| | 320×240 | | 192×144 | |
Bitrate	Mean	Std. Error	Mean	Std. Error
10	2.90	0.31	**3.55**	0.28
20	**5.10**	0.29	4.72	0.29
30	5.34	0.26	**5.48**	0.26
40	**5.90**	0.25	5.41	0.23
50	**6.27**	0.19	5.48	0.22
60	**6.34**	0.14	5.62	0.20

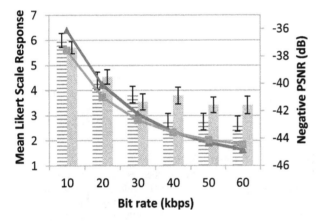

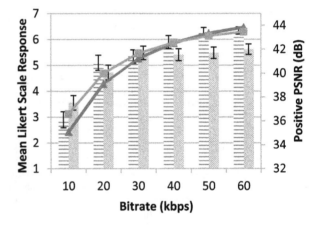

Figure 7: Double *y*-axis plot of 7-point Likert scale. Negative PSNR values of spatial resolutions and bitrates. Lower Likert scores correspond to less difficulty and lower PSNR values correspond to higher video quality. Notice a negative PSNR crossover point occurs at 40 kbps.

Figure 8: Double *y*-axis plot of 7-point Likert scale. Positive PSNR values of spatial resolution and bitrate. Higher Likert scores correspond to more ease and higher PSNR values correspond to higher video quality. Notice a positive PSNR crossover point occurs at 40 kbps.

5.2.1 Rating Difficulty of Comprehension

Recall that about half of the respondents saw a 7-point Likert scale concerning the *difficulty* of comprehension, ranging from 1 (strongly disagree), *i.e.*, less difficult to comprehend, to 7 (strongly agree), *i.e.*, more difficult to comprehend. Table 1 shows the mean Likert scale response for the difficulty of comprehending the ASL video transmitted at each bitrate and spatial resolution and displayed at 320×240 pixels.

Figure 7 is a double *y*-axis plot of the mean Likert responses and the negative PSNR values for each bitrate and spatial resolution. Notice that the PSNR values are *negative*, where *lower* values correspond to *higher video quality*.

Comprehension was significantly less difficult at 60 kbps for the 320×240 spatial resolution than the 192×144 spatial resolution (Z=35.0, *p*<.01). However, changing the spatial resolution within other bitrates did not indicate more difficulty in comprehension.

For example, Table 1 and Figure 7 indicated a large difference of mean Likert scores at 40 kbps, but changing the spatial resolution within that bitrate was not significant in affecting the difficulty of comprehension (Z=48.5, *n.s.*).

5.2.2 Rating Ease of Comprehension

Recall that about half the respondents saw a 7-point Likert scale concerning the *ease* of comprehension, ranging from 1 (strongly disagree), *i.e.*, less easy to comprehend, to 7 (strongly agree), *i.e.*, more easy to comprehend. Table 2 shows the mean Likert scale response for the ease of comprehending ASL video transmitted at each bitrate and spatial resolution and displayed at 320×240 pixels.

Figure 8 is a double *y*-axis plot of the mean Likert responses and the positive PSNR values for each bitrate and spatial resolution. Notice that the PSNR values are *positive*, where *higher* values correspond to *higher video quality*.

Transmitting at 320×240 spatial resolution rather than at a 192×144 spatial resolution at 50 and 60 kbps was significantly easier to comprehend (Z=100.0, $p<.001$ and Z=88.5, $p<.001$, respectively). This result is also shown in the PSNR curve in Figure 8; at 50 kbps and 60 kbps, the positive PSNR values were higher for the larger spatial resolution. However, changing the spatial resolution within other bitrates did not make the content easier to understand. Even though Table 2 and Figure 8 indicate a large difference of mean Likert score at 10 kbps, changing the spatial resolution within that bitrate was not significant in affecting comprehension (Z=45.5, *n.s.*).

6. DISCUSSION

We compared the video preference results from part 1 to PSNR measurements, which reinforced that PSNR may not accurately reflect subjective video quality. The PSNR values suggested that bitrates at 40 kbps and lower spatial resolution of 192×144 pixels had higher quality than the 320×240 spatial resolution; however, subjective user preferences revealed that at 20 kbps and higher, the larger spatial resolution was preferred. This finding is not unexpected since PSNR does not account for compression artifacts (blockiness and Gibbs's phenomena [23]). Also, visual inspection of each pair of videos showed that at bitrates 20 kbps and higher, enlarging the smaller spatial resolution to display at 320×240 pixels caused the video to appear more blurry than when simply transmitting the larger spatial resolution.

One might expect that the same bitrates and spatial resolutions indicated as preferred in part 1 would similarly influence comprehension of content; that is, that respondents would indicate greater ease (or less difficulty) of comprehension when shown video at a 320×240 spatial resolution at bitrates of 20 kbps and higher. However, transmitting either spatial resolution sent at 10-50 kbps had no effect on making comprehension more difficult. At 60 kbps only, respondents expressed that transmitting the larger spatial resolution made the content significantly less difficult to comprehend. This result was the same among the respondents who were asked to rate the ease (rather than the difficulty) of comprehension. Neither of the two spatial resolutions, at bitrates of 10 to 40 kbps, made comprehending the video easier. However, at 50 and 60 kbps, respondents did indicate that transmitting the larger spatial resolution made comprehension easier. When comparing these findings to the PSNR curves (Figures 8 and 9), we see that PSNR measurements may accurately reflect the perceived ease/difficulty at which respondents rated comprehension of ASL video. The PSNR curves showed a threshold where at 50 kbps and higher, transmitting the larger spatial resolution produces better video quality than transmitting and enlarging the smaller spatial resolution. The results of the survey agree with this and also indicate that at 50 kbps and higher, video comprehension was made easier.

These results suggesting that PSNR may be a reliable measure for comprehensibility of ASL video may be valuable in selecting the spatial resolution and bitrate for mobile video telephony. Having knowledge of how PSNR relates to comprehension, especially for sign language video, can influence how video is transmitted on mobile phones using 3G networks. When possible, selecting the smaller spatial resolution at the PSNR crossover point provides intelligible video while keeping computational complexity and cost of video transmission low. For MobileASL, transmitting video at 40 kbps at 192×144 spatial resolution would be sufficient to hold an intelligible conversation while saving limited computing resources.

7. CONCLUSION AND FUTURE WORK

In this work, we investigated how varying bitrates and spatial resolutions of ASL video affect subjective video quality (for both self-reported ASL speakers and non-ASL speakers) and comprehension of video content (ASL speakers only). We found that our respondents' preferences for video spatial resolutions at different bitrates did not agree with the results of the calculated PSNR values of measured video quality. Whether or not respondents were fluent in ASL did not impact their preference for bitrate and spatial resolution; both groups selected the 320×240 spatial resolution over the 192×144 spatial resolution at 20 kbps and higher. However, we did find a main effect where changing the spatial resolution and bitrate significantly impacted perceived ease/difficulty of comprehension. Closer inspection of which spatial resolution and bitrates significantly impacted comprehension revealed that the 320×240 spatial resolution sent at 50-60 kbps improved the ease of comprehension. A notable finding was that PSNR may correlate with rating the perceived ease/difficulty of comprehension at higher bitrates and spatial resolutions. Therefore, the recommendation for MobileASL is to transmit video at 192×144 spatial resolution at 40 kbps to provide intelligible sign language video while keeping computational costs low.

For future work, we would like to see how our findings can be applied to improve consumption of mobile phone resources such as battery life and data consumption of metered cell phone plans. We are particularly interested to learn if behavioral changes occur when users are aware of how they consume resources and, if given the option, would users elect to lower bitrates and spatial resolution to gain more battery life or conversation time.

9. ACKNOWLEDGEMENTS

Thanks to Anna Cavender, Jessica Belwood, Frank Ciaramello, Katie O'Leary, Sorenson VRS, and our respondents. This work was supported by the National Science Foundation under grant IIS-0811884.

10. REFERENCES

[1] Apple FaceTime. Retrieved 4 29, 2011, from Apple FaceTime: http://www.apple.com/mac/facetime/

[2] *MobileASL. University of Washington.* (2011). Retrieved from http://mobileasl.cs.washington.edu/

[3] Aimar, L., Merritt, L., Petit, E., Chem, M., Clay, J., Rullgrd, M., et al. (2005). x264 - a free h264/AVC encoder.

[4] Bae, S., Pappas, T., & Juang, B. (2006). Spatial Resolution and Quantization Noise Tradeoffs for Scalable Image Compression. *IEEE International Conference Acoustics, Speech, and Signal Processing.*

[5] Cavender, A., Ladner, R., & Riskin, E. (2006). MobileASL: Intelligibility of Sign Language Video as Constrained by Mobile Phone Technology. *Proceedings of ASSETS 2006: The Eighth International ACM SIGACCESS Conference on Computers and Accessibility.* Portland, OR.

[6] Cherniavsky, N., Chon, J., Wobbrock, J., Ladner, R., & Riskin, E. (2007). Variable Frame Rate for Low Power Mobile Sign Language Communication. *Proceedings of ASSETS 2007: The Ninth International ACM SIGACCESS*

Conference on Computers and Accessibility, (pp. 163-170). Tempe, AZ.

[7] Ciaramello, F. & Hemami, S. (2011, January). Quality versus Intelligibility: Studying Human Preferences for American Sign Language Video. *Proceedings in SPIE Volume 7865, Human Vision and Electronic Imaging.*

[8] Feghali, R., Speranza, F., Wang, D., & Vincent, A. (2007, March). Video Quality Metric for Bit Rate Control via Joint Adjustment of Quantization and Frame Rate. *53*(IEEE Transactions on Broadcasting).

[9] Friedman, M. (1937). The use of ranks to avoid the assumption of normality implicit in the analysis of variance. *Journal of the American Statistical Association 32* (200), 675-701

[10] *Fring*. Retrieved 4 29, 2011, from http://www.fring.com/

[11] Girod, B. (1993). What's wrong with mean-squared error? *Digital images and human vision*, 207-220.

[12] Hooper, S., Miller, C., Rose, S., & Veletsianos, G. (2007). The Effects of Digital Video Quality on Learner Comprehension in an American Sign Language Assessment Environment. *Sign Language Studies, 8*(Sign Language Studies), 42-58.

[13] Huynh-Thu, Q., & Ghanbari, M. (2008). Scope of validity of PSNR in image/video quality assessment. The Institution of Engineering Technology.

[14] ITU. (September 1999). p.910: Subjective video quality assessment methods for multimedia applications.

[15] Jumiski-Pyykko. (2005). Evaluation of Subjective Video Quality of Mobile Devices. *Multimedia Proceedings of the 13th annual ACM international conference on Multimedia .* Singapore.

[16] Lin, W., & Dong, L. (2006, September). Adaptive Downsampling to Improve Image Compression at Low Bit Rates. *IEEE Transcations on Image Processing. 15.*

[17] Masry, M., & Hemami, S. (2003, January). CVQE: A metric for continuous video quality evaluation at low rates. *Proceedings in SPIE: Human Vision and Electronic Imaging.*

[18] Nemethova, A., Ries, M., Zavodsky, M., & Rupp, M. (2006). PSNR-Based Estimation of Subjective Time-Variant Video Quality for Mobiles. *Measurement of Audio and Video Quality in Networks.*

[19] Nguyen, V., Tan, Y., Z, & Lin, W. (2006). Adaptive Downsampling/Upsamping for better video compression at low bit rate. *IEEE International Symposium on Circuits and Systems.*

[20] *Purple VRS on Your Devices.* (Purple Communications.) Retrieved 7 31, 2011, from http://www.purple.us/

[21] *Qik.* (Qik, Inc.) Retrieved 4 29, 2011, from http://qik.com/

[22] Reiter, U., & Korhonen, J. (2009). Comparing Apples and Oranges: Subjective Quality Assessment of Streamed Video with Different Types of Distortion. (IEEE).

[23] Radaelli-Sanchez, Baraniuk, R. (2010). Gibbs's Phenomena. http://cns.org/content/m10092/latest

[24] Richardson, I. (2004). vocdex: H.264 tutorial white papers.

[25] Thu, H., & Ghanbari, M. (2008). Scope of Validity of PSNR in image/video quality assessment. *44.*

[26] Tran, J. J., Johnson, T. W., Kim, J., Rodriguez, R., Yin, S., Riskin, E., Ladner, R., Wobbrock. J., (2010). A Web-Based User Survey for Evaluating Power Saving Strategies for Deaf Users of MobileASL. *Proceedings of ASSETS 2010: The 12th International ACM SIGACCESS Conference on Computers and Accessibility.* Orlando, FL.

[27] Vision Sytems Design. Retrieved 5 03, 2011. Understanding image-interpolation techniques.

[28] VQEG. (2003, September). Final report from the video quality experts group on the validation of objective models of video.

[29] Wang, R. Chien, M., Chang, P. Adaptive Down-Samping Video Coding. VQEG. (2010). *Proceedings in SPIE 7542.*

[30] Wang, Z., Bovik, A., & Lu, L. (2002). Why is Image Quality Assessment so Difficult? *IEEE Acoustic, Speech, and Signal Processing.*

[31] Wang, Z., Lu, L., & Bovik, A. (2004, February). Video quality assessment based on structural distortion measurement. *19*(Signal Processing: Image Communication special issue on Objective video quality metrics), 121-132.

[32] Wiegang, T., Schwarz, H., Joch, A., Kossentini, F., & Sullivan, G. (2003). Rate-constrained coder control and comparison of video coding standards. *IEEE Transactions Circuits Systems Video Technology, 13*(7), 688-703.

[33] Wilcoxon, F. (1945). Individual comparisons by ranking methods. *Biometrics Bulletin 1* (6), 80-83.

[34] Winkler, S., & Faller, C. (2005). Audiovisual Quality Evaluation of Low-Bitrate Video. *SPIE/IS&T Human Vision and Electronic Imaging, 5666*, pp. 139-148. San Jose.

[35] Winkler, S., & Faller, C. (2005). Maximizing Audiovisual Quality at Low Bitrates. *Workshop on Video Processing an Quality Metrics for Consumer Electronics.* Scottsdale, AZ.

[36] *ZVRS.* (ZVRS Communication Service for the Deaf, Inc.) Retrieved 7 31, 2011, from http://www.zvrs.com/z-series/

Annotation-based Video Enrichment for Blind People: A Pilot Study on the Use of Earcons and Speech Synthesis

Benoît Encelle
Université de Lyon,
CNRS Université Lyon 1, LIRIS,
UMR5205, F-69622, France
benoit.encelle@liris.cnrs.fr

Magali Ollagnier-Beldame
Université de Lyon,
CNRS Université Lyon 1, LIRIS,
UMR5205, F-69622, France
mbeldame@liris.cnrs.fr

Stéphanie Pouchot
Université de Lyon,
Université Lyon 1, ELICO,
EA 4147, F-69622, France
stephanie.pouchot@univ-lyon1.fr

Yannick Prié
Université de Lyon,
CNRS Université Lyon 1, LIRIS,
UMR5205, F-69622, France
yannick.prie@liris.cnrs.fr

ABSTRACT

Our approach to address the question of online video accessibility for people with sensory disabilities is based on video annotations that are rendered as video enrichments during the playing of the video. We present an exploratory work that focuses on video accessibility for *blind people* with *audio enrichments* composed of speech synthesis and earcons (i.e. nonverbal audio messages). Our main results are that earcons can be used together with speech synthesis to enhance understanding of videos; that earcons should be accompanied with explanations; and that a potential side effect of earcons is related to video rhythm perception.

Categories and Subject Descriptors

H.5.2 [**User Interfaces**]: Auditory (non-speech) feedback, Evaluation/methodology; K.4.2 [**Social Issues**]: Assistive technologies for persons with disabilities.

General Terms

Design, Experimentation, Human Factors

Keywords

Video accessibility, accessibility for blind people, video annotation, video enrichment, audio notification.

1. INTRODUCTION

Accessibility to digital information for all, including people with disabilities, is one of the major social challenges of our society. Laws were voted to support this idea, e.g. "section 508" in the USA or a 2005 law in France. The United Nations also adopted the Convention on the Rights of Persons with Disabilities [31] in 2006. However, while efforts have been made to improve the accessibility of some types of electronic content (e.g. global accessibility of Web pages – Web Accessibility Initiative [33]), other types still suffer from a lack of accessibility solutions. As the amount of video available on the Web is continually growing and as its consumption is continuously increasing, video content appears as a first-choice medium to share information. In this context, the 21st Century Communications and Video Accessibility act signed in October 2010 into US law promotes expanded access to internet-based video programming. New technical solutions that allow people with sensory disabilities (hearing/visually impaired, deaf and blind people) to access this kind of content need therefore to be developed.

The ACAV project (Collaborative Annotation for Video Accessibility) addresses these problems by exploring how accessibility of online videos can be improved by developing free Web applications intended for a large audience. Our approach is based on video annotations rendered as video enrichments during the playing of the video stream. In this article we present an exploratory work that focuses on video accessibility for *blind people* with *audio enrichments* composed of speech synthesis and earcons (i.e. nonverbal audio messages). Our main results are that earcons can be used together with speech synthesis to enhance understanding of videos; that earcons should be accompanied with explanations; and that a potential side effect of earcons is related to video rhythm perception.

Section 2 presents the scientific and technical context of the ACAV project. The related work (section 3) focuses on blind people and audio enrichments. Section 4 deals with questions concerning information access and understanding, associated with audio enriched videos. Section 5 introduces our technical proposal for enriching video with audio elements –including earcons– and focuses on the experiments we conducted with blind people in order to determine the utility and the usability of these earcons.

2. CONTEXT

2.1 Video accessibility and video enrichment

Classical techniques for improving video accessibility for people with sensory disabilities include the audio-description of key visual elements for visually impaired/blind people, and the subtitling/close-captioning and/or the sign translation of key audio elements for hearing impaired or deaf people. Deaf-blind people need a combination of these two techniques and, in some cases, with descriptions presented on a Braille display.

Concerning particular cognitive and neurological disabilities [32], some individuals may process information aurally better than by reading text: audio descriptions of text embedded in a video can be needed. For autism, the content should be customizable and well designed so as to not be overwhelming. Media adaptation has then to focus on the purpose of the content and has to provide alternative content in a clear and concise manner. Such alternative content could for instance present the key points of the video (e.g. key educational messages, important verbal communications, etc.). Another issue for autism could be to present social stories (a series of pictures, supported by simple text to describe the actions, behavior, and outcomes that some quite visual individuals might learn effectively from). A combination of pictures and synchronized text or audio could then be added to the video in order to improve its accessibility.

For all these disabilities, additional content has to be associated to the whole video or to some parts of it and presented over it using one or several modalities. We call this approach *video enrichment*. Its underlying concepts and the associated formats, tools and recommendations are detailed in the following section.

2.2 Enriching videos

Enriched videos are videos augmented with various elements, such as captions, images, audio, hyperlinks, etc. The goals are here either to *translate* parts of its content so that people who cannot fully understand it visually or aurally can apprehend it; or to *complement* it with additional information in order to enhance the watching experience. Two types of users are basically involved in a video enrichment process: users who enrich videos, namely the enrichment producers, and end-users who watch enriched videos.

Several technical recommendations, initiatives and formats related to videos enrichment have been issued recently. The Web Accessibility Initiative (WAI) advocates in one recommendation (WCAG) [34] the development of different versions of given temporal content, e.g. audio versions using audio-description of visual content, etc. Mozilla Foundation [26] advocates the usage of the Ogg open video format with multiplexed specialized tracks for video accessibility. In the same way, the HTML Accessibility Task Force suggests adding several tracks to a video content, e.g. a subtitle track, an audio-description track, etc. These "enrichment" tracks would be represented as HTML 5 *Track* elements inside a *Media* element (*Video* or *Audio* element). As an alternative to this expected notion of track in HTML 5, SMIL (Synchronized Multimedia Integration Language) can be used for synchronizing different multimedia contents (e.g. a video synchronized with an audio file containing an audio-description and with a subtitle file).

Full-featured tools for making accessible video are not yet available. Several subtitling tools nevertheless exist, such as MAGPie, Nico Nico Douga or YouTube subtitler[1]. Tools for audio-describing visual content are even less common, though MAGPie permits the recording of audio elements while playing the video.

2.3 Annotation based video enrichment

Most of the preceding formats or tools use "direct" enrichments: the added elements are presented without a change in their original modalities (e.g. by captioning a textual element or playing a sound element). Our approach is different in that it separates the content used for enrichment from its rendering. As a result, not only "direct" enrichments but also "indirect" enrichments (e.g. speech synthesizing a textual content) can be provided. In our opinion, this separation –similar to the one suggested in the document-engineering field– has good properties. It can for instance foster innovation by allowing different people independently create content or content rendering, for example in a collaborative process. It also allows performing "live" video enrichment according to end-user preferences that can change during the rendering itself, paving the way to real-time adapted enrichments.

Accordingly, the ACAV project general workflow is made up of two main steps: an annotation step and a rendering one (cf. Figure

---

[1] http://ncam.wgbh.org/invent_build/web_multimedia/tools-guidelines/magpie
http://www.nicovideo.jp
http://yt-subs.appspot.com

1). The first step consists in annotating the video. An *annotation* is defined as *any information associated to a fragment of a video*.

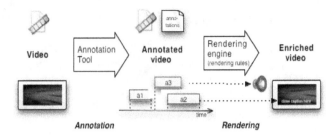

Figure 1: annotating videos for enriching their playing

For instance, a text describing an action can be associated to a temporal fragment (defined by two timecodes) during which this action occurs. The second step consists in rendering annotation data in order to enrich the video. Annotation rendering for accessibility presents the content of an annotation using one or several adequate presentation modalities. As a result, a video can be enriched using three main kinds of elements: visual enrichments (captions, still images, video fragments, etc.), audio enrichments (voices, sounds) or tactile enrichments (using vibrating or Braille devices).

Before we present the data models used for representing the contents of enrichments and their renderings, we first describe a general user–oriented overview of the ACAV system (Figure 2).

2.4 Towards collaborative video enrichment

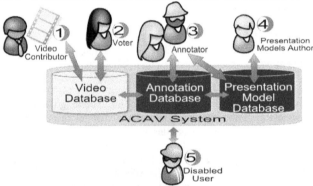

Figure 2. ACAV system and users

The ACAV system defines several workflows that were initially defined with accessibility experts and sensory disabled people. A vote system allows determining a priority order for videos that have to be made accessible (i.e. enriched) for various audience(s) (visually disabled and/or hearing disabled people). Disabled users, their friends/relatives can thus use this vote system (2). As a result, a producer of enrichments (more precisely here an annotator) can view this list of requests and start the annotation step. She also can invite other annotators (i.e. collaborators) to help her (3). After this stage, she can specify a presentation model for rendering these annotations for a given disability. She also can share her annotations with other people, for instance authors of presentation models (4).

Next, users with disabilities can query the video database and find enriched videos adapted to their interests and disabilities, view enriched videos and personalize the presentation of some kinds of enrichments (e.g. change the average rate of the voice synthesis, enlarge font sizes, etc.) (5). If an end-user encounters troubles during the visualization of an enriched video, he can use the feedback system to inform enrichment producers (back to 3/4).

2.5 Annotation and rendering models

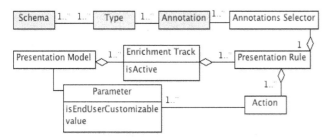

Figure 3. Main elements of annotation and rendering models

The annotation model used in ACAV (Figure 3, grey) is an adaptation of a more general model for video annotation proposed in [1]. *Annotations* are the key elements of the model. Basically, an annotation has a unique id, a content and is associated to a temporal interval. *Annotation Types* classify annotations by describing their semantics and constraining and structuring their content. Each annotation is associated to a given type (e.g. annotations of type *Character*, of type *Action*, etc.). An *Annotation Schema* embodies a particular annotation practice and is composed of several types. For example, one could define a schema for describing the dialogues of a video, another schema for the musical part, and yet another one for the shots.

The annotation-rendering model (Figure 3, white) is based on the notion of enrichment tracks (cf. section 2.2) to describe the way annotations are to be rendered. A *presentation model* contains one or several enrichment tracks. An *enrichment track* contains one or several presentation rules. A *presentation rule* is made up of two parts: an annotation selector and one or several presentation actions. An *annotation selector* is the expression of constraints that filter the annotation set. These constraints could be structural (for selecting annotations associated with one or several schemas, types) and/or intrinsic (for selecting annotations based on properties of their content). A *presentation action* indicates the modality that has to be used for rendering the contents of selected annotations. Possible presentation actions are:

- For visual disabilities-adapted renderings: *oralize* (using a text-to-speech engine), *display in Braille* (integral or contracted form), *use a Braille Symbol*, *play a sound*
- For hearing disabilities-adapted renderings: *display as a subtitle, display as a close-caption, display a shape*, etc.

A presentation action can be parameterized and related values could be, if indicated, end-user customizable. Enrichment tracks and their parameters are all that end-users can manipulate by activating or deactivating tracks or changing their parameters.

3. RELATED WORK

Having presented our general approach for video enrichment for accessibility in the ACAV project, we focus here on audio enrichment for blind and visually impaired people.

Audio-description is a means of providing access to theatre, television and film for blind or visually impaired people. For videos, the audio-description process consists in describing the visual elements of a film to give essential keys for its understanding. The recorded text is aligned with gaps in the original soundtrack of the video, and mixed with it. The fundamentals of audio-description for theater can be found in [3]

and [28], while numerous standardization documents exist for video [19, 24, 27, 30]. [23] gives the core information categories that must be described for movies: *characters* (appearance/role) and their interrelations, *actions* and the *sets* used in the filming. They underline that the importance of the descriptions both depends on the type of the film and the time that is available for description.

Audio-description has its limits. First, not all the visual content is described. For instance visual editing information is generally not indicated despite the fact it can be important for understanding the story. Moreover, audio-description only uses the audio verbal modality. As a consequence, parallel communication possibilities offered by multimodal communications are unavailable. In addition, making an audio-description is money and time consuming (for instance, audio-describing a 90 min movie in France costs more than 5000 Euros (7300 USD) and takes one month). [22] also highlights the fact that audio-description should be personalized, contrary to a "one size fits all" approach, a remark that is coherent with the general approach of the ACAV project for video on the web accessibility.

Audio enrichments for the blind consist in the addition of audio information to a film sound track. Different kinds of enrichments can be added: pre-recorded audio files, vocal synthesis, or audio notifications (auditory icons and earcons). The E-inclusion project [8, 22] aims to assist humans in generating and rendering video description for people who are blind or visually impaired. The E-inclusion prototype uses computer-vision technologies to automatically extract visual content, associate textual descriptions and add them to the audio track with a synthetic voice [13]. This work is different from our: there are no annotation/presentation models, no usage of different modalities (E-inclusion only uses the vocal synthesis), and no usage of audio notifications.

Audio notifications. *Auditory icons* [15, 16] are everyday sounds that convey information about events by analogy to everyday sound-producing events (e.g. the sound of crumpling paper for indicating the event "trash can empty"). Good mappings between sounds and associated meanings should therefore be easy to learn and remember. However, auditory icons *"lack flexibility, as metaphoric mappings are not always easy to find"* [14] and *"can be confused with actual environmental sounds"* [10].

Earcons are defined in [4] as *"nonverbal audio messages used in the user-computer interface to provide information to the user about some computer object, operation or interaction"*. This definition is extended to *"abstract, musical tones that can be used in structured combinations to create auditory messages"*, *"composed of short, rhythmic sequences of pitches with variable intensity, timbre and register"*. The main advantage of earcons is their flexibility and the fact that they *"can be designed in families so that they represent hierarchies, by controlling or manipulating their different parameters (e.g. timbre and pitch)"*. However, earcons suffer from a lack of meaningful relationship with their referent: end-users have to learn and memorize mappings between sounds and associated meanings.

Audio notifications have to be sparingly used as they could cause annoyance if too frequent [5]. With regards to the learning of mappings between audio notifications and associated meanings, auditory icon notifications are generally found to be easier to learn and retain in comparison with earcon notifications [4,6,7,12,17,21]. Audio notifications have been used for *conveying information that has a strong spatial component* to blind and visually impaired people. For instance, they were used for improving orientation and mobility skills of blind people (in conjunction with haptic feedback) [29], for improving objects localization [11] or for enhancing accessibility to mathematical material such as equations with fractions (two dimensional objects) [25] or graphs [9] using "graph sonification". Audio notifications have been also frequently used for *improving accessibility of Human-Computer Interface components*: e.g. audio menus and scroll bars [35], mobile service notifications [14]. However, as far as we know, audio notifications have been never used to try to convey information related to videos.

4. QUESTIONS ASSOCIATED WITH THE USE OF AUDIO NOTIFICATIONS

Several general *perception issues* are related to the use of audio information for enriching videos, with regards to information access and understanding. First, *low level perception* issues are a) the need to assess the cognitive (over)load engendered by the added sounds, and b) the need to test their discriminability, i.e. the difference from the original soundtrack (important parameters for discrimination are volume, sound duration, etc.). These issues are all the more important when added audio information pertains to various semiotic modalities [2], such as audio linguistic (speech synthesis) or audio non linguistic (audio notifications). This is the case in our research where we hypothesize that using *bi-modal* video enrichments associating earcons with speech synthesis is possible.

Second, one important question we have to face concerns *high level perception*: *how to reach integrated perception* for the users? Audio enrichment of video needs to ensure that a) audio notifications help the understanding of the video, while at the same time, b) every enrichment (including audio notifications) is smoothly integrated into the whole so as to reach a "unity of the video support". Jaskanen [20] refers to the tension between these aims with the term 'paradox'. In our context, this tension can only be clarified by qualitative experiments.

Finally, we need to question *earcons' utility* for film enrichment, in relation to the kind of video information they are useful for (Characters? Actions? Sets?). Earcons are used in operating systems to represent specific and important events, such as the end of an operation or ruptures in a temporal stream (the arrival of a mail or chat message, an error, etc.). For video enrichment, we hypothesize that, and will try to assess whether, they are useful to transmit spatial and temporal information (here we will focus on set changes indicated by earcons).

5. EARCONS AND SPEECH SYNTHESIS FOR AUDIO ENRICHMENT

We carried out several experiments using a mixed approach, combining quantitative and qualitative methods. Using an inductive methodology, we worked step by step: the conclusions from a preliminary experiment allowed us to design a second experiment and to refine our results. Section 5.1 deals with the production of our experiments material (enriched video for the blind). Sections 5.2 and 5.3 present the preliminary and the principal experiments (all the experimental material is available at: http://www.advene.org/acav/assets11). All experiments were conducted using the Advene platform (advene.org).

5.1 Experimental material: enriched videos

We defined several presentation models (see section 2.5) upon one simple annotation schema in order to produce audio enriched videos for blind people. Annotation schemas indicate what to describe of the visual content of videos and rendering models specify means of presenting the resulting descriptions, as described below.

Annotation schema. Visual information is described in an annotation schema called *VisualBase* made up of the annotation types *Action* and *Set* (corresponding to the key visual information identified by [23] minus *Character*), complemented with a *TextOnScreen* annotation type to represent text appearing on the screen (e.g. opening or closing credits).

We used the *VisualBase* schema to annotate the videos we used in the tests. We used two short humorous videos V1 (3') and V2 (1'45). V1 was described by 54 annotations (average length: 8 words) describing sets, characters' actions and text on screen. V2 was described by 24 annotations (average length: 6 words). We used the following audio-description rules: annotations should 1) be brief and not tell too much, in order to preserve the original work; 2) not overlap important parts of the soundtrack; 3) be as neutral as possible. Examples of annotations are: "*in front of the stage*" (Type: *Set*), "*Ben is showing the coffee table*" and "*The girl is standing by him, is showing the table and the socks*" (Type: *Action*), "*MyBox Production presents… interpreted by… realized by…*" (Type: *TextOnScreen*).

Presentation models. Audio notifications have to be sparingly employed in order to avoid end-users annoyance (cf. section 3), and only a small number of them can be learned. Because there usually are less different sets than actions and because their succession rhythm goes generally slower, using earcon audio notifications for *Set* annotations was considered as a potentially relevant and innovative rendering.

As presented in Table 1, we produced several presentation model variations with different kinds of bi-modal audio enrichments (speech synthesis and earcons). In addition to the rendering of annotations when playing the video, we also added a prologue for each video. Figure 4 illustrates these various notions focusing on the presentation model for one particular situation.

Our goal was to study two types of enrichments: earcons and speech synthesis. More precisely, we wanted to:

- Verify that our descriptions of video content actually helped blind persons understand it.
- Identify which verbosity level is better adapted to action descriptions: simplified (C1) or detailed (C2)
- Validate the fact that the association of earcons and speech synthesis does not create too much a cognitive load that would prevent video understanding.
- Confirm that users can handle as much as 6 different earcons, a number we had estimated based on an unpublished experiment.

Participants were individually shown (on a computer) V1 and V2, both annotated with the *VisualBase* schema and audio-enriched with earcons for *Sets* and speech synthesis for other annotations (cf. PM-S0 in Table 1). As there are 2 sets in V1 (actions take place either in front of a theater stage or in a lounge), we used 2 different earcons. For the 6 different sets in V2 (6 places in one apartment), we used 6 earcons. Videos do not have the same rhythm: V1 has much more rapid rhythm than V2. After each film, participants answered 21 questions related to their perception of the audio enrichments and their understanding of the story. At the end they all participated to a focus group.

Table 1. Five presentation models for rendering annotations during the playing of a video

	PM – S0	PM – S1	PM – S2	PM – S3	PM – S4
PROLOGUE					
Video Metadata	-	Synthesize Speech for Synopsis			
Set	-	Synthesize speech for lexicon	-		
ENRICHED VIDEO RENDERING					
Action, TextOnScreen	Speech Synthesize content of the annotation				
Set	Play Earcon associated with content *then* Synthetize speech for content if first occurrence	Play Earcon associated with content	Play Earcon associated with content *then* Synthetize speech for content if first occurrence	Play Earcon associated with content *then* Synthetize speech for content if asked by the user	Play *unique* Earcon *then* Synthetize speech for content of the annotation

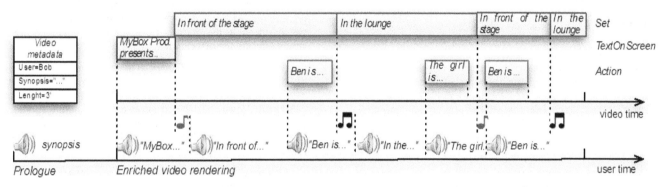

Figure 4. An illustration of audio enrichment of a video with Presentation Model S2

Our enrichment proposal received a warm welcome from the participants. Results from questionnaires showed that video understanding was very good, meaning that our annotations are relevant, but sometimes too long and sometimes overlapping the dialogues (even a little overlap was distracting).

They also showed that the better speech synthesis enrichment is the simplified one (C1), because it contains nearly all the useful information and is shorter than the detailed one. So the criteria of shortness and respect of the original soundtrack are more important than the 'exhaustiveness' one (description with a lot of details). From the focus group, the participants' comments show that earcons are well adapted to communicate time and space change information. The benefits for understanding are clear, as participants were very positive on this point: "*Hum, I found that the sounds were very interesting to mean set changes*", "*Just the small beep for the change of scene it's good.*", "*I prefer audio icons than speech synthesis (…). An icon is short, while speech synthesis encroaches a lot upon the soundtrack*". As to the number of different earcons, questionnaires and focus group showed that 6 earcons could be handled. Focus group also showed that earcons are easy to learn, that their speech synthesis explanation (just after the first time an earcon is played) is useful.

These findings clearly revealed the potential of earcons for video enrichment, and showed that mixing earcons and speech synthesis could be useful. Moreover, as blind persons are used to speech synthesis and audio-description, we considered (a) that audio-enriched videos should contain audio-description, and (b)

that the use of earcons alone for audio-enrichments is not conceivable yet, as a prerequisite would be societal agreement on their meaning. So we decided to focus on the way earcons and speech synthesis can be combined to express one category of description (*Sets*) while keeping "classical" audio-description for *Actions*. We then conducted a more substantial experiment with new objectives and hypotheses aimed at studying this combination in enriched videos.

5.2 Combining earcons and speech synthesis for presenting sets

Our objective here was to evaluate and compare four kinds (S1-S4) of bimodal enrichment presentation models as described in Table 1. Earcons are used each set change. Speech synthesis is used to present both the actions of the characters and the text on screen (e.g. title of the video). It is also used to pronounce some text accompanying earcons and explaining them. Here, we hypothesized that:

- H1: Earcons are perceived as additional elements to the video. This hypothesis concerns the low-level perception of earcons.
- H2: Earcons (combined with speech synthesis) help participants to understand the elements of the story they describe (here *Sets*).
- H3: Earcons help participants perceive narrative "meta-information". Earcons here indicate set changes, and should lead to high-level perception of the number of different sets and of the frequency of set changes.

Our pilot study also suggested to us that it might be useful to include a short oral overview of each video, at the beginning.

5.2.1 Protocol and experimental conditions

The protocol of this experiment is quite similar to that of the pilot study with some minor adjustments regarding both video enrichment and questionnaires.

For each video, a *prologue* part (cf. Table 1 and Figure 4) was added, that consisted of a short synopsis. Besides a "control" situation with no enrichment, we distinguish four "situations" (S1…S4), ways of using the earcons. In S1, S2 and S3 we used as many earcons as there are sets in the videos, with these differences:

- S1: a lexicon presenting earcons was presented before the video begins, and after the synopsis.
- S2: synthesized speech explained what each earcon corresponded to just after it was used for the first time.
- S3: the speech explanation for the last earcon heard was accessible by typing the F1 key of the keyboard.

S1, S2 and S3 are situations where speech synthesis has a "supporting" role to the earcons; speech is used here to explain sounds. But we wanted to explore a second type of combination: in S4, a unique earcon was used for every set change and a short speech synthesis was systematically associated to it as explanation (e.g. "♪/ kitchen"; "♪/ bathroom"; etc.). Earcons here show that the following descriptions concern sets and not action, they act as "semantized audio onsets" for the following speech.

These four *situations* should not be confused with more "classical" experimental *conditions* that would be set up to study the effect of variables on other variables. We aimed to investigate the possible useful earcons / speech synthesis combinations, and our quantitative results are mainly guides to assess the good ones.

Situations 1, 2, and 4 are 'theater situations', ones that could be used with an audience of many people. Situation 3 is more individualized: videos are showed on a personal computer, with each participant listening to the soundtrack with headphones. In this paper we present data comparing the three "theater" situations, S1, S2, and S4; S3 will be the subject of future work.

5.2.2 Participants and data collection

We recruited 21 unpaid legally blind volunteers (23-72 years old) with the help of an association for blind people. One of them did not watch the first video (V1). Six participants contributed to S1 (V1 and V2), eight participants to S2 (V1 and V2), six participants to S4 (V1) and seven participants to S4 (V2). All are traditional media consumers: they watch TV and listen to the radio. A few go to the movies. Some watch DVD and all agree that the use of DVD players is difficult for them and they need help to access the audio-description functions. Some of the participants have good computer skills, while others are not familiar with Internet and do not use it. For each situation, after each video, participants answered 21 questions (being helped to fill the questionnaires) about both the earcons (perception, understanding, quality of the enrichment) and their understanding of the story itself. The questions concerning the story understanding improvement thanks to earcons were 'closed' questions: 4 questions for V1 (Qa…Qd), 3 questions for V2 (Qe…Qg). These questions concerned 'facts' in the story. For example 'Where does Ben install his piece of furniture?'. These questions thus had expected answers. At the end they all

took part in a focus group that we recorded. We collected our data in the projection room of the association.

5.2.3 Results

Although the results we present here only concern S1, S2 and S4, we already have interesting elements. Three volunteers participated to a control condition (video without enrichments). Their answers to questionnaires were logically "reconstructed" and they said they missed information to fully understand the video, particularly concerning sets (about 50% of expected answers). They were also favorable to an earcons-based enrichment.

Concerning H1, for both videos, it appears that 85 % of the participants heard the earcons, thus confirming that earcons are readily perceptible.

More precisely, the distribution of the perceptions shows a perfect perception for S1. This leads us to further hypothesize that a preliminary presentation of icons and their meaning is effective on the future perception of earcons. Situation 2, which we considered as the "most difficult" situation, does not show a strong effect in the perception.

Our second hypothesis H2 aimed at assessing the understanding of the sets-related elements of the story. Overall, this understanding was good (Table 2). Our hypothesis is thus confirmed. However, the performance varied across questions (see discussion). Situations were grouped in this analysis, as there was no apparent effect of the situation on the understanding of the video story.

Table 2: Amount of good answers to set-related understanding questions regarding to expected answers

	Video 1 (V1)				Video 2 (V2)		
Question	*Qa*	*Qb*	*Qc*	*Qd*	*Qe*	*Qf*	*Qg*
S1, S2, S4	14/20	16/20	17/20	8/20	10/21	18/21	10/21
Total	55/80 - 69%				38/63 - 60%		

The third hypothesis H3 was related to the global understanding of 'meta-information' about the narration, earcons acting as indicators of the number of sets and the frequency of set changes. Regarding the evaluation of the number of sets, participants did not have the exact answer most of the time, though they were close for V1 (2 sets), and under the exact number for V2 (6 sets).

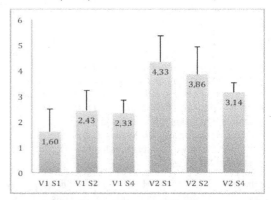

Figure 5. Means of perceived number of set changes

Figure 5 shows inter-individual agreement in S4 (where the name of the set is repeated each time), with better answers for

V1 than for V2. Regarding frequency of set changes, the results did not show much, but suggested that earcons give saliency to visual elements that where not deemed significant by non visually-impaired viewers (see discussion). Overall, our third hypothesis is not verified though there is a potential effect of the repetition of the sets' names on remembering them.

Participants also answered a questionnaire to evaluate the enriched videos they had been presented. They gave their opinion using a Likert satisfaction scale. Answers to these questions show three interesting points. First, the majority of the participants (65%) found that enrichments helped them understand videos. It is interesting to note that it is in situations 2 and 4 that the help was considered the most useful. Secondly, nearly half of the participants (46%) declared that the enriched videos had pleased them. The distribution of these answers is very uneven and the majority of S2 participants declared having appreciated the video. This is strengthened by the answers to another question which concerned boredom: all the subjects of S2 said they did not get bored, while in the other situations there were only a third. Finally, nearly half of participants (44%) found that it was easy to adapt themsleves to the enrichment, except in S1 where we had 8 negative answers of 12.

6. DISCUSSION

Our first question was about low-level perception of earcons. H1 was confirmed and the best results were obtained with S1 (preliminary presentation of earcons significations in a lexicon). Focus groups confirmed the sensitivity of blind people to the quality of earcons and their discriminability in the soundtrack. S1 obtained the best qualitative answers ("agree") to the question on easiness of perception of the enriched content. **We think the preliminary presentation of earcons has an effect on their later perception.** Focus group also brought information on how to improve the lexicon for earcons' preliminary presentation: "*we could put twice the beep then its meaning*". Another S1 participant would have preferred the lexicon was associated with a repetition of all earcons and meanings for each occurrence: "*if there are many earcons, it would be necessary to verbalize every time*". So **the lexicon must be refined and improved. In the future accessibility tool, lexicon apparition should be user customizable.**

Our second question was about high-level perception of earcons. Our third hypothesis (H3: earcons help participants perceive narrative "meta-information") was not confirmed. However it mainly showed that participants evaluated V2's rhythm as fast while we considered it medium, meaning that blind persons did not share our rhythm judgment. Using earcons for sets may lead to distorting the perception of the video rhythm, because earcons draw the attention to set changes (discontinuity). This illustrates Jaskanen paradox, leading us to state that **earcons must be perceived but they must not perturb.** A S2 participant asserted that "*it has to be non intrusive; we have to be able to make our own idea of the image*". Hence, **earcon enrichment of videos can have side effects, leading to modifications in the perception of video rhythm, possibly not desirable.** So video enrichment based on automatic video segmentation based on set classification should be used with care.

Our third question concerned the utility of earcons associated to speech synthesis. Participants' answers show a good global understanding. **Earcons associated with speech synthesis are useful for the understanding of sets-related information.** Besides we must be attentive to the contents of annotations: as the results of the pilot study show, **the criterion of conciseness dominates the criterion of exhaustiveness.** We had several comments in this direction. An S1 participant asserted: "*You should not enrich too much. Some sounds are self-sufficient and it is not necessary to describe them with speech synthesis*". Another comment from S4: "*you should not look for too much coverage, otherwise it is too heavy. It is not necessarily annoying if we do not understand locations exactly. It is not necessary to detail all the sets*".

Besides, the prologue was well received for both films in all situations and considered very useful in the focus groups. We think **that presenting a video synopsis as a prologue is beneficial for understanding.**

Our experimental results will help us specify elements of **good practices** for annotating videos and designing rendering. When the annotation platform comes on-line (beta version) for advanced annotators, we will be able to clarify and refine these recommendations that will later serve for less advanced annotators. We are confident that with the adoption of annotation and rendering tools, practices will evolve and stabilize so as to support new standard ways of audio-enriching videos with earcons. As a participant stated, "*Sure, it will be necessary to normalize, and then perhaps it will be possible to increase the number of earcons*". All these results show the importance of taking into account aspects related to user experiencing. They also emphasize the core issue of personalization research for accessibility.

7. CONCLUSION

In this paper we have presented the ACAV project for enhancing video accessibility on the web, together with concepts related to annotation-based enriched videos: annotations, annotations schemas and presentation models. Focusing on audio-enrichment of videos for blind people, we presented a series of questions we wanted to tackle, and two studies in which we tested different ways of combining speech synthesis and earcons. Main results show that earcons are readily perceived; that earcons and speech synthesis can be used to enhance the understanding of videos; that earcons should be accompanied with synthesized speech, prologue lexicon and explanations during the play; and that a potential side effect of earcons is related to video rhythm perception. This exploratory work is a first investigation of model-based video enrichment for accessibility, focused on the use of earcons as a way to complement speech synthesis for conveying visual information. Another key modality in annotation-based video enrichment, to be studied in the future, will be Braille display.

8. ACKNOWLEDGMENTS
This paper was supported by the French Ministry of Industry under contract 09.2.93.0966, ACAV "Collaborative Annotation for Video Accessibility" project. We thank Olivier Aubert, the main engineer of the Advene project and our mentor for their help. We are indebted to the experiment participants; to Cité Scolaire René Pellet in Villeurbanne and Association Valentin Haüy (AVH) in Lyon for providing local arrangements; to A. Carlier who helped us to validate the questionnaire; and to the students who provided help for data collection.

9. REFERENCES
[1] Aubert, O., Champin, P.-A., Prié, Y. and Richard, B. 2008. Canonical Processes in Active Reading and Hypervideo Production. *Multimedia Systems*, 14(6), 427–433.

[2] Baker, M. 1998. Routledge Encyclopedia of Translation Studies. Routledge. London.

[3] British Journal of Visual Impairment. 1985. The Play's the Thing - Audio description in the theatre, 3(3).

[4] Blattner, M. M., Sumikawa, D. A. and Greenberg, R. M. 1989. Earcons and Icons: Their Structure and Common Design Principles. Human Computer Interaction, 4(1), 11–44.

[5] Block Jr F.E., Nuutinen L. and Ballast B. 1999. Optimization of Alarms: A Study on Alarm Limits, Alarm Sounds, and False Alarms, Intended to Reduce Annoyance. Journal of Clinical Monitoring and Computing, 15(2), 75–83.

[6] Bonebright, T.L. and Nees, M.A. 2007. Memory for Auditory Icons and Earcons with Localization Cues. In Proc. ICAD 2007, 419–422.

[7] Bussemakers, M.P. and De Haan, A. 2000. When it Sounds Like a Duck and it Looks Like a Dog ... Auditory icons vs. earcons in multimedia environments. In Proc. ICAD 2000, 184–189.

[8] Chapdelaine, C. 2010. In-situ study of blind individuals listening to audio-visual contents. In Proc. ASSETS 2010, 59–66.

[9] Choi, S. H. and Walker, B. N. 2010. Digitizer Auditory Graph: Making graphs accessible to the visually impaired. In Proc. CHI 2010, 3445–3450.

[10] Cohen, J. Monitoring Background Activities. 1994. In G. Kramer (Ed.), Auditory Display: Sonification, Audification and Auditory interfaces, 499–522.

[11] Crommentuijn, K. 2006. Designing Auditory Displays to Facilitate Object Localization in Virtual Haptic 3D Environments. In Proc. ASSETS 2006, 255–256.

[12] Edworthy, J. and Hards, R. 1999. Learning Auditory Warnings: The Effects of Sound Type, Verbal Labelling and Imagery on the Identification of Alarm Sounds. International Journal of Industrial Ergonomics, 24(6), 603–618.

[13] Gagnon, L., Foucher, S., Heritier, M., Lalonde, M., Byrns, D., Chapdelaine, C., Turner, J., Mathieu, S., Laurendeau, D., Nguyen, N.-T. and Ouellet, D. 2009. Towards computer-vision software tools to increase production and accessibility of video description for people with vision loss. Univers. Access Inf. Soc., 8(3), 199 –218.

[14] Garzonis, S., Jones, S., Jay, T. and O'Neill, E. 2009. Auditory icon and earcon mobile service notifications: intuitiveness, learnability, memorability and preference. In Proc. CHI 2009, 1513–1522.

[15] Gaver, W. W. 1986. Auditory icons: using sound in computer interfaces. Human-Computer Interaction, 2(2), 167-177.

[16] Gaver, W. W. 1989. The SonicFinder: an interface that uses auditory icons. Human-Computer Interaction, 4(1), 67-94.

[17] Graham, R. 1999. Use of Auditory Icons as Emergency Warnings: Evaluation within a Vehicle Collision Avoidance Application. Ergonomics, 42(9), 1233-1248.

[18] Hoggan, E., Raisamo R. and Brewster, S. Mapping information to audio and tactile icons. 2009. In Proc. of the 2009 international conference on Multimodal interfaces (ICMI-MLMI '09), 327–334.

[19] ITC UK. 2000. ITC Guidance on standards for audio description. Technical Report: Independent Television Commission. 16 pp.

[20] Jaskanen, S. 1999. On the inside track to Loserville, USA: strategies used in translating humour in two Finnish versions of "Reality Bites", MA essay, Univ. of Helsinki.

[21] Leung, Y. K., Smith, S., Parker, S. and Martin, R. 1997. Learning and Retention of Auditory Warnings. In Proc. ICAD 1997, 288-299.

[22] Mathieu, S. and Turner, J. 2007. Audio description for indexing films. World Library and Information Congress (IFLA), Durban (South Africa).

[23] Mathieu, S. and Turner, J. 2007. (FRENCH) Audiovision ou comment faire voir l'information par les personnes aveugles et malvoyantes : lignes directrices pour la description d'images en mouvement. Congrès annuel de l'ACSI, McGill University, Montréal.

[24] Morisset, L. and Gonant, F. 2008. (FRENCH) Charte de l'audiodescription. Technical Report: Ministère des Solidarités et de la Cohésion sociale. 7 pp

[25] Murphy, E., Bates, E. and Fitzpatrick, D. 2010. Designing auditory cues to enhance spoken mathematics for visually impaired users. In Proc. ASSETS 2010, 75–82.

[26] Pfeiffer, S. and Parker, C. 2009. Accessibility for the HTML5 <video> element. In Proc. W4A 2009, 98–100.

[27] Piety, P. J. 2003. Audio description, a visual assistive discourse: an investigation into language used to provide the visually disabled access to information in electronic texts. Master of Arts thesis. Washington: Georgetown University.

[28] Piper, M. 1988. Audio Description: Pioneers Progress, British Journal of Visual Impairment, 6(2).

[29] Sanchez, J. and Tadres, A. 2010. Audio and haptic based virtual environments for orientation and mobility in people who are blind. In Proc. ASSETS 2010, 237-238.

[30] The American Council of the Blind. The Audio Description Project. Online: http://www.acb.org/adp/. Accessed 04/21/2011.

[31] United Nations. 2006. Convention on the rights of persons with disabilities. Convention: UN. New York.37 pp.

[32] W3C. Media Accessibility User Requirements. Online: http://www.w3.org/WAI/PF/HTML/wiki/Media_Accessibility_Requirements. Accessed 04/21/11

[33] W3C. Web Accessibility Initiative (WAI): strategies, guidelines, resources to make the Web accessible to people with disabilities. Online: http://www.w3.org/WAI/ Accessed 04/21/11.

[34] W3C, Web Content Accessibility Guidelines (WCAG) 2.0. Online : http://www.w3.org/TR/WCAG20/ Accessed 04/21/11.

[35] Yalla, P. and Walker , B.N. 2008. Advanced auditory menus: design and evaluation of auditory scroll bars. In Proc. ASSETS 2008, 105-112.

Developing Accessible TV Applications

José Coelho,[1] Carlos Duarte,[1] Pradipta Biswas,[2] and Patrick Langdon[2]

[1]LaSIGE, University of Lisbon, PT
Campo Grande Edifício C6 Piso 3
1749-016, Lisboa
+351 21 750 05 32
jcoelho@lasige.di.fc.ul.pt, cad@di.fc.ul.pt

[2]Department of Engineering, University of Cambridge, UK
15 JJ Thomson Avenue
Cambridge CB3 0FD
+44 1223 766959
pb400@cam.ac.uk, pml24@eng.cam.ac.uk

ABSTRACT

The development of TV applications nowadays excludes users with certain impairments from interacting with and accessing the same type of contents as other users do. Developers are also not interested in developing new or different versions of applications targeting different user characteristics. In this paper we describe a novel adaptive accessibility approach on how to develop accessible TV applications, without requiring too much additional effort from the developers. Integrating multimodal interaction, adaptation techniques and the use of simulators in the design process, we show how to adapt User Interfaces to the individual needs and limitations of elderly users. For this, we rely on the identification of the most relevant impairment configurations among users in practical user-trials, and we draw a relation with user specific characteristics. We provide guidelines for more accessible and centered TV application development.

Categories and Subject Descriptors

H.5.2 [**Information Interfaces and Presentation**]: User Interfaces – *input devices and strategies, voice I/O.* K.4.2 [**Computers and society**]: Social issues – *assistive technologies for persons with disabilities.*

General Terms

Design, Experimentation, Human Factors.

Keywords

Accessible applications, elderly, multimodal, simulation, GUIDE.

INTRODUCTION

Modern research in multimodal interactive systems can offer valuable assistance to elderly and disabled population by helping them to engage more fully with the world. Additionally, systems and services developed for elderly or disabled people often find useful applications for their able bodied counterparts. The early attempts at designing systems for people with disabilities were confined to developing isolated systems like blind access via Optacon, special video card for low vision access or switch access software for motor impaired users. From late 90s, researchers started to take a more holistic approach like developing Accessibility APIs (e.g. Microsoft Accessibility API) and standardizing guidelines like Web Content Accessibility

Guidelines (WCAG). However services and products for people with disabilities still lag behind mainstream systems.

As new developments in technology are responsible for new TV hardware and software, the elderly are having more difficulty in interacting with their own TV sets and getting almost nothing out of this progress. Also, as new technology is available, application developers are not interested in developing new applications targeting only this specific population (or even developing different versions of the same application). However, if not much additional effort would be required for the development of specific User Interfaces (UIs), developers would increase their application's accessibility to include a wider range of users.

Because the elderly can exhibit so many different disabilities, and a single person can have several disabilities at the same time, adaptation to user differences can be very difficult, and has to rely on many different levels. If an elderly person has visual difficulties, information has to be retrieved in redundant modalities (e.g., audio and visual information at the same time), or somehow complemented by adapting the visual components (e.g., increasing the size of the buttons). If this type of adaptation can be achieved automatically, elderly users would want and be capable to interact with new TV systems.

The GUIDE (Gentle User Interfaces for Elderly People) project [6] adopts multimodal interaction as a natural interaction approach to give its target users a simple and more intuitive way of controlling TV based applications. By using several different modalities in a parallel or alternate way, elderly users can avoid errors, and react to interaction situations where they would be blocked if interacting only with a Remote Control. GUIDE will also provide a toolbox to assist in the development of accessible TV applications. It will offer a simulation mechanism letting developers understand the effects of any impairment on the perception of a rendered UI (during design) and supporting an adaptive mechanism capable of adjusting or replacing UI components to fit specific user characteristics.

In this paper, after presenting related work, we present how GUIDE approaches can help in the development of accessible TV applications. We complement and attest these approaches with the results of a user study consisting of a survey and a technical user-trial. Before concluding, we describe implications of this study on the development of accessible applications from the developer and GUIDE framework points of view. The paper's main contributions are the results of user studies conducted with over 60 participants, and the implications for the design of accessible TV applications drawn from those results, which can nevertheless be extended to other classes of applications.

RELATED WORK

Multimodal Interaction

Multimodal interfaces aim to provide a more natural and transparent way of interaction with users, and making use of several modalities like gestures (and pointing), speech, gaze, etc. They have been able to enhance human-computer interaction (HCI) in many ways, including:

User satisfaction: studies revealed that people favor multiple-action modalities for virtual object manipulation tasks [10, 24]; Oviatt [24] has also shown that about 95% of users prefer multimodal interaction over unimodal interaction; **Robustness and Accuracy:** Keates and Robinson (1998) asserted that "using a number of modes can increase the vocabulary of symbols available to the user" [14], leading to increased accessibility. Oviatt stated that multiple inputs have a great potential to improve information and systems accessibility, because by complementing each other, they can yield a "highly synergistic blend in which the strengths of each mode are capitalized upon and used to overcome weaknesses in the other" [25]; **Efficiency and Reliability:** Multimodal interfaces are more efficient than unimodal interfaces, because they can in fact speed up tasks completion by 10% [23]. This improvement can be justified by the fact that an interface can exploit the potential for simultaneously-performed mode-specific input actions [3, 19]. Also, multimodal interfaces have been shown to improve error handling and reliability: users made 36% fewer errors with a multimodal interface than with a unimodal interface [23]; **Adaptivity (Increased flexibility):** Keates and Robinson argued that multimodal interfaces offer an increase in flexibility and adaptivity in interaction because of the ability to switch among different modes of input, to whichever is more convenient or accessible to a user [14]. Brewster investigated the use of auditory feedback as an addition to combat menu usability problems [4], or drag-and-drop tasks [3], finding that it produced better user task performance compared with the basic visually enhanced versions of these tasks. Researchers also investigated the performance value of supplementing visual feedback with haptic feedback for several tasks, including selecting menu items using scroll bars [22]. So, users with physical or cognitive limitations can benefit from multimodalities [14]. However, Vitense [30] illustrates the need for additional research in multimodal interaction, especially involving elderly people with visual impairments.

User Interface Adaptation

Interface adaptation or personalization is mainly explored in the domain of content personalization and developing intelligent information filtering or recommendation systems based on user profiles. Still, too little research work has been done beyond content personalization. A few representative and significant projects on interface personalization are the SUPPLE project at University of Washington [8] and AVANTI project [28] for people with disabilities.

The SUPPLE project personalizes interfaces mainly by changing layout and font size for people with visual and motor impairment and also for ubiquitous devices. However, it does not consider visual and motor impairment in detail and thus works for only loss of visual acuity and a few types of motor impairment. The AVANTI project [28] modeled an assistive interface for a web browser based on static and dynamic characteristics of users. The interface is initialized according to static characteristics (such as age, expertise, type of disability and so on) of the user. During interaction, the interface records users' interaction and adapts

itself based on dynamic characteristics (such as idle time, error rate and so on) of the user. This model works based on a rule based system and does not address the basic perceptual, cognitive and motor behavior of users and so it is hard to generalize to other applications. Apart from full scale systems, there are also a few approaches which tried to adapt pointing devices like Gravity Well [12], SteadyClicks [29] and adapting pointing [15] by changing control-display ratio of a gesture based system.

Simulation of User Impairments

There is also not much reported work on systematic modeling of assistive interfaces. McMillan [20] felt the need to use HCI models to unify different research streams in assistive technology, but his work aimed to model the system rather than the user. A few researchers also worked on basic perceptual, cognitive and motor aspects. The EASE tool [19] simulates effects of interaction for a few visual and mobility impairments. However the model is demonstrated for a sample application of using word prediction software but not yet validated for basic pointing or visual search tasks performed by people with disabilities. Keates and colleagues [13] measured the difference between able-bodied and motor impaired users with respect to the Model Human Processor (MHP) [5] and motor impaired users were found to have a greater motor action time than their able-bodied counterparts. The finding is obviously important, but the KLM model itself is too primitive to model complex interaction and especially the performance of novice users. Gajos et all [8] developed a model to predict pointing time of users with mobility impairment and adapt interfaces based on the prediction. They estimated the movement time by selecting a set of features involving target distance and width and found that movement patterns of different users inclined to different functions of distance and width of targets. Serna and colleagues [26] used ACT-R cognitive architecture [1] to model progress of Dementia in Alzheimer's patient. They simulated the loss of memory and increase in error for a representative task at kitchen by changing different ACT-R parameters [1]. The technique is interesting but their model still needs rigorous validation through other tasks and user communities.

Use of Interaction Filters

Users with a number of different motion impairment conditions (e.g. Parkinson's disease, strokes and severe arthritis etc.) cannot cope with current computer input systems. However, computer access may be improved through the use of software based techniques such as damping and smoothing, gravity well attractors and trajectory filtering [9, 16]. Performance in pointing tasks is most commonly evaluated using speed and accuracy. However, differences in cursor movement between people, devices, and conditions can exist in a variety of ways. Although traditional measures may show that a difference exists between conditions, establishing why they exist is more likely to be accomplished by analyzing the path of movement throughout a trial. For this reason, MacKenzie et al [18] proposed new accuracy measures for evaluating computer pointing devices. However, for a user who must continue to navigate to the target after a spasm has driven the cursor to a far corner of the screen, a measure based on the cursor's initial position has little meaning. A speed versus accuracy sub-movement analysis designed for able-bodied movement may be an appropriate model for motion-impaired interaction [21]. In these models it is assumed that users perform as well as they can under stochastic conditions of task and system noise. They may trade speed against accuracy, achieving an optimized number of sub-movements that is often about two with able-bodied subjects. Such a model may be applicable to the analysis of modified cursor movements [16, 11] where motion is often laborious and characterized by multiple trajectories separated by user assessment of their own performance under perturbation from their own motor coordination system.

GUIDE APPROACHES

To support accessibility in TV application development, GUIDE bases itself on multimodal interaction and adaptation to user characteristics, as well as in the use of a mechanism which simulates the user's impairments as a way to give developers insight on how their applications are perceived by the users. Additionally GUIDE uses interaction filters to increase the accessibility of pointing based interaction.

Multimodal Interaction and Adaptation

Proper interaction with traditional TV systems is very difficult for the elderly because of typical impairments (e.g. limitations on upper limbs movement can prevent the use of a remote control). A unimodal system also restricts presented information to a single modality excluding those who suffer from impairments affecting the sensory channel needed to perceive that modality (e.g. a blind person cannot see graphical information and a deaf person cannot hear sounds). GUIDE offers multimodality as the way to address this issue, allowing presenting the same information (and giving feedback to the user) in different modes, compensating sensorial impairments and offering users the possibility to interact in the most suitable way (choosing from a range of alternative devices of interaction). All these features are extremely valuable to improve the accessibility of applications. GUIDE employs multimodal interaction and makes adaptation possible in the following ways [6]:

1) GUIDE supports the use of speech commands, finger pointing, remote control, gesture and tablet PC interaction to control interaction with a TV; 2) GUIDE makes use of sound and visual elements, as well as an Avatar persona and haptic feedback to present information to its users; 3) The first time a user interacts with GUIDE, a User Initialization Application (UIA) is presented. The UIA guides the user through different tasks, comprising a tutorial on how to use the system and the available devices. At the same time sensorial and preference data about the user is collected. Using the information collected by the UIA, GUIDE assigns a User Profile (UP) to the user depending on user abilities and preferences; 4) For each application, GUIDE adapts the UI elements and interaction to fit user's characteristics. This is done by providing the application developers with three possible levels of adaptation: "Augmentation" (keeps the visual presentation as specified by the developer, and augment it with content in other modalities), "Adjustment" (adjusting several parameters of the UI visual rendering and applying augmentation also) and "Replacement" (adaptation is made by transforming application content, layout configuration and presentation styles, and also performing augmentation and adjustment).

Simulation of User Impairments

Existing accessibility guidelines are not adequate to analyze the effects of impairment on interaction with UIs and devices. GUIDE developed a simulation system [2] that helps to develop inclusive systems by providing simulation features and application support tools that allow the developer to evaluate his UI design considering virtual user feedback from a simulation. The developer can perceive an interface as if he was impaired (figure 1, top). This can complement the functionality of existing accessibility validation schemes and tools. Additionally, the

simulator can predict the likely interaction patterns when undertaking a task using a variety of input devices, and estimate the time to complete the task in the presence of a specific user model (or user profile) (figure 1, bottom).

Figure 1: Simulation of user visual impairments (top images) and estimating cursor movement and times (down images)

Use of Cursor Smoothing Techniques

One of the important requirements of the GUIDE project is to offer a robust way of gathering high-quality user input data typically measured in terms of speed and accuracy of the communication. Elderly users potentially have a wide range of impairments that hinder their ability to communicate their intentions to an application. In some cases these impairments can be severe, and significantly affect the speed and accuracy leading to an inefficient or even undesirable interaction with an application. The use of cursor smoothing techniques in GUIDE consists in processing the raw user input to obtain a filtered input. This requires the usage of efficient statistical signal processing schemes to estimate the user's intended operations in real time. Basically it consists of the application of corrective forces and forcing relatively smooth paths in a cursor interaction as well as assigning attraction fields to UI elements [9, 16].

Methods: The following graphical UI 'tweaks' or filters have been tested within the GUIDE project.

1. Exponential averaging: this modification calculates the cursor position p_i as $p_i = \alpha x_i + (1-\alpha)p_{i-1}$, where x_i is the user input, p_{i-1} is the previous cursor position and $\alpha \in [0,1]$ is a parameter determining how strong the user input influences the cursor position. This method produces smooth cursor traces but has the drawback that it can produce a delay between user's intended position and the actual position.
2. Damping: This method introduces a quadratic force that opposes the velocity of the cursor.
3. Gravity well: This method warps the cursor space, generating attractive basins to ease the selection of visual targets.

STUDY DESCRIPTION

To identify the most relevant UI component configurations and user impairments, as well as to understand elderly user's typical patterns when performing unimodal and multimodal interaction, concrete and practical user-trials were conducted. Both initial user survey (before the user-trials) and analysis of the user trial videos constitute the main study described next.

GUIDE Survey

As a first stage in this project an exhaustive survey (or interview process) was developed. The aim of this survey was to obtain data from each one of the participants to help develop a user model based on extensive user data and by dividing users in several clusters, each one with different characteristics. This survey is the first step for making adaptation of UI elements to users possible.

Participants

We recruited 46 elderly people (30 female and 16 male) with different disabilities. Their ages varied from 41 to 81. The average age was 70.5. They all participated voluntarily and we contacted them from different associations in San Sebastian (Spain) like IZA and ONCE. The survey data was recorded by means of an audio recording and analysed after the survey. All the activities under this study involving end users have been safeguarded from the ethical point of view.

Procedure

The survey was administered by psychologists with background in neuropsychology discipline as a face-to-face 15 minutes interview, individually administered. The survey was administered to every person in order to know the profile of the participant, and questions involved more than 100 items, combining objective and subjective assessment of the user capabilities. This survey collected information in the following areas: Socio-demographics; Attitudes towards technology; Coping styles with new technologies; Attributional styles toward technological devices; Daily living activities; Vision; Hearing; Mobility; Cognition; and Personality traits.

GUIDE User-Trials

The user trials (figure 2) were a primary source of user requirements engineering, with the aim of observing elderly users in a lab situation interacting with a prototype of a system application, gathering quantitative and qualitative data. It allowed the identification of viable usage methods (gestures, command languages, etc.) of novel and traditional UI paradigms for the different impairments in the target groups.

Participants

Seventeen people (4 male and 13 female) between the ages of 55 and 84 years old (average age 65.8) participated in the user-trials. All of them were recruited in Spain and presented different levels of expertise in technology, as well as different physical and cognitive characteristics or impairments. Also all of them were on the initial pool of 46 who were surveyed.

Procedure

In each user-trial every user was presented with all possibilities of interaction (pointing with the hand, Wii remote, voice or TV remote control) and asked to perform a series of tasks related with TV interaction. The tasks were divided into several scripts concerning different types of interaction or different UI elements:

Visual: The TV screen presented buttons on different locations. Participants were encouraged to say which button location, size and inter-spacing would suit their preferences. Afterwards, they were asked to select their colour preferences according to the button and background. Subsequently, they were requested to read some texts with different size fonts and comment which one they would prefer. For each task they were required to point at a concrete button on the screen using their preferred modality.

Audio: Participants heard different messages at different volumes. They were asked to repeat what they heard and finally to select the most appropriate volume for them. This was asked also while watching TV (with the sound on). Additionally, female and male voices were compared, and participants reported their preference.

Motor: In order to examine which gestures participants prefer, they were requested to perform a variety of gestures in the air (with one or both hands) and also on a tablet PC. Finally, they reported which ones they were comfortable performing. Participants also had to select different buttons on the screen using either a conventional remote control or their fingers. They reported which one suited them better taking into account the button placement on the screen: bottom or top, right or left. Participants were also asked to interact with Tablet PC applications, entering numbers in a visual keyboard and controlling virtual maps. At last, they performed pointing selections interacting with a gravity-well filter and without any filter to understand if there were big differences.

Cognitive: Cognitive tests in the form of "games" were performed to evaluate participants' visual memory and attention capacity. Images were shown on the screen, and participants were requested to memorize them. The images then disappeared and participants were asked to select the location where a specific image was. Time of selection was measured.

Avatar: The same message was presented to participants, either by an avatar or by an audio voice. Participants then reported their preference. This was also done for Avatar and text. Finally users were asked to choose one of three types of avatars (face avatar, half-body avatar and full-body avatar).

Multiple modalities: Participants were asked to perform several selections using only one modality or several modalities at the same time. This was asked also while simulating different contexts of interaction, and while interacting from different locations in the room. Participants were also asked which way of presenting information they preferred, combining presentation in one modality and in several modalities at the same time.

The measurements taken in this study were the number of errors, the time rate, and observation of participant's actions and behaviours. Every user-trial lasted around 60 minutes and during the trials, participants had to sit down in front of the screen ensuring that the distance was the same for every user. Every assessment was recorded with two cameras, one of them focused on the user and the other on the TV screen. Analysis of the user-trials was made from analysis of these videos.

Figure 2: User-trials photos. Colour selection screen (on the left), and an elderly user using a Wii remote (on the right).

RESULTS

Analysis of the results of both user survey and user-trials are essential to support the GUIDE approaches described. Both quantitative and qualitative results are now reported.

Survey Results (Quantitative Data)

The full survey data set contained a very large number of variables (over one hundred). Since a large number of these variables are related (the sets addressing vision for example) and the number of cases small, a two stage process of analysis was adopted to reduce the variable set. Firstly, the initial set was poorly configured for factor or principal component analysis so a simple correlation threshold was applied. Cross (self) correlations were calculated for all variables. The highly correlated variables were then subjected to k-means cluster analysis [2] for each modality, again because of the large numbers of variables and this subsequently allowed the removal of variables that did not significantly contribute to the clustering.

In defining the user profiles we have used k-means clustering with a value of $k=3$. K-means clustering algorithm works like an Expectation Maximization (EM) algorithm, which partitions n observations into k clusters in which each observation belongs to the cluster with the nearest mean. Each cluster centre defines a profile and we have only used the significant variables ($p<0.01$) to define the profiles. Table 1 uses the result of the k-means clustering to characterize what a typical member of three different impairment groups would be capable of, based on the calculated cluster1, cluster2 and cluster3 centres. The profiles of users will ultimately be formed by a combination and grouping of all modalities simultaneously such that a specific grouping may represent capability on users perceptual, cognitive and motor capability ranges. Clearly a particular user may present, for example, low vision, medium cognition and high motor capability levels and it's this that will be initially used to index the GUIDE user profiles following a successful initialization application interaction. Following this, adaption may utilize more accurate quantitative data to further locate the user's profile. This may entail a short visual acuity, cognition, physical or hearing test.

Table 1: K-Means Cluster Centres for visual, hearing, cognitive and motor variables

Vision	Cluster1	Cluster2	Cluster3
Close vision: level able to read perfectly	20/20	20/60	20/80
Distant Vision: level able to read perfectly (metres)	5	5	20
general eyesight	good	excellent	normal
seeing at distance	good	poor	poor
seeing at night	normal	poor	poor
colour perception	good	bad	bad
Hearing	**Cluster1**	**Cluster2**	**Cluster3**
Able to hear a sound of 500Hz?	Yes	Yes	No
Able to hear a sound of 2Khz?	Yes	Yes	Yes
conversation from a noisy background	excellent	normal	normal
Cognition	**Cluster1**	**Cluster2**	**Cluster3**
TMT (seconds)	30	49	136
Cognitive executive function	(no impairment)	(low impairment)	(high impairment)
Motor	**Cluster1**	**Cluster2**	**Cluster3**
mobility diagnosis	none	hernia / slipped disc	none
muscular weakness	never	A few occasions	Frequently
write	No difficulty	No difficulty	Mild

			difficulty
Tingling of limb difficulty	No	Mild	Mild
Rigidity difficulty	No	Mild	Moderate

Quantitative Results from the User Trials

Button Configuration: Users preferred big buttons (83%), well-spaced between each other (83%) and centered on the screen (65%). Also, there is no clear preference regarding color of buttons, with the exception of all users preferring high contrasts between the button background color and button text color.

Text Configuration: From six sizes of fonts presented to users, almost 50% of them preferred the third largest, and the rest of them divided themselves between the second (18%) and fourth (24%) largest fonts. No one chose the two smaller text sizes and only one user chose the biggest one. Also, more than 50% of users with minor vision difficulties (users who can't see all sizes of text presented) prefer the second and third largest sizes, and 90% of users who don't have any vision difficulties prefer the third and fourth largest sizes. Additionally, for dark background colors more than 75% of users prefer white text, and vice-versa. As for colored backgrounds there is a division in the preference of text color, from white (32%) to black (31%) to dark blue (25%).

Audio Configuration: From five different volumes presented, almost 65% of the users preferred the second loudest, and the rest of them divide themselves by the first (12%) and third (18%) loudest. No one chose the fourth and fifth volumes. Also, 100% of users with minor hearing difficulties (users who can't hear all volumes presented) prefer the first and second loudest. All users who don't have any hearing difficulties preferred the second and third loudest. Regarding the genre of the voice of the audio feedback, there is no clear preference between male and female voices (6 preferred male voices, with 4 preferring female voices, and 7 having no preference).

Gesture Configuration: Users had to choose from swipe, pinch and circle gestures, with one and two hands. When making gestures on air, the preference has gone to the one-hand-swipe (47%) and two-hand-swipe (or clapping) (47%) gestures, while two-hand-circle or any variation of pinch weren't chosen by any user. 12% of users didn't like to interact using gestures on air. Regarding the gesture interaction with the tablet PC the same two gestures (swipe) were preferred, by the same order, but in different proportions (35% and 29% respectively). Also, gestures like two-hand-pinch and making a circle using both hands where not chosen by any user. However, 92% of the users liked interacting with gestures on tablet, as well as interacting with Tablet specific applications.

Filtering Options: All users who experienced interaction using the gravity well filter were able to make pointing selections more easily and faster than without this filter. Times of selection where measured resulting in an average of 5120 milliseconds to select a button using pointing without any filter algorithm and an average of 3515 milliseconds to do the same selection using the gravity-wells filter.

General Interaction: In these trials more than half of the users (53%) preferred to interact using speech and 35% preferred pointing. If not suggested, very few users (11%) will alternate hands or arms to make pointing interaction easier, and even when suggested only 2 in 6 tried it. From the two who tried it, no one continued the interaction with the opposite arm even after noticing improvements.

Multimodal Interaction: When buttons on a UI are labeled like "Button1", about half of the users when interacting with speech, and about one third when interacting multimodally (speech and pointing at the same time), said words like "One" or "The First" to select it, instead of reading what was written on it. With buttons labeled with content like "Kitchen" or "Football" this didn't happen once, and users always read what was written on the button. More than half of the users (53%) want both multimodal input and output when they are using the system (even if only in specific contexts of interaction). Moreover, 59% of users said they want to interact using more than one modality at the same time, leaving only 29% wanting to interact using one single modality. Additionally, 82% of users said they preferred multimodal feedback from the system, and only 18% say they wanted information present in only one way (just visual information, or just audio information).

Selection Preferences: From 11 users who performed pointing selection using the finger, all were right-handed and 9 (82%) preferred to make selections on the right side of the screen, with only two preferring to select on the left side (18%). Also when performing the same type of interaction, 9 from 11 users preferred to select buttons on the top of the screen, with only two preferring to point to the lower part of the screen.

Avatar and Interaction Preferences: When asked which type of Avatar they would prefer for presenting information, and guiding them through several tasks and demonstrations of interaction, 33% of users preferred a head-only avatar, the same percentage preferred a full-body avatar, and 27% liked the half-body avatar most. One user said the type of Avatar to be presented would depend on the application and interaction contexts. Also, users prefer the Avatar to present them information (53%) than this being presented only in text (18%). However for 12% of the users this would depend on the interaction context also. The Avatar is also preferred when compared to voice output (47% against 30%).

Qualitative Results

The following results from participant comments and behavioral patterns were observed in the user-trial videos.

Button Configuration: Big buttons are preferred by users because they are easier to see and elderly users typically have some kind of visual impairments. Also, they are easier to select because a bigger area is available for users to select when pointing with the finger, or using any other pointing tracking system. More space between buttons was preferred because it added more precision to pointing selection actions, and centered buttons were preferred because it was easier to point to the center of the screen, than to the peripheries. However, more than based on user abilities or preferences, the location of buttons on a UI is based on tasks being performed or the type of application being executed. For example, buttons centered on the screen can be less suitable while watching TV, but more suitable when using an application for exploring photos. Additionally, if the input recognition mechanisms are very accurate, less space between buttons would bring the advantage of having to travel less distance with the finger to make a selection.

Text Configuration: Users do not prefer the bigger text fonts because otherwise too much area would be taken on the screen, leaving no space for other UI components. Also, another reason for choosing smaller fonts is because they provide a more comfortable reading. However, smaller fonts are more difficult to read for people with visual impairments like the majority of the elderly participants, and that's the reason why a medium sized font is the best option for them.

Audio Configuration: It is evident that users with audio difficulties prefer higher volumes than users without, as it is also the inexistence of a preference regarding male and female voice for audio feedback. In addition, it was also clear in the analysis that no relation existed between the gender of the user interacting and the gender of the voice chosen, with both female and male users choosing both female and male voices for audio feedback.

Gesture Configuration: Users clearly prefer gestures easier to make, and have no problem whatsoever interacting by gestures. However, this type of interaction should not be imposed on the users, but be available as an intuitive option for interacting with the TV. The existence of specific gestures for specific tasks, like raising or lowering volume, is needed and should be explained to the user before he or she starts using the system.

Filtering Options: Times in selections with and without the gravity well filter clearly show how interaction filters can ease and speed the interaction, especially for users with slow movements. However, the use of an interaction filter can result in some awkwardness at the beginning (because the pointer the user is controlling is pushed to different locations on the screen while the finger doesn't move accordingly), and may require some initial training by the users.

General Interaction: It is evident that alternative ways of interacting with the TV (speech and finger pointing) are preferred to the traditional way (remote control interaction). Also, training makes pointing interaction more efficient as the user learns what is required to move the cursor on the screen to each button or menu. Support for interaction from different locations (front or side to TV) and positions (sitting or standing) will be necessary, because the user may need (or want) to perform several tasks in different situations. If users don't intuitively alternate between hands to perform better pointing interaction, than it can't be imposed on them. Also, users won't change the hand they're interacting with if they can interact well in every task with the one they are used to. Neither will they do it when they can't select a button that is on the opposite side of the hand they are using while interacting.

Multimodal Interaction: Every user is able to interact multimodally with the system and combine speech and pointing, even when they prefer only one modality. Users exhibited different multimodal interaction patterns during the trials. For instance, in a first interaction, a user can speak first and point afterwards, and in the next interaction do the opposite, or point and speak at the same time. There is no specific multimodal interaction pattern for each user. Even if most of the times a user interacts in the same manner, there is no certainty he or she will do it every single time. Users can also change the way they interact depending on the type of feedback given while interacting. Regarding user preferences in input and output modalities, there are clear differences between what users say they prefer, and what users really ask for when interacting. In fact, 100% of the users want multimodal output every time information is presented to them, because every user who said to prefer only one type of feedback admitted differently when in specific interaction contexts. The same happened concerning input modalities, with almost half of the users admitting they were wrong when they said to prefer only one modality.

Preferences in Selection: There exists a strong relation between the arm used for interacting when pointing with a finger to the screen, and the preferred area of selection (right-arm interacting almost always means preference in selecting items or buttons in the right area of the screen). This, however, needs to be validated with a sample of left-handed users.

CONCLUSIONS

One of the most conclusive results from the GUIDE user-trials is that elderly users want to interact using several modalities at the same time. Even users who said they would prefer using only one modality for input or output, when confronted with specific interaction contexts they chose to interact multimodally. Also, elderly users are characterized by being very different between each other. These facts allied with the big range of preferences registered for input modalities, or output ways of presentation, attests the necessity of having a system capable of doing adaptation to different user characteristics. Additionally as developers are not interested in developing different versions of the same application, the type of UI adaptation supported by GUIDE is essential to the development of TV applications accessible to all elderly users.

The motor-behavior module of the simulator shows pointing time increases with distance for touch screen interfaces which mean users prefer centrally located target than targets at the periphery of the screen. This module also shows that buttons should be sufficiently large to accommodate random cursor movement during pointing interaction. Similarly, the visual impairment module [2] shows white text in blue background remains legible for all dichromatic color blindness. At last, results from the simulation say that fonts should be big to accommodate slight visual acuity loss resulting from aging. For all these reasons, we can say that user-trial results on user preferences regarding button layout, color combinations, font size, and use of interaction filters, attest the GUIDE approach on making use of a simulator of user impairments, as results are in total accordance with the solutions proposed by this mechanism.

In GUIDE user-trials both exponential averaging and gravity well filters have been introduced in user interaction, and compared in terms of performance with a "normal" interaction using none of the filters. Despite exponential averaging having not worked well enough to make any comparison, there is a clear preference on interacting using the gravity wells filter, as an average of 1605 milliseconds were gained in any selection made using this filter. This is clear evidence that GUIDE approach on using interaction filters can in fact increase the accuracy and efficiency of users interacting with TV applications, increasing accessibility.

Implications for Development

Quantitative and qualitative results described in this paper have clear implications in the development of accessible applications for elderly users. These implications can be relevant to developers as well as to the GUIDE framework points of view:

Button configuration: Applications, should always present a short number of interactive elements for each screen, focusing on big buttons. If developers make complex UIs, GUIDE has to be capable of dividing one screen in multiple screens (and provide navigation through them), or present options to user in alternative modalities.

Text and audio configuration: Applications should make sure both text size and audio volume are configurable by the user at the beginning as well as at middle of an interaction. If the application by itself doesn't offer this option, GUIDE UI adaptation should offer this possibility.

Gesture configuration: In GUIDE the existence of specific gestures to perform specific tasks should be a reality, but all gesture interaction should be explained to the user as he is introduced to the system or to a specific application. The studies also have shown to be possible the development of applications fully controlled by gestures, as elderly users like this kind of interaction.

Filtering options: User interfaces with a lot of buttons, or small buttons (or both) are difficult to interact without any pointing filter, and in this, selection of items/buttons should be made by target approximation or making use of interaction filters. Also, for users with movement impairments or difficulties, GUIDE should be capable of recognizing difficulties in pointing interaction (for example by measuring long periods of screen navigation without any selection occurring) and adapt the interaction by applying interaction filters.

General interaction: TV applications should always provide different modalities of interaction, and GUIDE has to ensure that users can control the system even they are not in front of it, or in a sited position. For this to be possible, recognition mechanisms like recognition of pointing coordinates, have to be capable of recognizing user specific traces. This is also true, to ensure that a user can continue interacting even when another person is standing at his side. Additionally, and for preventing too many errors every time an interaction context changes, speech interaction (and pointing interaction) should be activated by GUIDE specific phrases or words, like "GUIDE, SELECT", or "GUIDE, THIS".

Multimodal interaction: When interacting with a GUIDE application, a set of speech commands should be recognized every time the user says them. Words like "Select", "This", "Yes", "No" and "Confirm", should be included in a speech recognizer dictionary, with the objective of helping in the selection of a button or option to where the user is pointing when the command is issued. The system should also recognize the number or order for selecting buttons presented on the screen. "One", "Two", "Three", "First", "Second", "Third", etc., should represent keywords, supporting redundancy in the selection when a user is pointing to an element on the screen, or used alone when the user is interacting with using only speech.

Preferences in selection: The existence of a strong relation between arm and item location on screen, will influence the way developers design the layout of their applications, as it also affects the configuration and parameterization of GUIDE simulator, as both have to contemplate the existence of this user-UI relation.

Preferences in interaction: If system feedback and presentation could only be performed in one modality (Avatar, Audio or Visual information), the way to do it would depend on the interaction and application context. This is also true for the type of Avatar: head-only avatar would be more suitable for talking with the user or giving simple feedback, while half and full-body Avatar would be suitable for instructing the user on how to do certain gestures, or on how to perform certain tasks. However, and independently of which output modality chosen, output should be repeatable every time the user asks for it again, solving problems derived from lack of attention or changes in the context of interaction.

Additionally, the use of GUIDE's simulation mechanism also has implications in the development of accessible applications. Developers, by having at their disposal a tool that simulates user impairments, and gives them a preview on how their application UI will be perceived by different users, have the opportunity of changing UI characteristics, or giving GUIDE the freedom to augment, adjust or replacing UI elements.

Future Work

In the future, performing user-trials with a bigger number of users will be a priority, since until now the clustering process only used data from the surveys, as data from 17 people (user-trial participants) would be insufficient for a good clustering, and the quality of data possible to collect from these type of user-trials would enrich greatly this process. Also, as GUIDE project continues performing more user trials with its end-users for the purpose of testing the use of specific applications (like the UIA), more results and findings can have a positive influence on the user clustering process, as it could also influence the use of the simulator, or its parameterization. More data from user interaction patterns and preferences will result in better (and more distinct) user profiles, with the possibility of resulting in the creation of more than three clusters of users, as differences between users grow or become more defined.

ACKNOWLEDGMENTS

The research leading to these results has received funding from the European Union's Seventh Framework Programme (FP7/2007-2013) under grant agreement n°248893.

REFERENCES

1. Anderson J. R. and Lebiere C. The Atomic Components of Thought. Hillsdale, NJ, USA: Lawrence Erlbaum Associates, 1998.

2. Biswas, P., Robinson, P., and Langdon, P.: Designing inclusive interfaces through user modelling and simulation. International Journal of Human Computer Interaction, Taylor & Francis. ISSN: 1044-7318

3. Brewster, S. A. (1998a). Sonically-enhanced drag and drop. ICAD'98, Glasgow, UK.

4. Brewster, S. A., & Crease, M. G.: Correcting menu usability problems with sound. Behavior and Information Technology, 18(3): 65–177, 1999

5. Card S., Moran T. and Newell A.: The Psychology of Human-Computer Interaction. Hillsdale, NJ, USA: Lawrence Erlbaum Associates, 1983.

6. Coelho, J., Duarte, C.: The Contribution of Multimodal Adaptation Techniques to the GUIDE Interface. HCII2011, Orlando, Florida, USA

7. Dunaway J., Demasco, P., Peischl, D., and Smith, A.: A pilot study for multimodal input in computer access. RESNA '96

8. Gajos K. Z., Wobbrock J. O. and Weld D. S.: Automatically generating user interfaces adapted to users' motor and vision capabilities. ACM symposium on User interface software and technology 2007. 231-240.

9. Godsill S. J. and Vermaak, J.: Variable rate particle filters for tracking applications. IEEE Stat. Sig. Proc.2005, Bordeaux, France.

10. Hauptmann, R., and McAvinney, P. Gesture with speech for graphics manipulation. International Journal of Man-Machine Studies 38(2):231-249. 1993.

11. Hwang F, Keates S, Langdon P, Clarkson PJ: Mouse movements of motion-impaired users: a submovement analysis. ASSETS 2004. New York, USA.

12. Hwang F. et. al.: Cursor Characteristics And Haptic Interfaces For Motor Impaired Users. Cambridge Workshop on Universal Access and Assistive Technology 2002. 87-96.

13. Keates S., Clarkson J. and Robinson P.: Investigating The Applicability of User Models For Motion Impaired Users. ACM/SIGACCESS'2000.

14. Keates, S., and Robinson, P.: The use of gestures in multimodal input. ASSETS'98, Marina del Rey, CA.

15. Konig W. A. Et. al.: Adaptive Pointing – Design and Evaluation of a Precision Enhancing Technique for Absolute Pointing Devices, INTERACT'09.

16. Langdon, P.M. and Godsill, S. and Clarkson, P.J.: Statistical estimation of user's interactions from motion impaired cursor use data. ICDVRAT 2006, Esbjerg, Denmark

17. Langdon, P.M., Hwang, F., Keates, S., Clarkson, P.J. and Robinson, P.: Developing Assistive Interfaces For Motion-Impaired Users Using Cursor Movement Analysis In Conjunction With Haptic Feedback. ICDVRAT 2002, Veszprem, Hungary.

18. MacKenzie I. S., Kauppinen T., and Silfverberg M.: Accuracy measures for evaluating computer pointing devices. *CHI 2001*, New York, USA.

19. Mankoff J., Fait H., Juang R.: Evaluating accessibility through simulating the experiences of users with vision or motor impairments. IBM Sytems Journal 44.3 (2005).

20. Mcmillan W. W.: Computing For Users With Special Needs And Models of Computer-Human Interaction. ACM/SIGCHI'92.

21. Meyer, D.E., Abrams, R.A., and Wright, C.E.: Speed-accuracy tradeoffs in aimed movements: toward a theory of rapid voluntary action. In *Attention and Performance XIIII*, Hillsdale, NJ: Lawrence Erlbaum (1990) 173-226.

22. Oakley, I., Brewster, S. A., & Gray, P. D.: Solving multi-target haptic problems in menu interaction. CHI'01, Seattle, USA.

23. Oviatt S. L. Multimodal interactive maps: Designing for human performance. Human-Computer Interaction, 12(1):93–129, 1997.

24. Oviatt, S. L., DeAngeli, A. & Kuhn, K. Integration and synchronization of input modes during multimodal human-computer interaction. CHI '97, New York, USA.

25. Oviatt, S.L.: Mutual Disambiguation of Recognition Errors in a Multimodal Architecture. CHI'99, Pittsburgh, USA

26. Serna A., Pigot H. and Rialle V. Modeling the progression of Alzheimer's disease for cognitive assistance in smart homes. User Modeling and User-Adapted Interaction 17 (2007): 415-438.

27. Smith, A., Dunaway, J., Demasco, P., and Peichl, D.: Multimodal input for computer access and alternative communication. ASSETS'96, Vancouver, Canada.

28. Stephanidis C. et. al.: Adaptable And Adaptive User Interfaces for Disabled Users in the AVANTI Project. Intelligence In Services And Networks, LNCS-1430, Springer-Verlag 1998. 153-166.

29. Trewin s. et. al.: Developing steady clicks:: a method of cursor assistance for people with motor impairments, ASSETS 2006

30. Vitense, H. S., Jacko, J. A., and Emery, V. K. Multimodal feedback: An assessment of performance and mental workload. Ergonomics 46, pp. 66-87, 2003.

Accessibility of 3D Game Environments for People with Aphasia: An Exploratory Study

Julia Galliers[1], Stephanie Wilson[1], Sam Muscroft[1],
Jane Marshall[2,] Abi Roper[2], Naomi Cocks[2], Tim Pring[2]

[1]Centre for HCI Design
School of Informatics
City University London
Northampton Square
London EC1V 0HB, UK
jrg@soi.city.ac.uk

[2]Dept of Language and Communication Science
School of Health Sciences
City University London
Northampton Square
London EC1V 0HB, UK
j.marshall@city.ac.uk

ABSTRACT

People with aphasia experience difficulties with all aspects of language and this can mean that their access to technology is substantially reduced. We report a study undertaken to investigate the issues that confront people with aphasia when interacting with technology, specifically 3D game environments. Five people with aphasia were observed and interviewed in twelve workshop sessions. We report the key themes that emerged from the study, such as the importance of direct mappings between users' interactions and actions in a virtual environment. The results of the study provide some insight into the challenges, but also the opportunities, these mainstream technologies offer to people with aphasia. We discuss how these technologies could be more supportive and inclusive for people with language and communication difficulties.

Categories and Subject Descriptors

H.5.m [Information Systems]: Information Interfaces and Presentation — *Miscellaneous*.

General Terms

Human Factors, Design.

Keywords

Aphasia, stroke, 3D games, virtual environments, accessible interaction design.

1. INTRODUCTION

Aphasia is a language disorder caused by damage to the areas of the brain that are responsible for language. It is most commonly caused by a stroke. People with aphasia have difficulty with all aspects of language: speaking, reading, writing and understanding. The negative impact of this can be immense for the individual,

their family and social circle. Aphasia has profound implications for quality of life [11]. Those affected report loss of family roles, friendships and employment [19]. Aphasia affects substantial numbers of people. There are currently about 250,000 people living with aphasia in the UK [21], with approximately 45,000 new cases each year, and an estimated 1 million people with aphasia in the US [15].

With computing technologies, in a myriad of forms, becoming increasingly pervasive and embedded within the everyday lives of many people, it is valuable to consider how accessible these technologies are to people with aphasia. At present, interaction with most computing technology still requires the expression and comprehension of language. Yet many people with aphasia struggle in these areas. For example, they struggle to comprehend spoken and written language, particularly when the material is long or complex [4], meaning that access to technology such as the Internet and recreational computer games is reduced [7] or denied.

In this paper, we report a study undertaken to investigate the experiences of people with aphasia when interacting with state-of-the-art computing technology in the form of 3D game environments. Our aim was to explore both the challenges and the opportunities afforded by these environments for people with language communication difficulties. There has been some previous research that indicates the positive effects of computer games in the rehabilitation of motor performance following a stroke [1, 2 and 8] but we have found no similar work related to the use of computer games specifically by people with aphasia.

The study described here was undertaken in the context of the GReAT project (Gesture Recognition in Aphasia Therapy) [10], an interdisciplinary research collaboration between Human-Computer Interaction (HCI) researchers and Language and Communication Science researchers. The eventual goal of this project is to develop and trial a prototype gesture therapy software package that will support people with aphasia in practicing a number of communicative gestures. The project has a strong commitment to user participation and recruited five people with aphasia to work as consultants. The consultants worked with the project researchers in exploratory evaluations of a range of technologies, including the work reported here, both as a precursor to the design of the therapy package and, more broadly, to help us understand the interaction needs of this user group.

We firstly summarize related research into the design and evaluation of computing technologies for people who have had a stroke and people with aphasia. Sections 3, 4 and 5 then report the study that we undertook to investigate how people with aphasia interact with game technologies (i.e. the hardware devices) and 3D game environments, thereby providing some insight into the challenges and the opportunities that these technologies offer to people with aphasia. The main findings are organized as a series of "lessons learned", focusing on key themes that emerged from the data. The findings have immediate implications for the design of game environments, suggesting ways in which these mainstream technologies could be more supportive and accessible for people with language and communication difficulties. However, it is our belief that many of our results have broader implications and are applicable not just to 3D game environments but also to other forms of interactive computing technology. They offer insight into effective interaction design for this user population that is of direct relevance to projects like GReAT.

2. BACKGROUND

Previous research into computer game technologies for people who have had a stroke has focused largely on physical rehabilitation rather than communication difficulties. For example, Alankus et al [1] describe the adaptation of existing games to enable practice of nine different types of arm movement. They used Wii technologies and a webcam application that tracked a coloured sock worn or held by the user to effect changes in 3D scenes. They report lessons learned about developing games for this group of users, such as the need to support multiple modes of user input, the need for direct and natural mappings between input actions and effects, the importance of utilising audio as well as visual feedback and of including non-player characters and storylines, amongst others. Some of these lessons are confirmed in the study reported in this paper, although our focus is on people with aphasia rather than stroke itself.

The same team report lessons learned about home-based, repeated game-based rehabilitation from a case study involving a 62 year old woman, seventeen years post-stroke, who played motion-based therapeutic games over a six week period [2]. They found that their video-based game approach improved her motivation to do the therapy and she consequently made significant progress resulting in improved motor control. Additional effects included the fact that the games helped her to channel her frustration.

There are other examples of physical rehabilitation via games following stroke. Jung et al [12] developed a virtual reality game called 'The Reaching Task' which integrated 3D stereo visualization and a tracking system for an interactive virtual environment; users wore active liquid crystal shutter eyewear with an emitter to perceive the 3D stereo effect and distinguish difference in depth among virtual targets which they had to reach for. Flynn et al. [8] describe using the Sony PlayStation 2 Gaming Platform with one individual post-stroke to show the positive motivational element of game playing and how it enabled practice of certain physical movements, which led to some clinical improvement. [23] is a website set up by a physiotherapist and dedicated to rehabilitative games for all sorts of disabilities, including stroke, using the Wii.

Most computer-based applications specifically for people with aphasia are concerned with assisting communication. For example, Daeman et al created a storytelling application in which people with aphasia could create and share their stories from pictures they took themselves [5]. The Aphasia project developed

PDA applications for people with aphasia to independently manage appointments and communicate via an individualized store of frequently used phrases. PhotoTalk, another application from the same project, allows people with aphasia to capture and manage digital photographs to support face-to-face communication [3]. A number of therapeutic applications have also been developed, such as SentenceShaper [16], which supports the composition of grammatical language, and AphasiaScripts [13], which provides a platform for conversation practice. There are also a few commercially available communication aid technologies specifically for people with aphasia, such as Dynavox [6], Lingraphica [14] and Touchspeak [22]. The focus of these is on icons and pre-loaded phrases or sentences for mobile devices such as PDAs.

We have found no previous research that is specifically concerned with developing a general understanding of the competencies and limitations of people with aphasia when interacting with computing technologies. Nor have we found any studies that investigate 3D game environments for people with aphasia. The latter is the focus of the study reported here, but we believe that the results contribute towards understanding the interaction needs of people with aphasia more generally.

3. METHOD

We undertook an exploratory study to investigate how people with aphasia interact with and respond to 3D game environments and individual elements of such environments. The study was run as a series of participatory workshops.

3.1 The Participants

Five people with aphasia participated in the study. As mentioned in section 1, these participants were recruited as consultants to the GReAT project. They were recruited on the basis of all being at least several years post stroke, but otherwise representing a range of people with aphasia. They varied in terms of age, gender and the difficulties they experienced with language. (Pseudonyms are used throughout this paper in referring to the consultants.)

Sarah was the youngest consultant. She was in her early twenties, had a stroke three years prior to our study and was able to use one or two words at a time. She understood what was said to her and could read individual words. She was familiar with computer technologies and had an iPhone. She could use only her left hand.

Tanya was in her thirties, had her stroke nine years previously and spoke in short sentences. She could not read or write and sometimes struggled to understand but generally got the gist of conversations. She used Skype regularly and also viewed photos on Facebook. She could use only her left hand.

Ann was in her sixties, had her stroke many years ago and generally understood what was said to her but struggled to speak words. She used a (paper) 'communication book' in which she kept photos and pictures. She was able to use both hands. Ann was not a user of technology.

Tom was in his sixties, had his stroke three years previously and communicated with few words but he drew pictures. He could read clear text and understood what was said to him. He was able to use both hands.

Martin was in his seventies, had his stroke two and a half years previously and could use one or two words at a time but found communicating very difficult. He did not always understand what was said to him. Martin was able to use both hands.

3.2 Participatory workshops

The exploratory study reported here was undertaken as a series of twelve participatory workshops over a six month period. Each workshop had a specific research question to explore, such as which mode of presenting instructions or providing feedback was the most effective. The workshops lasted approximately two hours and each consultant attended seven of these workshops, referred to as sessions 1-7 in the description below. The first workshop was an introductory session attended by all five consultants; subsequent workshops were attended by either 2 or 3 consultants. A speech and language therapy (SLT) researcher and two human-computer interaction (HCI) researchers facilitated all the workshops.

All workshops followed the same structure. Each commenced with some introductory, non-computer-based activity, often in the form of a round-the-table game. The main activity then involved the consultants individually (and sometimes collaboratively) interacting with a 3D game environment or elements of such environments. These activities were videoed for later analysis, yielding rich observational data. Finally, to supplement the observations with the consultants' perceptions, the sessions ended with individual interviews with the SLT researcher. Interviews were supported by the use of paper-based rating scales. Consultants were asked to rate aspects of their experience on a scale from 1 – 5, shown with a thumbs-up sign at one end of the scale and a thumbs-down sign at the other end which they could point to, or pictures which they could rank in order of preference. For example, in session 2 which explored Nintendo's Wii Sports, the consultants were asked about the instructions, the weight and feel of the Wiimote controller, use of its buttons - whether these were easy or hard and what they liked or did not like about them. Visual aids such as the controller itself and screenshots were used to assist with recall and to focus attention. The consultants were also asked to rank how 'fun' they found the session. The interviews were videoed.

All session videos (including introductory activities, main activities and interviews) were reviewed carefully afterwards by one of the HCI researchers and the SLT researcher, and a detailed summary was written for each session. The more quantitative data from the rating activities was also summarized. The reflections in this paper are based on both the observational data and the quantitative data.

3.3 Workshop sessions

The seven sessions attended by each consultant were as follows:

Session 1: Introductory session. First, the consultants were introduced to the project. The consultants and researchers then spent some time getting to know each other through one-to-one discussions focused around a set of pre-determined topics. (Given the language difficulties that all the consultants experienced, the "discussions" involved much gesturing, drawing and referring to physical artefacts such as photos and notes, as well as limited verbalisations.) Name badges were used at this and every subsequent session.

Session 2: Nintendo Wii Sports. This exploratory session introduced the consultants to the Wii 3D environment and avatars (digital characters). The main activity investigated the consultants' interaction with two games from Nintendo's Wii Sports: tennis and bowling. We were interested in how the consultants handled the Wiimote controller (especially in view of movement limitations post-stroke), their understanding of the

controls on the controller, their understanding of the mappings between their movement of the controller and the resulting changes on the screen, their perceptions of the different screens, their understanding of instructions, and whether they enjoyed the games or not.

Session 3: Gesture recognition technologies. Many game environments take users' gestures as input (e.g. Microsoft's Kinect) and this session investigated two different approaches to gesture input and recognition. The first was a vision-based gesture recognition technology that used a webcam with OpenCV [18], an open source library of functions and algorithms for real time computer vision including hand-shape recognition and motion tracking. We had trained OpenCV to recognize five different hand shapes, e.g. scissors and stone. The second was the Wiimote again, but this time it was used as an input device in combination with wiigee, an open-source, gesture recognition library for accelerometer-based gestures [24]. We had defined and trained wiigee to recognize four gestures: watch, triangle, an S shape and a tennis serve.

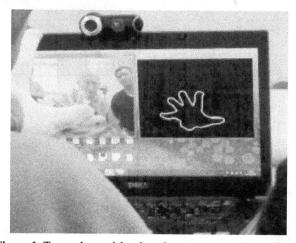

Figure 1. Tom using a vision-based gesture recognition system

The introductory activity involved showing five pictures and teaching the consultants the corresponding gestures. A gesturing game was also played. This served the purpose of showing everyone the gestures to be used and provided a fun and easy way of re-familiarizing everyone (memory being an associated issue for people with aphasia) and getting everyone relaxed. The main activity was making the gestures with the two different gesture recognition technologies (Figure 1).

Sessions 4-7: Explorations of 3D game environments. We developed several prototype 3D game environments using the Unity 3D [23] game development tool and incorporating the vision-based gesture recognition method developed using OpenCV software. Figures 2 and 3 show two of these environments: a town environment and a beach environment.

These environments were used to explore different aspects of interaction. Over several sessions, the participants repeatedly played a game in which a character travelled along a path in a 3D world. At certain points, the character stopped and the participants were presented with instructions to gesture. Making the correct gesture (successfully recognized) moved the game on. We explored different worlds of varying interest and complexity (hills, beach, a matrix, a town, rooms of a house), different methods of presenting gesturing instructions, different ways of giving feedback about the gestures that users had made, different methods and positions for representations of the gestures and pictures of the objects being gestured, different congratulatory messages, motivational scoring, a story line, and less or more control by the user in navigating the character through the world.

Figure 2. The 'town' world

Figure 3. The 'beach' world

4. RESULTS: THE TECHNOLOGIES

We first provide a summary overview of what happened in the sessions, describing our observations and the reactions of the consultants to the various technologies. Then, in section 5, we consider these reactions in terms of the issues they raise. We present these as a number of "lessons learned" regarding interaction design for people with aphasia.

4.1 Nintendo Wii and Wii Sports (Session 2)

All the consultants enjoyed playing the Wii Sports games. Tanya reported afterwards that she would now have the confidence to join in when her nephews played at home, whereas previously she had merely watched them play.

Handling the Wiimote – the weight, the shape, the buttons - was not a problem. With repetition and sufficient time, all the consultants learned to use the buttons, in particular the thumb and finger buttons, in the way the games required. However, sequences of actions, such as holding and then releasing buttons at a certain point, took some practice. Similarly, all the consultants found it much more difficult to hold two buttons at the same time than to use just one button. Two of the consultants needed to be reminded regularly about this, in particular after a short break. In

the bowling game, all consultants understood the direct mapping between left and right buttons and the movement of a red line on the screen showing which direction the ball would be bowled, but only Sarah understood how to elicit spin from the same buttons. (Sarah had played the game before). They all liked having their own characters.

The screens for the games were generally understood. The only problem was when we offered Tom and Sarah, who were able to play the tennis game very effectively, a two-person game with a split screen. This was too confusing for both of them. Tanya and Martin only played games where the characters were viewed from a first person perspective. Tom and Sarah did not seem to find first or third person any more or less difficult. Some aspects of the games were too quick for Martin – he needed more time to be able to react.

4.2 Accelerometer-based gesturing with Wiimote and wiigee (Session 3)

Gesture recognition with this technology was unreliable for our purposes, even when the consultants gestured reasonably accurately. This method requires a level of precision and conformity in the way gestures are made. Hence, although holding the Wiimote was not a problem, and holding down the button was not a problem (although most of the consultants needed reminding to do this at some point), the variations in the way individual consultants made the shapes in terms of size, speed and orientation meant a lot of failure and minimal positive feedback; this was very evidently disheartening. For example, at one point, Martin made an S shape back to front after having previously made it the right way round. One of his triangle shapes was only two-sided. Although Tom and Tanya were more consistent in the shapes they made, they too were frustrated and disheartened by the variability of response. All reported this as 'less fun' than the more reliable vision-based technology described in 4.3.

Two of the consultants, Sarah and Martin, tried using the Wiimote strapped to their arm in a purpose-built wrist strap as an alternative to holding it in the hand. They found it wobbly and awkward (and it could not be put on one-handed).

4.3 Computer vision-based gesturing with OpenCV (Session 3)

This technology does not use a controller as an input device. Instead, the OpenCV software recognizes hand shapes made in front of a webcam. In order for the gesture recognizer to readily separate the user's hand from other objects in the scene, we had trained it to pick out the colour yellow. The consultants were each given a yellow cotton glove to wear (see Figure 1) which they found fun and, thankfully, were mostly able to put on with ease - even Tanya and Sarah who had to do this one-handed. (We have since devised a very simple technique for putting on the glove one-handed, using a clothes peg and a clip board.)

Gesture recognition with this software was an instant 'hit' with the consultants. They all reported having fun whilst using it. They could see themselves and a contour of their hands, the yellow colour allowing a very clear separation from background details for their own visual feedback (as well as for the software). It is not the focus of this paper to describe the nature of the recognition algorithms we developed, but the fact that they were robust and more 'forgiving' than those described in section 4.2 allowed for greater variation in the way the gestures were made.

4.4 Exploring 3D game environments (Sessions 4-7)

The first time they saw the virtual worlds, Tanya and Sarah responded very positively, noting various features. For example Tanya pointed to tables and chairs outside a café, saying "I like this". Sarah indicated her preference for the beach world on more than one occasion. The other 3 consultants got on with performing the tasks of the game without reference to the background (until asked later in the interviews). We wondered whether this was due to Sarah and Tanya being younger, or possibly the fact that Sarah and Tanya were the most able at gesturing and so needed less concentration on the task, leaving them freer to notice other things. Tom did indicate in the interviews that he was busy focusing on performing the tasks he had to do and had not noticed when the world that he was playing in changed. The observations confirmed this; Ann, Tom and Martin were all very focused on the tasks. It appeared to require a lot of concentration from them. However, all said the game was fun and all engaged well with it.

Sarah and Tanya definitely liked having a character (which Sarah wanted to be female but Tanya did not mind). Ann answered that she too liked the character and did not mind if it was male or female. Martin rated the character at 2 (i.e. he liked it, but not at 1) and Tom said he would be just as happy without a character. He was also troubled by a change in perspective when the character stopped; the scene would change and appear as seen through the character's eyes. This was indicated by seeing the back of his head. 'What?' he asked, whilst pointing.

5. LESSONS LEARNED

The issues identified in this exploratory study can be usefully organized into two main categories: factors that impacted upon the consultants' motivation and enthusiasm for using the technology and factors arising from the design of the technologies that gave rise to specific interaction difficulties.

5.1 Motivation

A successful game is fun; players want to play it. Motivation is crucial for any game or other activity that we want people to engage in independently at home. The following four factors emerged as key with regards to how motivating (or de-motivating) the consultants found the game technologies and 3D game environments.

5.1.1 Reliability

A fun game reliably does what is expected (even when the "expected" is some element of surprise). As reported in section 4.2, recognition of gestures with the Wiimote and wiigee library was unreliable. Even when the consultants made the gestures apparently consistently, the software did not always recognize them and all the consultants reported finding this less fun than using the computer vision-based recognition with the glove. Tanya said at one point that it was a "stupid idea".

It was very obvious that when the consultants did not understand what was happening or why something was (or was not) happening, they quickly became de-motivated. Tom and Tanya expressed this by asking 'Why?' or 'What?' quite vehemently (see section 5.1.3 below on anger and frustration). In session 2, whilst using the Wiimote and wiigee library, all consultants expressed this via some aspect of their body language – slumping or shaking of the head, frowning, shrugging. Some of them then stopped trying.

5.1.2 Feedback and reassurance

One of the sessions with the 3D game environments was devoted to investigating the best method of presenting instructions from within the game. We presented instructions for five gestures (previously unseen) in a number of different ways that all included a picture of the object together with either: a video of a speech and language therapist (SLT), a cartoon avatar of the SLT, a video of a disembodied gloved hand, or a video of a contoured hand. These were presented randomly. The consultants were asked to copy the gestures as and when instructed. The researchers observed the activity but did not participate to avoid influencing the consultants' behaviour.

Initially, all the consultants copied quite well, though sometimes looking confused, sometimes hesitant. However, very quickly, the gesturing of some of the consultants deteriorated. They became frustrated, unsure whether what they were doing was correct or not. At one point, when one consultant in particular became upset and gave up, we interrupted the session and the SLT researcher presented the gesture in the same way as in the video, but face-to-face. As the consultant attempted to copy the gesture, the SLT researcher provided additional instructions such as, 'now lift your little finger'. The consultant was looking intently at the SLT's face, receiving feedback from her facial expressions and whether or not she chose to correct him. His anger and frustration were instantly defused. This incident exemplified the importance of reassurance and feedback and how de-motivating it can be when it is not there.

Similarly, in other sessions, before we had correctly adjusted the timing in the games between the recognition of a correct gesture and the story moving on, the consultants were unsure whether or not they had done it correctly. They looked to us for reassurance, querying or uttering 'Oh!'

We determined that it was insufficient for the game simply to move on after the user had taken some action, hence *implying* that the task in the game had been completed correctly (and this is how interaction proceeds in many game environments). In contrast, very definite, positive feedback - either visual or auditory - was also required.

5.1.3 Anger and frustration

Anger and frustration are natural side effects of not being able to communicate. Some of the consultants would become quite overtly frustrated when things did not work as expected or things happened that they could not understand. For example, this frustration was triggered by sudden changes in perspective, or by unexpected changes in the position of things on the screen (see section 5.2.4). At such points, one must assume that if they were playing the game at home, they would have simply given up. In our sessions, with full and patient explanations from the SLT researcher, understanding was achieved and the consultants were happy to continue with the session.

This indicates the importance of ensuring that games incorporate an appropriate level of challenge. Certain kinds of interaction design (see section 5.2) can in themselves pose challenges for people with aphasia in addition to the challenge of the game itself. More general design principles here are that there must always be a way of escaping from the game world and of obtaining help.

5.1.4 Positive effects

Playing games and achieving a result is rewarding. All the consultants enjoyed playing the games and noticeably gained confidence from participating in the sessions. As mentioned earlier, after the session with Wii Sports, Tanya commented that she would now be able to join in when her nephews played; previously she had just watched. Sarah and Tom particularly liked playing competitively against each other. The 'fun' rating that each consultant gave at the end of every session was consistently high.

As described in section 4.4, the consultants who found the games easier were more open to noticing the different game environments and commenting on features such as tables and chairs, or hills. Whenever a new environment was introduced, Tanya and Sarah in particular, pointed to features and made comments such as, '[I] like that'. Alternatively, Sarah said the matrix world was 'boring'. Liking the world appeared to increase the level of motivation with the game. However, those who had to concentrate more on performing the tasks in the game environments, such as Ann, Tom and Martin, did not comment on the worlds until they were more familiar and confident with what they needed to do.

Tom was very enthusiastic about playing tennis on Wii Sports. He indicated by making a tennis serve movement and pointing to himself, that he used to play before his stroke. Although he struggled at times to co-ordinate and remember the two simultaneous actions required when using the controller (see section 5.2.5) he was evidently motivated to keep trying and definitely enjoyed himself. He enjoyed the bowling less, whereas this situation was reversed for Martin (for reasons explained below).

5.2 Interaction

The following five issues relating to interaction with the game technologies and environments emerged as particularly important.

5.2.1 Controlling the pace

The pace of interaction with the 3D game environments was a theme that emerged from many of the sessions. There is a general expectation that people with communication difficulties will need extra time to interact with computers and play games. This was certainly true in some cases. For example, we observed Martin struggling with the pace of balls in the tennis game. However, interestingly there are also times when they may want things to move faster. For example, Tom thought the character walking between gesturing points took too long in the 3D worlds. Similarly, when playing Wii Sports, he thought the clapping and cheering when a point was scored was a distraction. He was much happier once told that by pressing the thumb button, he could cut short the celebratory feedback and allow the game to continue. Sarah already knew to do this. Martin and Ann however, seemed content to use such episodes as 'breathers' between tasks. The design principle here is that control is important; players should be able to pace the game themselves. When that control is not provided, the interaction can be incredibly frustrating.

5.2.2 Reminding

A key deficit in aphasia is the loss of access to words [17] and in some cases this is accompanied by difficulties with other symbols [20]. The consultants therefore needed regular reminders of people's names, how to use buttons and how to make gestures. The 'round-the-table' games, away from the computer, that started each session were very helpful in serving this purpose.

When playing the gesturing game in our 3D game environments (sessions 4-7), there were a couple of occasions when Ann took time with a particular gesturing task and then forgot what she was supposed to be gesturing. This led us to keep a constant visual reminder on the screen of where the player is in the course of the game. This is, of course, consistent with general HCI design principles about making the state of the system visible to the user, but it is a principle that is sometimes deliberately flouted in game environments.

In the Wii Sports session, most of the participants (except Sarah who had played before) needed repeated reminders and explanations, especially when complexity of the task increased. The consultants found it challenging to remember the sequences of button presses that were sometimes required to trigger an action in the game world. For example, when more than one button on the controller had to be pressed simultaneously, or when more than one move was required in a sequence such as holding the finger button, moving the controller and then letting go.

In general, it is important for aphasic users that instructions and required action sequences should be short and straightforward. Where feasible, compound action sequences should be replaced by single actions, such as only needing to press one large and obvious button, for example to both start a game and to respond within it, and that help be available at all levels.

5.2.3 Mapping and consistency

People with aphasia often find it hard to deal with abstract information [9]. The mapping between input actions and their effects on the screen therefore needs to be intuitive. In the Wii Sports bowling game for example, it was possible to alter the angle of the ball by pressing on 'left' and 'right' buttons on the controller. These buttons were obvious and, because of their positioning on the controller, their use was intuitive. A red line showing the angle shifted left or right on screen simultaneously with the user pressing the relevant button. The consultants found this easy to use. However, using the same buttons to spin the ball was not intuitive and proved too complex for most of the consultants. Likewise, when playing tennis, several of the consultants had difficulty remembering the combination of button presses required; there was no intuitive mapping between the buttons and their effect on the environment and no prompt on the screen. A similar finding is reported in [1].

Perspective also proved to be an issue in the games. Initially, when the character stopped in the 3D game environments and an action was required, the perspective would change and the environment would appear as if seen through the character's eyes. This confused several of the consultants. Some of the Wii Sports tennis games do the same. It appeared that it was the change in perspective that was confusing. There was no overall preferred perspective; it was consistency that was required.

Consistency in general was another aspect of the 3D environments that was very important to the consultants. They became familiar with the position of certain things on the screen, how instructions and feedback were represented, and how tasks were to be performed. When we explored alternative screen positions for objects (such as pictures of a target gesture), the main message that came through from the consultants was that they just needed these to be consistently in the same place.

5.2.4 Complexity, distraction and 'noise'

In general, the lighter the cognitive load in performing a task, the better it was for the consultants. For example, simply using a gloved hand to gesture was better than having to remember to simultaneously hold a button down on a controller such as the

Wiimote. In addition, keeping the screen (and 3D environment) relatively empty and navigation as simple as possible, was also effective in enhancing interaction. These are general guidelines for good interaction design, but they are especially important for people with aphasia who can be easily overwhelmed by too much complexity. In particular, including verbal or textual information is especially difficult for people with language and communication difficulties. Additional support can be made available [7] but there is also a conflict between offering support and this too being a distraction.

For example, certain clues, such as seeing a picture of the target gesture whilst making their own gestures, were helpful for some of the consultants. However, Tanya, one of the more competent gesturers, found this a distraction (because she did not need it). Ann, Tom and Martin, however, found the additional clue a great help. So what is a distraction for one individual is not necessarily for another.

Therefore, another design implication to result from these observations is that the system should provide the facility to switch certain support materials on and off, ideally whilst simultaneously trying to comply with another general principle of having no more than two (for our consultants) elements on the screen requiring attention at any one time.

5.2.5 Individual differences
In general, people vary in what they want from a game, what they like and how long they take to process what is required of them. So, while the preceding discussion has focused on issues experienced in common by the consultants, there were, of course, many individual differences. Effective and motivating interaction design must be sensitive to these also. For example, Sarah was the only consultant who persistently expressed a preference for a female avatar. This could have been because she was already familiar with games such as Wii Sports where a character can be created in one's own image.

Another case was reaction time. Martin, for example, understood exactly what he needed to do in the WiiSports tennis game, but could not react quickly enough, whereas the other consultants did not experience the same difficulty. The bowling game, on the other hand, was paced appropriately and gave him sufficient time to respond.

People with aphasia have very individual difficulties with language and these extend to their experience with interactive computing technologies. They may well change over time. The requirement to handle these variations, as well as to respond to personal preferences, means that it is crucial that many aspects of systems should be tailorable to reflect an individual's preferences and abilities. Similarly, as discussed in section 5.2.4, the level of support needed to perform a task will vary. Alternative levels of support should be available at all levels of the game.

6. CONCLUSIONS
People with aphasia can feel isolated and excluded from technology. Yet our study clearly demonstrated that the consultants were able to have fun and gain confidence whilst playing games in 3D environments. We said in the introduction that our aim was to provide some insights into the challenges and opportunities for people with aphasia interacting with 3D games. We want to suggest ways in which these mainstream technologies could be more supportive and accessible for people with language

and communication difficulties. In summary, our exploratory study has led us to the following suggestions:

- Characters, story lines, patterns of navigation or of progression, feedback, etc, all need to behave reliably and consistently. Items on the screen should appear in consistent locations. All aspects of the game and the 3D environment should conform to players' expectations.

- Non-textual, visible reminders are important. For example, to show the current state of interaction, to show the player where he/she is in the course of the game.

- Positive, explicit feedback (visual and auditory) is crucial for maintaining confidence and motivating the player to continue. The player needs to be reassured that what he/she has done is correct.

- 3D game environments for people with aphasia should contain minimal distractions, allowing them to focus on the primary game task.

- Players should be able to progress through a game (or any other application) at their own pace, which means that they can speed up, as well as slow down, the course of the game. This needs to be achieved without adding complex layers of navigation.

- The mappings between input actions (e.g. using controls on hardware input devices or gestures) and effects within the 3D environment must be direct and intuitive. Compound sequences of actions should be avoided.

- Players have very individual preferences which should be catered for. For example, the capability to select characters of different genders, and game worlds that contain different elements to reflect the user's individual interests.

- Similarly, there should be the facility to change certain settings, for example, to accommodate different reaction times.

- Additional support should be available, but it should be possible to switch this off. Supports that are not needed are a distraction.

- It should be possible to escape from the game world and get help at any time by one simple action.

- Verbal instructions should be kept to a minimum.

In conclusion, the study reported here has focused on developing an understanding of the interaction needs of people with aphasia, attending to issues related to the challenges they face in using language rather than challenges arising from other post-stroke deficits such as movement limitations. Through a series of workshops, we have investigated how people with aphasia interact with 3D game environments, considering where interaction design is effective and where it is less so. The findings are making an important contribution to the design of the gesture-based therapy tool for the GReAT project, providing a solid foundation for our design decisions. However, reflecting upon the principles for interaction design given in the list above, we would argue that these results are not limited to 3D game environments but have broader applicability. These principles offer insights that should help enable effective and accessible interaction design for this user population with all manner of other applications, and, in so doing, enhance and enrich lives.

7. ACKNOWLEDGMENTS

This work was funded by the Research Councils UK Digital Economy Programme (EPSRC grant EP/I001824/1). We would like to express our gratitude to our collaborators, The Stroke Association, and the five consultants who participated in the study.

8. REFERENCES

[1] Alankus, G, Lazar, A., May, M. and Kelleher, K. 2010. Towards Customizable Games for Stroke Rehabilitation. In *Proceedings of the 28th International Conference on human factors in computing systems,* (Atlanta USA, April 2010) CHI'10. ACM, New York, NY. 2113-2122. DOI= http://doi.acm.org/10.1145/1753326.1753649

[2] Alankus, G., Proffitt, R., Kelleher, C., and Engsberg, J. 2010. Stroke Therapy through Motion-Based Games: A Case Study. *In Proceedings of the 12th international ACM SIGACCESS conference on computers and accessibility.* (Orlando, Florida, USA October 25th – 27th, 2010). ASSETS'10. ACM, New York, NY, 219- 226. DOI= http://doi.acm.org/10.1145/1878803.1878842

[3] Allen, M., McGrenere, J., and Purves, B. 2007. The Design and Field Evaluation of PhotoTalk: a digital image communication application for people with aphasia. *In Proceedings of the 9th international ACM SIGACCESS conference on computers and accessibility.* ASSETS'07. ACM, New York, NY,. DOI= http://doi.acm.org/10.1145/1296843.1296876

[4] Berndt, R.S. 1998. Sentence processing in aphasia. In *Acquired Aphasia* (3rd Edition), M. Sarno, Ed. Academic Press, New York.

[5] Daeman, E., Dadlani, P., Du, J., Li, Y., Erik-Paker, P., Martens, J., and De Ruyter, B. 2007. Designing a free style, indirect, and interactive storytelling application for people with aphasia. *Human Computer Interaction – INTERACT 2007*, Lecture Notes in Computer Science, 2007, Volume 4662/2007, 221-234, DOI: 10.1007/978-3-540-74796-3_21 221--234.

[6] Dynavox company homepage, 2010. Retrieved May 5th, 2011, from DynaVox Mayer-Johnson: http://www.dynavoxtech.com/

[7] Egan, J., Worrall, L., and Oxenham, D. 2004. Accessible internet training package helps people with aphasia cross the digital divide. *Aphasiology,* 18, 3, 265 – 280.

[8] Flynn, S., Palma, P., & Bender, A. 2007. Feasibility of Using the Sony PlayStation 2 Gaming Platform for an Individual Poststroke: A Case Report. *Journal of Neurologic Physical Therapy,* 31, 4, 180-189.

[9] Franklin, S., Howard. D., and Patterson, K. 1994. Abstract word meaning deafness. *Cognitive Neuropsychology*, 11, 1 – 34.

[10] GReAT project homepage, 2011. Retrieved 27th April, 2010, from School of Informatics, City University London: www.soi.city.ac.uk/great

[11] Hilari K. and Byng S. 2009. Health-related quality of life in people with severe aphasia. *International Journal of Language and Communication Disorders*, 44, 2, 193-205.

[12] Jung, Y., Yeh, S., and Stewart, J. 2006. Tailoring virtual reality technology for stroke rehabilitation: a human factors design. *In Proceedings of the CHI '06 extended abstracts on Human factors in computing systems*, ACM 2006, 929-934. DOI= doi>10.1145/1125451.1125631.

[13] Lee, J., Kaye, R. and Cherney, L. 2009. Conversational script performance in adults with non fluent aphasia: Treatment intensity and aphasia severity. *Aphasiology*, 23, 7/8, 885 – 897.

[14] Lingraphica company homepage, 2009. Retrieved May 5th, 2011, from Lingraphicare America, Inc.: http://www.aphasia.com/

[15] Living with Stroke: Aphasia Information, 2010. Retrieved May 4th, 2011, from Internet Stroke Center at UT Southwestern Medical Center: http://www.strokecenter.org/patients/aphasia.html

[16] McCall, D., Virata, T., Linebarger, M., and Berndt, R.S. 2009. Integrating technology and targeted treatment to improve narrative production in aphasia: A case study. *Aphasiology*, 23, 4, 438- 462.

[17] Nickels, L.A. 1997. *Spoken word production and its breakdown in aphasia.* Hove, UK : Psychology Press.

[18] OpenCV programming library, 2011, Retrieved 27th April, 2011, from OpenCVWiki: http://opencv.willowgarage.com/wiki/

[19] Parr, S., Byng, S. and Gilpin, S. 1997. *Talking About Aphasia.* Buckingham: Open University Press.

[20] Rose, M. 2006. The utility of gesture treatments in aphasia. *Advances in Speech Language Pathology*, 8 (2), 92-109.

[21] Speakability charity homepage, 2011. Retrieved 27th April, 2011, from Speakability: www.speakability.org.uk

[22] Touchspeak company homepage, 2007. Retrieved May 5th, 2011, from Touchspeak: http://www.touchspeak.co.uk/

[23] Unity company homepage, 2011. Retrieved 27th April, 2011, from Unity Technologies USA http://unity3d.com

[24] Wiigee open-source gesture recognition library, 2008. Retrieved 27th April, 2011, from Benjamin Poppinga and Thomas Schlömer, University of Oldenburg, Germany: http://wiigee.org

[25] Wiihabilitation project homepage, 2010. Retrieved May 5th, 2011, from wiihabilitation.co.uk: www.wiihabilitation.co.uk)

The Interplay Between Web Aesthetics and Accessibility

Grace Mbipom
School of Computer Science
University of Manchester
England, M13 9PL, UK
grace.mbipom@cs.manchester.ac.uk

Simon Harper
School of Computer Science
University of Manchester
England, M13 9PL, UK
simon.harper@manchester.ac.uk

ABSTRACT

Visual aesthetics enhances user experience in the context of the World Wide Web (Web). Accordingly, many studies report positive relationships between Web aesthetics and facets of user experience like usability and credibility, but does this hold for accessibility also? This paper describes an empirical investigation towards this end. The aesthetic judgements of 30 sighted Web users were elicited to understand what types of Web design come across as being visually pleasing. Participants judged 50 homepages based on Lavie and Tractinsky's *classical* and *expressive* Web aesthetics framework. A cross-section of the homepages were then manually audited for accessibility compliance by 11 Web accessibility experts who used a heuristic evaluation technique known as the Barrier Walkthrough (BW) method to check for accessibility barriers that could affect people with visual impairments. Web pages judged on the classical dimension as being visually clean showed significant correlations with accessibility, suggesting that visual cleanness may be a suitable proxy measure for accessibility as far as people with visual impairments are concerned. Expressive designs and other aesthetic dimensions showed no such correlation, however, demonstrating that an expressive or aesthetically pleasing Web design is not a barrier to accessibility.

Categories and Subject Descriptors

H.5.2 [**Information Interfaces and Presentation**]: User Interfaces (D.2.2, H.1.2, I.3.6) - Evaluation/Methodology, User-centred design; K.4.2 [**Computers and Society**]: Social Issues-Assistive technologies for persons with disabilities

General Terms

Design, Experimentation, Human Factors

Keywords

User Experience, Visual Aesthetics, Web Accessibility

1. INTRODUCTION

The increasing levels of competition among organisations with an on-line presence has facilitated the need for sophisticated and fanciful visual designs. Sometimes, in a bid to attract on-line visitors, the visual appearance of a Web page is placed ahead of its functionality. How to maintain a balance between form and function has been a long standing issue for disciplines with elements of visual design [7]. The present study seeks to address a case of this design dilemma by investigating the interplay between visual aesthetics and accessibility considerations in the context of the Web.

Although visually attractive sites enhance Web experience for sighted users [10, 28, 30], these sort of sites are speculated to hinder people with disabilities, especially those with visual impairments[1] [31]. On the other hand, most Web designers perceive the accessibility initiative to be restrictive creativity-wise [24, 27]. Web accessibility practitioners' efforts to mediate between these two extremes have met with challenges, primarily because the current state of affairs seem not to support claims that appealing Web designs can go hand in glove with accessibility [27]. The nature of the interaction between the use of Web aesthetics and accessibility still remains unclear. A proper understanding of this interaction will help address some of the misconceptions that surround accessible designs. These misunderstandings have slowed down the advancement of inclusive Web design.

To aid to our investigation, the following research questions were considered: i) What types of Web design come across as aesthetically pleasing to sighted users? In order to answer this first question, Lavie and Tractinsky's Web aesthetics framework was used to classify Web pages. They found that perceived visual aesthetic aspects of the Web are "bi-dimensional", with classical and expressive aspects. The first dimension represents early visual design principles rooted in clarity and orderliness, while the second dimension highlights designs which showcase a Web designer's ingenuity [15]. ii) What is the relationship between Web aesthetics and accessibility? To answer this second question, manual accessibility audits were performed on Web pages whose aesthetic quality had already been determined in (i). Web accessibility experts examined a cross-section of the Web pages for accessibility barriers which could affect people with visual impairments. We did not employ user-testing, another effective manual accessibility evaluation technique for the following reasons: It is expensive [19]; It is also difficult to find people with disabilities of the same degree, who have

---

[1]Visual impairments here include blindness, low-vision and colour-blindness.

the same level of computing expertise [14, 25]; A person with disabilities may have more than one disability. As a result, such a person may be affected by multiple Web accessibility barriers which an evaluator may not be able to account for in one go [25, 34]; People with disabilities have different assistive technologies and personal adaptations. An evaluator may not be able to create the same environment [25]; The user's ability to use the assistive technologies available is another issue [14, 32]. We reckoned that the level of subjectivity would be greater if user-testing was employed, compared with the use of Web accessibility experts. It is important to note that no one evaluation method can identify all the accessibility issues on a Website [19, 29]. Hybrid approaches are agreed to be the most effective. In particular, expert reviews have been shown to be very effective when multiple evaluators are involved, and a combination of techniques are used [19]. We employed 11 experts, and they made use of a combination of accessibility evaluation tools and techniques.

The study reveals the relationship between Web aesthetics and accessibility to be a rather complex one. Web pages judged on the classical dimension as being visually *clean* were more readily accessible, while expressive Web designs (*fascinating* and *creative*) and other aesthetic dimensions showed no significant relationships with accessibility.

2. AESTHETICS AND WEB EXPERIENCE

The effect of visual aesthetics on user experience has been widely investigated in Web domains. Most studies report a positive relationship between Web aesthetics and the facet of user experience which they investigate. In general, Web users perceive visually attractive Websites to be more credible [13, 28], usable [1, 10, 26], useful [8, 12] and desirable [30], compared with sites that are not as visually adorned.

In the usability case, however, while some studies report a straightforward strong positive relationship, because Websites which users perceive to be aesthetically pleasing are also perceived to be easy to use (e.g [1, 12, 16, 26]). Other studies relay a more complex interaction, as such strong positive associations exist given certain conditions only. For example, when the aesthetic quality of Web pages are considered under 'classical' or 'expressive' dimensions as defined in [15], Web pages preferred on the classical dimension show stronger positive relationships with usability. Classical designs are simple and clear. Expressive designs which are usually more sophisticated in nature tend to be less closely related with usability [9, 11, 15]. This insight is particularly important for our study, since usability and accessibility are considered to be closely related facets of user experience.

Very few studies explicitly address the relationship between visual design and accessibility. In one of such studies [27] where the state of affairs in accessible design was discussed, the author highlighted the gaps between visual designs and Web accessibility, and the challenges which accessible designs present to Web designers. The study was based on the author's industrial design experiences, and the outcomes were mostly advisory in nature. No empirical data was gathered as such. In another closely related study [24] which was empirical in nature, 3 out of 100 Websites ascertained to be highly accessible by people with disabilities were also shown to have complex visual designs. The authors concluded that accessibility considerations do not prevent Web designers from creating Websites with complex visual designs. Along with the limited number of case studies

employed, their work highlights one aspect of visual designs which is complexity. Visual complexity, however, happens to be a rather weak indicator of aesthetic pleasure in Web domains [23, 33]. As such, questions regarding the relationship between the use of Web aesthetics and accessibility remain unanswered. The closest to our study is our earlier work [20] in which we established that there was a link between Web aesthetics and accessibility which required further investigations. In that preliminary study, an automated accessibility checker, Cynthia Says[2] was used to examine Web pages whose aesthetic quality had already been determined. We found that Web pages which were rated by sighted users as being *clean, clear* and *organised* significantly violated fewer checkpoints specified in Web Content Accessibility Guidelines (WCAG) 1.0 [6]. Web pages rated as being *beautiful* or *interesting* showed no significant relationships with the number of accessibility checkpoints violated.

The present study extends our previous work and closely related studies in a number of ways: i) More Web pages were examined here for their aesthetic quality, compared to our previous study. As such, a wider range of Web designs were taken into account considering the subjectivity of aesthetic preference ii) A more reliable method for measuring Web accessibility is employed here as well. Manual accessibility evaluations were conducted by Web accessibility experts who are well versed in the field iii) The manual evaluation technique employed here distinguishes between disability types, and takes into account the severity of accessibility barriers found a Web page, whereas automated checkers do not and finally iv) Our work extends the aforementioned closely related studies by adopting an empirical approach and a widely validated framework for Web aesthetics respectively, in order to explain the interplay between Web aesthetics and accessibility as it affects people with visual impairments.

3. STUDY 1 - AESTHETIC JUDGEMENTS

The aim of this study was to investigate how sighted users rate the visual quality of Web pages. This facilitated the classification of Web pages based on five design dimensions: *clean, pleasing, fascinating, creative* and *aesthetic*. Design features which moderated users' judgements were also elicited.

3.1 Participants

Thirty-two (32) participants, 25 males and 7 females were recruited for the study. Two persons (males) had invalid responses, so their data were not included in the final analysis. Consequently, there were 30 participants with valid responses, 23 males and 7 females with ages ranging from 16 to 41 and over. Twenty six (26) were undergraduate and postgraduate students from computing and life sciences departments, while 4 were professionals with nursing, teaching, veterinary medicine and engineering as their backgrounds. All the participants were frequent Web users. One person reported a mild case of colour blindness. Interviews before and after the task confirmed that the impairment he claimed did not affect the purpose of the experiment. Moreover, the inclusion or removal of his data did not influence the means or standard deviations for the participants' ratings significantly, hence, his data was included. From a cultural point of view, there were 16 Whites (British), 5 Blacks, 3 Asians, 2 Chinese, and 4 others (2 Arabics, 1 German, 1 Iraqi).

---

[2]Cynthia Says - http://www.cynthiasays.com/

3.2 Stimuli

Fifty (50) homepages were used for the study. This allowed for the investigation of a wide variety of Web designs. Homepages were used because they represent gateways to Websites. In agreement with Pandir and Knight [23], we judged that the use of visual aesthetics may be more crucial for homepages. The Web pages were randomly selected from the top 100 UK Websites as ranked by Alexa[3]. We also used randomly selected Web pages from the winners and nominees list for the Webby awards[4] under the best visual aesthetic design and home/welcome page categories for years 2005 to 2009. All the Web pages from Alexa were downloaded on the 10th of November, 2009, while the Web pages from the Webby award's Website were downloaded on the 23rd of November 2009, and then merged together to form a pool. The 50 Web pages were stored locally, and presented together with all their interactive features to the participants. The Web pages represented news, sports, entertainment, education, blogging, search, government, social networking, e-commerce and leisure genres among others.

3.3 Task and Procedure

Participants were first made to read an information sheet outlining the aim of the study. On agreeing to participate, a consent form was signed and a demographic form filled. The task was to judge the visual quality of 50 homepages. Participants were shown a homepage for 4 seconds, and were free to scroll up or down the page as they would normally do when browsing. However, they could not navigate away from the homepage. This was to ensure stimulus uniformity. After 4 seconds, another page was shown instructing participants to rate the Web page they had just seen based on the 5 design dimensions under investigation. A 7-point Likert scale was used, and the scores were written on a paper questionnaire. After rating a Web page, participants then clicked the 'next' button. This made another homepage appear for 4 seconds as before, after which a page with instructions to rate followed. The viewing time was set to 4 seconds because we were interested in visceral responses. Previous studies report viewing times ranging from 50 milliseconds [17] to 7 seconds [21] for gathering visceral responses. The pages were ordered in two different ways to counter balance any position effects, and participants had to rate twice.

Judgements were based on Lavie and Tractinsky's Web aesthetic dimensions [15], and the adjectives *clean, pleasing* and *fascinating, creative* were selected to represent the two dimensions respectively. Participants also gave an overall score under the term *beautiful/aesthetic*. A close examination of Lavie and Tractinsky's framework will reveal that some of their terms are very much related. For example, the following pairs are synonyms: clean and clear; original and creative. Hence, we chose a subset of terms that were semantically disparate. Their framework has also been criticized for the inclusion of the term 'aesthetic', firstly as a design dimension of aesthetics [17], and secondly under the classical dimension only [22]. Consequently, we gathered the overall judgements of the participants under the term 'aesthetic'. Also, the word 'beautiful' was used alongside 'aesthetic' in the questionnaire to aid people who were not familiar with the word 'aesthetic'. As we had users with differing back-

grounds in mind, we did not make use of a more technical design dimension like 'symmetrical' from their framework. Qualitative feedback was gathered after the experiment. Experiment sessions lasted between 30 minutes and 1 hour depending on the participants' judgement speed, and after task discussions. The participants were paid £10 for their time.

3.4 Results

Means and standard deviations were computed for each of the 50 homepages based on the participants' ratings for the pages, given the 5 design dimensions. This allowed the Web pages to be ranked under the different aesthetic dimensions. A Pearson correlation analysis was performed between each of the four design dimensions and the overall term 'aesthetic' using the mean ratings given by the participants. Figure 1 and Table 1 show that visual cleanness had the least positive correlation with the term 'aesthetic', suggesting the term 'clean' to be most unlike the other design dimensions. Clean homepages were found to have a simple and less-dense compositional layout, usually with one main image and a mostly white background. While cluttered homepages had a complex, dense look and feel, with heavy text presence and/or segmentation of the layout.

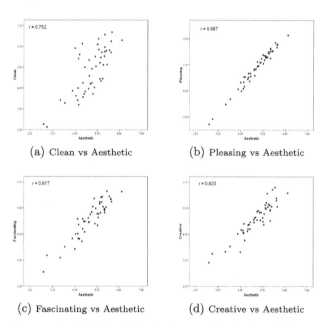

(a) Clean vs Aesthetic (b) Pleasing vs Aesthetic

(c) Fascinating vs Aesthetic (d) Creative vs Aesthetic

Figure 1: Relationship between the design dimensions investigated and the term 'aesthetic'

Table 1: Pearson correlation matrix for Figure 1

r	Clean	Pleasing	Fascinating	Creative	Aesthetic
Clean	1.000	0.781	0.471	0.513	0.752
Pleasing		1.000	0.898	0.891	0.987
Fascinating			1.000	0.958	0.917
Creative				1.000	0.920
Aesthetic					1.000

All correlations are significant at the 0.01 level (2-tailed)

Expressive aspects (fascinating and creative) had a stronger positive relationship with the term 'aesthetic'. Expressive Web designs made use of moderate to heavy animations and were very colourful. They also contained more images than

[3]http://www.alexa.com/topsites/countries/GB
[4]http://webbyawards.com/

clean homepages. The term 'pleasing' had the strongest relationship overall with the term 'aesthetic'. Perhaps the participants perceived the term 'pleasing' to be a general design dimension as well. Recall that the participants were asked to give an overall visual quality score under the term 'aesthetic'. It was particularly difficult to determine Web page attributes which moderated participants' ratings for the design dimensions 'pleasing' and 'aesthetic'. The Web pages which topped the chart in these two categories exhibited a combination of characteristics found in the other design dimensions. A similar concern is raised in [22].

In general, if a page received a high rating for one design dimension, it was likely to receive similar ratings for other dimensions, suggesting a positive link between the terms. The correlation analysis in Table 1 confirms this. However, this was not always the case for homepages which topped the chart as being visually clean. Some of them performed poorly in the expressive design realm, hence the moderate correlations between the design dimensions *clean* and *fascinating* (r = 0.471), as well as *clean* and *creative* (r = 0.513).

4. STUDY 2 - ACCESSIBILITY AUDITS

The purpose of this study was to investigate the accessibility level of a cross-section of homepages whose visual aesthetic quality had been determined in Study 1. Based on insights gained from the usability case discussed earlier in the background and related work section (Section 2), we conjectured that Web pages preferred on the classical dimension were likely to have fewer accessibility barriers, compared with Web pages classed as being expressive in their designs.

4.1 Participants

Nineteen (19) judges were contacted by e-mail. They were people who currently work in the accessibility area, and belong to research groups that focus on inclusive design across academia and industry. Seventeen (17) of them volunteered to do the study, but 12 judges carried out the accessibility audits and returned their completed evaluation results. Others sent in their apologies. One (1) out of the 12 had invalid questionnaire responses, hence the associated data was not used. There were 8 males and 3 females with ages ranging from 26 to 50 years (Mean = 36.2 and SD = 7.76). All the judges were fluent in English language except one judge who had intermediate skills. The judges had experience working in the accessibility area for number of years ranging from 1 to 15 (Mean = 7.5 and SD = 4.76). None of the evaluators were beginners to the Web accessibility area, they rated themselves as having intermediate or expert skills in the area. Six (6) rated themselves as intermediate, while 5 rated themselves as experts. Four (4) of the judges had worked as Web accessibility consultants in the past. The judges evaluated one or more Web pages, depending on how much time they were willing to spare.

4.2 Stimuli

Sixteen (16) out of 50 homepages which had previously been rated for their aesthetic quality were selected for Study 2. Ten (10) pages were first chosen by arranging all 50 homepages in descending order of their overall aesthetic quality, and choosing every fifth page. The selected pages therefore spanned the best, average and worst pages in terms of aesthetic quality. Six (6) extra pages were then added to the list. These were pages which were consistently in the top

or bottom positions under the visual design categories (i.e clean, pleasing, fascinating, creative and aesthetic) previously investigated. This was to enable us report findings on the interplay between various Web design dimensions and accessibility as well. Table 2 contains the selected Web pages, together with their study IDs and Web addresses.

Table 2: Web pages with their study IDs and Urls

Page Name	PageID	Web address
Villa San Michelle	ID1	http://www.villasanmichele.com/web/ovil/villa_san_michele.jsp
Google UK	ID2	http://www.google.co.uk/
Good things-Orange	ID3	http://awards.goodthingsshouldneverend.com/
Full Sail University	ID4	http://www.fullsail.edu/
Whalehunt	ID5	http://thewhalehunt.org/
BBC	ID6	http://www.bbc.co.uk/
Askjeeves	ID7	http://uk.ask.com/?o=312&l=dir
Solar System-NASA	ID8	http://solarsystem.nasa.gov/index.cfm
Wordpress	ID9	http://wordpress.com/
MSN	ID10	http://uk.msn.com/
Virgin Media	ID11	http://www.virginmedia.com/
Rapidshare	ID12	http://www.rapidshare.com/
Gumtree	ID13	http://www.gumtree.com/
Directgov	ID14	http://direct.gov.uk/en/index.htm
Money Saving Expert.com	ID15	http://www.moneysavingexpert.com/
Ezine Articles	ID16	http://ezinearticles.com/

4.3 Task and Procedure

On agreeing to participate, the judges were assigned a judge number and sent the study materials via e-mail. The study pack comprised of a Participant Information Sheet (PIS), demographic information sheet, Web page(s) to be evaluated, barrier-checklist spreadsheet(s) and a post-evaluation questionnaire(s). The judges were instructed to read the PIS which outlined the aim of the study and further instructions.

The following user categories were selected for investigation after discussions between 4 of the judges: *Blind*: people who cannot see and have to use screen readers to access the Web; *Low-vision*: people who see partially and require screen magnifiers, accessibility features offered by operating systems and maybe screen readers to access the Web; *Colour-blind*: people who cannot distinguish between certain colours [2]. The user categories chosen for investigation were restricted to people with visual impairments, because they represent a large population of people with disabilities who have access to the Web [19]. Other disability types were not considered, because we did not want to overburden the judges. Manual accessibility audits are very time consuming. The evaluators were asked to imagine that the user goal was browsing or information search. The evaluators judged the Web pages independently, and in their own work environment using the Barrier Walkthrough method.

The Barrier Walkthrough (BW) method: is an accessibility evaluation method adapted from heuristic evaluation techniques widely used in usability engineering [2]. The heuristics used as checkpoints in the usability case are replaced with *barriers* in the BW method. An *accessibility barrier* prevents a person with disabilities from achieving his/her set goals when interacting with a Web application. Barriers are derived from known accessibility guidelines, and can be described in terms of i) user category, ii) assistive technology used, iii) goal/task being hindered and iv) Web page features which trigger the barrier in question. A BW evaluator must take the following steps: i) define of the user category (e.g blind, deaf, mobile device user e.t.c), ii) define user goals (e.g casual browsing, e-shopping e.t.c), iii) check the selected Web pages for barrier presence and iv) determine the severity of each barrier as {0,1,2,3}, meaning *none*, *minor*, *significant* or *critical*. According to Brajnik [3], the

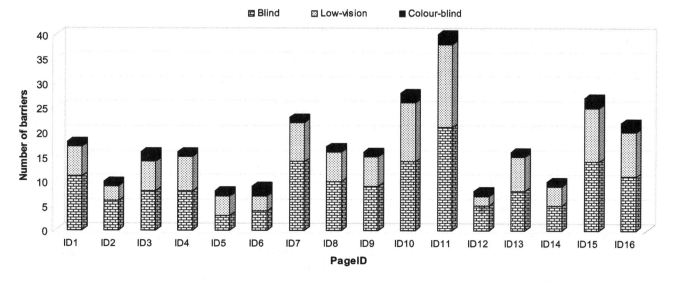

Figure 2: Accessibility barriers found on the Web pages based on average severity ratings

Table 3: Correlation between the aesthetic dimensions, number of barriers and other subjective quantities

r	Clean	Pleasing	Fascinating	Creative	Aesthetic	Barriers	Time	Confidence	Effort	Productivity
Clean	1.000	0.868^a	0.637^a	0.594^b	0.835^a	-0.501^b	-0.246	0.033	-0.417	0.047
Pleasing		1.000	0.930^a	0.898^a	0.994^a	-0.342	-0.228	-0.118	-0.184	-0.011
Fascinating			1.000	0.972^a	0.947^a	-0.158	-0.120	-0.218	0.011	-0.049
Creative				1.000	0.921^a	-0.129	-0.137	-0.266	0.008	-0.065
Aesthetic					1.000	-0.294	-0.218	-0.139	-0.163	-0.022
Barriers						1.000	0.378	-0.433	0.783^a	-0.439
Time							1.000	-0.220	0.517^b	-0.378
Confidence								1.000	-0.547^b	0.740^a
Effort									1.000	-0.655^a
Productivity										1.000

a is significant at the 0.01 level, while b is significant at the 0.05 level (2-tailed).

the BW method is believed to be educative for novice evaluators. It is also effective in identifying severe accessibility issues and reducing false positives in the evaluation process. However, like many other heuristic evaluation techniques, the BW method suffers from an evaluator effect [5, 35].

On completing the manual accessibility audits, the judges were required to fill a post-evaluation form. The form captured the time taken to do the evaluations, the judges' confidence in auditing the Web page(s), the effort required and their productivity levels. The completed accessibility audits were then e-mailed back to the principal investigator.

4.4 Results

We received 37 valid BW reports for the 16 Web pages investigated. Figure 2 shows the number of barriers found on a Web page which received an average severity rating of at least 1 from the judges which examined the page in question. The highest number of barriers were found on ID11, while the least numbers were found on ID5 and ID12. From the BW reports, 'spaced titles', 'ASCII art' and 'pages without titles' were the 3 accessibility barriers capable of affecting people with blindness that were not found on any of the examined Web pages. 'Widely formatted forms' were not found on any page examined for barriers which could affect

people with low-vision. The most common barrier found which could affect persons with blindness across the Web pages was 'generic or ambiguous links', while 'insufficient visual contrast' was the most common barrier found which could affect people with low-vision and colour-blindness. In general, more barriers were found capable of affecting people with blindness, followed by low-vision and colour-blindness.

Table 3 shows a Pearson correlation analysis which was performed between the aesthetic dimensions (ratings obtained from Study 1), the number of accessibility barriers found and other subjective ratings given by the judges. Although all the aesthetic dimensions showed negative relationships with the number of barriers found on the examined homepages, only visual cleanness had a moderate significant correlation with the number of barriers found. Visually clean homepages had fewer accessibility barriers. Furthermore, the number of barriers found on a Web page was positively related with the effort required to perform the accessibility evaluations. The time taken for the accessibility evaluations was positively related with the effort required to do the evaluations. The judges' confidence in identifying the accessibility barriers was negatively related with the effort expended, and positively related with productivity. Effort expended was negatively related with productivity.

Quality Assessment (QA): It is also important that we evaluate the effectiveness of the BW method here. One way of doing this is through a reliability test. Reliability is the extent to which independent accessibility audits produce the same results [4]. One way of measuring reliability is by the coefficient of variation (cv). It is defined as $\frac{SD}{M}$, where SD is the standard deviation and M is the mean of the number of correctly identified barriers. The smaller the *cv* value, the more reliable the audit results. Whenever the cv value exceeds 1, it depicts low reliability as SD is greater than M. Similar quality assessment measures are used in [4, 5, 35]. The cv value here measures the variation between the barrier severity ratings given by different judges for barriers on the same Web page, and for different disability types. It is represented by the triple (barrier type, disability category, page). Since this value can be influenced by the number of evaluators, we performed the reliability tests with the same number of judges per page. Two judges were chosen per page. For Web pages which had evaluations from more than two judges, two sets of audits were randomly chosen. ID4 and ID10 had lone evaluations due to invalid questionnaire responses from the second judge who was assigned the Web pages in question, hence no reliability checks could be performed. The results for the QA are shown in Table 4.

Table 4: Coefficient of variation (cv) among judges for the Web pages evaluated both at the page level and for the three disability types investigated - Blind (BL), Low-Vision (LV) and Colour-Blind (CB)

PageID	Page	BL	LV	CB
ID1	0.21	0.26	0.16	0.24
ID2	0.23	0.29	0.10	0.70
ID3	0.21	0.22	0.17	0.70
ID4	n/a	n/a	n/a	n/a
ID5	0.13	0.12	0.15	0.00
ID6	0.15	0.06	0.17	1.40
ID7	0.27	0.32	0.17	0.70
ID8	0.17	0.18	0.14	0.35
ID9	0.26	0.25	0.22	0.70
ID10	n/a	n/a	n/a	n/a
ID11	0.50	0.47	0.55	0.35
ID12	0.11	0.13	0.05	0.70
ID13	0.29	0.29	0.29	0.14
ID14	0.22	0.20	0.21	0.70
ID15	0.47	0.49	0.46	0.24
ID16	0.27	0.18	0.30	1.40

At the page level, we observe reasonable variations between the independent accessibility audits performed by the judges. The highest variation between judges was observed for ID11. The Web page in question had the highest number of barriers with an average severity rating of at least 1. Accordingly, we would expect greater variances in the opinions of the judges involved. When split between disability types, the results show reasonable variations for the blind and low-vision categories. The cv values are rather high for colour-blindness on some of the homepages. This is because the BW method specifies only two types of barriers capable of affecting people with colour-blindness, which are 'color is necessary to understand information' and 'insufficient visual contrast'. Whenever the judges disagreed on the barrier severity ratings for this user category the effect was greater. Going by

the page level reliability scores, the accessibility audits are quite reproducible among judges. This also boosts our confidence in the audits performed on ID4 and ID10, as the lone judge with valid questionnaire responses also helped in evaluating the accessibility levels of other Web pages.

In one study [5] where the role of expertise in Web accessibility evaluations was investigated, the authors found that a lone expert judge was capable of identifying 70% of the problems on a Website. With 2 judges 94% of the problems were covered and 3 judges covered all. While more than one expert judge per Web page is encouraged, they also found that the reproducibliity of the accessibility evaluations reduce as the judge numbers per page increase. This is due to the increased subjectivity arising from the many different opinions. Although the authors point out that not all of their study outcomes are generalizable, as they either apply to the experts they employed or the Websites evaluated. Their findings still give us an idea of the effect of expertise on our own studies, especially as we employed some of the Web accessibility experts that they used for their work.

5. DISCUSSION

The overall objective of this paper was to investigate the interplay between Web aesthetics and accessibility as it affects people with visual impairments. In the usability case discussed in the background section (Section 2), Web pages on the classical dimension were perceived to be easier to use, while expressive Web designs were perceived to be more difficult to use, because of their complex and sophisticated visual designs [9, 11]. We had speculated that a similar situation will hold for accessibility, since usability and accessibility are closely related facets of user experience. Results from Study 2 show the relationship between Web aesthetics and accessibility to be rather complex. The only design dimension that showed significant relationships with accessibility was visual *cleanness*. We observed a moderate significant negative correlation between the design dimension *clean* and the number of accessibility barriers present on a Web page. So, the cleaner the homepage, the fewer the accessibility barriers. Perhaps this outcome is due to the small number of HTML elements required to build visually clean Web pages. A Web page with a simple HTML code base is more likely to have fewer accessibility issues, because the Web designer typically has fewer bytes of code to mind. A similar outcome is reported in [18] where a correlation was observed between Web page complexity levels (measured by the number of HTML elements present) and accessibility quality. Web pages with fewer HTML elements had better accessibility quality. The authors believe that simplicity minimizes the occurrence of accessibility issues, and makes verification of accessibility compliance manageable during Web development.

The other classical design dimension investigated, 'pleasing' showed no significant relationships with accessibility. We had established in Study 1 that it leaned more towards the expressive, because it showed strong positive correlations with expressive design dimensions (*fascinating* and *creative*), and the overall term 'aesthetic'. In the original aesthetics framework developed by Lavie and Tractinsky, the design dimensions clean, pleasing and aesthetic all come under classical aesthetics. Notice that in Table 3, 'pleasing'(r = -0.342) and 'aesthetic' (r = -0.294) follow up closely behind 'clean' (r = -0.501) on their correlation with the number of barriers present. However, our study reveals the design dimension *clean* to be most unlike the other two investigated. Hence, its unique relationship with accessibility here. In our previous study [20], significant correlations were also observed between similar design dimensions (clean, clear and organised) and accessibility. This class of Web designs are characterised by simplicity and minimalism. They primarily address design clarity rather than appeal or affective aspects. It may be this simplicity that the design community struggles with or misunderstands. It is commonly believed that accessible Websites are boring, because of the perceived minimalistic undertone to their designs [24, 27]. Many Web designers fail to see simplicity as an aesthetic notion [13].

Our findings do not fully support a closely related study where highly accessible Websites were also shown to have complex visual designs [24]. In our case, it was more common for simple Web designs to have fewer accessibility issues. A similar situation to ours is reported in [18]. Expressive designs which would normally come across as being more complex and sophisticated showed no significant relationships with accessibility. However, further studies would be required to draw stronger conclusions across related studies. Consequently, this does not rule out the fact that fanciful or expressive Web designs cannot be created in an accessible fashion. Our data here, and indeed from our previous study [20] only shows this to be less the case presently. Expressive designs are not necessarily a barrier to accessibility. Since the relationship between classical aesthetics and functionality is more consistently established across studies, Web designers need to embrace simplicity in visual design. We also acknowledge the fact that there may be other factors moderating the interplay between Web aesthetics and accessibility which we did not investigate here. Some examples include the tools used for Web development, the Web designer's background and level of accessibility awareness, and an individual's or organisation's adherence to accessibility guidelines, either for business or legal reasons.

Furthermore, our findings suggest a link between the visual appearance of a Website and its underlying functionality. At a very high level, the way a Web page looks could be used to predict how easy or difficult Web users would find the Web page in question. Existing studies establish links between perceived aesthetic aspects of Web pages and their perceived usability [1, 12, 16, 26]. However, none of these studies explore the possibility of predicting functionality based on visual appearance. Such a system is diserable, as it could provide a rough overview of any functionality issues, before actual user evaluations are employed. Our study suggests visual cleanness to be a suitable proxy measure for accessibility, compared with other aesthetic dimensions. It is important to note, however, that we do not suggest that such a system replaces manual accessibility evaluations.

6. CONCLUSION

Using two sets of studies, this work provides empirical evidence for the interplay between visual aesthetics and accessibility in the context of the Web. In the first study, we elicited the aesthetic judgements of sighted Web users in order to understand what types of Web pages were aesthetically pleasing or displeasing. The adjectives *clean, pleasing, fascinating, creative* and *aesthetic* were used to categorize Web pages. In the second study, a cross-section of the Web pages from the first study were examined by experts for accessibility barriers which could affect people with visual

impairments. This was to enable us understand the interactions between the use of Web aesthetics and accessibility.

Our results show only one aesthetic dimension, *clean* to be significantly related with accessibility. Clean Web designs were characterised by simplicity and minimalism. They had fewer accessibility barriers compared with the other aesthetic dimensions investigated. Our data suggests this design dimension to be a suitable proxy measure for accessibility as far as people with visual impairments are concerned. This research contributes to our knowledge by further lending support to the existing relationship between classical aesthetic aspects and functionality, in this case accessibility.

As a next step, we intend to build a tool which is capable of predicting the accessibility level of Web pages based on the clarity of their visual designs. A further evaluation will also be undertaken to investigate the efficacy of our tool. Further details on the studies can be found in their associated technical reports available on-line at http://weleprints.cs.manchester.ac.uk/view/subjects/eivaa.html

7. ACKNOWLEDGEMENTS

We would like to thank the anonymous reviewers for their useful feedback. We also would like to thank all the participants, especially the volunteers who took time off their very busy schedules to do the manual accessibility audits. Special thanks to Giorgio Brajnik for answering all our queries on the Barrier Walkthrough method. The first author is also grateful to AKUTECH, Nigeria for their support.

8. REFERENCES

[1] L. Brady and C. Phillips. Aesthetics and Usability: A Look at Color and Balance. *Usability News, February,* 5 (1), 2003.

[2] G. Brajnik. Barrier Walkthrough: Heuristic Evaluation Guided by Accessibility Barriers. *Available Online at http://sole.dimi.uniud.it/ giorgio.brajnik/projects/bw/bw.html (Accessed 08 September, 2010).*

[3] G. Brajnik. Web Accessibility Testing: When the Method is the Culprit. *Lecture Notes in Computer Science, Springer Berlin / Heidelberg,* pages 156–163, 2006.

[4] G. Brajnik. A Comparative Test of Web Accessibility Evaluation Methods. *In Proceedings of the 10th international ACM SIGACCESS conference on Computers and accessibility, Nova Scotia, Canada,* pages 113–120, 2008.

[5] G. Brajnik, Y. Yesilada, and S. Harper. The Expertise Effect on Web Accessibility Evaluation Methods. *Human Computer Interaction, Taylor and Francis,* 2011.

[6] W. Chisholm, G. Vanderheiden, and I. Jacobs (Eds.). Web Content Accessibility Guidelines 1.0. *W3C Recommendation 5th May, 1999. http://www.w3.org/TR/WAI-WEBCONTENT/,* 1999.

[7] R. Crozier. Manufactured Pleasures: Psychological Responses to Design. *Manchester University Press,* 1994.

[8] D. Cyr, M. Head, and A. Ivanov. Design Aesthetics Leading to M-loyalty in Mobile Commerce. *Information and Management, Elsevier B.V.,* 43 (8):950 – 963, 2006.

[9] A. De Angeli, A. Sutcliffe, and J. Hartmann. Interaction, Usability and Aesthetics: What Influences Users' Preferences? *In Proceedings of the 6th Conference on Designing Interactive Systems, University Park, PA, USA, ACM Press*, pages 271 – 280, 2006.

[10] J. Hartmann, A. Sutcliffe, and A. D. Angeli. Investigating Attractiveness in Web User Interfaces. *In Proceedings of the SIGCHI conference on Human Factors in Computing Systems, San Jose, California, USA*, pages 387 – 396, 2007.

[11] J. Hartmann, A. Sutcliffe, and A. D. Angeli. Towards a Theory of User Judgment of Aesthetics and User Interface Quality. *ACM Transactions on Computer-Human Interaction (TOCHI), Article No. 15, ACM New York, NY, USA*, 15(4), 2008.

[12] H. Heijden. Factors Influencing the Usage of Websites: The Case of a Generic Portal in the Netherlands. *Information and Management, Elsevier Science B.V.*, 40 (6):541 – 549, 2003.

[13] K. Karvonen. The Beauty of Simplicity. *In Proceedings Conference on Universal Usability, Arlington, Virginia, USA, ACM Press.*, pages 85 – 90, 2000.

[14] B. Kelly, D. Sloan, L. Phipps, H. Petrie, and F. Hamilton. Forcing Standardization or Accommodating Diversity? A Framework for Applying the WCAG in the Real World. *In Proceedings of the International Cross-disciplinary Workshop on Web Accessibility (W4A), Chiba, Japan, ACM*, pages 46 – 54, 2005.

[15] T. Lavie and N. Tractinsky. Assessing Dimensions of Perceived Visual Aesthetics of Web Sites. *International Journal of Human-Computer Studies, Academic Press, Inc. Duluth, MN, USA*, 60(3):269 – 298, 2004.

[16] Y.-M. Li and Y.-S. Yeh. Increasing Trust in Mobile Commerce Through Design Aesthetics. *Computers in Human Behaviour, Elsevier Ltd.*, 26 (4):673 – 684, 2010.

[17] G. Lindgaard, G. Fernandes, C. Dudek, and J. Brown. Attention Web Designers: You Have 50 Milliseconds to Make a Good First Impression! *Behaviour and Information Technology. Taylor and Francis*, Vol. 25, No. 2:115–126, 2006.

[18] R. Lopes, D. Gomes, and C. Luis. Web Not For All: A Large Scale Study of Web Accessibility. *In Proceedings of the International Cross Disciplinary Conference on Web Accessibility (W4A)*, 2010.

[19] J. Mankoff, H. Fait, and T. Tran. Is Your Web Page Accessible?: A Comparative Study of Methods for Assessing Web Page Accessibility for the Blind. *In Proceedings of the SIGCHI conference on Human factors in computing systems, Portland, Oregon, ACM Press*, 41 - 50, 2005.

[20] G. Mbipom. Good Visual Aesthetics Equals Good Web Accessibility. *ACM SIGACCESS Newsletter, January 2009*, 93:75 – 83, 2009.

[21] E. Michailidou, S. Harper, and S. Bechhofer. Visual Complexity and Aesthetic Perception of Web Pages. *In Proceedings of the 26th ACM International Conference on Design of Communication, Lisbon, Portugal, ACM*, pages 215 – 224, 2008.

[22] M. Moshagen and M. Thielsch. Facets of Visual Aesthetics. *International Journal of Human-Computer Studies, Elsevier Ltd*, 68 (10):689–709, 2010.

[23] M. Pandir and J. Knight. Homepage Aesthetics: The Search for Preference Factors and the Challenges of Subjectivity. *Interacting with Computers, Elsevier Science Inc. NY, USA*, 18(6):1351–1370, 2006.

[24] H. Petrie, F. Hamilton, and N. King. Tension, What Tension? Website Accessibility and Visual Design. *In Proceedings of the international cross-disciplinary workshop on Web Accessibility (W4A), New York city, New York*, 63:13 – 18, 2004.

[25] H. Petrie, F. Hamilton, N. King, and P. Pavan. Remote Usability Evaluations with Disabled People. *In Proceedings of the SIGCHI Conference on Human Factors in Computing Systems, Montréal, Québec, Canada*, pages 1133 – 1141, 2006.

[26] C. Phillips and B. Chaparro. Visual Appeal vs. Usability: Which one Influences User Perceptions of a Website More? *Usability News, October*, 11 (2), 2009.

[27] B. Regan. Accessibility and Design: A Failure of the Imagination. *In Proceedings of the international cross-disciplinary workshop on Web accessibility (W4A), New York, ACM Press*, 63:29 – 37, 2004.

[28] D. Robins and J. Holmes. Aesthetics and Credibility in Web Site Design. *Information Processing and Management: An International Journal*, 44(1):386–399, 2008.

[29] M. Rowan, P. Gregor, D. Sloan, and P. Booth. Evaluating Web Resources for Disability Access. *In Proceedings of the 4th International ACM Conference on Assistive Technologies, Arlington, Virginia, USA, ACM*, pages 80 – 84, 2000.

[30] B. Schenkman and F. Jönsson. Aesthetics and Preferences of Web Pages. *Behaviour and Information Technology*, 19 (5):367–377, 2000.

[31] D. Sloan, P. Gregor, M. Rowan, and P. Booth. Accessible Accessibility. *In Proceedings Conference on Universal Accessibility, Arlington, Virginia, USA*, pages 96 – 101, 2000.

[32] D. Sloan, A. Heath, F. Hamilton, B. Kelly, H. Petrrie, and L. Phipps. Contextual Web Accessibility - Maximizing the Benefit of Accessibility Guidelines. *In Proceedings of the International Cross-disciplinary Workshop on Web accessibility (W4A), Edinburgh, UK, ACM*, 134:121–131, 2006.

[33] A. Tuch, J. Bargas-Avila, K. Opwis, and F. Wilhelm. Visual Complexity of Websites: Effects on Users' Experience, Physiology, Performance, and Memory. *International Journal of Human Computer Studies*, 67 (9):703 – 715, 2009.

[34] M. Vigo, A. Kobsa, M. Arrue, and J. Abascal. User-tailored Web Accessibility Evaluations. *In Proceedings of the eighteenth conference on Hypertext and Hypermedia, Manchester, UK*, pages 95 – 104, 2007.

[35] Y. Yesilada, G. Brajnik, and S. Harper. How Much Does Expertise Matter?: A Barrier Walkthrough Study With Experts and Non-experts. *In Proceedings of the 11th international ACM SIGACCESS Conference on Computers and Accessibility, Pittsburgh, Pennsylvania, USA*, pages 203 – 210, 2009.

How Voice Augmentation Supports Elderly Web Users

Daisuke Sato   Masatomo Kobayashi   Hironobu Takagi   Chieko Asakawa   Jiro Tanaka[†]

IBM Research – Tokyo

1623-14, Shimo-tsuruma, Yamato City,
Kanagawa Pref. 242-8502 Japan

+81 46 215 {4793, 4679, 4557, 4633}

{dsato, mstm, takagih, chie}@jp.ibm.com

[†]University of Tsukuba

1-1-1, Tenno-dai, Tsukuba City,
Ibaraki Pref. 305-8573 Japan

+81 29 853 5343

jiro@cs.tsukuba.ac.jp

ABSTRACT

Online Web applications have become widespread and have made our daily life more convenient. However, older adults often find such applications inaccessible because of age-related changes to their physical and cognitive abilities. Two of the reasons that older adults may shy away from the Web are fears of the unknown and of the consequences of incorrect actions. We are extending a voice-based augmentation technique originally developed for blind users. We want to reduce the cognitive load on older adults by providing contextual support. An experiment was conducted to evaluate how voice augmentation can support elderly users in using Web applications. Ten older adults participated in our study and their subjective evaluations showed how the system gave them confidence in completing Web forms. We believe that voice augmentation may help address the users' concerns arising from their low confidence levels.

Categories and Subject Descriptors

H.5.2 [**Information Interfaces and Presentation**]: User Interfaces; K.4.2 [**Computers and Society**]: Social Issues – *Assistive Technologies for Persons with Disabilities.*

General Terms

Experimentation, Human Factors

Keywords

Older adults, Web accessibility, voice-based augmentation

1. INTRODUCTION

The United Nations has reported that elderly people (60 or older) constitute 11% of the world's population and 21% of the population of developed regions, and the percentage of older people is continuing to rise [1]. People experience degenerative effects of ageing in their senses of vision and hearing, in their psychomotor abilities, and in their attention and memory [2]. Even people who are happily using the Web now may face problems in the future, because the technologies are evolving and the new technologies will be different [3]. The Web has become an essential tool and online applications have made our daily lives

much more convenient. Everyone, including the elderly and people with disabilities, should be equally able to use the Web.

Unfortunately there are many webpages that are not friendly for seniors, including Web applications for our daily lives such as online banking and online shopping. Although the elderly may be gradually losing some of their cognitive and physical abilities, they can still learn new technologies. Kolodinsky et al. reported that the most significant problems for elderly Web users are not age-related functional impairments, but fears of the unknown and of the consequence of incorrect actions that inhibit exploration [4]. Many older adults offered such comments as "We can use new applications if we get used to them" or "The problems are in the initial attempts." This same kind of feedback also comes from visually impaired users.

This paper describes how a voice-based augmented interface can make elderly users more confident in completing tasks with online Web applications. This voice augmented interface was originally evaluated for people with visual impairments. Those results showed that the second channel for voice guidance increases blind users' confidence in navigating in Web applications [5]. We assume that although the main channels of the user interfaces are different (voice vs. graphics), the second channel using voice may help older adults complete the tasks in Web applications by increasing their confidence in their operations. Proper support can reduce their cognitive load and help them remember and learn. For example, some new home electrical appliances have function to provide voice guidance about proper usage. Users can operate such an appliance without any manual, and such appliances are increasingly popular with the elderly, though most Web applications still lack corresponding approaches to customer support. This is primarily because the Web tends to be designed by and for younger people, a situation that is steadily changing. That is why we are investigating new ways to apply voice augmentation methods to operations in Web applications.

One of the advantages of voice augmentation approach is that voice support can provide additional content for existing Web applications, extending the lives and utility of those applications. Of course voice augmentation can coexist with other alternative interfaces and just provide the basic components for such groups as older adults or novice users.

This paper describes two experiments after reviewing related work. The first experiment focused on online banking and shopping applications to observe the behavior of older adults and assess the effects of voice augmentation. The other experiment evaluated relative performance in completing Web forms with and without voice augmentation, comparing younger and older adults.

155

The results and future possibilities are discussed in the concluding section.

2. RELATED WORK

Ageing societies have been a focus for some years now. This section mainly describes studies of older adults using the Web. In addition, we cover studies of user interface agents that augment voice-based user interfaces.

2.1. Studies for Elderly Users

There have been many field studies with older adults. [6,7] cover the differences between younger and older adults in their Web navigation behaviors. Meyer et al. [6] conducted a study with thirteen older and seven younger adults. They reported that the older group needed more steps to find information, but both groups decreased their steps after a hands-on tutorial session. One of the interesting behaviors of older adults reported in this study is returning back to a "home" location if they became disoriented during navigation. Fairweather [7] reports that older adults tended to use the least risky method in navigating. Chadwick-Dias et al. [8] studied how Web experience influenced the behavior of users on the Web. They report Web experience is the same as Web expertise, but older adults take more time to develop their Web expertise. They concluded that older adults need more opportunities for collaborative learning with other people to learn Web navigation techniques.

[9,10,11] presented observations of older adults using existing systems. Sayago and Blat [9] conducted a 3-year study of everyday interactions with the Web and reported that problems with remembering steps, with understanding Web and computer jargon, and with using the mouse are more significant than problems with perceiving visual information, with understanding icons, or with using the keyboard. Akatsu and Miki [10] studied the unexpected behaviors of older Japanese adults using Automated Teller Machines (ATMs). Some users overreacted to certain voice messages or repeated the same error when they couldn't understand the situation. Leitner et al. [11] found that older adults do not show major differences from younger people in their needs and preferences related to an online ticket service.

Hanson et al. [12] evaluated a voice browsing application that provides functions to interact with the browser using speech. Inexperienced users tended to use long commands instead of the brief voice commands that the system could easily recognize.

2.2. Guidelines for Elderly Users

Many studies about ageing Web users have been conducted and many guidelines for Web content have been published to improve accessibility. The Web Accessibility Initiative (WAI) of the World Wide Web Consortium (W3C) discussed accessibility for older adults in their three-year WAI-AGE project that contributed to the Web Content Accessibility Guidelines (WCAG) 2.0 in 2010. Web accessibility for people with disabilities has gradually improved due to guidelines and new accessibility technologies. In addition, work continues on new assistive technologies for older adults. ISO IEC Guideline 71 [13] also requires considering the needs of the elderly and of persons with disabilities. This guideline affects local standards that implement accessible designs such as JIS X8341, which is also based on the WCAG.

The SPRY Foundation published a Web guideline for older adults in 1999 [14]. This guideline mainly focuses on vision, cognition, hearing, and motor skills. The criteria of this guideline are very similar to WCAG. Newell and Dickinson [15] used a case study

approach to the development of a simple Web application for elderly users. Chandwick-Dias et al. [16] studied how older users surf and their problems with the accessibility of Web 2.0 content. They found that each functional impairment of elderly people was relatively smaller than the corresponding impairment of people who need special support. Most of the special needs guidelines are easily applicable for elderly people. In addition, we need to address problems related to memory and learning to support older adults, limitations that have rarely been considered in accessibility technologies to date.

2.3. Assistive Technology for Elderly Users

Although there is no prior study that supports older adults in navigating Web applications by themselves while using audible user interfaces, there are many assistive approaches for older adults. BrookesTalk is an audible Web browser designed for people with visual impairments. A BrookesTalk extension called Voice Help provides guided support for older people with visual impairments [17]. It provides the status of the applications and lists of possible next actions in a way similar to the interface of IVR. Zajicek and Morrissey [18] used BrookesTalk to study the effects of multimodality with older adults. They reported that long instruction messages interfered with the correct operations and the users preferred text instructions rather than mixed text and speech. They also mentioned that older adults found synthesized voices hard to understand.

Hailpern [19] proposed a wizard interface that tracks the current status of elderly users. The system provides a simple interface within a single window and uses a history list to recognize the status of users. Milne et al. [20] proposed a minimal application interface for senior users. Their prototype browser has only five buttons and highly intuitive labels. For example they used "look up" and "look down" for "page up" and "page down". Muta et al. [21] developed a Web browser extension for older adults. It provides functions to read the selected content out loud, to magnify it, or to manage the colors to improve the contrast of the text and background.

Some online shopping applications use online support systems with chat, telephone support, or special applications for remote control by an operator [22,23]. Basically these forms of help are provided by humans, but some systems include intelligent agents combined with frequently asked questions. These applications target novice users (including older adults) who are customers or potential customers.

2.4. User Interface Agents with Voices

Maes [24] talked about the concepts of interface agents to help users reduce their efforts and avoid information overload. Bederson [25] created an automated tour guide prototype that uses audio to guide tourists. Sawhney and Schmandt [26] worked on Nomadic Radio, an agent system to decide how to most effectively present information to the user based on the context, interruption settings, and automatic text understanding. Wagner and Lieberman [27] introduced Woodstein, which predicts and assists the next user action based on analysis of collected sequences of previous actions on the webpages. Roth et al. [28] created an agent to provide audio feedback for the user's cursor location. Yu et al. [29] designed context-aware Web agents to provide audio and haptic feedback for the user's cursor location in a screen reader. Dontcheva et al. [30] created a Web agent that can help record and organize user sessions for comparison and analysis. The authors reduced the users' memory load and

The transaction menu is located at left side. You can select a menu …

What should I do?

Voice Augmentation

Figure 1. Concept of voice-augmented Web browsing

Table 1: Experience with online banking and shopping. "*" indicates that the user has experience with the specific application that was used in the task for our research.

User ID	Age-group	Experience with online banking	Experience with online shopping
1	60-64	Yes	Yes
2	60-64	No	Yes *
3	65-69	No	Yes
4	65-69	Yes	Yes *
5	65-69	No	Yes
6	70-74	No	Yes *
7	70-74	No	No
8	70-74	No	Yes
9	70-74	No	Yes *
10	75-79	Yes	Yes

simplified their tasks. Hartmann et al. [31] described Augur, a context-based smart agent that can highlight, suggest, and automate by analyzing the context data with pre-defined rules.

3. VOICE-AUGMENTED WEB

The voice output we tested is a very simple concept to support operations in Web applications (see Figure 1). The voice can provide instructions for users even when they visit an application for the first time. During the processing of each Web form in the application, the voice repeats the user's input and tells the user about the next action. Users can be notified of errors that are augmented with voices or sounds more easily than by error text alone. Such a voice can be pre-recorded or synthesized. Older adults prefer a pre-recorded voice to a synthesized voice, but that approach is less flexible and more expensive. Although we have developed a voice-based augmented interface for people with visual impairments, a system for older adults requires different type of augmentation, so we investigated the use cases and categorized the augmentations into four types: confirmation, notification, contextualization, and summarization.

Confirmation provides confirmation of a user's input. It reads all types of form fields such as text, radio buttons, and so on, checking whenever the value of the field is changed.

Notification makes users aware of a status change on a webpage, such as errors in a form (e.g., incorrect input) and the progress of content loading.

Contextualization suggests the next action a user should perform in a situation, such as the choices that can be performed and operational tips. For example, "Press the search address button to input the address automatically using the postal-code". The system can also explain the results of some actions.

Summarization explains choices available on a page, summarizes the page structure, or lists the steps to be performed by the user.

4. STUDY 1: BANKING AND SHOPPING

Our first study observed how users interacted with unfamiliar Web applications and how they felt about voice augmentation with a Wizard of Oz implementation [32].

4.1. Participants

Ten older adults participated in this study. Half of them were in their 60s and the other half were in their 70s. They were familiar with computers because they had retired after working for IT

companies. Some of them were engineers and others were in sales. Since current employees are quite experienced with computers and the Web, we believe that our participants typify the older population of the future. Table 1 summarizes their experiences with online Web applications, online banking, and online shopping. Most of them were experienced online shoppers but only three had experience with online banking. The participants without online banking experience said they felt it was insecure, they were satisfied with ATMs, and that it was too much trouble to sign up for and learn how to use new services and applications.

4.2. Procedure

Each user was asked to perform two tasks with Web applications: (1) a fund transfer using an online banking application, followed by (2) a purchase using an online shopping application. Table 1 shows the experience of each user. For each task, the observer first told the user about the task and then the user attempted to perform the task without voice augmentation or human assistance. The observer manually recorded the user's behavior, including the page navigation history, struggles, errors, and so on, as precisely as possible. After the task was finished, the user was asked about the task with reference to the recorded notes about the session.

The three users with experience using online banking had not used the specific application used in this study. The four users with experience in online shopping had used the same application as the study (the *s in Table 1). It was not feasible to register for the online banking application for each user in this study, so the authors provided two online banking accounts and the participants transferred money from one account to the other. This gave the users an authentic feeling of making transactions on the Web. In contrast, the purchases were not executed, but the users were told to stop just before clicking on the last button in the ordering process.

After doing the two tasks without voice augmentation, the user and the observer walked through the tasks again with voice augmentation using a Wizard of Oz protocol and the user was interviewed again. The observer manually used a text-to-speech application to play predefined messages suitable for the user's operations. Typical messages were (Japanese) instructions such as "Please click the red login button on the right side of this page to start online banking", "Please input your account number and the password", or "Please click the Continue button. The transaction will not be executed yet."

4.2.1. Task 1: Online Banking

First the user was given an account card that describes the user ID with a table of random numbers, the password for the account, and the account information for the recipient of the transfer. Next the user was asked to open the webpage of the banking application[1] based on the observer's instructions. Then the user was told to transfer a specified amount of money from the account to the recipient. Here are the required steps for the task.

1. Click the "login" button at the top right of the webpage to open a new window for the transaction. The user must do all of the banking transactions in this new window. The window will initially be 700 pixels wide and 600 pixels high (though users can resize it).

2. Input the user ID and password for the account to get to the account page.

3. Click on the "transfer" menu at the top left of the account page.

4. Select the "new recipient" button after scrolling down approximately one screen (for the initial window size).

5. Select the bank of the recipient and click on the button with the first letter of the branch of the recipient account to navigate to the next page.

6. Select the proper branch from a combobox and select the account type, and input the account number and the amount of money. Then click on the "next" button to confirm the information.

7. Check the information and input two requested random characters from the table on the account card. Finally click on the "execute" button to finish the transfer.

4.2.2. Task 2: Online Shopping

Here are the required steps for this task, starting after the user had opened a product page on the shopping website[2].

1. Put the item into the shopping cart to open the page of the shopping cart.

2. Click the "proceed to checkout" button for the next page.

3. Input the user's name, address, and e-mail address and click the "next" button to open the next form.

4. Select a payment option and a delivery option using radio buttons and click the "next" button to open the last form

5. Confirm the information for the order but stop before clicking the "order" button.

4.3. Observations

Here are some characteristic observations from the sessions. Most of these points are addressable by voice augmentation. Some items confirm findings from earlier studies.

---

[1] Bank of Tokyo-Mitsubishi UFJ: http://direct.bk.mufg.jp/, the experiment was conducted during April 18-22, 2011.

[2] Rakuten Ichiba: http://www.rakuten.co.jp/, the experiment was conducted during April 18-22, 2011.

4.3.1. Could not grasp content structure and meaning

Participants struggling with a task tend to read and reread content that was not relevant to the task, and scanned the content sequentially seeking the correct path for the task. A participant might scroll up and down rapidly looking for a target. Such behaviors were described in earlier studies. Participants sometimes lost their partial work on a task because of confusion about their status.

They often failed to select required radio-button options in the shopping application. The form of application was hard to understand because a needed set of radio buttons could not be seen within the initial window because the descriptions of the options were too long. In addition, most of the participants with problems overlooked the error messages that appeared at the top of the page when the incomplete form was submitted. In addition, some participants were confused by the expired-page warning that appeared if the browser "back" button was used within the form.

4.3.2. Did not understand widgets

Participants in their 70s tended to click on non-clickable elements, being misled by bright colors or disabled radio buttons. They also tried clicking on unneeded buttons or links even when they had figures showing how to use the application. They could not understand the meaning of some widgets by looking at them.

One user sometimes clicked (left and right) on some breadcrumb navigation links with a distinctive background to try to input the information. This was because the default-size window was too small and users had to scroll down to complete the transaction.

4.3.3. Did not know the function of the application or understand the general GUI metaphors

About half of participants were not aware of standard functions that are generally used in Web applications, such as a function to search for an address from a postal code. Some participants needed a long time to understand the functions needed for the application, such as how to use the table of randomized numbers. One user quickly found the login button and succeeded in logging in, but after that he returned to the initial page because he accidentally clicked outside of the new window. He said "The window disappeared" in the interview. After that he assumed that he had logged into the application and he searched for "transfer", but got lost in a FAQ page that describes how to transfer funds.

4.3.4. Anxiety Interference

One user, whenever he tried to click a link or button for the next action seemed to nervously confirm the action to himself. Also he said "What?" and struggled with a page for a while when the behavior of the application was different from his expectations.

The top page of the banking application provides a menu with over 20 items, various types of statuses and notifications for the account, and also advertisements for some financial products. A participant said about this page "I feel that [this] important thing (banking) was done as an advertisement leaflet."

5. STUDY 2: WEB FORM

Operations with a Web form are likely to cause errors because users must input or select values that are acceptable to the application. Errors include typos, long or short input, illegal characters for a text field, null selections, and so on. Another reason is that older adults tend to type keys while looking at the keyboard instead of the screen. Our hypotheses were that the

Table 2: A translation of the items from the questionnaire

Label	Question
Accurate	Compared to the normal mode, I found voice augmentation to be more accurate for input
Fast	Compared to the normal mode, I could input faster with voice augmentation
Comfortable	Compared to the normal mode, I felt sure that I would finish with voice augmentation
Distracting	Compared to the normal mode, I could not concentrate on the tasks with voice augmentation

voice augmentation could enhance their focus and help support their accurate input, thus reducing errors and increasing the confidence of the users.

The users were asked to fill out several types of forms in two modes, one without voice (normal) and one with voice. The forms are: input a number (task-1), input a user's name in Japanese (task-2), input a bank account type and number (task-3), and choose a valid option (task-4). The voice assistant read aloud each key when the user typed the forms in the first three tasks. After a short delay, the assistant would read all of the input text. For example, a user would input "1000" into a text field and the assistant read "one, zero, zero, zero, (pause), one thousand". For task-4, the voice read the current status. For example if there was an unchecked checkbox by the words "mail notification", then the voice read a phrase such as "mail notification is off". Users had a practice session before the actual experimental session.

The users first did the tasks without the voice, followed by the tasks with the voice for training. Then users were asked to input 8 things in each task. In total, 8 × 4 tasks × 2 modes = 64 actions were to be performed. The order of the tasks was randomized. After finishing all of the tasks, we used a survey with seven-point Likert items from -3/definitely-disagree to +3/definitely-agree to compare the test conditions. Table 2 shows a translation of the items from the questionnaire related to accurate, fast, comfortable, and distracting.

5.1. Participants
Five younger adults and ten older adults participated in this study. The younger adults are all in their 30s and are all familiar with computers and have advanced computer skills. The older adults were the same participants from Study 1.

5.2. Apparatus
For this study, we implemented a simple Web form application with voice augmentation using Eclipse ACTF [33] and a Japanese male synthesized voice. All events from the mouse and keyboard were recorded by the application. The application was running on Windows, in an A4 notebook with a Japanese keyboard. The users could point with the trackpoint on the notebook or with a USB mouse with a scroll wheel.

5.3. Results
Figure 2 compares the average task completion times for each participant group (30s, 60s, and 70s) for each task. The overall average values without the voice augmentation were 6.67 (SD = 3.82), 10.17 (SD = 4.86), and 13.57 (SD = 6.20) seconds for 30s, 60s, and 70s, respectively. The values with voice were 6.72 (SD =

3.72), 10.47 (SD = 5.04), and 15.77 (SD = 9.47) seconds. Obviously the task completion times are increasing with age. In addition, they tend to slightly increase with the voice augmentation for people in their 70s.

Three-way mixed ANOVA showed significant main effects on the task completion times of the age ($F_{2,12}$ = 43.05, $p < .001$), the task ($F_{3,924}$ = 309.48, $p < .001$), and the mode ($F_{1,924}$ = 10.52, $p < .005$). It also showed significant interaction effects of the age and the task ($F_{6,924}$ = 9.66, $p < .001$) and the age and the mode ($F_{2,924}$ = 6.78, $p < .005$). Only the participants in their 70s were significantly slowed down by the voice augmentation ($F_{1,924}$ = 23.65, $p < .001$). A post-hoc analysis found that the participants in their 30s were significantly faster than those in their 60s ($p < .005$) and 70s ($p < .001$) while the 60s were significantly faster than the 70s ($p < .005$). We also found that task-3 took significantly longer than the other three tasks ($p < .001$) while task-4 took significantly less time than the other three tasks ($p < .001$).

Figure 3 compares the error rates of each group on each task and the overall error rates. The overall values without the voice augmentation were 2.5%, 4.4%, and 4.4% for 30s, 60s, and 70s, respectively. The values with voice were 2.5%, 0.6%, and 3.8%. Three-way mixed ANOVA showed a significant main effect of the task on the error rate ($F_{3,924}$ = 4.43, $p < .005$). The age and the mode had no significant main effects. A post-hoc analysis found that task-4 caused significantly more errors than task-1 or task-2 ($p < .05$).

Figure 4 shows a comparison of the average scores for the subjective questionnaires. For the question on "accurate", the values were 1.2 (SD = 0.98), 1.6 (SD = 0.49), and 2.4 (SD = 0.8) for 30s, 60s, and 70s, respectively. For "fast", the values were 0.2 (SD = 0.75), 1.2 (SD = 0.75), and 2 (SD = 1.10). For "comfortable", the values were 1 (SD = 0.90), 1.4 (SD = 0.8), and 2.6 (SD = 0.49). For "distracting", the values were -2 (SD = 1.10), -0.6 (SD = 1.36), and -2.2 (SD = 0.4). The respondents in their 70s gave relatively more positive scores for each question. Based on the recorded times, the participants in their 70s took longer with voice than with the normal mode, but they said they could input faster and did not need more time with voice than with the normal mode.

6. DISCUSSION
6.1. Tradeoff of Confidence for Speed
The participants, especially those over 70, reported that the voice augmentation sped up their operations. However, the actual task-completion times increased in spite of their own reports. These results were surprisingly contradictory. We believe this shows that participants had increased confidence in their operations due to the support of the voice augmentation. However the actual time increased, because participants listened to the voice while pausing in their operations which could be observed in logged events. The time seemed shorter because of their higher confidence. It is known that stressful situations lengthen subjective time [34]. Some of the participants' comments support this interpretation, such as "The voice makes us feel relaxed", "It is useful on the first attempt", "I'm sure the input is correct with the voice", and "I could confirm the input without watching the screen". The participants also reported that they could do the tasks more accurately, but there was no significant difference in the actual error rates. Given the relatively small number of errors in the

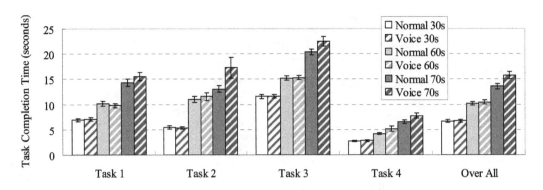

Figure 2: Comparison of task completion times

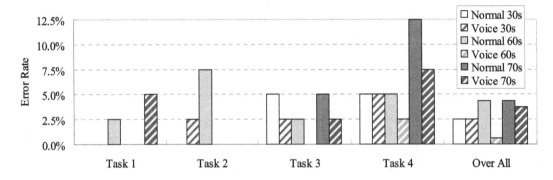

Figure 3: Comparison of error rates of tasks

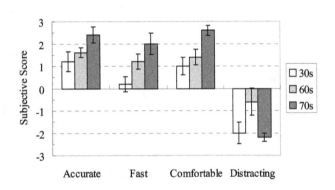

Figure 4: Subjective scores for the questions

experiments, more experiments and observations are required to determine how voice augmentation affects accuracy.

It is known that there are generally small correlations between empirical measurements (speed and accuracy) and subjective evaluations [35]. Since many elderly people tend to resist using technologies due to their fears [4], we believe that subjective factors should be regarded as more important than objective performance in the design and development of senior-friendly applications.

The participants in their 30s and 60s also reported they could input accurately and felt comfortable. Although their subjective scores are relatively lower than those of the participants in their 70s, they were also confident about using voice augmentation compared to the normal condition. They tended to click on the complete button before the confirmation message was finished (which stopped the voice), therefore there was no significant difference in their task completion times. The final message began 1.5 seconds after the final key was pressed for the normal speech rate. Using a faster speech or and shorter pauses for the confirmation messages linked to the user's input speed might change the results.

6.2. Another Way to Gain Confidence

The participants in their 70s tended to first focus on the most appealing content or on the content located at the center of the screen without grasping the structure of the page. Especially with the small window, the buttons the participants must click are located elsewhere and scrolling is needed. This often worried the older participants. They tended to try to read all of the visible content (which was mostly a warning statement about the timing of the transfer). One participant tried to click on an unclickable element without scrolling down.

The next element that should be focused on by the user can be identified for most of the webpages used here. The voice augmentation can say where the next focal element is located. Also visual feedback with highlighting using dynamic HTML technologies would help the users more effectively than voice augmentation alone and would give them more confidence. Participants also commented about such support, with comments such as "The element mentioned by the voice should be highlighted" while the content that should be focused on by the user in that status could be changed according to the user's intention. For example, though the user wants to transfer money, it may be hard for the system to anticipate the user's intention. An instruction for the page structure can help in such a situation, with a message such as "A transaction menu is located at the top left of this page."

6.3. Will They Want to Stop the Assistant?

Many people have bad memories of Microsoft's "Clippit" or "Clippy" (a dolphin in Japanese versions), an intrusive assistant avatar for a user interface agent for GUI applications, and a frequently asked question was "How to disable Clippy?" That strongly indicated that users want to control the assistance shown to them based on the context and their own skills.

Out of four types of voice augmentation, **repetition** and **notification** seem acceptable in many situations for older adults, giving them confidence in completing forms. **Contextualization** and **summarization** mainly support users in constructing mental models of the applications. Therefore they may stop supporting and start interfering with the users as they try to complete the Web forms. More investigation is needed to answer such questions as how older adults learn about applications, how long they remember what they have learned, and how can we assess the mental models of the users from their behaviors. Studying the navigation history in a Web application and the interaction events may help in understanding the users.

Appropriate analysis of a user's behavior and skills may be useful in deciding on the proper presentation for that user. For example a financial Web application may offer a new financial product to a user, based on frequent visits to the application, and lead the user to contact a sales representative.

6.4. Possible Implementations

Sloan et al. [36] reported on the potential of adaptive assistive technology for people whose abilities are gradually declining. In their study, they proposed a new application architecture that provides on-demand assistive technologies for each level of impairment (e.g. vision, hearing, motor, and so on). Instead of providing OS-dependent assistive technologies for certain impairments, users could be supported by multiple forms of assistance running within applications.

The most important component of our system is the voice output component. A prerecorded voice is one solution to provide good voice quality and it is preferred by older adults over a synthesized voice. However, synthesized voices are needed for a voice augmentation system because the Web content is dynamic and fluid and users can input text freely. Synthesized voice is mainly provided by library applications installed in a client system, while some applications provide synthetic voices through the Internet. Client-side voices have advantages in reduced response latency. Server-side voices have disadvantages in latency but the users don't need to install any voice libraries. WebAnywhere [37] is an audible Web browser that provides a server-side synthesized voice through the Internet. This system tries to predict the user's next action to reduce the latency of the speech response by analyzing the keyboard events with a hidden Markov model. Although synthesized voices are disliked by older adults [18], most of the participants could understand the synthesized voice messages. Several of them complained about the quality of voice and could not understand the meaning of the sentence until they heard it a second time. They said "Hmm?" or "What?" to ask for a repetition of the sentence, which could provide feedback to a speech recognition component. [18] also mentioned that a deeper male voice is generally easier for older adults, while some participants suggested a female voice would be better.

Most participants reported the voice did not distract their attention from the input, though two participants in their 60s reported they were distracted during the task. They disliked the timing of the voice presentation, which again indicates that the voice presentation should be optimized to consider the user's typing speed or some other criteria.

7. CONCLUSION

We investigated a voice augmentation system that supports elderly people in online banking transactions and online shopping. Subjective evaluations showed that the system made them feel confident (especially for people in their 70s) when they needed to accurately fill out electronic forms for online banking. This means the voice augmentation succeeded in reducing the mental barriers for using Web forms, giving the users confidence in their accuracy. The results of the experiment showed that the voice augmentation system can to encourage elderly Web users in using Web services even if their abilities are declining. Further exploration is required to clarify how the voice augmentation system might help elderly users navigate and complete forms in heterogeneous applications.

8. ACKNOWLEDGMENTS

We'd like to express appreciation for the participation of retirees of IBM Japan and to Oyagamo-kai.

9. REFERENCES

[1] United Nations. World population ageing 2009. 2010. http://www.un.org/esa/population/publications/WPA2009/WPA2009-report.pdf.

[2] Harper, S. and Yesilada, Y. *Web accessibility: a foundation for research*. Springer, 2008.

[3] Hanson, V.L. Age and Web access: the next generation. *Proceedings of the 2009 International Cross-Disciplinary Conference on Web Accessibility (W4A)*, ACM (2009), 7–15.

[4] Kolodinsky, J., Cranwell, M., and Rowe, E. Bridging the generation gap across the digital divide: Teens teaching Internet skills to senior citizens. *Journal of Extension 5*, 10 (2002), 2.

[5] Sato, D., Zhu, S., Kobayashi, M., Takagi, H., and Asakawa, C. Sasayaki: augmented voice Web browsing experience. *Proceedings of the 2011 Annual Conference on Human Factors in Computing Systems*, ACM (2011), 2769–2778.

[6] Meyer, B., Sit, R.A., Spaulding, V.A., Mead, S.E., and Walker, N. Age group differences in World Wide Web navigation. *CHI 1997 Extended Abstracts on Human Factors in Computing Systems: Looking to the Future*, ACM (1997), 295–296.

[7] Fairweather, P.G. How older and younger adults differ in their approach to problem solving on a complex website. *Proceedings of the 10th International ACM SIGACCESS Conference on Computers and Accessibility*, ACM (2008), 67–72.

[8] Chadwick-Dias, A., Tedesco, D., and Tullis, T. Older adults and Web usability: Is Web experience the same as Web expertise? *CHI 2004 Extended Abstracts on Human Factors in Computing Systems*, ACM (2004), 1391–1394.

[9] Sayago, S. and Blat, J. About the relevance of accessibility barriers in the everyday interactions of older people with the web. *Proceedings of the 2009 International Cross-Disciplinary Conference on Web Accessibility (W4A)*, ACM (2009), 104–113.

[10] Akatsu, H. and Miki, H. Usability research for the elderly people. *Oki Technical Review (Special Issue on Human Friendly Technologies) 71*, 3 (2004), 54–57.

[11] Leitner, M., Subasi, Ö., Höller, N., Geven, A., and Tscheligi, M. User requirement analysis for a railway ticketing portal with emphasis on semantic accessibility for older users. *Proceedings of the 2009 International Cross-Disciplinary Conference on Web Accessibility (W4A)*, ACM (2009), 114–122.

[12] Hanson, V.L., Richards, J.T., and Lee, C.C. Web access for older adults: voice browsing? *Proceedings of the 4th International Conference on Universal Access in Human Computer Interaction: Coping with Diversity*, Springer-Verlag (2007), 904–913.

[13] ISO/IEC. ISO/IEC Guide 71:2001 - Guidelines for standards developers to address the needs of older persons and persons with disabilities. 2001. http://www.iso.org/iso/catalogue_detail?csnumber=33987.

[14] SPRY Foundation. SPRY's Work: Education - A Guide for Web Site Creators. 1999. http://www.spry.org/sprys_work/education/web_guide.html.

[15] Newell, A.F., Dickinson, A., Smith, M.J., and Gregor, P. Designing a portal for older users: A case study of an industrial/academic collaboration. *ACM Transaction on Computer-Human Interaction 13*, 3 (2006), 347–375.

[16] Chadwick-Dias, A., Bergel, M., and Tullis, T.S. Senior Surfers 2.0: a re-examination of the older Web user and the dynamic Web. *Proceedings of the 4th International Conference on Universal Access in Human-Computer Interaction: Applications and Services*, Springer Berlin Heidelberg (2007), 868-876.

[17] Gregor, P., Newell, A.F., and Zajicek, M. Designing for dynamic diversity: interfaces for older people. *Proceedings of the Fifth International ACM Conference on Assistive Technologies*, ACM (2002), 151–156.

[18] Zajicek, M. and Morrissey, W. Multimodality and interactional differences in older adults. *Universal Access in the Information Society 2*, 2 (2003), 125-133.

[19] Hailpern, J.M. WISE: a wizard interface supporting enhanced usability. *Proceedings of the 8th International ACM SIGACCESS Conference on Computers and Accessibility*, ACM (2006), 291–292.

[20] Milne, S., Dickinson, A., Gregor, P., Gibson, L., McIver, L., and Sloan, D. Not browsing, but drowning: designing a Web browser for novice older users. *Proceedings of HCI International*, (2005), 7 pages.

[21] Muta, H., Ohko, T., and Yoshinaga, H. An activeX-based accessibility solution for senior citizens. *Proceedings of the Center on Disabilities Technology and Persons with Disabilities Conference 2005*, (2005).

[22] Dell. DellConnect™. http://support.dell.com/support/topics/global.aspx/support/en/dellconnect.

[23] Citrix Online. Remote Support And Remote Support Services | GoToAssist. http://www.gotoassist.com/.

[24] Maes, P. Agents that reduce work and information overload. *Communications of the ACM 37*, 1994, 30–40.

[25] Bederson, B.B. Audio augmented reality: a prototype automated tour guide. *Conference Companion on Human Factors in Computing Systems*, ACM (1995), 210–211.

[26] Sawhney, N. and Schmandt, C. Nomadic Radio: speech and audio interaction for contextual messaging in nomadic environments. *ACM Transaction on Computer-Human Interaction 7*, 3 (2000), 353–383.

[27] Wagner, E.J. and Lieberman, H. Supporting user hypotheses in problem diagnosis. *Proceedings of the 9th International Conference on Intelligent User Interfaces*, ACM (2004), 30–37.

[28] Roth, P., Petrucci, L., Pun, T., and Assimacopoulos, A. Auditory browser for blind and visually impaired users. *CHI 1999 Extended Abstracts on Human Factors in Computing Systems*, ACM (1999), 218–219.

[29] Yu, W., McAllister, G., Strain, P., Kuber, R., and Murphy, E. Improving Web accessibility using content-aware plug-ins. *CHI 2005 Extended Abstracts on Human Factors in Computing Systems*, ACM (2005), 1893–1896.

[30] Dontcheva, M., Drucker, S.M., Wade, G., Salesin, D., and Cohen, M.F. Summarizing personal Web browsing sessions. *Proceedings of the 19th Annual ACM Symposium on User Interface Software and Technology*, ACM (2006), 115–124.

[31] Hartmann, M., Schreiber, D., and Mühlhäuser, M. AUGUR: providing context-aware interaction support. *Proceedings of the 1st ACM SIGCHI Symposium on Engineering Interactive Computing Systems*, ACM (2009), 123–132.

[32] Dahlbäck, N., Jönsson, A., and Ahrenberg, L. Wizard of Oz studies -- why and how. *Knowledge-Based Systems 6*, 4 (1993), 258-266.

[33] ACTF. Accessibility Tools Framework Project Home. http://www.eclipse.org/actf/.

[34] Droit-Volet, S. and Gil, S. The time–emotion paradox. *Philosophical Transactions of the Royal Society B: Biological Sciences 364*, 1525 (2009), 1943 -1953.

[35] Hornbæk, K. and Law, E.L.-C. Meta-analysis of correlations among usability measures. *Proceedings of the SIGCHI Conference on Human Factors in Computing Systems*, ACM (2007), 617–626.

[36] Sloan, D., Atkinson, M.T., Machin, C., and Li, Y. The potential of adaptive interfaces as an accessibility aid for older Web users. *Proceedings of the 2010 International Cross-Disciplinary Conference on Web Accessibility (W4A)*, ACM (2010), 35:1-35:10.

[37] Bigham, J.P., Prince, C.M., Hahn, S., and Ladner, R.E. WebAnywhere: a screen reading interface for the Web on any computer. *Proceedings of the 2008 International Cross-Disciplinary Conference on Web Accessibility (W4A)*, ACM (2008), 132–133.

Monitoring Accessibility:
Large Scale Evaluations at a Geo-Political Level

Silvia Mirri
Department of Computer Science
University of Bologna
Via Mura Anteo Zamboni 7
40127 Bologna (BO), Italy
+39 0547 33813

silvia.mirri@unibo.it

Ludovico A. Muratori
Department of Computer Science
University of Bologna
Via Mura Anteo Zamboni 7
40127 Bologna (BO), Italy
+39 0547 33813

ludovico.muratori2@unibo.it

Paola Salomoni
Department of Computer Science
University of Bologna
Via Mura Anteo Zamboni 7
40127 Bologna (BO), Italy
+39 0547 33813

paola.salomoni@unibo.it

ABSTRACT

Once we assumed that Web accessibility is a right, we implicitly state the necessity of a governance of it. Beyond any regulation, institutions must provide themselves with suitable tools to control and support accessibility on typically large scale scenarios of content and resources. No doubt, the economic impact and effectiveness of these tools affect accessibility level. In this paper, we propose an application to effectively monitor Web accessibility from a geo-political point of view, by referring resources to the specific (category of) institutions which are in charge of it and to the geographical places they are addressed to. Snapshots of such a macro level spatial-geo-political analysis can be used to effectively focus investments and skills where they are actually necessary.

Categories and Subject Descriptors

H.5.4 [**Information Interfaces and Presentation**]:
Hypertext/Hypermedia – *User issues*; K.4.2 [**Computers and Society**]: Social Issues – *Assistive technologies for persons with disabilities; Handicapped persons/special needs*.

General Terms

Measurement, Design, Human Factors.

Keywords

Web Accessibility, Automated Evaluation, Accessibility Evaluation, Monitoring Accessibility.

1. INTRODUCTION

Nowadays dynamism and wideness of the Web represent critical parameters whenever content and services become the target of a certain control or any regulation has to be applied to them. This is the case of Web accessibility compliance to the national laws some countries have enacted since the last „90s. The number of Web pages and services to be evaluated may be actually

prohibitive, even by reducing any assessment to a particular Public institution. Many evaluation activities were conducted in recent years, focusing on different realms, starting from the Riga Dashboard (involving 34 European countries [7]) to local monitoring actions. All these evaluations are used to be sporadically done on a Web sites sample, which is small enough to be manually checked. The macro-level analysis about Web sites accessibility and its geo-political localization require a different approach. It is worth noting that these points of view are strategic as it concerns to investment and resource saving by public administrations and institutions.

To actually measure the accessibility of a Web page, an in-depth evaluation is required, which must include also manual controls. Despite guidelines and regulations about accessibility have been present on the world wide scenario for many years, sites are still afflicted with automatically detectable errors, which can completely compromise their accessibility. The provision of automatable assessments would guarantee time and resource saving, thereby opening the evaluation to larger sets of URLs and allowing more frequent controls. Moreover, the automatic monitoring of Web accessibility, whether it were done in time and according to some classifications (e.g. spatial, geo-political or by role) on the dominion of controlled institutions, would represent a great support to a deeper manual evaluation. A Web sites accessibility monitoring application can be really effective in such a context, since it greatly supports human operators in evaluating a large scale amount of Web pages.

In order to be effectively used in a wide range of monitoring actions, an automatic monitoring application needs to be tailored to different aspects, such as: (i) sets of URLs (and their related classification criteria) to be controlled; (ii) guidelines and requirements (or subset of them) to be checked; (iii) frequency of evaluations; (iv) spatial and geo-political reports and analysis of results.

Design and development of the above tool imply some open issues to be faced. First of all, evaluations must be as exhaustive and in-depth as possible. This means that the monitoring system should be based on an accurate evaluation tool which is not prone to false positives and negatives. In turn, the evaluation tool should provide controls based on the largest variety of accessibility guidelines and regulation requirements. Finally, it should maximize the checks which may be automatically conducted. Indeed, available automatic validation tools do not perform some complex checks. As an instance, none of the existing tools completely analyze XHTML and CSS codes in order to verify the color contrast on a whole Web page, by exploiting the cascading characteristics of style sheets and the inheritance of their rules. In fact, available color contrast analyzers usually perform evaluations on single couples of background and foreground colors, which have to be manually specified by users. Further complex checks should be performed by automatic tools, such as the correct usage of headings structure.

On the one hand, many efforts have been done to provide evaluate-and-repair tools focusing on single URLs or pages. On the other hand, an approach to give a snapshot about any set of URLs, according to suitable criteria, has not been faced yet. This macro level point of view could be useful to Web site commissioners and public institutions in managing investment and resources. Summing up a "resolution-independent" system – i.e. integrating a big picture with in-depth analysis capabilities – would represent the best solution in such a context.

In this paper we will present an application (named AMA, which stands for Accessibility Monitoring Application) which has been designed and implemented to gather accessibility status of large collections of Web sites according to different guidelines and regulations (including WCAG 2.0 [18], U.S. Section 508 [15] and Italian Stanca Act Requirements [10]). Such a tool is a part of the VaMoLà project [1], [12], which was born from a collaboration between the Emilia-Romagna Region and the University of Bologna. Both these institutions are Italian Public Administrations and their Web sites have to be made compliant with the Stanca Act [11]. This law imposes that Italian public Web services and information should be accessible, that employers with disabilities should be provided with adequate assistive technologies and accessible applications and the public Procurement of ICT goods and services should always take accessibility into account [11].

AMA periodically validates a set of URLs (by means of different automatic evaluation tools) and reports the accessibility level of the Web sites they address to. Obviously, only a subset of the guidelines and requirements are fully automatable. On the current official version of AMA, checks that require manual controls and human judgment are not taken into account. Nevertheless, a prototype devoted to collect, record and report manual evaluation results has been designed and developed and it is going to be integrated into AMA. Some of its features will be described in the following.

AMA obtains data which clearly depict a significant status of accessibility barriers, based on certain errors (i.e. absence of alternative to images, controls without labels, not enough color contrast). Hence, our monitor provides a meaningful and structured screening of accessibility level and trend, by showing the number of detected errors. In fact, AMA is not devoted to evaluate and repair single Web sites, but its goal is to capture a snapshot of a situation. It is worth mentioning that URLs that fail automatic evaluation are certainly inaccessible, while those which pass it may be accessible. Hence we can provide an optimistic accessibility evaluation with automated controls. Currently, the Emilia-Romagna Region and other public institutions are using AMA for their periodical Web sites monitoring activities.

The remainder of this paper is organized as follows. Section 2 (*Background and related work*) will introduce main related work, with the aim of comparing them with our system. Section 3 (*Design issues*) will describe the main goals of the project and the system features while Section 4 (*Architecture*) will depict the whole system, its components and configuration issues. Section 5 (*System at a glance*) will present main features of an instance of the system at work (analyzing some European public institutions Web sites) and some evaluation results. Finally Section 6 (*Conclusions*) will close the paper, by presenting some final considerations and future work.

2. BACKGROUND AND RELATED WORK

In the field of accessibility monitoring some tools are available, but all of them are devoted to monitor just single Web sites. Moreover, most of such applications are pay services, provided by software houses. The different aims (evaluate-and-repair Web site vs. providing accessibility evaluation from macro-level and geo-political point of views) and the different level of results presentation (report about a single Web site vs. report about large scale accessibility evaluations) make our system novel and unique in such a context.

Thus far, several national and international studies on Web accessibility have been conducted [2]. Some of them are devoted to identify and to monitor the accessibility level of different kinds of Web sites (e.g. governmental, Public administration, higher education) according to national or international guidelines. Such studies are mainly based on accessibility monitoring activities which are conducted by human operators (who have been supported by automatic and/or semi-automatic evaluations tools). Hence these are time-consuming activities that cannot involve a large set of Web pages and that cannot be often and regularly performed. In the following we present some international works which deal with the accessibility evaluation and monitoring of Public administrations and governmental Web sites, by summarizing their main results.

In 2006, the United Nations has commissioned the "United Nations Global Audit of Web Accessibility" [13]. In such a study 100 Web site homepages were evaluated, in order to present an indication of the existing Web accessibility level. The homepages were chosen from twenty countries around the world, five for each country and, in turn, one of them was from the Public administration (very often the main governmental Web site home page was selected to be evaluated). This study was conducted by testing only the homepage of each Web site, using both automated and manual techniques, according to the WCAG 1.0 AAA conformance level [17]. Each checkpoint was given a *pass*, *fail* or *not applicable* status. The resulting report presents detailed analysis for each country and shows that only 3% of the analyzed Web sites (all from the European Public sector) were found to meet WCAG 1.0 level A, while none of the sites were WCAG 1.0 level AA or AAA compliant. The use of a tool like our system would make possible a similar, but wider and deeper study. In particular, our application is capable to check a larger set of homepages and it allows wider and more detailed evaluations, by automatically controlling also other pages of each Web site. Its Web interface can provide the same kind of comparisons which are shown on [13], from a geographical point of view, and it is also capable to show them as they change in time. In addition, it provides evaluations based on different guidelines, not only as it concerns to the WCAG 1.0.

In 2007, the "Assessment of the Status of eAccessibility in Europe" study has been commissioned by the European Community [5]. The main aim of this work (called MeAC, which stands for "Measuring progress of eAccessibility in Europe") is to follow up on previous researches and support the future development of European policy in the field of eAccessibility. A certain number of Web sites were chosen from each EU member state, plus USA, Canada and Australia. Overall, 336 Public and private Web sites were evaluated by using a combination of automated and manual testing procedures to assess WCAG 1.0 level A. In particular, 25 pages were collected from each site with an automated retrieval process and then they were automatically and manually analyzed. In few countries, the majority of tested Public Web sites met the standards, while in most of them none of the sites did. In order to control accessibility evolution, one year later a similar and consequent study has been conducted, involving only 10 of the original 28 countries (9 EU member states plus USA) [4]. The results show that the situation was generally improving, but only the accessibility of Web sites in USA was significantly increased. Another study has been conducted in 2009 with the aim of analyzing the Web accessibility level of compliance with WCAG 2.0 in the European countries [3]. Results of this study report that none of the analyzed Web sites achieved WCAG 2.0 compliance and none of them achieved full WCAG 1.0 compliance (by taking into account both automatic and manual testing). Also in this case, the use of AMA would make possible a similar study, with some additional features, such as comparisons among results based on both geographical and temporal dimensions. Our system would also guarantee the possibility of conducting evaluations on the basis of different guidelines and requirements.

Another study about accessibility monitoring of European Web sites was conducted by the European Internet Accessibility Observatory (EIAO) [2] in 2008. The EIAO is an implementation of the automated monitoring application scenario of UWEM (Unified Web Evaluation Methodology) [16]. UWEM describes methods for the collection of evaluation samples, test procedures according to WCAG 1.0 level AA, and several different reporting options. In [2] a comparison between the EIAO study results and the MeAC ones is presented: there is a positive trend of the overall level of accessibility of European governmental Web sites, even if it is rather poor.

Finally, in [14] a large-scale study of Web accessibility is presented. Such a study has been conducted over a set of Portuguese Web sites with the aim of discovering Web pages quality according to 39 checkpoints from WCAG 1.0 (priority 1 and 2). The study has confirmed that simpler and smaller Web pages tend to have a higher accessibility quality, even if accessibility communication must be improved, as well as the diffusion of accessibility culture. The authors indicate this study as an ongoing work, since they are planning to evaluate the same set of URLs in next years (in order to study the evolution of accessibility guidelines compliance by providing temporal comparisons) and to report some specific Web sites categories results.

As it concerns the studies mentioned above, our system would provide accessibility evaluation from macro-level and geo-political point of views. This could be strategic to Web site commissioners and public institutions in managing investment and resources. In addition, our system provides more features, allowing evaluations on the basis of different guidelines, requirements and comparisons among results, which could be based on different criteria, such as geographical and temporal dimensions. This means that, as an instance, the same evaluation of the same set of URLs can be conducted in two different periods and results can be compared in order to show accessibility

improvements or worsening. In other words, our system would support different kind of accessibility evaluations (e.g. large set of URLs, in-depth evaluation of a single Web site, comparisons from different point of views, and so on) with great benefits in terms of effective interventions by their public institutions.

3. DESIGN ISSUES

The main goal of AMA is storing and providing data related to accessibility evaluation about large sets of URLs in order to provide macro-level, spatial and geo-political analysis. Public Administrations and institutions ought to periodically perform large scale accessibility evaluation of their Web sites, which could be not enough in terms of depth, wideness and frequency, due to the large amount of required resources. In order to provide an effective support to this process, AMA repeatedly performs automatic checks of URLs stored in its database and it presents analysis results by means of a Web based interface.

In such an application:

A. Data automatic evaluation and storage are periodically and automatically performed by the system, without any human activity. The system checks all the pages from the database and stores results into it.

B. Quantitative synthesis of evaluation results can be extracted from the database. This may be done by browsing the Web interface or through direct queries.

Periodical evaluations (A) permit to outline the accessibility macro-level trend for each URL from the database. Thanks to the automatic storage, AMA can evaluate pages by considering several sets of guidelines or requirements, including WCAG 1.0 [17], WCAG 2.0, Section 508 and Stanca Act. We have chosen the WCAG 2.0 because they are the most recent W3C guidelines. Evaluations according to the Stanca Act Requirements have been included because AMA is currently used by some Italian Public Administrations (in particular, by the Emilia-Romagna Region) to monitor Web sites which are under their authority (e.g. Provinces, Municipalities, schools, public health institutions). Through the Web interface users can choose also to check according to WCAG 1.0 guidelines and Section 508 regulation. Evaluations according to other regulations (i.e. the German BITV) could be added, since AMA is extensible. Obviously, a wide check requires a strong computational effort and it can consequently take long evaluation time for each URL. Moreover, the larger the set of evaluated guidelines is, the bigger the database storing results will be.

Complexity and database dimension are also related to the number of evaluated Web sites. Furthermore database dimension depends upon frequency of evaluations, which are configured by the system administrator (by means of a suitable Web interface). Finally, for each URL, AMA can evaluate one or more pages, going in depth from the home page. A configuration file (defined by the system administrator) sets the level of the pages AMA has to evaluate (the first level is the home page, the second level is represented by all the URLs directly linked from the home page, and so on). Anyway, through the configuration file, it is also possible to set a maximum number of pages to evaluate per single Web site.

For each evaluation (A), the system saves into the database the following data:

- the evaluation date;
- the evaluated URL;

- for each evaluated guideline: the number of errors generated by the evaluation system, the number of manual controls to do, which are suggested by the evaluation system, the number of potential errors detected by heuristics performed by the evaluation system and the number of checks which were done for each kind of error (computed by the evaluation system).

The system supports geo-political referenced URLs, with the aim to spatially explore (B) data into the database. This feature is specifically designed to support the quantitative synthesis in geographically distributed administration. URLs and their geographical and geo-political data have to be manually inserted into the database through a specific Web interface by admin users. URLs can be categorized on the basis of groups of interest, such as government, municipality, region, province, university, health board, etc.

AMA is a multi-user application, so users can access it by logging in through username and password. The end-users could create and exploit their accessibility reports (B), according to some options they could set. Setting options is a fundamental element in AMA interface. The Options Menu permits to set some preferences (related to the Web sites to evaluate and to the evaluation itself) so as to customize reports.

In particular, it is possible to select:

- the guidelines and requirements, in order to verify the checked URL conformity according to them.

- The categories and the sub-categories of the Web sites that the end-users want to evaluate.

- A previous date, in order to compare the correspondent accessibility level with the current one.

- The geographical area to monitor.

Once the above elements have been set, a complex set of queries can be performed on the database. Evaluation data are provided through tables and though a mash-up with Google Maps.

Data presented to users through the Web interface are the percentage of pages without any error (for the former and the current evaluation) and the average number of errors detected per page (for the former and the current evaluation). In addition for each analyzed group of sites, the AMA Web interface shows the number of checked pages, the number of checked pages without any error, the percentage of pages without any error, the total errors number and the average number of errors detected per page.

AMA has been developed in PHP and the system which interacts with end-users generates XHTML 1.0 Strict Web pages. Data are stored in a MYSQL database. An instance of AMA is available at this URL: http://polo-rer.polocesena.unibo.it/v3ama_bif (username: guest, password guest). It has been customized as follows:

- it uses a database storing main URLs which are related to the main European public institutions (154 Web sites, about 5 for each European country plus some European Union ones, including National Parliaments, Governments, Presidents and Prime Ministries Web sites); for each URL the system can provide accessibility monitor results of the home page (level 0), of all the pages directly linked from the home page (level 1) and of all the pages directly linked from the level 1 pages, according to end-user's selection;

- it supports access to data by using a geo-referenced interface;

- it validates WCAG 1.0, WCAG 2.0 checkpoints, Section 508 rules and Stanca Act Requirements;

- it provides a Web interface in Italian language and in English;

- it records evaluations results since July 2010.

Fig. 1 - A screenshot of an AMA instance

Figure 1 shows the home page of such an instance of the application. AMA source code is distributed under UEPL open source license. We have chosen such a license because of a local regulation which bound the Emilia-Romagna region in delivering this kind of permissions about intellectual properties.

4. ARCHITECTURE

AMA is composed of two main components:

(i)   an Evaluation Manager, based on a script in charge of storing data from periodical evaluations in a database;

(ii) a Results Manager which lets users to exploit and navigate accessibility reports.

In addition, a simple Users Manager provides support to user access. The whole system architecture is depicted in Figure 2.

The Evaluation Manager selects a set of sites from the URLs-DB and evaluates them by using (through Web Services) an external accessibility validator, called Accessibility Validation Application (AVA). This system outputs results of an analysis about actual and potential barriers it has found on the basis of several guideline and requirements (currently Stanca Act, WCAG 1.0, WCAG 2.0 and Section 508 [15]). Moreover, AVA exploits some external evaluation systems to respectively validate HTML and CSS code and verify color contrast. AVA is an open source software, derived from AChecker [9], available both as Web service and as a Web based application which can be used by end users through its Web interface. More details on AVA design issues and implementation can be found in [1] and in [12]. AChecker has been chosen because at the moment it is the only automatic accessibility evaluation tool which controls also WCAG 2.0 and some other national requirements (including the Italian Stanca Act

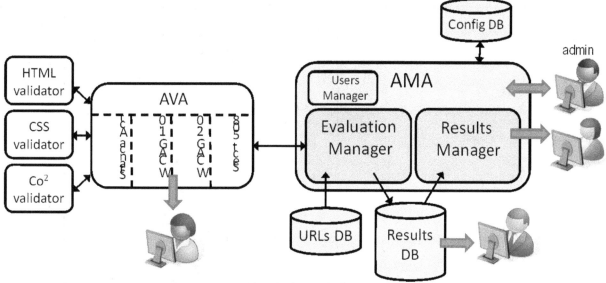

Fig. 2 - System Architecture

and the German BITV). This means that it is not possible to provide a comparison among AChecker and other automatic accessibility evaluation tools, because none of them check Web resources according to WCAG 2.0 success criteria. AChecker is an open source software and it is expansible, thus it is possible to add new guidelines and requirements, in order to provide a more complete monitoring application. More details about AChecker and the accuracy of its evaluations can be found in [9] and in [8].

Colors are verified by means of an application called Co2 Validator (COlor COntrast Validator) we have designed and implemented to estimate contrasts. Since color differences between foreground and background must be measured for every textual element, a recursive, crossed control has been provided. In fact, the cascading characteristics of style sheets (which are actually imposed for separating presentation from content) implies suitable inferences on XHTML pages and CSS documents, thereby allowing for inheritance and exceptions. Cross-browsing features (implicitly stated by the law) further restrict the possibility of omitting text/background colors which have to be always identified and compared. Due to the intrinsic complexity of crossed measures, parallelization of the process, as well as other techniques for optimization, have been taken into account.

Let us notice that such an approach to the colors contrast assessment sets aside from the Italian regulations and can be assumed as a general principle for accessibility.

Results from AVA are stored by the Evaluation Manager into the Results-DB. Checks are performed periodically, according to the frequency settings, previously declared into the Config-DB.

Further configurations are related to maps and shapes to be used in case of geo-referenced analysis and to guidelines and requirements to be considered in the evaluation. All configurations are set by the administrator of the AMA instance, who is responsible also for the user management.

Data stored in the Result-DB can be (i) browsed through the Web-based interface of the Result Manager, which permits to select main synthesis and produces results on a tabular form (available also as a map-based graphical representation in case of geo-referenced sites); (ii) directly queried from the Results-DB in order to obtain more detailed or more specific synthesis.

5. SYSTEM AT A GLANCE

In this section we will describe some main features of the AMA system, by referring to the instance described at the end of Section 3 and depicted in Figure 1.

5.1 Options Selections

The AMA Web interface provides an Options Menu which can be exploited by the user in order to choose some options and customize the monitoring activities as well as the presentation of report results. User can choose the guidelines which will drive the evaluation (e.g. WCAG 1.0, WCAG 2.0, Section 508 and Stanca Act). For each of this set of guidelines it is possible to select the level (if any is available, e.g. level A, AA or AAA) and one or more requirements or success criteria. This means that it is possible to conduct evaluations according to specific accessibility issues, such as the presence of alternatives to non-textual content, or the correct use of labels in forms, etc.

Moreover, user can choose the categories of Web sites to be evaluated (e.g. municipalities, provinces, states, governments, education, public health and so on). User can also set a previous date in order to compare most recent evaluations results with previous ones in a temporal dimension and the depth of the evaluations. In particular, in this AMA instance, user can choose to check the accessibility level of home pages (level 0), of all the URLs directly linked from the home page plus the previous levels pages (level 1), or of all the URLs directly linked from the level 1 pages plus the previous levels pages (level 2).

Finally user can choose the spatial-geo-politically related information, in order to enjoy accessibility evaluations results related to a specific area. In this AMA instance, default configuration is set to show results of European Web sites.

Detailed about all the European countries Web sites are available and related accessibility evaluations results could be browsed through this menu section and through the map. The AMA system can provide and manage results for the following geo-political levels: continents, countries, states, regions, provinces and municipalities.

Figure 3 depicts the Options Menu related to our AMA instance.

Fig. 3 Options Menu

5.2 Browsing and presenting report results through maps

In the AMA system URLs-DB is geo-referenced. Consequently, data in the Results-DB can be exploited through a map, providing a macro-level and a spatial-geo-political accessibility point of view. Figure 4 shows the map related to the evaluation of the main European public institutions Web sites according to Level A of WCAG 2.0 success criteria.

Different colors in the map highlight different accessibility levels of monitored Web sites: the lighter is the color of an area in the map and the higher is the level of accessibility of Web sites in that area (expressed as the number of evaluated pages without errors

according to the selected guidelines and requirements). On the contrary, a dark color means a low percentage of Web sites with no errors according to the selected Guideline(s). A script based on a map "mouseover" event allows the visibility of a tooltip with the percentage of Web sites without errors in an area. Moreover, clicking on a specific country area allows user to evaluate detailed accessibility report results about that country, browsing to a different geo-political level of the monitoring application.

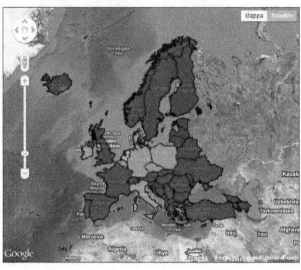

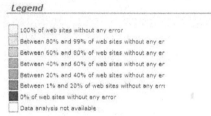

Fig. 4 – Screenshot of the map which shows accessibility evaluation results

5.3 Detailed results and temporal comparisons

Despite a map is a good way to provide an easy-to-read spatial and geo-political report, it is obviously not enough to offer detailed data about accessibility evaluations and it is worth mentioning it is not accessible to users with visual disabilities. To overcome this, the AMA web interface provides detailed data through tables. A summary table of the main analyzed geo-political entity (in our instance the European continent) is shown before the map, in order to provide data about the number of evaluated Web sites, the number of Web sites without any error, the total number of errors and the average number of errors per Web site. The map is followed by a table which reports summarized data for every country of the continent. In particular, such a table shows for each country the percentage of Web sites without any error and the average number of errors per Web site. The table is navigable (as well as the map) and it is possible to access to specific country data by clicking on its name. More detailed results are available for each country at the end of the page, showing: the number of evaluated Web sites, the number of Web sites without any error, the percentage of Web sites without any error, the total number of errors and the average number of errors per Web sites. Moreover, for each evaluated requirement or success criterion, a table is shown in order to provide information about certain errors and the number of evaluated Web pages for each Web site (which can be directly opened). An example of these latter detailed tables is shown in Figure 5.

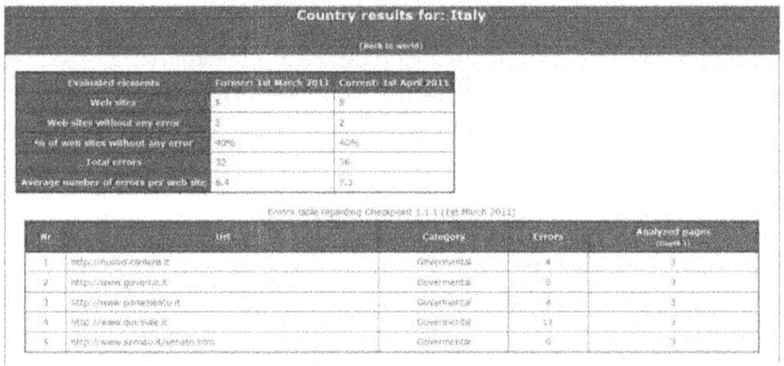

Fig. 5 Table showing detailed accessibility evaluation results related to the Italian country

All these tables can show a temporal comparison between the last conducted evaluation and a previous one, if the user chooses it by means of the Option Menu. All the shown data are available into the instance described in section 3 "Design issues". It is worth noting that Netherlands provides the highest percentage of Web sites without any error (66.67%), while Ireland provides the lowest average number of errors per page (2.00), according to WCAG 2.0, Level A (evaluating all the success criteria).

5.4 Evaluating technological barriers

In order to measure accessibility levels, several metrics have been defined. Some of them are based on the number of errors per page, some other ones require complex manual evaluations. A short summary of main metrics can be found in [12]. With the aim of measuring the accessibility barriers impact in a feasible and effective way on a large scale sample of Web sites, we have defined and added a new metric to our system. The BIF (Barriers Impact Factor) metric is computed as follows (on the basis of WCAG 2.0):

$$BIF(i) = \sum_{error} \#error(i) * weight(i)$$

Where i represents the assistive technologies/disabilities affected by detected errors; $BIF(i)$ is the Barrier Impact Factor affected the i assistive technology/disability; $error(i)$ represents the number of detected errors which affect the i assistive technology/disability; $weight(i)$ represents the weight which has been assigned to the i assistive technology/disability.

The lowest value of BIF could be 0 and this represents the absence of barriers. The higher is the BIF value and the higher is the impact of a certain barrier on a specific type of assistive technology/disability. Barriers have been grouped into 7 sets, which impact in the following assistive technologies and disabilities: screen reader/blindness; screen magnifier/low vision; color blindness; input device independence/movement impairments; deafness; cognitive disabilities; photosensitive epilepsy. AMA shows also evaluation results based on aBIF, which is the average barriers impact factor on the whole set of barriers. For the sake of simplicity, the weights have been defined as follows: the weight of each error which requires a manual control is 0; the weight of each certain level AAA error is 1; the weight of each certain level AA error is 2; the weight of each certain level A error is 3. Different weights could be computed on the basis of experiments with users. To obtain data results related

to the barrier impact evaluations, users can select "Barriers (WCAG 2.0)" as guidelines in the Option Menu into the AMA Web interface. Users can select the level of conformity to WCAG 2.0 (level A, level AA and level AAA) and one or more types of assistive technology/disability which have to be investigated. When the user chooses to evaluate Web sites according the Barriers Impact Factor, two data are added at the table which shows the analysis results: the total barrier impact factor and the average barrier impact factor. Data about Barrier Impact Factor provides more significant results and can sketch the accessibility level of a large sample of Web sites in a better way. Let us note that the BIF results on screen reader/blindness are very high, as we could expect it. In fact, barriers which impact on screen reader are more frequent and automatically detectable, without a manual evaluation.

5.5 Recording manual evaluations

In monitoring large scale accessibility Web sites from a macro level and spatial-geo-political point of view, evaluating certain errors can capture a snapshot of a situation and it is an effective way to provide results about those sites which are surely inaccessible (because they do not pass the automatic evaluations), since our application is not an evaluate-and-repair tool. Obviously this is not enough to offer a view of accessibility level which includes also manual controls and results about warning which should be checked by a human operator. In order to overcome this lack we have designed and developed a prototype which allows users managing and storing manual evaluations results. Such a prototype downloads Web pages code and allows user deciding about the actual presence of an error whenever a warning occurs in evaluating the accessibility of a specific URL (see Figure 6). For each warning user can browse the downloaded Web page which shows a marker corresponding to that warning. Currently the recording manual evaluations prototype Web interface is available in Italian language. The recording manual evaluations prototype is going to be integrated into the AMA system and to be translated in English language, so as to allow a more complete monitoring activity.

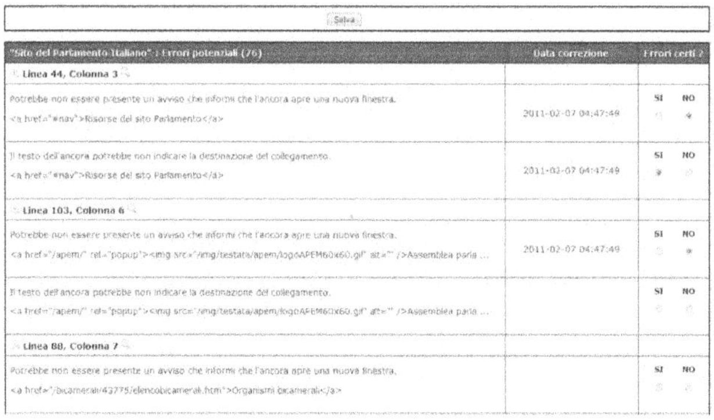

Fig. 6 The recording manual evaluations prototype Web interface

5.6 The Emilia-Romagna Region case study

Currently some Italian public administrations are using AMA instances in order to monitoring related public Web sites. In particular, the Emilia-Romagna Region [6] is monitoring the Regional, Provinces and Municipalities Web sites. The Emilia-Romagna Region AMA instance regularly evaluates a group of 376 Web sites (about 4,000 pages) and periodically monitors their accessibility level. Such AMA instance is available at the following URL: http://polo-rer.polocesena.unibo.it/vamola-monitor/ (username: guest; password: guest). It validates the WCAG 1.0, WCAG 2.0 checkpoints and the Stanca Act requirements (storing evaluations results since July 2010). Details about evaluations report results can be browsed and enjoyed on the basis of the following geo-political entities: Provinces and Municipalities. Analyzing Stanca Act requirements compliance results about the last year (from July 2010 to July 2011) we can observe a general positive trend: Web sites without any error is increased (from 2.64% to 4.51%) and the average number of errors per Web sites is decreased (from 147.87 to 143.30).

6. CONCLUSIONS

We designed and developed AMA to provide a macro-level and spatial-geo-political accessibility monitoring application. Its aim is supporting Web site commissioners and public institutions in managing investment and resources and in facing issues and shortcomings, in order to increase their Web pages accessibility level, rather than providing an evaluation-and-repair tool. In our application a set of parameters are customizable, according to end-users expectations and preferences. The presented case study is meant to show that the results reports, provided by AMA, represents a suitable cue for any aimed intervention, with the consequent resources saving (from a human and economical point of view). We have designed and developed a prototype which allows users manually adding checked errors to the Results-DB (URL by URL), thereby offering support to an integrated automatic/manual monitoring action. An integration phase is planned and it is going to be managed so as to provide a more complete monitoring application. Our system is currently used by the Emilia-Romagna Region and some other Italian public institutions, to support the periodical evaluation action, which is formally established by this institution.

7. ACKNOWLEDGMENTS

The authors would like to thank Giovanni Grazia and Jacopo Deyla (from the Emilia-Romagna Region), Marina Vriz and Ennio Paiella (from ASPHI) and Gregory R. Gay (from IDI, Ontario College of Art and Design).

8. REFERENCES

[1] Battistelli, M., Mirri, S., Muratori, L.A., Salomoni, P., Spagnoli, S. Avoiding to dispense with accuracy: A method to make different DTDs documents comparable. In *Proceeding of the 25th Symposium On Applied Computing (SAC2010)* (Sierre, Switzerland, March 22-26, 2010). ACM Press, 2010.

[2] Bühler, C., Heck, H., Nietzio, A., Goodwin Olsen, M., and Snaprud, M. Monitoring Accessibility of Governmental Web Sites in Europe. In *Proceedings of the International Conference on Computers Helping People with Special Needs (ICCHP 2008)* (Linz, Austria, July 9-11, 2008). Springer, Lecture Notes in Computer Science, 2008, 410-417.

[3] Cullen, K., Kubitschke, L., Boussios, T., Dolphin, C., and Meyer, I. Web accessibility in European countries: level of compliance with latest international accessibility specifications, notably WCAG 2.0, and approaches or plans to implement those specifications. Available at: http://ec.europa.eu/information_society/activities/einclusion/lib rary/studies/docs/access_comply_main.pdf, 2009.

[4] Cullen, K., Kubitschke, L., and Meyer, I. eAccessibility status follow-up 2008. Available at: http://ec.europa.eu/information_society/activities/einclusion/do cs/meac_study/meac_follow-up_2008.pdf, 2008.

[5] Cullen, K., Kubitschke, L., and Meyer, I. Assessment of the status of eAccessibility in Europe. Available at: http://ec.europa.eu/information_society/activities/einclusion/lib rary/studies/meac_study/index_en.htm, 2007.

[6] Emilia-Romagna Region. ERMES. Available at: http://www.regione.emilia-romagna.it, 2010.

[7] European Commission, DG Information Society and Media. Measuring progress in e-Inclusion Riga Dashboard 2007. Available at: http://ec.europa.eu/information_society/activities/einclusion/do cs/i2010_initiative/rigadashboard.pdf, 2007.

[8] Gay, G.R., Li, C. AChecker: Open, Interactive, Customizable, Web Accessibility Checking. In *Proceedings 7th ACM International Cross-Disciplinary Conference on Web Accessibility (W4A 2010)* Raleigh (North Carolina, USA), April 2010, ACM Press, New York, 2010.

[9] IDI, Ontario College of Art and Design, AChecker. Available at: http://www.atutor.ca/achecker/index.php, 2011.

[10] Italian Parliament. Decreto Ministeriale 8 luglio 2005 - Annex A: Technical assessment and technical accessibility requirements of Internet technology-based applications. Available at: http://www.pubbliaccesso.it/normative/DM080705-A-en.htm, 2005.

[11] Italian Parliament. Law nr. 4 – 01/09/2004. Official Journal nr. 13 – 01/17/2004, January 2004.

[12] Mirri, S., Muratori L., Roccetti, M. and Salomoni, P. Metrics for Accessibility: Experiences with the Vamolà Project. In *Proceedings 6th ACM International Cross-Disciplinary Conference on Web Accessibility (W4A 2009)* Madrid (Spain), April 2009, ACM Press, New York, 2009, pp. 142-145.

[13] Nomensa. United Nations global audit of Web accessibility. Available at: http://www.un.org/esa/socdev/enable/documents/fnomensarep. pdf, 2006.

[14] Rui, L., Gomes, D., Carrico, L. Web not for all: a Large Scale Study of Web Accessibility. In *Proceedings 7th ACM International Cross-Disciplinary Conference on Web Accessibility (W4A 2010)* Raleigh (North Carolina, USA), April 2010, ACM Press, New York, 2010.

[15] U.S. Rehabilitation Act Amendments. Section 508. Available at: http://www.webaim.org/standards/508/checklist, 1998.

[16] Web Accessibility Benchmarking Cluster. Unified Web Evaluation Methodology (UWEM 1.2 Tests). Available at: http://www.wabcluster.org/uwem1_2/UWEM_1_2_TESTS.pd f, 2007.

[17] World Wide Web Consortium. Web Content Accessibility Guidelines (WCAG) 1.0. Available at: http://www.w3.org/TR/WCAG10/, 1999.

[18] World Wide Web Consortium. Web Content Accessibility Guidelines (WCAG) 2.0. Available at: http://www.w3.org/TR/WCAG20/, 2008.

A Mobile Phone Based Personal Narrative System

Rolf Black, Annalu Waller
University of Dundee
School of Computing
Dundee DD1 4HB, Scotland
+44 1382 386530

{rolfblack, awaller}
@computing.dundee.ac.uk

Nava Tintarev, Ehud Reiter
University of Aberdeen
Department of Computing Science
Aberdeen AB24 3UE, Scotland
+44 1224 273443

{n.tintarev, e.reiter}
@abdn.ac.uk

Joseph Reddington
Royal Holloway
Computer Science
Egham TW20 0EX, England

joseph@cs.rhul.ac.uk

ABSTRACT

Currently available commercial Augmentative and Alternative Communication (AAC) technology makes little use of computing power to improve the access to words and phrases for *personal narrative*, an essential part of social interaction. In this paper, we describe the development and evaluation of a mobile phone application to enable data collection for a personal narrative system for children with severe speech and physical impairments (SSPI). Based on user feedback from the previous project "How was School today...?" we developed a modular system where school staff can use a mobile phone to track interaction with people and objects and user location at school. The phone also allows taking digital photographs and recording voice message sets by both school staff and parents/carers at home. These sets can be played back by the child for immediate narrative sharing similar to established AAC device interaction using sequential voice recorders. The mobile phone sends all the gathered data to a remote server. The data can then be used for automatic narrative generation on the child's PC based communication aid. Early results from the ongoing evaluation of the application in a special school with two participants and school staff show that staff were able to track interactions, record voice messages and take photographs. Location tracking was less successful, but was supplemented by timetable information. The participating children were able to play back voice messages and show photographs on the mobile phone for interactive narrative sharing using both direct and switch activated playback options.

Categories and Subject Descriptors

K.4.2 [**Computers and Society**]: Social Issues – Assistive technologies for persons with disabilities; D.2.2 [**Software Engineering**]: Design Tools and Techniques – User interfaces; H.1.2 [**Models and Principles**]: User/Machine Systems – Human factors; H.5.2 [**Information Interfaces and Presentation**]: User Interface – User-centered design; I.2.7 [**Artificial Intelligence**] Natural Language Processing – Language generation.

General Terms

Design, Experimentation, Human Factors.

Keywords

Augmentative and Alternative Communication (AAC), Personal narrative, Language development, Accessibility, Assistive technology, Disability, Cerebral Palsy, Mobile phone application, Voice output communication aid (VOCA), Speech Generating Device (SGD), User centered design

1. INTRODUCTION

In the "How was School today...?" (HwSt) project we have successfully developed a new personal narrative tool for children with severe speech and physical impairments (SSPI) [1, 2]. HwSt is the first step towards our goal of developing AAC tools that support storytelling and social dialogue. The proof of concept prototype of the system was able to collect sensor data, record voice messages from school staff and use other information, such as the timetable, to generate narratives automatically that children with SSPI could use to talk about their day. The system uses data-to-text natural language generation (NLG) technology to generate the appropriate utterances forming the narrative [3]. A graphical user interface, accessible both directly via touch screen and indirectly via switch scanning access, allowed the children firstly to personalise the stories through editing and then share them with adults and peers. The system was evaluated with three participants but needed substantial technical support to run.

In this paper, we describe key stages in designing and testing a data gathering module in form of a mobile phone application. It is part of a follow-on system that was anticipated to be usable by staff in a special school with limited technical support given over a longer period with several participants. This next generation prototype system uses the mobile phone to facilitate and expand the data collection. Additional data collected include photographs that can be linked to the voice message sets, and the ability to read 2D barcodes and Radio Frequency ID (RFID) tags to identify both interactions and locations. Data collected with the mobile phone are transferred automatically to a remote server, and can be used for the generation of narratives on the child's voice output communication aid (VOCA). School staff and students have both been involved in the design of the system.

At the end of the first HwSt project a questionnaire was given to staff to collect feedback on the use of the initial prototype. Parents were also given a questionnaire with questions about the use of AAC and their expectations on future devices. Feedback indicated the need for: (a) access to older narratives than just the previous day; (b) access to narratives directly after data collection (e.g. to tell the class about an experience after coming back from therapy or a special event); (c) smaller devices with better battery power; (d) the ability to print the generated narratives. In our current 18 months project, we have aimed to address all but the last of these issues.

2. BACKGROUND

Augmentative and Alternative Communication (AAC) technology can help individuals without speech to communicate with their environment. Since its early days in the 60s and 70s, AAC has seen dramatic changes in the technology used – from letter and phrase boards to gaze controlled computer access[1] or mobile phones with dedicated AAC software[2], both with natural sounding voice output technology [4]. However, most commercially available technology has been designed mainly to support transactional communication such as voicing needs and wants ("I am thirsty") and computing power is mainly used to enable physical access (e.g. to support eye gaze) or to improve voice output (via Text-to-Speech technology). Word selection and phrase construction, the storing and retrieving of content with all their associated cognitive requirements are still mainly left to the user [5].

For human beings, personal narrative is one of the main ways to access social communication. When we talk about our experiences we translate the things we know into narratives [6] which can help us to shape our language development [7]. Additionally, the telling and re-telling, structuring and re-structuring of our personal stories, enable us to reflect on our life and helps us to develop a sense of self [8]. Through the sharing of stories we make new friends and sustain current relationships.

Some AAC research projects have developed prototype systems which attempt to facilitate personal narrative, e.g. by providing users with fixed conversational utterances that can be selected with some support for conversational moves and spoken using synthesised speech [5, 9, 10]. However, these systems all need to be authored ahead of any conversation by the user (or their carer) in a laborious time consuming process.

Other research systems use Natural Language Processing technology to provide users with computer generated messages and support in accessing and selecting appropriate messages [11, 12]. However, these systems tend to be literacy based and are not necessarily appropriate for children or non-literate users.

Current commercially available VOCAs or AAC software applications for mainstream technology only partly support personal narrative interaction. Most devices allow the user or carer to save collections of utterances about personal experiences on the device for later retrieval. However, the process of organising the storage (in folders or so called 'notebooks') is left to the user or the user's carers and there is little support to edit the stories on the fly to accommodate interactive narrative where communication partners alter their stories to suit the conversation.

As an example, devices without a graphical interface such as sequential voice recorders (e.g. Step-by-step[3]) allow the user to record voice message sets which can be accessed sequentially or individually to talk about an experience.

A common way to enable users with a VOCA with graphical interface to speak about a personal experience is creating a photograph album with added annotations which the user can play back as a slide show. Photographs can also be used as visual scene displays by adding hot-spots with individual messages to the image. However, devices usually require advanced programming of the device in order to allow the user to access utterances other than the initial captions of the photograph[4].

All currently available applications have to be updated manually, i.e., the user or carer needs to decide what narrative to store on a device [13]. There is little or no opportunity to edit a story interactively during narration, and there is no support in retrieving situation or interaction appropriate stories. Technical abilities of new mainstream hardware, such as GPS for location detection on the iPhone and other smart handheld devices have been used to support retrieval of situational vocabulary, but the use of this technology has been limited, to date, to needs based communication such as ordering a meal at a restaurant[5].

3. USER CENTRED DESIGN PROCESS

Developing systems and interfaces for assistive technology is particularly challenging from an HCI perspective. What would work for a general population cannot be assumed for the intended user groups. It is particularly important to work with the users and their carers to develop something that works for them.

Several information gathering methods were used during the design of the original proof of concept (PoC) prototype [1]: (a) interviews were conducted and informal feedback gathered from speech and language therapist/pathologists, teachers and parents; (b) an ethnographic study over two weeks was conducted, shadowing the three participating children throughout their day to collect information about daily activities, interaction with staff and peers and the location of the children; (c) further information such as the children's timetable, lunch menu, current use of AAC equipment, literacy/symbol use and access methods were noted [14].

This information was used, together with ongoing feedback during the iterative design process, to ensure the development of a system that would fit into the school environment. The evaluation of the original PoC prototype showed that the system's output successfully supported personal narrative for the participating children. However, using the system was not practical on a day to day basis by staff without extensive support from the researchers (e.g. staff were unable to update the system, several hardware components had to be mounted and un-mounted on the user's wheelchair on a daily basis).

The follow-on project is set in a different special school. This school has less experience in AAC than the original school and therefore needed more input from the research team on the use and concept of supporting personal narrative of children with severe speech and physical impairments.

In the next sections, we describe the user-centred design process from information gathering to evaluations of the mobile phone prototype.

3.1 Information gathering

The researchers spent several weeks at the new special school to establish routines and identify possible participants for the evaluation.

The school caters for children with social, emotional and behavioural difficulties, profound or complex learning needs and physi-

---

[1] See http://cogain.org/ for examples

[2] E.g. http://www.proloquo2go.com/

[3] Trademark of http://www.ablenetinc.com/

[4] E.g. http://dynavoxsys.custhelp.com/ci/fattach/get/536/, retrieved 11 August 2011

[5] E.g. http://myvoiceaac.com/ or http://locabulary.com/

cal and sensory impairment and has about 60 pupils in nursery, primary and secondary classes. About half of the pupils are non-speaking and many use a combination of un-aided AAC (such as Makaton[6]) and 'low-tech' AAC (such as symbols or photographs) for communication. 'Low-tech' VOCAs are used for curriculum support, but are not widely used for communication support.

In collaboration with staff at the school, eight possible participants were identified on the basis of their communication and/or intellectual impairments; some of the children exhibited a desire to share their experiences, for others it was felt by staff that the children might benefit from participation. A bigger pool of potential participants allowed us to prepare for drop-outs due to illness or other issues (such as key staff leaving) which are common when working with individuals with severe disabilities. After drop-outs, we continued the evaluation with two children with very diverse profiles in particular in terms of mobility and age (See Section 5.1 for a description of our participants).

3.2 Workshop sessions at the school

A major factor for the successful use of a narrative tool using voice recordings which was identified in the original PoC project was staff experience and skills in using VOCAs to support personal narrative. The collaborating school in the current project had only one 'high-tech' AAC user at the time and used voice recording devices mainly to support curriculum activities rather than communication. To address the issue of building up skills on how to use AAC devices to support narrative, the research team, together with Nicola Grove[7], led a workshop on personal narrative for individuals with learning disabilities over two evenings for the teachers at the school. During the workshop, staff were encouraged to express expectations and possibilities for supporting personal narrative for the students at the school.

In order to support the data collection using the system, a further workshop on the use of voice message recording AAC devices (such as Step-by-Step voice recorders) was held as part of an in-service training day at the school.

3.3 Hardware Requirements

The following requirements list for the portable data gathering device was compiled from information gathered during the project and from feedback from the previous project:

(a) Accessible to individuals with reduced dexterity;

(b) Remotely accessible for individuals using switch access, e.g. via cable or Bluetooth;

(c) Audio recording and playback capabilities with sufficient playback volume;

(d) Inbuilt camera accessible for photograph taking and barcode detection;

(e) Data transfer via Wifi or 3G (UMTS) mobile phone network;

(f) Running Windows for mobile operating system to be able to run Wifi tracking client (we used a Windows Mobile based commercial system, see Section 3.4.3);

---

[6] Makaton uses signs together with symbols and speech to support communication for individuals with communication and/or learning difficulties. http://www.makaton.org/

[7] Nicola Grove, Director of the Openstorytellers, a professional group of storytellers with learning disabilities

(g) Sufficient battery life, i.e. at least 2 days stand-by with active Wi-Fi and 3G network to avoid running out of battery during data gathering.

At the time, the most suitable device appeared to be the HTC Touch2 mobile phone with a touch screen. The choice was justified by the fact that this device would support all technical requirements mentioned above. The touchscreen would allow switch-like access for users with reduced dexterity by creating whole screen buttons and Bluetooth keyboard support would allow remote switch access for head switch users via adapted Bluetooth keyboards. Later, we had to switch to a Nokia 6212 Classic due to hardware as well as software implications described in Section 3.4.2.

3.4 Data collection trials

Interface design scenarios based on the information gathering described earlier were drawn up to inform the design of a Power-Point mock-up graphical user interface (GUI). The mock-up interface could run on the HTC Touch2 for initial user feedback.

The interface mock-up allowed for recording sets of voice messages (similar to Step-by-Step voice recorders), taking photographs (e.g. to accompany the recordings), or detecting barcodes for interaction tracking.

3.4.1 Voice recording trial

A first working prototype running on the touch screen mobile phone (HTC Touch2) was set up to allow recording of voice messages only, and feedback was collected for the ease of input and the user interface. During a data gathering trial, researchers trained staff in the use of the device. Advice was given on strategies for recording voice messages designed to support interactive narrative. This advice included: dividing stories into several recordings to facilitate interactive conversation (i.e., time for the communication partner to comment and ask questions), using statements that will prompt comments or questions by the communication partner which can be anticipated and reacted to by the subsequent recording (e.g. "I played some music." would probably result in the conversation partner asking "What did you play?". Even if the question were not asked, the subsequent message would make sense, "I played the drums!"). Staff at that point were not routinely using voice message recording devices. Voice recordings were taken by both researchers who shadowed children during the day and staff under the instruction of the researchers.

After a day of recording, messages were transferred from the phone to a laptop, transcribed and played back to the children, using a Text-to-speech (TTS) engine reading the transcripts. The participating children were able to access the messages using a single switch for sequential playback. The mobile phone was used for very limited playback since none of the identified participants had enough dexterity to be able to access the phone via the touchscreen in a meaningful way. Playback via TTS using the transcription of the audio recordings meant that the utterances from voice recordings and the automatically generated messages by the system would all be spoken in the same voice (we aim to address this in a future project). Recordings were used for the design of the narrative structuring algorithm used for automatic narrative generation [15].

3.4.2 Barcode interaction tracking using the HTC Touch2

Initial trials with the HTC Touch2 suggested that using QR code technology for barcode detection was unreliable, with at best 10%

of barcodes being recognised. Users had to take several photographs before the software would recognise the barcode, often with no reliable readings, due to the low resolution available to the program written in Java. It was decided to change data collection to RFID sensor technology which worked reliably in the previous project. The only phone with an inbuilt RFID sensor available on the market at the time was a classic keypad phone, the Nokia 6212 Classic.

3.4.3 Location tracking using Wifi tracking with EKAHAU Wifi tracking software

In order to detect the location of the user we experimented with Wifi tracking software. In order to keep software development efforts to a minimum, we trialed an 'off-the-shelf' system that used extrapolation of readings rather than simple triangulation to avoid 'ghost' errors. The software is functional and the technology is rapidly maturing; however commercial solutions, e.g., EKAHAU, are intended to locate items (or staff members) for security applications or for periodic location updates. The data density and reliability required in this context is at the very limit of current technology. A practical application usable in a school environment did not seem achievable during this project and it was decided to explore other location tracking methods (See Section 4.1).

4. THE HwSt-itW MOBILE PHONE

In this section we describe the motivation and functionality of the mobile phone used to collect data.

The original HwSt PoC prototype allowed for the recording of voice messages onto the child's VOCA. These messages successfully augmented the narratives generated from on the sensor data. However, access to the narratives was limited due to (a) message generation only at the end of the day and (b) the nature of VOCAs taking a long time to boot up and set up at home or in school. Alternative 'low-tech' and 'mid-tech' communication aids, such as Step-by-step (SBS) voice recorders, are recommended as quickly accessible alternatives for situations where a VOCA is impractical [16]. However, messages used on an SBS are limited and usually replaced by newer messages; older messages are therefore not available for long term use. Using a mobile phone for data collection would allow for quick access to all voice recordings independent of the child's VOCA. This supports spontaneous narrative interaction. The phone can also wirelessly transmit the collected data to a remote database for automatic story generation on the user's VOCA.

4.1 Data collection methods

Different methods for data collection (interaction with people and objects, location data and voice recordings) were trialed:

4.1.1 Tagging of objects, people and locations using 2D barcode (Quick Response, QR) stickers

Sufficient camera resolution using the Nokia 6212 Classic allowed for reliable use of 2D QR barcodes (See Figure 1). These were mainly used to identify any unexpected locations of the participants. Staff took a photograph ("New picture" option, see Figure 2) of a QR code on an A4 poster located in every room of the school when the participant was in this location, if it conflicted with his/her timetable's location (e.g., the participant went to the hall for a theatre presentation rather than staying in class for the timetabled lesson). The QR codes contained a unique 2-digit decimal or 8-digit hexadecimal code and a text string with type of

interaction information (object, person, location) for database retrieval.

Figure 1. QR barcode, encoding the text "15:object".

4.1.2 Tagging of objects, people and locations using Radio Frequency Identification (RFID) tags

Objects that were regularly used by the participants were tagged with near field communication (NFC) tags; these are RFID tags which can be detected by the Nokia 6212. Staff cards with NFC tags were prepared for teachers, Special Learning Assistants (SLA) and other people the participants were likely to interact with (e.g., kitchen staff, visitors or friends). The tags contained information about the nature of the tagged object (person, object or location) which was registered by the phone together with the tag's 8-digit unique hexadecimal code for identification via database entries.

4.1.3 Voice recordings

The mobile phone's interface allowed for multi-part voice message recordings (voice message sets). Feedback from staff using both the initial "voice recording" application on the mobile and Step-by-Step AAC devices was used to design an interface that allows for: (a) sequential recording of voice messages; (b) playback and limited editing of message sets (adding to or deleting of recordings of an existing set); (c) adjusting the timestamp of a recording for recordings taken at the end of the day; (d) adding a photograph to a recording.

4.2 Equipment setup

A Nokia 6212 classic is used for data collection by staff, carers and parents. The 6212 is a classic design with a 16-key keypad, additional navigation keys and colour screen, equipped with a front and back camera and an RFID/NFC sensor (see Figure 2). Communication with the system server runs via a 3G network[8].

Interaction and location data are acquired by (a) holding the inbuilt sensor at the top end of the phone to an NFC tag or (b) taking a photograph of a QR barcode using the camera mode (New Picture Menu, see Figure 2). Both tags and QR code stickers were attached to objects, location posters or a person's name badge.

To support immediate story sharing the phone is connected to a small external battery powered loudspeaker which can be used when accessing voice recordings stored on the phone. Stories, which consist of a voice message set, are selected by staff and can be played back either using the large centre key on the navigation keypad (see Figure 2) or using a modified NFC card connected to a switch. Pressing the switch closed the circuit of the tag antenna

---

[8] The used phones contain a pay-as-you-go SIM card for network access. Data transfer is minimal and during the whole project not more that £1 of the SIM card balance was used up (Three.co.uk Network).

which had the same effect as swiping the tag on the phone (see Figure 3).

Figure 2. Main mobile phone interface with links to voice recorder, camera, and collected data (left). Photograph display during voice recording playback (right)[9].

Future systems will allow users to select a story themselves without support. However, many of the anticipated users will have some degree of learning disability which means they will need carer's support when choosing a story.

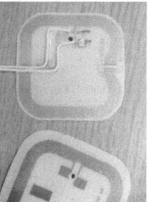

Figure 3. Modified tag attached to mobile phone cradle with connected switch (left). NFC tag with attached cable for switch connection (top right) and original tag (bottom right).

The mobile phone automatically sends all collected data to a remote server, checks for successful data transfer and attempts to resend in case of connection failure. A particularly pleasing use of this functionality occurred when one of our participants went on holiday abroad – the pictures were sent on their return to the UK.

5. EVALUATION AND PRELIMINARY RESULTS

The prototype system was implemented in the collaborating school to assess if it could be used for collecting and telling stories under realistic school conditions. Teachers and other school staff were equipped with NFC staff cards for interaction tracking. All locations/ rooms accessible to the students/ participants were

---

[9] The authors have permission from the participating children's parents and staff to show their photographs.

tagged with a location poster (A4 size) containing the symbol used in the school for this location and a QR code image. Objects used regularly by the participants (phonic book, computer, standing frame, etc.) were also tagged using NFC stickers for interaction tracking.

All staff were introduced to the mobile phone and a researcher was with staff for the first two weeks to train them in using it. One-page manuals were handed out to the class explaining the handling of the phone. Participants took their phone home with them to play back and record new messages about interesting events at home. So, parents of the participants were also trained in the use of the phone for recording and playback of messages.

5.1 Participants

Two participants in two separate classes were equipped with a mobile phone and the appropriate accessories. Both used home/school diaries routinely for information transfer between school and the parents. The mobile phone was handled by staff (teachers and special learning assistants) for data collection and selection of voice message sets for playback.

5.1.1 Peter[10]

Peter was a student at primary four class. At the beginning of the project he was 10:2 (years:months) old and had been at the school since nursery.

Peter has athetoid cerebral palsy. He is not ambulatory and is not independently mobile in the school. He arrives in a manual wheelchair which he is not able to wheel himself and is transferred into a special chair for class. He has very little functional speech. Peter is a friendly boy and is easy to engage with in interaction. He uses gestures and head pointing in his environment for communication as well as an E-Tran[11] folder for aided communication. The vocabulary folder (in symbols) is prepared by class staff. He has some emerging literacy, being able to recognise whole words and letters. Peter can work on a computer using his hands to select up to two switches for binary access using a combination of ballistic and fine motoric movements. He can only use this access method very ineffectively. Peter is in a class with five peers. Three of his class peers have no functional speech and two are not ambulant.

As part of the HwSt project Peter was equipped with a Step-by-Step device to support personal narrative for six months prior to the mobile phone prototype use. He used the device enthusiastically with recorded messages from both school and home.

For the evaluation, Peter used the mobile phone with the cradle (see Figure 5) mounted on his tray (attached to his standing frame or wheelchair). He was able to play back messages pre-selected by staff by pressing the switch attached, but he was unable to navigate to the messages by himself.

5.1.2 Martin

Martin is a student in his final year at the special school. He is a 17:0 year old teenager who has been at the school since nursery.

---

[10] All names mentioned have been changed to ensure anonymity.

[11] Eye-Transfer (E-Tran) systems are "low tech" AAC devices using eye pointing for spelling or access to words and phrases. The user first selects one of 4 or 6 color coded groups and selects the item with a second gaze at the appropriate color.

Martin has a chromosomal disorder. He is ambulatory and is independently mobile in the school. He has no functional speech with some single words and a mild movement disorder which results in an uncoordinated walking gait and reduced dexterity. He can use a computer using a touch screen. Martin is a friendly teenager and is easy to engage with in interaction. He sometimes displays behavioural difficulties which usually result in physical contact against weaker peers. He uses Makaton gestures and pointing at his environment as well as visual supports (photos and symbols) for communication. Martin has a GoTalk 9+[12] 'mid-tech' VOCA. However, in the past he only used the device for accessing requests and answers to curriculum questions, and then only very ineffectively. He preferred using a BigMAC single message voice recording switch which he sometimes took home to bring back messages from the weekend. Martin was in a class with five peers. Three peers are ambulant with functional speech. Two peers need a wheelchair for getting around and have no functional speech.

As part of the HwSt project Martin had been equipped with a Step-by-Step (SBS) device. When Martin had an accident at school resulting in a black eye, he used his SBS for several days when asked about the story behind his disfigurement: "Guess what happened to me. Look! – I tripped over my big feet and hurt my elbow my knee and my eye. – I had to go to the nurse and get an ice pack. But it wasn't too sore."

For the evaluation, Martin either carried his mobile phone which was attached to a lanyard around his neck or the phone was carried by the school staff who were supporting him. He was able to play back messages by pressing the centre navigation button on the phone, but had little concept of navigating to the messages by himself and needed support from staff to select stories he might have wanted to tell.

5.2 Example datasets

5.2.1 Voice recordings from school

Staff in the classes of both participants ensured that the mobile phone was always with the participants during the school day. Tables 1 and 2 show examples of multi voice messages from both participants.

Table 1. Voice Recordings for School, Martin

#	Photographic Image	Voice Recordings
1	No image.	Message 1: "I was so excited when I got into class today." Message 2: "Because Ms ____ (class teacher) was back."

5.2.2 Voice recordings from home

Both participants took their mobile phone home during term time and holidays to collect stories to tell when back at school. Parents of the participants were given a short training session on what kind of stories to record and on how to illustrate them with photographs which they could take after recording a story. The following examples (Tables 3 and 4) show multi voice messages from both participants.

---

[12] The GoTalk 9+ can store 12 voice recordings that can be accessed by pressing a symbolised button for each message on the device.

Table 2. Voice Recordings from School, Peter

#	Photographic Image	Voice Recordings
1		Message 1: "I have just come back from swimming this morning I had good fun." Message 2: "I started off getting weights put on my legs so I could practice walking in the pool" Message 3: "Then I get the helmet on and the weights are taken of and some floats so I can swimming on my own which I like doing. Message 4: "When I was swimming so first of all the funniest thing of the day was when ____ (peer) came over and tried to give me a big kiss."

Table 3 gives examples of voice recordings by Martin's parents with and without photographs taken. Martin lives on a sheep farm, and he sometimes stays in respite care over night or during the weekend. The first example recording was taken during the Easter holidays, the second one before a weekend in respite care. Messages were not always about Martin's experiences, but to inform staff and the research team about use of the system (see Table 3, Example 3).

Table 3. Voice Recordings from Home, Martin

#	Photogr. Image	Voice Recordings
1		Message 1: "Guess who I like feeding on the Farm!" Message 2: "Yes, you've guessed it, the little lamb."
2	No image	Message 1: "Guess where I 'm going tonight!" Message 2: "I'm going to ____ Cottage – for the weekend. I'm quite excited."
3		Message 1: "Dad says he's going to have to phone Rolf because he can't hear my messages from school. He thinks the speaker's not working."

Example 1 and 2 in Table 3 use the pattern of building up anticipation by asking a question and giving the answer in the following message. This was a pattern demonstrated during the introduction of the mobile phone and Step-by-Step devices as an example of how to support an interactive conversation using sequenced voice recordings. Any recording should aim to make it easy to predict the response by the conversation partner. This way following messages can be recorded to help the conversation flow because they can respond to the predicted communication partner's response of the conversation. However, the use of photographic images makes this more difficult because in many cases the image already contains the answer to a question (Example 1).

Recording 3 is an example of using the voice recordings for messages to the carer or parent that would usually be given by a home/school diary entry.

The first voice recording in Table 4 illustrates the learning process for the person making the recordings. Messages should be recorded as if they were spoken by the user. The example is the first message recorded by Peter's uncle which became one of Peter's favourite messages.

The recording time (which is displayed on the mobile phone with each recording) indicated that this recording and other similar recordings were recorded in the morning after the event before setting off to school.

Table 4. Voice Recordings from home, Peter

#	Photogr. Image	Voice Recordings
1	No image	Message 1: "Hey, Peter got home . I got home and I . eh . met my uncle and ma mum and ma wee sister and ma big sister . eh (short laugh, then giggling by two people)"

5.3 Example interaction

Martin is using the mobile phone at home to tell his parents about a stray cat that had been at the school. The phone displays a photograph of the cat at the window during message playback.

```
M - participant Martin
P - voice recording in phone accessed by Martin
Mum - Martin's mum
RA - researcher
[] - parallel events
{} - non verbal
(...) - unintelligible
```

M: Hoooo
P: I went to Mr _____ for Eco . and we went outside to clear the tubs . then I saw a cat from the neigbourhood and I chased it
Mum: Ooooh Martin you didn't chase the pussycat
M: Hoooo
Mum: you would as well cause he chases anything that moves
RA: ah
M: hoo
      (interruption of conversation)
Mum: What else did you do with Mr _____?
M: {turns to his mum, shakes his head} hoohooo {folds his arms}
Mum: Were you taking all the roots out of the tubs {gestures pulling roots out of tubs}
Mum: Gettin them ready for plantin up in the spring
M: Huhoo {points at biscuit box and signs food}

Mum: No . no more biscuits . You're maybe gettin one later . don't tell you've had a biscuit
M: {shakes head, signs - index finger on side of palm: television} hooo
Mum: I'll put the telly on for you in a wee minute
M: {turns to RA, presses play button, turns back to mum,
M: [{signs "home"}
P: [Then I was told by Mr _____ and Mrs (...) to leave the cat alone and carry on with the gardening
Mum: Listen . did you get a row for chasing the cat (phone rings)
M: {nods, signs "phone"}
Mum: Dad's gettin it through there

6. NEXT STEPS

The mobile phone currently allows the staff, and to a limited extent the children, to access the stored voice recordings and photos for personal narrative interaction. However, the main functionality of the mobile phone is to collect data that can be used a) to automatically generate utterances to augment the voice messages and b) to identify interesting stories and allow computational support to the user when searching for stories they want to tell. We had partly realised these aims in our original PoC prototype [17]: the system created messages such as "Martin was there" from interaction data and was able to recognise exceptions and use them to identify interesting stories (e.g. from location data and timetable information: "I went to the hall this morning during English class").

We have now set up the automatic generation of narratives on the participants' PC based VOCA systems (DynaVox Vmax and Tobii C12[13]). The data recorded by the phone is automatically transferred to a remote server linked to a database. All the data sent are encrypted and identified with unique identifiers. That way, even if the data were to be intercepted and decoded, most of it would not be intelligible. The database saves all interactions logged by the phone. These include location, object and people interactions (both 2D barcodes and RFID), voice recordings (single, multipart) and photographs (stand-alone or associated to voice recordings).

Early trials used The Grid 2 VOCA software[14] to display and access messages and recordings which were manually transferred onto grid pages. Figure 6 shows the interface for Peter, a page to access the messages of a specific event (green fields, from top left): location message ("I was in the gallery"); people interaction message ("Peter, Paul and Mary were there"); object interaction message ("I used my reading book"); and four voice messages, labelled with photographs taken at the time of recording. The page also contains evaluation messages (such as "I liked it") and buttons for navigation ("back to day overview", top left), editing ("hide this event", middle left) and link to the user's regular AAC method (bottom left). Martin tried a similar setup but had difficulties navigating and preferred using a single switch for accessing stories as sequentially played back messages to selecting individual messages via the touchscreen.

A Java programmed interface which used automatic transfer to the VOCA system was trialled. This interface was adaptable to the

---

[13] http://dynavoxtech.com/, http://tobii.com/

[14] http://sensorysoftware.com/thegrid2.html

user skills and allowed access to narratives from the current and previous days. Results from the evaluation of this trial will be published in a separate paper.

There are plans to implement search algorithms to present a personalised selection of narratives such as the most told narratives ('Favourites') or include links to related narratives that have an overlap in content (e.g. in the given example the system would present other stories containing the gallery, any of the people or the objects interacted with) [18].

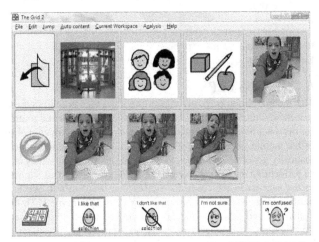

Figure 6. Wizard of Oz VOCA Interface using The Grid 2 software to display and access recordings and automatically generated massages based on collected data.

7. ACKNOWLEDGMENTS

The authors would like to thank the children, their parents and school staff, who participated in this study and who so willingly gave us their time, help and support. We would also like to thank Steven Knox and Alan Clelland for their work on programming the mobile phone application.

We would like to thank DynaVox Inc. for supplying the Vmax communication devices to run our system on and Sensory Software Ltd for supplying us with The Grid 2 VOCA software to enable the manually prepared access to the narratives.

This research was supported by the Research Council UK's Digital Economy Programme and EPSRC (Grant numbers EP/F067151/1, EP/F066880/1, EP/E011764/1, EP/H022376/1, and EP/H022570 /1).

8. REFERENCES

[1] Reiter, E., et al., *Using NLG to Help Language-Impaired Users Tell Stories and Participate in Social Dialogues*, in *ENLG2009*. 2009, Association for Computational Linguistics: Athens, Greece.

[2] Black, R., et al., *"How was School Today...?" Evaluating the Personal-Narrative-Telling Prototype: Preliminary results*, in *Communication Matters Symposium 2009*. 2009, Communication Matters: Leicester.

[3] Reiter, E. *An Architecture for Data-to-Text Systems*. in *ENLG-2007*. 2007.

[4] Vanderheiden, G.C., *A journey through early augmentative communication and computer access*. Journal of Rehabilitation Research and Development, 2002. **39**(6): p. 39-53.

[5] Waller, A., *Communication Access to Conversational Narrative*. Topics in Language Disorders, 2006. **26**(3): p. 221-239.

[6] McCabe, A. and C. Peterson, *Getting the story: A longitudinal study of parental styles in eliciting narratives and developing narrative skill*, in *Developing narrative structure*, A. McCabe and C. Peterson, Editors. 1991, Lawrence Erlbaum Associates: Hillsdale, NJ. p. 217-253.

[7] Quasthoff, U.M. and K. Nikolaus, *What makes a good story? Towards the production of conversational narratives*, in *Discourse Processing*, A. Flammer and W. Kintsch, Editors. 1982, North-Holland Publishing Co.: Oxford.

[8] Polkinghorne, D.E., *Narrative configuration in qualitative analysis*, in *Life history and narrative*, J.A. Hatch and R. Wisniewski, Editors. 1995, Routledge: London. p. 5-24.

[9] Todman, J., et al., *Whole utterance approaches in AAC*. Augmentative & Alternative Communication, 2008. **24**(3): p. 235–254.

[10] Todman, J. and N.A. Alm, *Modelling conversational pragmatics in communication aids*. Journal of Pragmatics, 2003. **3**: p. 523-538.

[11] Dempster, M., N. Alm, and E. Reiter, *Automatic generation of conversational utterances and narrative for Augmentative and Alternative Communication: a prototype system.* , in *Proceedings of NAACL-10 Workshop on Speech and Language Processing for Assistive Technology*. 2010: Los Angeles, USA.

[12] McCoy, K., C. Pennington, and A. Badman, *Compansion: From research prototype to practical integration*. Natural Language Engineering, 1998. **43**(73-95).

[13] Beukelman, D.R. and P. Mirenda, *Augmentative and Alternative Communication: Management of Severe Communication Disorders in Children and Adults*. 3rd ed. 2005, Baltimore: Paul H. Brookes Publishing Co.

[14] Black, R., et al., *Tell me about your day: creating novel access to personal narrative*, in *Communication Matters Symposium 2008*. 2008, Communication Matters: Leicester.

[15] Reddington, J. and N. Tintarev, *Automatically generating stories from sensor data*, in *Proceedings of the 16th international conference on Intelligent user interfaces*. 2011, ACM Palo Alto, CA, USA.

[16] Musselwhite, C., K. Daswick, and S. Daswick. *Self-Constructed Scripts*. Tip of the Month 2005 [cited 2010 8 February]; Available from: http://www.aacintervention.com/selfconstructing%20scripts.pdf.

[17] Black, R., et al., *A New Tool to Support Interactive Narrative Experience for Children with Communication Disorders*, in *14th Biennial Conference of the International Society for Augmentative and Alternative Communication*. 2010, International Society for AAC: Barcelona, Spain.

[18] Black, R., et al. *Using NLG and Sensors to Support Personal Narrative for Children with Complex Communication Needs*. in *First Workshop on Speech and Language Processing for Assistive Technologies (SLPAT), Human Language Technologies: The 11th Annual Conference of the North American Chapter of the Association for Computational Linguistics*. 2010. Los Angeles.

Blind People and Mobile Touch-based Text-Entry: Acknowledging the Need for Different Flavors

João Oliveira   Tiago Guerreiro   Hugo Nicolau   Joaquim Jorge   Daniel Gonçalves

IST / Technical University of Lisbon / INESC-ID
R. Alves Redol, 9
1000-029 Lisbon, Portugal
+351 21 4233565

jmgdo@ist.utl.pt, {tjvg, hman}@vimmi.inesc-id.pt, {jaj, daniel.goncalves}@inesc-id.pt

ABSTRACT

The emergence of touch-based mobile devices brought fresh and exciting possibilities. These came at the cost of a considerable number of novel challenges. They are particularly apparent with the blind population, as these devices lack tactile cues and are extremely visually demanding. Existing solutions resort to assistive screen reading software to compensate the lack of sight, still not all the information reaches the blind user. Good spatial ability is still required to have notion of the device and its interface, as well as the need to memorize buttons' position on screen. These abilities, as many other individual attributes as age, age of blindness onset or tactile sensibility are often forgotten, as the blind population is presented with the same methods ignoring capabilities and needs. Herein, we present a study with 13 blind people consisting of a touch screen text-entry task with four different methods. Results show that different capability levels have significant impact on performance and that this impact is related with the different methods' demands. These variances acknowledge the need of accounting for individual characteristics and giving space for difference, towards inclusive design.

Categories and Subject Descriptors

H.5.2 [**Information Interfaces and Presentation**]: User Interfaces – *Input devices and strategies, User-centered design.*

General Terms

Design, Experimentation, Human Factors.

Keywords

Blind, Mobile, Touch screens, Text-Entry, Individual Differences.

1. INTRODUCTION

Touch-based phones have paved their way into the mobile scene and turned the richness of the user interfaces into a differentiating factor between brands. Further, multi-touch surfaces played a

Figure 1 – A blind user entering text in a touch screen device

paramount role in these gadgets extraordinary adoption both by manufacturers and end-users. Touch-based devices present a wide set of possibilities but a comparable number of new challenges. These devices have incrementally decreased the number of tactile cues and simultaneously amplified the interaction possibilities, thus increasing the visual demands imposed to their users.

While a blind person is likely to be able to interact with a keypad-based phone to place a call without the need for any assistive technology, it would be a herculean task to do so with today's touch screen devices. The magnitude of this problem increases as we load the screen with interface elements, as happens with text-entry interfaces, where all letters are placed onscreen. Assistive screen reading software, like Apple's VoiceOver, enables a blind person to overcome these issues by offering auditory feedback of the visual elements onscreen. Still, as aforementioned, mobile interfaces are extremely visual and a large amount of information is lost in this visual-audio replacement. Possible examples are the need of a good spatial ability to have a notion of the device and the interface components therein, or cognitive capabilities to memorize letter placement on screen. Visual feedback makes these attributes dispensable or less pertinent, while its absence makes them relevant and worthy of consideration.

Our goal is to identify and quantify the individual attributes that make a difference in a blind user when interacting with a mobile touch screen. The mapping between individual capabilities and interface demands will then enable us to suggest the best interface for a particular individual or inform designers about the most promising methods and attributes, thus promoting inclusive design. In this paper, we focus our attention on mobile touch-based text-entry, a very visual, common, useful and demanding task. We present four different non-visual text-entry methods and evaluate them with 13 blind users (Figure 1). Results showed that different methods present different advantages and disadvantages and that these are related with users' individual abilities. Spatial ability, pressure sensitivity and verbal IQ were revealed as determining characteristics to a particular user's performance and good indicators of the suitable methods for each person.

2. RELATED WORK

In this section we present and discuss previous work on touch-based mobile text-entry solutions for blind people. Also, we look into individual differences and how they have been addressed in the past in different contexts.

2.1 Touch-based Text-Entry Solutions

In the past five years, several manufactures have included basic screen reading software in their touchscreen devices. Apple's VoiceOver[1] is a successful example. Users can explore the interfaces' layout by dragging their finger on the screen while receiving audio feedback. To select the item, the user rests a finger on it and taps with a second finger (i.e. split-tapping [6]) or alternatively lifts up the first finger and then double-taps anywhere on the screen. This approach is application independent, allowing blind people to use traditional interfaces with minimum modifications.

While we acknowledge that progresses on assistive technologies have been made, users still face some several problems when interacting with touch interfaces [7]. One of the major issues relates to text-entry. This is one of the most visually demanding tasks, yet common on innumerous mobile applications (e.g. contact management, text messages, email).

Indeed, several authors have been approaching this problem. Yfantidis and Evreinov [14] proposed a new input method, which consists in a pie menu with eight alternatives and three levels. Users can select each letter by performing a gesture on one of the eight directions of the layout. The character is read and users accept it by lifting the finger. The remaining levels of the interface are accessed by moving the finger towards some character and dwelling until it is replaced by an alternative letter. The interface layout and letter arrangement can be edited to accommodate the users' needs and preferences.

NavTouch [4] also uses a gesture approach, allowing blind users to navigate through the alphabet using only four directions. One can navigate horizontally or vertically, using vowels as shortcuts to the intended letter. Speech feedback is constantly received and split or double-tap is used to confirm a selection. To complement navigation, special functions (e.g. erase, menu) were placed on screen corners.

More recently, Bonner et al. [1] presented No-Look Notes, a keyboard with large targets that uses an alphabetical character-grouping scheme (similar to keypad-based multitap approaches). The layout consists in a pie menu with eight options, which are read upon touch. Split-tapping a segment sends the user to a new screen with that segment's characters, ordered alphabetically from top to bottom. Users select the desired character in a similar way to group selection. Performing a swipe to the left or right, allows the user to erase or enter a space, respectively.

Overall, there has been an effort to provide blind and visually impaired users with alternative touch-based text-entry methods. In fact, different interaction techniques are used, from single to multi-touch primitives, directional and scanning gestures, fixed and adaptive layouts. However, there is no knowledge of which

methods are better for each individual user. Most approaches neglect the individual differences among blind people and how they relate to users' performance.

2.2 Acknowledging Individual Differences

Current mobile devices force users to conform to inflexible interfaces, despite their wide range of capabilities. Users must struggle to use the interface as-is, and may or may not surpass their difficulties. Several design approaches have highlighted this issue in order to offer users better and more adequate interfaces.

Gregor and Newel [3] go beyond this idea and stated that while it is important to understand that a user is different from the next one, even for a single user, his capacities and needs are likely to diverge across time (dynamic diversity). Persad et al. [10] also acknowledge this diversity proposing an analytical evaluation framework based on the Capability-Demand theory, where users' capabilities at sensory, cognitive and motor levels, are matched with product demands. More recently, Wobbrock et al. [13] introduced the concept of ability-based design, which consists in an effort to create systems that leverage the full range of human potential. Our work extends all this knowledge in a way that both the users' capabilities as the device demands should be explored to foster inclusive mobile design. By doing so we will be able to provide more inclusive devices and adapt interfaces accordingly to the variations within the users, maximizing each individual performance. In this sense, a previous experiment [5], where we interviewed psychologists, occupational therapists, rehabilitation technicians, and teachers that work daily with blind users, suggested that individual differences between blind people are likely to have a wider impact on their abilities to interact with mobile devices than among sighted people. Tactile sensibility, spatial ability, verbal IQ, blindness onset age and age are mentioned as deciding characteristics for mobile performance.

When considering blind people, a capability that should not be ignored is tactile sensibility. Besides being crucial to capture information at the expense of vision, approximately 82% of all people who are blind are aged 50 or more [16] and as diabetes is one the main causes of blindness, changes in this sensorial capability are fairly common and should be accounted for. In [8] several physical requirements were identified in order for mobile devices to be accessible with limited sensibility for older adults. Despite the fact that these studies acknowledged key requirements, these characteristics were not quantified nor related with the different users' abilities.

Cognitive capabilities such as short-term memory, attention and spatial ability should also be meaningful when developing interfaces for the blind. Mobile interaction requires a cognitive effort that, for someone lacking sight, is much more demanding. Although there are studies that relate cognitive ability with mobile device usage for sighted older adults [2], there is an enormous gap in terms of studies relating cognitive ability and mobile phone interaction of a visually impaired person. The research reported in this paper tries to overcome this gap by studying the impact of individual differences among the blind on mobile touch-based text-entry tasks.

3. EVALUATION

Touch-based interfaces still pose several challenges to blind users. Recently, a number of efforts have been made to make these devices more accessible, particularly several text-entry methods have been proposed. Although each one present their own

---

[1]   http://www.apple.com/accessibility/iphone/vision.html (last visited on 03/05/2011)

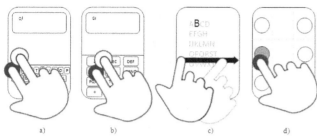

Figure 2. From left to right: QWERTY, MultiTap, NavTouch, and BrailleType.

advantages and limitations, to our knowledge there are no comprehensive studies that relate them to blind users' individual capabilities. Our goal was to relate text-entry demands with the individual differences among blind people.

3.1 Research Goals

The main purpose of this study is to understand the relation between a blind person's individual attributes and mobile touch interface demands, particularly in a text-entry context. In detail, we aim to answer the following research questions: 1) Which are the method's advantages and disadvantages? 2) How are individual differences related with each method and its demands?; 3) Which individual differences have greater impact in user abilities and performance?.

3.2 Text-Entry Methods

In this study, we sought for a set of text-entry methods that could highlight different users' capabilities. This set includes fixed and adaptive layouts, different target sizes and number of on-screen keys, scanning and gesture approaches, and multiple selection mechanisms. We then studied blind people using those methods and report their performance, highlighting some individual differences at sensory, cognitive and functional ability.

All text-entry methods, and their characteristics, used in this evaluation are described in Table 1. *QWERTY* and *NavTouch* have been previously presented elsewhere. *MultiTap* and *BrailleType* are presented here first hand. These two methods intend to explore the user's acquired knowledge both in terms of mobile keypads and Braille usage. All methods provide text-to-speech and audio feedback to the users' interactions.

The **QWERTY** text-entry method is identical to Apple's VoiceOver and consists in the traditional computer keyboard layout with a screen reading software (Figure 2-a). Users can focus the desire key by touching it (*painful exploration* [1]), and enter the letter by split-tapping or double tapping anywhere. On the strong side, this method enables blind users to input text similarly to a sighted person with a simple screen reading approach. On the other hand, it features a large number of targets of small size, which can be difficult to find, particularly for those who are not proficient with the QWERTY layout.

The **MultiTap** approach uses the same exploration and selection mechanism of the previous method. However, the layout presented is similar to keypad-based devices. We chose this method since this is a familiar letter arrangement to most users. There are twelve medium size buttons, each one featuring a set of characters, thus reducing the number of targets on screen. To enter a letter, users must split or double tap multiple times, according to the character position in that group (Figure 2-b).

NavTouch [4] is a gesture-based approach with adaptive layout, i.e. users can perform gestures anywhere on the screen, therefore

not being restricted to a fixed layout. This method is based on a navigational approach: gestures to left and right navigate the alphabet horizontally (Figure 2-c); while gestures up and down navigate vertically (i.e. between vowels). Vowels are only used as shortcuts to the intended letter, thus users can choose whatever path they feel more comfortable. Speech feedback is given as users navigate the alphabet. To select the current letter users can perform a split or double tap.

BrailleType takes advantage of the capabilities of those who know the Braille alphabet. The touch screen serves as a representation of the Braille cell, having six large targets representing each of the dots positions. These targets were made large and mapped to the corners and edges of the screen to allow an easy search. Users can perform a *painless exploration*, while receiving auditory feedback about each dot they are touching. To mark/clear a dot, a long press is required (Figure 2-d). After marking all the necessary dots for a Braille character, in whichever order the user desires, a double-tap in any part of the screen accepts it. A swipe to the left clears the Braille cell if one or more dots are marked or erases the last entered character if the matrix is empty. As *MultiTap*, this method seeks to provide a less stressful first approach with touch screen devices by reducing the number of onscreen targets.

Table 1. Text-entry methods' characterization

Method	Layout	Size	Explor.	Selection
QWERTY	Fixed	Small	Scan	Split/double tap
MultiTap	Fixed	Med.	Scan	Split/double tap
NavTouch	Adaptive	-	Gesture	Split/double tap
BrailleType	Fixed	Large	Scan	Long press and double tap

3.3 Procedure

The study comprised two phases: one to portray the users, their attributes and abilities, and a second one to analyze their speed and accuracy, capabilities and limitations, with the aforementioned text-entry methods. All the evaluations were performed in a formation centre for the blind.

3.3.1 Individual attributes and abilities

The characterization phase encompassed an oral questionnaire, sensory (pressure sensibility and spatial acuity), cognitive (verbal IQ and spatial ability), and functional (braille, mobile keypad and computer writing performance) evaluations.

To assess the participants' tactile capabilities, two different components of tactile sensibility were measured. Pressure sensitivity was determined using the Semmes-Weinstein monofilament test (Figure 3) [11]. In this test, there are several nylon filaments with different resistance levels, bending when the maximum pressure they support is applied. This way, if a user can sense a point of pressure, his pressure sensibility is equal to the force applied by the filament. Five monofilaments of 2.83, 3.61, 4.31, 4.56 and 6.65 Newton were used, starting the stimuli with the least resistant one. Pressure was applied in the thumb, index and middle fingers in random order, so we could prevent arbitrary identification of a stimulus by the person being tested.

Spatial acuity was measured using a Disk-Criminator (Figure 3) [9]. This instrument measures a person's capability to distinguish one or two points of pressure on the skin surface. The Disk-Criminator used is an orthogonal plastic instrument that has in each side a pair of metal filaments with relative distances ranging from 2 to 15 mm, with 1mm increments. Each of these filament pairs was, applied randomly in the aforementioned three fingers. There were made 10 stimuli per finger, randomly, alternating between a pair of filaments and a unique filament. The participant had to indicate when he/she felt one or two points of pressure. When he/she was able to correctly identify 7 out of 10 stimuli, his/her level of spatial acuity was the distance between filaments.

The cognitive evaluation focused two components of the cognitive ability, a verbal and a non-verbal. The verbal component was evaluated in terms of working memory: short-term memory and main responsible for the control of attention. The non-verbal component, which consists of abilities independent of mother language or culture, was evaluated in terms of spatial ability: the ability to create and manipulate mental images, as well as maintain orientation relatively to other objects.

To evaluate working memory, the subtest Digit Span of the revised Wechsler Adult Intelligence Scale (WAIS-R) was used [12]. In a first phase, the participant must repeat increasingly long series of digits presented orally, and on a second, repeat additional sets of numbers but backwards. The last number of digits of a series properly repeated allows calculation of a grade to the participant's working memory and, subsequently, to the user's verbal intelligence quotient (Verbal IQ). Spatial ability was measured using the combined grades of the tests Planche a Deux Formes and Planche du Casuiste (Figure 3). These two tests are part of a cognitive battery for vocational guidance [15]. Their goal is to complete, as fast as possible, a puzzle of geometrical pieces.

To assess previous device-wise functional abilities and experience, the users were asked to input text with a mobile phone, a Perkins Braille typewriter and a personal computer. All users were asked to write three individual sentences in each of the devices. The Perkins typewriter and personal computer were made available by the researchers. The computer keyboard featured silicone marks on letters 'F' and 'J' to ease exploration. The mobile task was performed with the user's own device. All participants, excepting two, owned a device with a screen reader.

3.3.2 Experimental evaluation

The evaluation was set up with a within-subject design where all participants were evaluated with all four text-entry methods, one method per session, with one week recess between sessions. In all sessions, with the help of the experimenter, participants started by learning each method and interacting with it for 15 minutes. They were encouraged to ask questions and allay all doubts. If by the end of 15 minutes the participant was unable to write his name or a simple, common four-letter word, the evaluation was halted.

After the tutorial, participants were instructed to write a set of five sentences as fast and accurately as they could (no accentuation or punctuation). Each sentence comprised 5 words with an average size of 4.48 characters. These sentences were extracted from a written language *corpus*, and each one had a minimum correlation with language of 0.97. The sentences' selection was managed by the application and randomly presented to the user to avoid order effects. The order in which the sessions (methods) were undertaken was also decided randomly to counteract order effects.

All focused and entered characters were registered by the application. The option to delete a character was locked. If a participant made a mistake or was unable to input a certain letter, she/he was told not to worry and simply carry on with the next character. It was made clear to all participants that we were testing

Figure 3. Individual abilities: Semmes-Weinstein test (left); Disk-Criminator (middle); Planche a Deux Formes (right).

the system and not their writing skills. Upon finishing each sentence, the device was handed to the experimenter to load the next random sentence and continue with the evaluation. The session ended with a brief subjective questionnaire on the text-entry method. All these steps were repeated in all sessions (methods).

Table 2. Participant's characterization. U[User]; G[Gender];A(O)[Age(Onset);PS[Pressure Sensitivity in Newton];SA[Spatial Ability];VIQ[Verbal IQ];MP[Mobile Phone in WPM]; PC[Computer in WPM];BR[Braille Reading in WPM];BW[Braille Writing in WPM]. The lower the PS, the better the tactile sensitivity. The opposite for SA and VIQ.

U	G	A(O)	PS	SA	VIQ	MP	PC	BR	BW
1	M	26(10)	3,61	1,8	105	15,8	45,8	49,4	26,4
2	M	32(15)	2,83	10,0	111	11,9	44,6	21,3	13,4
3	F	52(5)	4,31	10,0	78	4,0	11,5	8,8	14,9
4	F	34(27)	4,31	8,5	99	12,6	41,8	2,6	8,2
5	M	24(2)	3,61	5,5	65	14,2	45,3	63,7	27,3
6	M	45(20)	2,83	7,8	114	6,7	21,8	9,4	11,6
7	M	62(3)	4,31	4,8	104	7,9	23,7	64,7	25,8
8	F	46(25)	3,61	6,2	84	7,7	20,3	26,5	17,8
9	M	60(0)	4,31	4,0	134	9,6	24,8	80,8	13,4
10	M	48(26)	4,31	4,8	84	10,6	33,9	19,2	22,0
11	M	49(34)	4,31	3,3	78	N/A	N/A	N/A	N/A
12	F	49(17)	4,31	5,5	78	7,1	26,7	3,8	7,9
13	M	46(3)	4,31	7,0	84	N/A	4,7	9,0	11,7

3.4 Apparatus

We used the Samsung Galaxy S touch screen device, which runs Android operating system. This device features a 4 inch capacitive touch screen with multi-touch support. No tactile upper and bottom boundaries were created. All text-entry methods were implemented as Android applications. All audio feedback was given using SVOX Classic TTS, Portuguese language pack. In BrailleType, a timeout of 800ms was used to accept a selection. An application to manage text-entry methods, user sessions and sentences required to type was also implemented. This application informed which sentence to type and logged all the participants' interactions (focus and entry), for later analysis.

3.5 Participants

Thirteen blind participants (light perception at most) were recruited from a formation centre for visually impaired people. The participant group was composed of 9 males and 4 females, with ages ranging from 24 to 62 (M=44). All of the participants knew the Braille alphabet, although one user stated that he did not know how to write with a Perkins Braille typewriter and was not able to read due to poor tactile sensitivity and lack of practice. This same user does not use a computer or send text messages on a mobile phone. With the exception of another user, who was not able to write text on a mobile phone as well, all of the participants, with more or less difficulty, write text messages on their mobile phones and use the computer. Only one of the users had previous experience with mobile touch screen devices. Their characterizations are depicted in Table 2.

4. Results

The goal of this study was to assess the advantages and limitations of different touch-based text-entry approaches, and to acknowledge if in fact, and how, different blind people, with different individual attributes, can benefit from a method over others. We start by analyzing the different methods from the standpoint of user performance and preference. Then we focus on individual characteristics and how they diverge across methods, finishing with some case studies, thus giving us a better insight on why certain methods are better suited to a particular person.

4.1 Methods

In this section we focus on the different text-entry methods through the analysis of the users' performance in terms of speed and accuracy. We also examine their preference, opinions and frustrations regarding the presented methods.

4.1.1 Text-entry Speed

To assess speed, the words per minute (WPM) text entry measure calculated as *(transcribed text – 1) * (60 seconds / time in seconds) / (5 characters per word)* was used. One participant, after 15 minutes in the practice session was still struggling with the QWERTY and the MultiTap methods, so he did not perform the test with these two methods.

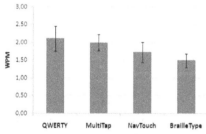

Figure 4. WPM (average) across the different methods. Error bars denote 95% CI.

Figure 4 shows the users' average WPM with the four methods. QWERTY was the fastest method (M=2.1, SD=0.7) followed very closely by MultiTap (M=2.0, SD=0.48). BrailleType was the slowest of the methods (M=1.49, SD=0.43) with NavTouch being a little faster (M=1.72, SD=0.55). Given the normality of the data (according to the Shapiro-Wilk normality test) a one-way repeated measures analysis of variance was conducted to see if these differences were significant. There was a statistically significant difference of Method on Text-Entry Speed (Wilk's Lambda=0.29, $F_{3,58}$=45.54, p<.01). A Bonferroni post-hoc comparison test indicated that QWERTY and MultiTap techniques were significantly faster than NavTouch and BrailleType. QWERTY did not differ significantly from MultiTap, but NavTouch was faster than BrailleType. Even though QWERTY and MultiTap require searching for a specific character or group of characters along the screen, they still proved to be faster as they offer a more direct mapping between input and desired output. Both NavTouch and BrailleType require multiple gestures and inputs to access a

specific character, which resulted in slower performances. BrailleType, besides having multiple inputs per character, was hindered by the fact that it uses a timeout system, an aspect that contributed for making the method the worst in terms of speed.

4.1.2 Text-entry Accuracy

Accuracy was measured using the the MSD Error Rate, calculated as *MSD (presentedText, transcribedText) / Max(|presentedText|, |transcribedText|) * 100*. Figure 5 presents the MSD Error Rate of the participants in the different methods. Since the data did not present a normal distribution, the Friedman test was used verify statistically significant differences among the methods. Results indicated that there was a statistically significant difference in Text-Entry Accuracy between the Methods (X^2(3)=15.27, p<.01). A Wilcoxon Signed Rank Test was used between each pair of methods to understand where these differences resided.

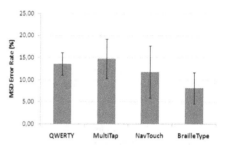

Figure 5. MSD Error Rates. Error bars denote 95% CI.

BrailleType was significantly less error prone than both QWERTY and MultiTap. NavTouch was only significantly different from MultiTap. The fastest methods were also the most error prone, while BrailleType, the slowest method, was the one with the best results accuracy-wise.

4.1.3 Users' Feedback

User feedback was registered through a brief questionnaire at the end of each session. This questionnaire was composed of four statements to classify using a five-point Likert scale (1=strongly disagree, 5=strongly agree). The participants' ratings to the several methods are shown in Table 3. The Wilcoxon Signed Rank Test was used to assess significant differences.

Table 3. Questionnaire results for each method (Median, Inter-quartile Range). '*' indicates statistical significance.

Method	Easy to comprehend*	Easy to use*	Fast method	Would use
QWERTY	4.0 (2)	4.0 (2)	4.0 (3)	3.0 (3)
MultiTap	4.0 (2)	4.0 (1)	3.5 (2)	4.0 (3)
NavTouch	5.0 (1)	4.5 (2)	3.0 (3)	3.0 (2)
BrailleType	5.0 (1)	5.0 (1)	3.0 (1)	3.5 (1)

Participants strongly agree that Navtouch is an easier method to understand than MultiTap (Z=-2.26, p=.024) and that BrailleType is also easier to understand than both MultiTap and QWERTY methods (Z=-2.21, p=.027 and Z=-2.058, p=.040). Users also strongly agree that NavTouch is easier to use than the QWERTY technique (Z=-1.98, p=.047) and that BrailleType is easier than both QWERTY and MultiTap (Z=-2.24, p=.025 and Z=-2.07, p=.039). BrailleType and NavTouch, the methods where users performed less mistakes, were also the slowest in terms of WPM, which was reflected in the questionnaire.. In terms of preference,

MultiTap was the elected followed by BrailleType, probably due to the resemblance to the traditional and familiar multi-tap and Braille methods. However, if we observe the Inter-quartile range values, we can see that there wasn't a consensus on most methods, in fact, only with BrailleType users seem to collectively agree that they would use the system.

The questionnaire was also composed of an open question about the difficulties faced and general opinion on the text-entry methods. Table 4 shows the main difficulties observed as well as mentioned by the users on each method.

Table 4. Main difficulties observed and perceived by users.

Method	Difficulties
QWERTY	Targets small and close, split-tapping near edges.
MultiTap	Split multi-tapping
NavTouch	Accidental touches, lose track of text
BrailleType	Timeouts, lose track of text

With QWERTY, the main cause of errors and frustration were the proximity and small nature of the targets. Most users found them to be a bit too tiny and close to each other, making it hard to select and split-tap the desired one, especially when the user has large fingers. Since most users would grab the device with the left hand, and use the other to interact, searching with the index finger and split-tapping with the middle finger, targets near the right edge would also become hard to split-tap. Dexterity problems and some indecision on how to hold and interact with the mobile phone were apparent on some users.

With MultiTap most errors occurred due to difficulties in multi-tapping, more specifically in finding the right timing to navigate between characters of a group. This was particularly apparent in the beginning, as some users would tend to not time well their taps, resulting in accepting undesired characters. Even though most are perfectly accustomed to multi-tap on their mobile keypads, some users had difficulty adapting this technique to a sensitive touch device. These adaptation difficulties were also apparent with the NavTouch method. Users would frequently touch/rest their fingers on the screen resulting in errors. Some users would also accidently fail doing the directional gestures, tapping the screen instead of actually doing fling gestures. A concern of some users was the difficulty they found in keeping track of the current text, as they would tend to get confused or even forget the current state of the text as they navigated through the alphabet.

BrailleType, in spite of being the method where fewer errors were committed, they would still happen and their main cause were timeouts. Since focusing each target would read their cell number, but not actually select it until a pre-determined time elapsed, confident users, wanting to write faster, would forget to actually wait for the timeout to select the targets. This resulted in trying to accept incorrect Braille cells. It was evident that most users by the end of the last sentence wanted a shorter timeout, or possibly none whatsoever.

Besides these particular difficulties on each method, common problems such as figuring how to properly hold and interact with the device, as well as involuntary touches were frequent on every method. The general opinion on the methods was in line with what we expected. Users seemed to agree that NavTouch and BrailleType were simpler, easier and safer systems albeit slower

(too slow for some participants). On the other hand, the QWERTY and MultiTap methods were perceived as slightly more complex, where errors are more frequent, but that allow writing at a faster pace. It is worth remembering that one participant was unable to use both the QWERTY and MultiTap methods, but had no problems using the other two methods.

4.2 Individual Differences

Now that we have observed how the different methods fared against each other, we will take a closer look at some individual traits to try to understand if they can explain the differences in the users' performance. In this section, we center our attention in three main groups of characteristics: age related, sensory, cognitive, and a more functional group based on the experience in mobile devices, computer and Braille.

4.2.1 Age Related Differences

In terms of WPM, younger users always performed better than older users, independently of the text-entry method used. This difference was statistically significant for QWERTY ($F_{1,58}$=6.67, p<.05) and MultiTap ($F_{1,58}$=23.12, p<.05) methods. It is interesting to note that although younger users were always faster, the difference between the two age groups is less pronounced on NavTouch and BrailleType methods. In terms of accuracy, younger users also performed better, committing fewer errors whatever the method tested. This difference, however, was only statistically significant for MultiTap method (X^2(1)=4.75, p<.05).

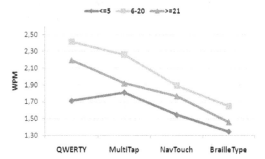

Figure 6. Age of onset impact on WPM.

Users, who were blind before the age of 6, had the slowest performance across all methods, as seen in Figure 6. This difference was statistically significant for QWERTY ($F_{2,57}$=6.096, p<.05) and MultiTap ($F_{2,57}$=5.31, p<.05), with the post-hoc Tukey HSD multiple comparisons test revealing significant differences between the early blind and users who lost their sight between 6 and 20 years of age. NavTouch and BrailleType methods seem to get smaller differences in performance on different age of onset groups, than the other two methods. The MSD Error Rate of the different groups was significantly different only for QWERTY (X^2(2)=13.53, p<.01), with users with the oldest age of onset committing fewer errors than the earlier blinds. Just like with the WPM metric, congenitally blind users or that acquired blindness at a very early stage of their lives had the worst performance across all methods.

4.2.2 Sensory and Cognitive Differences

Figure 7 shows the differences of WPM, for users with different levels of pressure sensitivity. There was a significant statistical difference on the MultiTap method ($F_{1,58}$=11.54, p<.01), as users with better pressure sensitivity performed far better. This was probably due to a combination of the very sensitive nature of the screen and the need for multiple touches of the multi-tap technique. No statistically significant results were found for the MSD Error Rate measure.

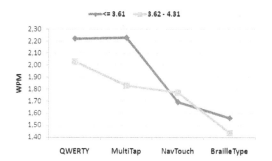

Figure 7. Pressure sensitivity impact on WPM.

For QWERTY and MultiTap, two methods where exploration of the screen is vital, spatial ability was significant ($F_{2,57}=4.43$, p<.05 and $F_{2,57}=9.95$, p<.01, respectively). Participants with the best spatial ability values performed much better than the others, a gap non-existent on NavTouch and BrailleType methods (Figure 8). Users with better spatial ability also committed significantly fewer errors on MultiTap ($X^2(2)=12.35$, p<.01).

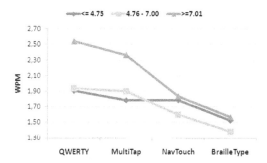

Figure 8. Spatial ability impact on WPM.

Users with a verbal IQ inferior to 85 were always slower independently of the method. This was significant across all methods (QWERTY: $F_{2,57}=4.33$, p<.05; MultiTap: $F_{2,57}=7.08$, p<.01; NavTouch: $F_{2,63}=3.66$, p<.01; BrailleType: $F_{2,63}=6.89$, p<.01). Users with smaller values of verbal IQ also committed significantly more errors on MultiTap ($X^2(2)=12.56$, p<.01) and NavTouch ($X^2(2)=6.81$, p<.05) methods. These two methods seem to have had a greater impact of short term memory and attention.

4.2.3 Functional Differences

There wasn't a statistical significant difference on the QWERTY method, in terms of speed and accuracy, on users with different levels of computer experience. The same is applied to the MultiTap method when comparing users with different levels of mobile device experience. This result suggests that the knowledge acquired from button-based devices do not transfer to their touch counter-parts. However, experience in Braille was significant in terms of Braille reading experience, on the speed of the users with the BrailleType method ($F_{2,57}=3.60$, p<.05). Faster users at reading Braille, and thus knowing extremely well the Braille alphabet, were faster than the others.

4.3 Case Studies

To understand specific behaviors when performing text-entry tasks, in this section we highlight some key observations about specific participants. Starting by looking at the most critical user (Participant 7), the one who was unable to do the test with the QWERTY and MultiTap methods, even after all the practice session time and help from the experimenter. He was an older person, the oldest of the group of participants (62 years old), with an early age of onset (3 years old), bad pressure sensitivity (4.31) and although he had a good verbal IQ (104), he had poor spatial ability (4.75). As we have seen before, these characteristics were significantly related with inferior performances, especially on the two methods the user couldn't cope with, so their combined effect must have contributed for this inability. He was the only user who didn't perform the test in these two methods and, coincidently or not, he was the only user in our study that had this combination of traits. We could argue that maybe he is a *Luddite* or a technophobe, however the mobile and computer assessments made beforehand would state otherwise (7.9 and 23.7 WPM respectively). The user does have experience with technology, and yet his individual attributes seem to put him in a disadvantage, especially when facing certain methods.

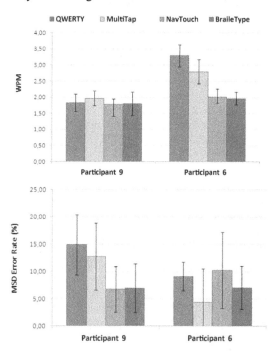

Figure 9. Two users' WPM (top) and MSD ER (bottom).

The impact of individual differences can be observed in more cases. Figure 9 shows the performance of two participants with clearly different outcomes both speed-wise and in terms of accuracy. Participant 9 is a congenital blind, with poor pressure sensitivity (4.3) and spatial ability (4.0). These characteristics certainly influenced his performance as he got much better results with NavTouch and BrailleType. In terms of WPM he was constant in all methods, an indication that he had more difficulty with QWERTY and MultiTap, as the other two are clearly slower methods. Although maintaining speed across methods, Participant 1 performed far more errors on the more demanding methods.

Participant 6, however, is the opposite: has an older age of onset (20 years old) and much better tactile sensitivity (2.83) and spatial ability (8.0). This is reflected in the results, since he was faster with the more demanding methods, and made as much errors, if not less, with these than with the "safer" methods. The performance on MultiTap, a method highly demanding on spatial ability and pressure sensitivity is a good example of the impact of these individual characteristics, especially if we compare the performance of the two participants. These examples illustrate how important individual attributes are in regards to what methods are most accessible to a certain user.

4.4 Discussion

After analyzing each method in detail and revealing individual differences with impact in user's performance we answer the proposed research questions as follows:

1) Which are each method's advantages and disadvantages?

A parallel contribution of this paper comes with the presentation and comparative evaluation of four different text-entry methods. QWERTY (similar to Apple's VoiceOver) and MultiTap (the touch screen counterpart of the original keypad text-entry method) presented themselves as faster input methods. NavTouch (a directional approach) and BrailleType (a coding approach), less direct methods, provide a slower but less erroneous experience.

2) How are individual differences related with each method and its demands?

Results showed that text-entry interfaces with a large number of onscreen elements, like QWERTY and MultiTap, are more demanding to what concerns spatial ability. Users with low spatial skills are likely to perform poorly or even be unable to use those methods. On the other hand, NavTouch and MultiTap, are more demanding to what concerns to memory and attention, as the user has to keep track of the evolution within a selection. Also, results suggest that users with low pressure sensitivity have problems with repeated multi-touch interactions (e.g.,multi split-tapping).

3) Which individual differences have greater impact in user abilities and performance?

Spatial ability, pressure sensitivity and verbal IQ play an important role in the blind user's ability to use and perform accurately with a touch screen and particularly with touch-based text-entry methods. Also, age and age of blindness onset seem to have an impact in users' overall abilities. Previous experience with mobile and other input devices seem to have a reduced impact, or none, in the users' skill to use a new text-entry method.

5. CONCLUSIONS

Individual differences among the blind have a great impact on the different mobile interaction proficiency levels they attain. General-purpose interfaces and assistive technologies disregard these differences. In this paper, we argue that both the users' capabilities as the interaction demands should be explored to foster inclusive design. By doing so, we will be able to provide more inclusive devices and interfaces accordingly to the variations within the users, maximizing each individual performance.

Results in a comparative text-entry method evaluation showed that different methods pose different demands. How these demands are surpassed depends on specific individual attributes. This indicates that different designs suit different blind people. It is paramount to understand these relations and provide informed design diversity to account for individual differences.

6. ACKNOWLEDGMENTS

We thank all the users and Dr. Carlos Bastardo for his insights and support. This work was supported by FCT through PIDDAC Program funds. Nicolau and Guerreiro were supported by FCT, grants SFRH/BD/46748/2008 and SFRH/BD/28110/2006.

7. REFERENCES

[1] Bonner, M. et al. 2010. No-Look Notes: Accessible Eyes-Free Multitouch Text-Entry. *Pervasive Computers*, 409-426.

[2] Czaja, S. and Lee, C. 2007. The impact of aging on access to technology. *UAIS*, 5(4):341-349.

[3] Gregor, P. and Newell, A. 2001. Designing for dynamic diversity: making accessible interfaces for older people. In *Proceedings of the 2001 EC/NSF work-shop on Universal accessibility of ubiquitous computing*, 90-92.

[4] Guerreiro, T., et al.. 2008. From Tapping to Touching: Making Touch Screens Accessible to Blind Users. *IEEE Multimedia*, 15, 4, 48-50.

[5] Guerreiro, T., et al. 2010. Identifying the individual ingredients for a (in)successful non-visual mobile experience. *Proc. of ECCE'10*.

[6] Kane, S., et al., 2008. Slide Rule: Making Mobile Touch Screens Accessible to Blind People using Multi-Touch Interaction Techniques. In *Proceedings of ASSETS*, 73-80.

[7] Kane, S., et al. 2011. Usable Gestures for Blind People: Understanding Preference and Performance. In *Proc.of CHI*.

[8] Kurniawan, S. 2007. Mobile Phone Design for older persons. *Designing for seniors: innovations for graying times*, 24-25.

[9] Mackinnon, S., Dellon, A. Two-point discrimination tester. Journal of Hand Surgery. 10A:906-7, 1985.

[10] Persad, U., et al. 2007. Characterising user capabilities to support inclusive design evaluation. *UAIS*, 6(2):119-135.

[11] Tremblay, F., Mireault, A.C., Dessureault, L., Manning, H., Sveistrup, H. Experimental Brain Research : 155-164, 2004.

[12] Wechsler, D. Wechsler Adult Intelligence Scale - Revised. San Antonio, TX: Psychological Corporation; 1981.

[13] Wobbrock, J., et al. 2011. Ability-Based Design: Concept, principles and examples. ACM Trans. on Access.Computing.

[14] Yfantidis, G., and Evreinov, G. 2006. Adaptive Blind Interaction Technique for Touchscreens. *UAIS*, 4, 328-337.

[15] Xydias, N. Tests pour l'orientation et la selection professionnelle des aveugles. Ed.Sc. et Psych, 1977.

[16] Zajicek, M. Design principles to support older adult. 2004. Springer Berlin/Heidelberg, 111-113.

Automatically Generating Tailored Accessible User Interfaces for Ubiquitous Services

Julio Abascal, Amaia Aizpurua, Idoia Cearreta,
Borja Gamecho, Nestor Garay-Vitoria, Raúl Miñón
University of the Basque Country/Euskal Herriko Unibertsitatea
Laboratory of HCI for Special Needs. Manuel Lardizabal 1
20018 Donostia, Spain
+34 943018000
{julio.abascal, amaia.aizpurua, idoia.cearreta, borja.gamecho, nestor.garay, raul.minon}@ehu.es

ABSTRACT

Ambient Assisted Living environments provide support to people with disabilities and elderly people, usually at home. This concept can be extended to public spaces, where ubiquitous accessible services allow people with disabilities to access intelligent machines such as information kiosks. One of the key issues in achieving full accessibility is the instantaneous generation of an adapted accessible interface suited to the specific user that requests the service. In this paper we present the method used by the EGOKI interface generator to select the most suitable interaction resources and modalities for each user in the automatic creation of the interface. The validation of the interfaces generated for four different types of users is presented and discussed.

Categories and Subject Descriptors

D.2.2 [**Design Tools and Techniques**]: User Interfaces. H.1.2 [**User/Machine Systems**]: Human Information Processing; Human Factors. H.5.2 [**User Interfaces**]: Evaluation/Methodology; Theory and Methods. H.5.3 [**Group and Organization Interfaces**] Evaluation/Methodology; Theory and Methods; Web-based Interaction.

General Terms

Design, Experimentation, Human factors, Verification.

Keywords

Adaptive Systems, Accessible User Interfaces, Ubiquitous Computing, Automatic User Interface Generation.

1. INTRODUCTION

Recent developments in wireless networking and ubiquitous computing, among other technologies, have made possible the creation of Ambient Intelligence environments aimed at assisting people that occasionally or frequently access such environments. Intelligent environments offer ubiquitous services to the users, allowing them access (through their mobile devices) to information kiosks, vending machines, Automated Teller Machines (ATMs), ticketing machines or elevators, for instance. These services allow users to access such devices and machines.

In these types of intelligent environments there is a middleware layer that *discovers* and introduces incoming mobile devices by establishing communications between them and the available services in a way that is transparent to the user. Hence, when a person enters an intelligent environment, information about the local services available is displayed on the user device. If the user requests one of these services, the system downloads its user interface to the user's device. This interface allows the user to access and interact with the selected service. In addition, the middleware layer plays a key role, making possible the interoperation of diverse types of networks with different protocols. Paradoxically, the lack of generally accepted middleware standards is one of the biggest barriers to the deployment of the Ambient Intelligence concept.

People with disabilities can benefit from the previously mentioned ubiquitous services for performing tasks that might otherwise present barriers for them. Users with disabilities often have their own mobile devices customized to their needs. Therefore, granting them access to services through their own devices, instead of them having to interact directly with the machines that offer these services, can very much enhance their user experience.

Unfortunately, in such ubiquitous environments the interface that is downloaded to the user's mobile device is usually the same for all users and hence frequently inaccessible for many of them. Most Human-Computer Interaction (HCI) researchers think that a single user interface cannot fit all users' needs. The Universal Accessibility philosophy requires each user to be provided with a user-tailored interface based on his or her characteristics, needs and preferences [1].

To this regard, the INREDIS project [2] created a ubiquitous architecture aimed at people with physical, sensory and cognitive disabilities. The goal was to grant access to intelligent machines located in INREDIS-sites for users with disabilities provided with customized mobile devices. At the end of the project, a number of prototypes were developed to demonstrate the main outcome of this project: a comprehensive architecture that provides accessible ubiquitous services.

Trying to advance in this direction, and starting from the experience gained through participation in the INREDIS project, our Laboratory has developed EGOKI, a system that generates accessible user interfaces adapted for people with disabilities in order to grant them access to ubiquitous services.

In this paper we will focus particularly on the procedures followed by EGOKI to select and adapt to each user the most suitable interaction resources, considering the modalities used to transmit information. The reason is that one of the key issues related to the accessibility of multimedia interfaces is the provision of appropriate interaction modalities and resources [3].

In the next section, related work is presented. In section 3, the adaptive interface generation mechanism created for EGOKI is described. Section 4 shows the validation of the system, while the last section presents several conclusions and outlines future work to be carried out.

2. RELATED WORK

In recent years, personal computing has evolved from laptops to ubiquitous interactions with handheld devices. Ubiquitous services are usually provided by means of generic interfaces that may contain barriers for people with disabilities. To overcome this problem, the use of adaptable or adaptive user interfaces is recommended. Adaptable interfaces allow the user to tune certain system parameters. For instance, User Interface Facades [4] allows end-users to quickly, flexibly and seamlessly change the interface of any application without manipulating its code. Meanwhile, adaptive interfaces are able to automatically adapt themselves to the user's characteristics [5]. For instance, the latter approach was adopted by Savidis and Stephanidis (2009) [6], who describe ways to automatically adapt interfaces to users by considering their requirements, capabilities and preferences, as well as the interaction context. Leonidis et al. (2011) propose a toolkit for rapid prototyping, in order to ease the design of adaptive widget-based interfaces [7].

The massive expansion of the Internet has promoted the application of adaptive interaction methods for accessing the Web. These methods focus on adapting the navigation, content and presentation schemes [8]. What is not so common in this field is to find systems where the adaptations are aimed at people with disabilities. The AVANTI project [9] provided users with special needs with hypermedia information by adapting the content, navigation and presentation. Another instance is the SADIe *transcoder* [10], which adapts news websites for blind users. In this line, one of the specificities of our system, EGOKI, is that it adapts the user interface to the capabilities of people with special needs, selecting the most appropriate media resources to allow the user interaction.

Nevertheless, the requirements of the adaptive web differ significantly from those needed for accessing ubiquitous services. In the former case the main goal is to navigate and to present information to the user, whereas in the latter case the objective is to manage a local service. Although both types of interfaces can be coded using the same technology, their aims, structure and organization are different. In addition, most of the above-mentioned systems adapt a previously existing user interface, whereas for other applications (such as ubiquitous access) it is common to start from an abstract description of the functions of the interaction. The SUPPLE system [11] is an interesting instance of interface generator. SUPPLE generates graphic user interfaces, primarily for people with motor impairments. These interfaces are intended for stand-alone applications, such as desktop applications. Another user interface generator for ubiquitous services is the ViMos framework [12], which provides an architecture to dynamically generate interfaces that allow the visualization of service information available in a particular context.

In ubiquitous environments, each user interface will have a specific configuration depending on the services offered by the environment and the features of the user. A good approach to univocally describe the structure of the interface is to use a user interface description language (UIDL) [13]. These languages allow the construction of abstract user interfaces that are independent of the modality and the platform used. This is the approach adopted by EGOKI.

Starting from this background and from our previous experience in INREDIS, we can conclude that a new approach is required in order to allow people with disabilities to interact with an accessible ubiquitous environment offering diverse services. This approach has to combine two techniques: user interface adaptation and automatic generation of user interfaces for ubiquitous services. Such a system has to meet some specific requirements:

- Universal accessibility: the system should be accessible for all users, although the design is focused on people with special needs.

- Technological independence: it should be independent of the technology, the network and the middleware layer of the ubiquitous environment.

- Abstraction: Since a wide range of services can be provided, they have to be described in a generic way. This will allow the system to generate adapted interfaces regardless of the service type. A UIDL can be used for this purpose [13].

- Resource availability: each service provider is responsible for supplying the resources associated with each service (images, texts, audio, etc.) in order to allow the system to generate the final adapted interface. As a result, the greater the number of alternative resources provided for each interaction element, the higher the probability of meeting the specific user's needs. For instance, a label can be displayed as text or as an image on the user interface. In this case the interaction resource is the label and the alternative resources are text and image. Moreover, it is highly recommended to provide other specific resources such as signed and captioned videos, audio descriptions, high contrast images, etc.

3. EGOKI ADAPTIVE SYSTEM

Let us briefly describe the structure of the EGOKI adaptive system that generates adapted accessible user interfaces (see figure 1), before going into the details of the interface generation mechanisms.

EGOKI takes into account the user capabilities and the interaction elements that best suit the users' needs. These parameters constitute the knowledge base (KB), built as an ontology. The KB performs the functions of storing, updating and maintaining the models and, in addition, it provides the necessary rules for reasoning and extracting information from the ontology.

EGOKI also considers the services functionalities and characteristics specified by means of a user interface description language, UIML, as detailed in the following section. These files provide independence of the modality and the platform and represent the different layers of the service, including structure, style, content and behaviour.

Both information from the ontology and the UIML files are the inputs to EGOKI. To summarize the process: first, the Resource Selector module selects the most appropriate resource for each interaction element for the specific user and the specific service, as described in the section 3.3; and then, the Adaptation Engine module performs the necessary transformations and adaptations to generate a final user interface with the selected resources. These adapted user interfaces are created by means of XSL transformations and are enhanced with non-intrusive JavaScript code, CSS style-sheets and the resources supplied by the service provider.

In addition, these UIs are able to interact with the available services through an interoperability framework that provides the middleware functions. Furthermore, it ensures the *discovery* of incoming mobile processors and the communication and interoperation between the diverse computers and wired and wireless networks of the ubiquitous environment. We adopted UCH [14], an implementation of the standard URC [15], in order to ensure portability to other ubiquitous environments.

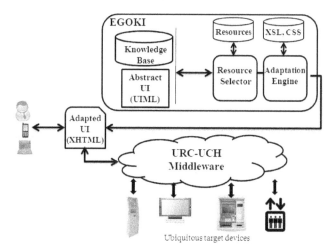

Figure 1.Architecture of the system

3.1 Matching user capabilities and interaction resources

Most web adaptive systems adapt previously developed web-based user interfaces. Although we start from this experience, for EGOKI we adopted a different approach more appropriate for ubiquitous computing. As previously stated, EGOKI starts from an abstract specification of the user interface supplied by the service provider. We currently use a UIDL called User Interface Modelling Language (UIML) [16]. From this UIML description of the service functionality, and taking into account the user characteristics, EGOKI selects the most suitable interaction resources from those supplied by the service provider in order to complete the final user interface. The success of the resource selection depends on the availability of appropriate interaction resources for the specific user accessing the service.

EGOKI uses the Knowledge Base (KB) for the resource selection. Different types of resources and possible adaptations are modelled in the KB, based on users' capabilities (rather than users' disabilities). For each media[1] type that the service provides, it is possible to choose the most appropriate alternative resource and adaptations for each person, independently of his or her limitations. For this purpose, the KB contains an ontology, where user capabilities are modelled. Among other parameters, the users' capability level[2] is defined (high, low, null) for each

communication modality[3]. We currently use three levels of capability, since a more detailed classification does not mean a more specific adaptation (due to the limitations of the current user interface technology). However, capabilities could be defined in greater detail in the future by including more discrete categories to cover the needs of diverse users.

In any case, this ontology represents the users' profiles by indicating their capabilities for using the previously mentioned communication modalities. In other words, it does not indicate their disabilities by creating generalized stereotypes. Thus, the personalization of the interfaces is based on what the users can do, instead of what they cannot do. The ontology includes combinations of capabilities that are associated with alternative resources and adaptations for each media type. In total, there are 125 different combinations (from 5 communication modalities with 3 levels). Each combination of capabilities can be considered as an instance of a user profile, since users with the same characteristics will obtain the same interface for the same service and access device. Table 1 shows two of these combinations for generating two interfaces for two different users. The first row matches a user with a high level of auditory, cognitive, motor and speech capabilities, but with no visual capability. The second row matches a user with low vision but with a high level in the other capabilities.

Table 1. Examples of two combinations of capabilities integrated in the ontology. They are associated with a blind user and a user with low vision, respectively (N: Null; H: High; L: Low; A: Audio; V: Video; I: Image; T: Text; B: Background colour; S: Structure)

Visual	Auditory	Cognitive	Motor	Speech	Media type	Layout	Resource	Adaptation
N	H	H	H	H	A	-	text	-
					V	-	text	-
					I	-	text	-
					T	-	text	-
					-	B	-	-
					-	S	-	navigation support; headings inclusion
L	H	H	H	H	A	A	audio	-
					V	V	video	-
					I	I	high contrast	enlarge image
					T	T	text	enlarge text
					B	B	-	high contrast
					S	S	-	-

For the first user, instead of selecting images (audio or video), alternative text will be selected as the resource for the screen reader. In addition, EGOKI applies two adaptations in relation to the structure: a navigation support adaptation for a better structure of the interface, and a headings inclusion adaptation for a better use of the screen reader. For the second user, EGOKI can include any type of media but selects high contrast images so that the user can see them better. In this case the user needs adaptations for

---

[1] Media are the channels used to deliver information by presenting content such as text, graphics, animation, video, audio, etc.

[2] The user capability level is considered as the degree of ability that a given user has for using a certain modality.

[3] In human-computer interaction, a modality is a sense through which the human can receive the output of the computer. The most common are vision, audition, and haptic modality.

enlarging the font size and the images as well as for adjusting the background colour. The contrast is changed for better visualization of the interface elements.

Each UIML document provides EGOKI with the resources available for a specific service. Service designers are required to specify priorities for the different media types, in order to allow EGOKI to select the most suitable resources. Priorities must be set for each function provided by a service represented in the UIML; for instance, the text media type is suitable for representing the information about a bus timetable, whereas the image media type is appropriate for showing the route of a bus line. The UIML vocabulary was extended to fulfil this need.

3.2 Selection of the most suitable interaction resources at the design phase

In order to establish alternatives and adaptations that are properly suited to people with special needs and accordingly design the KB, a Heuristic Walkthrough [17] was performed at the design phase. Two usability experts played the role of users in eight different scenarios simulating diverse disabilities (colour blindness, repetitive stress injury, deafness, blindness, attention deficit, and three combinations thereof). In each scenario, they had to complete a list of tasks on a satellite television service. The main goal was to check whether the resources and adaptations selected for each interface were appropriate for each scenario. This Heuristic Walkthrough exercise provided us with valuable feedback about resource types as well as usability issues with the user interfaces, which were subsequently considered in the improvement of the the EGOKI system.

3.3 Automatic Tailored Interface Generation

As previously stated, the adapted user interface generation process is based on the selection of appropriate resources and the application of the required adaptations. Since the process does not start from a previously designed interface, in order to automatically generate adapted user interfaces EGOKI needs the following elements as input:

1. *An abstract description of the service requested by the user.* This is a UIML document that represents all functions offered by the target and the list of resources associated with each function, including the priorities set for each modality. Taking an elevator service as an example, the corresponding functions would be *Going up*, *Going down* and *Select floor*. In this case, the *Select floor* function would have different media types associated with it, such as text or images.

2. *User capability for each communication modality.* From the information in the ontology, EGOKI can determine if a media type can be offered to a certain user or if he or she requires the inclusion of an alternative resource or the application of an adaptation.

With this information the user interface generation process can start. The objective is to generate an interface adapted to the user's needs by transforming the abstract description into a final interface. The key issue is selecting the appropriate resources and applying the required adaptations. By "appropriate resources" we mean that they have to consider users' needs as well as the priorities established by the service designer regarding functions. For instance, in the case of the elevator the designer may assign the highest priority to images for representing the numbers corresponding to the floors. However, images will be only selected if the user is able to see them. Otherwise, EGOKI will use an alternative resource to the image media type; for example

audio instructions. However, if the service designer does not offer any audio cue for the function, EGOKI selects the media type with the next highest priority. Since EGOKI cannot create resources on the fly, it is necessary that each provider offers sufficient resource options.

The following heuristic is used to select the most appropriate resource for a specific functionality:

For each function in UIML
    Select the media type with the highest priority:
        1 - *Query* the ontology about the resource associated with the media type according to the user's capability levels.
            - *If* the resource associated with that media type does not exist in the UIML:
                • *select the media type with the next highest priority*
        2 - *Query* the ontology about the adaptations required for that media type according to the user's capability levels.

When the appropriate resources for each function of the service have been selected, EGOKI generates a final user interface in XHTML with all the resources integrated in the code. Using XSL transformations, the abstract interface coded in UIML is converted into a final interface. Afterwards, if the user requires personal adaptations these will be applied to the final interface. This will allow tuning for qualitative differences; such as in the case of low vision, given the various forms it may take [18]. In this case, personal adaptations are added as code fragments using Cascading Style Sheets (CSS). It should be noted that the automatically generated user interface is totally functional. Moreover, in this regard the extension of the UIML vocabulary allowed us to describe the behaviour of the user interfaces.

Since the EGOKI system is part of a ubiquitous environment within a more general architecture (see Figure 1) the following requirements must be met:

- *User identification/authentication*: the user must be logged in to use any service provided through the proposed architecture.

- *Ontology population*: the information about the user and his/her communication capabilities must be previously collected and stored in the model.

- *Service description*: each service offered through the system must have an associated UIML document, where information on the functionalities and resources provided by the service is contained. Every UIML document, for a target service, must at least offer textual resources. Service providers are responsible for handing the UIML description as well as offering diverse types of resources.

- *User device*: The user's device must run a JavaScript-enabled browser in order to be able to interact with the user interface generated. It is also assumed that users who want to access these services have their mobile devices adapted to their needs; for instance, a blind person should have a screen reader or a Braille line installed.

In order to reduce the workload of the service designer, we plan to develop a wizard tool [19] that will have a double objective: firstly, it will allow service designers to create valid UIML documents, and secondly, it will assist them in the selection of appropriate resources for the abstract user interface. This implies that the service provider does not need any technical background to develop services compliant with EGOKI.

4. VALIDATION

Although the EGOKI system was not yet fully complete, we believed that it was necessary to validate the current prototype at that stage in order to detect functionality flaws and accessibility barriers. Thus, the validation had a twofold goal: firstly, to verify that the interaction resources selected for each user interface were fully accessible for the target user; and secondly, to check whether the interfaces performed all available functions correctly.

To have a reference point, we decided to compare the interfaces generated by EGOKI with the interface generated by Webclient, in order to estimate the improvements involving the adaptation in this context. Webclient is a JavaScript library that includes an automatic interface generator used by UCH to test the ubiquitous services that are added to the environment. This generator provides interfaces in HTML with JavaScript to control ubiquitous applications. Webclient is designed to serve as a tool for testing and helps the developer responsible for adapting a URC/UCH ubiquitous application.

4.1 Barrier Walkthrough

To fulfil the first objective (i.e. to verify that the interaction resources selected for each interface are accessible to the intended users) we conducted a Barrier Walkthrough exercise [20]. This method is an adaptation of the Heuristic Walkthrough for usability inspection, where the principles are replaced by barriers. A barrier is any condition that hinders the user's progress towards achievement of a goal, when the user is a person with disabilities.

The scenario was a ubiquitous service that allows people to buy underground tickets, which are downloaded to their mobile devices after payment has been made. EGOKI generated four different interfaces for four user categories. In order to be able to compare it with other alternatives, we also used the interface generated by UCH/Webclient for this same service.

The ticketing service has the following options:

- Selection of the type of ticket: one way, round trip, 10 trips

- Selection of the number of zones to which one can travel: 1, 2 or 3 zones

- Payment

The interface also provides information on:

- The price of the "ticket type" and "number of areas" combination chosen by the user

- Whether the payment has been successfully made

4.1.1 Procedure

We followed the procedure proposed by Brajnik [20]. To this end, we turned to four PhD students who had completed a course on web accessibility and had experience in using this method. We had previously defined the scenarios; i.e. user categories, goals and possible barriers. In order to apply the method, four user categories were considered for the experiment: blind users, users with low vision, users with motor impairment, and people with cognitive disabilities.

User categories

Blind users
- Users of screen readers or of speaking browsers; sometimes also users of Braille readers.

Users with low vision
- Users with screen magnifiers; sometimes they only use the accessibility features offered by the operating system, such as reducing screen resolution, increasing font size, contrast levels and colour polarity.

Users with motor impairment
- Users who do not have complete control of their upper body, arms and/or hands due to Parkinson's disease or repetitive stress injury.

Users with cognitive disabilities
- Users with limited ability to process and memorize information, to take decisions or to learn; these include learning disabilities (affected by dyslexia and dysgraphia), attention disorders, developmental disorders (Down's syndrome, autism) or neurological disorders (Alzheimer's).

- This category could also include people that have to use a service under stressful conditions (e.g. in a hurry, in a noisy or distracting environment, while carrying out some other important task).

Aims

The user interface for the ticketing service provides two main functions: firstly, to check the price of three different ticket types for three transport areas; and secondly, to buy a ticket.

Possible barriers

The possible barriers for each user category were collected from the tables proposed by Brajnik [20].

The four evaluators were provided with the documentation required to perform the Barrier Walkthrough exercise. As there was more than one evaluator, they proceeded as in heuristic evaluations:

- Since the user categories and scenarios were previously defined, the evaluators did not have to agree on these issues

- Each evaluator explored both user interfaces for each user category (the one generated by UCH/Webclient and the adapted one generated by EGOKI) and familiarised themselves with the possible goals and interaction mechanisms of the interfaces

- Each evaluator, independently of the others, crossed all barriers for each of the two different interfaces, in order to compare them, and rated the severity of each barrier

- Finally, the evaluators met once more and merged their problems into a single list by assigning a single severity score to each problem.

4.1.2 Results

The outcomes are presented in the tables 2 and 3. Table 2 shows the summary of the barrier types identified for each user category. As can be seen in this table there were generally fewer barriers found in the interface generated by EGOKI than in the one generated by UCH/Webclient (6 vs. 18 barriers identified). Table 3 shows the list of the barrier types identified for each user category with the severity assigned according to Brajnik's classification [20]. Comparing each user interface generated by EGOKI for each user category with that generated by UCH/Webclient, the former has less barriers for all user categories except in the case of users with low vision.

Table 2. Barrier Types for all users on different user interfaces (B-blindness, L-low vision, M-motor impairment, C-cognitive disability, X-barrier found)

Interface generated by	UCH/Webclient				EGOKI			
Barrier type	B	L	M	C	B	L	M	C
Mouse events	X		X					
Forms with no LABEL tags	X		X					
Layout tables	X							
Page without titles	X							
Language markup	X				X			
No page headings	X			X	X			X
Dynamic changes	X	X			X	X		
Missing layout cues						X		
Links/buttons that are too close to each other			X					
Links/buttons that are too small			X					
Missing icons				X				
Complex text				X				
Complex site				X				
Text fields with no example				X				
Acronyms and abbreviations without expansions				X				

For blind users, 7 barriers were identified in the UCH/Webclient interface while there were 3 barriers in the EGOKI interface. For example, the former contains "mouse-oriented events" in the form controls, so the interaction was not equivalent when using a mouse or a keyboard. Furthermore, these controls had no labels. It also contained a table for layout purposes, and the title of the page was not meaningful "URC Generic Web Client". Barriers shared by the two interfaces were a lack of language tags (i.e. the "lang" attribute in the HTML element), so the English speaking screen reader sometimes said something with a Spanish accent. A lack of headings was also identified in both interfaces. Although the interfaces are not complex, at least one H1 element should have appeared. The most critical factor was that there were dynamic paths that the user was not able to perceive; e.g. when the user chose a type of ticket he/she was not aware that the fare zone at the bottom of the interface changed. These changes were not detected by the screen reader either.

For people with low vision, two barriers were identified in the EGOKI interface and one in the UCH/Webclient interface. The former lost its shape when it was expanded. Despite the fact that it had a flexible design and the elements did not overlap, it could be confusing for users.

Regarding motor impairments, we did not identify any barriers in the interface generated by EGOKI but we did in the interface generated by UCH/Webclient (four barriers). The presence of "mouse events" gave problems in the tab navigation. The payment was triggered by passing over the payment button with the tab key without pressing the enter key. In addition, the button was too small to be easily activated by using the mouse, although there was no problem when using the tab key. In regard to cognitive impairment, the only barrier found in the EGOKI interface was connected to the headings. Although it was not properly marked by H1, there was a title informing the user of the content of the page. The UCH/Webclient interface had 6 barriers. One of the most significant was the lack of icons. The interface lacked icons

Table 3. Barrier Types for all users on all different user interfaces with corresponding severity ratings (B: blindness, L: low vision, M: motor impairment, C: cognitive disability; I: Impact, P: Persistence, S: Severity, - : non: existent barrier, c: critical, s: significant, m: minor)

Interface generated by		UCH/Webclient			EGOKI		
Cat.	Barrier type	I	P	S	I	P	S
B	Mouse events	3	3	c	-	-	-
	Forms with no LABEL tags	1	3	s	-	-	-
	Layout tables	1	3	s	-	-	-
	Page without titles	2	3	c	-	-	-
	Language markup	2	2	s	2	2	s
	No page headings	1	3	s	1	3	s
	Dynamic changes	3	3	c	3	3	c
L	Missing layout cues	-	-	-	2	2	s
	Dynamic changes	2	3	c	2	3	c
M	Mouse events	3	3	c	-	-	-
	Links/buttons that are too close to each other	3	3	c	-	-	-
	Links/buttons that are too small	3	3	c	-	-	-
	Forms with no LABEL tags	1	3	s	-	-	-
C	Missing icons	3	3	c	-	-	-
	Complex text	2	3	c	-	-	-
	Complex site	3	3	c	-	-	-
	Text fields with no example	2	2	s	-	-	-
	No page headings	1	3	s	1	3	s
	Acronyms and abbreviations without expansions	1	1	m	-	-	-

4.1.3 Discussion

The first surprising issue is the low number of barriers that were detected in general. This may be because the interfaces did not have much content; that is, although they were based on web technology, we validated interfaces specifically designed to access services, not common web pages. Analyzing the tables we found fewer barriers in the interfaces generated by EGOKI than in the one generated by UCH/Webclient, except in the case of users with low vision. Since EGOKI generated a different interface for each user category while UCH/Webclient generates a single interface for all, it is clear that the user-adapted interfaces included greater variety of resources. At least we can say that the resources selected for each category are more accessible than those allocated in UCH/Webclient, since the interfaces presented fewer barriers.

The application of the Barrier Walkthrough method also helped us to discover that the interfaces generated by EGOKI were not completely accessible, because they contained some accessibility barriers. In this sense, the results of the Barrier Walkthrough were also useful for improving the EGOKI interface generation system.

4.2 Case Study

As a second aim of the validation, we wanted to prove the correct functionality of the interfaces that EGOKI generates automatically. To this end, we conducted a case study, which is a detailed examination of specific situations. In this case a qualitative analysis of an instrumental single case study was performed with a blind user in a ubiquitous environment set up in our laboratory. Although a single participant does not provide a comprehensive picture of the needs of blind people, we thought that research on her interaction would lead to valuable insights that may apply to other blind people. This person used her laptop with JAWS 11 and Firefox 4 configured, since she did not have a mobile device adapted to her needs. She had to perform several tasks using both interfaces, the one generated by UCH/Webclient and the other from EGOKI, in order to compare them. Although the service was the same one used for the Barrier Walkthrough exercise (the underground ticketing service), the user interface was updated. Based on the results from this exercise we improved the system by applying some changes to the transformation rules, in order to generate interfaces without barriers.

4.2.1 Procedure

The participant was given the instructions and documentation required to conduct the session. To start the session she was asked to perform four tasks using the UCH/Webclient interface (see Figure 2). After that, she had to perform the same tasks using the interfaces generated by EGOKI (see Figure 3). The tasks that the participant had to complete were checking the price of two specific ticket types and buying another two particular ticket types.

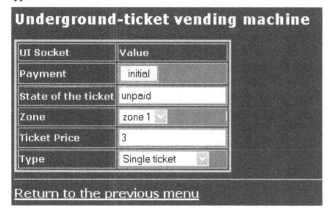

Figure 2.Automatically generated interface by UCH/Webclient.

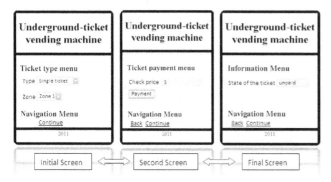

Figure 3. Navigational interfaces automatically generated by EGOKI for a blind user.

After performing each task, the participant was asked to answer a short survey in order to let us know about issues such as the difficulty of the task or the barriers found, if any. The entire session lasted 45 minutes and it was recorded, with the consent of the participant. We asked the participant if she could turn the speaker on while using the service so we could analyze the behaviour of the Jaws screen reader in the recording afterwards. It should be noted that she was allowed to wear the headphones when completing the survey in order to have total privacy to answer the questions.

4.2.2 Results

In order to obtain the results, the participant's answers and the recording were analysed.

In the case of the interface generated by UCH/Webclient, the participant said that she had completed one out of the four tasks. However, we noticed that this was not actually true. This interface presented some problems that did not allow her to fully accomplish the tasks. For instance, the 'Payment' option was unintentionally selected by the participant when she passed over the button with the tab key. Furthermore, values changed on the interface without properly informing the participant. Thus, she believed that she had finished the task successfully. The participant wrote that she had had problems with the tab key. That is why she preferred to use the arrow keys for navigation. Regarding the other three tasks, she could not finish them due to similar accessibility barriers.

In contrast, when using the interface generated by EGOKI, the participant had no problem in completing all the tasks. In this case she was able to select every option, check the prices and buy tickets correctly.

4.2.3 Discussion

Although the type of resource used was the same in both interfaces (text), the case study showed that only the user interface generated by EGOKI was successfully used. The participant was able to correctly perform the tasks set, since all the elements of the interface were accessible by her screen reader. Moreover, the EGOKI interface was generated in such way that it was possible to avoid some of the barriers found in the UCH/Webclient interfaces. As previously mentioned, these barriers were overcome thanks to the conclusions obtained in the Barrier Walkthrough exercise performed. To avoid the problems related to dynamic changes, EGOKI divides the interface into three screens in which the participant can navigate in order to complete her goals. In the initial screen, she can choose the type of ticket in the desired zone using two completely accessible "select" areas; in the second screen, she can check the price of that ticket and purchase it using a button that works correctly; in the final screen, the participant is informed of the purchase status (in the case of performing the request in the second screen, the participant is informed that the ticket has been paid for; otherwise, she is informed that the ticket has still not been paid for). In this way, thanks to the adaptation applied by EGOKI (see navigation support in Table 1), the functions offered by the service are suitably structured and organized. Moreover, the barrier of dynamic changes in the interface has been overcome, as demonstrated in the validation of the single case with the blind person. In addition, the screen reader navigation with the EGOKI interface is appropriate since an adaptation has been applied to correctly include the headings (see headings inclusion in Table 1).

Therefore the analysis of the case study suggests that the interface elements generated by the adaptations and transformations performed in EGOKI are appropriate. At least in the case of blind users, the selection of resources allows them to interact appropriately with the service.

5. CONCLUSIONS AND FUTURE WORK

In this paper we have presented EGOKI, an automatic user interface generator aimed at adapted interaction with ubiquitous services, accessible for people with disabilities provided with suitably adapted mobile devices. We have specifically concentrated on describing the selection of the most appropriate interaction resources and modalities taking into account the user's communication capabilities. The feedback obtained from the validation of the current prototype indicates that the user interfaces automatically generated by EGOKI are fully functional and additionally, that selected communication elements and resources are accessible for each type of user. These tests have been useful in detecting a number of flaws in EGOKI and as a concept proof. Nevertheless, a complete accessibility and usability evaluation will be required when the EGOKI system is complete.

We are currently working on the extension of the quantity and complexity of the ubiquitous services available. In addition, since the communication resources are selected by EGOKI from the palette created by the service designers, we plan to design a well-defined vocabulary of resources that can be used by the designers. We also plan to design a tool to assist service designers to select the appropriate interaction elements and resources. This tool will provide a graphical user interface, independent of the UIML language, to ease this task.

6. ACKNOWLEDGMENTS

This research work has been partly funded by the Department of Education, Universities and Research of the Basque Government. In addition, A. Aizpurua, B. Gamecho and R. Miñón enjoy PhD scholarships from the Research Staff Training Programme of the Department of Education, Universities and Research of the Basque Government. We thank the INREDIS project, which has been the foundation for this work. The authors are grateful to the anonymous reviewers' valuable comments, which have helped to improve this paper.

7. REFERENCES

[1] Sloan, D., Atkinson, M.T., Machin, C. H. C., and, Li, Y. 2010. The potential of adaptive interfaces as an accessibility aid for older web users. In *Proceedings of the 2010 International Cross Disciplinary Conference on Web Accessibility (W4A'10)* (Raleigh, North Carolina). Article 35, 10 pages.

[2] INREDIS: INterfaces for RElations between Environment and people with DISabilities. http://www.inredis.es/Default.aspx.

[3] Obrenovic, Z., Abascal, J., and Starcevic, D. 2007. Universal accessibility as a multimodal design issue. *Communications of the ACM,* 50, 5 (May 2007), 83-88.

[4] Stuerzlinger, W., Chapuis, O., Phillips, D., and Roussel, N. 2006. User interface façades: towards fully adaptable user interfaces. In *Proceedings of the 19th annual ACM symposium on User interface software and technology* (Montreux, Switzerland), 309-318.

[5] Fink, J., Kobsa, A., and Nill, A. 1998. Adaptable and adaptive information provision for all users, including disabled and elderly people. *New Review of Hypermedia and Multimedia*, 4, 163-188.

[6] Savidis, A., and Stephanidis, C. 2009. A unified software architecture for user interface adaptation. In *The Universal Access Handbook*. Stephanidis C., Ed. CRC Press, 21, 1-17.

[7] Leonidis, A., Antona M., and Stephanidis, C. 2011. Rapid Prototyping of Adaptable User Interfaces. *International Journal of Human-Computer Interaction* (to appear).

[8] Peter Brusilovsky, Alfred Kobsa, and Wolfgang Nejdl (Eds.). 2007. *The Adaptive Web: Methods and Strategies of Web Personalization*. Springer-Verlag, Berlin, Heidelberg.

[9] Stephanidis, C., Paramythis, A., Sfyrakis, M., and Savidis, A. 2001. A study in unified user interface development: the AVANTI web browser. In *User Interfaces for All: Concepts, Methods and Tools*. Stephanidis, C., Ed. Lawrence Erlbaum Associates, NJ. 525-568.

[10] Lunn, D., Bechhofer S., and Harper, S. 2008. The SADIe transcoding platform. In *Proceedings of the 2008 international cross-disciplinary conference on Web accessibility (W4A'08)* (Beijing, China), 128-129.

[11] Gajos, K.Z., Weld, D.S., and Wobbrock, J.O. 2010. Automatically generating personalized user interfaces with SUPPLE. *Artificial intelligence* 174, 12-13, 910-950.

[12] Hervás, R., and Bravo, J. 2011. Towards the ubiquitous visualization: Adaptive user-interfaces based on the Semantic Web. *Interacting with Computers*, 23, 1, 40-56.

[13] Guerrero-García, J., González-Calleros, J.M., Vanderdonckt, J., and Muñoz-Arteaga, J. 2009. A theoretical survey of user interface description languages: Preliminary results. In *Proceedings of the Latin American Web Congress (la-web 2009)* (Mérida, México), 36-43.

[14] Universal Control Hub Reference Implementations. http://myurc.org/tools/UCH/

[15] Vanderheiden, G., Zimmermann G., and Trewin S. 2005. Interface Sockets, Remote Consoles, and Natural Language Agents. A V2 URC Standards Whitepaper. V1.8, Rev Feb 2005. http://myurc.org/whitepaper.php

[16] OASIS User Interface Markup Language (UIML). http://www.oasis-open.org/committees/tc_home.php?wg_abbrev=uiml

[17] Sears, A. 1997. Heuristic Walkthroughs: Finding the Problems without the Noise. *International Journal of Human-Computer Interaction*, 9, 3, 213-234.

[18] Theofanos, M.F., and Redish, J.C. 2005. Helping low-vision and other users with web sites that meet their needs: Is One Site for All feasible? Technical Communication 52, 1, 9-20

[19] Miñón, R., and Abascal, J. 2011. From Ubiquitous Computing to User Interface Description Language: Tool Support. Internal Technical Report No. EHU-KAT-IK-02-11. University of the Basque Country. http://sipt07.si.ehu.es/rminon/SPA4USXML.pdf

[20] Barrier Walkthrough. http://users.dimi.uniud.it/~giorgio.brajnik/projects/bw/bw.html

Improving Calibration Time and Accuracy for Situation-Specific Models of Color Differentiation

David R. Flatla and Carl Gutwin

Department of Computer Science, University of Saskatchewan
110 Science Place, Saskatoon, Canada, S7N 5C9

david.flatla@usask.ca, gutwin@cs.usask.ca

ABSTRACT

Color vision deficiencies (CVDs) cause problems in situations where people need to differentiate the colors used in digital displays. Recoloring tools exist to reduce the problem, but these tools need a model of the user's color-differentiation ability in order to work. Situation-specific models are a recent approach that accounts for all of the factors affecting a person's CVD (including genetic, acquired, and environmental causes) by using calibration data to form the model. This approach works well, but requires repeated calibration – and the best available calibration procedure takes more than 30 minutes. To address this limitation, we have developed a new situation-specific model of human color differentiation (called ICD-2) that needs far fewer calibration trials. The new model uses a color space that better matches human color vision compared to the RGB space of the old model, and can therefore extract more meaning from each calibration test. In an empirical comparison, we found that ICD-2 is 24 times faster than the old approach, and had small but significant gains in accuracy. The efficiency of ICD-2 makes it feasible for situation-specific models of individual color differentiation to be used in the real world.

Categories and Subject Descriptors: K.4.2 [**Social Issues**]: Assistive technologies

General Terms: Human Factors

Keywords: Color vision deficiency (CVD), color blindness, color differentiation, adaptation tools, modeling

1. INTRODUCTION

Approximately ten percent of people [23] have some form of color vision deficiency (CVD - commonly called color blindness). People with CVD experience *color confusion*, in which they cannot distinguish between colors that are distinct for individuals without CVD. Color confusion leads to difficulties understanding information that is encoded using color. These difficulties range from annoyances (e.g., not being able to distinguish visited from unvisited hyperlinks), to critical safety issues (e.g., distinguishing traffic signs and signals, recognizing warning messages).

In the digital domain, color confusion problems can be at least partially addressed through adaptation tools that recolor images. These tools modify images to use colors that are more differentiable for individuals with CVD; in order to do this, they rely on models of color differentiation, both to identify problem colors and to find replacement colors.

Traditional differentiation models rely on many assumptions about the user and the environment that greatly limit their applicability. For example, these models assume that the user has a particular type of color vision deficiency called dichromatism, and that the user is working in an environment with constant and controlled lighting – assumptions that do not hold for other types of CVD or other environmental situations.

A new approach that solves the problem of assumption-based models is called *situation-specific modeling (SSM)* [8]. This technique builds the color-differentiation model not from assumptions, but from empirical data gathered from the user in the actual environment where they will use the model. SSM uses performance or judgment tasks to determine exactly what the user can and cannot differentiate in the current setting, thus implicitly accounting for all factors that affect the user's color vision. SSM is far more sensitive than assumption-based models [8]; however, the main limitation of the approach is that the accuracy of the model degrades as conditions change (e.g., as the user becomes tired, or lighting changes in the room), and eventually another calibration must be carried out. The best current SSM technique (called ICD [8]), however, requires more than thirty minutes for calibration, limiting the applicability of the approach.

To address this problem, we have developed a new SSM model (ICD-2) that requires a much shorter calibration. The new model is a substantial improvement because it is based on a much more complete understanding of the mechanics of color vision than the previous model's RGB color space. The old model measured minimum differentiability on each of the red, green, and blue channels, and working solely in RGB space means that many such measures must be taken because RGB is not *perceptually uniform* (i.e., the RGB difference between any two colors does not correlate with their visually-perceived difference). ICD-2, in contrast, represents color differences using the LUV color space (which is perceptually uniform), allowing the measurements for a single color to be generalized to all other colors. In addition, ICD-2 measures color differentiation abilities in terms of *color confusion axes*, which embody the exact color confusion difficulties experienced by individuals with CVD [28]. These two underlying changes to the approach mean that ICD-2 requires only eight color differentiation measurements, compared with the 192 measurements needed by the previous model.

To validate ICD-2, we compared it to the old ICD model in a study with both CVD and non-CVD participants. The study calibrated and built both the old and new models for each person, and then tested the color-differentiability predictions generated by the models against a ground truth set established by the participant. We found that calibration with ICD-2 was 24 times faster than with the old model (2.17 minutes vs. 52.6 minutes), and that the ICD-2 model was modestly but statistically significantly more accurate (78.7% vs. 76.1%).

We make three main contributions in this paper. First, we demonstrate that the situation-specific modeling approach can be feasible and practical if it has an efficient model such as ICD-2. Second, we show how calibration time and model accuracy can be traded off, which provides an additional degree of flexibility for SSM. Third, we improve the understanding of how different types of color-differentiation models affect the larger problems of recoloring and reducing color confusion for people with CVD.

2. BACKGROUND

2.1 Color Vision Deficiencies

There are several sources of color vision problems, ranging from genetic disorders to acquired deficits to situation-specific environmental factors.

- *Genetic Factors* can cause anomalies or deficiencies in the three types of color-sensing cells of the retina (cones). Different types of cones are sensitive to different parts of the visible spectrum: *protan* cones for long-wavelength, *deutan* cones for medium-wavelength, and *tritan* cones for short-wavelength light. *Anomalous trichromacy* can result if these wavelength sensitivities are shifted for some cones. If all cones of a certain type are missing, *dichromacy* can result. In rare cases, people can be missing two types of cones (*cone monochromacy*) or all color-sensing cells (*rod monochromacy*), limiting perception to shades of grey [1][5].

- *Acquired Deficits* involve damage to the vision system from external events such as accident, disease, or exposure to harmful chemicals. Retinopathy occurs when a portion or all of the photoreceptors of the retina die – e.g., resulting from diabetes or long-term exposure to styrene. When photoreceptors die, color perception can be drastically altered [14]. Aging can also bring changes to color vision: for example, yellowing of the lens and cataracts both modify the light entering the eye.

- *Situational Effects* are factors in the user's local environment that cause temporary changes to color perception; if the resulting effect causes problems, these are known as 'situationally-induced disabilities' [22]. These factors can be of many different types, and can include characteristics of the color source (e.g., the quality and calibration of the monitor that displays the colors), physical characteristics of the environment (e.g., the amount of ambient light in the room, or glare from light striking the display), or the state of the user (e.g., the presence of drugs such as Viagra or antidepressants).

All types of CVD cause similar problems for our purposes – they make it difficult for people to differentiate among colors that can be distinguished in other circumstances or by other users. The use of color in digital information displays is ubiquitous, and many presentations require that the user be able to tell different colors apart. For example, information visualization uses color for categorical encoding, highlighting, popout, and representation of continuous variables [24][27]. Everyday interfaces also use color extensively – for example, to show visited links in web pages, or to clearly indicate alerts and warnings.

2.2 Color-Adaptation Systems and Models

Several systems exist to aid the problem of color differentiation in digital displays. These techniques select colors in an image that are likely to be problematic for the user, and switch these to different colors that are more likely to be differentiable. From an early proposal by Meyer and Greenberg [16], several methods have been developed including SmartColor [26] and a number of techniques for dealing specifically with photographic images (e.g., [12][19][20]). In some cases the user can participate in the recoloring process – for example, some forms of CVD (such as anomalous trichromatism) are less severe than dichromatism, and an interactive system can allow these users to guide the recoloring process [10][11].

Regardless of their approach, all recoloring techniques rely on an underlying model of the user's color differentiation abilities, and most current models are based on an early assumption-based algorithm [4][16][25]. This algorithm allows the simulation of dichromatic color perception for individuals without CVD: it first transforms an image from RGB to the Long-Medium-Short (LMS) cone stimulation color space, then removes appropriate wavelength information for the desired type of dichromatism (e.g., long-wavelength for protanopes), then translates the modified LMS colors back to RGB. The algorithm can be used to detect color confusion by comparing colors in the original and modified images – if regions that were different colors become the same, the colors will not be differentiable.

This algorithm uses several assumptions, however, that limit the applicability of the model. The transformation to LMS requires that the emission spectra for the monitor are known (which varies widely across monitor technologies), and that the monitor is calibrated in terms of white balance and gamma. The transformation also assumes a 'representative' human color vision system, but individual differences are common [17]. Most importantly, the model does not deal with the variability seen in CVD users (e.g., in anomalous trichromats), nor does it handle other forms of CVD such as extreme anomalous trichromacy [3] or monochromacy. It also does not take into account any of the acquired or situational causes of CVD as described above. There is at least one model proposed that handles anomalous trichromacy [15], but it requires details about how far the peak wavelength of the photoreceptor of interest has been shifted, which is not easily obtained.

To address these limitations, Flatla and Gutwin [8] developed *situation-specific models* of color differentiation. SSMs account for all of the factors affecting a user's color perception, by testing their differentiation abilities in the actual scenario and environment of use, with performance or judgment tests. More details about this approach will now be presented.

3. COLOR DIFFERENTIATION MODELS

Color differentiation models provide information about the differentiability of colors. This can be accomplished through a simple API that provides a single function:

boolean : areDifferentiable(Color c1, Color c2)

This function accepts two colors and returns true if the model predicts that they are differentiable and false otherwise. To accomplish this, the function predicts the set of colors that are not differentiable from c1, and then checks to see whether c2 is in this set. If it is not in the set, then the colors are differentiable.

Certain color spaces (e.g., RGB, CIE XYZ, CIE LUV) all exhibit a property that is beneficial for identification of these 'not differentiable' sets. Considering color spaces as physical spaces (in which each color occupies a unique location) allows the metaphor of movement through a color space. As one moves away from any particular color, increasingly different colors are encountered. While moving on any path away from a color, a point will eventually be reached at which the colors that are being encountered transition from not differentiable to differentiable, in reference to the starting color. This transition is called a psychometric function, which can be described mathematically using a sigmoid function. For simplicity, many models (including ICD and ICD-2) approximate the psychometric function as a step function, which transitions from 'not differentiable' to 'differentiable' in a single step (Figure 1). When reasonable paths are chosen, these transition points (called *differentiation limits*) can be used to define a volume around the starting color. All colors within this volume are predicted to be not differentiable from the starting color, and all colors outside the volume are predicted to be differentiable.

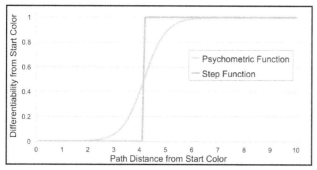

Figure 1. Approximation of a normalized psychometric sigmoid function with a simple step function.

3.1 Original ICD Model (the 'old model')

The situation-specific model proposed in [8] (ICD, here referred to as the 'old model') relies exclusively on the RGB color space, in which each channel (red, green, and blue) defines an orthogonal axis in a 3D space. For any particular color, six lines extend out from the color, two for each channel axis (one in the increasing direction, the other in the decreasing direction). Along each of these lines, a differentiation limit can be identified where the colors along the line become differentiable from the original color. These six limits (one for each line) are used to define a box around the original color. Colors within this box are considered not differentiable from the original color, and colors outside are considered differentiable.

3.1.1 How to calibrate the old model?

As RGB is not a perceptually uniform color space, the differentiation limits for one color do not generalize well to other colors. To calibrate the old model, therefore, differentiation limits are measured for many colors (64) uniformly spread through the RGB color cube. To measure a single differentiation limit, binary search is used along the color channel line described above. The user is presented with a rectangular field of dots on a black background (Figure 2). One half of the dots are the starting color (the color for which differentiation limits are needed). The other half of the dots are a color that lies along the line between the original color and the extreme value for the channel involved. The user responds with either 'not different' or 'different' depending on whether he/she sees a difference between the two colors. If the user says 'not different' then the colors are made more different and redisplayed. If the user says 'different' the colors are made less different and redisplayed. This is repeated in a binary search pattern, until the differentiation limit is identified.

This binary search process requires approximately ten presentations (taking about one second each) before a single

differentiation limit is identified. For reasons presented in [8], only increasing differentiation limits are required for calibration, giving three limits per calibration color (of which there are 64). As a result, calibrating the old model requires 64x3x10=1920 samples – if each takes one second, a total of 32 minutes.

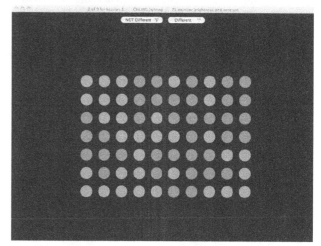

Figure 2. Screen presented during original calibration. User responds with 'not different or 'different' [8].

3.1.2 How to make predictions?

To answer an 'areDifferentiable(Color c1, Color c2)' query, the model uses trilinear interpolation to estimate the differentiation limits for one of the parameters. The other color parameter is then tested to see whether it is inside or outside of the box defined by these interpolated limits.

3.2 ICD-2 Model

The old model requires a lengthy calibration because differentiation limits are required for 64 RGB colors. As identified above, this is because RGB is not perceptually uniform. By using a perceptually uniform color space (CIE LUV [6]), the number of limits necessary for calibration can be drastically reduced.

Images are encoded using the RGB space in digital environments, so moving colors in RGB space to LUV space is necessary for using the LUV color space in the new model. To accomplish this, we use the sRGB transform provided by [13] to move between RGB and CIE XYZ, and transforms from the same source to move between XYZ and LUV. As a result, transformations from RGB to LUV (and back again) can be accomplished.

CIE LUV is a color space that is perceptually uniform and separates the description of a color into a luminance axis (L – ranging from 0-100) and two chromaticity coordinates (U,V – centered at 0). This allows colors of equal luminance to be found simply by holding L constant and varying U and V. When U and V equal 0, the color is achromatic (black, grey, or white).

In the LUV color space, the differentiation abilities of an individual can be described well using a *discrimination ellipse* when only colors of identical luminance are considered [21]. For a given color, a discrimination ellipse can be found that surrounds the color. Those colors outside the ellipse are differentiable and those inside are not differentiable from the original color. To extend this to a three-dimensional shape, *discrimination ellipsoids* [18] are used in the ICD-2 model. The discrimination ellipsoid is defined using the discrimination ellipse and two points above and below the equal luminance plane. The ellipsoid that matches the ellipse and intersects the two points is the ellipsoid used.

To find the discrimination ellipse, six discrimination limits are measured via a calibration procedure. Instead of finding these limits along RGB channel axes, as in the old model, we find these limits along three *lines of confusion* [28]. A line of confusion is defined by a base color and a *copunctal point*. The colors that lie along each line are not differentiable for individuals with dichromatic CVD (Figure 3) and there is one copunctal point for each type of dichromacy. Each line gives two differentiation limits, one moving from the base color to the copunctal point, and one moving from the base color away from the copunctal point, resulting in six differentiation limits. These six limits are then used to generate the best-fit ellipse using approaches outlined in [7] and [9]. The half lengths of the major and minor axes of this best-fit ellipse are then used to find the ellipsoid.

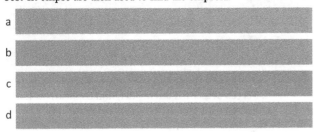

Figure 3. Confusion line colors for individuals with tritanopia (blue-yellow dichromatic CVD) using the base color for the ICD-2 model: a) confusion colors toward the tritan copunctal point, b) tritan simulation of (a), c) confusion colors away from the tritan copunctal point, d) tritan simulation of (c).

To find the two points above and below the luminance plane, two additional discrimination limits are measured via the calibration procedure. These limits correspond to the amount of luminance that needs to be added and subtracted from the base color in order for the user to perceive a difference.

An ellipsoid can be described using the following formula:

$$\frac{x^2}{a^2} + \frac{y^2}{b^2} + \frac{z^2}{c^2} = 1$$

where a is the best-fit ellipse major axis half length, b is the best-fit ellipse minor axis half length, and c is the amount of luminance that is added or subtracted, as described above. This formula is used in ICD-2 to internally represent the discrimination ellipsoid.

3.2.1 How to calibrate ICD-2?

To calibrate the ICD-2 model, eight discrimination limits are needed for a single base color. These limits are found in a similar manner as the old model, but the technique has been modified so that the user no longer provides a judgment about the differentiability of the two colors presented, but rather performs a task. If the user can perform the task, then it is interpreted that the user can see the difference between the two colors. If they cannot do the task, then it is interpreted as the user not being able to differentiate between the two colors. The base color was chosen to be the color represented by the LUV coordinates L=50.0, u=0.0, v=0.0, which is a mid-luminance grey. These LUV coordinates map to RGB color (118,118,118) using the sRGB transform described above.

This performance task involves the user identifying the orientation of a circle with $1/8^{th}$ of its perimeter missing (Figure

4). The circle is presented to the user, and if they can identify the location of the gap, they press a correspondingly labeled key on the numeric keypad. If they see no gap, the user presses the space bar. A binary search approach is used to find the differentiation limit, where the difference between the circle and the background is increased when the user sees no difference, and decreased when they see a difference.

To facilitate the performance task, the presentation of the colors to the user has been modified to approximate the approach used in [21] to determine discrimination ellipses. A 400x400 pixel region on a black screen is presented to the user. This region is filled with a regular pattern of small (4-pixel diameter) circles, with black between the circles. The gapped circle introduced above is superimposed on this background of small circles, such that the background is the base color, and the gapped circle is a color along the confusion line (or luminance line) for which a discrimination limit is desired (Figure 4). The numeric keypad of the keyboard was modified with labels such that the labels matched the possible orientations of the gapped circle.

When two colors are placed directly adjacent to each other, any differences in luminance between the two colors results in the user seeing a difference between the two colors, even though this difference may go away as soon as a small gap is introduced between the two colors. To offset the effect of luminance contrast, temporal random luminance noise [1] was applied to the entire presentation (background and gapped circle). This noise produces colors with identical LUV UV coordinates (chromaticity), but varying L values (luminance). The black space between the small circles further reduces the effects of luminance contrast.

When a differentiation limit has been identified, its Euclidean distance in LUV space is recorded. This gives a distance along each confusion line (6 measures) and distance in luminance above and below the base color (2 measures).

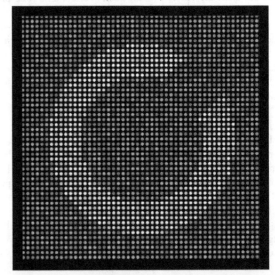

Figure 4. Screen presented during ICD-2 model calibration. User presses numeric keypad key that matches the rotational orientation of the gapped circle, or space if they see nothing.

3.2.2 How to make predictions?

To answer an 'areDifferentiable(Color c1, Color c2)' query, the model first converts both colors to LUV color space (using the default sRGB transform mentioned above), and determines which is closer to the base color using Euclidean distance. The closest color is chosen because the discrimination limits for the base color are known, and if the LUV color space is not perceptually uniform for those with CVD, then the discrimination limits for the color that is closest to the base color should be more similar to the base color differentiation limits. The parameter nearest to the base color is called the primary color, the other parameter is called the secondary color. To determine an appropriate discrimination ellipsoid, the differentiation ellipsoid for the base color needs to be transformed to fit the primary color.

To save computation, before the discrimination ellipsoid is transformed, a luminance comparison is performed. Using the luminance thresholds determined during the calibration for the base color, luminance bounds for the primary color are determined. If the luminance of the secondary color is outside of these bounds, the query returns 'differentiable'. If the luminance of the secondary color falls within these bounds, then the transformation is performed.

To transform the discrimination ellipsoid of the base color to the primary color, the confusion lines for the primary color are found (between the primary color and the copunctal point). As confusion lines are defined by the copunctal point and another point, they are not rotationally invariant as different 'other' points are selected. Once the color confusion lines for the primary color are found, the algorithm walks along each confusion line away from the primary color until the LUV distance just exceeds the differentiation limit LUV distance found during the calibration. The LUV coordinates for the color at this point on the confusion line are then used to specify six points in the UV plane for the primary color. These six points are used to find the best-fit ellipse.

Using the luminance of the secondary color, the best-fit ellipse is resized to be the discrimination ellipse for the primary color, but at the secondary color's luminance, by using modifications of the formula for an ellipsoid given above to find the adjusted half major and half minor axis lengths for the resized ellipse:

$$a' = \sqrt{a_p^2 - \frac{a_p^2 * (L_s - L_p)^2}{c_p^2}} \qquad b' = \sqrt{b_p^2 - \frac{b_p^2 * (L_s - L_p)^2}{c_p^2}}$$

Figure 5. Formula for the resized half major axis length (left) and the formula for the resized half minor axis length (right).

Once the resized ellipse is found, its center, dimensions, and orientation are used to transform a unit Java Ellipse2D.Double object. When transformed, this object is defined by a Path2D.Double object, which provides a contains(Point2D.Double) method, which determines if the given point is within the ellipse. The LUV UV coordinates for the secondary color are packaged into a Point2D.Double object and passed as a parameter to the 'contains' method. If the point is in the ellipse, then the query returns 'not differentiable', otherwise it returns 'differentiable'.

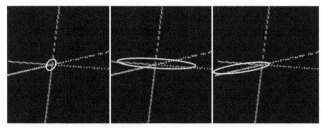

Figure 6. Three examples of the ellipses found by ICD-2: normal color vision (left), protan CVD (middle), deutan CVD (right). Colored lines indicate confusion axes.

4. EVALUATION

We compared the ICD-2 model to the original ICD model [8] (here called the 'old model') in an empirical study. There were two main goals of our evaluation – first, to confirm that calibration of ICD-2 is in fact faster than the old model (and to determine the actual reduction in time), and second, to determine ICD-2's accuracy compared with the existing approach.

4.1 Study Methods

To compare the ICD-2 model with the old model, we conducted a user study with 16 male participants (mean age 33.8 years) - eight who self-identified as having CVD (mean 39.0 years) and eight who self-identified as not having CVD (mean 28.7 years). As both the old model and ICD-2 are general models of color differentiation, we did not perform any tests to assess the type or severity of participant CVD. We constructed a custom Java application using the Processing libraries for displaying visual content to the screen (processing.org). The study ran in a single location on a Windows 7 machine using a 20-inch 1600x1200 Dell 2001fp monitor.

During the study, participants performed two tasks. The first task collected calibration data for generating both models. In the second task, 'ground truth' responses were collected from the participant to evaluate each generated model.

4.1.1 Calibration Task

As the study was designed to compare the models to each other, identical calibration procedures were used for the old model and the ICD-2 model. We opted to use the calibration procedure with the gapped circle (described above) for both models. The procedure was modified for the old model in order to gather increasing and decreasing differentiation limits on RGB channels.

As the old model calibration is time consuming, a reduced set of old model calibration points was gathered to reduce study run time. Nine points were chosen in RGB space to approximate the uniform spread of the 64 calibration points in the true calibration of the old model. These were (118,118,118), and eight additional colors, one halfway along each ray from this start color to the eight corners of the RGB color cube. This gave the following nine colors: grey, black, green, yellow, red, blue, purple, cyan, and white. For each of these, six differentiation limits were collected from the user, for a total of 54 differentiation limits. To calibrate the ICD-2 model, the standard eight differentiation limits around (118,118,118) were collected. This gave a total of 62 differentiation limits.

The order of these limits was randomized and presented to the participant sequentially. When the participant supplied a response (either the space bar for 'no circle visible,' or the appropriate numeric keypad key) the difference between the background and the circle was adjusted accordingly and the limit was reinserted into the sequence. If an incorrect numeric key was pressed, it was interpreted the same as pressing the space bar. Once the participant had given a response for each of the 62 limits, the order was shuffled and presented sequentially to the participant again. This was repeated until the binary search for each limit converged on a single value. For the old model, this value was reported as a raw RGB channel difference. For the ICD-2 model, this value was converted into its equivalent LUV Euclidean distance from the base color. The entire calibration required about 400 presentations to the participant, taking approximately 30 minutes. The participant could take a break at any time, but was encouraged to take at most 3-4 seconds per presentation.

The total time to collect each differentiation limit was recorded as well. With this time data, the total time to gather the 54 old model differentiation limits, and the total time to gather the eight ICD-2 calibration differentiation limits was measured. As the original old model requires 192 calibration limits, the actual time to collect the 54 limits was scaled up (192 * time / 54) to reflect the original calibration time.

4.1.2 Evaluation Task
Once the calibration data was collected, the participant took a short (~5 minute) break to rest their eyes. Once finished, the experimenter conducted the evaluation test. At the beginning of this task, the calibration data from the first session was used to generate the old model and the ICD-2 model. These models were then used to generate evaluation trials as described below.

Any two RGB colors selected randomly have a high probability of being differentiable. We wanted to use evaluation data that would provide a more uniform chance of each model predicting that the colors would be differentiable or not. To accomplish this, the models based on the calibration data for each participant were used to generate the evaluation trials for that participant. Using the nine RGB colors mentioned above (grey, black, green, yellow, red, blue, purple, cyan, white), each model was asked to generate two sets of 15 colors – one that the model predicts as being differentiable from the supplied color and one that the model predicts as being not differentiable from the supplied color. To accomplish this, colors were uniformly randomly selected from a volume twice as large as the old model box or ICD-2 ellipsoid. Each color selected was then predicted as differentiable or not differentiable and added to the appropriate set. The sets were returned when they were both full. This resulted in 15x2x2x9=540 trials for the evaluation session. These trials were randomly presented to the participant using the same test procedure (with the gapped circle) as the ICD-2 calibration. If the participant correctly identified the orientation of the gapped circle, then the colors were recorded as 'differentiable'; otherwise 'not differentiable' was recorded. This was used to establish a 'ground truth' set of color comparisons. For each of these responses, each models' differentiability prediction was also recorded.

4.2 Study Design
Our evaluation used a repeated-measures factorial design with two factors: *model type* (old model or ICD-2) and *CVD presence* (normal color vision or CVD). The CVD-presence factor was used only to check for interactions in the other analyses.

Four dependent variables were recorded by the system. *Calibration time* was gathered from the calibration task as described above. The remaining three variables were calculated from the raw correct / incorrect data gathered from comparing the predictions to ground truth: *overall accuracy* (number of correct predictions over total trials), *false positive rate* (proportion of predictions that incorrectly suggested that colors were differentiable), and *false negative rate* (proportion of predictions that incorrectly suggested that colors were not differentiable).

Our analysis used repeated-measures ANOVAs to test the effects of model type on these four dependent variables, and to look for interactions with CVD presence.

4.3 Results
4.3.1 Calibration Time
We recorded the time needed to carry out the entire calibration with both the old and new models, and scaled the old model calibration time to reflect the true calibration procedure for the old model (from 54 to 192 limits). As shown in Figure 7, calibration time for ICD-2 (mean of 2.17 minutes) is dramatically lower than for the old model (mean 52.6 minutes). Not surprisingly, the effect of model type is significant ($F_{1,14}=123.46$, $p<0.001$); there was no interaction with CVD presence ($F_{1,14}=0.077$, $p=0.78$). The 24-times improvement is proportional to the reduction in the number of calibration trials (from 192 to 8). It should be noted that these times are for the 'gapped circle' calibration technique, which is slower than the old calibration technique (see Figure 2); with the old technique, it is likely that the calibration time for ICD-2 will be even lower.

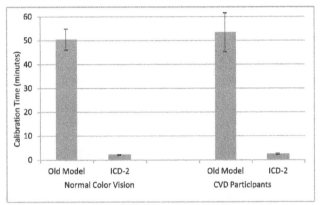

Figure 7. Calibration time ±s.e, by CVD status and model.

4.3.2 Model accuracy
As described above, we tested the accuracy of the models' predictions by comparing them to the ground truth of the 540 evaluation trials collected from participants.

Overall Accuracy. The overall mean accuracy for the old model was 76.1%, and for ICD-2 was 78.7% (see Figure 8). ANOVA showed that model type had a significant main effect on accuracy ($F_{1,14}=5.13$, $p<0.05$), with ICD-2 at approximately 2.6% higher accuracy. There was no interaction with CVD presence ($F_{1,14}=1.15$, $p=0.30$).

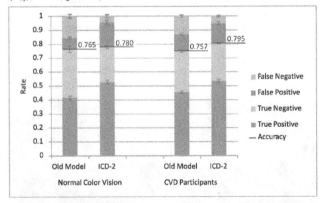

Figure 8. Model accuracy ±s.e, by CVD status and model (true positive rate + true negative rate = overall accuracy).

False Positive Rate. The mean false positive rate for the old model was 10.01%, and for ICD-2 was 16.02%. ANOVA shows that this difference is significant ($F_{1,14}$=64.19, p<0.001); ICD-2 had approximately 6% more false-positive errors. In addition, there was a significant interaction between model type and CVD presence ($F_{1,14}$=22.16, p<0.001). As shown in Figure 8, the false-positive difference between the old and new models is larger for participants with normal color vision than for CVD participants. We discuss the implications of these differences below.

False Negative Rate. Mean false negative rates were 14.18% for the old model and 4.75% for ICD-2. This difference is also significant ($F_{1,14}$=154.17, p<0.001). There was no interaction with CVD presence ($F_{1,14}$=4.23, p=0.059).

5. DISCUSSION

Our evaluation of ICD-2 provided four main results:

1. Calibration of ICD-2 is dramatically faster than the old model, requiring 1/24 the time of the old calibration;
2. ICD-2 is significantly more accurate than the old model, with a 2.6% improvement in overall accuracy;
3. ICD-2 does show a higher rate of false positives (although primarily for participants with normal color vision).

In the next sections we provide explanations for these results, discuss their implications for the feasibility of recoloring tools based on ICD-2, and outline ways in which the model could be improved and extended.

5.1 Explanation of main results

Calibration Time. The reason for the reduced time to calibrate ICD-2 is simple – using the perceptually uniform LUV color space and basing the discrimination volume on known color confusion lines means that ICD-2 requires far fewer calibration samples than the old model. These changes show the value of building the model on principles that more completely characterize human color perception. The short calibration time of ICD-2 (just over two minutes) means that we can even consider taking additional samples to further improve accuracy (as discussed below).

Overall Accuracy. The increase in accuracy for ICD-2 compared with the old model was modest (2.5%), so it is difficult to conclusively determine the source of the improvement. However, we believe that the change from a bounding box (in the old model) to an ellipsoid (in ICD-2) is the main reason for the better performance: previous research has shown that an ellipsoid better matches the way that humans perceive color and the way that individuals with CVD have difficulty with differentiation [18].

Higher False Positive Rate for Normal Color Vision. The ICD-2 model showed a 6% higher false-positive rate than the old model, for participants with normal color vision. False positive errors are more serious for recoloring tools than false negatives, since false positives lead to situations where the recoloring algorithm is not able to identify problem colors (because two colors that are actually not differentiable are predicted to be). The seriousness of these situations is compounded further if the recoloring tool proposes replacement colors that are not in fact differentiable by the user. The higher false positive rate is directly caused by the model ellipsoid being smaller than it should be; the reasons why the model chose too-small ellipsoids, however, are not clear. One possibility is that the step between colors along the color confusion lines is too large. As these colors were pre-computed (to save processing time), it is possible that the chosen step was too large. This could result in the calibration returning a differentiation limit that was on the 'not differentiable' side of a

step, even though the true differentiation limit was somewhere in the middle of the step. This would result in unnecessarily small differentiation limits, leading to a small ellipsoid.

A step size that is too large would also explain the difference in false positives between CVD and non-CVD participants. The error introduced by this problem would have an additive (not multiplicative) effect on the volume of the resulting model. Smaller volumes (e.g., for non-CVD users) would be more greatly affected by reducing their axes by a fixed amount than larger volumes (e.g., for CVD users).

5.2 Generalization

Application to Recoloring Tools. The problem of false positives can be dealt with through an 'offset factor' that arbitrarily increases the size of the ellipsoid (this factor was also needed for the old model [8]). The size of this offset differs per user, but can be easily calculated when the model is built. We note that the overall accuracy of the situation-specific modeling approach is such that even a liberal offset value will not greatly reduce the number of colors available to a recoloring algorithm.

Generalizing to Other Situations and Users. ICD-2 is able to generate different ellipses for different types of users; for example, Figure 6 shows ellipses for a normal user, a user with protan CVD, and a user with deutan CVD. This variation in generated models (and the associated accuracy results) present a strong argument that this modeling approach is applicable to many individuals with a variety of color differentiation abilities. In the future, we plan to examine how ICD-2 generalizes to different environmental situations, as well as internal variations, such as those associated with aging. The evaluation did include two individuals with CVD who were older (63 and 67 years old, one diagnosed with cataracts), who both experienced gains in accuracy from the old model to ICD-2 (3% and 2%, respectively). These results suggest that the model will generalize well, at least with regard to internal variations such as age and illness.

5.3 Improving and Extending the Model

Two main approaches present themselves for improving ICD-2, both of which involve the collection of more calibration points.

Increasing the Number of Differentiation Limits. The three confusion lines introduced above give rise to six differentiation limits defining the discrimination ellipse. To improve the shape, location, and size of the ellipse, additional differentiation limits at different points can be collected. These would be along lines of a different rotational orientation. Each new line would introduce two additional discrimination limits, so the accuracy of the model can be balanced against calibration time.

Increasing the Sampling of Single Differentiation Limits. For the eight differentiation limits used to define the ellipse, we noted above that we use step functions to approximate the true psychometric sigmoid function (Figure 1). If repeated samples of differentiation limits were collected, then the nature of this sigmoid could be determined. This would give two main benefits. First, the true sigmoid function could be used to overcome the 'step size' issue presented as an explanation for the increased false positive rate. Setting the differentiation limit to be the point where the sigmoid function levels off (at 1.0 differentiability), allows a false-positive-reducing ellipsoid to be constructed. Second, knowing the sigmoid function allows the model to provide a confidence score with each prediction. The model would have 100% confidence for where the sigmoid is 0.0 (not differentiable) and 1.0 (differentiable). In the region where the sigmoid rises from 0.0 to 1.0, the confidence can be determined by:

$$confidence = 4 * (sigmoid - 0.5)^2$$

Extending the Approach to Other Color Problems. The situation-specific modeling approach also shows promise for other kinds of color problems experienced by users with CVD. Two problems in particular that can use similar techniques are color matching and the effects of simultaneous color. Color matching is the task of finding a color that has been identified in another part of a display (e.g., using a legend in a bar chart to look for a particular data category). Simultaneous color issues arise when colors (and color differentiability) are affected by the presence of surrounding colors (e.g., colors on a dark background look lighter than they do on a light background). Performance-based SSMs can model both of these tasks and can further help designers to choose colors that work well both for CVD users and those with normal color vision. These models would also allow more broadly-applicable recoloring tools by providing the necessary information to successfully recolor images that contain matching and simultaneous contrast color use.

6. CONCLUSION & FUTURE WORK

Situation-specific modeling is a calibration-based approach to building empirical models of a user's color-differentiation ability. This approach is able to account for all of the factors affecting a person's CVD, including genetic, acquired, and environmental causes. The main difficulty with current situation-specific techniques is that the calibration procedure takes a long time, which is a problem because calibration must be carried out whenever the user's situation changes. In this paper we described a new SSM technique called ICD-2 that makes several improvements on the current state of the art. ICD-2 is based on a perceptually uniform color space that better matches human color perception, and so requires far fewer calibration steps than the old model; in addition, the change in color space also allows us to use known CVD color confusion lines to select our calibration points. We compared ICD-2 to the existing model in a controlled experiment, and found that ICD-2 was both dramatically faster for calibration and significantly more accurate than the old model. The efficiency and performance of ICD-2 makes it now feasible for situation-specific models of individual color differentiation to be used for recoloring tools in the real world.

Our future work in this area will follow three main directions. First, we plan to build and deploy a recoloring tool based on ICD-2, and test its performance in real-world use. Second, we plan several additional improvements to the model, including the development of confidence scores as discussed above. Third, we will extend our performance-based approach to other dimensions of color perception, such as color recognition or recall.

7. ACKNOWLEDGMENTS

Our thanks to Hervé Bitteur for providing the library for finding the best-fit 2D ellipse for a set of points.

8. REFERENCES

[1] Birch, J., Barbur, J., Harlow, A. New Method Based on Random Luminance Masking for Measuring Isochromatic Zones Using High Resolution Colour Displays. *Opthal. Physiol. Opt.* 12(2), 1992, 133-136.

[2] Birch, J. *Diagnosis of Defective Colour Vision.* 2nd ed., 2001.

[3] Birch, J. Extreme Anomalous Trichromatism. In Mollon, Pokorny, and Knoblauch, eds., *Normal and Defective Colour Vision.* Oxford University Press, 2003, 364-369.

[4] Brettel, H., Viénot, F., Mollon, J. Computerized Simulation of Color Appearance for Dichromats. *J. Opt. Soc. Am. A.,* 14(10), 1997, 2647-2655.

[5] Cole, B. The Handicap of Abnormal Colour Vision. *Clinical and Experimental Optometry*, 87(4-5), 2004, 258–275.

[6] Commission Internationale de l'Eclairage (CIE). *Colorimetry*, 2nd ed., CIE Publication 15.2, 1986.

[7] Fitzgibbon, A., Pilu, M., Fisher, R. Direct Least Squares Fitting of Ellipses. *Trans. PAMI,* 21(5), 1999, 476-480.

[8] Flatla, D. R., Gutwin, C. Individual Models of Color Differentiation to Improve Interpretability of Information Visualization. *Proc. CHI 2010,* 2563-2572.

[9] Halir, R., Flusser, J. Numerically Stable Direct Least Squares Fitting of Ellipses. *Proc. WSCG 1998,* 59-108.

[10] Jefferson, L., Harvey, R. Accommodating Color Blind Computer Users. *Proc. ASSETS 2006,* 40-47.

[11] Jefferson, L., Harvey, R. An Interface to Support Color Blind Computer Users. *Proc. CHI 2007,* 1535-1538.

[12] Kuhn, G., Oliveira, M., Fernandes, L. An Efficient Naturalness-Preserving Image-Recoloring Method for Dichromats. *IEEE Trans. Vis. and Comp. Graphics* 14(6), 2008, 1747-1754.

[13] Lindbloom, B. Website: www.brucelindbloom.com. Last accessed May 6th, 2011.

[14] Lomax, R., Ridgway P., Meldrum M. Does Occupational Exposure to Organic Solvents Affect Colour Discrimination? *Toxicological Reviews,* 23(2), 2004, 91-121.

[15] Machado, G., Oliveira, M., Fernandes, L. A Physiologically-based Model for Simulation of Color Vision Deficiency. *IEEE Trans. Vis. & Comp. Graph.* 15(6), 2009, 1291-1298.

[16] Meyer, G., Greenburg, D. Color-Defective Vision and Computer Graphics Displays. *IEEE Comp. Graph. & Appl.,* 8(5), 1988, 28-40.

[17] Neitz J., Jacobs, G. Polymorphism of the Long-Wavelength Cone in Normal Human Colour Vision. *Nature,* 323, 1986, 623-625.

[18] Poirson, A., Wandell, B. The Ellipsoidal Representation of Spectral Sensitivity. *Vision Research,* 30(4), 1990, 647-652.

[19] Rasche, K., Geist R., Westall, J. Detail Preserving Repro-duction of Color Images for Monochromats and Dichromats. *IEEE Comp. Graph. & Appl.,* 25(3), 2005, 22-30.

[20] Rasche, K., Geist R., Westall, J. Re-coloring Images for Gamuts of Lower Dimension. *Computer Graphics Forum,* 24(3), 2005, 423–432.

[21] Regan, B., Reffin, J., Mollon, J. Luminance Noise and the Rapid Determination of Discrimination Ellipses in Colour Deficiency. *Vision Research,* 34(10), 1994, 1279-1299.

[22] Sears, A., Lin, M., Jacko, J., Xiao, Y. When Computers Fade: Pervasive Computing and Situationally-Induced Im-pairments and Disabilities. *Proc. HCI Int.* 2003, 1298-1302.

[23] Stone, M. *A Field Guide to Digital Color.* 2003.

[24] Tufte, E. *Envisioning Information.* 10th ed., 1990.

[25] Viénot, F., Brettel, H., Ott, L., Ben M'Barek, A., Mollon, J. What Do Colour-Blind People See? *Nat.* 376, 1995, 127-128.

[26] Wakita, K., Shimamura, K. SmartColor: Disambiguation Framework for the Colorblind. *Proc. ASSETS 2005,* 158-165.

[27] Ware, C. *Information Visualization: Perception for Design.* 2000.

[28] Wyszecki, G., Stiles, W. *Color Science: Concepts and Methods, Quantitative Data and Formulae.* 2nd ed., 2000.

Supporting Blind Photography

Chandrika Jayant[†], Hanjie Ji[‡], Samuel White[‡], and Jeffrey P. Bigham[‡]

Computer Science and Engineering[†]
University of Washington
Seattle, Washington 98195
cjayant@cs.washington.edu

Computer Science, ROC HCI[‡]
University of Rochester
Rochester, NY 14627
{hanjie.ji,swhite,jbigham}@cs.rochester.edu

ABSTRACT

Blind people want to take photographs for the same reasons as others– to record important events, to share experiences, and as an outlet for artistic expression. Furthermore, both automatic computer vision technology and human-powered services can be used to give blind people feedback on their environment, but to work their best these systems need high-quality photos as input. In this paper, we present the results of a large survey that shows how blind people are currently using cameras. Next, we introduce EasySnap, an application that provides audio feedback to help blind people take pictures of objects and people and show that blind photographers take better photographs with this feedback. We then discuss how we iterated on the portrait functionality to create a new application called PortraitFramer designed specifically for this function. Finally, we present the results of an in-depth study with 15 blind and low-vision participants, showing that they could pick up how to successfully use the application very quickly.

Categories and Subject Descriptors: H.5 [Information Interfaces and Presentation]: User Interfaces

General Terms: Design, Human Factors

Keywords: camera, blind, visually impaired, photography

1. INTRODUCTION

Photography has been an important part of mainstream culture for over 100 years, helping people preserve memories, socialize, and express creativity. Blind people want to take photographs for the same reasons as everyone else, and blind photographers around the world serve as a testament to the importance of photography for blind people. The online presence of blind photographers is strong, with hundreds on Facebook, Flickr, blind photography websites and galleries, and blogs. Photographs can also serve as a way for blind people to get feedback on their environment, through automatic or human-powered interpretation (e.g., recognizing text, identifying products, locating objects). Applications

like EasySnap and PortraitFramer, both introduced in this paper, seek to aid this process with framing and environmental information provided to the blind user to be used as they see fit.

How does a blind person take a photograph? To understand what real blind photographers are doing now, and to hear other blind and low-vision people's opinions and issues, we conducted an online survey with 118 blind people, which demonstrated the extent to which blind people are already taking photographs, and want to take more. To explore a general paradigm that can assist blind photography for a broad selection of tasks, we developed EasySnap, an audio-feedback camera application on the iPhone platform, and tested it out with six people. We also created a more in-depth portrait framing application, PortraitFramer, which helps frame and orient multiple people in a photograph, with different audio and vibrational cues. This was to get more detailed feedback related to a specific application, and to conduct visual observations with 15 subjects. The subjects expressed a positive reaction to this application, and all successfully used the PortraitFramer to take framed portraits with only a few minutes of training. We chose faces to use as the subject matter in order to simplify the computer vision problem and concentrate on interactions. This was also motivated by the popularity of blind people taking photographs of other people, as expressed in the survey results. Of the 118 people surveyed, 84 had recently taken photographs. Of those photographs, 52 (62%) were of friends and family, the majority of photos taken.

The contributions of this paper include: (i) an empirical foundation for understanding the need for accessible photography for blind people and demonstration that they already use cameras, (ii) the creation of a multi-modal application to get more consistent photo results given specific tasks, (iii) the creation of an accessible interface to take portraits, and (iv) usability studies to evaluate the camera interfaces.

2. RELATED WORK

Although there have not been explicit studies on blind and low-vision users' interaction with a camera, many projects and papers have mentioned the need for this type of research [20, 21, 4, 3, 30]. Usually the focus is on the computer vision algorithms and camera technology itself, while the more practical interaction techniques for picture composition are not discussed or analyzed. Exploring interaction techniques is a central feature of our work.

There has been a lot of research the last two decades in how to use computer vision techniques for applications for the visually impaired. These projects include sign recognition [28], way-finding with environmental markers [13], shopping assistants like Grozi [18], currency recognition [26], text detection and optical character recognition (OCR) [12], and street sign and scene detection [30]. Other areas like robotics, not necessarily in the accessibility domain, use some of the same computer vision strategies [17, 16].

There are statistics that indicate that more than 100,000 blind and visually impaired individuals currently own an Apple iPhone, since the introduction of the VoiceOver screen-reader in 2007 [27]. Android phones have become increasingly more accessible as well. There is a growing number of accessible applications on mainstream devices that could benefit from some added accessibility with the camera. Some applications employing the camera already exist, such as the Looktel currency reader [29], the shopping and visual information tool oMoby [2], remote sighted assistance with VizWiz [11], and various OCR applications like the knfbReader Mobile [5].

Blind and low-vision people taking photographs may surprise many sighted people, but there is a whole community based around it. Blind photography is researched, explored, and celebrated in books (e.g., Deifell's 'Seeing Beyond Sight'), movies ('Proof' (1992) and 'A janela da alma' (2003)), news articles, websites, and art exhibits all over the world, not just in the US— from Ukraine to China, India to Israel [9, 10]. Communities such as Flickr, Facebook, myspace, Twitter, and more comprise over hundreds and thousands of interested people and blind photographers [7]. There are many websites dedicated to these groups or to particular artists. For decades, there have been, and still are, classes and books that teach blind people about cameras and how to use them [8, 15, 14].

Blind people who take part in photography consist of not only people with limited and highly attenuated sight, but also those with no sight or light perception at all. Blind and low-vision people have come up with some do-it-yourself ways to make their cameras more accessible, including adding tactile buttons or raised dots, using a sonified viewfinder, and using a viewfinder enlarger, to name a few mentioned in our survey. Such modifications often only make menus and buttons more accessible and have little to do the photo-taking composition and process. Adapted viewfinders can assist with composition in certain situations, but those discussed in our survey were for expensive digital cameras and used by professionals. Some prototype cameras have been created for blind people [19, 6], but they also concentrate on making the hardware accessible and changing the output (e.g. sounds, tactile prints, vibrations). The devices do not address the interactive photo-taking process. An everyday blind person should be able to quickly take snapshots on an accessible mainstream device just as sighted people have the opportunity to.

3. CAMERA SURVEY

We conducted an accessible online survey on camera usage that was sent out to various blind organizations, mailing lists, and companies, receiving 118 responses. The average age of the survey respondents was 40.0. There were 55 females and 63 males. When asked directly about their vision, 66 identified as totally blind, 15 had only a small amount of light perception, and 37 identified as generally low vision and legally blind. About half the respondents (56% of blind and

Figure 1: Percentage of how many blind and low-vision respondents had used a camera recently (out of 118 total). Of these respondents, 71% had recently taken photos.

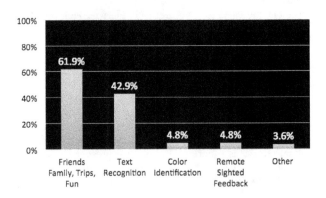

Figure 2: Reasons for recent camera usage, by percentage (out of 84 respondents who had taken photographs recently).

52% of low-vision respondents) carried an internet-enabled cell phone and an audio player with them on a daily basis.

When asked whether being able to use a camera accurately would be useful for them, 90 respondents said yes (76.3%), two said no (1.7%), and 26 were not sure (22.0%). 84 respondents (71.2%) had used a camera (including those on cell phones) recently. 34 (28.8%) had not (18 of whom were completely blind). See Figure 1 for an overview. Some reasons cited for not using the camera included "I can't use the camera," to "I'm curious but I haven't tried." Inaccessible phone cameras were another reason to not take photos. Only two people said they did not think they could at all. Of those 84 respondents who said they had used a camera recently, the main reason for using one was to take photographs of friends, family, trips, and events (see Figure 2). Of the respondents who were totally blind, 48 had taken photos (of 66), and 18 had not. The majority of all respondents took photos as a hobby or experiment (52 of 84). Other cited reasons were for text recognition (36) and remote sighted identification (4), of which one example was taking a photo of a vending machine control and sending it to a spouse to get information about it.

The next portion of the survey posed an open-ended ques-

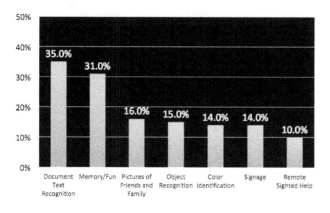

Desired uses for camera

Figure 3: Imagined and desired uses for a camera in daily life, shown by percentage of respondents (118 total).

tion asking the respondents if they could use a camera, what they would use the camera for in their daily lives. Results are shown in Figure 3. The top two uses desired were for document text recognition and for fun, memory, and creativity. Next, respondents were asked to check off at most three daily tasks from a list that they could use help with in their daily life (in terms of priority and usefulness). Reading digital appliances and street signs were the top choices, at 66% and 61%, respectively.

Next, respondents were asked what type of cues they would expect to be most useful, if there was a program to help them position a camera. Choices were: Phone Vibrations (28), Audio Instructions (e.g., "Move Left," "Move Up") (55), and Audio Tones (Pitch) (29). Some open-ended suggestions given included using a complex 3D tone system for the three axes, combining some or all of the mentioned three methods, using a focal plane meter, and simply having the camera auto-shoot when "enough" of the desired object is in view (the knfbReader tells the user what percent of the page is in the view-frame, and could automatically shoot if it got to the correct percentage). One subject noted that it would really depend on what he is using the camera to do. Another wanted to be able to choose what information she received and how, and have different modes (e.g., meeting mode).

The survey results show a large desire for blind and low-vision people to take photographs, even in the absence of accessible cameras. Many people with disabilities are known to create their own interesting do-it-yourself workarounds that show a lot of creativity and reflect user diversity [23]. A surprisingly large percent of the survey respondents, even those totally blind, had taken photographs recently. Taking personal photographs (e.g., family, friends, vacations, pets) was the top reason blind people were taking photographs. This interest has not been addressed by camera phone technology. The survey gives a glimpse into the excitement, curiosity, and creativity of blind people with photography. By using the camera on mainstream phones along with computer vision, accessible cues, and/or remote human or automatic services, many daily issues of concern could be resolved or at least addressed; it seems that blind people would be very

receptive to try out such applications judging by their responses.

4. EASYSNAP

Bearing the needs of blind photography in mind, we developed EasySnap, an iPhone application that assists with blind photography and provides an accessible photo album that helps users review and share pictures non-visually. It provides non-visual support to help with image framing, exposure, and blur detection. EasySnap successfully achieves two goals: (i) real-time feedback while taking a picture and (ii) generality in assisting a broad definition of photographs.

4.1 EasySnap Application

EasySnap has three modes: "Freestyle", "People", and "Object". The simplest mode is "Freestyle" mode, which functions like an ordinary camera, providing no audio feedback. With no constraints, simply by point-and-shoot, users are given the most freedom in taking pictures. Users are still given feedback regarding blur and darkness, which earlier work has shown are common problems [11]. "People" mode and "Object" mode provide a real-time status report of the person or object that one wants to take a picture of while moving the camera to frame the view.

"People" mode is specifically designed to take pictures of a person. It detects whether there is a face in the view of the camera, and tells users its location and size. Once the mode is activated, users move the camera slowly around the general direction of the person that they would like to get in the photo. If there exists a face in the frame, the real-time feedback reports how much the face takes up the screen, its location in the frame, and how the phone is angled. Otherwise, it reports "Searching" every two seconds. In this case, the generic face detection algorithm from the OpenCV library is used and well-tuned– using a bigger search window and limiting the smallest face that can be found– for high speed performance on the iPhone. The algorithm uses a cascade of boosted classifiers working with Haar-like features, which are trained with pictures of front faces as positive examples [1].

"Object" mode is designed to help take pictures of objects in the environment (e.g., a book, a cup, a piece of furniture). In this mode, users first take a picture of the object up close, and then EasySnap will provide audio feedback to help make sure the object stays in the frame as users move back to frame or change the point of view of the camera. The feedback, which is reported every three seconds, consists of three parts: the current position of original view, how much the original view is taking up the screen, and the phone orientation with respect to gravity. Here is an example of the feedback: "Bottom right, 60 percent, slightly angled down." The feedback functions as a useful input to the users instead of an explicit instruction so that they can autonomously adjust their framing according to their artistic or practical needs.

Instead of using complex and un-robust computer vision methods such as image segmentation, a light-weight tracking algorithm is employed to generate real-time framing feedback of the present view. Specifically, the close-up picture is captured as the initial view, from which a set of SURF feature points is calculated and continuously tracked in the subsequent frames by the Lucas-Kanade optical flow method. A bounding box of the tracked points is generated in each

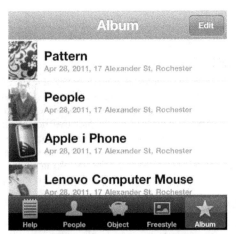

Figure 4: An example of part of EasySnap's photo album - photos are tagged with a descriptive label, and the time and location where they were taken.

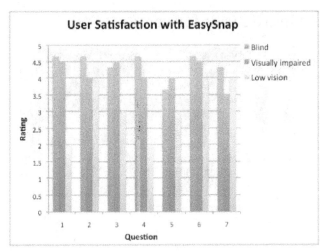

Figure 5: Likert scale results from 1 (disagree strongly) to 5 (agree strongly). (1) It is difficult for me to take pictures normally. (2) EasySnap helped me take better pictures. (3) I understood the directions that EasySnap gave me. (4) EasySnap helped me take pictures of objects. (5) EasySnap helped me take pictures of people. (6) The photo album was easy to use. (7) I would use EasySnap if it was available. Results demonstrate participants found EasySnap useful in assisting photography (2,3,4,7).

frame. A percentage that indicates the area ratio of the original bounding box to the new bounding box is reported to users. From this number users are able to infer how far they have gone away from the subject and how much the object is taking up the screen. The object location is calculated based on the coordinates of the bounding box and is reported back to users in one of the following position feedback: "top left", "top", "top right", "left", "center", "right", "bottom left", "bottom", "bottom right". The application also warns users when the phone is angled down or angled up with respect to gravity using the accelerometer built in the iPhone. This series of operations runs at 4-5 frames per second.

The final images captured in "Object" and "People" mode are checked for proper exposure and sharpness. Exposure detection takes precedence and works by creating a grayscale histogram to check for any large concentrations of dark pixels indicating insufficient lighting. Sharpness is estimated by computing the mean and standard deviation of an image from its binary map and evaluating these values using a set of pre-built covariance matrices created from images known to be blurry or sharp [24]. At the user interface level, users are warned with an audio alert after successfully capturing a photo if it may be too blurry or too dark, and are requested to retake the picture or continue.

EasySnap also implements an accessible album (See Figure 4). After each image is taken, the GPS coordinates of the phone are sent to Google Maps to fetch the location, and the image is sent to IQEngine [2] to recognize its content. Both location and content are leveraged to automatically label the images in a timely fashion, which can greatly help people with vision loss to browse the album.

4.2 Study

To explore the effectiveness of EasySnap in assisting blind photography, we conducted a study with six people (three blind people, two visually impaired, and one low vision) ranging in age from 19 to 60. Before the study, the participants were briefed on the idea of the application and its interface, tried out iPhone gestures and VoiceOver (if the user had never used iPhone before), and familiarized themselves with each mode by shooting two pictures in each

mode, respectively. In the formal study, they were asked to take three photos in each of "People" and "Object" mode, along with corresponding pictures with "Freestyle" mode for comparison. In "Object" mode, three objects of three different sizes were randomly picked from the environment. To alleviate short-term memory of the position where they just took the pictures, the picture taking order is randomized to create unbiased comparison pairs. See Figure 6 for an example.

4.3 Results and Discussion

At the end of the study, participants were asked to take a short survey (See Figure 5). The results show that most of the participants agreed that EasySnap helped their photography and found it easy to use, and that the two blind participants, in particular, thought so more than others. In addition, one of them left the following comment, "I have no idea what [it] is going to be when I walked in, but it actually works. It feels like having a 'cane' while taking pictures."

Besides the direct positive feedback from the study participants, we were also interested to see what "unbiased" viewers would think about the effectiveness of EasySnap. To this end, we put the pictures taken by the participants onto a web page and presented them in random order to 31 people, who judged which of each of the pairs of photographs they preferred based on the framing criteria (i.e., the picture is better centered, the picture is taken at a better distance). In total, for the 36 pairs of images (18 for "Object", 18 for "People") we collected 1116 evaluations, 58% of which are better with EasySnap's feedback, 29% are better without feedback, and 12% are neutral. With a close look at the results we found that both "Object" and "People" modes with feedback have achieved around a 60% success rate in assisting photography (See Figure 7).

(a) With "Freestyle" mode. (b) With "Object" mode.

Figure 6: An example of two photographs of the same object (a stuffed panda) taken with 2 modes of EasySnap. a) Photo of object taken in "Freestyle" mode. b) Photo of object taken in "Object" mode.

Figure 7: EasySnap evaluation results.

(a) Original Photo

(b) With Framing Boxes   (c) High Contrast Faces

Figure 8: Steps of PortraitFramer application. a) Photo taken (background removed for clarity). b) Faces found. c) If there are faces, PortraitFramer announces the number of faces, and vibrates where those faces are on the touchscreen while also showing them as high contrast circles. When each face circle is touched, it plays a short, distinct pitch. Instruction mode can be turned on to provide directional instructions. The user can accept this photo and save it, or try again, by swiping left or right respectively.

5. PORTRAITFRAMER

Motivated by the results of the aforementioned survey, along with EasySnap we concurrently designed a group portrait application for phones running on the Android platform (1.6+) because of Android's text-to-speech API. The interface is a self-voiced portrait taker that provides interaction cues for a blind or low-vision person as an additional tool to help shoot "well-framed" photographs of people. Face detection uses fairly straightforward computer vision compared to identifying general objects or reading text, therefore allowing us to hone in on the interaction issues. While EasySnap works with one person, PortraitFramer works with groups of people as well.

The application starts by asking the user to click the camera button to take a photo. The user is told how many faces are in the camera's sight. Concurrently, there is a screen that comes up which is black, with the face areas in white (Figure 8(c)). The visible cues are suitable only for those with some limited vision. Touching the "face areas" causes the phone to vibrate, so the user can explore the touchscreen and get a sense of where the faces are in their camera view frame. Users might just want access to the information and decide themselves where they want to position the people in the photograph, using audio and/or haptic cues. No directions are given about the z-axis, or distance to the scene; however, the user can feel or see how large the white "face areas" are to get a sense of their distance from the subject.

Other information that can be accessed through the interface is the face borders (including overall framing border, see Figure 8(b)) and the actual size of the face areas in relation to the screen view, similar to EasySnap's "People" mode.

5.1 First Study Setup

To get user feedback on the design of PortraitFramer, formative user studies were conducted with eight blind and low-vision people. After ten minutes of training, the participants were asked to take three photos using the PortraitFramer application. They were asked to go through their steps verbally. Three cardboard cutouts were set up in an office, to simulate people (See Figure 8(a)). Naturally, the human to human interaction part of the photo-taking experience is extremely important, with communication between the photographed and the photographer possibly changing both the location of the people or the aim of the photographer. However, for this initial formative study, we wanted to have all the participants taking photos of the same setup to more easily notice differences. The task was to try to take a centered photo of the three cutouts. All photographs with face framing were saved to the phone to see the progression of localizing the faces (See Figure 8 for one example). After about 20 minutes of taking photos, we asked their overall thoughts about the software, if it seemed useful, and what problems and suggestions they had.

5.2 Results

Our subject pool consisted of four males and four females, and the average age was 48.1. Three of the participants were fully blind. For those with low-vision, vision problems included having poor light/dark perception, only being able to see blurry shapes, having no peripheral vision, and being born blind and regaining some sight. Five participants had used a camera before. Participants ranged from low to high-tech, in terms of the devices they carried around with them. Four had previously used a camera. Participants were asked what would be motivating uses of the camera for them, if any. Three mentioned OCR for text documents, street and office signs, and unfamiliar documents while on the go (e.g., airplane magazine, menu). One man regretted not chronicling the last 10 years of his life. Two participants wanted to be able to send a photo to a remote human service or family member to get it identified. Four were eager to take photographs of their friends and family. Beauty, creativity, and art (e.g., architecture, sunset) were reasons expressed by four participants. One woman wanted to take photographs to study up close later to come up with characters for her novels. One subject said she only saw using a camera for OCR, but then mentioned that she had wished she could take photographs at her family reunion to show her mother.

All eight study participants successfully centered the faces after getting vibration and overlay cues from the application. Figure 8 shows the succession of photos taken from one subject. The average amount of time to take a successful photograph was 13 seconds. All participants took a successful photograph within three attempts. Success was measured by having the bounding box of three faces touch all the quadrants of the screen, but not overflow it.

5.2.1 Space and Pose Estimation

Space issues were the most difficult to predict or understand. Five participants started off with a discussion of basic camera skills and their understanding of how a camera works. Three people were confused that distance made a difference; they had to think for awhile before understanding that the further away they took the picture, the more people could fit into the photo. Blind people have a very different sense of space than sighted people, especially having to do with perspective [22]. Three participants had an excellent sense of distance. Two had a little trouble holding the camera vertically straight. All but two moved the phone along the x-y plane when trying to take a more accurate picture according to the program's feedback; the other two tilted the phone (from the same center point) around the x and y axes. It was difficult for one of the blind participants to understand the mapping between the vibrations and the physical scene they were photographing. We had to explain that we were only simulating localized vibration, and that the whole phone would actually vibrate when the faces were touched. One subject had no touchscreen or smartphone experience but had used the Optacon, which allowed her to easily grasp the concept of the screen layout relating to the physical world (the Optacon raises the shapes of letters that it sees through the camera [25]). For two participants, it was difficult to distinguish between the various spots that caused vibrations, especially if two face areas were close. Study participants could tell the difference between small and larger face areas by sight or vibration.

5.2.2 Suggested Cues

There were many suggestions given by the participants in terms of what cues they would like from the software. Two participants suggested using musical tones or different types of vibrations instead of the same vibrations to indicate which part of screen has a face, in order to find the spots which were hard to localize for two participants. One subject suggested using volume to indicate the size of the head and proximity of the person. Three participants strongly preferred to have speech directions. One was concerned about having too many noises when they were out in public, but acknowledged that often earbuds were used regardless while using the phone (one in, one out). Two low-vision participants wanted options for seeing a more contrasted framing overlay over the actual video screen, and wanted zoom ability with holistic context. One person wanted the camera to beep when it was at the "right" distance away from the subject and automatically take the photo then.

5.2.3 Reactions and Public Attitudes

Two participants said they would be uncomfortable with obvious verbal cues spoken out in public from the application. One subject felt the opposite, and thought that it could explain to people what was going on, and spur interesting conversations. Reactions were overall extremely positive. Only one subject was skeptical and said he did not see himself excelling in taking pictures of people. One was visibly excited about the practicality and potential of this application and wanted to use it right away. "This is something I can imagine blind and low-vision people using right out of the box. People who decided pictures were no longer for them would say "Now I can take a picture"." Other comments were that the application was "cool," "cute," and "very easy to use." In response to the statement "I liked this application," on a Likert scale from 1 to 7 (1 being strongly disliked it, 7 being loving it), the average response was 5.5. In response to the statement "I would use this application," (1 being never, 7 being very often), the average was 3.9. One participant thought his vision was not bad enough to need the application, and one subject mentioned she only wanted to use OCR and never take photographs of people. When asked about what reactions sighted people might have, seeing a blind person using a camera, two people were worried that it would seem they were faking being blind; with both a cane and a camera, one woman felt very self-conscious and encouraged us to talk to sighted people about their opinions.

5.3 Second Study

Based on the results of this study, we changed a few parts of the PortraitFramer application for a second iteration to make its likelihood of adoption potentially higher. Changes included adding in quick swiping gestures for saving photos or trying again, adding in pitches to the vibrations of the faces (each face would give emit a different pitch when touched, to distinguish between them all), a tilt correction option, and an option to have the program explicitly tell you how to move the camera in order to center the faces.

This study was similar to the first one, in which it was a formative study and participants were asked to take photos of the three faces and center them. We tested this out using instructions as well as the freeform option (no instructions, but still with vibration, pitch, and overlay cues).

5.4 Results

There were seven subjects for this study, with an average age of 40.1. Subjects did not overlap between studies. There were five females and two males. One subject was completely blind, five had severe low-vision with barely perceptible light perception, and one was low-vision but could see shapes. Five had used a camera before. One said that when taking portraits, "I aim it at the sound." Another said, "When I take pictures of my grandkids, my daughter tells me "Higher, higher!" or helps with where to aim." Using the instruction mode, all participants took a successfully centered photo within five seconds (average 3.2) and three tries (average 2.8).

When showed the tilt option, no one in this study found that they would want to use it, having no trouble keeping the phone straight up and down. All of the participants seemed to be good at layout concepts (e.g., face is in the left of screen, so move the camera left, or whether to move forward or backward to change size of faces). When touching the screen to find the faces, one user was extremely methodical (up/down then horizontal), one used a seemingly arbitrary approach of exploring the screen, and the remaining five lay somewhere in between.

Six participants liked having the addition of pitch to the vibration of the faces, for added verification and for situations like crowds. Three preferred using the instruction option: "As much detail as possible is great" said one. Two liked explicit verification of success: "Great, take a photo!" Another subject felt the opposite saying the less information he could get away with, the better, for the sake of simplicity, speed, and autonomy.

There were four user-suggested interaction techniques that came out in the post-study interview. One of them would announce the general size of each face when it was touched on the screen (i.e. "small," "medium," "large"). Another suggestion was similar but would give even more detail, speaking the percentage each face took up of the screen. I had been using random pitches for each of the faces when touched, instead of ordering them left to right or up to down in terms of pitch, which was suggested. Another suggestion was to give each face a spoken number from left to right when touched, so that the user would have a more absolute understanding of where each face was in the screen, and not relative in terms of pitch. One participant wanted an option to toggle between "point and shoot" mode and "more detailed instruction" mode. The two youngest participants expressed a desire for being able to use this application to help them tag their friends in Facebook pictures, and two participants wanted to be able to either tag already existing photographs, or to be able to name and annotate photographs before saving them. Three other participants expressed a desire for facial recognition to be built into this application as well.

Reactions to the application were all positive and excited, even with one subject who came into the study quite skeptical. "It's cool, I like it!" "It's fun. I would use it on my phone." The "app makes me feel confident that i didn't chop the heads off." "I could take pictures of my friends for fun and put it on my Facebook". We asked the same questions as in the first study based on a Likert scale of 1 to 7. For the first statement, averages were around 5.5 for the first version and 6.2 for the second version of PortraitFramer. These numbers were quite high, and didn't have large standard deviations. However, the second statement resulted in much more varied responses. The first version had an average score of less than 4, while the second version was closer to 6. Not only that, but in the first version, four participants gave very low scores, while in the second one, everyone scored at least a 5. The change in results for statement 2 was significant, using a standard t-test ($t = 2.15, DF = 13, p < .05$). This is promising in terms of adoption of this application in real life.

6. DISCUSSION

The fact that so many blind people already take photographs was surprising to us, even though we knew there was a growing community. We had also expected most photographs to be for practical matters, such as OCR or barcode scanning. A lot of practical task applications using cameras and computer vision have not gotten good enough to be consistently used and trusted by blind and low-vision people, and our EasySnap results show promise for aiding in the framing process.

The desire and excitement for taking photographs of people in their lives from the survey was a strong motivation to come up with an application to do so, and does not require heavy computer vision. All of the fifteen blind and low-vision study participants picked up on how to use PortraitFramer within mere minutes.

The importance of customization and user preference options became quite clear through our studies. There were some strong reactions about sighted people's potential reactions to seeing a blind person taking a photograph, which begs more research as mainstream technology is becoming more and more accessible and universal. Themes of security and privacy, responsibility, independence and autonomy, convenience, personal expression, and social acceptance need to be considered in the design process and will result in better technology and experiences for all, not just blind people. Balancing an effort between the user and technology, with the constraints of the users' preferences in mind, is a large but important task for future human computer interaction. Customization is key, and the user can and should decide how much or how little information they want and how they want it presented to them.

While the target user base in this work is blind and low-vision people and has been designed with them in mind, many of these ideas can be considered for different user groups in different situations. Novel input and output methods for people with different situational impairments, preferences, and abilities should be studied in general.

7. CONCLUSION AND FUTURE WORK

In this paper, we have contributed an empirical foundation for understanding the need for accessible photography for blind people and demonstrating that they already use cameras, the creation of two accessible interfaces to take pictures of objects and people by blind people, and usability studies to evaluate these interfaces. Many blind and low-vision people are already using what resources they have to be a part of the world of photography. Given the desire for more accessible camera applications and the prevalence of relatively cheap, accessible mainstream phones, we should leverage the opportunity to include future blind users into the design of novel interactive user interfaces for taking photographs. Taking portraits is one of the more popular reasons blind people already use cameras, and creating an accessible interface on mainstream technology to help do so as well as help framing other practical task-oriented applications, has the potential to have a large effect, even bringing in those blind people who did not think they could ever take a photograph before.

More in-depth studies are presently being conducted on what types of interaction cues on mobile devices work best for different tasks in terms of speed and preference. A plethora of specific task-oriented applications (e.g., recognizing street signs, qr codes, text, and faces) could benefit from better framed photographs taken by their blind and low vision users. The rise of programmable cameras comes at the perfect time where we can make sure to include blind and low vision users in the design loop and provide more universal customization options for future users.

8. ACKNOWLEDGMENTS

The authors would like to thank all the survey and study participants and Professor Ladner at the University of Washington. This work has been supported by Google and NSF Award #IIS-1049080.

9. REFERENCES

[1] http://opencv.willowgarage.com/wiki/facedetection.

[2] http://www.iqengines.com/.

[3] *A Video Based Interface to Textual Information for the Visually Impaired.* IEEE Computer Society, 2002.

[4] *Trinetra: Assistive Technologies for Grocery Shopping for the Blind*, 2007.

[5] knfbreader mobile, knfb reading technology, inc. http://www.knfbreader.com/products-mobile.php, 2008.

[6] Touch sight, camera for the blind. http://www.yankodesign.com/2008/08/13/this-camera-is-outta-sight/, 2008.

[7] Blind photographers. http://blindphotographers.org/, 2010.

[8] Blind with camera school of photography. http://blindwithcameraschool.org/, 2010.

[9] Quiet-light photography. http://www.quietlightphoto.com/, 2010.

[10] Tim o'brien's photos. http://www.timobrienphotos.com/, 2010.

[11] J. Bigham, C. Jayant, H. Ji, G. Little, A. Miller, R. Miller, A. Tatrowicz, B. White, S. White, and T. Yeh. Vizwiz: Nearly real-time answers to visual questions. *UIST 2010*, 2010.

[12] X. Chen and A. Yuille. Detecting and reading text in natural scenes. In *IEEE Computer Vision and Pattern Recognition*, pages 366–373, 2004.

[13] J. Coughlan and R. Manduchi. Color targets: Fiducials to help visually impaired people find their way by camera phone. *EURASIP Journal on Image and Video Processing*, 2007.

[14] G. Covington. Let your camera do the seeing: the world's first photography manual for the legally blind, 1981.

[15] G. Covington. *Access to Photography*, pages 26–30. National Endowment for the Arts, 1989.

[16] B. Deville, G. Bologna, M. Vinckenbosch, and T. Pun. Guiding the focus of attention of blind people with visual saliency. In *Workshop on Computer Vision Applications for the Visually Impaired*, 2008.

[17] M. Dixon, C. Grimm, and W. Smart. Picture composition for a robot photographer. In *Technical Report WUCSE*, 2003.

[18] G. Foo. Summary 2009 grocery shopping for the blind/visually impaired. National Federation of the Blind, 2009.

[19] N. Haidary. Camera for the blind. http://nadeemhaidary.com/camera.html, 2009.

[20] E. Horvitz. Principles of mixed-initiative user interfaces. In *Proceedings of the SIGCHI conference on Human factors in computing systems*, pages 159–166, 1999.

[21] J. Ivanchenko V., Coughlan and H. Shen. Crosswatch: A camera phone system for orienting visually impaired pedestrians at traffic intersections. In *Computers Helping People with Special Needs*, pages 1122–1128, 2008.

[22] B. Jones. Spatial perception in the blind. *British Journal of Pyschology*, 66(4):461–472, 1976.

[23] S. Kane, C. Jayant, J. Wobbrock, and R. Ladner. Freedom to roam: a study of mobile device adoption and accessibility for people with visual and motor disabilities. ACM, 2009.

[24] J. Ko and C. Kim. Low cost blur image detection and estimation for mobile devices. In *Proc. of the 11th international conference on Advanced Communication Technology - Volume 3*, ICACT'09, pages 1605–1610, Piscataway, NJ, USA, 2009. IEEE Press.

[25] J. Linvill and J. Bliss. A direct translation reading aid for the blind. volume 54, pages 40–51, 1966.

[26] X. Liu. A camera phone based currency reader for the visually impaired. pages 305–306, Halifax, Nova Scotia, Canada, 2008. ACM.

[27] U. B. of Engraving and Printing. Bureau of engraving and printing launches eyenoteapp to help the blind and visually impaired denominate us currency, 2011.

[28] P. Silapachote, J. Weinman, A. Hanson, M. Mattar, and R. Weiss. Automatic sign detection and recognition in natural scenes. In *Proc. of the IEEE Computer Society Conference on Computer Vision and Pattern Recognition*, volume 3. IEEE Computer Society, 2005.

[29] J. Sudol, O. Dialemah, C. Blanchard, and T. Dorcey. Looktel: A comprehensive platform for computer-aided visual assistance. *CVAVI Workshop Proceedings of CVPR*, 2010.

[30] M. Vazquez and A. Steinfeld. An assisted photography method for street scenes. *Proceedings of the 2011 IEEE Workshop on Applications of Computer Vision*, 2011.

On the Intelligibility of Fast Synthesized Speech for Individuals with Early-Onset Blindness

Amanda Stent
AT&T Labs Research
180 Park Ave., Bldg. 103
Florham Park, NJ 07932
stent@research.att.com

Ann Syrdal
AT&T Labs Research
180 Park Ave., Bldg. 103
Florham Park, NJ 07932
syrdal@research.att.com

Taniya Mishra
AT&T Labs Research
180 Park Ave., Bldg. 103
Florham Park, NJ 07932
taniya@research.att.com

ABSTRACT

People with visual disabilities increasingly use text-to-speech synthesis as a primary output modality for interaction with computers. Surprisingly, there have been no systematic comparisons of the performance of different text-to-speech systems for this user population. In this paper we report the results of a pilot experiment on the intelligibility of fast synthesized speech for individuals with early-onset blindness. Using an open-response recall task, we collected data on four synthesis systems representing two major approaches to text-to-speech synthesis: formant-based synthesis and concatenative unit selection synthesis. We found a significant effect of speaking rate on intelligibility of synthesized speech, and a trend towards significance for synthesizer type. In post-hoc analyses, we found that participant-related factors, including age and familiarity with a synthesizer and voice, also affect intelligibility of fast synthesized speech.

Categories and Subject Descriptors

K.4.2 [**Social Issues**]: Assistive technologies for persons with disabilities; I.2.7 [**Natural Language Processing**]: Speech recognition and synthesis

General Terms

Experimentation, Human Factors

1. INTRODUCTION

People with visual disabilities increasingly use text-to-speech synthesis rather than Braille as a primary output modality for interaction with computers. In fact, they probably represent the second largest user population (after developers of interactive voice-response systems) for text-to-speech synthesis. As they become expert users of synthesized speech, they typically listen to the speech at speeds multiple times real time [2]. Consequently, they may have different performance metrics for text-to-speech systems than other user populations (e.g. they tend to prefer intelligibility

over naturalness). They tend to have strong preferences for a particular synthesizer and voice[1], based partly on familiarity but also perhaps on suitability of the engine or voice for their needs. Although some studies have analyzed the intelligibility of fast speech in general (e.g. [11, 12, 14, 15, 20]), there has been no comprehensive research on the performance of text-to-speech systems for people with visual disabilities.

In this paper we report the results of a pilot experiment evaluating, for individuals with early-onset blindness, the intelligibility of synthesized speech across text-to-speech synthesis engines, voices and approaches. The goals of our research are to:

- Empirically identify the best text-to-speech engines for people with visual disabilities who listen to fast synthesized speech.

- Identify whether the method of synthesizing speech affects intelligibility of fast synthesized speech.

- Identify whether gender of the voice affects intelligibility of fast synthesized speech.

- Identify good metrics for evaluating the quality of text-to-speech synthesis for people with visual disabilities.

We hope that the answers to these questions will help drive research on text-to-speech synthesis for this user population.

The rest of this paper is structured as follows: In Section 2, we summarize the findings of previous work on the intelligibility of fast synthesized speech. In Section 3, we present the design of our pilot study, and in Section 4 we present the results. In Section 5 we conclude and summarize our current work and ideas for future research in this area.

2. RELATED WORK ON FAST SPEECH

Research on the intelligibility of fast speech in individuals with normal vision has shown that:

- Natural speech is more intelligible than synthesized speech [18].

- Linearly time compressed synthesized speech is more intelligible than both uncompressed fast natural speech and 'naturally compressed' synthesized speech [11] (cf. [15], who used subjective judgments rather than recall to evaluate intelligibility).

---

[1] See, for instance, the blog post by Sean Randall titled "Being eloquent about Eloquence: a formant toast", published January 31, 2009 at http://randylaptop.com/blog/being-eloquent-about-eloquence-a-formant-toast/.

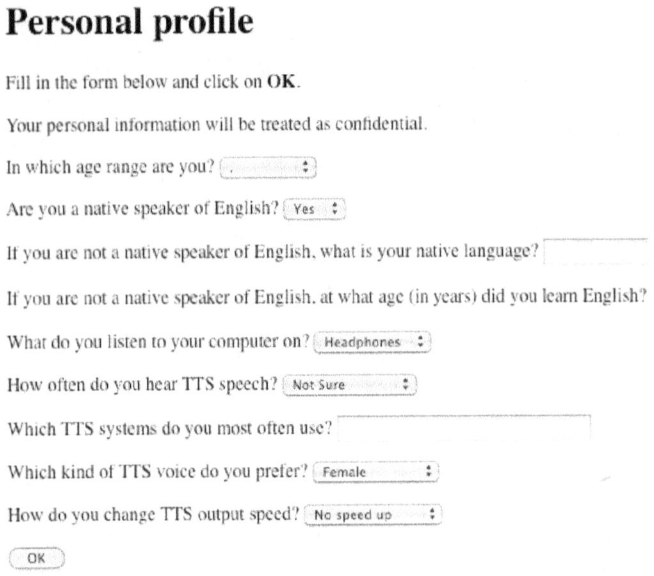

Personal profile

Fill in the form below and click on **OK**.

Your personal information will be treated as confidential.

In which age range are you? [⇕]

Are you a native speaker of English? [Yes ⇕]

If you are not a native speaker of English, what is your native language? [   ]

If you are not a native speaker of English, at what age (in years) did you learn English?

What do you listen to your computer on? [Headphones ⇕]

How often do you hear TTS speech? [Not Sure   ⇕]

Which TTS systems do you most often use? [   ]

Which kind of TTS voice do you prefer? [Female   ⇕]

How do you change TTS output speed? [No speed up   ⇕]

[OK]

Figure 1: Demographic survey, including questions about participant age, English speaking ability, and experience with text-to-speech synthesis systems

- Linearly time compressed natural speech is more intelligible than linearly time compressed synthesized speech [14].

- The intelligibility of fast speech can be affected by listener-related factors including age, hearing ability, language fluency, and familiarity with the synthesis engine and voice [12, 20].

In recent work, Papadopoulos *et al.* show that individuals who are blind are better at understanding synthesized speech than individuals who are sighted [18]. Individuals who are blind are also more likely to use synthesized speech as a primary output modality than individuals who are sighted, due to the widespread use of screen readers such as JAWS and WindowEyes. When used as a primary output modality in a screen reader, synthesized speech is often sped up to multiple times real time. However, surprisingly little research has been done on the intelligibility of fast speech for individuals who are blind.

Asakawa and colleagues performed an experiment on the intelligibility of linearly time compressed natural speech in listeners who are blind [2]. They used a recall-based experimental methodology. Their experiment involved only a small number of participants, but they were able to divide their participants into two groups: expert users of synthesized speech and novice users of synthesized speech. They found that expert users can recall 90% of SUS (semantically unpredictable sentence) content at about 2.5 times, and novice users at about 1.6 times, the default speaking rate of a Japanese TTS system.

Moos and Trouvain compared fast synthesized speech to linearly time compressed natural speech in sighted listeners and blind listeners who were proficient users of a formant-based synthesizer [16]. In contrast to other research, they found that intelligibility of fast synthesized speech was higher than that of linearly time compressed natural speech for

Intelligibility Evaluation

Click here if you need to recap the instructions

1 of 60

Just listen once to this utterance: [Play]

Write down what you heard:

[   ]

(If absolutely unable to guess a word, type xxx for that word.)

[Continue]

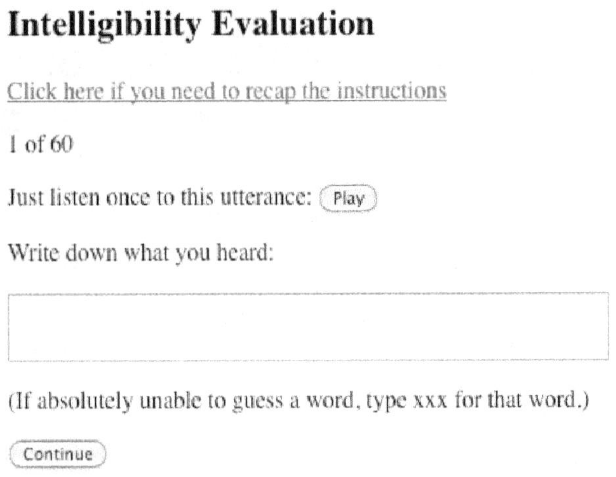

Figure 2: SUS screen, which contains a link to the experiment instructions, a button to play the SUS speech, and a text area to type the transcription of the SUS speech

blind listeners (however, it was lower for sighted listeners). However, their method for evaluating intelligibility was via subjective judgments rather than recall, and listeners may not be very good at judging intelligibility. Also, the sighted listeners listened to slower speech than the blind listeners.

Nishimoto *et al.* compared several methods of synthesizing fast speech using a hidden Markov model (HMM) based synthesizer that separately models F0 and phone duration. They compared models trained on fast natural speech and normal-rate natural speech, used in combination with a rapid speech model, which can produce speaking rates from real time to 1.6 times real time. Their experiments included 4 individuals who are blind. They found that models trained on fast natural speech produce more intelligible speech than models trained on normal-rate natural speech as the speaking rate increases [17]. None of these models correspond directly to linearly time compressed speech, so the results are not directly comparable to the other work mentioned here.

In summary, although we have some information about how people who are sighted and people who are blind process fast natural speech and fast synthesized speech, previous research does not give a user or developer of speech synthesis technology guidelines about choosing the "best" synthesis approach or engine, or about where to focus development efforts to get the biggest performance improvement of synthesis systems for individuals with visual disabilities.

3. EXPERIMENT

In this section, we describe the pilot experiment we ran. We followed a proposed standard developed for testing text-to-speech intelligibility by the Acoustical Society of America's TTS Technology standards committee (S3-WG91).

3.1 Task

We used an open-response recall task for this experiment. In this type of task, participants listen to a spoken stimulus once and then transcribe what they think they heard. In order to prevent participants from using context and

Synthesizer	Type	Bandwidth	Voice	Number of participants
CTTS1	concatenative unit-selection	16 bit, mono 16kHz	F	7
			M	6
CTTS2	concatenative unit-selection	16 bit, mono 1600 Hz	F	1
			M	1
FTTS1	formant	16 bit, mono 11025 Hz	F	2
			M	5
FTTS2	formant	16 bit, mono 11025 Hz	F	6
			M	8

Table 1: Synthesizers used, with number of participants per voice per synthesizer

inference to identify words, rather than simply transcribing what they hear, we used **semantically unpredictable sentences** (SUSs) as stimuli. These sentences are grammatically correct but semantically meaningless. Examples include *A polite art jumps beneath the arms* and *The law that finished shows the boots.*

The experiment was web-based. Participants were presented first with a screen containing experimental instructions, second with a form requesting demographic information (see Figure 1), then with 6 training SUSs, and finally with 198 experimental SUSs. Each SUS was presented on its own screen (see Figure 2). The participant clicked on a button linking to an audio file to hear the SUS, and then typed the transcription in the text box, using 'xxx' to indicate regions of unintelligible speech.

3.2 Synthesis Engines

We tested two popular approaches to text-to-speech synthesis: formant-based and concatenative unit-selection. A *formant-based synthesizer* generates speech by systematic variation of parameters – including formant frequencies and amplitudes, voicing, and noise – to synthesize audio for each phoncme in the input. Formant synthesizers are widely used in screen readers, and are thought by many in the blind user community to be 'clearer' than other synthesizers. Well-known formant synthesizers include eSpeak [6], ETI-Eloquence [9] and DECTalk [8].

A *concatenative unit-selection synthesizer* operates by selecting and concatenating speech units (uniform- or variable-length speech segments) from a speech database to match the input. Generally speaking, concatenative unit-selection synthesizers produce more natural-sounding speech. However, signal processing is required to speed the output of a concatenative unit-selection synthesizer beyond rates that a human speaker can produce. Well-known concatenative unit-selection synthesizers include AT&T Natural Voices [3] and IVONA [10].

Both approaches to speech synthesis typically incorporate additional processes, e.g. to assign prosody or pronunciations to input text, and to speed up output speech before play-back. These processes may have substantial impact on the quality of the output speech, so it is hard to isolate the performance of the synthesis algorithm from the performance of the synthesis engine as a whole.

3.3 Participants

Participants were recruited via email and the web. We sent email announcements to numerous organizations including the American Foundation for the Blind and the Na-

tional Federation of the Blind; some of these organizations graciously shared our announcement with their membership.

We restricted participation in this experiment to individuals with early-onset blindness (onset at less than seven years of age), because such individuals are likely to have different hearing abilities from those with late-onset vision impairment [7].

Thirty-six participants completed our pilot study. Four were under 25 years of age, twenty-five were between 25 and 50 years of age, and seven were between 51 and 65 years of age. Four described themselves as using text-to-speech synthesis systems 'never' or 'occasionally', four as using them 'frequently', twenty-five as using them 'very frequently', and three were not sure. The most commonly listed text-to-speech engines used were ETI-Eloquence (fourteen participants), JAWS (which comes with ETI-Eloquence by default, nine participants), and Apple VoiceOver's default voice, Alex (six participants). Thirty-four self-reported as being native speakers of English. Thirteen listened using speakers, while twenty-three used headphones.

3.4 Materials

For this experiment, we used two widely-available formant based synthesizers and two widely-available concatenative unit-selection synthesizers (see Table 1). Because male and female voices have different characteristics which may affect intelligibility [13], we used male and female American English voices for each synthesizer.

We used the University of Delaware SUSgen system [4] to generate our SUSs. We used 204 SUSs (6 training SUSs, 198 test SUSs) covering the full range of phonemes observed in English. SUS length ranged from 5 to 7 words with a maximum of 10 syllables. Sentence frames included a variety of syntactic structures.

Each synthesizer produced speech for each SUS at six different speeds ranging from 300 to 550 words per minute at intervals of 50 words per minute. This corresponds to roughly 1.5 times real time to 3 times real time (where 'real time' is the synthesizer and voice's default speaking rate). SUSs were saved as .wav files and played back through the browser in a pop-up window that opened when the participant clicked a link in the SUS screen (see Figure 2). The assignment of test SUSs to speeds, and the order of SUSs, was randomized across participants. The test progressed in blocks of 33 SUSs from 300 words per minute to 550 words per minute in 6 50 word-per-minute steps. Listeners were assigned a text-to-speech system and voice according to a predetermined round-robin order.

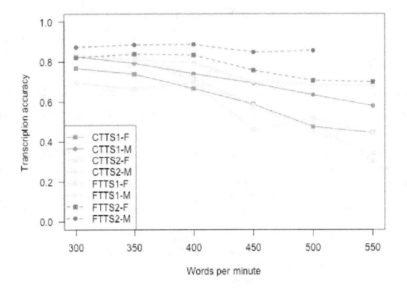

Figure 3: Line graph showing transcription accuracy by synthesizer, voice gender and speaking rate

3.5 Data Processing

The transcriptions were automatically processed to remove punctuation and replace upper case letters with lower case letters. For the analysis reported in Section 4.1, the transcriptions were also automatically processed to remove typographic errors and unify spelling of homophones, using a word list constructed by hand by one of the authors.

3.6 Issues With Experimental Design

Participants faced several issues with this experimental design. The three biggest issues had to do with audio playback and experiment length. Numerous participants dropped out of our pilot study due to these issues, giving an unbalanced data set.

The first issue related to the interaction between screen reader speech and SUS playback. Participants could only listen to each spoken SUS once. Unfortunately, many screen readers indicate using speech that a link has been clicked on, and this speech would overlap with the SUS speech. We solved this by forcing a 5-second pause between link clicking and start of audio playback; this time is long enough for the screen readers used by our participants to finish speaking.

The second issue was the length of the experiment. It takes about one hour to listen to all 198 test SUSs. This is quite a long time for a web-based experiment; furthermore, due to the cognitive load of listening to and transcribing semantically unpredictable sentences while interacting with a screen reader and various pop-up windows, participants were strongly encouraged to break up the task into multiple sessions. In our current version of this experiment (see Section 5), we have reduced the task length to 60 test SUSs.

4. RESULTS AND DISCUSSION

In this section, we report the results of our pilot study for our main variables of interest (synthesizer type, voice gender and speaking rate). We also report informal post-hoc

analyses of participant-related factors, and a comparison of alternative methods for computing transcription accuracy.

4.1 Experiment Results

For our pilot experiment, we measured transcription accuracy using the cosine similarity between a reference transcription for each SUS and the participant's post-processed transcription for the SUS (see Section 4.3). Figure 3 shows a plot of results by synthesizer type and voice. FTTS2 appears to perform the best, with transcription accuracy over 0.8 for the male voice across all speaking rates. By contrast, FTTS1 shows the steepest rate of decline as speaking rate increases, from above 0.8 at 300 words per minute to below 0.4 at 550 words per minute for both male and female voices. Performance for CTTS1 and CTTS2 also declines as speaking rate increases, though less than for FTTS1. Except for FTTS1, transcription accuracies appear to be higher for the male voice for all synthesizers.

We ran a three-way mixed Anova with two between subjects variables: synthesizer type (2 levels, formant and concatenative unit-selection) and voice gender (2 levels, M and F), and one within subjects variable: speaking rate (5 levels, words per minute ranging from 300 to 500 at intervals of 50[2]). There was a significant main effect for speaking rate, $F(4, 5760) = 59.9759$, $p < .001$, such that transcription accuracy decreased as speaking rate increased. In addition, there was a trend towards a main effect for synthesizer type, $F(1, 5760) = 3.2563$, $p = .08$. There was no significant main effect for voice gender, and there were no significant interaction effects.

Looking at Figure 3, we see that one of the formant-based synthesizers outperforms the other three, while the other

---

[2]Due an error in the experimental setup, we are missing data for the 550 words per minute setting for CTTS1-M, so we excluded all the 550 words-per-minute data from this analysis.

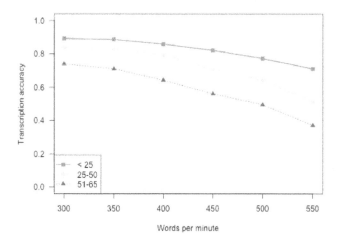

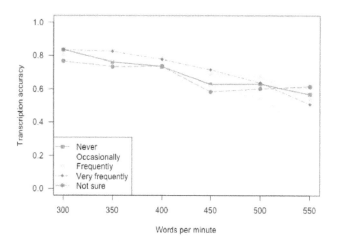

Figure 4: Line graph showing transcription accuracy by speaking rate for different participant age ranges: under 25, 25-50, and 51-64

Figure 5: Line graph showing transcription accuracy by speaking rate for expert and non-expert users of text-to-speech synthesizers

formant-based synthesizer shows the steepest decline in performance as speaking rate increases. The performance of the male voice for one of the concatenative unit-selection synthesizers is similar to that of the female voice for the best-performing formant-based synthesizer. We did post-hoc analyses using t-tests to compare the performance of individual synthesizers, and found significant differences in performance between FTTS1 and FTTS2 (df = 2143, p < .001), between CTTS2 and FTTS2 (df = 443, p < .001), and between CTTS1 and FTTS2 (df = 4190, p < .001).

In general, Figure 3 seems to show that the male voices outperform the female voices for all synthesizers except the poorer-performing formant-based synthesizer. The lack of a significant main effect for voice gender may be due to the unbalanced nature of our data.

Interestingly, although a speaking rate of 500 words per minute is 2.5 times real time, transcription accuracies for all synthesizers were still at or above 50%, in the range Asakawa *et al.* define as acceptable [2].

4.2 Participant-Related Factors

We did post-hoc analyses to see if participant-related factors mentioned in the literature also played a role in text-to-speech intelligibility in our data.

Figure 4 shows average transcription accuracy across different speaking rates for different participant age ranges. Participants under 25 years of age had the highest transcription accuracies, and transcription accuracy declined more gradually as speaking rate increased (from 0.89 at 300 words per minute to 0.71 at 550 words per minute). Participants over 51 years of age had the lowest transcription accuracies, and transcription accuracy declined more rapidly as speaking rate increased (from 0.74 at 300 words per minute to 0.37 at 550 words per minute). These results agree with those reported in the literature (e.g. [12]).

Figure 5 shows average transcription accuracy across different speaking rates for expert and non-expert users of text-to-speech synthesizers. Participants who used synthesized

speech 'frequently' or 'very frequently' had the highest transcription accuracies from 350 words per minute (0.83) to 500 words per minute (0.66). Participants who 'never' or 'occasionally' used synthesized speech, or who were not sure, had lower transcription accuracies from 350 words per minute (0.76) to 500 words per minute (0.59).

Nine of the participants assigned to one of the voices of FTT2 self-reported as using FTT2. This may partly explain the very good results for FTT2. In fact, familiarity with a synthesizer may negate or severely retard the negative impact on intelligibility of speaking rate; for the FTT2 male voice, transcription accuracy remains above 0.8 even at 500 words per minute.

Figure 6 shows average transcription accuracy across different speaking rates for native and nonnative speakers of English. Native speakers of English achieved higher transcription accuracies at every speaking rate; furthermore, transcription accuracy declined more slowly as speaking rate increased. At 550 words per minute, the transcription accuracy of native speakers of English was higher than that of non-native speakers of English at 400 words per minute.

Figure 7 shows average transcription accuracy by listening equipment used by the participant across different speaking rates. The lines are very similar, diverging only at 550 words per minute. The potential impact of equipment appears to be small except at the fastest speaking rates. It may be that participants who regularly use screen readers have good sound equipment.

4.3 Measuring Transcription Accuracy

Transcription accuracy can be measured as orthographic accuracy (ability of the listener to reproduce exactly the words that form the stimulus), corrected orthographic accuracy (ability of the listener to reproduce the words that form the stimulus, post-corrected for typographic errors and for homophones), or phonetic accuracy (ability of the listener to reproduce the sounds in the stimulus). Furthermore, there are multiple different ways to compare a reference transcrip-

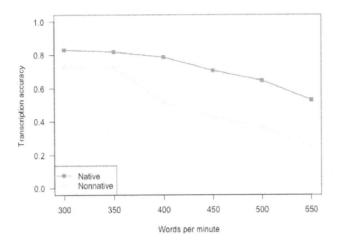

Figure 6: Line graph showing transcription accuracy by speaking rate for native and nonnative speakers of English

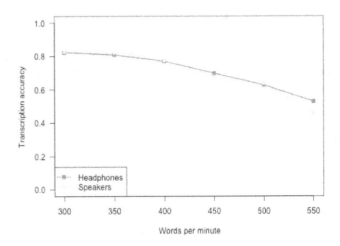

Figure 7: Line graph showing transcription accuracy by listening equipment (headphones or speakers) and by speaking rate

tion (orthographic or phonetic) with a listener's transcription. In the analyses above, we used corrected orthographic accuracy, measured using cosine similarity. However, in order to do this we had to post-process the transcriptions to account for homophones (e.g. *pear, pair, pare*) and spelling errors (e.g. *against, againest, aginst* or *apartment, appartment*). Participants in this study frequently made spelling errors that involved dropping a letter or doubling a letter, perhaps because they were listening to a screen reader repeat each character they typed. It takes time for an experimenter to construct a list of permissible substitutions to post-process a set of transcriptions, and even then, word boundary errors (e.g. *about* vs. *a boat*) persist[3].

We explored using other measures of orthographic or phonetic accuracy. To compute a quasi-phonetic representation of the transcriptions, we used Double Metaphone [19], as implemented in the Apache commons codec [1]. To compute accuracy, we tried the following metrics, all implemented in the freely-available Simmetrics package [5]:

- **Cosine similarity** – a word-based similarity metric that computes the cosine distance between two vectors representing the input strings.

- **Dice** – a character bigram-based similarity metric; given input strings s_1 and s_2, the dice coefficient is $\frac{2*|common\_bigrams(s_1,s_2)|}{(|bigrams(s_1)||bigrams(s_2)|)}$

- **Jaro Winkler** - a character-based similarity metric that takes into account transposition errors; given input strings s_1 and s_2, the Jaro Winkler score is $1/3*(\frac{|matching\_chars(s_1,s_2)|}{|chars(s_1)|}+\frac{|matching\_chars(s_1,s_2)|}{|chars(s_2)|}+\frac{(|matching\_chars(s_1,s_2)|-|transpositions(s_1,s_2)|)}{|matching\_chars(s_1,s_2)|})$

---

[3]The Acoustical Society of America's TTS Technology standards committee's proposed standard calls for word boundary errors to be counted as errors.

- **Levenshtein distance** - a character-based similarity metric that counts the number of insertions, deletions and substitutions required to turn input string s_2 into input string s_1.

We note that any character-based metric can be made word-based by segmenting on word boundaries rather than between characters. Also, while the default implementation of cosine similarity is order-invariant, so can only be used if the input strings contain no repeated words, an order-preserving version can easily be obtained by indexing the words in each string. In all cases, we used versions of these metrics normalized to the length of the reference transcription.

We automatically processed each participant's transcription to obtain:

- **Ortho-plain** – a minimally-processed orthographic transcription (remove punctuation and replace upper with lower case).

- **Ortho-processed** – similar to ortho-plain, except that a hand-created list of permissible substitutions covering common typographic errors and homophones was also applied.

- **Phono-plain** – a double-metaphone representation of ortho-plain.

Since Double Metaphone produces a single word as output, and represents the order of phonemes in the transcription, it does not make sense to use any metrics other than Levenshtein on the phono-plain version of a transcription. In addition, since we hope to replace a manually-constructed list of substitutions with a robust similarity metric, it only makes sense to compute Cosine on the ortho-processed version of a transcription. Consequently, we computed similarities as shown in Table 2.

The **Cosine** metric represents our best human-aided effort at a similarity metric, so we are looking for an alternative metric that is very closely correlated with **Cosine**.

216

Metric	Transcription Type		
	Ortho-plain	Ortho-processed	Phono-plain
Cosine	Cosine-plain	Cosine	
Dice	Dice-plain		
Jaro Winkler	JaroWinkler-plain		
Levenshtein	Levenshtein-plain		Levenshtein-phono

Table 2: Similarity computations made

	Cosine-plain	Dice-plain	JaroWinkler-plain	Levenshtein-plain	Levenshtein-phono
Cosine	.982	.982	.699	.911	.897

Table 3: Correlation between Cosine and other similarity computations summarized in Table 2

Table 3 shows the Pearson correlations between **Cosine** and the other similarity computations summarized in Table 2[4]. The good news is that both **Cosine-plain** and **Dice-plain** are highly correlated with **Cosine**; this means that we probably do not need to hand-author lists of spelling corrections and homophone substitutions. **JaroWinkler-plain** has the lowest correlation with **Cosine**: participants in this experiment tended to drop or repeat letters, not swap them. **Levenshtein-plain** is highly correlated with **Cosine**, but not as highly as **Cosine-plain** or **Dice-plain**.

Levenshtein-phono is also highly correlated with **Cosine**, though not as highly as we might expect. An examination of the data indicates that the rules Double Metaphone uses to create a quasi-phonetic representation of a string are over-generous for our purpose, for example mapping word-final /d/ and /t/ to the same character (while we want, e.g. *send* and *sent* to be treated as different words). This means that the phono-plain representations of two quite different strings will be quite similar: consider *why should the velmas in the mont* vs. *why should the bell miss an amount* (**Cosine**: .463; **Levenshtein-phono**: .857), or *the bags left between a small coat* vs. *the bags leapt beneath the small coat* (**Cosine**: .617; **Levenshtein-phono**: .75). In future work, we may consider more direct phonetic representations, such as a phonetic transcription from the input to a text-to-speech synthesizer not included in our experiments.

5. CONCLUSIONS AND FUTURE WORK

In this paper, we report the results of a pilot study examining the impact of synthesis method, voice gender and speaking rate on intelligibility of fast synthesized speech for individuals with early-onset blindness. We found a significant effect of speaking rate and a trend towards significance for synthesizer type. In post-hoc analyses, we found that participant-related factors also affect intelligibility of fast synthesized speech. In particular, we confirmed prior research showing that age affects ability to understand fast speech. We also found evidence that familiarity with a synthesizer and voice may ameliorate the negative impact of speaking rate on intelligibility of synthesized speech.

We are currently conducting an experiment that uses a modified version of the methodology used in our pilot study. In particular, we have corrected issues pertaining to interference between a screen reader and stimulus playback, and have reduced the number of test SUSs from 198 to 60. We are also including text-to-speech engines that use a third synthesis method: Hidden Markov Model (HMM)-based synthesis [21]. We intend to collect data for this experiment until we have a balanced data set involving participants not familiar with the engine to which they are assigned, and covering two voices (male and female) for each of at least two synthesizers for each of these three approaches to text-to-speech synthesis. The Acoustical Society of America's TTS Technology standards group is conducting a parallel study (using the same experimental methodology) with participants who do not have early-onset blindness.

In future work, we would like to further separate the synthesis method from other components of the text-to-speech synthesizer, particularly the signal processing for speeding up speech. We can do this by collecting speech at a single rate from multiple synthesizers (and, optionally, a human speaker) and speeding it up as a separate process using different methods, including linear time compression and linear time compression excluding pauses [16].

In this experiment, we evaluated intelligibility using a recall task, which is an approximation of close reading of a text. People with visual disabilities who use text-to-speech synthesis as a primary output modality also use the speech stream for skimming/gisting (e.g. skimming through emails, skimming through a news story) and for search. It would be interesting to look at whether the synthesis method or method of speeding up speech affect usability of synthesized speech for these and other alternative use cases. For example, a study could be run in which participants are asked to listen for a particular phrase or topic and then stop the playback as soon as possible. Perhaps skimming and searching are possible at higher speaking rates than close reading. We leave these questions for future research.

6. ACKNOWLEDGMENTS

We thank the members of the Acoustical Society of America's TTS Technology standards committee (S3-WG91) for providing their proposed standard method for evaluating TTS intelligibility, and for letting us borrow their materials for our study. We thank the individuals who contributed text-to-speech synthesis output for our experimental materials. We also gratefully acknowledge the experimental participants, who not only worked patiently through our long experiment but also sent us detailed feedback on the interactions between the experiment pages and their screen readers.

---

[4]The order of similarity of the other metrics to **Cosine** remains the same when Spearman rank correlations are used as the measure of similarity.

7. REFERENCES

[1] Apache commons codec. http://commons.apache.org/codec/apidocs/overview-summary.html.

[2] C. Asawka, H. Takagi, S. Ino, and T. Ifukube. Maximum listening speeds for the blind. In *Proceedings of the International Conference on Auditory Display*, 2003.

[3] M. Beutnagel et al. The AT&T next-gen TTS system. In *Proceedings of the Joint Meeting of the ASA, EAA and DAGA*, 1999.

[4] H. T. Bunell and J. Lilley. Analysis methods for assessing TTS intelligibility. *Presented at the 6th ISCA Workshop on Speech Synthesis*, 2007.

[5] S. Chapman. Simmetrics. http://staffwww.dcs.shef.ac.uk/people/S.Chapman/simmetrics.html.

[6] eSpeak. http://espeak.sourceforge.net/.

[7] F. Gougoux et al. Neuropsychology: Pitch discrimination in the early blind. *Nature*, 430, 2004.

[8] W. Hallahan. DECtalk software: Text-to-speech technology and implementation. *Digital Technical Journal*, 7(4), 1995.

[9] S. Hertz, R. Younes, and N. Zinovieva. Language-universal and language-specific components in the multi-language ETI-Eloquence text-to-speech system. In *Proceedings of the 14th International Congress of Phonetic Sciences*, 1999.

[10] IVONA. http://www.ivona.com/.

[11] E. Janse. Word perception in fast speech: artificially time-compressed vs. naturally produced fast speech. *Speech Communication*, 42:155–173, 2004.

[12] E. Janse, M. van der Werff, and H. Quené. Listening to fast speech: aging and sentence context. In *Proceedings of the 16th International Congress of Phonetic Sciences*, 2007.

[13] D. Klatt and L. Klatt. Analysis, synthesis, and perception of voice quality variations among female and male talkers. *Journal of the Acoustical Society of America*, 87(2):820–857, 1990.

[14] J. Lebeter and S. Saunders. The effects of time compression on the comprehension of natural and synthetic speech. *Working Papers of the Linguistics Circle of the University of Victoria*, 20:63–81, 2010.

[15] D. Moers, P. Wagner, B. Möbius, F. Müllers, and I. Jauk. Integrating a fast speech corpus in unit selection synthesis: experiments on perception, segmentation, and duration prediction. In *Proceedings of Speech Prosody*, 2010.

[16] A. Moos and J. Trouvain. Comprehension of ultra-fast speech - blind vs. "normally hearing" persons. In *Proceedings of the 16th International Congress of Phonetic Sciences*, 2007.

[17] T. Nishimoto et al. Effect of learning on listening to ultra-fast synthesized speech. In *Proceedings of the IEEE Engineering in Medicine and Biology Conference*, 2006.

[18] K. Papadopoulos, E. Katemidou, A. Koutsoklenis, and E. Mouratidou. Differences among sighted individuals and individuals with visual impairments in word intelligibility presented via synthetic and natural speech. *Augmentative and Alternative Communication*, 26(4):278–288, 2010.

[19] L. Phillips. The double metaphone search algorithm. *C/C++ Users Journal*, 18(6):38–43, June 2000.

[20] B. Sutton, J. King, K. Hux, and D. Beukelman. Younger and older adults' rate performance when listening to synthetic speech. *Augmentative and Alternative Communication*, 11(3):147–153, 1995.

[21] K. Tokuda, T. Yoshimura, T. Masuko, T. Kobayashi, and T. Kitamura. Speech parameter generation algorithms for hmm-based speech synthesis. In *Proceedings of ICASSP*, 2000.

A Straight-Talking Case Study

Annalu Waller
University of Dundee
School of Computing
Dundee DD1 4HB, Scotland
+44 1382 388223
awaller
@computing.dundee.ac.uk

Suzanne Prior
University of Dundee
School of Computing
Dundee DD1 4HB, Scotland
+44 1382 386539
sprior
@computing.dundee.ac.uk

Kathleen Cummins
University of Dundee
School of Computing
Dundee DD1 4HB, Scotland
+44 1382 384677
kcummins
@computing.dundee.ac.uk

ABSTRACT
The Straight-Talking User Group within Dundee University's School of Computing aims to create a place where adults with complex disabilities can meet to explore technology and where they can work with researchers to develop better technology. A pilot project has shown the potential for this type of centre is terms of increasing the self-esteem and motivation of participants and raising expectations of what people are able to achieve.

Categories and Subject Descriptors
H.1.1 [**Models and Principles**]: User/Machine Systems – *human factors.* K.4.2 [**Computing Milieux**]: Computers and Society - *Assistive technologies for persons with disabilities.*

General Terms
Design, Human Factors.

Keywords
Augmentative and Alternative Communication (AAC), Severe Speech and Physical Impairments (SSPI), Computing, Voice Output Communication Aid (VOCA), User-Centred Design.

1. INTRODUCTION
The School of Computing has a long history of developing technology for older or disabled people [1] and has a unique in-house user centre where older adults meet with HCI researchers and students [2]. The members of the user centre develop their computing skills, while providing a valuable resource for researchers by providing feedback on their work. The concept of having such a resource within a computing department has been extended to people with severe speech and physical impairments (SSPI). The Straight-Talking User Group was established as a pilot project in September 2010 with five adult volunteers with SSPI. This paper describes the experience of running the user group and discusses the challenges and successes of the first ten months of this unique group.

2. BACKGROUND
Augmentative and Alternative Communication (AAC) attempts to compensate (either temporarily or permanently) for the impairment and disability patterns of individuals with severe expressive communication disorders [3]. AAC technology in the form of voice output communication aids (VOCAs), in particular, provide people with Severe Speech and Physical Impairments (SSPI) with access to spoken and written communication. In addition to a physical impairment, individuals with SSPI will have

a moderate to severe communication impairment, accompanied by physical, sensory and/or cognitive impairment. It is estimated that there are 365,000 adults with SSPI in the United Kingdom [4] and this number is growing.

While Assistive Technology has the potential to greatly improve the quality of life and independence of people with SSPI, but has a high rate of abandonment; estimated to be as high as 58% [5]. One of the major reasons for abandonment is poor usability [6]. Previous projects with technology disenfranchised groups have seen improvements in the usability of devices when the end users have been included in user centred design [7].

2.1 User Centred Design & Adults with SSPI
A recent study has shown that with the appropriate support adults with SSPI are able to act as co-designers in the creation of technology and can make a valuable contribution in this process [8]. The participants in the study also showed an increase in self-confidence, communication ability and desire for inclusion in the community. The study took place at the participants' current day and residential support centres. While the pilot was successful it also showed that these centres are not ideally suited to this work. There are often difficulties in finding space to work with participants away from the activity of the main rooms in the centre and it proved challenging to set up technology in the centre [8].

3. ESTABLISHING AN AAC USER GROUP
The first author delivers a five week research module on AAC for final year computing students at Dundee University. This experience led to the establishment of the Straight-Talking User Group in September 2010. The group meets in the School's User Centre. This is a space on the ground floor of the Queen Mother Building which is home to the School of Computing at Dundee University. The space has access to a kitchenette area and there are two accessible washrooms in close proximity. There is ample room to manoeuvre although conventional furniture does make it difficult for people who use wheelchairs to access appropriate table space.

The user group is currently composed of 4 members (3 female and 1 male). All of the members had previously been involved in research projects within the School of Computing and were known to the research staff. All four participants have cerebral palsy, use motorised wheelchairs and use varying types of AAC.

The participants were formally invited to join the user group via a letter. The residential participant's care team was approached prior to sending the letter to confirm that the participant would be able to join the group.

4. THE FIRST TEN MONTHS

It was hoped that eventually the participants would take increasing responsibility for the group in a similar way to the older user group. The first meeting was therefore designed to discuss the focus of the group and to decide upon a name for the group. This discussion was in the form of an adapted focus group [8]. The members chose the name "Straight-Talking" and one participant offered to produce a logo.

Three aims were suggested and the group created a calendar of events which reflected these aims:

- To train members in becoming "expert end users"
- To raise awareness in wider community of AAC
- To provide a social space for members to meet

One of the aims of the User Group is to provide students and researchers with access to 'expert users'. This involves interacting with others who may not have had any prior experience of people with SSPI. It was therefore decided to give the members an introduction to different HCI techniques, e.g., heuristic evaluations, and to give them techniques to work with students.

The group has been involved in:

- Working with MSc students to identify requirements for a team HCI project;
- Evaluating prototypes for a talking photograph album developed by a final year computing student;
- Providing feedback to a design team from England on a workshop plan for people with SSPI.
- Working with a doctoral student to develop a communication device;
- Providing consultancy on the design of health questionnaires

5. CHALLENGES

Although the goal of developing a resource for researchers and students within a computing department mirrors that of the older user group, the management of the AAC group has different challenges. Staffing has been a challenge running the group requires additional staffing; participants need support and guidance to engage in activities. A staff member acts as manager. It is her job to 'keep the diary' and arrange sessions. The demand on the group is increasing and the manager must ensure that participants are not overused. Other staff members within the AAC research group volunteer to support participants.A further challenge is finance, the participants cannot be paid for their work due to benefit constraints. However, travel costs can, and should be reimbursed and these can be high. We are beginning to consider charging researchers who commission work with the group.The final challenges relate to ethical issues.We are finding that obtaining consent for each different project is time consuming and exasperating for users. Consent is normally obtained using a modified consent form whereby users are asked to confirm each question with a yes/no response. We are now considering consenting three or four times a year and using shorter forms for actual projects.

6. BENEFITS

The benefits can viewed in terms of benefits for participant, researchers; and technology development.

In the ten months of running the centre, we have seen a marked change in the participants in terms of self-esteem and self-

confidence. There has been 100% attendance at sessions apart from times when transport has let the participant down. The participants consider their involvement in the centre to be their "work" and are taking increased responsibility in setting the agendas for sessions. Participants are motivated to engage in sustained activity. This contrasts with a high level of inactivity for some participants in their usual environments.Participants exhibit insight into the needs of other disabled users and are able to reflect on design issues from different perspectives. E.g., one participant was able to navigate an interface but noted that a friend would not because he could not handle a mouse.

7. CONCLUSION

The AAC user centre is still in its infancy, but this pilot has shown that the concept of such a user centre could be of benefit to developers as well as the participants themselves. The users are keen to engage in a variety of activities and they wish to bring their own skills to the group (e.g. through creating logos or assisting with the scenario acting). Providing a challenging environment for adults with SSPI has the potential to provide people with the motivation and opportunity raise the expectations of both participants and social care professionals to participate in viable employment.

8. ACKNOWLEDGEMENTS

This work is funded in part by Capability Scotland.

9. REFERENCES

[1] Newell, A., et al., *Information technology for cognitive support*, in *The Human-Computer Interaction Handbook*, J. Jacko and A. Sears, Editors. 2008, Lawrence Erlbaum: New Jersey, USA. p. 811-828.

[2] Forbes, F., et al., *Dundee user centre: a space where older people and technology meet*, in *Proceedings of the 11th international ACM SIGACCESS conference on Computers and accessibility*2009, ACM: Pittsburgh, Pennsylvania, USA.

[3] Glennen, S. and D. Descoste, *The Handbook of Augmentative and Alternative Communication*1997: Thomson Delmar Learning. 795.

[4] Holmes, K., S. Judge, and J. Murray. *Communication Matters - Research Matters: an AAC Evidence Base*. in *Commuication Matters*. 2010. Leicester.

[5] Riemer-Reiss, M.L. and R. Wacker, *Factors Associated with Assistive Technology Discontinuance among Individuals with Disabilities*. The Journal of Rehabilitation, 2000. **66**(3): p. 44-50.

[6] Prior, S., *HCI methods for including adults with disabilities in the design of CHAMPION*, in *Proceedings of the 28th of the international conference extended abstracts on Human factors in computing systems*2010, ACM: Atlanta, Georgia, USA. p. 2891-2894.

[7] Eisma, R., et al., *Early user involvement in the development of information technology-related products for older people*. Universal Access in the Information Society, 2004. **3**(2): p. 131-140

[8] Prior, S., *Towards the Full Inclusion of People with Severe Speech and Physical Impairments in the Design of Augmentative and Alternative Communication Software*, in *School of Computing* 2011, University of Dundee: Dundee

A Tactile-Thermal Display for Haptic Exploration of Virtual Paintings

Victoria E. Hribar
Virginia Commonwealth University
401 West Main Street
Richmond, Virginia 23284
001-804-828-7839

hribarve@vcu.edu

Dianne T.V. Pawluk
Virginia Commonwealth University
401 West Main Street
Richmond, Virginia 23284
001-804-828-9491

dtpawluk@vcu.edu

ABSTRACT

To enable individuals who are blind and visually impaired to participate fully in the world around them, it is important to make all environments accessible to them. This includes art museums which provide opportunities for cultural education and personal interest/enjoyment. Our interest focuses on the portrayal of paintings through refreshable haptic displays from their digital representations. As a complement to representing the structural elements (i.e., objects and shapes) in a painting, we believe it is also important to provide a personal experience of the style and expressiveness of the artist. This paper proposes a haptic display and display methods to do so. The haptic display consists of: (1) a pin matrix display to the fingers to relay tactile texture information about brushstroke, (2) a thermal display on which the warm-cold spectrum of colors is mapped, and (3) the sensing of location within the painting used to change tactile and thermal feedback to create contrasts within a painting.

Categories and Subject Descriptors

K.4.2 [**Computing Milieux**]: Social Issues– *Assistive technologies for persons with disabilities.*

General Terms

Design, Human Factors

Keywords

Haptics, art, visually impaired, assistive technology

1. INTRODUCTION

The loss of vision limits the access of individuals who are blind and visually impaired to environments such as museums and aquariums which provide both informal learning opportunities and personal enjoyment. In particular, this work focuses on providing access to both the learning and enjoyment of art museums which are not fully attainable to these individuals. Related work has focused on the presentation of 3-D form to museum visitors through The Museum of Pure Form Project (www.pureform.org/project.htm). Here, we focus on paintings.

An already customary method to increase accessibility to paintings is to relay the content of a painting with an audio-recorded description to the user. This method, while informative, does not always allow the user full understanding of the carefully crafted style and mood the artist has captured through use of brushstrokes, choice of colors, and contrast. This method also prevents the user from forming a personal interpretation of the artwork, arguably the main purpose individuals choose to view art. Some museums do also offer a tactile representation that can be printed (e.g., www.artbeyondsight.com), however, these are limited to the depiction of objects and shapes in the painting. In these pictures, the textures used are meant to differentiate different objects but potentially mislead a user about an artist's style.

To describe the style and mood of a painting, we based our method on portraying pictorial attributes that are used in the annotation of Medieval and Modern paintings (Leslie et al., 2007). These include: brushwork concepts, color temperature and palette, and color contrast. From the visual brushwork concepts, we determined the importance of describing texture in terms of its stroke width, length and directionality, as well as the use of color contrasts. Similar aspects can be relayed tactually as well. From the color concepts, we focused on color temperature (i.e., the warm cold spectrum) which appeared to have a strong relationship to the emotional quality of the picture. As it appeared to us that thermal temperature had similar and corresponding emotional qualities, we chose to display color with a thermal display. Color contrasts can then be realized by the juxtaposition of thermal patches.

2. RELATED WORK

Several pin matrix displays have been developed (e.g., Levesque and Hayward, 2008; Garcia-Hernandez et al., 2010; Headley and Pawluk, 2010) that could be used to present brushstroke information. In fact, the first two papers examined the discrimination of spatial wavelength and orientation with these displays. Their results indicate the plausibility of using this type of display to relay brushstroke information, albeit more crudely than for vision. There have also been several different groups (e.g. Ho and Jones, 2007; Yang et al., 2007) that have developed thermal displays (the latter being a mechanical and thermal display). However, their focus has been on simulating thermal properties of materials rather than displaying temperature directly.

3. INTERVIEWS ON THE DESIGN

Subjective data on the concept of this device was collected through one-on-one discussions with two visually impaired individuals and one blind individual. The interviewer described the idea of creating a haptic display to depict virtual paintings as well as the approach to provide tactile and thermal feedback to the fingertips or palm of one or both hands. Following this brief description and an opportunity to clarify any concepts, the subjects responded to a series of questions. All users agreed that they would use this device if it were accessible for free in a museum, school, or other facility and were open to trying this new technology. Two subjects emphasized that they believed this device would be more fun to use and more educational than established methods for the blind and visually impaired to experience art. The third subject felt the audio-descriptions provided an enjoyable and educational experience already, but would like to use this system to experience art in a new way.

4. DEVICE DESIGN

For the display of physical brushstrokes, we have created a haptic display device, which senses the location of the display on the virtual painting and then provides tactile feedback in mechanical texture form [4]. Our computer mouse-like haptic display device is built around four main commercially available components: a Braille cell (P16, Metec AG), a 200 V power supply (Metec AG), a digital I/O board (National Instruments USB-6501), and a graphics tablet (currently an Adesso CyberTablet 12000). The Braille cell, which houses a 2x4 pin array constituting the tactile interface of the device, is situated inside of a commercially-available mouse casing. Also contained in the casing is an RF transmitter tuned to communicate absolute position information to the graphics tablet. The coil of the transmitter is centered under the pin array of the Braille cell. The digital I/O, power supply, and driving electronics are contained within an electronics module. Brushstrokes are created by specifying local square patterns corresponding to the appropriate stroke size and orientation.

For the thermal display, the computer senses the haptic display position (as described above) on the virtual painting and then provides thermal feedback to the user through the thermal display based on this location. The system consists of several components: a Peltier thermoelectric module, a temperature sensor, such as a thermocouple or thermistor, a power supply and an analog input with digital input/output USB board. The specified local temperature is controlled by a PD controller, which reduces the error between the sensed and commanded temperature. Rather than using an analog amplifier between the computer and the thermoelectric device, PWM (pulse-width modulation) is used to drive the device to reduce cost. An algorithm is currently being developed to display the temperature of the color along the warm-cool spectrum based in the amount of red and blue in the local screen area (in RGB) and the brightness of the color.

The actual devices being used are described in Figure 1. A block diagram of the haptic device is shown in Figure 2.

5. FUTURE INVESTIGATIONS

In the near future, we hope to perform human factors testing of different methods to convey the individual aspects of brushstroke and color to determine which are most effective. We then intend to assess the use of the combined methods in a tactile display to convey the style and mood of a virtual painting. Ultimately, we hope to develop a display system, display methods and picture conversion methods to display paintings found in public and private art galleries. This would include complementary diagrams for depicting structural aspects of a painting and its mood and style, as well as zooming techniques to investigate details. The system could then be made available in kiosks in Art Museums or available for home use on the World Wide Web.

Figure 1. Current Devices Being Used

(a) tactile display, (b) thermal display

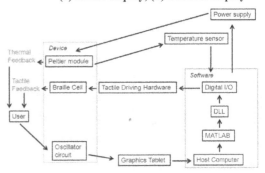

Figure 2. Haptic Device Block Diagram

6. ACKNOWLEDGMENTS

We thank Patrick Headley for his support. We also thank the VCU HHMI Summer Scholars program and the VCU Undergraduate Research Opportunities Program. This work is funded by NSF CBET Grant #0754629.

7. REFERENCES

[1] Leslie, L., Chua, T-S. and Jain, R. (2007). Annotation of Paintings with High-level Semantic Concepts using Transductive Inference and Ontology-based Concept Disambiguation. MM '07 Sep 23-28, Augsburg, Germany.

[2] Levesque, V. and Hayward, V. (2008). Tactile graphics rendering using three laterotactile drawing primitives. Proceedings of the 16th Haptics Symposium, March 13-14, Reno, Nevada, 429-436.

[3] Garcia-Hernandez, N., Tsagarakis, N., Sarakoglou, I. and Caldwell, D. (2010). Psychophysical evaluation of a low density and portable tactile device displaying small-scale surface features. Eurohaptics, 50-57.

[4] Headley, P. and Pawluk, D. (2010). A Low-cost, Variable-amplitude Haptic Distributed Display for Persons who are Blind and Visually Impaired. ASSETS '10, Orlando, Florida.

[5] Ho, H-N and Jones, L. (2007). Development and Evaluation of a Thermal Display for Material Identification and Discrimination. ACM Trans. on Applied Presentation, 4(2).

[6] Yang, G-H., Kim, S-C, Kwon, D-S and Kang, S-C (2007). Compact Tactile Display for Fingertips with Multiple Vibrotactile Actuator and Thermoelectric Module. IEEE Intl. Conference on Robotics and Automation, Roma, Italy, 1-14 April, 491-496.

Access Lecture: A Mobile Application Providing Visual Access to Classroom Material

Stephanie Ludi, Alex Canter, Lindsey Ellis, and Abhishek Shrestha
Rochester Institute of Technology
Dept. of Software Engineering
Rochester, NY USA
+1 585.475.7407

salvse@rit.edu, ajc2760@rit.edu, lle6138@rit.edu, axs1430@rit.edu

ABSTRACT

Following along with course lecture material is a critical challenge for low vision students. Access Lecture is a mobile, touch-screen application that will aid low vision students in viewing class notes in real-time. This paper presents the system overview, features, and initial feedback on the system. Current status and next steps are also presented.

Categories and Subject Descriptors

K.4.2 **[Computers and Education]** - Social Issues – assistive technologies for persons with disabilities, K.3.2 **[Computers and Education]** - Computer and Information Science Education – computer science education.

General Terms: Design, Human Factors

Keywords

Mobile systems, visual impairment, programming, tablet.

1. INTRODUCTION

The inability to view the whiteboard while an instructor explains the written material puts low vision students at a severe disadvantage. This problem is amplified in math and science courses, as real-time example-problems and diagrams are frequently used. Access Lecture aims to provide a solution to this problem through the use of wireless, real-time capture and annotation on a mobile device.

Throughout the project the attributes of portability, accessibility and discretion remain goals. Common approaches such as the SMART Board [5] is an example of a pre-existing system that does not provide portability. The system requires a full-sized electronic whiteboard device to function, making it only practical for a single room. Discretion is also considered a key factor as many students would prefer to use a system that would not single them out or draw negative attention to them.

2. PROJECT SUMMARY

Access Lecture is a mobile, touch-screen application which aims to aid low vision students in viewing class notes in real-time. For the proof-of-concept system, the instructor uses the Mimio system to write on the whiteboard. Special sleeves envelope the markers and are placed on the eraser, enabling the instructor to write naturally. Mimio Capture bar (affixed magnetically) uses infrared and ultrasonic sensors to sense where the pens are and transmit the pen/eraser strokes wirelessly to the receiving computer in real time (< 1s latency). For the prototype the computer is capturing the content, but eventually a more ubiquitous approach will be used.

The student's iPad app connects to the computer and requests the lecture stream, which is saved locally to the iPad, enabling the user to zoom in/out with either multitouch (pinching) or icons, adjust contrast, and take notes on the ongoing lecture (which can be saved). The student navigates the whiteboard by moving the area being focused on with a finger. Notes can be written digitally, with a keyboard or with a stylus. Additional preferences can be set for note taking colors, thickness, along with zoom speed. The Access Lecture app is implemented in Objective C. Initial surveys of visually impaired college students provided feedback on the breadth of customizations needed in addition to the likelihood of the use of the a system.

The Apple iPad was selected because of its generous 10-inch screen size, native touch/gesture support, accessibility features, and portability. The iPad is a mainstream device that can also be used for other purposes, and many feel more comfortable using one as assistive technology [2].

The Mimio was selected for the proof-of-concept means of capturing written material due to its portability and low cost. In addition, the capture of the strokes in the marker/eraser requires less bandwidth than capturing the entire whiteboard at once (as a camera would do). Such stroke-based capture also mitigates issues with glare, position of the teacher or accommodating obstacles which can impact capture of material with a camera.

3. REQUIREMENTS GATHERING

To establish the fundamental system requirements instructors and low vision students, representing the university and secondary school levels, were contacted. Interviews were conducted with 10 instructors from varying stages of education in the subject areas of math, science, and programming. Online surveys were conducted with 11 low vision university students from 3 US universities, representing diversity in visual acuity and program of study.

Instructors and students made it clear that viewing the course material in real-time, is critical. All but two of the students reported that they have had difficulty viewing whiteboard notes.

Survey respondents noted concerns about currently used assistive technologies taking up space, portability, standing out in class, or a lack of accessibility features. They also noted desired features such as saving lectures, recording audio, being able to take notes with the system, and the ability to make color adjustments.

Features were then designed that can be customized for the user's needs. For example, the use of multi touch (pinching) to zoom in and out offers a fine-grained level of adjustment that can be executed quickly. Otherwise, zoom in and out icons can be used that adjust zooming in increments. Icons for tasks such as saving notes, zooming in or out, or to go in or out of the note taking mode are large and simple, facilitating identification. Note taking required multiple rounds of usability testing. The icons were also tested with users for ease of identification.

4. USABILITY TESTING

After the real time presentation of the lecture material was validated technically and initial feedback by two visually impaired stakeholders was considered, the team wanted to ensure that Access Lecture app's user interface is visually accessible and the tasks of following a short lecture and taking notes on the lecture can be completed with user satisfaction.

During the initial round of testing, nine university students with uncorrected vision that is considered to be low vision provided feedback. Ten more students from the same population provided feedback after revisions were completed from the initial set of feedback. In both cases, a pre-survey gathered background information (e.g. visual acuity, use of accessibility features, use of mobile devices) while a post-survey focused on user preferences regarding the icons and tasks. During each user session, the participants were asked to complete a set of tasks while a member of the team served the role of instructor, providing a short (5 min.) talk on a science topic and a math problem. The app also captured the participant's notes.

4.1 Methodology

Each test session was divided into three parts. The initial survey gathered general user information and recorded their level of exposure to smart phones and iOS devices. For the hands-on portion of the test, two different versions of the prototype were used. Each version had a different method of zooming and a different set of icons. For each version, the users were asked to perform a fixed set of tasks (identifying the different icons and their purpose, feature navigation, content zooming, and typing notes with both a virtual and physical keyboard). Afterwards, a post survey was conducted to capture the user's experience with different usability aspects of the application and preferences.

4.2 Results

The usability testing helped refine the app's user interface. During the first round of testing, 75% of users found that the pinching method for zooming was considered to be the best gesture for magnification. Regardless of either the physical or virtual keyboard, all participants were unsatisfied with the note taking aspect of the application and wanted to directly annotate the lecture notes (especially given the need to capture formulae). As a result of the first round of feedback, the save and note taking icons were further simplified and the ability to directly draw notes on a live lecture was added. Options to adjust zooming speed and transparency of the tool bar were added to increase lecture real estate. The second round of testing affirmed the value of pinching for zooming, and all users found the revised icon set clear, easy to select and identifiable. Nine out of ten participants said they

could zoom in enough to read the lecture material for both the written text and diagrams. Four out of ten found the zooming buttons useful, including the double-tap shortcut to zoom out to hasten moving around the whiteboard. All participants would want to use it for notes and liked the option to use their finger or a stylus to take notes, and most liked the ability to write on the ongoing lecture. However, none of the participants liked how Access Lecture facilitated note taking. For example, the eraser icon was not clear enough and over time, the teacher's writing clashes with the notes (thus needed a way to manage the notes so that they are triggered on screen or available temporally while being visually differentiated from the instructor's writing.

5. FUTURE DEVELOPMENT

Additional refinement and testing is still needed. While the basic features and settings have been implemented, there are more that can be added or refined. The note taking features still needs refinement. A confirmation of saving notes has been added, as has clearer "wipe" transition between the note taking and lecture mode. New features will be color mapping for the marker strokes in the live lecture presentation, better storage for the lectures over time, time shifting for recordings, and the audio recording of the lecture. The application also needs further testing in a classroom.

The other major area where development is still needed is refinement of the capture hardware. Currently the Mimio system is being used, but ultimately specialized hardware for Access Lecture will be developed to support blackboards and the capture of projected material, as many pre-college classrooms still use blackboards.

6. ACKNOWLEDGEMENTS

Thank you to the CRA for their support and our participants.

7. REFERENCES

[1] Dymo Mimio, 2011. Mimio Interactive Teaching Technologies. http://www.mimio.dymo.com

[2] Hager, E. 2010. 1-10. IPad Opens World to a Disabled Boy. The New York Times.

[3] Hayden, D., Colbry, D., Black, J., and Panchanathan, S. 2008. Note-taker: enabling students who are legally blind to take notes in class. In *Proceedings of the 10th international ACM SIGACCESS conference on Computers and accessibility* (Halifax, Nova Scotia, October 12-15, 2008). Assets '08. ACM, New York, NY, USA, 81-88.

[4] Kane, S., Jayant, C., Wobbrock, J., and Ladner, R. 2009. Freedom to roam: a study of mobile device adoption and accessibility for people with visual and motor disabilities. In *Proceedings of the 11th international ACM SIGACCESS conference on Computers and accessibility* (Pittsburgh, PA, USA, October 26-28, 2009). Assets '09. ACM, New York, NY, USA, 115-122.

[5] Smart Technologies, 2011. Home- SMART Technologies. http://smarttech.com

An Integrated System for Blind Day-to-Day Life Autonomy

Hugo Fernandes
UTAD, Portugal
hugof@utad.pt

José Faria
UTAD, Portugal
jfaria@utad.pt

Hugo Paredes
GECAD/UTAD, Portugal
hparedes@utad.pt

João Barroso
GECAD/UTAD, Portugal
jbarroso@utad.pt

ABSTRACT

The autonomy of blind people in their daily life depends on their knowledge of the surrounding world, and they are aided by keen senses and assistive devices that help them to deduce their surroundings. Existing solutions require that users carry a wide range of devices and, mostly, do not include mechanisms to ensure the autonomy of users in the event of system failure. This paper presents the nav4b system that combines guidance and navigation with object's recognition, extending traditional aids (white cane and smartphone). A working prototype was installed on the UTAD campus to perform experiments with blind users.

Categories and Subject Descriptors

H.5.2 [**Information Interfaces and Presentation**]: User Interfaces—*Interaction styles*; K.4.2 [**Computers and Society**]: Social Issues—*Assistive technologies for persons with disabilities*

General Terms

Human Factors

Keywords

Mobile technology, assistive technology, blindness.

1. INTRODUCTION

Autonomy can be defined as a *"capacity for detachment, critical reflection, decision making and independent action"* [5]. For making decisions and performing actions, people need to have knowledge about the environment, usually gathered with natural senses. Blind people lack a major surrounding knowledge gatherer: vision. To equalize this shortcoming, blind people developed their other senses, particularly hearing, to create mental models of the environment. Moreover, they attend to known places and usually study the routes previously before moving. Regarding day to day objects, they know their typical location in order to ensure their autonomy. Technology can be used to help blind people in their day-to-day life. Examples of these technologies are: navigation systems, mostly based on GPS and restricted to outdoor usage; audio signage systems, that are limited concerning the availability of information and location accuracy;

and the talking labeling system, which requires a specific device for locating objects and does not associate objects to their locations and day-to-day activities.

This paper presents the nav4b system, a technological solution to support the day-to-day life of the blind users. The infrastructure of the system is based on electronic trails and tags, complemented by non-technological solutions to ensure system redundancy and user autonomy in case of system failure. On the core of the infrastructure is the Radio Frequency IDentification (RFID) technology, which is the common technology base of the system. From the blind user's perspective, the system design takes into account ergonomics and ubiquity, using typical blind aids: a white cane, which is instrumented to accommodate the necessary components for interfacing with the infrastructure; a smartphone, hosting the software application that enables the system operation; and bone-conduction headphones, to ensure the transmission of information to the user without hearing interference. A prototype was installed on UTAD campus to perform tests and experiments with blind users.

2. BACKGROUND

In the last decade several projects have emerged aiming to use of RFID technology for the navigation of the blind. The BIGS System, proposed Na[6], includes an infrastructure, the smart floor, and a portable terminal unit. A more complex system was presented by Ding [2] consisting of RFID tags, a portable reader which can be integrated into the white cane, a mobile phone, a Call Center and a central information server. Recently, Chen [1] proposed the inclusion of pre-built RFID tags in blind pathways. Moreover, the SmartVision project aims to develop a system for assisting the blind navigate autonomously, integrating GPS, Wi-Fi, RFID and computer vision technology [3]. In a complementary perspective, the TANIA system, which was originally developed to provide the blind with a navigation device, was extended with an RFID reader or the recognition of tagged objects [7]. The integration of navigation and object recognition was previously explored by Hub et. al[4].

3. NAV4B ARCHITECTURE

To create an integrated system that ensures day-to-day life autonomy of blind people there are a set of requirements that should be taken into account. One of the main requirements of the system regards the recognition of the environment and the surrounding objects that the blind needs in his daily routine, such as a bottle of milk or a box of medicines. The system should be able to distinguish similar objects in order to give accurate information to the user. Usually objects are placed on a specific spot and do not move. So, if the system has the ability to associate an object to a location, navigation can be provided. Ergo, guidance and navigation are also key requirements. This feature must ensure the ability to guide the blind on a route with accurate information about the environment, including points of interest and interactive objects, such us traffic lights. However, the user should not be overloaded with audio messages which may interfere with his perception of the environment. A last requirement regards the robustness and redundancy of the system, so that in case of technological failure, a minimum level of autonomy can be ensured.

Based on the presented requirements an architecture was developed with two major building blocks: infrastructure and user equipment (Figure 1). Regarding the infrastructure,

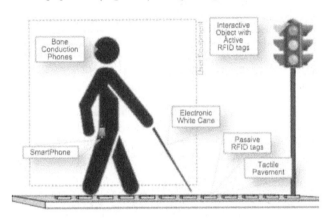

Figure 1: nav4b system architecture

the architecture endows traditional blind aids with passive RFID tags, creating electronic paths in the tactile pavement and electronic identifiers on tagged objects. Additionally, interactive objects can be equipped with active RFID technology to interact with the system. The user equipment consists of three elements that nowadays are typically used by blind people: white cane, SmartPhone and headsets. The white cane is instrumented with: an RFID reader and two antennas, a bluetooth communication module, a control module, a vibration module and power supply (Figure 2). The handgrip of the cane also includes a joystick to control the application installed on the SmartPhone. This application, implemented in the Android platform, is the functional core of the system, receiving information from the RFID readers on the cane. The application implements algorithms to plot routes using a set of maps of the areas housing the infrastructure. The data layer of the application is ensured by a geo-referenced database and connectors to external data sources, such as the SmartPhone agenda. The information

Figure 2: Electronic white cane model

tracking the route is usually transmitted by vibration on the handgrip of the cane. This information can be complemented by audio information for path correction or points of interest, via bone conduction headphones, ensuring the full hearing of the user without restrictions.

4. FINAL REMARKS

The progresses that have been made recently in technology allowed the creation of a system prototype using a common platform based on RFID technology providing autonomy to the blind. However there are some refinements that should be made in the prototype implementation regarding some particular issues on the range of RFID readers. Concerning future developments of the system we expect to carry out experiments with blind users to enhance and refine the prototype, as well as setting guidelines for tag placement, taking into consideration current standards and guidelines for tactile pavement installation.

5. ACKNOWLEDGMENTS

This research was supported by the Portuguese Foundation for Science and Technology (FCT), through the project RIPD/ADA/109690/2009 – BLAVIGATOR: a cheap and reliable navigation aid for the blind.

6. REFERENCES

[1] J. Chen, Z. Li, M. Dong, and X. Wang. Blind path identification system design base on rfid. In *Electrical and Control Engineering (ICECE), 2010 International Conference on*, pages 548 –551, june 2010.

[2] B. Ding, H. Yuan, X. Zang, and L. Jiang. The research on blind navigation system based on rfid. In *Wireless Communications, Networking and Mobile Computing, 2007. WiCom 2007. International Conference on*, pages 2058–2061, 2007.

[3] J. H. du Buf, J. Barroso, J. M. Rodrigues, H. Paredes, M. Farrajota, H. Fernandes, J. JosÃl', V. Teixeira, and M. Saleiro. The smartvision navigation prototype for blind users. *JDCTA*, 5(5):351–361, 2011.

[4] A. Hub, J. Diepstraten, and T. Ertl. Design and development of an indoor navigation and object identification system for the blind. In *Proceedings of the 6th international ACM SIGACCESS conference on Computers and accessibility*, Assets '04, pages 147–152, New York, NY, USA, 2004. ACM.

[5] D. Little. *Learner Autonomy: Definitions, Issues and Problems*, volume 1. Authentik Language Learning Resources Ltd, Dublin, Ireland, 1991.

[6] J. Na. The blind interactive guide system using rfid-based indoor positioning system. In K. Miesenberger, J. Klaus, W. Zagler, and A. Karshmer, editors, *Computers Helping People with Special Needs*, volume 4061 of *Lecture Notes in Computer Science*, pages 1298–1305. Springer Berlin / Heidelberg, 2006. 10.1007/11788713 187.

[7] B. Schmitz and A. Hub. *Combination of the Navigation System TANIA with RFID-Based Initialization and Object Recognition*, page 2. 2009.

Audio Haptic Videogaming for Navigation Skills in Learners Who are Blind

Jaime Sánchez
Department of Computer Science and Center
for Advanced Research in Education (CARE),
University of Chile
Blanco Encalada 2120, Santiago, Chile

jsanchez@dcc.uchile.cl

Matías Espinoza
Department of Computer Science and Center
for Advanced Research in Education (CARE),
University of Chile
Blanco Encalada 2120, Santiago, Chile

maespino@dcc.uchile.cl

ABSTRACT

The purpose of this study was to determine whether the use of audio and a haptic-based videogame has an impact on the development of Orientation and Mobility (O&M) skills in school-age blind learners. The video game Audio Haptic Maze (AHM) was designed, developed and its usability and cognitive impact was evaluated to determine the impact on the development of O&M skills. The results show that the interfaces used in the videogame are usable and appropiately designed, and that the haptic interface is as effective as the audio interface for O&M purposes.

Categories and Subject Descriptors

K.4.2 [**Computers and Society**]: Social Issues – *Assistive technologies for persons with disabilities, Handicapped persons/special needs.*

General Terms

Human Factors.

Keywords

Haptic and Audio Interfaces, Orientation, Mobility, People Who Are Blind.

1. INTRODUCTION

For people who are blind, navigation through unfamiliar spaces can be a complex task compared to a sighted person. In order to achieve orientation & mobility (O&M), people who are blind need to use other resources to receive feedback from the environment, such as sounds or textures (haptic feedback). Various virtual environments have been designed in order to train people who are blind, and to assist them with the development of O&M skills [1][2][3].

The purpose of this study was to determine whether the use of an audio and haptic-based videogame has an impact on the development of O&M skills in school-age learners who are blind. A video game untitled Audio Haptic Maze (AHM) was developed from previous video game design experiences [2][3]. AHM was designed to be used by school-age learners who are blind either autonomously or with the supervision of a facilitator in contexts of research and practice. Initially, we evaluated the usability of

AHM to determine how well it maps the mental model of users who are blind. Then, we evaluated the cognitive impact of using AHM on the development of O&M skills.

AHM allows a school-age blind learner to be able to navigate through a series of mazes from a first-person perspective, obtaining feedback from the game through the use of three kinds of interfaces: haptic, audio and haptic plus audio. In order to escape from a maze, the player must find jewelry boxes spread throughout several corridors and rooms, which contain keys and treasures. The interaction with AHM is carried out through the use of a standard computer keyboard. In the case of the audio-based interface, all of the user's immersion is achieved through the use of stereo sound. In the case of the haptic-based interface, the Novint Falcon device was used for haptic feedback, which works as a three dimensional pointer that allows for an interaction with 3D volumes and generating force feedback.

2. USABILITY EVALUATION

A second set of usability evaluations of AHM was implemented. An initial usability evaluation was previously implemented during the development of the videogame [3]. A sample consisting of 10 school-age learners who are blind with ages ranging from 9 to 17 years old was selected. None of these research participants have any additional associated disabilities other than visual impairment. All the users' prophile fitted the the target user of AHM.

Software Usability Elements (SUE) questionnaire allowed to quantify the degree to which the sounds and haptic feedback used in the videogame were recognizable.

The Open Question Usability (OQU) questionnaire allowed to collect knowledge regarding aspects related to O&M that represent the focus of the AHM videogame, as well as regarding the use of the controls, the information provided by the software, and the user's navigation in the virtual environment.

In general, the videogame was well accepted by end-users. One relevant aspect regarding the use of the audio-based interface was the user comments mentioning that the interaction experience was very enriching, but not necessarily because of the capacity to convey information from the virtual environment to the user; rather users noted that, in part, the sound provided by AHM helped to generate a context and environment that is more associated with what they would expect from a videogame.

Once the corrections and redesign of the software had been carried out considering the results obtained from the administration of the SUE and OQU questionnaires, Sánchez's Software Usability for Blind Children (SUBC) questionnaire [4]

was administered. This questionnaire allowed to perform an evaluation of the software's usability according to the user's satisfaction. In order to perform the evaluation, the three kinds of interfaces involved in the videogame were analyzed: haptic, audio and haptic plus audio.

The results show that the mean level of the dimension "users' satisfaction" was 7.0, 8.5 and 7.1 points respectively for each kind of interface, on a scale with a maximum of 10 points. Regarding the dimension "Control and Use" the mean scores were 6.7, 7.5 and 7.8 points respectively, using the same score scale. The mean level of the "Audio" dimension was 10 and 7.7 points respectively for audio and haptic plus audio interface (the haptic interface did not apply for this dimension). And finally, the mean level of the "Haptic" dimension was 9.0 and 7.7 points respectively for haptic and haptic plus audio interface (the audio interface did not apply for this dimension).

3. COGNITIVE IMPACT

A second set of cognitive impact evaluations of AHM was performed. A pilot first evaluation for the ongoing study was introduced in [3]. An intentional sample was made up of 7 school-age learners who are blind (3 females, 4 males), all from Santiago, Chile, belonging to the Santa Lucia School for the Blind. These learners were not the same of those that participated in the usability evaluation. The requirements to participate were: Be between 10 and 15 years of age; present total blindness; be enrolled between third and eighth grade. These requirements fitted the user prophile that targeted AHM.

A cognitive impact evaluation instrument was applied individually to each user during the pretest and posttest. In between a cognitive intervention was implemented to determine whether the use of the videogame has impacted the development of O&M skills. This instrument was designed and validated by special education teachers who are specialists in visual disabilities. For this purpose two O&M skills checklists were created for two sample groups: a checklist was adapted to the O&M skills of users between 10 and 12 years of age (4 users from the sample) and a second checklist was adapted to the O&M skills of users between 13 and 15 years of age (3 users from the sample).

The results obtained from the evaluation of the two sample groups showed an increment in the pretest/posttest performance mean scores in all dimensions covered by the checklists: Sensory perception, tempo-spatial development, and O&M skills.

The results of the dimensions for the 10-12 year old age sample group were: "Sensory perception" (scale ranging from 0 to 72 points, pretest mean = 65.75, posttest mean = 70.75), "Tempo-spatial development" (scale ranging from 0 to 34 points, pretest mean = 24.45, posttest mean = 28.75) and "O&M skills" (scale ranging from 0 to 52 points, pretest mean = 32.31, posttest mean = 48.75). A student-t test was applied. The "O&M skills" dimension was statistically significant ($t = -4,323$; $p < 0.05$).

The results of the dimensions for the 13-15 year old age sample group were: "Sensory perception" (scale ranging from 0 to 68 points, pretest mean = 59.00, posttest mean = 68.00), "Tempo-spatial development" (scale ranging from 0 to 34 points, pretest mean = 33.33 points, posttest = 34.00), "O&M skills" (scale ranging from 0 to 44 points, pretest mean = 34.00 points, posttest

mean = 43.76). A student-t test was applied. The "Sensory perception" dimension was statistically significant ($t = -5,197$; $p < 0.05$).

4. CONCLUSIONS

The purpose of this study was to determine whether the use of an audio and haptic-based videogame has an impact on the development of O&M skills in school-age learners who are blind. For this reason, first, the AHM videogame was designed and developed. Second, the usability of AHM was evaluated to establish how well it maps the mental model of users who are blind. Third, the cognitive impact of the videogame in terms of the development of O&M skills was determined.

Regarding the usability, both the haptic and the audio-based interfaces were effective to provide adequate feedback to the user within the virtual environment. The use of the haptic and audio interfaces together allows the blind user who is navigating the videogame's virtual environment to be able to form a better perception of distances, shapes and the orientation of the objects on the map when updating his position. Due to this fact, the users could navigate through all of the areas that make up the maze, making intelligent decisions regarding what direction to follow in order to go from point A to point B thanks to the information provided.

Regarding the cognitive impact, the results of this study show that all the audio and haptic icons were useful for establishing navigational paths in the virtual environment. The users developed their orientation and mobility skills as a result of their interaction with the AHM videogame which is directly related to the efficiency of the user's movements when navigating within the videogame's virtual environment.

Finally, as a future work, more in-deph long-term study evaluations involving a large sample to obtain more deep and complete results in all dimentions studied.

5. ACKNOWLEDGMENTS

This report was funded by the Chilean National Fund of Science and Technology, Fondecyt #1090352 and Project CIE-05 Program Center Education PBCT-Conicyt.

6. REFERENCES

[1] Lahav, O. and Mioduser, D. (2008). Haptic-feedback support for cognitive mapping of unknown spaces by people who are blind. Int. J. Hum.-Comput. Stud. 66, 1 (Jan. 2008), 23-35.

[2] Sánchez J., Tadres A., Pascual-Leone A., and Merabet L., (2009) Blind children navigation through gaming and associated brain plasticity, in Virtual Rehabilitation International Conference, pp. 29-36.

[3] Sánchez, J., & Tadres, A. (2010) Audio and haptic based virtual environments for orientation and mobility in people who are blind. The 12th International ACM SIGACCESS Conference on Computers and Accessibility, ASSETS 2010. USA, Orlando (FL), October 25-27, 2010, pp. 237-238.

[4] Sánchez, J., (2003) Software Usability for Blind Children Questionnaire (SUBC), Usability evaluation test, University of Chile, 2003.

Automatic Sign Categorization using Visual Data

Marek Hrúz

Department of Cybernetics, Faculty of Applied Sciences, University of West Bohemia
Univerzitni 8, Pilsen 306 14, Czech Republic
mhruz@kky.zcu.cz

ABSTRACT

This paper presents a method of visual tracking in recordings of isolated signs and the usage of the tracked features for automatic sign categorization. The tracking method is based on skin color segmentation and is suitable for recordings of a sign language dictionary. The result of the tracking is the location and outer contour of head and both hands. These features are used to categorize the signs into several categories: movement of hands, contact of body parts, symmetry of trajectory, location of the sign.

Categories and Subject Descriptors

I.2.10 [**Computing Methodologies**]: Vision and Scene Understanding—*Video analysis*

General Terms

EXPERIMENTATION, LANGUAGES

Keywords

sign language, visual tracking, sign categorization

1. INTRODUCTION

There is a lot of sign language corpora that exist for linguistic purposes (for example [1, 2]). The corpora usually consist of video recordings from one ore more cameras in various environments. It is common that these data are provided with additional information in the form of annotation. These annotations describe the performed signs from a linguistic point of view and are created by an expert. The annotations can be biased because of different perception of different annotators. On the other hand there are computer vision techniques that can analyze video sequences automatically. These methods provide features that can be used to describe the movements and other phenomena for subsequent recognition of signs [4]. The advantage is that the algorithms are deterministic (there is only one result for one video) but can fail. In this paper we address two issues: finding a robust method for visual tracking in defined conditions and using the results to categorize the signs.

Figure 1: Example of considered data and tracking result.

2. DATASET

It is very hard to design a system of visual tracking in general environments for general purposes. The existing tracking methods have problems with occlusions, clutter and mimicking. The system has to be modified to work in a limited environment or under defined conditions.

Our dataset consists of recordings of sign language in the form of isolated signs. Furthermore, these recordings are designed for on-line dictionary. This delimits the conditions to: *constant lightning conditions, uniform background, long sleeves, low number of interpreters, starting and ending pose are defined.* An example from the dataset is shown in Figure 1. These conditions allow us to use relatively simple methods of image segmentation and tracking.

3. VISUAL TRACKING

The tracking process is based on skin-color image segmentation, object detection and their scalar description used in discriminative measurements. In every video frame a set of objects is detected using a skin-color look-up-table. For now the look-up-table is of size 128 by 128 by 128 defined in RGB color space. For every 2 by 2 by 2 cluster of 8 colors a likelihood is defined which represents the likelihood of the given color to be skin. The look-up-table was trained from various examples of skin-color. These examples were used for the training of a Gaussian Mixture Model using Expectation Maximization algorithm. After skin-color segmentation is performed the objects (connected components) are detected and filtered to refuse improbably large or small

Table 1: The sign categories chosen for the experiment.

Hand movement	Body contact	Hand location
one handed	no contact	at waist
two handed	contact of head and right hand	at chest
symmetric	contact of head and left hand	at head
non-symmetric	contact of hands	above head
	contact of everything	

objects. In the first frame the objects are identified as individual body parts according to the known starting position. In the next frame, every object is described by a set of scalar features and compared to the last known features. The comparison involves computing the absolute difference of the scalar features, performing template matching and contour matching. Then we evaluate the probability of a feature vector constructed from the differences and measurements. For further details read [3]. The tracking process is actually identification of unknown objects. There are lot of features that can be extracted from the objects. In our experiments we use the trajectory and information about occlusion of objects.

4. SIGN CATEGORIZATION

The categorization of signs can be used for various purposes. Our main goal is to describe the video recordings published in an on-line sign language dictionary with general terms rather then numeral features. These terms or categories can be used to find a particular sign when the user does not know the translation into the natural (spoken) language but remembers into which category it belongs. For now we consider the categories summarized in Table 1. To determine the category of a sign we make use of the features from the tracking process. Consider a vector of 2D positions of one body part. Lets call the vector a trajectory. Then the sum of variance of x and y components of the trajectory determines whether the sign is one handed or two handed. If the variance is sufficient enough it means the hand has moved. To determine the symmetry of the trajectory we compute the sum of absolute values of Pearsons correlation coefficients for x and y positions of both hands. If the trajectories are correlated enough (better than 0.89 each dimension) we claim the sign trajectories are symmetric. The absolute value of the correlation coefficient reflexes the anti-symmetry that occurs in symmetric signs. The location of hand symbolizes what space relative to the location of the head has the hand occupied the most. We compute a histogram of relative y positions of hands consisting of 5 bins. The bins are chosen so that they correlate with the categories. Then the category connected to the most occupied bin is chosen. This approach can fail if the sign duration is relatively small to the video duration. That is why we consider only the segment of the video where the hands are moving and are out of starting position. The last category is contact of the body parts. For now we can only tell when more objects merge into one. This means that the objects occlude each other relative to the camera or touch each other. This is a necessary condition for the body parts contact, but not sufficient because occlusion does not imply contact. Further experiments are needed. The merging of

objects occurs when two trackers identify the same object as the tracked one.

In practice there are two applications that are needed to determine the category. First program tracks the body parts in a video. We support most formats of video that can be decoded by OpenCV. OpenCV is used for all image processing routines and I/O routines. The features are stored in a file or standard output stream which becomes the input for the second program. This program analyses the features and resolves the category of the sign. It is important to mention that the tracking process can fail. In our experiments 95% of video recordings (out of 560) were tracked correctly. The analysis of the results of categorization is a very difficult process. The difficulty lies in the fact that only experts can confirm the correctness of the categorization. But since we analyze video files we can only categorize the actual performed sign in the video. The sign itself can behave in a way that some category is not important and can be different in different performances of the same sign.

5. CONCLUSION

We have presented an approach for automatic sign categorization. It consists of two parts. First part is to track individual body parts in a video recording from a sign language dictionary. Such data need to have the background distinguishable from the foreground by color. We have achieved 95% success rate. The second part is to analyze the features provided by the tracking process and decide into which category the performed sign falls. This categorization enables one form of sign searching. These categories are not linguistic categories but rather intuitive categories that can differentiate signs from one another. In the future more sophisticated categories can be proposed when we take the shape of the hands into account. These categories need to be consulted with sign language linguists.

6. ACKNOWLEDGMENTS

This research was supported by the EU and the Ministry of Education of the Czech Republic, project No. CZ.1.07/2.2.00 /07.0189 and by the Ministry of Education of the Czech Republic, project No. ME08106.

7. REFERENCES

[1] P. Campr, M. Hrúz, and M. Železný. Design and recording of czech sign language corpus for automatic sign language recognition. *Proc. of Interspeech 2007*, pages 678–681, 2007.

[2] O. Crasborn and I. Zwitserlood. The corpus ngt: an online corpus for professionals and laymen. *Proceedings of the sixth Conference on Language Resources and Evaluation (LREC 2008)*, pages 44–49, 2008.

[3] M. Hrúz, Z. Krňoul, P. Campr, and L. Müller. Towards automatic annotation of sign language dictionary corpora. *Lecture Notes in Artificial Intelligence*, LNAI 6836, in press, 2011.

[4] J. Trmal, M. Hrúz, J. Zelinka, P. Campr, and L. Müller. Feature space transforms for czech sign-language recognition. In *In ICSLP*, 2008.

Click Control: Improving Mouse Interaction for People with Motor Impairments

Christopher Kwan, Isaac Paquette, John J. Magee, Paul Y. Lee, Margrit Betke
Image and Video Computing Group
Department of Computer Science, Boston University
111 Cummington Street, Boston, MA 02215 USA
{ckwan, paquette, mageejo, luc2pl, betke}@cs.bu.edu

ABSTRACT

Camera-based mouse-replacement systems allow people with motor impairments to control the mouse pointer with head movements if they are unable to use their hands. To address the difficulties of accidental clicking and usable simulation of a real computer mouse, we developed Click Control, a tool to augment the functionality of these systems. When a user attempts to click, Click Control displays a form that allows him or her to cancel the click if it was accidental, or send different types of clicks with an easy-to-use gesture interface. Initial studies of a prototype with users with motor impairments showed that Click Control improved their mouse control experiences.

Categories and Subject Descriptors

K.4.2 [**Computers and Society**]: Social Issues—*assistive technologies for persons with disabilities*; H.1.2 [**Models and Principles**]: User/Machine Systems—*human factors*; H.5.2 [**Information Interfaces and Presentation**]: User Interfaces—*input devices and strategies*

General Terms

Human Factors

Keywords

Accessibility, assistive technology, Camera Mouse, human computer interaction, mouse gestures, mouse-replacement system, video-based interface

1. INTRODUCTION

For users with motor impairments who cannot use their hands to operate a computer mouse, camera-based mouse-replacement systems, e.g. [1, 2, 3, 4], have been developed to allow control of the mouse pointer with head movements.

One difficulty in using these systems is accidental clicking. If a user is not attentive to whether or not the system is in a clicking-state, e.g. because his or her attention is elsewhere or because there is insufficient feedback, items may be selected unintentionally (especially in systems that require a user to keep the mouse pointer still for a period of time to simulate a click). A lack of precision in using the system,

e.g. due to tracking limitations or movement abilities, may also cause a user to select wrong neighboring targets.

Difficulties can also arise when using these systems to simulate the capabilities of a real computer mouse, e.g. left and right-clicking, double-clicking and dragging. For this functionality, some systems impose additional requirements on a user's movement abilities, e.g. certain movements with the nose [2] or winking with both eyes [3]. Also, when using the Camera Mouse [1] with tools[1] for additional mouse functions or the system of Varona *et al.* [4], a user must first move the mouse pointer to an external window at a fixed location to select a command and then must move the mouse pointer back to the target to issue the command. This can be frustrating if a user sends the command to the wrong target (common in cluttered areas like the desktop) and tiring if he or she must repeatedly move the mouse pointer back and forth between the target and the command window.

To address these difficulties, we developed Click Control, a tool that augments the abilities of camera-based mouse-replacement systems. Click Control: (1) works with any system that allows control of mouse pointer movement, (2) provides visual feedback to notify a user before clicks will occur and allows him or her to dismiss unintentional clicks, and (3) simulates the commands of a real computer mouse using a gesture-based approach that does not impose requirements on a user's movement abilities.

2. CLICK CONTROL FEATURES & USAGE

A user launches Click Control as a separate application along with his or her mouse-replacement system (we used Camera Mouse [1]). Click Control waits in the background until the user tries to perform a mouse command. By default, Click Control is triggered by the MouseDown event sent by the mouse-replacement system to the operating system. However, this trigger could be changed to another binary switch, e.g. a keypress, voice command or physical input.

When the user triggers that they want to perform a mouse command, Click Control stores the current location of the mouse pointer and displays a gesture form (Fig. 1) near that location. The semi-transparent gesture form displays a crosshair to show the user exactly where the command will be sent and displays a set of buttons with which he or she can perform "gestures" to send different types of mouse commands. The form serves as an indicator that the system

---

[1]ClickAid (http://www.polital.com/ca), Point-N-Click (http://www.polital.com/pnc), Dwell Clicker (http://www.sensorysoftware.com/dwellclicker.html)

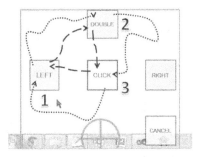

Figure 1: Double-clicking on the sunflower icon on the taskbar with the gesture form. Dashed and dotted lines show two different mouse trajectories.

is about to click, giving the user both visual feedback and the opportunity to cancel the action if it was unintended.

A "gesture" entails moving the mouse pointer over the buttons on the form in a certain order. E.g., a left-click is sent if the user touches the left then center buttons; a double-left-click is left, top, then center (Fig. 1). Once a valid gesture is recognized, the associated mouse command is sent to the previously stored mouse pointer location. If the click was accidental and the user does not wish to send any command, he or she can dismiss the gesture form or wait until it automatically disappears. We define "gestures" as touching targets rather than following a specific trajectory so as to not constrain the movements a user must be able to make. The gestures were designed to be easy to perform, requiring only the ability to move the mouse pointer and explicit in that they are unlikely to be performed unintentionally.

We implemented Click Control for Windows using the open source Global Mouse and Keyboard Library[2] to capture the `MouseDown` events that trigger the gesture form and to simulate mouse events after gestures are performed.

3. INITIAL USER STUDIES

We conducted a study of Click Control with C, a high school student with cerebral palsy. In previous sessions, C was able to use Camera Mouse along with the external tools for additional mouse functionality. However, C had difficulties knowing when the system was in a clicking-state and as a result would end up clicking on things unintentionally. Also, since it was difficult for C to make very precise movements with Camera Mouse, he would often accidentally send mouse commands to unintended targets in cluttered areas.

We introduced Click Control to C and he was able to understand its usage within a few minutes of experimenting. C was now notified by Click Control before Camera Mouse was about to click, so that he could react appropriately. When trying to click on targets in cluttered areas, C was able to quickly cancel clicks to unintended targets. C was also able to use the gesture form to send left and double-clicks to targets of various sizes. He was able to perform tasks that were previously difficult for him, such as opening files on the desktop and manipulating an online video.

C believed that Click Control improved his experience with Camera Mouse. He commented, "I am not struggling as much as before...now it feels like a real mouse."

[2]http://www.codeproject.com/KB/system/
globalmousekeyboardlib.aspx

We also worked with F, a speech language pathologist, to conduct a study with two middle school students with cerebral palsy. In previous studies, the students were able to use Camera Mouse to interact with several custom applications but were often interrupted by accidental clicks.

Click Control was able to alleviate the problem of accidental clicking. The gesture form would appear before the system was about to send a click, at which point the students dismissed the click if it was accidental. The students were also able to perform gestures to send left-clicks but often needed guidance from F.

The students were able to use Click Control but it may not have been intuitive to them. They seemed to understand F's analogy that it was like a teacher asking "Are you sure?" One student told us, "I liked it...I know what I'm doing but it's confusing." To make Click Control more usable to these students, F recommended using images with the gestures and creating a mode where users could confirm or cancel only left-clicks with simplified gestures.

4. ONGOING WORK

We plan to conduct user studies to see how Click Control affects interactions in the longer-term. We will take quantitative measurements of its usage, such as how its use affects the completion time and error rate of performing various mouse-based tasks. We also plan to verify its compatibility with other mouse-replacement systems and to add customization options for gestures. Click Control will be improved from feedback and eventually available for download.

5. ACKNOWLEDGMENTS

We thank the participants of our studies and also Robin Berghaus, Danna Gurari, Fletcher Hietpas, Tessa Skinner, and Ashwin Thangali. We also thank the reviewers for their insightful feedback. Funding was provided by the NSF (HCC grants IIS-0910908, IIS-0855065, and IIS-0713229).

6. REFERENCES

[1] M. Betke, J. Gips, and P. Fleming. The Camera Mouse: Visual tracking of body features to provide computer access for people with severe disabilities. *IEEE Transactions on Neural Systems and Rehabilitation Engineering*, 10(1):1–10, Mar. 2002.

[2] D. Gorodnichy, E. Dubrofsky, and A. A. Mohammad. Working with a computer hands-free using the Nouse Perceptual Vision Interface. In *Proceedings of the International Workshop on Video Processing and Recognition*, VideoRec'07. NRC, May 2007.

[3] E. Missimer and M. Betke. Blink and wink detection for mouse pointer control. In *Proceedings of the 3rd International Conference on PErvasive Technologies Related to Assistive Environments*, PETRA '10, pages 23:1–23:8, New York, NY, USA, 2010. ACM.

[4] J. Varona, C. Manresa-Yee, and F. J. Perales. Hands-free vision-based interface for computer accessibility. *J. Netw. Comput. Appl.*, 31:357–374, November 2008.

Design of a Bilateral Vibrotactile Feedback System for Lateralization

Bernd Tessendorf,
Daniel Roggen,
Michael Spuhler,
Thomas Stiefmeier,
Gerhard Tröster
Wearable Computing Lab,
ETH Zurich, Switzerland
{lastname}@ife.ee.ethz.ch

Tobias Grämer
Laboratory for
Experimental Audiology
University Hospital Zurich
Tobias.Graemer@usz.ch

Manuela Feilner,
Peter Derleth
Phonak AG
Stäfa, Switzerland
{firstname.lastname}@phonak.com

ABSTRACT

We present a bilateral vibrotactile feedback system for accurate lateralization of target angles in the complete 360°-range. We envision integrating this system into context-aware hearing instruments (HIs) or cochlear implants (CIs) to support users that experience lateralization difficulties. As a foundation for this it is vital to investigate which kind of feedback and vibration patterns are optimal to provide support for lateralization. Our system enables to evaluate and compare different encoding schemes with respect to resolution, reaction time, intuitiveness and user dependency. The system supports bilateral vibrotactile feedback to reflect integration into HIs or CIs worn at both ears and implemented two approaches: Quantized Absolute Heading (QAH) and Continuous Guidance Feedback (CGF). We provide a detailed description of our hardware that was designed to be also applicable for generic vibrotactile feedback applications.

Categories and Subject Descriptors

H.5.2 [**User Interfaces**]: Haptic I/O

General Terms

Design, Experimentation

1. INTRODUCTION

Hearing impairment increasingly affects populations worldwide. In developed countries about 10% of the adolescents experience hearing impairment and the tendency is growing [2]. Being able to localize a sound is an essential part of the human auditory perception and allows the listener to turn towards an interesting sound source to maximize intelligibility or to get quickly and safely out of harm's way. Lateralization is the localization of sound sources in the horizontal plane and is challenging for listeners with a strong asymmetric hearing loss, e.g. unilateral deaf, unilaterally implanted CI, and also for listeners with bilaterally implanted CIs. Fewer difficulties are observed for milder or more symmetric types of hearing impairment. However,

listeners with a central (high up in the auditory pathway) hearing loss can have substantial difficulties in localization abilities. Especially in noisy settings hearing impaired people cannot lateralize at all depending on the SNR and kind of hearing impairment. Additionally, the signal processing in HIs can cause distortion of the cues human lateralization relies on and, thus, lead to decreased lateralization performance. Since people with lateralization difficulties are often wearing HIs or CIs and these devices are in the course of becoming multimodal interaction interfaces, we are investigating ways to address the lateralization problem by an alternate feedback modality. In particular, bilateral vibrotactile feedback integrated into HIs or CIs can support the hearing impaired with lateralization or at least provide the side of the most prominent sound source around. In this paper we present a system that allows to investigate the possibilities and limitations of bilateral vibrotactile feedback for lateralization.

2. RELATED WORK

In [5] the authors present a device to be placed inside the ear channel to transduce sound intro vibration. In [3] research regarding tactile sensitivity at the head is presented. They found frequencies around 32 Hz to be optimal for perception and concluded that the part around the ears are one of the most sensitive head regions for vibrotactile stimulation. A pair of glasses enhanced with 4 vibrators and 3 microphones with the purpose to locate sound sources for visually and hearing impaired people is presented in [1]. The approach doesn't focus on integration into HIs but the user is required to wear special goggles. In [4] the authors use a vibrotactile waist belt to provide vibrotactile feedback at 8 locations to allow navigation in unfamiliar places for blind people.

3. VIBROTACTILE FEEDBACK SYSTEM

We chose shaft-less coin vibrators with a diameter of 10 mm from *Precision Microdrives* designed for vibrotactile feedback in handheld applications. To emulate the integration of bilateral vibrotactile feedback into HIs we chose to enhance a pair of glasses with the miniaturized vibration motors at each of the sidepieces. We use the pair of glasses just as an mounting mechanism with a good pressure point to the mastoid bone to effectively conduct vibrations. To power

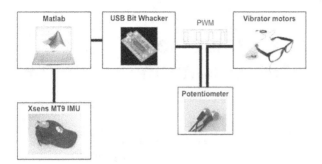

Figure 1: Block diagram of the bilateral vibrotactile feedback system for lateralization.

and drive the vibrators we use an *USB Bit Whacker* module combined with a motor driver module (TI ULN2803A). With potentiometers the supply voltage is adjusted. We control the hardware via the serial interface of a desktop computer and use pulse width modulation (PWM) to control the vibrator's intensity for different vibration patterns. The motors are connected with cables from off-the-shelf earphones. We attached an inertial measurement unit (Xsens MT9 IMU, angular accuracy $+\text{-}0.5°$) on a baseball cap to track the user's head yaw angle relative to the virtual target in the horizontal plane. With a common software framework we present the vibrotactile stimuli for the virtual target angle, retrieve user feedback from a GUI, control of the vibrators and head tracker and measure the user's response time and the resulting angular error. Figure 1 depicts the overall system.

4. BILATERAL VIBROTACTILE ENCODING OF LATERAL TARGET ANGLES

Quantized Absolute Heading Figure 2 depicts two example patterns implemented by our vibrotactile feedback system. For the first pattern we divided the lateral 360°-range into four base segments: front (red), left (green), right (purple) and back (black), each with a size of 90°. For each segment, the left (L) and right (R) motor are either on (1) or off (0). We encoded the back segment with a a double click (D) pattern consisting of an on-off-on-off sequence. The second example pattern represents a possible refinement of the preceding one and reduces the segment size to 45°.

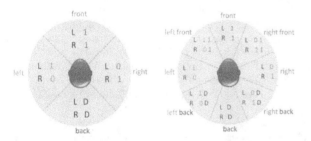

Figure 2: QAH: Two example patterns of different complexity and angular resolution.

Continuous Guidance Feedback Opposed to QAH that *informs* the user about the target location the continuous guidance feedback (CGF) *guides* the user with continuous vibrotactile feedback until the user has successfully turned the head to the target. We track the current angle to the target by measuring the user's head yaw angle with

an inertial measurement unit (IMU). In a HI application the current angle to the target can be calculated using sound localization, taking over the function of the head tracker. By vibrating on the corresponding side of the target, the system indicates the user to turn the head to the corresponding side of the target. The presented vibrotactile feedback is continuously updated based on the current angle to the target. The encoding is performed with two intensity levels as illustrated in Figure 3: If the target is near, meaning in the range of 20°, the vibration intensity is halved. The vibrotactile feedback stops when the user has moved the head to the target within a tolerance of 5°.

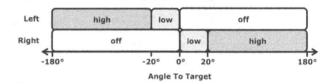

Figure 3: CGF: Continuous encoding of target angles based on the user's current angle to the target. 'Low' and 'high' stand for vibration at half and full intensity, respectively.

5. CONCLUSION AND OUTLOOK

As a foundation for integration of vibrotactile feedback into HIs or CIs our bilateral vibrotactile feedback system enables to evaluate and compare different encoding schemes with respect to resolution, reaction time, intuitiveness and user dependency. In addition to lateralization of sound sources vibrotactile feedback could extend HIs or CIs functionality with additional features, e.g. alerting the user in emergency situations and complement or substitute notification sounds of the state of the art sound-based HI user interfaces that indicate changing volume, low battery, alternative acoustic source, or incoming call.

In a planned study we will investigate combined acoustic and vibrotactile feedback to further evaluate the benefit of the system for hearing impaired listeners. We expect a high benefit especially in noisy settings. A further next step is to encode the distances of targets and to investigate the minimum required level of vibration intensity for the patterns in daily settings.

6. REFERENCES

[1] E. Borg, J. Ronnberg, L. Neovius, and T. Lie. Vibratory-coded directional analysis: Evaluation of a three-microphone/four-vibrator DSP system. *J. of rehabilitation research and development*, 38(2), 2001.

[2] S. Kochkin. MarkeTrak VIII: 25-year trends in the hearing health market. *Hearing Review*, 2009.

[3] K. Myles. Guidelines for Head Tactile Communication. Technical report, Army Research Lab Aberdeen Proving Ground Md Human Research And Engineering Directorate, 2010.

[4] M. Straub, A. Riener, and A. Ferscha. Route guidance with a vibro-tactile waist belt. In *4th European Conference on Smart Sensing and Context*, 2009.

[5] J. Weisenberger, A. Heidbreder, and J. Miller. Development and preliminary evaluation of an earmold sound-to-tactile aid for the hearing-impaired. *J Rehabil Res Dev*, 24:51–66, 1987.

Displaying Braille and Graphics on a Mouse-like Tactile Display

Patrick C. Headley
Virginia Commonwealth University
401 West Main Street
Richmond, Virginia 23284
001-804-828-7839

headleypc@vcu.edu

Victoria E. Hribar
Virginia Commonwealth University
401 West Main Street
Richmond, Virginia 23284
001-804-828-7839

hribarve@vcu.edu

Dianne T.V. Pawluk
Virginia Commonwealth University
401 West Main Street
Richmond, Virginia 23284
001-804-828-9491

dtpawluk@vcu.edu

ABSTRACT

For presenting graphics on small, moveable tactile displays such as those that resemble computer mice, word labels can be as important as the diagram itself. In addition, the ability to present Braille with these displays offers an alternative for accessing full pages of Braille with a cost effective system. In this work, we consider the inherent difficulties arising from presenting Braille on these displays and propose algorithms to circumvent these problems. Lastly, we present preliminary results from individuals who are visually impaired that suggests the promise of this approach.

Categories and Subject Descriptors

K.4.2 [**Computing Milieu**]: Social Issues – *Assistive technologies for persons with disabilities, Handicapped persons/special needs.*

General Terms

Design, Human Factors

Keywords

Haptics, haptic mouse, visually impaired, tactile graphics, Braille

1. INTRODUCTION

Graphical visual information has always been important for conveying a variety of information, and is increasingly being used at school, work and in daily living. Unfortunately, individuals who are blind and visually impaired do not have direct access to this information. Although summary word descriptions can be used, many aspects of using pictures, such as the ability to discover patterns and spatial relationships, are lost. An alternative to this approach is to use tactile diagrams. Particularly if many diagrams are needed, refreshable graphics displays can be more cost-effective, less cumbersome, and less time consuming than traditional methods of creating tactile diagrams.

Two different types of mechanical refreshable displays have been developed. The first type is "full page" pin displays which consist of a large matrix of pins that can move up and down (e.g., hyperBraille, Metec AG). Due to the large number of pins needed, these displays can be costly and difficult to maintain, while still covering a relatively small total area. Their pin spacing (i.e., 2.5 mm for the hyperBraille) is also limiting for presenting graphics. Alternatively, smaller tactile displays (e.g., Levesque et al., 2007; Rovira and Gapenne, 2009; Headley and Pawluk, 2010) can be used that move with the user's hand over a virtual diagram. The span of the diagram accessible is only limited by the position

tracking system used, while being more cost effective and easier to maintain. In addition, these devices have the ability to resolve significantly finer position information, through motion of the hand. In this work we will consider the issues involved in presenting Braille on these displays. (It should be noted that although the VT Player by virTouch is a similar type of display, albeit with poor position tracking, for Braille it was only used in a similar manner to a single line Braille display rather than allowing free exploration over a page with the hand.)

The presentation of Braille is important even for presenting graphics, as the word labels used can be as important in interpreting a diagram as the graphics themselves. Currently, labels are commonly presented in multimedia systems through audition (e.g. Talking Tactile Tablet, Touch Graphics; Petit et al., 2008). However, there are several limitations to the use of speech: (1) it precludes access to labels for individuals who are deaf-blind, a small but underserved group; (2) if headphones are used in an open office environment, they can isolate the individual from the remainder of the office; (3) if headphones are not worn, the speech can annoy officemates and embarrass users; and (4) a strong correlation has been shown between employment and using Braille in one's daily life (NFB Website). Therefore, being able to clearly interpret Braille on graphics displays is an important issue. In addition, for small moveable displays, if Braille is easily read, these devices can be used to access virtual, full pages of Braille at a much lower cost than traditional Braille displays.

2. PROBLEMS WITH BRAILLE

Unfortunately, we noticed two inherent problems when displaying Braille on a small, moveable display. First, even with Braille dots represented as 1.5 mm diameter circles, it is very difficult to read the Braille. This is likely due to the fundamental difference between moving a hand over a static refreshable Braille display as compared to moving a Braille cell *with* the hand. In the former case, each Braille dot has a prolonged period of contact with the finger as it scans across it. In the latter case, because what is experienced is only through individual points on the hand, there is much briefer contact. We found that increasing the dot diameter only confused matters more as it did not clearly distinguish between dots. Levesque and his colleagues (2007) actually increased both the diameter of the dots and their spacing; however, the average success in a letter identification task was on average only 57%.

The second problem is that the Braille can easily be confused with textures presented in the graphics. Textures are often used to convey meaning in tactile graphics (e.g., Petit et al., 2008), and Burch and Pawluk (2011) have found that using them to encode information can significantly improve performance. Therefore, a method needs to be developed that will allow Braille and textures to coexist while providing for each to be easily identifiable.

3. GRAPHIC DESIGN

To improve performance when presenting Braille on a moveable display, we chose not to represent Braille characters as graphical elements. Instead, we had two "layers" to our virtual diagram. The first layer contained the graphic and the second layer indicated boxes, approximately 100 pixels by 100 pixels, corresponding to the relevant Braille character. If the position of the moveable display moved within a boxed area on the virtual diagram, the tactile display would present the appropriate Braille character. The display would remain fixed while inside the box, which allowed the character to stay on the finger for a much longer period of time, while not blurring between elements. This improved the legibility of the Braille characters significantly.

To discriminate between the graphics and textures within these diagrams, we chose to represent the graphics and the Braille at two different amplitude levels. The Braille was chosen to be at the highest level, and the graphics at a lesser amplitude approximately mid-way between the highest level and 0.

4. DISPLAY DESIGN

Although displays that can vary continuously in amplitude do exist (e.g., [4]), they require expensive amplifiers to work. We instead used a haptic display system previously developed in our laboratory (Headley and Pawluk, 2010) that uses photorelays to display one of four possible amplitudes for each actuated pin. The main components of the device are: a Braille cell (P15, Metec AG) which houses a 2x4 pin array constituting the tactile interface, a RF transmitter directly underneath the pin array to keep track of absolute position, and a mouse casing (Figure 1). The maximum amplitude level and the minimum amplitude level are fixed, set by the maximum voltage (200V) and minimum voltage (0V) applied to the device. The middle two amplitudes can be selected for an individual mouse by the user: for both, a potentiometer is used in the voltage divider to adjust the voltage to apply to a pin.

Figure 1. Haptic Mouse.

5. PILOT TESTING

A total of 3 participants who were visually impaired participated in a pilot study. All participants had previous experience with the device but not with using it to perceive Braille. Each participant was presented with four maps, one at a time. Each map contained five 3 letter abbreviations (where the letters were not repeated between labels of a single diagram), several textured areas, and boundaries between "countries". Participants were asked to find the Braille labels on the diagram. The time to find and read each Braille label, and whether the participant correctly found the Braille and read the Braille was recorded for each diagram. At the end of the experiment, each participant was also asked their opinion, on a Likert scale from 1 to 10, where 1 meant extremely easy and 10 meant extremely difficult, on how easy it was to find and read the Braille labels.

It was found that all participants were able to successfully find the Braille labels amongst the textures and borders of countries. On average, they were also able to correctly identify a letter 97% of the time. This was much more effective than for the method found in (Levesque et al., 2007). The average time to find and read all five Braille labels in one diagram was about 9.4 minutes. However, it should be noted that the second participant took significantly longer on average than the other participants; this was likely due to a poor exploration strategy in which the participant repeatedly explored the same areas of the diagram rather than moving the mouse to new areas. In terms of ease of use, not surprisingly, the second participant found it very hard to find the Braille. The average rating for the other 2 participants was 4 for finding Braille. For reading Braille, the average for all 3 participants was 3.3. These results show promise in using the methods developed to access Braille.

6. FUTURE WORK

The methods presented here appear to be effective in presenting Braille on a moving tactile display. Future work will more fully assess these methods and compare them to alternate methods that would not have to use more than 2 amplitudes: the latter is desirable, as it would simplify the driving electronics when extending the display to multiple fingers. In addition, further consideration of the importance of training on how to use the display on the participant's resulting performance will also be considered.

7. ACKNOWLEDGMENTS

This work is funded by NSF CBET Grant #0754629.

8. REFERENCES

[1] Headley, P., and Pawluk, D. 2010. A Low-Cost, Variable Amplitude Haptic Distributed Display for Persons who are Blind and Visually Impaired. ASSETS'10, October 25–27, Orlando, Florida.

[2] K. Rovira and O. Gapenne. 2009. Tactile Classification of Traditional and Computerized Media in Three Who Are Blind. Journal of Visual Impairment and Blindness. July, 430-435.

[3] Petit, G., Defresne, A., Levesque, V., Hayward, V. and Trudeau, N. 2008. Refreshable Tactile Graphics Applied to Schoolbook Illustrations for Students with Visual Impairment. ASSETS 2008, October 13-15, Halifax, Canada.

[4] Levesque, V., Pasquero, J. and Hayward, V. 2007. Braille Display by Lateral Skin Deformation with the STReSS2 Tactile Transducer. World Haptics, March 22-24, Tsukuba, Japan.

[5] National Federation of the Blind. General Braille Information Center. Accessed June 28, 2011 at: http://www.nfb.org/nfb/Braille_general.asp

[6] Burch D. and Pawluk, D. (2011). Using Multiple Contacts with Texture-Enhanced Graphics.World Haptics, June 21-24, Istanbul,Turkey.

Do Multi-touch Screens Help Visually Impaired People to Recognize Graphics?

Ikuko Eguchi Yairi, Kumi Naoe, Yusuke Iwasawa and Yusuke Fukushima

Graduate School of Science and Technology, Sophia University

7-1 Kioicho, Chiyoda-ku Tokyo, 102-8554, Japan

i.e.yairi@sophia.ac.jp, k.r.naoe@gmail.com, iwasawa@yairilab.net, yfukushima@sophia.ac.jp

ABSTRACT

This paper introduces our research project for developing a novel graphic representation method with touch and sound as the universal designed touch-screen interface for visually impaired people to understand graphical information. Our previous works on single-touch screens clarified the problems about the low recognition rate of curves. To solve this, an improved graphical representation interface for multi-touch screens were implemented and evaluated.

Categories and Subject Descriptors

H.5.2[User Interfaces]:*Haptic I/O,* Auditory (non-speech) feedback

General Terms: Design, Human Factors.

Keywords

Visual impairment, graphic, recognition, touch-screen.

1. INTRODUCTION

Toward the upcoming ubiquitous computing and networking era, the digital divide problem of visually impaired people tends to be focused on the access difficulties of graphical information today. Our research goal is to propose the novel graphic representation method with touch and sound as the universal designed touch-screen interface for visually impaired people. The proposed method and interfaces are basic techniques for developing plug-ins which help blind people to use ordinary mass-produced computer devices with touch-screens, such as smart-phones and iPads. Our idea is so simple that musical scales enable users to trace graphics by their fingers and to memorize their position on the touch-screen. This paper introduces our previous work on single-touch screens and reports recent evaluation results on multi-touch screens.

2. OUR PREVIOUS WORK

We have been proposing "One Octave Scale Interface (abbr. OOSI)" as a graphical representation interface on touch-panels for visually impaired people. The OOSI is based on the view that all shapes of graphics are able to be divided into start/goal/relay points and line/curve segments. Each line/curve is divided into eight parts to be linked to a musical scale. When a user successfully traces a line/curve, continuous musical scale sound is played depending on the finger position as shown in Figure 1 [1]. For improving the performance of the OOSI as the single-touch screen interface, several experiments with visually impaired people were done for investigating the node number effect, the stereo sound effect and the node regulation effect

[2,3]. Figure 2 is the recognition results of the figures in three types of node regulation by eleven visually impaired people. In this figure, 'S' means the single-touch experiment, 'B' means the blind person, and 'L' means the low vision people. Despite these efforts of improving, the low recognition rate of curves still remained as unsolved problem. Looking at this problem from different angle, we decided to introduce the multi-touch screen in our development.

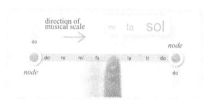

Figure 1 the One Octave Scale Interface.

	M	つ	⊐	⊐	⊃	N	ろ	几
SBa	M	⌐	⊐	⊐	⊃	N	ろ	▽
SBb	M	⊃	⊐	D	⊃	N	No answer	几
SBc	M	⌐	ろ	⊂	⊃	N	ろ	⌐
SDd	ʌ	⊃	⊃	⊐	⊐	L	∟	I
SBe	ʌ	Z	⊐	R	N	Z	⊃
SBf	⌐	⊃	⊐	D	⊃	N	ろ	几
SLg	M	ʔ	⋁	⌐	−	N	−	∧
SLh	M	⌐	⊐	⌒	⊃	N	∕	∧
SBi	M	⊃	ろ	R	⊃	N	ろ	几
SBj	I	⊐	⊐	▽	⊃	M	ろ	⌐
SLk	ʌ	ろ	ろ	⌐	ろ	N	ろ	几

Figure 2 Recognition Results of the Single-touch Experiment drawn by examinees

3. EVALUATION OF MULTI-TOUCH EFFECT

To enrich the OOSI as a multi-touch screen interface, using multi timbre will provide useful clues to find the location of each finger on a displayed graphic for users. We introduce the timbre of eight musical instruments into the OOSI's representation of lines and curves as shown in Figure 3(a). To evaluate the OOSI's multi-touch function, an application was written by Cocoa for iPad, which allowed us to develop an eleven finger multi-touch application. The application consists of a training graphic in Figure 3(b), and twelve graphics in three patterns as shown in Figure 3(c). The size of each graphic is 10cm x 10cm as same as the previous experiment in Section 2. Six blind people and five low vision people, who were staff members or former/recent students of braille training courses of Japan Braille Library, participated in our evaluation. People with low vision wore eye-masks, and all participants were given warm encouragement but no feedbacks about correct answers from examiners while evaluating. During the examination of each figure, examiners continuously asked examinees to tell everything what they felt. All figures were displayed in random order. Maximum time for examining one figure was strictly fixed at four minutes. After examining, the recognition result was presented by the examinee with fingertip drawing on a paper, and was traced by examiner with a pen. The recognition results by all participants are shown in Figure 4. By comparing the recognition results of the same figure " ∩ " in two experiments shown in Figure 2 and 4, the number of the perfect matching was zero in the single-touch evaluation and four in the multi-touch evaluation. Figure 5 shows trajectories of all fingers logged by our application. From left examples of perfect matching, examinees succeeded to find and touch whole sound area. Trajectories in right examples of partially/no matching indicate that the examinees touched screens as if they drew the same figure as the recognition results. The curve recognition ratio of single/multi-touch screens is compared in Table 1.

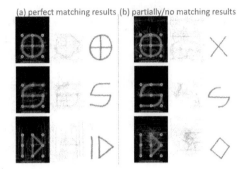

Figure 5 Comparison of Trajectories of Fingers

Table 1 the Curves' Recognition Ratio of Each Experiments

	The number of lines+curves	The number of curves	Recognition ratio of curves	Misrecognition ratio of curves	Absence ratio
Single	43	7	31.2%	50.6%	18.2%
Multi-Pat1	25	7	45.5%	23.4%	31.2%
Multi-Pat2	26	6	63.6%	9.1%	27.2%
Multi-Pat3	18	2	59.1.%	31.8%	9.1%

4. CONCLUSION

The title of this paper is our simple question. Maybe the results mentioned above give us an affirmative answer. The reason of this ambiguous expression is that the stringent comparison between the single-touch experiment and the multi-touch experiment is difficult because examined figures were different in each experiment. But based on the number of curves included in examined figures showed in Table 1, the difficulty level of examined figures in the multi-touch experiment was higher than in the single-touch experiment. And it is clear that the recognition ratio of curves is increased in multi-touch experiments. These results illustrated the possibility that our proposed graphic displaying interface for visually impaired using musical scales, the OOSI, will work better on multi-touch screens, and will enable the visually impaired to recognize more complicated figures.

5. ACKNOWLEDGMENTS

We are deeply grateful to Mr. Masamitsu Takano and all participants of our experiments. This work was supported by Grant-in-Aid for Young Scientists (B) No. 10358880 and Scientific Research (C) (General) No. 23500155 from the MEXT, Japan.

6. REFERENCES

[1] YAIRI, I.E., AZUMA, Y., AND TAKANO, M. 2009. The One Octave Scale Interface for Graphical Representation for Visually Impaired People. In *Proceedings of ASSETS2009*, pp.255-256, 2009.

[2] Kumi NAOE, Yoshiteru AZUMA, Masamitsu TAKANO and Ikuko Eguchi YAIRI, "Evaluation of Sound Effects and Presentation Position for Universal Designed Interactive Map with Due Consideration for Visually Impaired People", International Journal of Innovative Computing, Information and Control , Vol.7, No.5(B), pp.2897--2906, 2011

[3] Kumi NAOE, Masamitsu TAKANO, Ikuko Eguchi YAIRI, "Investigation of figure recognition with touch panel of visually impaired people from the perspective of braille proficiency", In Proc. SICE Annual Conference 2010, SB06.04, Taipei, Taiwan, August 18-21, 2010.

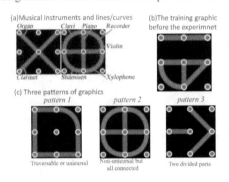

Figure 3 (a)Sound Mapping of Figures, (b) a Figure for Training and (c) Figures for Evaluation in three patterns.

Figure 4 Recognition Results of the Multi-touch Experiment drawn by examinees

E-Drawings as an Evaluation Method with Deaf Children

Ornella Mich
Fondazione Bruno Kessler
via Sommarive, 18
38123 POVO, TN, Italy
mich@fbk.eu

ABSTRACT

This paper describes a pilot test on the use of a drawing software program as an evaluation method for experiments with deaf children. As deaf children are visual learners, evaluation methods based on drawings seem to be a good alternative to traditional ones. We tested the effectiveness of such a method with a group of deaf children, all raised orally apparently without any knowledge of sign language, and a few hearing children, from eight to fourteen years old. As a testbed, we evaluated the readability of a set of stories, part of a literacy software tool for deaf children. All participants were relaxed and collaborative during the test. The results are promising.

Categories and Subject Descriptors

H.5.2 [**Information Interfaces and Presentation**]: User Interfaces—*Evaluation/methodology*.

General Terms

Experimentation

Keywords

evaluation methods, deaf children

1. INTRODUCTION

Involving deaf children in evaluation experiments may be not easy. As children, they approach technology differently with respect to adult users [3]. As deaf users, they may not have access to audio input/output material or to written material due to their literacy problems [6]. Therefore, adapted evaluation methods may be needed when involving them in an experiment. Methods based on drawings (see, for example, [9]) seem to be a good alternative to traditional methods, because deaf children are visual learners [7], and visual learners use images, colours and maps to organise knowledge and communication.

In this paper, we describe a pilot test aimed at verifying the applicability and effectiveness of a new evaluation method based on the use of digital drawings. As a testbed, we organised an experiment about the readability of a set of stories,

part of LODE[1], a literacy tool for deaf children [1].

In the following section, we analyse the advantages of an evaluation method based on e-drawings. After that, we describe the structure and the results of our experiment. Finally, we summarise conclusions and future work.

2. EVALUATING WITH E-DRAWINGS

One of the possible methods to use in evaluation sessions with children is that of inviting children to make a drawing after completing a given task [8, 9]. This method is suitable for children because, when drawing, children are relaxed and do not consider it a task or a duty, but rather a pleasure. Children's drawings embody a variety of information about the child himself/herself and on his/her experience [2].

Being deaf children who are visual learners, it seems worthwhile to adopt drawing-based evaluation methods when working with them. However, in our first attempt to use this method [4, p. 113], only one child in six wished to draw their experience during the test. Persuaded of the validity of the drawing-based evaluation method, we organised another experiment[2] where we proposed to deaf children the use of a drawing program, TuxPaint, instead of paper and felt tips, to describe their experience in the experiment. As a result, we expected a more active participation by deaf children, as they are generally very keen on using technological tools. We describe this test in the following section. Using drawing software programs in evaluation allows evaluators to directly obtain the drawings in digital format. Furthermore, a semi-automated procedure can be implemented to analyse drawings and extract info on colours used or on the drawing's content such as human faces, body or text. Even the comparison of images from different users becomes quicker.

3. OUR PILOT TEST

The aim of our test is to check if e-Drawings and comprehension exercises allow us to measure in the same way how much deaf children understood after reading a narrative text. If this is successful, it means that digital drawings can be used, in similar tasks, as an alternative to traditional comprehension exercises. Our test took place during a conference dedicated to families of deaf children. When parents attended the lectures, their children, with their parents' permission, were asked to participate in our evaluation. Parents

---

[1]LODE has been developed within a project founded by the Fondazione Caritro, Trento, Italy.

[2]A complete description of the test, the stories used and the produced drawings is reported in [5].

(a)
M., 9 years old
profoundly deaf
11/12 correct answers

(b)
T., 8 years old
hearing
11/12 correct answers

Figure 1: Drawings Examples.

filled out a questionnaire about their child's personal data. Fourteen Italian children, eleven boys and three girls, were involved. Among these were nine deaf children, all oralist, and five hearing children, siblings of the deaf children, involved as a small control group. We first asked the children to read a story, then complete a series of traditional comprehension exercises and finally create one or more drawings with TuxPaint to illustrate the story they read. A simple web application was designed to present the stories and the comprehension exercises to the participants. Before working on the story, children attended a short course (two hours) to learn how to use TuxPaint. After the test, we looked at the exercises' scores and at the drawings' content to measure the level of comprehension of the story read. For us, a child was demonstrated to have understood the narrative if he/she got a high percentage of correct answers on the comprehension exercises (above 70%) or if at least one of the main characters of the story and one of the main story actions were represented in his/her drawing. We can say that the e-Drawing evaluation method is a valid alternative to traditional comprehension exercises with deaf children, if drawing analysis and exercise results coincide. Eight participants, five deaf children and three hearing children finished the test. Three other kids attended the training with Tux Paint but refused to read the story. Two other children were not able to read, so we stopped their test. And finally, we missed the results of one child due to technical problems. Both deaf and hearing children gave almost all the answers to the comprehension exercises correctly (11/12 or 12/12); only one deaf child had a low answer rate (3 to 12). The drawings of three deaf children and of two hearing children clearly illustrate an action of the story and at least one of the story's main characters is represented. Following our criterion, this means that in these five cases the participants have understood at least part of the story read. This result is confirmed by the high number of correct answers (12/12 or 11/12) given in the comprehension exercises by all these five children. The drawing produced by another deaf child

did not represent the story; the same child got a low score in the comprehension exercises (3/12). In the remaining two cases, a deaf child and an hearing child, drawing analysis and exercises scores did not match. Figure 1 shows an example where drawing analysis and exercises' scores matched and an example where they did not: we had six out of eight cases where drawings and exercise scores matched.

4. CONCLUSIONS AND FUTURE WORK

The results of our pilot test are promising. It seems that the e-Drawings-based evaluation method is a valid alternative to traditional methods in reading comprehension tasks with deaf participants. We believe that improving the training with TuxPaint, including notions on how to create animations and videos, will give even better results. Future work will require the development of better scoring criteria for the drawings, so that it becomes possible to judge the children's reading comprehension more objectively. More research is needed to study which drawing's elements can give relevant information on reading comprehension level, in addition to information given by traditional comprehension exercises. Moreover, the proposed method requires testing of different tasks and with a more significant number of participants. The deaf world is heterogeneous and complex because there are different types of hearing loss, different family's backgrounds (deaf or hearing parents, for example), different types of physical solutions (CI, hearing aids, nothing) and several educational methods. Therefore, a larger and more representative population sampling of the deafness world than that involved in this preliminary study should be considered to get more significant results.

5. REFERENCES

[1] R. Gennari and O. Mich. Constraint-based Temporal Reasoning for E-learning with LODE. In *Proc. of CP*, 2007.

[2] R. Jolley. *Children and Pictures: Drawing and Understanding*. Wiley-Blackwell, 2010.

[3] P. Markopoulos, J. Read, S. MacFarlane, and J. Hoysniemi. *Evaluating Children's Interactive Products*. Morgan Kaufmann Publishers, May 2008.

[4] O. Mich. *Usability Methods and Deaf Children. The Case of the LODE e-Tool*. PhD thesis, 2010.

[5] O. Mich. Evaluating Readability of Stories for Deaf Children with a Drawing Program. FBK Technical Report, 2011.

[6] P. Paul. *Literacy and Deafness: the Development of Reading, Writing, and Literate Thought*. Allyn & Bacon, 1998.

[7] J. Reeves, P. Wollenhaupt, and F. Caccamise. Deaf Students as Visual Learners. In *Proc. of the Int. Congress on Education of the Deaf*, 1995.

[8] V. Scott and M. Weishaar. Talking Drawings as a University Classroom Assessment Technique. *The Journal of Effective Teaching*, 8(1):42–51, 2008.

[9] D. Xu, J. Read, G. Sim, and B. McManus. Experience It, Draw It, Rate It. Capture Children's Experiences with Their Drawings. In *Proc. of IDC*. ACM Press, 2009.

Enhancing Social Connections Through Automatically-Generated Online Social Network Messages

John J. Magee, Christopher Kwan,
Margrit Betke

Department of Computer Science
Boston University, Boston, MA, USA
{ mageejo, ckwan, betke } @cs.bu.edu

Fletcher Hietpas

Boston Public Schools
Boston, MA, USA
fhietpas@boston.k12.ma.us

ABSTRACT

Social isolation and loneliness are important challenges faced by people with certain physical disabilities. Technical and complexity issues may prevent some people from participating in online social networks that otherwise may address some of these issues. We propose to generate social network messages automatically from within assistive technology and augmentative and alternative communication software. These messages will help users post some of their daily activities with the software to online social networks. Based on our initial user studies, the inclusion of social networking connections may help improve engagement and interaction between users with disabilities and their friends, families and caregivers, and this increased interest can lead to the desire to use the assistive technology more fully.

Categories and Subject Descriptors

K.4.2 [**Social Issues**]: Assistive technologies for persons with disabilities; D.1.2 [**User/Machine Systems**]: Human factors; H.5.2 [**User Interfaces**]: Input devices and strategies

General Terms

Human Factors

Keywords

Online Social Networking, Automatic Message Generation

1. INTRODUCTION

We investigate the use of online social networks for people with moderate to severe motor disabilities and their families and caregivers. Online social networks may help overcome communication barriers, but there are still many challenges [3].

Online social networks can help alleviate problems of loneliness and isolation for people with disabilities, but only if the technology works for the individual [2]. Some of the challenges people with movement disabilities face when they attempt to use existing online networks are slow communication rates, inaccessible elements on web pages such as small

links or buttons, inability to personalize interfaces, low literacy, lack of privacy (the caregiver is always present), lack of autonomy [2, 3], and inadequate computer literacy of caregivers.

To address these challenges, we propose to generate messages automatically that would help answer the question "What did I do today?" The software can keep a log of the user's activities, e.g. what applications they use, what web pages they visit, what stories they read. The user can optionally annotate an activity or item to express their opinion about it (by applying a rating: like/dislike, thumbs up/thumbs down). At the end of the session, the user can update their social network with information and statistics about the session. This posting can include how much time the person used the computer and specific applications, what they liked or didn't like. This allows the user with disabilities to participate in social media and connect with family and caregivers without having to enter a lengthy message with an alternative text entry method.

We work with people who use a mouse replacement interface called the Camera Mouse [1]. This interface tracks head motion to move a mouse pointer on the screen. We have used it with a variety of accessible software designed for people who cannot use a typical keyboard or mouse interface.

2. PROTOTYPE SYSTEM DESIGN

The prototype system can integrate with several online social networks to post messages. Such integration is accomplished via publicly available Application Programming Interfaces (APIs). In order to generate messages, the software must also interface with other software that is being used on the computer. There are several ways this integration can be accomplished depending on the ability to modify the software.

Assistive software that we create can be designed with integrated social networking features to generate the most detailed messages. Some existing closed-source software may be modified or configured to produce logs that can be analyzed to create messages. In the worst case, proprietary software can be monitored for focus to measure how long it is used.

A flowchart of the proposed system is shown in Fig. 1. In the prototype system, the system is more limited: only one log file can be processed and the user interface presents the user with a choice of sending the message or not. Future work will expand the functionality of software to offer the user more options and more complex messages.

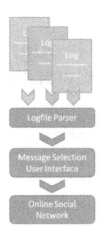

Figure 1: System flowchart. Each application produces logfiles, which are then parsed to present message options to the user. The selected message is then sent to the online social networking site.

3. CASE STUDIES

To observe how students might benefit from easier access to social network communication, we visited a public school over a 5-month period. Three female students with cerebral palsy, all age 13, participated in our study. We also visited a male high school student in his home. Students at the school are quite engaged with a "points economy," where they earn points for completing academic tasks. Language-impaired students would benefit greatly from having the ability to automatically post messages on social networks relating to their in-school achievements. Automatic message posting would enable many students to interact normally with the social network outside of their confined classroom.

We first conducted an evaluation of software usage with the Camera Mouse with participant T. Participants L and G, having seen T use the Camera Mouse and associated software, began asking to try it themselves. This positive social feedback cycle increased their engagement and desire to use the technology. L said "I saw $[T]$ using it and thought 'this looks like fun' so I wanted to try it." It is this social engagement we aim to foster in an online social network.

We observed L using the Camera Mouse to play the game EagleAliens, and then we showed her a potential social network posting (Fig. 2) and asked for her reactions. L does not use the internet at home and was intially not sure if she liked the idea. However, she indicated that she would want to share her game score or her work in class with her family or friends, adding "I think that would be cool, because then they would know how much work I did."

T had been out of school for 5 weeks and had used the Camera Mouse on her own during that time. She indicated that it would have been good to share what she was doing with her classmates while she was away. L said that if they could share their scores, "...she would know what I got, and I would know what she got..." and that would be good "...because we might have something in common." T indicated that she would be inspired if she saw online that her classmates had accomplished something.

All three participants expressed interest in sharing what they had done at school with family members who do not live

---

Post to Facebook:
Today I used the Camera Mouse for 20 minutes. I played the EagleAliens game for 15 minutes and my best score was 9/10 aliens at 2.3 seconds each!

Figure 2: We showed our study participants this simulated online social network posting and asked them for their reactions.

with them. G also indicated that she would try something new if she saw online that her classmates had tried it.

Participant C is a 16 year-old male high school student with cerebral palsy. After using the Camera Mouse with various software programs, we showed C the social networking posting message (Fig. 2). When asked if he would use this feature, he responded: "I would like it," but also expressed privacy concerns. C thought that it was important for users with disabilities to have an easy way to communicate their thoughts online. He said that people with disabilities have things to share and say, communicate and express.

Our discussion with a special education director indicated that her students with communication or transportation challenges would definitely benefit from enhancing social interactions through automatically generated social network messages that would keep them engaged with their peers. Our study indicates that such messages could be beneficial both to producers and consumers of the message.

4. FUTURE DIRECTION

We plan to conduct an expanded user study with a fully functioning system to analyze longer term usage trends and social interaction effects. We also plan to make a future version available as a download.

5. ACKNOWLEDGMENTS

The authors would like to thank their participants. Funding was provided by NSF, HCC grants IIS 0713229, 0910908, 0855065. Parental consent was obtained for minor subjects.

6. REFERENCES

[1] M. Betke, J. Gips, and P. Fleming. The camera mouse: Visual tracking of body features to provide computer access for people with severe disabilities. *IEEE TNSRE*, 10(1):1–10, 2002.

[2] L. Cooper, S. Baladin, and D. Trembath. The loneliness experiences of young adults with cerebral palsy who use alternative and augmentative communication. *AAC*, 25(3):154–164, 2009.

[3] M. Lewis. Cerebral palsy and online social networks. In *ASSETS 2010*, pages 243–244, Oct. 2010.

Evaluating Information Support System for Visually Impaired People with Mobile Touch Screens and Vibration

Takato Noguchi*, Yusuke Fukushima*, Ikuko Eguchi Yairi*
*Graduate School of Science and Technology, Sophia University
7-1 Kioicho, Chiyoda-ku, Tokyo, 102-8554, Japan
t-noguch@hoffman.cc.sophia.ac.jp,{yfukushima,i.e.yairi}@sophia.ac.jp

ABSTRACT
Throughout 6 months of blind user's touch panel usage interview, there were many problems of touch panel's audio assistant. The participant strongly demanded to improve the low accuracy and the slow software keyboard typing, and the poor understanding of the shape of the picture. She was also interested in recognizing the 3D shapes. Thus, we developed a fingertip tactile feedback system in order to indicate the "f" and "j" key for touch-typing and improved the speed of the software keyboard typing, and simplify the way to understand the 3D shapes. In this paper, we introduce and evaluate the recognition of the 3D shape by three participants using the system. The results showed that the proposed system succeeded in enabling the visually impaired participants to recognize the 3D shapes.

Categories and Subject Descriptors
H.5.2[User Interfaces]:*Interaction styles*, K.4.2[Social Issues]: *Assistive technologies for persons with disabilities*

General Terms
Design, Experimentation, Human Factors.

Keywords
Visually impaired, fingertip interaction, tactile feedback, touchscreens, tablet PCs.

1. INTRODUCTION
Touch screens have been rapidly growing popular and becoming the standard input methods of mobile devices, such as Android phones and iPads. However, because of the lack of tactile feedback, the impaired people have difficulties to use them. To solve this problem, we have been developing a support technique which has enabled visually impaired people to use touch screens easily. In this study, a blind female (BF) in her forties has been interviewed for 6 months every 2 or 3weeks since she bought iPad. She pointed out many problems of iPad's audio assistant "VoiceOver" function as follows: complicated music and video imports, low accuracy and slow input of software keyboard, and difficulty of understanding displayed figures and layouts. Among them the software keyboard problem was so serious that she couldn't surf internet and write e-mail freely. Also, understanding the figures and layouts should be easier in order to use millions of application which is made for touch screens. In an effort to address these issues, we developed and evaluated a tactile feedback system that was equipped on the fingers. This paper presents the system details and its evaluation which supports software keyboard typing and the 3D shape recognition.

2. The Fingertip Vibration Feedback System
There are previous approaches using vibration which increase the accuracy and the speed of touch screen display's software keyboard typing [1], and also make the touch screen feel like touching a physical button [2]. Although these approaches are optimized for sighted users with visual feedback, it is not suited for the visually impaired. In this study, we targeted the visually impaired and developed the Fingertip Vibration Feedback System (abbr. FVFS) which was equipped on a fingertip and made an intuitive control. The small and cheap TOUCH&MUSIC SPEAKER4580218305099 tactile actuator was chosen for the vibration device and was connected to the iPad 3.5-mm stereo headphone mini-jack. The tactile actuator has an advantage that can easily adjust the vibration level and the frequency level, and small enough to be attached on fingers. First, we developed an QWERTY keyboard application with vibration to indicate the "f" and "j" key written in Objective-C Cocoa which were important for touch-typing, shown in Fig. 1. This keyboard enabled BF to increase input accuracy and speed. She was also able to play a Ping-Pong game using the keyboard typing which required highly demanded accuracy and input time. For the second goal of the recognition of displayed graphic shape, BF and we were interested in not only the 2D shape, but also 3D shape. Thus, we used the vibration level to represent the depth information of 3D shape. To evaluate the 3D shape representation using the FVFS, multiple choice tests using the 10 misleading cardboard shapes were done by BF to show her recognition result of silhouette, and she explained the position of vertex and curve of lateral surfaces orally. The evaluation result showed that BF was able to understand the 3D shapes intuitively. A low vision male(LM) in his twenties participated in the evaluation, and were able to recognize each 3D shape correctly such as cube, circular cone, Tower of Honoi and so on. To quantify the effectiveness of 3Dshape recognition support, three visually impaired including BF, LM and a blinded male (BM) in his twenties took part in the evaluation shown in the next section.

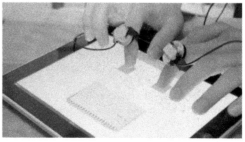

Fig. 1 The keyboard support experiment.

3.Evaluation of 3D Graphic Recognition
Fig. 2 describes the outline of evaluation systems. The FVFS are attached on the forefingers and connected to four iPads via audio mixer. The left iPad(iPad1) was used to present a shape, and participants must choose the same shape from other three

iPads(iPad2~iPad4). The 3Dshapes that were presented on each iPads were listed on fig. 3. In this study, we did three experiments as follows:

1) Every presented shape is triangular pyramid with the same silhouette, and the users verify the difference of each shape's highest vibration position.

2) All shapes of the vertex of highest vibration are the same, however, the corresponded shapes are 45degrees rotated and participants have to find the difference of silhouette of the shape. The presented shapes are rectangle, circle, and oval.

3) The four iPads present the same silhouette and the vertex, but each of the shape has different curves of lateral surfaces. Each curve of the lateral surfaces is linear function, quadratic function, and step function.

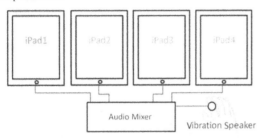

Fig. 2 The experimental setup with four iPads, Audio Mixer, and a Vibration Speaker.

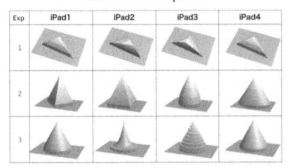

Fig. 3 3D figures

Fig. 4 shows the 3D shapes, the tracks of the finger, selected shapes, and the correct answers. The results showed that LM and BM selected the correct answers in the first and second experiments, which evaluated the recognition of the silhouette and vertex of the shape. BF selected the correct answer only in the third experiment which evaluated the recognition of curve of lateral surface. The tracks of the finger demonstrate that LM and BM employed tactics to find the feature of the shape like silhouette and vertex of the shape. On the other hand, BF had employed a tactic to move her finger fast, and tried to touch most part of the shape. While the tactics of LM and BM were suitable for the first and second experiments, the tactic of BF was suitable for the third experiment. She finally felt the difference of the sense of touch on lateral surfaces. The fact shows the effectiveness of the FVFS, because only a few times experiences of the FVFS enabled BF to understand the curves of lateral surfaces in intuitive way. Furthermore, from the analysis of tracks of the finger, even BM, the beginner of the FVFS was able to find the silhouette and the vertex of the shape correctly like LM who experienced the FVFS just once. There is a possibility that even the beginners can use the FVFS and recognize the characteristic of the shape intuitively.

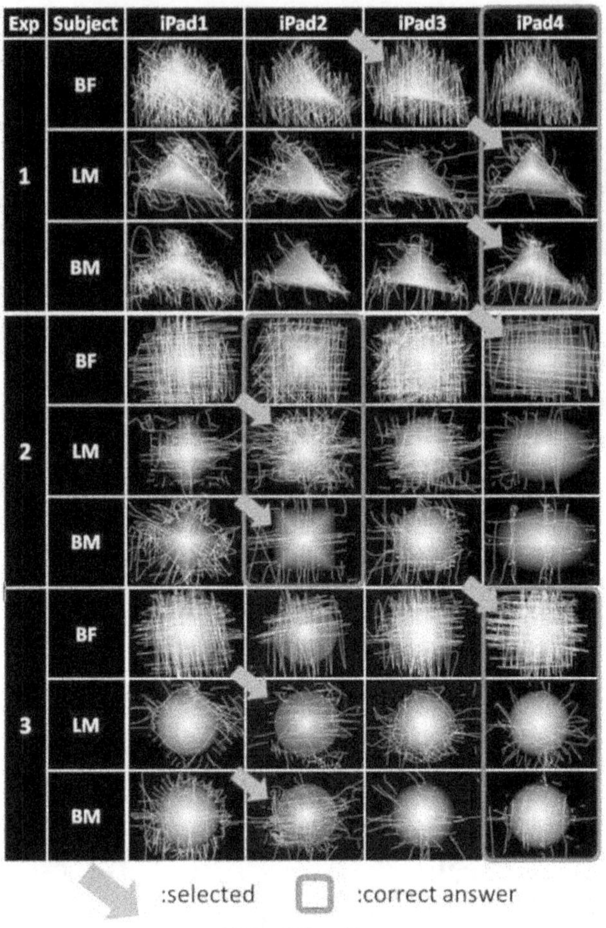

Fig. 4 Results

4. Conclusion

This paper proposed the fingertip vibration feedback system for visually impaired people to recognize 3D graphics on touch-screens, which is cheap, small and equipped easily by just connecting to headphone mini-jack. Results of the experiments showed that proposed system could also help visually impaired people to understand the difference of curves of lateral surfaces. Future research will be able to enhance the use of touch screens for the visually impaired. Using the multiple fingers may improve the results and have the possibility to recognize more complicated 3D shapes.

ACKNOWLEDGMENTS

The authors would like to thank to the participants for their efforts contributing to this work. This work was supported by Grant-in-Aid for Young Scientists (B) No. 10358880 and Scientific Research (C) (General) No. 23500155 from the Ministry of Education, Culture, Sports, Science and Technology of Japan.

REFERENCES

[1] E. Hoggan, S. A. Brewster and J. Johnston. Investigating the Effectiveness of Tactile Feedback for Mobile Touchscreens. In *CHI 2008 Proc. • Tactile and Haptic User Interfaces* p.1573-p.1582

[2] A. Nashel and S. Razzaque. Tactile Virtual Buttons for Mobile Devices. In *CHI 2003: NEW HORIZONS, Short Talks: Specialized Section* p.854-p.855

Exploring Iconographic Interface in Emergency for Deaf

Miriam Cabo
University of Trás-os-Montes e Alto Douro
Quinta de Prados, Apartado 1013
Vila Real, Portugal
al30041@utad.eu

Tânia Pereira
University of Trás-os-Montes e Alto Douro
Quinta de Prados, Apartado 1013
Vila Real, Portugal
al30046@utad.eu

Benjamim Fonseca
GECAD/UTAD
University of Trás-os-Montes e Alto Douro,
Quinta de Prados, Apartado 1013
Vila Real, Portugal
benjaf@utad.pt

Hugo Paredes
GECAD/UTAD
University of Trás-os-Montes e Alto Douro,
Quinta de Prados, Apartado 1013
Vila Real, Portugal
hparedes@utad.pt

ABSTRACT

In this demo, we present an application for mobile phones, which can allow communication between deaf and emergency medical services using an iconographic touch interface. This application can be useful especially for deaf but also for persons without disabilities that face sudden situations where speech is hard to articulate.

Categories and Subject Descriptors

H.5.2 [**Information Interfaces and Presentation**]: User Interfaces—Interaction styles; K.4.2 [Computers and Society]: Social Issues—Assistive technologies for persons with disabilities

General Terms

Design, Human Factors

Keywords

Deaf people; iconographic interface; medical emergency

1. INTRODUCTION

According to the World Report on Disability 2011 [1], the number of disabled people in the world is presently estimated in one billion, corresponding approximately to 15% of the current world's population. In Portugal, according to the 2001 census, there were 84,172 with hearing disability [2].

Currently there is only one possibility in Portugal to allow deaf people to request emergency services, by exchanging a series of SMS messages. These SMS will be received by the General Command of the GNR that will activate the necessary means [3].

With the advances in communication technologies, it is possible to create a mobile application that enables deaf people to quickly and easily request emergency services by selecting icons in a pictographic interface available in a smartphone touchscreen.

2. DESIGN AND IMPLEMENTATION

The main design requirements that guided the development were:

- Iconographic interface - the user interface should avoid the usage of text in order to allow all users to access emergency service calls. Large and accessible icons with high contrast should describe the situations. Icons should be selected from reference symbology.
- Touchscreen input - the input of information should be easy for people with mobility problems.
- Embedded emergency flow protocol - the application should allow the user to describe the situation with the highest detail possible, following the usual emergency protocols used by emergency control centers in order to facilitate the integration with existing systems.
- Low bandwidth communication with the emergency control center - the usage of the network bandwidth should be reduced to allow faster communication of the emergency situation.
- Automatic location of the incident (implicit or explicit).
- User call identification.
- Required user registration - registration of users will complement the identification of the caller and provide further information to prevent false calls, which can be complemented by users ranking.

For the prototype development we used the Windows Phone 7 platform, as it provides a basic set of hardware requirements that include assisted GPS and a touchscreen, as well as a quick prototyping cycle due to the development tools available.

This application generates a code that will be sent via SMS to the emergency services center. This code contains: User ID (Figure 1, left), required information about the victims (Figure 1, right), type (Figure 2) and location of occurrence.

Figure 1. User ID (left), information about the victims (right)

In the first use of the application, the user is asked to register (Figure 1, left) to avoid false alarms. The right side of Figure 1 shows the screen that is presented to the user to request information about the victim(s). To collect this information the user just needs to touch the appropriate option to select it.

Figure 2. Occurrences

After providing the necessary information about the victims, the user must select the type of occurrence. Initially a menu with the most common situations is shown (Figure 2, left) and if they do not correspond to the situation witnessed the user can access a second menu (Figure 2, right).

Figure 3. Specifying the type of occurrence

There are situations where it is important to note other information such as symptoms or the nature thereof.

Figure 4. Sending the message: confirmation of the occurrence (left) and code generated (right).

Finally, a message is shown to the user containing the textual description of the occurrence, enabling its confirmation or rollback for correction. After confirming, the code to be sent is shown, which includes the User ID and its current location, based on the GPS coordinates of the phone. This coding scheme is important to ensure that only one message is sent, because of the character limits of SMS.

3. FINAL REMARKS

So that all users to able to easily use this application we developed an iconographic interface. Given the large number of possible situations that can occur, it was impossible to cover them to avoid overloading the interface and making it too confusing. Thus, we grouped the various situations in broader groups of types of occurrences. The use of icons is intuitive and fast. This application is important for deaf people and also to other persons, in situations of panic or some other sudden incident that makes it difficult to articulate speech.

4. REFERENCES

[1] Organization, W.H., Bank, T.W.: World report on disability. WHO Press (2011)

[2] *PORDATA*. (n.d.). Retrieved Junho 2011, from http:www.pordata.pt

[3] O SMS ao serviço da igualdade. (2008, Julho 17). Retrieved Junho 2011, from A Nossa Opinião: http://opiniao.mai-gov.info/

Future Technology Oriented Scenarios on e-Accessibility

Christos Kouroupetroglou
ALTEC Software S.A.
M. Kalou 6
GR 546 29 Thessaloniki
+30 2310 595 646

chris.kourou@gmail.com

Adamantios Koumpis
ALTEC Software S.A.
M. Kalou 6
GR 546 29 Thessaloniki
+30 2310 595 646

akou@altec.gr

Dimitris Papageorgiou
Innovation Management
16 Dimitrakopoulou Str,
GR 546 55 Thessaloniki, Greece
+30 2310 422780

dimpap70@otenet.gr

ABSTRACT

This paper presents a set of future scenarios as a part of our study which explores and analyzes the relationships between the emerging ICT landscape in the European societal and economic context, and the development and provision of e-Accessibility, within a perspective of 10 years. Part of our study is the development and validation of various scenarios regarding the impact of new technologies in accessibility. This paper presents some draft scenarios that were produced by combining technologies referred by experts as crucial for the future of eAccessibility.

Categories and Subject Descriptors

H.5.2 [**User interfaces**]: Ergonomics, Theory and methods

General Terms

Design, Human Factors, Standardization, Accessibility.

Keywords

eAccessibility, scenario, future

1. INTRODUCTON

The study on e-Accessibility2020[1] ("Study on Implications from Future ICT Trends on Assistive Technology and Accessibility", SMART 2010/0077) aims to provide the European Commission with recommendations on future research policy, especially regarding Framework Programme 8 (ICT & FET) and the next Competitiveness & Innovation Programme (CIP). To achieve that, the study follows a data gathering process from various sources, such as scientific papers, past and running projects deliverables and interviews with experts. The object of this data gathering process is to identify key trends, micro-trends and weak signals on new technologies that will possibly affect the future of eAccessibility.

Having identified some of the key and micro trends in the data gathering process the study team developed a preliminary set of scenarios combining various technologies referred during the interviews. The aim of the paper is to present these scenarios in order to get feedback from experts on their plausibility and validity. It also aims to stimulate experts' thoughts for possible alternative scenarios.

2. THE DATA GATHERING

The data gathering process of the study is a process which is still in progress. However, it is in its final stages and its progress allowed us to use some preliminary outcomes in drafting the set of scenarios presented in this paper. Feedback from the respective poster presentation will be valuable for the next stages of our study and will be taken seriously under account in the project's

final report. The data gathering was based on two main axes: The desk research and interviews with experts.

2.1 Desk research

Desk research included reading and categorization of a large set of conference and journal research papers, EU funded RTD project deliverables and various trend analysis reports. The collected material was analyzed and categorized into groups according to the technology used, disability/ies addressed, and beneficiaries. In addition, during the desk research, the study team selected a set of 137 EU funded RTD projects relevant to eAccessibility and eInclusion as a base for other parts of the research. This analysis which is now in its latest stages produced some preliminary outcomes of technologies that seem possible to have an impact on accessibility in the future.

2.2 Interviews

Out of 137 projects related to eAccessibility and eInclusion the study team has selected a set of 46 projects relevant either to the projects goals or to technologies that were already identified as trends from the desk research. Next, we contacted about 130 persons that participated in those projects by email and asked for their participation in an interview regarding their views for the future of accessibility. Almost 30 of them replied and were scheduled for an interview. Until now 23 of them have already been conducted. Interviewees were also asked to review a summary of their interview as a follow up so that it could be used in official study reports. The interviews objective was twofold. The first one was to get the experts opinions in the future of their area of expertise in relation to eAccessibility. The second was to investigate experts' opinions on the future of eAccessibility in general.

3. SCENARIOS

The data gathering process which is now in its final stages has produced some preliminary outcomes about technology drivers for the future of eAccessibility. Based on them, the study team brainstormed on possible combinations of such technology trends in order to produce a set of draft technology oriented scenarios which are presented in this section.

3.1 Advanced dialog interfaces

Many of the experts referred to speech technologies as a crucial part of new technologies that can help in the future of eAccessibility. Looking at the possibility of having speech **recognition technology combined with Natural Language** Processing (NLP) technologies could produce quite accurate speech recognition of natural spoken language. Given the fact of the development of Information Retrieval (IR) systems and their integration with social networks and similar technologies could lead in personalized question answering systems for users. Combining speech recognition with NLP, so that machines can understand human language, and introducing modern IR systems in this combination, could lead to advanced personalized dialog interfaces used from a variety of devices such as mobile phones[2].

Thus, the scenario finally presented can be that of a blind user (and not only them) asking his/her mobile phone questions such as "What are my friends thinking about my new look?" and getting answers based on their personalized IR system.

3.2 Advanced hands-free interaction

One of the technologies identified also as a trend from our data gathering process was Brain-Computer Interfaces (BCI). Using our brain to control various computer functions seems possible in the future[3]. Another key trend identified in our interviews with experts was gesture based interfaces using technologies such as eye tracking, gesture recognition etc. Combining BCI with eye-tracking technologies could possibly lead to advanced hands-free interaction systems based on eye-tracking (as a pointing device) and BCI for declaring users' intent.

This can lead to the scenario of a person with serious mobility impairments using his/her laptop with integrated camera and a BCI device connected just by looking at it.

3.3 Automatic real time transcripts and audio description

Another technology trend identified by experts is the use of a variety of devices to access web content and services. People are interacting with web content and apps through their mobile phones, tablets, appliances, TVs etc. Combining the use of web services with new multimedia technologies such as new video formats embedded with metadata[4] can lead to a new generation of multimedia services[5].

The mixture of these metadata enabled multimedia formats with new speech technologies closer to human language understanding and advanced image recognition technologies could lead to the development of services that will automatically produce transcripts and audio descriptions for video and embed it in it in real time.

Thus, a possible future scenario could be a blind child watching the movies on their webTV together with his deaf grandma and having a similar experience.

3.4 Automatic adaptation of multimodal interfaces

The use of mobile devices is becoming more and more vital day by day. Modern smart phones can contain a lot of information about users, such as documents, music, preferences for various applications and so on. So, having a personal profile on a mobile device seems quite natural. In addition, mobile phones are enhanced with connectivity sensors which allow them to interact with other machines through WiFi, Bluetooth, NFC etc. Finally, they are also enriched with a variety of sensors, such as gps, camera, light sensors, movement sensor etc. which allow them to recognise the context where they are used.

One of the future trends in applications development mentioned by many experts is personalization according to users' needs. Joining personalization with multimodal interfaces[6] which also seem to be a trend for future applications, we can have applications that adapt their modality according to users' needs. Since users will need to interact with a variety of machines in the future and having said that they will probably carry a mobile device with their personal profile information in it, can lead to automatic connection of the mobile device with other devices and transfer of the user profile. This means that we could have a scenario of disabled users connecting automatically through their mobile devices to various machines and adapting their interface and modality according to their needs.

For example, a blind user's mobile phone having recognised the context of use and having stored the user's personal profile can communicate with a pc in a public library and force it to adapt its interface according to the user's needs (enable screen reading, enable key commands, enable use of headphones, disable speakers and voice commands since it is a public library etc.).

3.5 Easy development of accessible web apps

Our analysis also identified ubiquitous connectivity and network services as micro trends together with cloud based services and technologies. This means that in the coming years there will be an explosion of new web apps that will allow users to use a variety of services through web applications. The development of web apps is becoming easier by the years bringing even more developers to that area.

One of the ideas suggested by some experts is the movement of accessibility issues within deeper levels of application development. For example, instead of using a simple widget that you will have to adjust its functionality to make it accessible to disabled users you could use a similar widget which will be already properly adjusted to be accessible. This way, developers will not have to think about accessibility when developing their applications. They will just have to choose the appropriate set of already accessible widgets to work with and their new web apps will be accessible right from their birth.

4. ACKNOWLEDGMENTS

Our thanks to the group of experts working closely with us for the success of our assignment.

5. REFERENCES

[1] eAccessibility, http://www.e-accessibility2020.eu/ (accessed on 30/06/2011)

[2] Gilbert, M., and Junlan Feng, 2008, "Speech and language processing over the web", in *Signal Processing Magazine IEEE* Vol. 25 Issue:3 p18-28

[3] Brunner, P., Bianchi, L., Guger, C., Cincotti, F. and Schalk, G., 2011, "Current trends in hardware and software for brain - computer interfaces (BCIs)" in *Journal of Neural Engineering*, Vol. 8 Number 2

[4] WebVTT, http://www.whatwg.org/specs/web-apps/current-work/webvtt.html (accessed on 30/06/2011)

[5] Ogata, J., Masataka, G. and Kouichirou, E., 2007, "Automatic transcription for a web 2.0 service to search podcasts", In *INTERSPEECH-2007*, 2617-2620.

[6] Nicu, S., 2009, "Multimodal interfaces: Challenges and perspectives", in *Journal of Ambient Intelligence and Smart Environments*, IOS Press, Vol 1, Issue 1, p23-3

Guidelines for an Accessible Web Automation Interface

Y. Puzis, Y. Borodin, F. Ahmed, V. Melnyk, I.V. Ramakrishnan

Stony Brook University, Computer Science Department, Stony Brook, NY 11790-4400

{ypuzis, borodin, faiahmed, vmelnyk, ram}@cs.stonybrook.edu

ABSTRACT

In recent years, the Web has become an ever more sophisticated and irreplaceable tool in our daily lives. While the visual Web has been advancing at a rapid pace, assistive technology has not been able to keep up, increasingly putting visually impaired users at a disadvantage. Web automation has the potential to bridge the accessibility divide between the ways blind and sighted people access the Web; specifically, it can enable blind people to accomplish quickly web browsing tasks that were previously slow, hard, or even impossible to complete. In this paper, we propose guidelines for the design of intuitive and accessible web automation that has the potential to increase accessibility and usability of web pages, reduce interaction time, and improve user browsing experience. Our findings and a preliminary user study demonstrate the feasibility of and emphasize the pressing need for truly accessible web automation technologies.

Categories and Subject Descriptors

H.5.2 [**Information Interfaces and Presentation**]: User Interfaces; H.5.4 [**Information Interfaces and Presentation**]: Hypertext/Hypermedia – *navigation*

General Terms

Human Factors, Experimentation, Design

Keywords

Web Accessibility, Blind Users, Web Browser, Screen Reader, Macro Recorder, Macro Player, Non-Visual, Audio Interface

1   INTRODUCTION

The rapid progress in technology over the recent years has enabled web authors to create increasingly sophisticated web sites and web applications. Web interfaces are now reliant on visual presentation, geometric positioning, colors, shape, dynamic response to user actions, as well as visual clues about interface functionalities. Non-visual accessibility of web interfaces, however, receives significantly less attention, often leaving visually impaired users behind the technology curve.

Blind people typically access computers with the help of *screen readers* [5, 6], assistive technology software that narrates screen content and enables navigation over that content. While screen readers have made text-based web content accessible for blind people, the assistive technology is not offering adequate support of modern web interfaces and is quickly becoming obsolete.

Sighted users are able to visually review web pages and ignore any content that is of low interest (menu, advertisements, etc.). In contrast, screen-reader users remain confined to a very primitive click-and-listen mode of interaction with web pages reduced to a sequence of text, links, form fields, and other web objects.

The inability of screen-reader users to determine which content can be skipped before listening to it often causes *information overload*, which, in turn, impacts their browsing speed and their overall browsing experience. Observations of browsing behaviors of screen-reader users showed that, compared to sighted people, browsing for blind users is often more than 10 times slower [3]!

As a consequence of information overload, important parts of web page content and actionable objects (such as forms, "add to cart" buttons, etc.) become either difficult or impossible to discover and access [4]. This problem is further exacerbated while doing online transactions, such as shopping and bill payment, that usually span several web pages. Enabling accessible automation of web interfaces has the potential to empower blind users to interact effectively with very sophisticated visual web interfaces with the speed and precision matching or even exceeding that of sighted users. By making web content and functionality easier to discover and access, automation can significantly reduce the time and the effort needed for non-visual interaction with the Web.

2   GUIDELINES FOR AN ACCESSIBLE WEB AUTOMATION INTERFACE

Existing accessible web automation technology [1] still has a large barrier to entry for novice users requiring that they have special training on how automation works. Instead, the ideal automation interface should be intuitive, which means that it should not impose a high cognitive load and should not require training and specialized knowledge, and, especially, should not rely on instruction manuals, at least, for the basic functionality.

In accordance with the general good practice principles of user interface design, web automation tools need to be designed *top-down*, i.e., by first considering what types of users, use cases, and work flows are being targeted, then designing a user interface based on those assumptions, and only then designing the underlying algorithms that support the user interface.

We have identified the following characteristics of an ideal web automation interface: *easily discoverable*, *minimal*, and *highly controllable*. While some of these characteristics come directly from user interface design principles, we gain new understanding of these principles in the context of accessible web automation.

Browser users either know what they need to accomplish in advance (searching for a specific term, booking a hotel room, etc.), or are exploring web pages without a well-defined goal (reading news, visiting shopping web pages, etc.). Regardless of whether the user knows exactly what s/he wants to automate or whether the user should be hinted about what can be automated, the available automation needs to be *easily discoverable*. Interface discoverability is of the primary importance to blind users because they cannot just see what interface options are available.

Discoverability alone is not sufficient if the user is presented with too much information. Hence, the interface should minimize cognitive load on the user. Moreover, our target population is blind screen-reader users, and, compared to sighted people, interface interactions take blind people considerably longer [3]. Therefore, the design of the next-generation automation tool should be based on the "less-is-more" principle: one of the main design principles should be *minimizing* both the number of interface controls and the number of user interactions with those controls, regardless of whether those controls are based on speech, shortcuts, or GUI controls.

Today, many websites are very dynamic. The websites are constantly changed by website authors, as well as users (e.g., leaving comments in blogs). As a consequence, macros that were recorded on an earlier version of a website may not be reusable. Therefore, the user needs to have a *fine-grained control* over the automation process, i.e. needs to be able to confirm automated actions and perform the actions manually when automation fails.

3 INTERFACE DESIGN

We next describe an interface designed according to the proposed guidelines. The following are the key concepts of our design.

Let the browsing *state* be characterized by a sequence of visited URLs, loaded cookies, specific actions (e.g., fill out a form element, check a checkbox, submit a form, etc.) already executed by the user on the page. Our main observation is that *very few actions are applicable in a given state, and even fewer are reasonable/useful, i.e. can lead to a meaningful/desirable result.* An intuitive and accessible automation interface can then be based on the following approach: at any point of time, the user can (1) listen through a pseudo-natural language description of a set of actions applicable to the current state, and (2) select and confirm execution of a *single action* from that set. If the user is familiar with the actions that can be automated at that state, s/he can execute an action without listening to its description. The set of suggested actions should be minimal (preferably a single action), and it should be accessible through keyboard and/or a speech command. If necessary, the user can always interact with the webpage using the standard browser and screen-reader interface without the need to switch to some special mode of interaction.

The set of applicable actions can be inferred using a statistical model. The model can be based on the history of user's actions in the given state, and user's statistical profile (history of user's actions in any state). For example, one of the user's profile features can be user's gender, which can determine the correct selection in "gender" selection box. The exact details on how the system identifies the states and what are the statistical model and its features are subjects of future research.

The advantage of our design is the liberation of the user from the need to carefully craft, remember painstaking details of, and maintain an entire library of useful macros. The interface also provides a fine-grained level of control over the process of automation. There is no need to know if the macro is available for a given webpage, how to find it, if it will work in the current system state, or if the macro has finished replaying, and, if it did, what actually happened. There is no need for progress feedback and there is no danger that one or more steps will fail without the user realizing it. Finally, there is no need to explicitly start / stop recording a macro (because we often do not know if we need a macro), if the macro recorded correctly and is sufficiently general (or not general enough).

4 EVALUATION AND FINDINGS

We implemented an Automated Assistant interface and built it into the HearSay [2] non-visual web browser. We then validated the interface design in experiments with 17 visually-impaired screen-reader users, whose ages varied from early twenties to late fifties (gender representation was approximately equal). The subjects were asked to go through two realistic use scenarios ("reserving" a hotel room at hilton.com and "purchasing" an audio book at audible.com). In each scenario, subjects repeated the same tasks twice without (to account for learning effect, subtasks #1 and #2) and once with (subtask #3) the Automated Assistant. In every subtask, subjects were buying different books or reserving different hotel rooms. The order of the tasks was not randomized because we wanted to measure the learning effect between subtasks #1 and #2. The Automated Assistant led the subjects through subtask #3 prompting every step; so, familiarity with the website structure or the specific steps had no effect on the user performance in subtask #3. Finally, automation in subtask #3 was only possible after the user completed subtasks #1 and #2.

The results of the experiments showed that our approach can be very useful for both experienced and novice users. In the hotel reservation scenario, the average *interaction difficulty* (measured on the scale from 1-easy to 5-difficult) was 3.69, 2.75, and 1.56 for subtasks #1, #2, and #3 respectively. The average *interaction time* was 561 sec., 301 sec., 154 sec., for subtasks #1, #2, and #3 respectively. In the purchasing scenario, the difficulty was 3.12, 2.29, 1.65 and the timing was 440 sec., 242 sec., 120 sec. for subtasks #1, #2, and #3. In all cases the improvement between subtasks was statistically significant, with confidence level 0.01.

The vast majority of the test subjects were excited about the prospect of automating their interaction with the web using our approach. However, several subjects did not feel comfortable with relinquishing control of the browser to an automated system.

In the future, we will refine our approach and publish an expanded report of our findings. Looking forward, we see the need for an intelligent algorithm to power the Automated Assistant (or similar tools designed by the same principles). This includes correctly mapping actions that can be automated to the specific system state, ranking actions given history of user activity, handling the dynamic website updates and modifications made to the websites by their owners overtime.

5 ACKNOWLEDGEMENTS

We thank Terri Hedgpeth for help with experiments. This work was supported by NSF Awards IIS-0808678, and CNS-0751083.

6 REFERENCES

[1] Bigham, J.P., T. Lau, and J. Nichols, *Trailblazer: enabling blind users to blaze trails through the web*, IUI'09.

[2] Borodin, Y., F. Ahmed, M.A. Islam, Y. Puzis, V. Melnyk, S. Feng, I.V. Ramakrishnan, and G. Dausch, *Hearsay: a new generation context-driven multi-modal assistive web browser*, WWW'10.

[3] Borodin, Y., J.P. Bigham, G. Dausch, and I.V. Ramakrishnan, *More than meets the eye: a survey of screen-reader browsing strategies*, W4A'10.

[4] Islam, M.A., F. Ahmed, Y. Borodin, J. Mahmud, and I.V. Ramakrishnan, *Improving Accessibility of Transaction-Centric Web Objects*, SDM'10.

[5] JAWS. *Screen reader from Freedom Scientific*. Avaiable at: freedomscientific.com/products/fs/jaws-product-page.asp.

[6] NVDA. *NonVisual Desktop Access*. Available from: http://www.nvda-project.org/.

Helping Children with Cognitive Disabilities through Serious Games: Project CLES

Aarij Mahmood Hussaan
Université de Lyon
Université de Lyon 1, LIRIS
UMR5205, F-69622, France
+(33) 4 72 43 11 57

Aarij-mahmood.Hussaan@liris.cnrs.fr

Karim Sehaba
Université de Lyon
Université de Lyon 2, LIRIS
UMR5205, F-69679, France
+(33) 4 78 77 44 80

Karim.sehaba@liris.cnrs.fr

Alain Mille
Université de Lyon
Université de Lyon 1, LIRIS
UMR5205, F-69622, France
+(33) 4 72 44 58 24

Alain.mille@liris.cnrs.fr

ABSTRACT

Our work addresses the development of a Serious Game for the diagnostic and learning of persons with cognitive disabilities. In reality, many studies have shown that young people, especially children, are attracted towards computer games. Often, they play these games with great interest and attention. Thus, the idea of using serious games to provide education is attractive for most of them. This work is situated in the context of Project CLES. This project, in collaboration with many research laboratories, aims at developing an Adaptive Serious Game to treat a variety of cognitive handicaps. In this context, this article presents a system that generates learning scenarios keeping into account the user's profile and their learning objectives. The user's profile is used to represent the cognitive abilities and the domain competences of the user. The system also records the user's activities during his/her interaction with the Serious Game and represents them in interaction traces. These traces are used as knowledge sources in the generation of learning scenarios.

Categories and Subject Descriptors

I.2.1 [Applications and Expert Systems] *Games*

K.4.2 [Social Issues] *Assistive technologies for persons with disabilities, Handicapped persons/special needs*

General Terms

Performance, Design, Human Factors, Theory, Verification.

Keywords

Cognitive disability, Learning scenarios, interaction traces, serious games.

1. INTRODUCTION

The subject of helping persons in the situation of cognitive disabilities has been investigated by the researchers since long. Many tools has been created either to test the presence of a cognitive disability in a person or to help the person overcome these disabilities like in [1][2]. In this paper, we propose to use Serious Games as an educational medium to teach/help persons in situation of cognitive disabilities.

In this context, we focus to create a system that is capable of **generating learning scenarios keeping into account the learner's competencies and deficiencies along with the specificities of serious games**. These learning scenarios are composed of a suite of activities selected and parameterized by the system according to the learner's profile and learning objectives. Afterwards, these scenarios are presented to the learner via a serious game. These scenarios are dynamic in nature i.e. they are automatically adapted to the performance of the learner. The user's interaction traces [3] are used to analyze user's performance and accordingly update the user's profile.

Our research work is part of Project CLES[1]. The objective of this project is to create a serious game environment; this environment aims to support learning for children and adolescents with intellectual disabilities related to the following cognitive domains: perception, attention, memory, oral language, written language, logical reasoning, visual-spatial and transverse competencies. The details about this game are presented in [4].

2. PROJECT CLES

The Project CLES (Cognitive and Linguistic Element Stimulation) is financed by the French ministry and is conducted in partnership with the laboratories: EMC specializing in cognitive mechanisms study, LUTIN Laboratory for the usage of digital information techniques and the society GERIP specializing in the creation of digital solutions for cognitive sciences.

The main protagonist of this game is a person named "Tom 'O Connor". Tom is a relic hunter (much like Indiana Jones and Lara Croft). The user takes control of Tom in this game. Tom is assigned to search for a relic, which contains great mystical powers. On his mission, Tom is assisted by two of his colleagues. Their mission is to guide Tom throughout his journey by giving him tips and telling him what to do. In order to search for the relic, Tom is placed inside of a room. This room is attached to one or many other rooms. Tom needs to find the key in order to exit the room and enter the next one. Each room represents one of the eight cognitive domains (attention, perception, etc). Inside each room there are objects, with which Tom can interact and there are also some non-interactive objects as well. The rooms are depicted in the figures 1.

2.1 Examples of Games

In Figure 2 we present a mini-game called "Objets Entérmélés à Identifier" (Identify intermixed objects). The purpose of this game is to test the visual-perception of a child aged between 6-12 years. The game goes as follows: the learner is shown a "Model" which

---

[1] http://liris.cnrs.fr/cles

contains more than one element that is intermixed. s/he is also shown a number of single elements as responses possible.

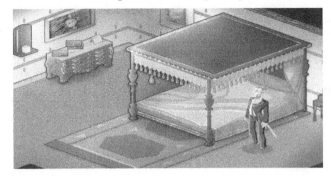

Figure 1: Room

The learner needs to identify, among the responses possible, the element which appears in the "Model". Furthermore, the learner has to do it in the allotted time.

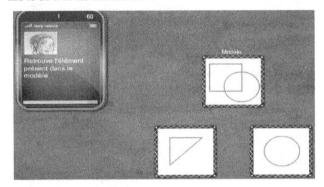

Figure 2: Mini Game

3. Knowledge Representation in System

As our objectives concern both the pedagogical domain and serious game specificities and also is to remain as reusable as possible, therefore it is necessary to identify and separate different aspects of the system. This separation on the one hand will let us to manage the information easily and on the other hand will make different aspects less dependable on other aspects thus, rendering our system more reusable.

We've identified three kinds of knowledge that is represented by our system. They are: 1) domain knowledge, 2) pedagogical resource, and 3) serious game resources. The figure 3 shows the interface for creating the domain's knowledge.

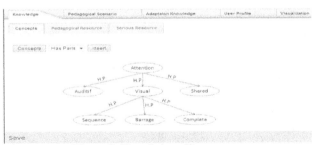

Figure 3: Knowledge editor screen

The first layer 'domain knowledge' represents two kinds of knowledge: the pedagogical knowledge of the domain to be taught, for example mathematics, physics, grammar, biology etc, and the physical and cognitive abilities of the learner, for example attention, perception, etc, this knowledge are composed of concepts and their sub-concepts. A concept is associated or linked with another concept via a *relation*. This relation tells what kind of impact a concept has on other concept. In our system we've identified four types of relations [4] Has-Parts, Required, Type-Of and Parallel.

The second layer contains the pedagogical resource knowledge. This is where all the pedagogical resources are located. All the pedagogical resources are associated with at least one pedagogical concept. A pedagogical resource can be associated with more than one concept. A pedagogical resource is atomic in nature i.e. it is not associated with other resources. The third kind of knowledge is the serious game resource. This represents the serious game resources like chairs, tables, Non Playing Characters, doors etc. A serious game resource is connected with one or more than one pedagogical resource and vice versa.

3.1 Scenario Generator

As the knowledge is divided into three layers, the generation process of the learning scenarios is also performed in three steps. Given the learning objectives (in the form of list of pedagogical concepts) and the user's profile, the first step consists in selecting the concepts from the knowledge domain that are necessary to achieve the learning objectives. This selection is done based on the user's profile.

In the second step, the pedagogical resources are selected for each knowledge concept selected in the previous step. This selection is also done on the basis of the user's profile. The profile tells which kind of resources a user prefers. In the third step, the serious game resources are selected based upon the pedagogical resources selected. These pedagogical resources are hidden behind the serious game resources in the game.

This three steps process is used by the system in achieving its objective of remaining reusable, by separating the generation of one kind of resources from others. Once generated the serious game resources with the pedagogical resources hidden behind them are shown to the user. The user interacts with these serious resources via the serious games. The moment the user is interacting with the game the user's interaction traces are generated and are used by the system to update the user's profile and to modify the generated scenarios if necessary.

4. References

[1] A. Diamond and P.S. Goldman-Rakic, "Comparison of human infants and rhesus monkeys on Piaget□s AB task: Evidence for dependence on dorsolateral prefrontal cortex," *Experimental Brain Research*, vol. 74, 1989, p. 24–40.

[2] M. Mody, M. Studdert-Kennedy, and S. Brady, "Speech perception deficits in poor readers: auditory processing or phonological coding?," *Journal of experimental child psychology*, vol. 64, Feb. 1997, pp. 199-231.

[3] K. Sehaba, B. Encelle, and A. Mille, "Adaptive TEL based on Interaction Traces," *In AIED 09 (14 International Conference on Artificial Intelligence in Education) workshop on "Towards User Modeling and Adaptive Systems for All (TUMAS-A 2009): Modeling and Evaluation of Accessible Intelligent Learning Systems,"* 2009.

[4] A.M. Hussaan, K. Sehaba, and A. Mille, "Tailoring Serious Games with Adaptive Pedagogical Scenarios A Serious Game for persons with cognitive disabilities," *ICALT '11*, 2011, p. 5.

Improving Accessibility for Deaf People: An Editor for Computer Assisted Translation Through Virtual Avatars

Davide Barberis, Nicola Garazzino, Paolo Prinetto, Gabriele Tiotto
Politecnico di Torino, Dipartimento di Automatica e Informatica
Corso Duca degli Abruzzi 24, 10129
Torino, Italy
{davide.barberis, nicola.garazzino, paolo.prinetto, gabriele.tiotto}@polito.it

ABSTRACT

This paper presents the ATLAS Editor for Assisted Translation (ALEAT), a novel tool for the Computer Assisted Translation (CAT) from Italian written language to Italian Sign Language (LIS) of Deaf People. The tool is a web application that has been developed within the ATLAS project, that targets the automatic translation from Italian written language to Italian Sign Language in the weather forecasts domain. ALEAT takes a text as input, written according to the Italian Language grammar, performs the automatic translation of the sentence and gives the result of the translation to the user by visualizing it through a virtual character. Since the automatic translation is error-prone, ALEAT allows to correct it with the intervention of the user. The translation is stored in a database resorting to a novel formalism: the ATLAS Written Extended LIS (AEWLIS). AEWLIS allows to play the translation through the ATLAS visualization module and to load it within ALEAT for successive modifications and improvement.

Categories and Subject Descriptors

K.4.2 [**Social Issues**]: Assistive technologies for persons with disabilities

General Terms

Experimentation, Human Factors, Languages

1. INTRODUCTION

The request for technology enabling people with disabilities to access services is more and more growing worldwide; in parallel new laws and rules are enforced in various countries to regulate the relationships between the governments and people with disabilities. E-inclusion has becoming one of the main issues to be undertaken by public administrations and government authorities. Approximately there are 60.000 Deaf or Hard of Hearing individuals in Italy [3]. 10% is hearing impaired [6] and severe deafness represents about 25%- 30% of the cause of disability.
Sign Languages (SLs) are the mean of communication of Deaf People. They allow Deaf People to acquire a full cognitive development within their community and to acquire a full access to education and culture, necessary prerequisites to a full inclusion into the working and social environment.

SLs rely on gestures instead of sounds to convey meaning. They combine shapes, orientation of hands, movements of the arms and facial expressions to convey syntactic and semantic content. Having the possibility to synthesize Sign Languages would be of great interest for Deaf People, as could improve their access to written content and to the spoken language of the hearing community.
Projects targeted sign language linguistics and resource creation for translation and find phenomena related to the language. DePaul University ASL synthesizer allows the visualization of signs in ASL [1], Signspeak [4] targets sign language recognition and translation, the DICTA-Sign project targets sign language recognition and synthesis [2]. VCom3D has developed a system for the creation of ASL signs sequence through a virtual character [5]. As demonstrated by the results of these international projects [9], virtual character based solutions are generally accepted by the deaf community and while some works revealed that this technology could give a satisfying level of understandability, additional work has to be done to improve the translation quality, in order to provide a sign language translation resorting to its grammar.
Computer Assisted Translation (CAT) systems have been proposed in [7], using statistical or pattern recognition methods to predict a best (or n-best) translation suffix(es) to complete the translation that is currently being performed. This paper presents a tool for the computer assisted (CAT) translation from Italian written language to Italian Sign Language (LIS) called ALEAT. ALEAT provides useful functionalities for sign language synthesis according to LIS grammar.

2. SIGN LANGUAGE ASSISTED TRANSLATION WITH ALEAT

The automatic translation is performed in the ATLAS system resorting to both statistical and rule based approaches. For each sentence in input, the corresponding translation is provided by both statistical and rule based modules and the best translation is chosen. The visualization process is performed by Donna, the ATLAS virtual interpreter, in two steps. First the Italian text is transformed/translated into AEWLIS, consisting of a sequence of signs and syntactic/semantic relationships among them. Then, a virtual character animates the AEWLIS content into a coherent LIS sequence. The module that is devoted to the visualization and synthesis of Donna is the Virtual Animator (henceforth Animator). The Animator relies on a Signary, and each sign is retrieved according to the sequence specified in the

AEWLIS produced by the translation modules. The architecture of the Animator includes two main components: *The Planner* which is based on linguistic plans, that describe how signs can be adapted to the context of a specific sentence (encoded in the AEWLIS representation), given the constraints given by the communicative situation and the interpreter's configuration (signing resources, availability of the resources, etc.). *The Executor* whenever receives a plan from the Planner, consults the Signary to replace each plan action with the definition of the corresponding sign. For each sign, it applies the matching animation mapping rule to obtain the animation language expression that describes how the sign is realized. The Sign-to-Animation mapping rules specify how a sign can be generated by using the animation data in the repository or by procedural functions (or a combination of the two). Then, a blending system creates the LIS by smoothly joining in real-time the existing animation clips through interpolation functions. A preliminary evaluation of the system shows that the virtual character is generally well accepted by deaf people even if they find it a little bit clumsy [8]. Given the error proneness of the automatic translation (while translating in a general linguistic domain), we developed an editor for Computer Assisted Translation, that allows providing a more robust translation even to other domains by easily expanding the Signary.

The user can manage the translation process sentence by sentence, saving the actual translation for a sentence and starting to work with another one. The translation process develops in the following steps:

- *Sentence Analysis.* The single sentence is given as input to an external module that is devoted to perform the morphological and syntactical analysis with the aim of automatically providing information about the syntax and the morphology. This information directly affect the translation as influence the virtual character by modifying how a sign is performed.

- *Sentence Modification.* The user performs some manual operations on the sentence Lemmas such as shifting, deletion and insertion.

- *Linking and Disambiguation.* This step is performed by taking effort of an Italian to LIS dictionary. The user associates each lemma to a sign and selects the right one in case of semantic ambiguity.

- *Tagging.* The user adds linguistic and articulatory information needed for the avatar to properly sign the translation.

When the tagging step is finished, the user saves the translation in AEWLIS XML format. It is automatically stored in the database and metadata are applied such as the user profile type, the name of the user, the time and date. The AEWLIS file can be visualized on demand. The ATLAS visualization module can export the translation as a video or as more low level animation file.

3. CONCLUSIONS AND FUTURE WORK

In this paper we presented ALEAT: a web based editor for the assisted translation from italian to LIS by means of a virtual character. The aim of this tool is to provide a robust translation of written content to be provided to Deaf People for improving their inclusion. The translation can be performed by a user which is proficient in both Italian Language and LIS.

A preliminary evaluation of the translation has been performed. Since some features of the target language are not implemented yet such as highly iconic structures, the visualization module has been evaluated by Deaf and the complete translation performed with ALEAT (from written text to synthesis with the visualization module) was evaluated by a native signer interpreter. The results shows as the quality of translation strictly depends on the quality of the animation clips stored in the Signary.

Future work aims at performing further evaluations of the translation and a comparison between the output of the automatic translation module with the output of ALEAT. We expect the ALEAT translation to be more reliable that the automatic one. The ATLAS Animator is being ported to Mobile and Digital Terrestrial Television platforms to visualize the translations of subtitles, announcements and written content in general. Moreover the Signary will be ported on the Web and Mobile devices as Italian-LIS Dictionaries.

4. ACKNOWLEDGMENTS

The work presented in the present paper has been developed within the ATLAS (Automatic Translation into sign LAnguageS) Project , co-funded by Regione Piemonte within the Converging Technologies Framework.

5. REFERENCES

[1] Depaul asl synthesizer webpage: http://asl.cs.depaul.edu/.
[2] Dicta sign web portal: Available at http://www.dictasign.eu/.
[3] Eud homepage: http://www.eud.eu/italy-i-187.html.
[4] Signspeak project webpage: http://www.signspeak.eu/.
[5] Vcom3d: Sign smith studio. available at http://www.vcom3d.com/index.php?id=ssstudio.
[6] D. Barberis, N. Garazzino, E. Piccolo, P. Prinetto, and G. Tiotto. A Web Based Platform for Sign Language Corpus Creation. *Computers Helping People with Special Needs*, pages 193–199, 2010.
[7] S. Barrachina, O. Bender, F. Casacuberta, J. Civera, E. Cubel, S. Khadivi, A. Lagarda, H. Ney, J. Tomás, E. Vidal, et al. Statistical approaches to computer-assisted translation. *Computational Linguistics*, 35(1):3–28, 2009.
[8] V. Lombardo, F. Nunnari, and R. Damiano. A Virtual Interpreter for the Italian Sign. In *Intelligent Virtual Agents: 10th International Conference, IVA 2010, Philadelphia, PA, USA. Proceedings*, page 201. Springer, 2010.
[9] C. Vogler and S. Goldenstein. Analysis of facial expressions in american sign language. In *Proceedings of the 3rd International Conference on Universal Access in Human-Computer Interaction*. Citeseer.

Improving Deaf Accessibility in Remote Usability Testing

Jerry Schnepp
DePaul University
243 South Wabash Avenue
Chicago, IL 60604
(312)362-8381

jschnepp@cdm.depaul.edu

Brent Shiver
DePaul University
243 South Wabash Avenue
Chicago, IL 60604
(312)362-8381

bshiver@cs.depaul.edu

ABSTRACT

For studies involving Deaf participants in United States, remote usability testing has several potential advantages over face-to-face testing, including convenience, lower cost and the ability to recruit participants from diverse geographic regions. However, current technologies force Deaf participants to use English instead of their preferred language, which is American Sign Language (ASL). A new remote testing technology allows researchers to conduct studies exclusively in ASL at a lower cost than face-to-face testing. The technology design facilitates open-ended questions and is reconfigurable for use in a variety of studies. Results from usability tests of the tool are encouraging and a full-scale study is underway to compare this approach to face-to-face testing.

Categories and Subject Descriptors

H.5.2 [**User Interfaces**]: Interaction styles (e.g., commands, menus, forms, direct manipulation)

General Terms

Measurement, Documentation, Design, Experimentation, Human Factors, Verification.

Keywords

Remote Usability Testing, Accommodations for the Deaf

1. INTRODUCTION

One barrier to better Deaf[1] accessibility to technology is the current process of usability testing itself. Members of the Deaf community in the United States use American Sign Language (ASL), not English as their preferred language. Although face-to-face usability testing protocols can incorporate certified ASL/English interpreters [1], barriers of scheduling, cost and localization remain. Hearing researchers must coordinate not only the schedules of their team and the schedules of the Deaf participants, but also the schedules of certified interpreters.

The cost of interpreters further confounds scheduling issues since rates for certified interpreters are typically $50.00 per hour with a

---

[1] The term "Deaf" with a capital "D" refers to the community that uses American Sign Language as their preferred language and shares a common culture, history and experience.

two-hour minimum. This motivates researchers to schedule back-to-back testing sessions, imposing further time constraints and stress on the test team. As previously noted [1], the resulting low numbers of participants can interfere with statistical analysis.

Localization is another challenge of face-to-face testing [2]. Testing of this kind typically draws users from a limited geographic area, which often results in an adversely small numbers of participants. Further, participants drawn exclusively from a particular locale may yield skewed results when compared to a more geographically diverse sample.

2. CHALLENGES OF REMOTE TESTING

In contrast, remote testing can be done asynchronously, easing the burden of scheduling [3], and has been used in recent years to evaluate web sites, virtual prototypes, and software [4]. This technology allows researchers to test with large, geographically diverse populations. Data are collected asynchronously over a network and stored in a central database, leading to faster collection and lower costs [5].

Remote testing holds the potential to tap a large, geographically diverse Deaf population in a more cost-effective manner [6], particularly since many members of the Deaf community have embraced the Internet as a preferred means of communication [7]. Through the use of webcams, the Deaf communicate directly in ASL and avoid the necessity of typing.

However a significant language barrier remains. Remote testing technologies designed for hearing audiences in the United States use written English. English is not a viable option because the average reading fluency of a Deaf adult is at the fourth-grade level [8]. American Sign Language (ASL) is the preferred language of the Deaf community, and differs radically from English. Asking Deaf participants to test with written English is asking them to test in a second language. This barrier motivates a new approach to remote usability testing.

3. A MORE DEAF-FRIENDLY APPROACH

To lower barriers and increase the size of the participant pool, we have developed a reconfigurable, web-based evaluation tool that uses ASL exclusively. The goal is to capitalize on the advantages of remote testing – flexibility of scheduling and lowered cost – but without the barriers posed by written English. All information and instructions in this new tool, from informed consent to post-test questionnaire, are presented in ASL.

Figure 1 shows the screen layout for a closed-ended question. Recordings of the test moderator appear in the upper right window and test stimuli appear on the left. The test participant views instructions from the test moderator and observes test stimuli. The participant can view a stimulus for as long as s/he wants and then answer questions in the response area on the lower right. Across the top of the screen is a progress indicator.

As is apparent in the figure, there are no labels associated with the response choices. Instead, the interface takes advantage of a unique visual aspect of signed language called *indexing* [9]. Indexing occurs in ASL when a person refers to an object or another person in the environment, and involves pointing at the entity. The signed instructions in this tool use indexing to refer to the response choices. This is analogous to asking a hearing person to respond to the choices of a Likert scale.

The tool also provides for open-ended questions via an innovative approach for capturing responses via the participant's webcam. The test moderator asks the participant to sign their response for the webcam. The response area changes to show webcam input, and a webcam control. The participant signs a response in ASL and clicks the control when done. The participants are comfortable with this due to their previous experience in using webcams and the assurances in the informed consent that the recorded responses are only used for collecting aggregate data and are destroyed at the end of the study.

Figure 1: A screenshot of the interface

4. ADVANTAGES
Interpreter costs are greatly reduced because it is only necessary to hire an interpreter to voice the responses to open-ended questions. This is a small fraction of the time required to interpret an entire session. Further, the researcher can wait until the testing is complete and hire the interpreter to voice all of the responses in a single session.

5. CONFIDENTIALITY
For data analysis, we only retain the voice recording of the interpreter and destroy the original video. This is analogous to destroying recordings of a face-to-face test. In fact, since the researchers never see the face of the participant, this method has an enhanced level of confidentiality.

6. CONFIGURABILITY
The tool is written in Adobe ActionScript and accommodates any number of test stimuli and most common formats for questions. To create a test, a Deaf researcher or certified interpreter records videos of informed consent, instructions, questionnaires, etc. and inserts them into the tool. Since the tool itself is language-neutral, it has the potential for use with any type of signed language, as well as for populations having low literacy levels.

7. RESULTS
Early results from usability testing (IRB# 101609JSCDMR1) are promising. Of a group of eight users, seven indicated that the indexing technique was easily or very easily understood, and all agreed or strongly agreed with the statement "ASL is better than English for this type of test." Participants described the test approach as "inspired", "excellent", "super-great", and "beneficial to the Deaf community". The most common suggestion was to include a way to replay the facilitator's instructions, and the authors are in the process of implementing this feature.

8. FUTURE WORK
We are collecting data with this new tool to compare with data previously collected via face-to-face testing. Ultimately, we want to make an open source version of this tool for distribution.

9. REFERENCES

[1] Roberts, V. and Fels, D. 2006. Methods for inclusion: Employing think aloud protocols in software usability studies with individuals who are deaf. *Int. J. Human-Computer Studies.* 64, (2006), 489-501.

[2] Tullis, T., Fleischman, S., McNulty, M., Cianchette, C, and Bergel, M. 2002. An empirical comparison of lab and remote usability testing of Web sites. *Proc. Usability Professionals Association Conference* (Orlando, FL, July 8-12, 2003), 26-33.

[3] Scholtz, J. 2001. Adaptation of traditional usability testing methods for remote testing. *Proc. Annual Hawaii International Conference on System Sciences* (Maui, HI, January 3-6, 2001), 8-15.

[4] Thompson, K., Rozanski, E., and Haake, A. 2004. Here, there, anywhere: Remote usability testing that works. *Proc. 5th Conference on Information Technology Education* (Salt Lake City, UT, October 28 - 30, 2004). CITC5 '04. ACM, New York, NY, 132-137. DOI=http://doi.acm.org/ 10.1145/1029533.1029567

[5] Hong, J., Heer, J., Waterson, S., and Landay, J. 2001. WebQuilt: A proxy-based approach to remote web usability testing. *ACM Transactions on Information Systems*, 19, 3, (July, 2001), 263-285. DOI=http://doi.acm.org/ 10.1145/502115.502118

[6] Petrie, H., Hamilton, F., King, N., and Pavan, P. 2008. Remote Usability Evaluations with Disabled People. *Proceedings of the SIGCHI Conference on Human Factors in Computing Systems.* (Montréal, Quebec, Canada, April 22-27, 2008). CHI'06 ACM, New York, NY, 1133-1141. DOI=http://doi.acm.org/ 10.1145/1124772.1124942

[7] Hogg, N., Lomicky, C. and Weiner, S. 2008. Computer-Mediated Communication and the Gallaudet University Community: A Preliminary Report. *American Annals of the Deaf.* 153, 1, (Spring 2008), 89-96.

[8] Erting, E. 1992. Deafness & Literacy: Why Can't Sam Read? *Sign Language Studies.* 75, (Summer, 1992), 97-112.

[9] Baker-Shenk, C. and Cokely, D. 1980. *American Sign Language: A Teacher's Resource Text on Grammar and Culture.* Gallaudet University Press, Washington, DC.

In-Vehicle Assistive Technology (IVAT) for Drivers Who Have Survived a Traumatic Brain Injury

Julia DeBlasio Olsheski, Bruce N. Walker, and Jeff McCloud
Sonification Lab, Georgia Institute of Technology
Atlanta, Georgia, USA
+1-404-894-8265
julia@gatech.edu, bruce.walker@psych.gatech.edu, jefferson.mccloud@gtri.gatech.edu

ABSTRACT

IVAT (in-vehicle assistive technology) is an in-dash interface borne out from a collaborative effort between the Shepherd Center assistive technology team, the Georgia Tech Sonification Laboratory, and Centrafuse™. The aim of this technology is to increase driver safety by taking individual cognitive abilities and limitations into account. While the potential applications of IVAT are widespread, the initial population of interest for the current research is survivors of a traumatic brain injury (TBI). TBI can cause a variety of impairments that limit driving ability. IVAT is aimed at enabling the individual to overcome these limitations in order to regain some independence by driving after injury.

Categories and Subject Descriptors

J.4 [**Computer Applications**]: Social and Behavioral Sciences – *Psychology*.

General Terms

Performance, Design, Human Factors

Keywords

Driving, Cognitive Limitations, TBI, Assistive Technology, Human Factors

1. INTRODUCTION

Millions of people incur, and then strive to recover from, traumatic brain injuries (TBI) each year. Following extensive rehabilitation, they are often able to reintegrate into daily life. The ability to drive a car unsupervised is often a critical factor in regaining independence. Unfortunately, many TBI survivors (and indeed people with various disabilities) have residual perceptual, cognitive, motor, or affect-control deficits that impact their ability to drive, among other activities. To assist people who have had TBI be better, more independent drivers, we have developed an in-vehicle assistive technology (IVAT). The system is, in fact, a framework for developing a range of assistive applications, each one tuned to the particular needs of the individual driver. In the current research, an in-vehicle PC is utilized with Centrafuse Application Integration Framework software that merges connected car technology and IVAT in a multimodal in-dash touch screen interface (see Figure 1). IVAT utilizes driver interaction and multimodal positive reinforcement to improve and sustain behaviors known to increase driver safety.

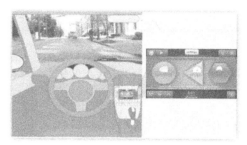

Figure 1. IVAT in-dash display.

2. TRAUMATIC BRAIN INJURY

2.1 TBI Classification

The level and type of cognitive limitations resulting from TBI depend on the injury details: severity, mechanism, and location. The most common causes of TBI include violence, transportation accidents, construction mishaps, and sports injuries [6]. Brain concussion, cortical contusions, intracranial hemorrhage, and axonal shear injury may occur with both open and closed head injuries. Classification is generally made using observational ratings such as the Glasgow Outcome Scale (GOS) or the Disability Rating Scale (DRS) [3]. These provide the criteria for TBI classification as mild, moderate, or severe. Classification into these categories allows determination of appropriate treatment and early identification of potential sequelae [6]. Even after rehabilitation, permanent cognitive impairment may or may not preclude an individual from becoming a safe driver [7]. Correct identification of unsafe drivers is of critical import for both the TBI survivor and his or her potential fellow drivers.

2.2 Driving After TBI

Driving after TBI has been identified as a critical component of achieving autonomy and reintegration into the mainstream community [2]. Despite great potential risks, the percentage of individuals who return to driving after TBI is believed to be as high as 60% [3] of the 2 million new cases in the U.S. each year [4]. Less than half of these (37%) ever receive professional driving evaluation [3]. Cognitive, behavioral, and physical sequelae commonly associated with TBI that have been shown to have negative effects on safe driving include: information processing speed, psychomotor speed, visuospatial ability, and executive function including meta-awareness of individual self limitations [7][1]. Assessment of these key symptoms has been shown to validly predict safe-driving ability after brain injury [7]. Successful rehabilitation must address these population-specific needs. Training that focuses on visual scanning, spatial perception, attention focusing skills, and problem solving is believed to significantly improve driver awareness of shortcomings and driving abilities (anosognosia) [7] Similarly, the Shepherd

Center rehabilitation hospital's driving evaluators report mirror scanning, space monitoring, and environmental awareness as the key skills that need to be trained in order to improve clients' defensive driving abilities [1]. For these reasons, the current iteration of IVAT focuses on these three driving skills.

2.3 A Shepherd Center Case Study

One challenge for driving evaluators stems from the tendency of TBI clients to be better able to remain focused on the driving task in the presence of the evaluator than when driving solo. As part of a limited self-awareness of individual deficits, many TBI survivors have a propensity to forget that they are driving, especially when alone. This can be observed by a 'glazed over' look and the onset of defensive driving practice neglect [1]. While working with one such individual who exhibited attention deficits, Shepherd Center evaluators noted that a lack of stimulation for 6-7 minutes resulted in swerving, disregard for traffic signals, and poor space management. The individual was capable of passing evaluation, but would then experience problems once returning home to a normal driving routine. This individual accumulated traffic violations and was in jeopardy of losing driving licensure.

In order to replicate the experience of driving with an evaluator, the Shepherd Center team designed a device they called the Electronic Driving Coach (EDC). The EDC is a three-button box that rests on the driver console. Each of the buttons is labeled to match the three tasks this individual most needed to remember to practice in order to be a safe driver: mirror scanning, speed maintenance, and space monitoring. Every time the individual noticed himself practicing one of these tasks, he was to push the corresponding button. The EDC would then give the driver auditory positive feedback. For instance, if the driver noticed that he was checking his speed and pushed the corresponding 'speed' button, the EDC might display, "Great job checking your speed! It's easy to accidentally drive faster than the posted limit." After a 3, 6, and 12-month re-evaluation, the individual's driving skills have been rehabilitated to a much safer level as evidenced by continued evaluations and the discontinuation of traffic violations.

3. IVAT
3.1 IVAT Design

The early success of the Shepherd Center's EDC with this initial individual and a handful of clients afterward motivated the current research project. Our goals were to: *1) Understand the variety and extent of disabilities affecting individuals with TBI*. The direction and methods of the design were informed by qualitative research. We conducted interviews with several physical therapists having at least two years of clinical experience with TBI clients. These interviews served to support the literature findings and provide design guidelines necessary for an effective assistive technology. *2) Create design guidelines to support the cognitive (dis)abilities of potential users.* The guidelines correlated data from the interviews with the framework established from our literature review. This further clarified the most common disabilities among individuals with TBI who still retain driving capabilities. Disabilities found to be common among these individuals highlighted the most relevant needs and critical elements necessary for an effective design. *3) Test the design's benefits on potential users of IVAT.* Focus groups consisting of therapists and TBI clients were shown example driving situation videos. Feedback was collected on the effectiveness of an assistive technology and modality preference for the design

concepts. *4) Design a prototype based on client feedback*. A demonstration video simulated the IVAT system in ecological driving conditions, with actual auditory and visual interfaces included. As part of the design prototype, a taxonomy of specific occurrences and notifications from the system to the driver were based on research and standards. This served as the criteria for the creation of the system. *5) Validate the design with the users and therapists.* A final focus group of therapists and potential TBI users saw the design prototypes and assessed the validity of the design. Focus group feedback is informing future developments and modules for IVAT.

3.2 IVAT Application Framework

The limitations of the physical button box are obvious. The potential (and need) for a more flexible software-based IVAT system became clear through our focus group efforts. Thus, using the research-informed prototype design, we created IVAT as an assistive technology plug-in architecture within Centrafuse. We also built the first AT plug-in module to mimic the original EDC button box enhanced by touch-screen software. In addition to the functionality of the original button box, IVAT features an in-dash touch screen display rather than the clunky box, is customizable for individuals with varying levels and types of cognitive and perceptual limitations, can log driving performance information, and merges with additional in-vehicle infotainment systems. A wide range of novel plug-ins may now be created and then deployed on a driver-by-driver basis depending on his or her particular diagnoses. The data logging capabilities inherent in the IVAT framework are also useful for evaluators who can track objective performance measures over time (e.g., between rehabilitative sessions). Currently, IVAT is fully functional as a Centrafuse application and we will begin running systematic empirical evaluations both in a simulator and in on-road vehicles in the near future. The initial population of interest has been TBI survivors, but in-vehicle assistive technology has potential benefits for other high-risk populations such as older adults and new drivers.

4. REFERENCES

[1] Anshutz, J. 2010. Personal communication.

[2] Brenner, L., Homaifar, B., & Schultheis, M. 2008. Driving, aging, and traumatic brain injury: Integrating findings from the literature. *Rehab. Psych., 53*(1), 18-27.

[3] Doig, E., Fleming, J., Tooth, L. 2001. Patterns of community integration 2-5 years post-discharge from brain injury rehabilitation. *Brain Injury, 15*(9), 747-762.

[4] Fisk, G., Schneider, J., Novack, T. 1998. Driving following traumatic brain injury: Prevalence, exposure, advice and evaluations. *Brain Injury, 12*(8), 683-695.

[5] Gerhart, K., Mellick, D., & Weintraub, A. 2003. Violence-related traumatic brain injury: A population-based study. *J. Trauma-Injury Infect. & Crit. Care, 55*(6), 1045-1053.

[6] Kushner, D. 1998. Mild traumatic brain injury: Toward understanding manifestations and treatment. *Arch. Inter. Med,* 158 (15): 1617–24.

[7] Schanke, A.-K., & Sundet, K. 2000. Comprehensive Driving Assessment: Neuropsychological Testing and On-road Evaluation of Brain Injured Patients. *Scand. J. Psych.,* 41(2), 113-121.

[8] Schultheis, M., & Mourant, R. 2001. Virtual reality and driving: The road to better assessment for cognitively impaired populations. *Presence, 10(4),* 431-439.

Increased Accessibility to Nonverbal Communication through Facial and Expression Recognition Technologies for Blind/Visually Impaired Subjects

Douglas Astler*, Harrison Chau, Kailin Hsu, Alvin Hua, Andrew Kannan, Lydia Lei,
Melissa Nathanson, Esmaeel Paryavi, Michelle Rosen, Hayato Unno, Carol Wang,
Khadija Zaidi, and Xuemin Zhang
Team F.A.C.E., Gemstone Honors Program, University of Maryland
College Park, MD, USA
face.gemstone@gmail.com

Cha-Min Tang
University of Maryland School of Medicine
Baltimore, MD, USA
ctang@som.umaryland.edu

ABSTRACT

Conversation between two individuals requires verbal dialogue; the majority of human communication however consists of non-verbal cues such as gestures and facial expressions. Blind individuals are thus hindered in their interaction capabilities. To address this, we are building a computer vision system with facial recognition and expression algorithms to relay nonverbal messages to a blind user. The device will communicate the identities and facial expressions of communication partners in realtime. In order to ensure that this device will be useful to the blind community, we conducted surveys and interviews and we are working with subjects to test prototypes of the device. This paper describes the algorithms and design concepts incorporated in this device, and it provides a commentary on early survey and interview results. A corresponding poster with demonstration stills is exhibited at this conference.

Categories and Subject Descriptors

A.1 [**Introductory and Survey**]: Miscellaneous; D.2.10 [**Software Engineering**]: Design

General Terms

Algorithms, design, human factors

Keywords

Assistive technologies, computer vision, blindness, face recognition, expression recognition

---

*Equal authorship shared by members of Team F.A.C.E.

1. INTRODUCTION

Humans rely on visual cues when interacting within a social context, and for those who cannot see, their lack of sight interferes with the quality of their social interactions [3]. Since the majority of non-verbal communication is comprised of facial gestures and expressions, blind individuals are at a disadvantage when engaging in interpersonal communication [3].

Since over 80% of human communication is actually carried out nonverbally [1], there is an opportunity to include image processing in assistive technologies. These missed messages include facial expressions, and hand gestures, which cannot be detected, and more importantly interpreted, without sight. With computer vision, an assistive device used by blind individuals can include algorithms designed to "read" faces. The design of our prototype includes realtime feedback for facial recognition in addition to algorithms built for identification of six different facial expressions.

2. ALGORITHMS

2.1 Facial Recognition

In the design of our device, fast recognition time is an important factor. A standard recognition system, under controlled conditions, can achieve a recognition rate of 99.2% in near realtime [5]. One system, developed by Krishna et al., uses a Principal Component Analysis (PCA) algorithm for facial recognition [3]. Our system uses a commercial solution (FaceSDK; Luxand, Inc., Alexandria, VA) for face recognition, matching images to user-built databases, and can provide audio or haptic feedback in realtime. We are pursuing interconnectivity with a user's facebook account to automatically populate the image database with the profile pictures of friends.

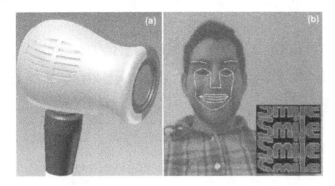

Figure 1: (a) Our design of a camera atop a standard white cane. (b) The expression recognition identifying a smile.

2.2 Expression Analysis

One classic expression detector is a parametric optical flow-based algorithm developed by Yacoob and Black in 1997. This computationally intensive algorithm tracks facial features in a sequence of images to detect the presence of six expressions [4]. These expressions are described according to the six universal expressions theory - happiness, anger, sadness, disgust, surprise and fear - as developed by Ekman and Friesen [2].

Many traditional expression detectors, including Yacoob and Black's, have been too slow to be used for realtime detection. In an effort to increase usefulness, our device has been designed to overcome the previous performance limitations. At the hardware level, a high speed IEEE-1394b camera is used to capture images at a very high frame rate while minimizing CPU load. We use commercial software (FaceAPI; Seeing Machines Inc., Canberra, Australia) to accurately track facial features in realtime. By analyzing the movement of facial features, we were able to find common trends in the same expressions among different individuals. We created computationally undemanding thresholding algorithms to classify expressions based on the detected trends. Using this method we have had success in detecting expressions at near 30 frames per second for happiness (Figure 1b), surprise, disgust, and anger.

3. INTERVIEWS AND SURVEYS

In addition to the hardware and software considerations, two societal concerns arise in the design of this device. The direct needs of the intended users must be considered, and that includes the perceptions of the sighted community, which may also be a concern for blind users. Our survey of over 200 sighted individuals showed agreement that there is a need for this device, but there is a jump in discomfort at the thought of facial analysis. Receptivity by the blind community was evaluated by interviewing nine subjects. We found that those who experienced blindness later in life expressed a greater interest in emotion recognition, while individuals with congenital blindness enthusiastically hailed both capabilities. One blind individual was quoted saying, "I lost my vision 14 years ago. I miss seeing people's faces. To see if they are angry, happy, or disgusted." Interviews also suggested features – such as mounting the system's camera atop a white cane (Figure 1a) – desired by the blind community.

4. DISCUSSION/FUTURE DIRECTIONS

Using data collected in surveys and interviews, we hope to tailor this device to the specific needs of all who will come in contact with it. In the next several months, we are working to have blind users test a prototype in a controlled environment. These experiments will allow us to evaluate the system's accuracy and usefulness. Whereas an assistive device to recognize people was met with predicted enthusiasm, one that analyzes facial features raises concerns of privacy and misinterpretations. Another issue is the effect on a user's standard behaviors while using the device. Combined, these factors could lead to an overall negative effect on communication. It is these elements that increase the challenge in developing an unobtrusive device as a social aid for the blind. Our goal is to develop an effective system to provide a blind user with the same analysis of faces that sighted individuals benefit from. As one sighted individual surveyed wrote, "The application of the [device] would be similar to another person looking at me and analyzing my facial expressions with his or her sight." While we cannot restore vision, we seek to balance communication between sighted and blind individuals, to enhance the quality of blind individuals' societal interactions, and to provide a device that fulfills all needs without interfering with comfort.

5. ACKNOWLEDGMENTS

Thanks is due to Team F.A.C.E.'s mentors and advisors Dr. R. Chellappa and Dr. C.M. Tang, and graduate advisor Mr. L. Stearns. We also thank the Gemstone Honors Program at the University of Maryland. Finally, we would like to thank the National Federation of the Blind for their support.

6. REFERENCES

[1] Argyle, M. Salter, U. Nicholson, H. Williams, M. Burgess, P. The communication of inferior and superior attitudes by verbal and non-verbal signals. *British Journal of Social Psychology*, 9:222–231, 1970.

[2] Friesen, W.V. Ekman, P. Constants across cultures in the face and emotion. *Journal of Personality and Social Psychology*, 17(2):124–129, 1971.

[3] Little, G. Black, J. Panchanathan, S. Krishna, S. A wearable face recognition system for individuals with visual impairments. In *7th Annual ACM Conference on Assistive Technologies*, pages 106–113, 2005.

[4] Yacoob, Y. Black, M.J. Recognizing facial expressions in image sequences using local parameterized models of image motion. *International Journal of Computer Vision*, 25(1):23–48, 1997.

[5] Yang, X.D. Xiao, Q. A facial presence monitoring system for information security. *IEEE Workshop on Computational Intelligence in Biometrics*, 2009.

MICOO (Multimodal Interactive Cubes for Object Orientation): A Tangible User Interface for the Blind and Visually Impaired

Muhanad S. Manshad and Enrico Pontelli
Department of Computer Science
New Mexico State University
mmanshad | epontell@nmsu.edu

Shakir J. Manshad
MATSD: Math Adoptive Technology Lab
for Students with Disabilities
New Mexico State University
smanshad@nmsu.edu

ABSTRACT

This paper presents the development of *Multimodal Interactive Cubes for Object Orientation (MICOO)* manipulatives. This system provides a multimodal *tangible user interface (TUI)*, enabling people with visual impairments to create, modify and naturally interact with diagrams and graphs on a multitouch surface. The system supports a novel notion of active orientation and proximity tracking of manipulatives against diagram and graph components. If the orientation of a MICOO matches a component, then a user is allowed to modify that component by moving the MICOO. Conversely, if a MICOO does not match orientation or is far from a component, audio feedback is activated to help the user reach that component. This will lessen the need for manual intervention, enable independent discovery on the part of the user, and offers dynamic behavior, whereas the representation interacts and provides feedback to the user. The platform has been developed and it is undergoing formal evaluation (e.g., browse, modify and construct graphs on a Cartesian plot and diagrams).

Categories and Subject Descriptors

H.5.2. [**INFORMATION INTERFACES AND PRE-SENTATION**]: Haptic I/O, Input devices and strategies

General Terms

Human Factors

Keywords

Haptic Feedback, Graphing, Accessibility, Blind and Visually Impaired, Multitouch, Multimodal, TUI, Diagrams.

1. INTRODUCTION

Through their K-12 years, blind and visually impaired students are taught to construct, manipulate and browse the physical world using the sense of touch through free hands. This method is ubiquitous in reading braille and in all learning interactions (Figure 1 and 2). Fundamentals of science and math are taught using simple inexpensive materials, requiring little to no learning curve. Dominant materials used in everyday classrooms are manipulatives, such as cubes, number lines, and combinations of corkboards, pins and rubber bands [7]. Manipulatives are tangible objects that are part of a hands-on learning environment. Through design and constant manipulation, a student is able to create mental models "images" of important concepts in algebra, geometry, measurements, and science. It is through multiple experiences that students gain true

conceptual understanding [7]. There are, however, several concerns. For example, each cube must be easily distinguishable, color properties have to be replaced by braille, and an unambiguous area for placement of cubes must be provided, to render interaction without distress for loss of position and proximity of cubes.

Figure 1: Two-handed uses for braille and manipulatives [7]

Another commonly used manipulatives relies on corkboards, pins and rubber bands (Figure 2). This form is used to create graphs, charts, and geometric shapes. This involves inserting pins on a wooden board with a raised grid and wrapping rubber bands around the pins to form a touchable graph. This is a simple method, but has several drawbacks. Pins can fall off if not placed correctly. If a pin is removed by mistake, the rubber bands can also fall off, causing the loss of the representation and possible injuries. The setup of this form is tedious and lacks feedback (e.g., audio) to denote correct or incorrect interactions. The static nature of manipulatives requires continuous manual intervention and validation (e.g., by the teachers).

Figure 2: Two-handed interaction when creating diagrams and graphs using corkboards, pins and rubber bands [7]

The emergence of digital manipulatives [5] offers a new approach to address some of these issues. These manipulatives are based on the concepts of *Tangible User Interfaces (TUIs)*, which provide a new compelling approach to enhance people's interaction with digital information [6]. The concept of TUI was first introduced in 1997, by Ishii and Ullmer – they define a user interface that can "augment the real physical world by coupling digital information to everyday physical objects and environments" [1]. TUIs naturally employ a two handed approach, which fits perfectly with the existing classrooms practices for blind and visually impaired students. However, the technological developments and the associated research implications of TUIs for these groups of students are still in their infancy. McGookin et al. developed a TUI system that tracks markers on a table-top surface [4]. Their results demonstrate the potential offered by this approach in providing non-visual access to charts. However, their system only allows for data browsing of statistical data, without construction and other types of interaction. Subjective workload evaluations were not provided.

In this project, we investigate TUIs for students with visual impairments further.

2. MICOO AND MULTITOUCH TUI

We have developed a collection of manipulatives called *MICOO (Multimodal Interactive Cubes for Object Orientation)* and *a custom multitouch table-top* to identify and track MICOO surface movements and interactions. This system renders active interactions by reading and tracking markers underneath MICOO. Once a marker is validated, it is immediately plotted on a Cartesian plane. The system supports the novel notion of *active orientation* and *proximity tracking* against components of interest (e.g., diagram relation markers, entities, or graphs). If the orientation of a MICOO matches a component, then a user is allowed to modify that component by moving the MICOO (Fig. 3). Conversely, if a MICOO does not match the orientation, or it is far from a component, the audio feedback will be activated to direct and help the user to reach that component. A user may also use his fingers to quickly touch and browse the surface while listening for audio feedback. If a component is found, a user may put a MICOO on that position. This notion is called "bread crumbs". As summarized in Fig. 3, multi-touch can be used to detect or create links among entities (e.g., connect two nodes in a graph) and to manipulate graphical structures.

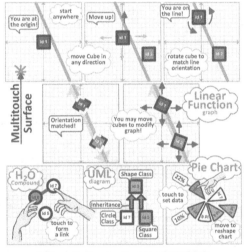

Figure 3. Example uses of MICOO

The design of MICOO is guided by the following criteria:

1. *Natural active interaction:* Any system will naturally require a learning curve. However, employing a two handed approach (natural to students with visual impairments) will yield a reduced learning curve.
2. *Multiple points of interaction:* Existing research has extensively investigated uses of haptic technology (e.g., Logitech Wingman, SensAble PHANToM, Novint Falcon). These devices require a user's whole palm and hand-grip, leaving other receptors on the hand unemployed (single point of interaction). Manshad and Manshad designed a haptic glove, which provides vibration feedback through natural movement and position [3]. Their evaluations highlight the significance of providing multiple points of interaction – students browsed a mathematical graph faster than using single point interaction. McGookin et al. evaluations also support this notion [4].

3. *Independence:* the system should provide active feedback in support of correct and incorrect interactions. This will lessen the need for manual intervention.

2.1 Hardware and Software Implementation

MICO has been developed from scratch, using affordable off-the-shelf hardware components. The system allows for natural interaction using MICOO on a multitouch surface. The surface is controlled through multiple infra-red cameras for MICOO movement tracking (Figure 4). Software implementation is a custom C# application which extends the open source reacTIVision TUIO framework [2]. Active proximity and orientation of MICOO against components of interest are calculated using special algorithms.

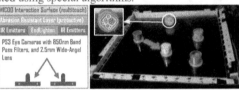

Figure 4. Side view layers (left) and current design (right)

3. CURRENT STATUS

A number of formal evaluation activities are currently underway to include: NASA TLX (Task Load Index) workload assessment, Neurosky's MindWave attention and meditation data. Current participants include students from the Alamogordo New Mexico School for the Blind and Visually Impaired. Participants will be tasked to: browse, modify and construct a graph (on a Cartesian plot) and a diagram. Completion times and errors will be recorded and analyzed. The initiative of MICOO is to develop a novel platform that adapts to a wide range of applications, particularly those found in everyday classrooms for blind and visually impaired students using manipulatives. The form and outer shape of MICOO is also meant to be adaptable and to serve as a generic platform for TUI-based interaction with graphical structures.

4. ACKNOWLEDGMENTS

Many thanks to the NUI Group Community forums for answering questions during the system building process.

5. REFERENCES

[1] Ishii h. and Ullmer B. 1997. Tangible bits: towards seamless interfaces between people, bits, and atoms. *CHI'97*.

[2] Kaltenbrunner M. 2009. reacTIVision and TUIO: a tangible tabletop toolkit. *Proceedings of ACM ITS'09*.

[3] Manshad M.S. and Manshad A.S. 2008. Multimodal vision glove for touchscreens. *Proceedings of ASSETS'08*.

[4] Mcgookin D.K., Robertson E., Brewster S.A. 2010. Clutching at straws: using tangible interaction to provide non-visual access to graphs. *Proceedings of CHI'10*.

[5] Resnick M., Martin F., Berg R., Borovoy R., Colella V., Kramer K., Silverman B. 1998. Digital manipulatives: New toys to think with. *Proceedings of CHI'98*.

[6] Shaer O. and Hornecker E. 2010. Tangible User Interfaces: Past, Present, and Future Directions. *Foundations and Trends in HCI*, v.3 n.1–2, p.1-137.

[7] Texas School for the Blind, 2011. Math Manipulatives for VI Students. www.tsbvi.edu/presentations.

Mobile Web on the Desktop: Simpler Web Browsing

Jeffery Hoehl, Clayton Lewis
Coleman Institute for Cognitive Disabilities
Department of Computer Science
University of Colorado
Boulder, CO 80309-0430 USA

{jeffery.hoehl, clayton.lewis}@colorado.edu

ABSTRACT

This paper explores the potential benefits of using mobile webpages to present simpler web content to people with cognitive disabilities. An empirical analysis revealed that the majority of popular mobile sites are smaller than their desktop equivalents with an average of half the viewable content, making them a viable method for simplifying web presentation.

Categories and Subject Descriptors

H.5.2 [**Information Interfaces and Presentation**]: User Interfaces – *Evaluation/methodology*.

General Terms

Measurement, Human Factors.

Keywords

Website simplicity, website complexity, mobile web, web accessibility, cognitive disabilities.

1. INTRODUCTION

People with cognitive disabilities often prefer simple presentation of information, and simple interactions, like many other people [3]. But how can these simple user experiences be provided? There are as yet no automatic means for simplifying an existing user interface. But as [4] points out, phone applications are naturally constrained to be simple in some key respects, because of severe limitations on available screen area. Could there be value in offering phone presentations to users who prefer simple user experiences? Of course users can get these experiences by using a phone, but the same small screens, and small keys, pose problems for many users. How about allowing users to see the interface offered to phone users, on their laptop or desktop screens? The presentation of mobile content in a desktop environment could benefit people with cognitive disabilities who find desktop-oriented websites confusing, cluttered, or distracting as well as people with physical disabilities that may find the use of a mobile device challenging or who use assistive technology that requires a desktop machine.

Although some work has evaluated the effectiveness of viewing a desktop-oriented website on a mobile device [6], the opposite has had little attention. We begin this work here, by investigating how Web applications delivered to phone browsers differ from those presented to desktop browsers.

When mobile versions of websites are created, they are often streamlined by removing features, simplifying content, removing advertisements, and reducing the number of interactive elements. This simplification of content can significantly reduce the amount of time required to complete simple tasks, but performance is largely dependent on the physical features of the device used, such as screen size and input method [5, 6]. Furthermore, some tasks can't be completed on a mobile-oriented site or require a much higher level of effort. By presenting mobile content on a desktop environment, these constraints are largely removed. For instance, when a task is not easily handled by the functionality on a mobile website, one can easily revert to and use the standard desktop-oriented site.

To determine the feasibility and potential benefits of presenting mobile webpages to desktop users, we analyzed current desktop and mobile webpages to see how often mobile-oriented alternatives are created, for popular sites, and how mobile-oriented sites differ from desktop-oriented sites.

2. METHODOLOGY

2.1 System Architecture

Servers deliver different versions of sites by examining the user agent string that is provided as part of the header of the request the server receives. To compare mobile and desktop sites, we created a custom web crawler, SimpleWebGatherer, that manipulates this request string, allowing us to receive the versions of sites that are generated for a number of different mobile and desktop browsers, as detailed below. Because modern Web pages are typically not loaded from static content, but rather are built up using scripts (JavaScript, AJAX), one cannot simply examine the response from the server to a request. Rather, our tool incorporates a so-called headless browser, HTMLUnit, which retrieves the pages, executes attached scripts, and saves the fully formed page for analysis. HTMLUnit, an open source project, is widely considered one of the most robust headless browsers, and incorporates Mozilla's Rhino JavaScript engine which is capable of handling many of the web's most popular JavaScript libraries (e.g. jQuery). For any particular website, our web crawler adjusts the user agent of the headless browser to mimic one of seven user agent types. These include 3 desktop variations (Firefox 3.6, Internet Explorer 7, Internet Explorer 8) and 4 mobile variations (Android 2.1, BlackBerry 5.0, iOS 4.3, Symbian 9.4).

We created a second custom tool that uses the jsoup HTML analysis library to produce a number of metrics for the pages retrieved by SimpleWebGatherer, including file size and character/word/sentence counts for both the page source as well as the content that would be seen by users of the page.

2.2 Determining Popular Websites

We studied a selection of the most visited websites in the United States, using the 63 sites that appear on both the Google and Alexa top 100 lists [1, 2]. Limitations in the headless browser in SimpleWebGatherer prevented us from including 4 of these sites, leaving us with 59 popular sites in our sample.

3. RESULTS

As expected, mobile sites differ considerably from desktop sites in most cases. For 41 of the 59 sites, the amount of text shown to users differed by 10% or more between the mobile and desktop sites. Across all 59 sites, the mobile versions presented only half as much text as the desktop versions. Figure 1 shows the comparison for all sites. Other measures, including total file size of the rendered page, show a similar pattern.

Interestingly, there are differences among the versions of sites sent to different phones. Across all of the sites, Android and iOS versions are comparable in size, but are about 50% larger than those for BlackBerry and Symbian. However, the amount of content itself was similar. In other words, the Android and iOS platforms seemed to contain much more HTML markup in their source code than BlackBerry and Symbian platforms, but all had nearly the same amount of actual usable content as shown to users.

This indicates that there are effectively three tiers of complexity among the versions of these sites. At the highest tier, desktop content provides the most complexity in terms of markup (111,156 bytes per file average) as well as the most content itself. The middle tier, represented by mobile sites delivered to Android or iOS, still provides some complexity in terms of markup (61,985 bytes per file) but provide less visible content. At the bottom tier, sites as delivered to BlackBerry and Symbian provide less markup (45,498 bytes per file) but about the same amount of visible content.

4. FOLLOW UP

Although our initial analysis has provided insight into how varied mobile and desktop sites are, there are several areas for further exploration.

First, our analysis has only included the homepages of the websites. For example, wikipedia.org is represented by its entry page, not any of its articles. But users spend more time on the subpages, or content pages, of sites, and an analysis of those pages would be important. For instance, comparing the mobile and desktop versions of a Google search results page, an Amazon product page, and a Wikipedia article could provide more practical insight into how mobile pages vary across the web.

Second, user testing needs to be conducted to determine if mobile pages are actually easier to use than desktop pages when presented on a desktop environment. Studies should include users with cognitive and physical disabilities and should focus on what properties of both mobile and desktop pages are the most helpful to users.

Lastly, a deeper analysis of the HTML markup would provide insight into how to better understand and process web data. Evaluations of the amount and types of controls on a page would be helpful in understanding how mobile pages differ from an interaction standpoint and could provide accessibility recommendations for web designers.

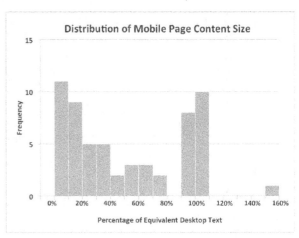

Figure 1. The distribution of mobile text content size as percentages of the equivalent desktop text.

5. CONCLUSION

Our comparisons of mobile and desktop sites indicate that there is a potential benefit to presenting mobile content on a desktop environment. Mobile sites provide less content to users and can benefit those with cognitive and physical disabilities by offering a simpler presentation of web content. Three tiers of web complexity were identified, suggesting that web content should not be seen as having just mobile and desktop variations, but a range of complexities that users can choose from to best suit their needs.

6. ACKNOWLEDGMENTS

We thank the Coleman Institute for Cognitive Disabilities, the RERC for Advancing Cognitive Technology, funded by NIDRR, and the Alliance for Advancing African American Research in Computing, funded by the NSF, for support. We also thank Damon Jones and Sarai Price for their valuable feedback and help in data analysis and preparation.

7. REFERENCES

[1] Alexa. *Top Sites in United States*. 2011; Available from: http://www.alexa.com/topsites/countries/US.

[2] Google. *The 100 most-visited sites: United States*. 2011; Available from: http://www.google.com/adplanner/static/top100countries/us.html.

[3] Lewis, C., *Simplicity in cognitive assistive technology: a framework and agenda for research.* Univers. Access Inf. Soc., 2007. **5**(4): p. 351-361.

[4] Markoff, J. *On a Small Screen, Just the Salient Stuff.* New York Times. 2008; Available from: http://www.nytimes.com/2008/07/13/technology/13stream.html.

[5] Schmiedl, G., M. Seidl, and K. Temper, *Mobile phone web browsing: a study on usage and usability of the mobile web*, in *Proceedings of the 11th International Conference on Human-Computer Interaction with Mobile Devices and Services.* 2009, ACM: Bonn, Germany. p. 1-2.

[6] Shrestha, S., *Mobile web browsing: usability study*, in *Proceedings of the 4th international conference on mobile technology, applications, and systems and the 1st international symposium on Computer human interaction in mobile technology.* 2007, ACM: Singapore. p. 187-194.

Multi-modal Dialogue System with Sign Language Capabilities

M. Hrúz, P. Campr,
Z. Krňoul, M. Železný
Department of Cybernetics,
Faculty of Applied Sciences,
University of West Bohemia
Univerzitni 8, Pilsen 306 14,
Czech Republic
{mhruz, campr, zdkrnoul,
zelezny}@kky.zcu.cz

Oya Aran
Idiap Research Institute
Martigny, Switzerland
oya.aran@idiap.ch

Pınar Santemiz
Computer Engineering
Department, Boğaziçi
University
İstanbul, Turkey
pinar.santemiz
@bound.edu.tr

ABSTRACT

This paper presents the design of a multimodal sign-language -enabled dialogue system. Its functionality was tested on a prototype of an information kiosk for the deaf people providing information about train connections. We use an automatic computer-vision-based sign language recognition, automatic speech recognition and touchscreen as input modalities. The outputs are shown on a screen displaying 3D signing avatar and on a touchscreen displaying graphical user interface. The information kiosk can be used both by hearing users and deaf users in several languages. We focus on description of sign language input and output modality.

Categories and Subject Descriptors

H.4.3 [**Information Systems**]: Information systems applications—*Communications Applications*

General Terms

EXPERIMENTATION, LANGUAGES

Keywords

sign language, visual tracking, sign categorization

1. INTRODUCTION

Deaf and hearing impaired users have limited possibility of communication with hearing people. This can be a problem especially in the case when communicating with authorities or information providers. These people also cannot use speech-based automatic information services. In these cases dialogue systems should be designed to be accessible by deaf users. Our goal was to design such a dialogue system and verify its functionality on an information kiosk for deaf people. The system uses sign language (SL) as one of the communication means in both directions.

The hardware setup of the information kiosk (Fig. 1) is a standard PC, a touch screen display, a large screen, a microphone and several cameras. The cameras capture the

body and facial gestures of the signing person, the large screen renders the SL output and the touch screen allows touch commands as an alternative input.

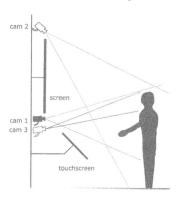

Figure 1: Setup of proposed information kiosk.

2. SIGN LANGUAGE RECOGNITION

The SL recognition system is intended for recognition of isolated signs. For this purpose a database was created using the described hardware setup. In total 338 files were recorded with one male and one female signer. The database contains 50 signs from Czech SL such as Czech towns, days etc. The constraining conditions were long sleeves, non-skin-colored clothes, uniform background and constant illumination. This is the first step towards an autonomous system. In the future much more data are required to train statistical models for recognition and less constraining conditions need to be applied. For tracking purposes we make use of joint particle filter that calculates a combined likelihood for all objects by modeling the likelihood of each object with respect to the others [1]. The filtering is done on a segmented image. We use skin-color segmentation to obtain the likelihood image. The result is shown in Fig 2.

The tracking provides coordinates of head and hands for each image from the camera. This information about trajectories is not sufficient for sign classification. In order to recognize the signs we also need shape information in addition to the tracking features. In order to describe the shape we have implemented five algorithms (3 based on Fourier

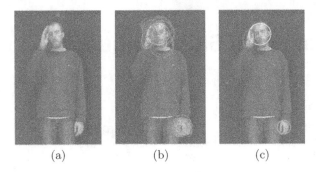

(a)   (b)   (c)

Figure 2: (a) Original image, (b) Particle distribution with joint PF, (c) Estimated hand and head positions

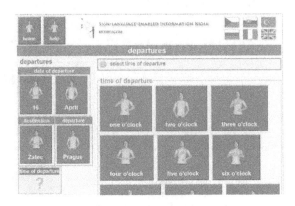

Figure 3: Sample screen of touchscreen graphical user interface.

descriptors, 1 based on Hu moments and last the one based on Discrete Cosine Transform, DCT). We tested their performances over the set of finger alphabet in Czech SL.

According to our results [1], DCT performed significantly better than the others. For the sign recognition from the calculated features we use Hidden Markov Model (HMM). The signs are modeled as an 8-state HMM (two of these states are non-emitting). Each state is modeled with a single Gaussian. This was due to the relative low amount of data. PCA and ICA were tested to reduce the dimensionality of the data and to align the data according to the feature space coordinate system. Both methods failed to improve the recognition rate since there were too few samples available. When more training data are available these methods should improve the recognition.

3. 3D SIGNING AVATAR

SL synthesis is used as the main output modality for the deaf users. We use the signing avatar animation in two forms. The first is an on-line generated avatar shown on the large screen that provides real-time feedback to deaf users. The second form is the pre-generated short movie clips inserted into the graphical user interface instead of text (see Fig. 3).

The animation model of the upper part of the human body is in compliance with the H-Anim standard. Currently, the animation model involves 38 joints and body segments. The talking head is composed from seven segments. The relevant body segments are connected by the avatar skeleton. For this purpose, one joint per segment is sufficient. The control of the skeleton is based on the rotation of segments (3 DOF per joint). The rotation of the shoulder, elbow, and wrist joints are computed by the inverse kinematics in accordance with 3D positions of the wrist and shoulder joints. The animation of the avatar's face, lips and tongue is rendered by the talking head system that performs local deformations of the relevant triangular surfaces.

For the manual component of the sign speech, the trajectory generator performs the syntactic analysis of HamNoSys symbolic strings. Since to define the rules and actions for all symbol combinations covering the entire notation variability is difficult, we have to make restrictions in order to preserve maximum degree of freedom. The trajectory generator currently involves 374 parsing rules. The structurally correct symbolic string is decomposed by the parsing rules to nodes of the parse tree. Two identical key frame data structures distinguishing the dominant and non dominant hand are used to describe the nodes. These data structures are composed from specially designed items. Firstly, the items of terminal nodes are filled from symbol descriptors stored in the definition file that currently covers 138 HamNoSys symbols.

Next, the nodes of the parse tree are processed by several tree walks whilst the rule actions are performed. We have defined 39 rule actions that are connected with each parse rule. The nodes are joined together and transformed to the control trajectories. The final trajectories of both hands are generated in the root node. The final step is the concatenation that puts together trajectories of hands with the articulatory trajectories generated by the talking head system and provides the control over a signed utterance. Reader can find more details in [2].

4. CONCLUSION

We have presented a dialogue system with SL capabilities. The system is able to track isolated signs and provide features for the recognizer. Significantly more data are needed for successful recognition. The system can be trained with signs from any topic. The system provides feedback in the form of a signing avatar. The dialogue is computer driven and suitable for different scenarios where the user answers queries with isolated signs.

5. ACKNOWLEDGMENTS

This research was supported by the Grant Agency of Academy of Sciences of the Czech Republic, project No. 1ET 101470416, by the Grant Agency of the Czech Republic, project No. GAČR 102/09/P609 and by the Ministry of Education of the Czech Republic, project No. ME08106.

6. REFERENCES

[1] P. Campr, M. Hrúz, A. Karpov, P. Santemiz, M. Železný, and O. Aran. Sign-language-enabled information kiosk. In *eNTERFACE'08*, 2009.

[2] Z. Krňoul, J. Kanis, M. Železný, and L. Müller. Czech text-to-sign speech synthesizer. In *Proceedings of the 4th international conference on Machine learning for multimodal interaction*, MLMI'07, pages 180–191, Berlin, Heidelberg, 2008. Springer-Verlag.

Multi-View Platform: An Accessible Live Classroom Viewing Approach for Low Vision Students

Raja Kushalnagar
Information and Computing Studies
Rochester Institute of Technology
rskics@rit.edu

Stephanie Ludi
Software Engineering
Rochester Institute of Technology
salves@rit.edu

Poorna Kushalnagar
Imaging Science
Rochester Institute of Technology
Poorna.Kushalnagar@rit.edu

ABSTRACT

We present a multiple-view platform for low vision students that utilize students' personal smart phone cameras and tablets in the classroom. Low vision or deaf students can independently use the platform to obtain flexible, magnified views of lecture visuals, such as the presentation slides or whiteboard on their personal screen. This platform also enables cooperation among sighted and hearing classmates to provide better views for everyone, including themselves.

Categories and Subject Descriptors

K.3.1 [Computers in Education]: Computer Uses in Education; K.4.2 [Social Issues]: Assistive technologies for persons with disabilities.

General Terms

Design, Economics, Human Factors.

Keywords

Blind, low-vision.

1. Introduction

Sighted people have a wide field of view that is at least 130° with a high resolution focus of about 2°. This high resolution focus is temporally multiplexed to give the illusion of high resolution focus everywhere, as shown in Figure 1. Most low vision people lack either a central high resolution focus (fovea), or a wide field of view with low resolution (peripheral vision) [1]. As a result, they struggle to cope with situations where both kinds of view are needed, such in classroom presentations that use many visuals such as whiteboards and slides. Traditional low-vision aids can improve either central or peripheral vision, but negatively impact the other. For example, magnifying devices for increase resolution of the lecture visual but reduce the field of view of the whole presentation. On the other hand, minifying devices increase the field of view and enable students to see the whole lecture at a glance, but reduce resolution of individual visuals [2].

Sighted people benefit from lectures that simultaneously transmit information visually and aurally, e.g., by listening to a presenter's explanation while reading the slide. A seminal paper by Mayer et al. [3] analyzed how the distribution of redundancy across two channels (visual and auditory) makes learning easier by processing in parallel in both channels and the effect is complementary. Presenters emphasize key terms or to explain in parallel. These words are usually dialogue-critical words and add meaning to the underlying visual representation [4], which reinforces importance of reading class visuals.

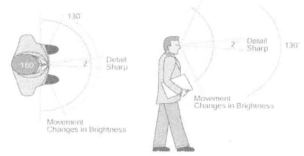

Figure 1: Field of View for Sighted People

We have implemented a multiple view approach that enables simultaneous views of both the wide field of view in the classroom and high resolution view of the presentation information sources. We utilize mobile devices so that the low vision student can independently and easily view the presentation. We developed a set of applications (capture, streaming and viewing) for Android smart phones and tablets. Our approach utilizes one or more smart phone cameras to record and stream the students' missing visual component, either the high resolution or wide field along with the other visual component. This also allows students to use or share smart phones in classroom environments. We focus on optimizing classroom learning views and comfort, with the goal of making them more effective, intuitive, and easy to use. Also, as smart phones are ubiquitous, i.e., easily available it is easy for low vision students to use these devices in the classroom without distracting other students.

2. Related Work

Pure optical solutions such as mounted monoculars like Designs for Vision [1], can aid low vision (resolution) students by magnifying lecture visuals so as to read the visual more easily. However, this approach incurs a trade-off; their field of view becomes narrow. Therefore the student has to continually shift view to scan and orient to classroom visuals, e.g., re-locating the professor after looking at the whiteboard notes.

Electronic optical solutions such PhotoNote [5] use multiple classroom camcorders and a high definition camera. However, these devices are bulky and require prior set up in classroom, and the recording is not viewable in real-time.

ClassInFocus [6] uses multiple webcam equipped laptops to record and stream the classroom visuals in real-time. However, ClassInFocus does not support magnification within the application; and it requires cooperation from the teacher and providers.

Note Taker [7] does not require classroom infrastructure or prior setup in a classroom and does not require the lecturer to adjust the presentation. Its main disadvantage is that there is only one camera view, and the camera location is limited by wiring to be close to the student. Moreover, the equipment is not ubiquitous and has to be brought separately.

Figure 2: Low vision student's magnified view of classroom visuals

The development and design for MVP for low vision students addresses the gaps identified by these studies listed above and addresses features that low vision students feel are important.

3. Development

Our Multiple View Platform incorporates the following design principles: 1) incorporate ubiquitous, cheap personal devices to record and view to optimize convenience and sharing; 2) utilize classroom visual properties to accommodate personal smart phones and tablets that are limited in bandwidth, resolution and battery life [8]; 3) use open source software (Android) to develop a flexible interface that students can customize to fit their widely varying needs; and 4) to design the view capture and presentation to correct for lighting and viewing angles through image processing, camera placement and built-in lighting.

As a result, we believe the platform is simple, ubiquitous and multifunctional, which enables students to use their own phone or classmates' phones as accessible technology devices that can be used anytime and anywhere with minimal set up.

Figure 2 shows the student viewing the slides and whiteboard in a classroom on an Android tablet (Motorola Xoom Wi-Fi). The student is viewing video streams that are being received from two Android phones aimed at the slides (HTC Evo 4G) and at the whiteboard (Samsung Galaxy Tab 7). The platform is standalone and independent in that the student can immediately place the phone recorders on the lecture podium or table to capture and stream the video. The student then uses a personal tablet computer view the streamed software, and can magnify within each video window as needed. With practice, this setup process takes about a minute, and can be done as the MVP software starts and synchronizes. All devices are standalone and can run on battery and in ad-hoc mode.

4. Evaluation

Figure 3 shows an MVP user-interface for students, which consist of up to four windows that can be viewed, magnified or contrast-adjusted. The student can pinch enlarge or tap create/remove a view. In addition, the student can record the lecture in real-time for future review.

Two low vision students evaluated the MVP user interface and platform. The first student commented that the most helpful features as compared to other low vision aids was the ability of the platform ability to adjust the video contrast and to use the smart phone LED lights so as to read slides that had poor contrast.

Figure 3: MVP Student View

The other student commented that the Android supported pinch-magnify feature was very helpful, but did not like the fingers getting in the way of reading the text. The student suggested inserting a magnify button at the bottom of the screen.

5. Summary

The MVP platform enables either low vision or deaf students to view multiple resizable visuals simultaneously on the same screen. As a result the student only needs to remember the location of each visual on the screen. This memorization eliminates search time and the student can rapidly switch between visuals and can magnify the visual as needed. The platform is scalable as it leverages general consumer smart phones to increase low vision students' classroom accessibility.

The larger project focuses on both deaf and low vision students. The user interface development for low vision students is an on-ongoing project with low vision students. Demonstrations will enable low vision accessibility researchers and users to give feedback on evaluating and extending usability and functionality.

References

[1] E. Peli, "Vision multiplexing: an optical engineering concept for low-vision aids," in *Proceedings of SPIE*, 2007, vol. 6667, p. 66670C.

[2] E. Peli, "Vision multiplexing: an engineering approach to vision rehabilitation device development," *Optometry & Vision Science*, vol. 78, no. 5, pp. 304-315, 2001.

[3] R. E. Mayer, J. Heiser, and S. Lonn, "Cognitive constraints on multimedia learning: When presenting more material results in less understanding.," *Journal of Educational Psychology*, vol. 93, no. 1, pp. 187-198, 2001.

[4] E. C. Kaiser, P. Barthelmess, C. Erdmann, and P. Cohen, "Multimodal Redundancy Across Handwriting and Speech During Computer Mediated Human-Human Interactions," *interactions*, pp. 1009-1018, 2007.

[5] G. Hughes and P. Robinson, "Photonote evaluation," in *Proceedings of the 9th international ACM SIGACCESS conference on Computers and accessibility - ASSETS '07*, 2007, pp. 99-106.

[6] A. C. Cavender, J. P. Bigham, and R. E. Ladner, "ClassInFocus," in *Proceedings of the 11th International ACM SIGACCESS Conference on Computers and Accessibility - ASSETS '09*, 2009, pp. 67-74.

[7] D. S. Hayden, L. Zhou, M. J. Astrauskas, and J. A. Black, "Note-taker 2.0," in *Proceedings of the 12th international ACM SIGACCESS conference on Computers and accessibility - ASSETS '10*, 2010, pp. 131-137.

[8] R. S. Kushalnagar and J.-F. Paris, "Evaluation of a scalable and distributed mobile device video recording approach for accessible presentations," in *Proceedings of the 29th International Performance Computing and Communications Conference (IPCCC)*, 2010, pp. 81-88.

Note-Taker 3.0, An Assistive Technology Enabling Students who are Legally Blind to Take Notes in Class

David Hayden,
Michael Astrauskas
CUbiC
Arizona State University
Tempe, AZ 85281

dshayden@asu.edu
trevie@asu.edu

Qian Yan,
Liqing Zhou
School of Industrial Design
Arizona State University
Tempe, AZ 85281

qian.yan@asu.edu
lzhou29@asu.edu

John Black

CUbiC
Arizona State University
Tempe, AZ 85281

john.black@asu.edu

ABSTRACT
While the Americans with Disabilities Act [2] mandates that universities provide visually disabled students with human note-takers, studies have shown that it is vital that students take their own notes during classroom lectures. Because students are cognitively engaged while taking notes, their retention is better, even if they never review their notes after class. However, students with visual disabilities are at a disadvantage compared to their sighted peers when taking notes - especially in fast-pace class presentations. They find it more difficult to rapidly switch back and forth between viewing the front of the room and viewing the notes they are taking. Currently available assistive technologies do not adequately address this need to rapidly switch back and forth. This paper presents the results of a 3-year study aimed at the development of an assistive technology that is specifically aimed at allowing students with visual disabilities to take handwritten and/or typed notes in the classroom, without relying on any classroom infrastructure, or any special accommodations by the lecturer or the institution.

Categories and Subject Descriptors
K.3.1 [Computers in Education] Computer Uses in Education
I.4.1 [Image Processing and Computer Vision] Digitization and Image Capture

General Terms
Design, Experimentation, Human Factors

Keywords
Note-Taker, Note Taker, note-taking, legally blind, low vision, Tablet PC, pen computer, classroom accessibility, STEM

1. INTRODUCTION
Education research has shown that secondary and post-secondary students benefit from taking notes, even when they don't subsequently review those notes [1]. However, students with visual disabilities, are at a severe disadvantage when taking notes in a classroom. Note-taking requires rapid switching between a near-sight task (viewing a writing surface and taking notes) and a far-sight task (viewing a distant board at the front of the room). For low-vision students, one or both of these tasks will usually require magnification. However, commercially available assistive technologies provide magnification for near-sight tasks, or for far-sight tasks, but are not designed to support rapid transitions between these two tasks.

2. THE NOTE-TAKER PROJECT
To allow students with visual disabilities to take notes in their classrooms, we have iteratively designed, prototyped, and tested, three generations of a portable, hardware/software assistive device that we call the *Note-Taker*. The first Note-Taker proof-of-concept Pan/Tilt/Zoom (PTZ) camera prototype was built from off-the-shelf components, and employed a rudimentary software application to display the video on a Tablet PC. The touch-sensitive surface of the Tablet PC provided incremental up/down/left/right buttons for aiming the camera, and a zoom slider for zooming in and out. The split-screen interface allowed students with visual disabilities to rapidly glance back and forth between the board and their notes, like their fully sighted peers. The Note-Taker 1.0 user interface is shown in Figure 1, and the Note-Taker 1.0 PTZ camera is shown in Figure 2.

Figure 1: The user interface for the Note-Taker 1.0 prototype

Figure 2: The Note-Taker 1.0 PTZ camera

3. NOTE-TAKER 2.0
Based on 150 hours of classroom testing of the Note-Taker 1.0 prototype, we then built and tested the Note-Taker 2.0 prototype [3]. One major complaint about the Note-Taker 1.0 PTZ camera was its imprecise positioning. To solve that problem we developed a servo-based camera positioner. Another complaint was that the incremental up/down/left/right buttons were tedious

to use, so we allowed the user to simply touch and drag within the video image to reposition the camera. We also allowed the user to tap on any feature of interest in the video frame to center the camera on that feature. A 36x optical zoom video camera was used to provide deep zoom, and handwritten or typed notes could be taken while viewing the zoomed video. (Typing was done with the display screen upright and the keyboard exposed, like a conventional laptop.) The Note-Taker 2.0 user interface is shown in Figure 3, and the Note-Taker 2.0 PTZ camera is shown in Figure 4. This Note-Taker 2.0 prototype won First Prize in the 2010 Microsoft Imagine Cup World Competition.

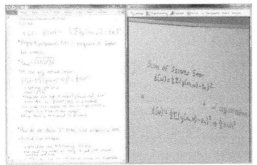

Figure 3: The user interface for the Note-Taker 2.0 prototype

Figure 4: The Note-Taker 2.0 PTZ camera

4. FIGURES/CAPTIONS

The Note-Taker 2.0 prototype was tested in a simulated classroom setting, with tasks that would be typical in a classroom. While users liked the new direct touch camera aiming method, it was rather slow, jerky, and not accurate enough. They also found that the pinch/unpinch gestures for controlling the zoom were not always recognized, due to problems with the Windows operating system.

To solve the positioning problems, we completely redesigned the PTZ camera to pivot around its own center of gravity, and also developed camera auto-calibration software. To solve the zoom control problems, we replaced the pinch/unpinch controls with a large vertical slider, which appears along the right edge of the video screen whenever it is touched. We addtionally made the camera safer and more aesthetic by constructing, assembling, and painting a hard-plastic shell from stereolithography.

In addition to these improvements, some new features were added. Color inversion and contrast enhancement is provided, to compensate for adverse classroom conditions (such as low-light, dusty chalkboards, faded whiteboard markers, and glare) that sometimes adversely affect board visibility. In the event that a professor obstructs an important region of the board, a "look back" feature allows the user to quickly scroll through recently cached video video frames, to find an unobstructed view. Finally, screen shots of the board can be dragged into the user's notes, and video/audio streams can be recorded for later review. The entire

system is battery-operated, fits into a backpack, and can be set up on the student's desk in less than a minute [4].

The Note-Taker 3.0 user interface is shown in Figure 5, and the Note-Taker 3.0 PTZ camera is shown in Figure 6. This Note-Taker 3.0 prototype won First Prize in the 2011 Microsoft Imagine Cup US Competition [5].

Figure 5: The user interface for the Note-Taker 3.0 prototype

Figure 6: The Note-Taker 3.0 PTZ camera and Tablet PC in use

5. CONCLUSION

The Note-Taker 3.0 prototype is undergoing additional user testing in a simulated classroom with 21 visually disabled students on the campus of Arizona State University. Three additional prototypes are under construction, and will be given to students to use in class during the Fall semester of 2011.

6. ACKNOWLEDGEMENTS

This material is based in part upon work supported by the National Science Foundation under Grant Number IIS-0931278. Any opinions, findings, and conclusions or recommendations expressed in this material are those of the author(s) and do not necessarily reflect the views of the National Science Foundation.

7. REFERENCES

[1] J. Hartley and I.K. Davies, "Note-taking: A critical review," *Innovations in Education and Teaching International*, vol. 15, 1978, p. 207.

[2] "Americans with Disabilities Act, Sec. 12189. Examinations and Courses. [Section 208]," 1990; http://www.ada.gov/pubs/ada.htm.

[3] D. Hayden et al. "Note-Taker 2.0: The Next Step Toward Enabling Students who are Legally Blind to Take Notes in Class", Proceedings of the 12th International ACM SIGACCESS Conference on Computers and Accessibility, 2010.

[4] http://www.youtube.com/watch?v=Ba6qHT3MGzk

[5] http://www.npr.org/2011/04/15/135442950/note-taking-made-easy-for-legally-blind-students

Participatory Design Process for an In-Vehicle Affect Detection and Regulation System for Various Drivers

Myounghoon Jeon[1], Jason Roberts[1], Parameshwaran Raman[2], Jung-Bin Yim[2], & Bruce N. Walker[12]

Sonification Lab, School of Psychology[1] & School of Interactive Computing[2]
Georgia Institute of Technology
654 Cherry Street Atlanta, GA USA
{mh.jeon, jyim}@gatech.edu, {robertsjasone, parameshr}@gmail.com, bruce.walker@psych.gatech.edu

ABSTRACT

Considerable research has shown that diverse affective (emotional) states influence cognitive processes and performance. To detect a driver's affective states and regulate them may help increase driving performance and safety. There are some populations who are more vulnerable to issues regarding driving, affect, and affect regulation (e.g., novice drivers, young drivers, older drivers, and drivers with TBI (Traumatic Brain Injury)). This paper describes initial findings from multiple participatory design processes, including interviews with 21 young drivers, and focus groups with a TBI driver and two driver rehab specialists. Depending on user groups, there are distinct issues and needs; therefore, differentiated approaches are needed to design an in-vehicle assistive technology system for a specific target user group.

Categories and Subject Descriptors

H.5.2 [**Information Interfaces and Presentations (e.g., HCI)**]: User Interfaces, user-centered design, voice I/O

General Terms: Design, Human Factors

Keywords

Participatory Design, Affect Detection, Emotion Regulation, Adaptive User Interfaces

1. PARTICIPATORY DESIGN

1.1 Emotion and Drivers with TBI

Even though affect-related in-vehicle assistive technology may be able to help various classes of drivers, those with Traumatic Brain Injury (TBI) are of primary interest. There are more than 5.3 million Americans with an identified traumatic brain injury and 1.5 million new brain injuries are reported per year [1]. In addition to cognitive and executive dysfunctions, they frequently show emotion regulation issues, such as a "*short fuse*", uncontrolled *aggression,* and *irritability* [2]. However, most TBI patients hope to continue independent driving to facilitate community reintegration [3].

1.2 Interviews with TBI Drivers and Driver Rehab Specialists

One TBI driver (male) and two driver rehab specialists (mean years of experience = 16) in the Shepherd Center rehabilitation hospital participated in three successive sessions. In these interviews, researchers demonstrated a prototype of the affect

detection system using facial expression [4] and obtained feedback for the system, general regulation approach, and plausible design directions. Participants generally favored the attempt to cope with emotional issues as well as cognitive issues and were satisfied with the current system's performance for facial detection. They suggested that the system would be more helpful if it could detect a "*black out*" state that TBI patients often show. They felt a speech based-system could also be useful because motivated TBI patients would like to talk through the system in order to engage more in driving. With respect to affect regulation, driver rehab specialists recommended direct mitigation (e.g., simple commands like "*take a deep breath*" or "*relax your grip on the wheel*" to help *anxious* drivers find a way to relax—complex commands might overwhelm them). Sometimes TBI patients get "*tunnel vision*" and focus only on a particular space. To avoid this, giving them prompts such as "*keep moving your eyes*" can help. Rehab specialists said to use female voices for perceived calming attributes. Also, a family member's voice has also worked well. Currently, we continue to collect data from TBI drivers through other TBI rehabilitation programs, such as "Pathways" and "Share".

1.3 Young Drivers

Research shows that young drivers are overrepresented in crashes involving excessive speeds, curves, alcohol, fatigue, distraction, and passengers [5]. Specifically, young drivers tend to engage in distracting activities while driving, such as texting [e.g., 6]. Moreover, young drivers are more likely to exhibit aggressive driving behaviors [7]. For example, young drivers low in emotional adjustment and high in sensation seeking showed high levels of aggressive driving and speeding in competition with others and accordingly, performed poorly in a simulated driving experiment [8]. All those reasons add to novice-level skills and coping strategies, and cause young and beginning drivers to be in a highly vulnerable group.

1.4 Focus Groups with Young Drivers

Twenty-one undergrads with a driving license and driving experience (12 female; mean age = 21.8; mean years of driving = 5.6) received course credit. A total of five focus groups were conducted, each with one to five participants.

Affective States Need to Be Regulated. First of all, participants commonly reported that they generally feel 'relaxed' while driving. For the affective states that need to be regulated while driving, they answered in the following order using 7-point scales (1 = "need not at all" and 7 = "need very much"): *urgent* (5.1), *angry* (5.1), *fearful* (4.4), *confused* (4.1), *bored* (3.9), *depressed* (3.4), *relieved* (2.9), *happy* (2.6), and *embarrassed* (2.5). In addition, they were encouraged to add other affective states to be regulated while driving. Answers included *fatigue* and *tired* (N = 7), *distracted* (N = 3), *excited* (N = 3), *preoccupied* (N = 2), *frustrated* (N = 2), and *stressed* (N = 2). Although most participants felt that positive emotions need not be regulated, several participants said that *'excited'* needs to be regulated because if a driver is too excited, he or she may be distracted from driving.

Current Regulation Strategies. When participants experience negative affective states, their regulation strategies involved *"rationalize their situations," "turn on music loud," "drive faster," "eat," "drink," "make myself uncomfortable in the seat," "talk with passengers," "pull over the car and take a rest or calm down,"* etc. Most agreed that having a passenger would be helpful. Nonetheless, they said that it depends on the person, with friends being more helpful than parents.

Plausible Issues of the Facial Detection System. Participants pointed to several issues, including individual differences in expressing one's emotions, *"some people are not very expressive, being reserved by nature,"* an aversion about machine's control, *"many people might not want an artificial system to take control of them and their emotions and it might get them even more angry,"* security and privacy, *"people might not want people/others to monitor their emotions,"* and *"who is getting this data and how will they use it?"* Additionally, some participants worried about reversal effects that might make drivers distracted or feel worse. We also discussed topics such as facial recognition in the dark, while wearing sunglasses, frowning due to sunlight, timing for detection and regulation, as well as basic issues such as system's discernability and accuracy.

Plausible Issues of the Speech Detection System. Music, conversation, or phone calls might interfere with voice commands and speech detection. Of note, all of our participants said they always listen to music while driving. How to overcome that situation using multimodal displays is one of the critical issues. Further, there is noise from the external environment of the car especially when the windows are open. Additionally, sensing grip pressure on the wheel and heart rate sensors similar to the ones used in treadmills were proposed by several participants.

Directions Regarding Regulation Interfaces. Investigators demonstrated four different types of regulating voice clips (male, female, male TTS, and female TTS) and a couple of music pieces. Participants preferred human voices over synthesized ones because they were more like a person, related better to the driver, and sounded nicer. Although the human voices were recordings of graduate students, participants said that they were acceptable. However, many participants felt that they would prefer voices of famous people over non-familiar voices or even family members. Female participants wanted a British-accented male voice. One participant suggested the system could tell the driver that his or her action is merely due to current emotions and not his or her ability to drive. Another proposed that when a driver is frustrated, the system could phone the driver's friend. In some cases, making a joke would also help. A previous study showed that an empathetic adaptive system that matched its prosody to the driver's emotion yielded better driving and higher subjective ratings [9], but most participants wanted a more consistent system, *"want static rather than empathizing," "when I am angry, I don't want another angry person or system in my car."*

Overall, participants rated the face recognition (M = 3.95 out of 5) method higher than speech analysis (M = 3.54) on the usefulness scale. For the regulation methods, participants preferred non-speech sounds including music (M = 3.65) over speech (M = 2.59). However, a non-speech approach also has to be cautiously used. Participants did not want their music to be changed into classics automatically. One said that synchronizing the music with the driver's favorite songs in the iPod would be a better alternative than playing predefined classics. Regardless of speech or non-speech, it should be optional, configurable, and easily turned off. Some participants recommended that this system be more useful for people with extreme emotional problems or drivers who have experienced accidents or are recovering from the aftermaths of seeing one.

2. DISCUSSION & FUTURE WORKS

In this participatory design loop, we attained invaluable suggestions and found that specific approaches are needed for different populations. For motivated TBI drivers, direct input from the speech-based system might be helpful, whereas for young drivers, the same method might make them feel as if the system is a back-seat driver. As stated at the outset, older drivers are also a vulnerable class and need to be considered. They know their physical limitations and regulate their emotional state better than young adults, but they still have a significantly higher rate of accidents due to other reasons. Based on this, we are devising a more robust affect detection and adaptive interface that can timely help various drivers. Also, we plan to conduct an in-car case study embedding our system as well as an in-lab simulation study.

3. REFERENCES

[1] K. Charle, "The right frame of mind," in *the Daily Checkup in the Daily News*, 2011.

[2] C. Hawley, "Return to driving after head injury," *Journal of Neurology, Neurosurgery and Psychiatry*, vol. 70, pp. 761-766, 2001.

[3] H. L. Lew *et al.*, "Predictive validity of driving-simulator assessments following traumatic brain injury: A preliminary study," *Brain Injury*, vol. 19, pp. 177-188, 2005.

[4] M. Jeon and B. Walker, "Emotion detection and regulation interface for drivers with traumatic brain injury," *CHI11*, Vancouver, 2011.

[5] S. A. Ferguson, "Other high-risk factors for young drivers-how graduated licensing does, doesn't, or could address them," *Journal of Safety Research*, vol. 34, pp. 71-77, 2003.

[6] M. E. Gras *et al.*, "Mobile phone use while driving in a sample of Spanish phone university workers," *Accident Analysis and Prevention*, vol. 39, pp. 347-355, 2007.

[7] G. Mathews *et al.*, "Driver stress and performance on a driving simulator," *Human Factors*, vol. 40, pp. 136-149, 1998.

[8] H. A. Deery and B. N. Fildes, "Young novice driver subtypes: Relationship to high-risk behavior, traffic accident record, and simulator driving performance," *Human Factors*, vol. 41, pp. 628-643, 1999.

[9] C. Nass *et al.*, "Improving automotive safety by pairing driver emotion and car voice emotion," *CHI05*, Portland, USA, 2005, pp. 1973-1976.

Peer Interviews: An Adapted Methodology for Contextual Understanding in User-Centred Design

Rachel Menzies, Dr Annalu Waller
School of Computing
University of Dundee
Dundee, DD1 4HN

rlmenzies, awaller@dundee.ac.uk

Dr Helen Pain
School of Informatics
University of Edinburgh
Edinburgh, EH8 9AB

helen@inf.ed.ac.uk

ABSTRACT

In User-Centred Design (UCD) the needs and preferences of the end user are given primary consideration. In some cases, current methodologies such as interviewing may be difficult to conduct, for example when working with children, particularly those with Autism Spectrum Disorders (ASD). This paper outlines an approach to understanding the end-users, context and subject matter through the use of peer interviewing. This is proposed as a viable adaptation to User-Centred methodologies for inclusion of children and those with ASD.

Categories and Subject Descriptors

D.2.1 [**Software Engineering**]: Requirements/Specifications – *Elicitation methods.*
D.2.10 [**Software Engineering**]: Design – *Methodologies.*

General Terms: Design, Human Factors.

Keywords: User-Centred Design, Software Design, Design Methods, Children, Interview, Autism, Requirements

1. AUTISM SPECTRUM DISORDERS

Autism Spectrum Disorders (ASD), affecting at least 500,00 people in the UK [1], is a continuum of developmental disorders of varying severity. Within each condition, the severity of symptoms may differ between individuals across the spectrum.

The typical trajectory of development is compromised, resulting in a lack of appreciation of the thoughts, beliefs and feelings of others (Theory of Mind) [2], with established difficulties in social interaction, social communication and social imagination. These difficulties often manifest as social anxiety [2], with the individual becoming distressed when dealing with new people, ambiguous situations or in discursive situations where the outcomes may not be predictable.

2. USER-CENTRED DESIGN

User-Centred Design (UCD) is a multi-disciplinary design methodology where the needs and preferences of users are given primary consideration. Efforts are made to fully identify and understand the end user demographics, their understanding of the use and purpose of the system and the context and subject matter of the problem area [3] with the benefits of user-centred design are frequently acknowledged in the literature. For example, the system produced will be more "useful" (effective and efficient) for the end users as it will be what they need rather than what the developers think they need.

The techniques and methodologies applied in a given development depend on the level of involvement of the user, as well as the users' individual capabilities. This means that it can be difficult for researchers to select an appropriate methodology for requirements analysis.

While it is not apparent what the best techniques in user participation are, there is an understanding in the field of technology development that early user involvement is crucial [6] and so the practice of user centred design continues to evolve. Despite this evolvement, children (particularly those with disabilities) are infrequently involved in the design and testing of computer systems [5].

3. INTERVIEWING

Interviewing is considered to be crucial in the implementation of user centred design. Through careful interviewing with varying levels of structure, researchers can gain a greater understanding of the user needs and concerns, their environment and, ultimately, their interaction with that environment in ways that can be meaningful for the development of research and design.

In some cases, traditional interviews may be difficult to conduct and lead to the researcher not fully understanding the problem space. In particular, there are a number of limitations that have been found when working with children. For example, children can be keen to give the "correct" answer and please adult researchers conducting the interviews [6]. In the case of requirements gathering, interviews are intended to be exploratory and, as such, there is no correct answer, and so the true opinions of the group being considered may not be reflected. This desire to please may result in anxiety. Good and Robertson [6] suggested that peer interviews could reduce this anxiety.

Furthermore, these limitations can be more pronounced in individuals with ASD. A lack of social imagination means that those with ASD may be averse to social communications (including an interview) with an unfamiliar adult, such as the researcher. This can lead to further increased angst and stress. In addition, those with ASD have a particular desire to provide a "correct" answer, and may struggle with exploratory interview situations where the answer is not clear.

This paper reports on the use of an innovative interview technique to aid the understanding of the context of use of the system being designed as well as the end-user and their knowledge of social situations.

3.1 Peer Interviews

One possible way of reducing these limitations is to employ peer interviewing. Peer interviewing is where an individual conducts an interview with a member of his or her peer group. To date, there is limited literature available in the use of this technique, with a focus currently being on the use of peer interviewing for review or employment purposes (e.g.[7]). This style of interviewing may be useful in overcoming the difficulties of traditional interviewing when working with children, particularly those with ASD.

4. PILOT STUDY

A pilot study was conducted to investigate the use of peer interviewing as a methodology for UCD. Peer interviews were conducted as part of the "understanding" phase of development and design. This was within research [8] to develop a social skills intervention to teach children, both Typically Developing (TD) and with ASD about sharing. As part of the UCD process, it was important to understand children's appreciation of sharing and their opinions about how and why to share. The peer interviewing methodology has been piloted with a TD participant group (n=27, aged 7-8 years). The purpose of this is to go some way towards to establishing the methodology before employing it with children with ASD. It is clear that there will be some changes in the precise implementation of the methodology with the ASD group due to the compromised development trajectory.

4.1 Methodology

Interviews were conducted within a local school as part of an ICT lesson. A visit to the classroom was arranged, whereby the researcher explained the interview process to the children and ensured that they were familiar with how to operate the video cameras. These instructions were printed onto a laminated sheet (complemented with photographs) along with the 10 interview questions (see figure 1). These interview questions were considered by the class teacher to be developmentally appropriate. The video cameras were left in the classroom for a period of one week. After completing classroom tasks, the children conducted a peer interview with a partner of their choosing.

What is your name? How old are you?

What is sharing? Why is it important?

Think of a time when you had to share something with a friend:

> Who was there?

> Where did it happen?

> When did it happen?

> Why did you have to share?

> What happened?

Figure 1. Interview Questions

4.2 Using the Results

Grounded Theory was utilised to extract themes from the interviews, with each theme relating to a concept of sharing. Each of these concepts is addressed in the development of the software system. This ensures that the software fits with the context of children's understanding of sharing.

5. POTENTIAL FOR USE IN ASD

From data gathered in the pilot study, there appears to be many potential benefits for the use of this technique by those with ASD. For example, the interview process is clearly structured with a well-defined start and end point. The child conducting the interview is in control of the situation and can determine the pace of the interaction. In addition, the nature of interviewing lends

itself well to turn taking. This is a type of interaction that children with ASD often find difficult [2] and so providing opportunities to experience this successfully is beneficial.

This opportunity for success can increase an individual's confidence, particularly if the peer that they are interviewing is familiar to them. From an educational perspective, the peer being interviewed may become progressively less familiar as the individual becomes more accustomed to the task of interviewing. Providing confidence-boosting opportunities in this way may be generalised across the curriculum. The use of technology (video cameras) is likely to be a motivator for children with ASD, due to the natural affinity they have with technology [9]. This can encourage them to participate in the activity.

5.1 Future Work

In this case study, the methodology was piloted and evaluated with TD children. This was important to ensure that the methodology was robust, so as not to cause any unavoidable increase in anxiety in the target group by presenting an interview process that was not complete. The peer interview methodology is currently being further investigated in a class of six children with ASD in a specialist provision school. These incoming results will be presented and will aim to fully assess the potential of this methodology for this unique group.

6. CONCLUSION

The use of peer interviewing has been successful in identifying the context of sharing within the TD population. Through the use of this technique, requirements have been gathered software focussing on improving children's understanding of sharing. The purpose of this study was to ensure that the methodology was feasible before expanding the participant group to include the target children with ASD. Current work comprises expanding the interviewing process to include children with ASD.

7. REFERENCES

[1] National Autistic Society, N. *Statistics: how many people have autistic spectrum disorders.* 2007 [May 2007 20th December 2009]; Available from: http://www.nas.org.uk/nas/jsp/polopoly.jsp?d=235&a=3527.

[2] Attwood, T., *The Complete Guide to Asperger's Syndrome* 2006: Jessica Kingsley Publishers.

[3] Schuler, D. and A. Namioka, *Participatory Design: Principles and Practices,* 1993, Hillsdale, NJ: Lawrence Erlbaum.

[4] Kujala, S., *User Involvement: a review of the benefits and challenges.* Behav Inform Technol, 2003. 22(1), pp1-16

[5] Druin, A., *The role of children in the design of new technology.* Behav Inform Technol, 2002. **21**(1): p. 1-25.

[6] Good, J. and J. Robertson, *CARSS: A Framework for Learner-Centred Design with Children.* Int. J. Artif. Intell. Ed., 2006. **16**(4): p. 381-413.

[7] Allen, S. and T. Thrasher, *Peer interviewing: Sharing the selection process.* Nursing Management, 1998. **29**(3): p. 46.

[8] Menzies, R., *Promoting sharing behaviours in children through the use of a customised novel computer system.* SIGACCES Newsletter, 2011(99): p. 30-36.

[9] Moore, D., P. Mcgrath, and J. Thorpe, *Computer-Aided Learning for People with Autism - a Framework for Research and Development.* Innovations in Educ. & Teaching Int., 2001. **37**(3): p. 218-22.

Reading in Multimodal Environments: Assessing Legibility and Accessibility of Typography for Television

Penelope Allen
BBC Research & Development
Dock House, MediaCityUK, UK
+447745309538
penelope.allen@bbc.co.uk

Judith Garman
Mindful Research
+447967688453
judith@mindfulresearch.co.uk

Ian Calvert
BBC Television Platforms
Dock House, MediaCityUK, UK
+ 441613358605
ian.calvert1@bbc.co.uk

ABSTRACT

Television viewing is accompanied by ever more complex supporting content: as interactive TV becomes more functional, it also becomes more multimodal. Television typography is no longer limited to teletext, subtitles and captions. It provides navigation, tickers, tabulated results, info-graphics and is embedded in videos and games. At the same time, screen resolution is improving, and the size of household screens are increasing. Currently, little is known about what user needs are associated with these advances. With the use of a customisation prototype, the research explores television typography by understanding the preferences of a variety of users; people with cognitive and sensory access needs, older users and users with no stated access needs. The results from the first study showed participants preferred a larger font size than the current television standard. This preference was particularly prevalent when text was presented along with other content elements demanding attentional focus. The font type Helvetica Neue was particularly favoured by participants with access needs. The second study aims to establish a further exploration into font size for differing interactive environments. We seek to develop the prototype to test and improve the accessibility of interactive TV services.

Categories and Subject Descriptors

H.5.2 [**Information Interfaces and Presentation**]: User Interfaces – *evaluation/methodology, screen design.*

General Terms

Measurement, Documentation, Performance, Design, Experimentation, Human Factors.

Keywords

Typography, Accessibility, Interactive TV, Font, Access needs.

1. INTRODUCTION

Research has shown that font typography affects legibility [3] and readability [2]. Previous research has focused on different aspects of typography to understand its role in legibility. Arditi [1] developed a font adjustment prototype, the Font Tailor, to assess the impact of customisable font settings on the legibility for low vision users. Participants were able to create their own font using the settings provided. He found that despite the high variance in fonts produced by the participants, letter spacing, aspect ratio and height impacted the legibility greatly. In fact a combination of customisations caused a 75% enhancement in legibility. These studies are limited to, for the most part, print and, more recently,

computer screen presented fonts; little research has focused on typography for television (TV). In 1998, The Royal National Institute of the Blind (RNIB) developed and tested a font that has become one of the most widely used and known accessibility fonts in the UK for TV subtitling [4]. Tested on visually and hearing impaired users, Tiresias was found to be most popular due to its clarity and reading ease. In addition to other stipulations, the research suggested a recommended minimum font size of 24pt to be used for TV. With the increase in text services, we feel it is the right time to revisit TV typography and explore different font settings in the TV environment.

This research seeks to expand the current typography research to include the consumption of text on TV in different reading contexts. Content on such services are provided to users combining a variety of forms; images, audio, video and text. Little is known about the impact of the current typographic choices within these text-inclusive services. Additionally, little is known about the impact of these services with regard to a variety of users with differing access needs. With the use of a typography customisation prototype, the current research seeks to explore how the accessibility of these services can be improved for a range of users.

2. DEMO

A prototype was built to provide customisable visual settings on the TV in different contexts.

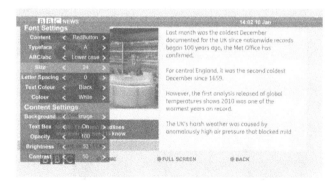

Figure 1: Prototype used to adjust settings in user test

Figure 1 shows the prototype with the customisable settings visible on the left hand side of the screen. There are a number of adjustable settings related to the text and the colours on the screen. The typographic elements that can be manipulated are relatively flexible to the needs of the study or user. The context in which the text is presented is utilised to explore text in multimodal environments incorporating video and images, this variable is referred to as the context condition.

We intend to use the demo session to explore the prototype and discuss ways in which it can be adapted to improve accessibility of interactive TV services. There is potential to deploy the customisation tool in a longitudinal large scale study in order to assess preferences over continued use. Currently the prototype is built in Flash and can be visible to or hidden from users for testing or use purposes. We will also discuss an adapted prototype and the findings from the current research and establish ways in which to improve testing accessibility on TV.

3. STUDY I
Exploring 4 existing fonts specific to BBC services we sought to lay the ground for further research. The study aimed to establish and compare the typography preferences, for font type and size in particular, for users with both sensory and cognitive conditions and those with no specified access needs. 20 participants were recruited, 11 male and 9 female, aged between 21 and 66 years. 10 participants had a specified condition which would strongly impact the way they read on television. 10 participants had no declared condition. The core access groups targeted in this user test were those with the cognitive conditions; ADHD, dyslexia and Aspergers syndrome and those with differing visual impairments and hearing loss.

3.1 Context Conditions
Five different task conditions were tested to establish the potential needs within differing reading contexts: Initial setup (text box on a background in which participants were required to select their initial preferences), BBC Red Button (See Figure 1: News story on red button service), Football Results Table (Premier league football scores in a table), News Ticker (Series of news headlines on a ticker at the bottom of the screen), and Strictly Results (Strictly come dancing results table for a selection of contestant pairs).

3.2 Main Findings
3.2.1 Preferred Font Size
Overall participants preferred a larger font size than the current standard for reading text on TV. There was no significant relationship between size preference and type of user, $x^2(1, N=20) = 0.88$, $p=0.05$, or the task condition, $x^2(4, N=20) = 3.56$, $p=0.05$. This suggests that overall participants wanted text larger in different contexts and this was true of participants with access needs and those with no access need.

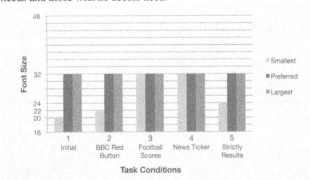

Figure 2: Smallest, preferred and largest font size for each context condition
Figure 2 shows the modes of the preferred font size as compared to the smallest and the largest size each participant was willing to accept for each task condition. The most preferred font size was 32pt and in context conditions with increased multimodal stimulus

levels was also the smallest acceptable size. This together with qualitative data suggests the font size variable is related to the context condition, with respect to the different modes of stimulus bidding for attentional focus.

3.2.2 Preferred Font Type
Helvetica Neue was the most preferred font for the access participants. Type of user has an effect on the preferred font type, $x^2(3, N=20) = 11.04$, $p=0.05$.

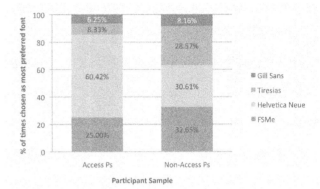

Figure 3: Distribution of most preferred font type for access and non-access participants.

Figure 3 shows the percentage of times a font was chosen as the most preferred for all task conditions. The graph compares access participants with non-access participants and shows a significant difference in font type preference between the 2 groups, in particular Helvetica Neue was considerably favoured by the access participants whereas there was no significant difference in preferred font type for the non-access participants between Tiresias, Helvetica Neue and FSMe. All participants disliked Gill Sans. Qualitative data suggests that Helvetica Neue was favoured for being unexceptional in way of appearing clear, and easy to read in terms of size and proportion.

4. STUDY II
The current study will develop the prototype in order to understand the font size variable. The first study findings suggest a relationship between context condition and font size. We aim to explore this relationship in a more controlled experiment using a participant group skewed to the older user.

5. REFERENCES
[1] Arditi, A. 2004. Adjustable typography: an approach to enhancing low vision text accessibility. *Ergonomics.* 47, 5, 469-482.
[2] Mackeben, M. 1999. Sustained focal attention and peripheral letter recognition. *Spatial Vision,* 12, 1, 51–72.
[3] McLean, R. 1980. *Thames & Hudson Manual of Typography,* Thames and Hudson, London.
[4] Silver, J., Gill, J., Sharville, J., Slater, J. and Martin, M. 1998. A new font for digital television subtitles. DOI= http://www.tiresias.org/fonts/screenfont/report_screen.htm

6. AUTHOR INFORMATION
4th Author; Jane Murison, BBC User Experience & Design, Dock House, MediaCityUK, Salford, UK, +447715479201

Self-Selection of Accessibility Options

Nithin Santhanam
Yorktown High School
Yorktown Heights, NY 10598, USA

seattle3@optimum.net

Shari Trewin, Cal Swart & P Santhanam
IBM Watson Research Center
P.O. Box 704, Yorktown Hgts, NY 10598, USA

{trewin, cals, pasanth} @us.ibm.com

ABSTRACT
This study focuses on the use of web accessibility software by people with cerebral palsy performing three typical user tasks. We evaluate the customization options in the IBM accessibilityWorks add-on to the Mozilla Firefox browser, as used by ten users. While specific features provide significant benefit, we find that users tend to pick unnecessary options, resulting in a potentially negative user experience.

Categories and Subject Descriptors
H.5.2 [**Information Interfaces and Presentation**]: User Interfaces

General Terms: Human Factors

Keywords
Web accessibility, customization, user study.

1. INTRODUCTION
Many tools and techniques are available to improve access to the web for people with visual and motor impairments. Some of the technology is built into operating systems, such as magnifiers, on-screen keyboards, etc. Many third party vendors provide countless additional software and hardware options. One example is the IBM accessibilityWorks software [1], which is an add-on to the Mozilla Firefox browser with features to assist with reading, viewing of images, legibility, etc. While providing more options increases flexibility, a criticism of such tools is that users may not choose an optimal configuration, or may even choose options that hinder, rather than help with usability.

There has been little research into the process of choosing accessibility options. As an example, an Accessibility Wizard in the Microsoft Windows 7 operating system asks questions to help select relevant options. Subtle differences between keyboard accessibility options are difficult to describe in words, and Trewin [2] proposed an automated configuration approach based on analysis of a user's typing. Options that have a visual effect on the user interface may be easier to understand, as their impact can be immediately seen. Occupational therapists use a formal process to select access options [3], focusing on large-scale adjustments such as seating, input devices, and positioning of devices. We claim that software configuration, and selection of assistive add-ons are more often done in the user's home context, perhaps with a friend or family member, and based largely on the individual's first impressions. Seniors used a variety of accessibilityWorks options, notably speech output, large fonts,

and screen magnification [4]. However, the performance impact of self-selected accessibilityWorks options has not been examined. This paper examines accessibilityWorks reading and visual access feature selections made by users, and their impact on performance.

2. THE USER STUDY
2.1 Participants
There were 10 participants (6 male, 4 female). Nine were wheelchair users. All had cerebral palsy, but the level of severity for each person was vastly different. Most had some level of visual impairment. Each participant had some computer experience and some were fairly advanced. Two of the participants had seen accessibilityWorks prior to this study.

2.2 User Tasks
Seven typical user tasks of increasing complexity were defined. They covered key aspects of effective web browsing representing a variety of skills needed. This paper presents three of these tasks, described in Table 1.

Table 1. Three user tasks and the interactions

Task	Description	User Interactions
1	Identifying and Hovering over nine 3"x 3" images on a grid	Mouse movement, mouse control, small amount of scrolling
2	Entering ten different letters into a text box	Clicking, reading small fonts
3	Finding times of movies at www.fandango.com	Clicking, reading, scrolling, looking for certain words

2.3 Methodology
The sessions took place at a United Cerebral Palsy center computer lab normally used by the participants for web browsing. Participants used a standard 14" laptop with Windows 7 operating system, the on-screen keyboard and a standard wireless mouse. A digital audio recorder and a screen recorder were used to record the session with each user, facilitating detailed analysis later. Users selected accessibilityWorks features based on oral descriptions and demonstrations. Each user performed the same set of tasks twice, with and without accessibilityWorks. The order of conditions was counterbalanced. The participants were free to stop during the trial whenever they chose. When a participant was unable to complete a task, the experimenter stopped the session and did not present the more difficult tasks. Participants were allowed to complete their tasks if they appeared confident. At the conclusion of all the tasks, each participant was asked to answer a survey on their favorite features and overall assessment of their experience. With this data, we measured the impact of

accessibilityWorks on the ability of the users to perform the tasks, both qualitatively and quantitatively.

3. RESULTS

3.1 The need for customization

Overall, each user selected from 1 to 8 features, with a mean of 3.6 and median of 3. Table 2 gives each accessibilityWorks feature with the number of users selecting it. Even though the average number of options selected was small, users sometimes appeared to select more options than they needed and in some cases the options introduced problems. For example, Participant 8 selected the one column option, which reformats a page into a single column on the left. This makes it easier to read but it requires more scrolling up and down. This increased the time on tasks due to the required scrolling. Participant 4 who had no difficulty viewing images, chose the image enlargement feature (which is meant for viewing an image through a separate window in the middle of the screen). Consequently, he had to keep closing the unnecessary windows to browse the rest of the content. These and several other examples during the study point to a clear need for a better customization procedure.

Table 2. accessibilityWorks Features & User Selections

Feature & Description	No. of Users
Large Cursor	8
Text Enlargement	6
Line Spacing	3
Word Spacing	2
Letter Spacing	4
One column rendering to avoid side scrolling	1
Image Enlargement on hovering	1
Speaking Text at Cursor Location	4
Hide/ Show Images	0
Keyboard entry using one hand	0
Banner Text Enlargement	3
Colors for better contrast	2
Changing text fonts	0
Visual Event Alerts of the computer	0
Visual Page History Trail	1

3.2 Qualitative and Quantitative Analysis

Participants 3 and 9 were unable to complete the tasks due to difficulty using the mouse and are excluded from the following analysis. Of the remaining eight, four participants were not able to complete all the tasks without accessibilityWorks. The common reasons for not completing a task were the inability to read small fonts and see small buttons making them difficult to click on. With accessibilityWorks, all the eight participants were able to finish all the tasks. Tasks that involved reading small fonts on the screen were easier with accessibilityWorks due to features such as the text enlargement and different line, letter and word spacing.

Table 3 shows the analysis of data taken for the three tasks performed by the eight participants with (aWrks) and without (dflt) accessibilityWorks. Where a participant was unable to complete a task, a time of 500 sec was used for the analysis. Due to the small sample size and non-normal distributions, median and

Inter-quartile range (IQR) are used for comparing times. Overall, task times are lower with accessibilityWorks. Table 3 also shows the results of the Wilcoxon Sign Rank Test with the associated p-values. It is evident that users performed Tasks 1 and 2 better with accessibilityWorks and Task 3 indicated some improvement. Without accessibilityWorks, Participant 6 could not complete task 2 and Participant 7 could not complete Task 3 in a reasonable time. Although these results indicate some benefit from using accessibilityWorks, further improvement is still needed.

Table 3. Analysis of task times of 8 users for the 3 tasks.

	Task1		Task 2		Task 3	
	dflt	aWrks	dflt	aWrks	dflt	aWrks
Median (sec)	53.5	46.5	398	107.5	186	158
IQR (sec)	47-83	41.5-56	99-500	57.5-152.5	118-500	89-214
p-value	0.019		0.012		0.176	

3.3 Results of the Participant Survey

In the survey, all the eight users expressed their overall positive experience with accessibilityWorks and identified Large Cursor, Text Enlargement, different spacing options and Speak Text (that mainly target tasks that involve reading) as the most helpful.

4. CONCLUSION

This paper describes a study to assess the benefit of the accessibilityWorks software for ten users with cerebral palsy, performing common web tasks. Using qualitative and quantitative methods, we have shown that the self-selected software features contributed positively to the user experience. However, this study points to the need for a better procedure to match the accessibility options to users' ability to maximize their overall user experience.

5. ACKNOWLEDGMENTS

We thank our participants and staff members at the United Cerebral Palsy Center in Suffolk, NY. This study was done as a part of the Yorktown High School Science Research program.

6. REFERENCES

[1] Hanson, V., Brezin, J., Crayne, S., Keates, S., Kjeldsen, R., Richards, J., Swart, C. & Trewin, S. (2005) Improving Web accessibility through an enhanced open-source browser, *IBM Systems Journal*, 44(3), pp. 573 - 588.

[2] Trewin, S. (2004). Automating accessibility: The dynamic keyboard. In *Proceedings of the Sixth International ACM/SIGCAPH Conference on Assistive Technologies*, Atlanta, Georgia, October 2004.

[3] Cook, A. M. & Hussey, S. (3rd Edition, 2007, Mosby) *Assistive Technologies: Principles and Practice*.

[4] Hanson, V., Snow-Weaver, A., and Trewin, S. (2006). Software personalization to meet the needs of older adults. *Gerontechnology* 5 (3), pp 160-169, International Society of Gerontechnology.

Sensing Human Movement of Mobility and Visually Impaired People

Yusuke Fukushima[†], Hiromasa Uematsu[§], Ryotarou Mitsuhashi[‡],
Hidetaka Suzuki[†] and Ikuko Eguchi Yairi[†]
Department of Information and Communication Sciences, Sophia University
7-1 Kioicho, Chiyoda-ku Tokyo, 102-8554, Japan
[†]{yfukushima, hideta-s, i.e.yairi}@sophia.ac.jp, [§]uematsu@yairilab.net, [‡]g.podden@gmail.com

ABSTRACT
This paper studies human movement of both mobility and visually impaired people using mobile sensing devices as the first step toward creating an accessible information base. Nine mobility impaired persons conduct an experiment of wheelchair moving, and the visualized sensing results mapped on Googlemap is compared with their subjective feelings. Also, one blind person conducts an experiment of walking with a walking assistant. The sensing results show that a single accelerometer enabled to detect walking, descending and waiting behaviors.

Categories and Subject Descriptors
K.4.2[Social Issues]:Assistive technologies for persons with disabilities

General Terms
Experimentation, Human Factors

Keywords
Sensing human behavior, mobility impairment, visually impairment.

1. INTRODUCTION
Human movement is the most basic physical function for independent living and dignified life, so, improving accessibility for both mobility and visually impaired people is desirable. A wheelchair is the best partner for mobility impaired people to control their movements by themself and to make the movements more freely. But, body vibration comes from the wheel rolling on uneven road surface evokes spasticity[1], and narrow road and illegally-parked bicycles or a people jam leading to narrow road make them nervous going outside. At the same time, a white cane is useful mobility tool for visually impaired people to detect obstacles on the ground by themself, and the sounds made by the cane hitting the ground help others to recognize them easily. But, it is not so easy to detect tiny bumps that increase risk of fall, and they can hardly explain where they are exactly when they have accidents, especially in the time of disaster. To improve road accessibility, most approaches focused on environmental modification techniques, such as revamping of roads surface and seating comfort; however, they are expensive and not always helpful for anybody because the degree of impairment and feeling of each person are apparently different.

Recently, several works creating database of any barrier objects in roads[2][3] are available. But, reuse of these personal feelings still remains unexploited because data conversion from subjective and individual feelings into generally needed objective and scientific data is difficult. Our goal is to reveal the facts of subjective

discomfort feelings in movement and to suggest accessible road. As the first step, this paper studies human mobility sensing of both wheelchair users and visually impaired people by using mobile devices with built-in sensors.

2. EXPERIMENT ON MOBILITY IMPAIRED PEOPLE
Nine human subjects with mobility impairment conduct an experiment of wheelchair moving around Akihabara Station in Tokyo. In order to obtain pure movement data, each human subject was asked to move their own wheelchair which is being used in their everyday life, and the vibration from wheelchair moving was obtained from a SunSPOT three-axis accelerometer of Sun Microsystems attached on the axle of the rear wheels. The moving vibration data was sent to a base station from the accelerometer and the location data obtained from a GPS receiver were automatically recorded into the laptop contained in the backpack attached to the back of each wheelchair (see Figure 1). The experiment was recorded by video taking, and each subject was asked his/her personal feeling through an interviewer.

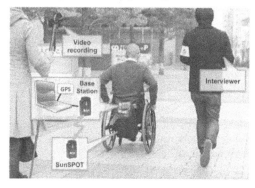

Figure 1: One of the human subjects moved with his manual wheelchair attached our sensing system.

To analyze the relation between physical vibration and subjective feeling, we employed vibration acceleration level (VAL) with unit decibel (dB) that is defined as $20 \log_{10}(a/a_0)$, where a and a_0 indicate the root-mean-square of three-axis acceleration values and a reference acceleration, respectively. a_0 is usually set to 10^{-5} m/s^2 by the Japanese Industrial Standards (JIS) C1510-1995. To find higher VAL on the route intuitively, we separated the moving route represented on Googlemap by every 20 *ms*, and each part of the route was painted with one of 13 colors according to the averaged VAL value, i.e. red color for VAL value over 116 dB. Notice that the location data obtained from the GPS receiver was revised by hand carefully to remove multipath effect.

Figure 2 shows the result of 50-year-old man subject who has about 40 years experience in using wheelchair. He has been using it both inside and outside all the time. In contrast, Figure 3 shows a whole picture of the visualized VAL of 30-year-old man subject who has about 10 years experience in using wheelchair. Since he usually plays kayak, a human-powered light narrow boat that has one or more covered cockpits, he enjoyed the wheelchair moving even when the body vibration turned to be so high. From those experiences, it can be observed the discomfort feeling in wheelchair moving does not only come from road surface, but also from the subject's feeling.

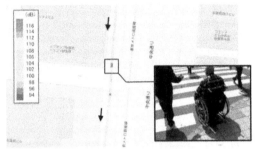

Figure 2: A 50-year-old man subject with rheumatoid and paralyzed arm moves his manual wheelchair. Although he tried to control his wheelchair carefully throughout this experiment, higher VAL values were detected at uneven road surface.

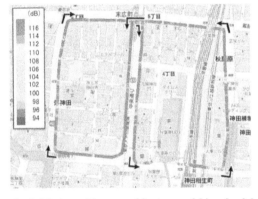

Figure 3: A 30-year-old man subject moved his wheelchair so fast, and higher VAL values were often detected. Anyway, he enjoyed his wheelchair moving.

3. EXPERIMENT ON VISUALLY IMPAIRED PEOPLE

One blind person conducted an experiment of walking around Yotsuya Station in Tokyo. In contrast with the previous experiment, it is rather difficult to fix the accelerometer. Hence, we put a smartphone with the built-in three-axis accelerometer, HTC Desire, into the coat pocket of each subject in which x-axis of accelerometer was set in vertical direction (see Figure 4). We also attached a Polar RS800CX heart rate meter to find out the relation of the human movement and the heart rate.

As shown in Figure 5, it can be observed the three basic behaviors like walking on a flat road or descending steps, or waiting at stoplights from detected vibrations. These three vibration patterns are apparently different. Moreover, since visually impaired people usually does not make quick movements such as running, so, we

can also detect some emergency movements out by comparing with vibration of three patterns above. For example, high vibration in y- and z-axis and small vibration in x-axis appeared when people bumped against the others or any objects.

Figure 4: A blind woman subject walks with a walking assistant on the steep downward slope.

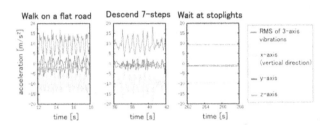

Figure 5: A blind subject walks around Yotsuya Station in Tokyo. Three types of walking behaviors can be detected by using the three-axis accelerometer in a smartphone, and also, even her steps and walking speed can be detected.

4. CONCLUSION

In this paper, we have conducted some experiments of human movement on both mobility and visually impaired people, and results show that human movement could be detected by using three-axis accelerometer sensors. Developing an index of subjective discomfort feeling when moving the wheelchair and classifying the human movements will be the next work.

5. ACKNOWLEDGMENTS

This work was supported by Research Grant of Support Center for Advanced Telecommunications Technology Research for FY2011 –FY2013 and Research Grant of Tateishi Science and Technology Foundation in FY2011.

6. REFERENCES

[1] S. N. W. Vorrink, L. H. V. V. der Woude, A. Messenberg, P. A. Cripton, B. Hughes, and B. J. Sawatzky. Comparison of wheelchair wheels in terms of vibration and spasticity in people with spinal cord injury. *J. Rehabil. Res. Dev.*, 45(9):1269–1280, 2008.

[2] M. Kurihara, H. Nonaka, and T. Yoshikawa. Use of highly accurate GPS in network-based barrier-free street map creation system. *In Proc. IEEE Syst. Man Cyb.*, volume 2, pages 1169–1173, October 2004.

[3] I. E. Yairi and S. Igi. Mobility support GIS with universal-designed data of barrier/barrier-free terrains and facilities for all pedestrians including the elderly and the disabled. *In Proc. IEEE Syst. Man Cyb.*, volume 2, pages 2909–2914, October 2006.

Smartphone Haptic Feedback for Nonvisual Wayfinding

Shiri Azenkot
Computer Science and Engineering
DUB Group
University of Washington
Seattle, WA 98195 USA
shiri@cs.washington.edu

Richard E. Ladner
Computer Science and Engineering
University of Washington
Seattle, WA 98195 USA
ladner@cs.washington.edu

Jacob O. Wobbrock
The Information School
DUB Group
University of Washington
Seattle, WA 98195 USA
wobbrock@uw.edu

ABSTRACT

We explore using vibration on a smartphone to provide turn-by-turn walking instructions to people with visual impairments. We present two novel feedback methods called *Wand* and *ScreenEdge* and compare them to a third method called *Pattern*. We built a prototype and conducted a user study where 8 participants walked along a pre-programmed route using the 3 vibration feedback methods and no audio output. Participants interpreted the feedback with an average error rate of just 4 percent. Most preferred the Pattern method, where patterns of vibrations indicate different directions, or the ScreenEdge method, where areas of the screen correspond to directions and touching them may induce vibration.

Categories and Subject Descriptors

H.5.2 [**Information Interfaces and Presentation**]: User Interfaces – *input devices and strategies*. K.4.2 [**Computers and society**]: Social issues – *assistive technologies for persons with disabilities*.

General Terms

Design, Human Factors.

Keywords

Haptic feedback, wayfinding, blind, accessibility.

1. INTRODUCTION

People with visual impairments experience challenges in wayfinding, the act of orienting and navigating in and through physical space. As such, many research and commercial systems have been developed to enable blind and low-vision people to navigate more independently. Most of these systems, however, primarily use speech output that can be distracting and difficult to hear in a loud environment. Since blind and low-vision people rely on their hearing to understand their surroundings, speech output can also be unsafe.

We explore ways of giving turn-by-turn routing instructions with haptic output, a safer and less distracting modality. We present our novel *Wand* and *ScreenEdge* feedback methods and evaluate them with the *Pattern* method, which is based on prior work [4,6]. All use the single vibration motor, compass, and touch screen on a relatively inexpensive smartphone. A navigation system can direct a user along a route with vibration using these methods instead of speaking the instructions. We built a prototype navigation system and conducted a user study with 8 blind people to compare Wand, ScreenEdge, and Pattern.

Our contributions include: (1) presenting two novel accessible techniques for providing navigation instructions (Wand and

ScreenEdge); and (2) empirically comparing these methods to Pattern with blind and low-vision users.

2. RELATED WORK

Most commercial and research wayfinding tools that provide nonvisual feedback use speech, but there has been some work on the use of haptic feedback for both blind and sighted users. Pielot and Boll [5] and Heuten *et al.* [3] used a tactile belt to convey directional feedback to users with visual impairments. Amemiya and Sugiyama [1] and Hemmert *et al.* [2] developed new vibrotactile feedback modalities to convey directions. Pattern, Wand, and ScreenEdge, in contrast, convey similar information but use commodity hardware that is cheaper and readily available. Jacob *et al.* [4] proposed using patterns to communicate directions but only described a case-study evaluation. Similarly, Pielot *et al.* [6] described using vibration patterns for sighted users. Our Pattern method is similar to methods used in [6] and [4] but the Wand and ScreenEdge methods are novel. Also, our work is the first to conduct a comparative evaluation of haptic wayfinding feedback for blind and low-vision users.

3. PROTOTYPE & FEEDBACK METHODS

In this section, we describe how the Wand, ScreenEdge, and Pattern methods provide navigation instructions to a user as she walks along a route. We built a prototype on a Motorola Droid phone. The built-in GPS is used to determine where the user is along a pre-programmed route and third-party routing API's are used to determine where she must turn at the nearest intersection. We focus on evaluating feedback methods, so our prototype is simple: it instructs the user which way to walk at the nearest intersection, assuming there are only four possibilities (forward, backward, right, or left). We defer incorporating vibration feedback into a more sophisticated navigation system to future work.

3.1 Wand

With the Wand technique, the user points the phone like a wand around him- or herself. When the top of the phone is roughly pointing in the direction where the user must walk, the phone will vibrate. The built-in compass is used to determine where the top of the phone is pointing.

3.2 ScreenEdge

The ScreenEdge method uses touch input and vibration output. With this technique, the user touches the screen near the four edges. The phone will vibrate when the user touches close to the edge that corresponds to the direction he or she must walk at the next intersection. For example, if the phone vibrates when the user touches close to the top edge of the screen, the user must walk forward; if the phone vibrates when the user touches the screen near the right edge, the user must turn right. Unlike the Wand, the ScreenEdge does not use the compass so the direction indicated is relative the previous leg of the route.

ASSETS'11, October 24–26, 2011, Dundee, Scotland, UK.
ACM 978-1-4503-0919-6/11/10.

Figure 1. A participant uses the phone to determine which direction to turn. The tape at the top and bottom of the phone tactually marks the edges of the screen. In the ScreenEdge image, the highlighted area shows which region of the screen will induce vibration when the user must turn right.

3.3 Pattern

The Pattern method simply vibrates for 1 to 4 pulses to indicate which way a user must turn at the nearest intersection. One pulse indicates the user must go forward, 2 pulses indicate the user must turn right, 3 pulses indicate the user must turn back, and 4 pulses indicate the user must turn left. The phone vibrates when the user presses one of the physical keys on the phone (we used the volume key in our implementation). As this method does not use the compass, Pattern indicates directions relative to the previous leg of the route.

4. EVALUATION

4.1 Participants and Methods

We conducted a within-subjects user study with 8 blind and low-vision participants (6 females, 2 males, mean age was 53) to compare the Wand, ScreenEdge, and Pattern methods. With each participant, we briefly explained each method, and conducted a lab test, a field test, and an interview.

During the lab test, each participant was asked to interpret feedback 4 times with each of the 3 methods while standing or sitting in one place. For example, we programmed our prototype to instruct the user to turn right using the ScreenEdge method, handed the phone to the participant, and asked him or her to tell us in which direction the phone instructed the participant to walk. We then conducted the field test, which involved walking along a pre-programmed route in a busy urban area. The route included 16 intersections where the participant used the phone to determine in which direction to continue walking. We used a different feedback method for each consecutive group of 4 intersections. We randomized the order of feedback methods to avoid bias. Finally, we conducted an interview with each participant that included the NASA-TLX tool for assessing the workload of using each feedback method.

4.2 Results

Accuracy was high for all methods. On average, participants erred 0.75 out of 8 times when using Wand (9%), 0.13 out of 8 times when using ScreenEdge (2%), and 0.13 out of 8 times when using Pattern (2%). Twenty-five percent of errors made when using the Wand occurred because the phone's compass was inaccurate in certain locations.

Four out of the 8 participants preferred using Pattern, while 3 preferred using ScreenEdge, and none preferred using Wand. One participant preferred either ScreenEdge or Wand. Participants felt that the Pattern method was fastest and some liked the tactile interaction in ScreenEdge. Moving the phone around in Wand was

uncomfortable for some participants, and they found this method less reliable. According to the NASA TLX questionnaires, all participants assessed the workload of Wand to be higher than that of ScreenEdge or Pattern, while workload assessments between the latter two methods varied. All participants indicated that they liked receiving navigation instructions through vibration and found all three methods to be effective.

5. CONCLUSION

We have developed and evaluated three methods for giving blind and low-vision people walking directions using vibration on a smartphone. Our user study demonstrates that all methods are viable means of communicating directional information without demanding a user's auditory attention or requiring special hardware. There were some reliability issues with the smartphone's built-in compass, however, which we hope to remedy in future work. Also, we plan to incorporate the methods presented here in a more sophisticated navigation system.

6. ACKNOWLEDGMENTS

The authors thank Shanthi Shanmugam. This work was supported in part by Google and by the US Department of Education under grant H327A100014.

7. REFERENCES

[1] Amemiya, T., and Sugiyama, H. (2010). Orienting Kinesthetically: A Haptic Handheld Wayfinder for People with Visual Impairments. *ACM Trans. Access. Comput.* 3, 2, Article 6.

[2] Hemmert, F., Hamann, S., Lowe, M., Zeipelt, J., and Joost, G. (2010). Weight-shifting mobiles: two-dimensional gravitational displays in mobile phones. *Proc. of the 28th of CHI EA 2010.* ACM, New York, NY, USA, 3087-3092.

[3] Heuten, W., Henze, N., Boll, S., and Pielot, M. (2008). Tactile wayfinder: a non-visual support system for wayfinding. In *Proc. of NordiCHI* 2008. ACM, New York, NY, USA, 172-181.

[4] Jacob, R., Mooney, P., Corcoran, P., and Winstanley, A. C. (2010). Haptic-GIS: exploring the possibilities. *SIGSPATIAL Special* 2, 3, 13-18.

[5] Pielot, M. and Boll, S. (2010). Tactile Wayfinder: Comparison of Tactile Waypoint Navigation with Commercial Pedestrian Navigation Systems. *The Pervasive Computing*, 2010.

[6] Pielot, M., Poppinga, B., Heuten, W., Schang, J. and Boll, S. (2011). A Tactile Compass for Eyes-free Pedestrian Navigation. *Interact* 2011.

Supporting Deaf Children's Reading Skills:
The Many Challenges of Text Simplification

Chiara Vettori
Institute for specialised communication and
multilingualism, EURAC research
39100 Bolzano, Italy   +39 0471 055 124,
cvettori@eurac.edu

Ornella Mich
Fondazione Bruno Kessler
38123 Povo, Italy
+39 0461 314 582
mich@fbk.eu

ABSTRACT

Deaf children have great difficulties in reading comprehension. In our contribution, we illustrate how we have collected, simplified and presented some stories in order to render them suitable for young Italian deaf readers both from a linguistic and a formal point of view. The aim is to stimulate their pleasure of reading. The experimental data suggest that the approach is effective and that enriching the stories with static and/or animated drawings significantly improves text readability. However, they also clearly point out that textual simplification alone is not enough to meet the needs of the target group and that the story structure itself and its presentation have to be carefully planned.

Categories and Subject Descriptors

H.5.2 [**User Interfaces**]: Natural language, Graphical User Interfaces.

General Terms

Experimentation.

Keywords

Deaf children, text simplification, reading comprehension.

1. INTRODUCTION

Most deaf children have substantial literacy difficulties [1]. This condition is due, on the one side, to the lack of exposure to oral language from birth and, on the other, to the type of educational intervention they are faced with, which accustoms them to decoding single words and isolated sentences, thus making it difficult for them to face the complexity of entire texts [2]. In order to support deaf children in improving their reading comprehension skills in Italian, we have developed a software literacy tool called LODE [3]. The child using LODE will read an entire story and then do a series of comprehension exercises which should help him/her to reason on the read text in its totality. To favour the child's focusing on the inference aspect and not on other factors involved in the reading comprehension skills [4], we have previously simplified the stories. In the present contribution, we describe the steps we undertook to select the stories to be published in LODE and how we simplified them on the basis of our target group's needs. Moreover, we discuss the results of an evaluation conducted in spring 2011 with Italian deaf children aged 8 to 14.

2. LITERACY AND DEAF CHILDREN

The term literacy refers to the ability to read and write at a level that lets one understand and communicate ideas in a literate society. Learning to read and write is extremely difficult for deaf

children because these activities are based on verbal language, which cannot be considered deaf people's first language. With regard to the reading ability of deaf children, they encounter difficulties at least at three levels of comprehension: lexical, morphological and inferential. At lexical level, they generally have a vocabulary limited to a few words and they tend to connect the meaning to the context, hardly ever generalizing it [5]. As a matter of fact, they often fail in detecting the meaning of idiomatic expressions, metaphors and allegories [6] and though they share the much of the same experiences as hearing people, deaf children do not rely on similar word knowledge. Moreover, some studies affirm that deaf pupils' education tends to focus on reading and writing tasks based on single sentences, so that the ability to infer information from the text itself develops with difficulty [7,8].

Information technology (IT) techniques are a great resource for those who work with deaf children. Characteristics such as high memory capacity, visualization abilities, hyperlink techniques as well as sophisticated artificial intelligence techniques can be exploited to build educational tools able to meet deaf children's needs in an effective way. Given that research consistently support the theory that those who read more become better readers [11], by combining both the attention for the language/content aspect of the story (re)writing and for the stories' formal presentation, LODE aims at supporting Italian deaf children's pleasure of reading.

3. THE LODE'S STORIES

There are two main aspects to be considered when looking for stories to be read by deaf children. First, stories should attract children's attention to help them maintain their concentration on what they are reading. Deaf children are generally untrained readers and get bored quickly, therefore the text's appeal becomes vital to keep their attention high and to. Second, stories should be suitable for the children's literacy levels. Indeed, too easy a story may bore the reader, whereas a too difficult one may be frustrating. Both aspects relate to the children's age and literacy level which do not correlate linearly. In fact, it is not infrequent that a deaf pre-adolescent is less literate than a younger child. To create the LODE's database of stories, we followed a four-step procedure: (1) we looked for suitable stories, (2) we annotated on the original version of each chosen story, (3) we simplified all the texts, reducing the number of subordinate clauses, of (multiple) pronouns and of clitics etc. and substituting with synonyms or paraphrases those words that are not included in the "Lessico elementare" [9], and (4) we classified and stored them in an electronic repository. The four steps are described in detail in [10].

4. STORIES' EVALUATION

To check if the LODE's stories are comprehensible to deaf children, we performed a test involving eighteen Italian deaf children, ten aged 8 to 11 (this group is indicated with yD in the following) and eight aged 12 to 14 (oD), and twelve Italian hearing children, eight aged 8 to 11 (yH) and four aged 11 to 14 (oH), as a control group. The aim of our test was to verify if the simplification operations we conducted on the stories have rendered the story texts easier to read and more understandable for our target group. We also aimed to test the effectiveness of using static and animated drawings to improve the readability of the simplified stories. An example is shown in Figure 1: when the child opens the page, he/she only sees the background image. Moving around the mouse, the user activates an animation; when clicking on it, the story text appears. Words with the yellow background are "active" words, i.e. they are linked to a dictionary proposing a textual definition, an example of use, an image and a video with the translation in Italian sign language (LIS).

We provided two sets of three stories each: one for younger and one for older children. Each child read three stories out of his/her set in the following progression: a story in its original version, a story simplified as explained above, and a simplified story illustrated with drawings and definitions. After reading each story, the child answered the eleven questions foreseen for the comprehension exercises. There is a significant difference among the responses to the sets of exercises related to the three types of stories in the yD group (F (330, 2) = 6.740; p < .001), but not in the oD group (F (264, 2) = 2.143; p=.119). In both cases there is an improvement of the correct answer mean from the original story (yD = 0.79; oD = 0.57) to the simplified illustrated version (yD = 0.88; oD = 0.70). Nevertheless, in the oD group the difference between the mean of correct answers given to the original story and the one relative to the simplified story is almost inexistent (0.57 versus 0.58). Moreover, in the yD group the mean of correct answers to the simplified story without images is lower (0.68) than the one achieved in the exercises to the other two story types. The main results are confirmed by the regression analysis which underlines that there is a significant difference among the three stories (i.e. the instrument fits the purpose) and that the third one always appears to be the most comprehensible for deaf children. Not surprisingly, the two hearing groups always perform better than the deaf ones, but the difference in terms of correct answer mean is bigger among the older children (0.295 versus 0.084).

The analysis show that the stories meant for the older children do follow the pattern we had intended (from the original, more difficult story to the simplified-illustrated, easier one) and that the slightly (though non significantly) better performance of the hearing children does not depend on the type of stories at all. As regarding the test's goals, we have verified that the simplified story with drawings and definitions is the most comprehensible for both yD and oD groups. Given these results we can therefore state that text simplification helps children to easily understand a story but, unfortunately, we cannot draw any firm conclusions about the simplification impact for the first, younger group, though the comparison with the control group's results do speak in favor of text simplification. Clearly enough, lexical and syntactic simplification alone is not sufficient to guarantee for the readability of a text by a deaf readership. The story's structure itself (event sequence, length etc.) has to be carefully designed in order to avoid confusion and boredom in the deaf reader, especially in the absence of drawings which help contextualize the events and information read.

5. CONCLUSIONS

The background, the process and the experimental data we have illustrated show that providing suitable stories for deaf children is in no way a simple task. The parameters and the factors to be managed and to be kept under control are diverse and numerous and reside in the target group's specifics – i.e. their specific needs - but also in the stories themselves – i.e. plot, climax, etc. -. Nonetheless, we have shown that though it might be challenging, it is possible to offer deaf children captivating stories they can easily understand and enjoy, with the aim of improving their motivation to read. Reading for pleasure will open up new worlds for them and help them develop better literacy skills.

Figure 1. The simplified illustrated story: an example of an animated drawing.

6. REFERENCES

[1] Wauters, L.N., van Bon, W.H.J. and Tellings, A.E.J.M. 2006. Reading Comprehension of Dutch Deaf Children. *Reading and Writing*. 19, 49-76.

[2] Banks, J. and Gray, C. and Fyfe, R. 1990. The Written Recall of Printed Stories by Severely Deaf Children. *British Journal of Educational Psychology*. 60, 192-206.

[3] Gennari, R. and Mich, O. 2007. Constraint-based Temporal Reasoning for E-learning with LODE. In *Proceedings of the 13th International Conference on Principles and Practice of Constraint Programming* (2007).

[4] Whitehurst, G. and Longian, C. 1998. Child Development and Emergent Literacy. *Child Development*. 69, 848-872.

[5] Fabretti, D., Volterra, V. and Pontecorvo, C. 1998. Written Language Ability in Deaf Italians. *J. of Deaf Studies and Deaf Education*. 3(3), 231-244.

[6] Rittenhouse, R K. and Stearns, K. 1982. Teaching Metaphor to Deaf Children. *American Annals of the Deaf*. 127(1).

[7] Arfé, B. and Boscolo, P. 2006. Causal Coherence in Deaf and Hearing Students' Written Narratives. *Discourse Processes*. 42(3), 271-300.

[8] Wilbur, R.B. 2000. The Use of ASL to Support the Development of English and Literacy. *J. of Deaf Studies and Deaf Education*. 5, 81-104.

[9] Marconi, L., Ott, M., Pesenti, E., Ratti, D.,a and Tavella, M. 1993. Lessico Elementare. *Dati statistici sull'italiano letto e scritto dai bambini delle elementari*. Zanichelli, Bologna.

[10] Mich, O., and Vettori, C. 2011. *E-Stories for Educating Deaf Children in Literacy. The DAMA Procedure*. Technical Report. FBK.

[11] Clark, C., and Rumbold, K. 2006. *Reading for pleasure. A research overview*. National Literacy Trust, London.

TapBeats: Accessible and Mobile Casual Gaming

Joy Kim
Computer Science & Engineering
University of Washington
Seattle, WA 98195

jojo080889@gmail.com

Jonathon Ricaurte
Computer Science & Engineering
University of Washington
Seattle, WA 98195

jonricaurte@gmail.com

ABSTRACT

Conventional video games today rely on visual cues to drive user interaction, and as a result, there are few games for blind and low-vision people. To address this gap, we created an accessible and mobile casual game for Android called TapBeats, a musical rhythm game based on audio cues. In addition, we developed a gesture system that utilizes text-to-speech and haptic feedback to allow blind and low-vision users to interact with the game's menu screens using a mobile phone touchscreen. A graphical user interface is also included to encourage sighted users to play as well. Through this game, we aimed to explore how both blind and sighted users can share a common game experience.

Categories and Subject Descriptors

H.5.2 [**Information Interfaces and Presentation**]: User Interfaces – *input devices and strategies, voice I/O.*
K.8.0 [**Personal Computing**]: General – *games.*

General Terms

Design, Human Factors

Keywords

Accessibility, blind, low-vision, audio games, mobile games, haptics and gestures, user interfaces, user centered design

1. INTRODUCTION

With the video game market placing an increased emphasis on graphics, the visual aspects of games are becoming more and more important. As a result, blind and low-vision people are often excluded from video game play [3]. In order to address this gap, we applied user centered design to create an accessible and mobile casual game for Android called TapBeats[1].

Tapbeats is based on audio cues so that blind and low-vision people can be included in game play. A gameplay screen with four buttons placed in each corner of the touchscreen is employed in different ways to provide various types of gameplay. Each of these buttons emits a different instrument sound when pressed. Blind and low-vision users are also able to navigate through the game menus through the use of text-to-speech and haptic feedback. TapBeats also includes a graphical interface to encourage play by sighted users as well.

There have been several attempts to design and build video games that are accessible to blind users, such as Blind Hero [4] and

AudiOdyssey [1]. Like these games, we aim to enable blind and low-vision people and sighted people to enjoy the same level and quality of gameplay, though by making TapBeats for a mobile device, players will be able to carry the game with them and play it whenever they want.

2. TAPBEATS

2.1 Menu Navigation and Accessibility

To give blind users the ability to interact with TapBeats via a mobile phone touchscreen, we developed a gesture system based on Slide Rule [2]. To explore menus and figure out the available options, the user can slide their finger around on the screen (Figure 1). As the user's finger touches a menu item, the phone will speak out the menu item name and generate a small vibration. Once the user hears the desired item, they can select it by double tapping anywhere on the screen. To return to a previous menu screen, the user can swipe with two fingers anywhere on the screen. The user can also use this gesture during gameplay to pause. Finally, if the user wants the game to speak out what menu screen they are currently on, they can double tap with two fingers.

Figure 1. The TapBeats Main Menu

2.2 Gameplay

2.2.1 The Gameplay Screen

TapBeats contains various types of gameplay based on this same gameplay screen (Figure 2). Each button on the screen makes a different percussion instrument sound and correlates to one of the corners of the phone so that it is easily findable by touch.

---

[1] http://mobileaccessibility.cs.washington.edu/tapbeats/

Figure 1. The gameplay screen.

2.2.2 Quick Play

In Quick Play mode, the player can pick directly between the four different types of gameplay TapBeats offers: Free Play, Memory Mode, Concert Mode, and Studio Mode.

Based on a preliminary review of our application by a blind colleague, we found that it was important for blind users to be able to explore and develop a feel for how the gameplay worked. Therefore, we added Free Play, where users can press the instrument buttons without the added stress of being recorded or having to correctly mimic patterns given by the game.

In Memory Mode, the user plays a game of Simon. Over several rounds, the phone plays a growing pattern of drum sounds the user has to copy. The game continues until the player makes a mistake.

Concert Mode is like Memory Mode, except that the phone and the user play drum sounds to the beat of a background song the user can choose. The game will play a pattern of drum sounds along with the rhythm for one measure, and in the following measure, the player is to mimic that pattern; this continues until the song finishes and the player receives a score. Concert Mode includes audio feedback to help the user figure out how well they are doing.

In Studio Mode, the player can choose a song to "freestyle" to, without having to mimic any patterns given by the game. As the music plays, the game records the player-created song by turning on the phone's microphone, which listens to the phone's speaker. The player can add more to their song by singing or playing other instruments into the microphone. Once the recording is completed, the user can choose to save the recording to later playback.

2.2.3 Career Mode

In Career Mode, the player follows the story of a drummer whose dream is to become a rock star. Career mode integrates the various modes of Quick Play into stages in which the player must complete objectives. For example, the objective for a stage may be to hit a certain number of correct notes while playing a song in Concert Mode. The story progresses as the player completes more stages.

3. USER FEEDBACK

We informally presented a previous version of TapBeats to blind and low-vision students at the Washington State School for the Blind in order to receive feedback on how fun and easy to use they found the game. The following is a concise list of features that were included in the version of TapBeats presented in this work as a result of their feedback:

- Including a Career Mode to act as a tutorial

- Changing the "error" sound from a cowbell noise to something more synthetic

- Using a two-finger swipe as a back gesture rather than a single finger swipe (which could accidentally happen if the user was exploring the menu)

- Adding the two-finger double tap as a "Where Am I?" gesture

Overall, however, students seemed to enjoy the idea of TapBeats and were able to figure out how to play with some guidance.

4. FUTURE WORK

There are several future features planned for TapBeats. We wish to allow user-created content, such as custom songs playable in Concert Mode or custom instrument sets to replace the default drum set. We also plan to add several multiplayer aspects to the game, including a mode where several players can use different instruments to play as a band. Lastly, we plan to run a formal user study in which we evaluate the gameplay learning curve, the enjoyment level of players, and the usability of the TapBeats interface and gesture system. With feedback from blind users, we hope to make TapBeats truly accessible and fun.

TapBeats is not only spontaneous and easy to play due to its mobility, but is also a casual game that both blind and sighted people can play. Through this application, we aim to create a game that allows players to share the same game experience.

5. ACKNOWLEDGMENTS

We would like to thank our mentor Shaun Kane, our instructor Richard Ladner, and our TAs Shani Jayant and Shiri Azenkot for their guidance and help. Special thanks to the University of Washington, UW Computer Science & Engineering, Google, Debbie Cook, and the Washington State School for the Blind.

6. REFERENCES

[1] Glinert, E. and Wyse, L. 2007. AudiOdyssey: an accessible video game for both sighted and non-sighted gamers. In *Proceedings of the 2007 conference on Future Play* (Future Play '07). ACM, New York, NY, 251-252.

[2] Kane, S.K., Bigham, J.P. and Wobbrock, J.O. 2008. Slide Rule: Making mobile touch screens accessible to blind people using multi-touch interaction techniques. In *Proceedings of the ACM SIGACCESS Conference on Computers and Accessibility* (Halifax, Nova Scotia, Canada, October 13 - 15, 2008). Assets '08. ACM, New York, NY, 73-80. DOI=http://doi.acm.org/10.1145/1414471.1414487

[3] Valente, L., Sieckenius de Souza, C. and Feijo, B. 2008. An exploratory study on non-visual mobile phone interfaces for games. In *Proceedings of the VIII Brazilian Symposium on Human Factors in Computing Systems* (Porto Alegre, Brazil, October 21 – 24, 2008). IHC '08.

[4] Yuan, B. and Folmer, E. 2008. Blind hero: enabling guitar hero for the visually impaired. In *Proceedings of the 10th International ACM SIGACCESS Conference on Computers and Accessibility* (Halifax, Nova Scotia, Canada, October 13 - 15, 2008). Assets '08. ACM, New York, NY, 169-176. DOI=http://doi.acm.org/10.1145/1414471.1414503

The CHAMPION Software Project

Suzanne Prior
University of Dundee
School of Computing
Dundee, DD1 4HN, Scotland
+44 1382 386539

seprior@dundee.ac.uk

Annalu Waller
University of Dundee
School of Computing
Dundee, DD1 4HN, Scotland
+44 1382 388223

a.waller@dundee.ac.uk

Thilo Kroll
University of Dundee
School of Nursing & Midwifery
Dundee DD1 4HB, Scotland
+44 1382 386539

t.kroll@dundee.ac.uk

ABSTRACT

A visit to hospital is traumatic for both a patient with disabilities and their family members, especially when the patient has no or limited functional speech [1]. For adults with Severe Speech and Physical Impairments (SSPI) being hospitalized presents particular challenges as hospital staff are often unaware of how the adult with SSPI communicates and what their basic care needs are.

The CHAMPION project aimed to develop a piece of software which would allow an adult with SSPI to input multimedia information on their care needs and on the "person behind the patient". It was hoped that the system could be used by the person with SSPI as independently as possible. The aim would then be for the information to be accessed in hospital.

The first stage of the process has now been completed with the input and output software developed using User Centred Design techniques. What is now required is an investigation into the efficacy of the software in the real life hospital setting.

Categories and Subject Descriptors

H.1.1 [Computer Applications]: Life and Medical Sciences – *Medical Information Systems.*

General Terms

Design, Human Factors,.

Keywords

Augmentative and Alternative Communication (AAC), Severe Speech and Physical Impairments (SSPI), Computing, User-Centred Design, Hospital, Multimedia

1. INTRODUCTION

There is increasing evidence in the literature that admission to hospital for adults with complex disabilities can be traumatic as they are separate from their usual caregivers who understand their many different care needs. This can be further compounded when a patient has a Severe Speech and Physical Impairment (SSPI). The term SSPI is used to indicate that the people concerned have severe physical impairments and will have significant problems in communication. They may also have some degree of cognitive impairment which can range from slight to profound [2].

This paper reports on the current progress of a software development project which is aiming to create a software system which will allow adults with SSPI to store their background

information through a variety of multimedia formats. To date the input section of the system has been developed and evaluated with a group of adults with SSPI.

2. BACKGROUND

When adults with SSPI are admitted to hospital it can be a difficult and traumatic experience for them and their family members [3]. Adults with SSPI, in particular those with cerebral palsy, are 2.2 times more likely to attend an outpatient clinic than their peers with no disability and have a 10.6 times higher risk of being admitted into hospital as an inpatient [4]. Recent research with adults who are unable to speak in hospital has indicated that hospitalisation presents special challenges to both the families and the staff who care for the patient with moderate to profound communication impairment [3]. Adults with SSPI are at higher risk of suffering from a preventable accident while in hospital [5].

Currently the most commonly used method for assisting medical staff is a paper care book compiled by the care attendants of the adult with SSPI, providing information on their needs and habits [6]. These have generally been overlooked by nurses, and patients themselves feel they are of little, if any use [7]. The use of multimedia as a form of advocacy is gaining popularity amongst adults with SSPI or learning disabilities, and has been well received by professionals using it to make decisions on care for the adult involved [8].

There have been a suggestion in the literature that Electronic Patient Communication Profiles could help with this problem [7]. The Communication Health And Multimedia Patient Information Organisational Networks (CHAMPION) project used User Centred Design techniques with four adults with SSPI to develop a software system to allow users to input multimedia information about themselves. The hope for the software is that an adult with SSPI could input information on their personal care needs ahead of a hospital admission and then when they were admitted to hospital this information would be available to medical staff through a touch screen tough book.

3. CHAMPION Input Software

The aim of the CHAMPION project was to allow adults with SSPI to input information on their care needs through a combination of text, video and photographs. The system could be compared to an internet file storage tool, however there are several key features which distinguish the software from other tools.

3.1 Scanning

Many adults with SSPI are unable to access computers using conventional peripherals. For some users, switches and scanning offer the best method of access. When scanning is used, the software moves through the objects on the screen, highlighting one at a time. Some users with SSPI will have specialized software installed on their computer which conducts the scanning for them, however this is not available as standard on personal computers. The CHAMPION software allows the end user to specify at start up which method of scanning they wish to use and also what speed of scanning they would like. For more experiences or confident users a faster scanning speed may be an advantage.

3.2 Information Topic Selection

Early in the development process a representative sample of end users were consulted on the information topics they would wish to share with medical staff in hospital. Seven medical professionals including both doctors and nurses were also involved in this process. In the final system there were a total of 45 topics of information. In order to customize the information topics to the end user as much as possible, the system used information such as the users gender to select some of the topics – for example topic number 24 would be "shaving" or "feminine" care depending on the gender selected when setting up the user profile.

End user participants were asked how much assistance they would want in selecting topics for information, and it was decided that when a user first created their personal profile a series of questions would be asked. The user could then chose to answer "Yes", "No" or "Maybe". This questionnaire was then used to determine which topics of information could potentially be of use to medical staff treating the end user. The end user then had the ultimate decision on whether to add information to the topic. The questionnaire would be completed when the user first created a profile, they would then be prompted to repeat the questionnaire every six months to see if the answers to questions had changed.

3.3 Symbols

Adults with SSPI are at a higher risk than the general population in having a literacy impairment [8]. For some this can mean that they will take longer to read a piece of text while for others this can mean they have no functional literacy. A variety of symbolic languages have been created to support adults with limited literacy. The CHAMPION system initially supported three of the main symbol sets – Picture Communication System (PCS), Rebus and Bliss. The end user could select the symbol set when they loaded up the software and the different symbols in the set would appear above the appropriate word in the system.

Later in the software development process it became evident that many of the end users used a combination of symbol languages in their daily life. The decision was made to allow the end user to swap between the symbol set used "in real time". On every software screen there was the option to change to a different symbol set.

3.4 Staff Selection

While this stage of the development was concerned with the input of information, the participants who were involved in the design were focused on the fact that the system would eventually used to retrieve information. There was a concern amongst participants about which members of staff would be able to see the different pieces of information. While an end user might be happy for the hospital porter to understand how to lift them onto a trolley, they might be less happy for the porter to be able to read about their toileting needs. The ability to select which members of staff (from

a selection of seven) could see the information was provided after the uploading of information.

Figure 1. An adult with SSPI using the CHAMPION Software

4. FUTURE STEPS

The initial usability evaluations of the system provided a positive response, the next stage in the development of the input system is to conduct a longitudinal study into the use of the system by a variety of users. At the same time the output system needs to be further developed with hospital staff. It is anticipated that in the future a larger evaluation of the effectiveness of the information system in the hospital will be able to be conducted.

5. ACKNOWLEDGMENTS

This work forms part of a doctoral study which was funded by Capability Scotland.

6. REFERENCES

[1] Bartlett, G., et al., Impact of patient communication problems on the risk of preventable adverse events in acute care settings. Canadian Medical Association Journal, 2008. 178(12): p. 1555-1562.

[2] Redmond, S.M. and S.S. Johnston, Evaluating the Morphological Competence of Children With Severe Speech and Physical Impairments, 2001. p. 1362-1375.

[3] Hemsley, B., et al., Nursing the patient with severe communication impairment. Journal of Advanced Nursing, 2001. 35(6): p. 827-835.

[4] Young, N., L., et al., Youth and Young Adults With Cerebral Palsy: Their Use of Physician and Hospital Services. Archives of physical medicine and rehabilitation, 2007. 88(6): p. 696-702.

[5] Zinn, C., 14000 preventable deaths in Australian hospitals. BMJ, 1995. 310(6993): p. 1487-.

[6] Millar, S., Personal Communication Passports, in SENSE Conference1997: University of Dundee.

[7] Prior, S., et al., Facilitating communication of people with complex communication needs in hospital: A review of the literature, in NHS Scotland Event 20092009: Glasgow, Scotland.

[8] Millar, S. and J. Kerr, Augmentative Communication and Literacy - the SAIL Kit Approach, in Augmentative Communication in Practice: an Introdcution, A. Wilson, Editor 1998, Call Centre: University of Edinburgh

The Effect of Hand Strength on Pointing Performance of Users for Different Input Devices

Pradipta Biswas
Engineering Design Centre
Department of Engineering
University of Cambridge, UK
E-mail: pb400@cam.ac.uk

Pat Langdon
Engineering Design Centre
Department of Engineering
University of Cambridge, UK
E-mail: pml24@eng.cam.ac.uk

ABSTRACT

We have investigated how hand strength affects pointing performance of people with and without mobility impairment in graphical user interfaces for four different input modalities. We have found that grip strength and active range of motion of wrist are most indicative of the pointing performance. We have used the study to develop a set of linear equations to predict pointing time for different devices.

Categories and Subject Descriptors

D.2.2 [Software Engineering]: Design Tools and Techniques – *user interfaces;* **K.4.2 [Computers and Society]:** Social Issues – *assistive technologies for persons with disabilities*

General Terms

Experimentation, Human Factors, Measurement

Keywords

Assistive Technology, Pointing, Hand strength, Usability Evaluation.

1. INTRODUCTION

Most existing application interfaces in modern electronic devices are based on graphical user interfaces. Pointing tasks form a significant part of human machine interaction in those graphical user interfaces. This work presents a set of models to predict pointing time for different input devices based on quantitative analysis of effect of impairments on pointing performance. Among a few similar notable works, Gajos and colleagues [6] found that different combinations of functions involving distance and width of target can predict movement time for different types of mobility impairment. Keates and colleagues [7] measured the difference between able bodied and motor impaired users with respect to the Model Human Processor (MHP) [4] and motor impaired users were found to have a greater motor action time than their able bodied counterparts. Laursen and colleagues [8] investigated differences in muscle activities in shoulder, neck and forearm during pointing and unsurprisingly concluded that motor impairment demands more motor activity. However they did not try to correlate any pointing parameter with human factors. Smits-Engelsman [10] found active range of wrist significantly correlate with Fitts' Law [5] constants in pointing tasks for children with congenital spas-

tic hemiplegia. Price and Sears [9] used motion based sensors to quantify users' upper limb dexterity and a subsequent regression model explained 92% of the variance in user capabilities. Though the measurement technique is promising but yet to be standardized through reliability analysis (test-retest values) like techniques used by ergonomist and occupational therapists. It should also be investigated that how virtual reality gaming glove affected natural interaction and works with people having severe spasm in finger that impedes them to straighten it. Balakrishnan and MacKenzie [1] measures bandwidth of finger, wrist and arms of able bodied users during pointing task but did not extend their study for motor impaired users. Our previous study [2, 3] also found that grip strength can be used to predict parameters of a pointing task using a mouse. In this study we analyzed pointing task for four different input modalities and investigated how hand strength affects performance for people with and without mobility impairment.

2. The Study

2.1. Participants

We collected data from 12 mobility impaired users and 13 able bodied participants. The disabled participants were recruited from a local centre, which works on treatment and rehabilitation of disabled people, and they volunteered for the study. All mobility impaired participants were expert computer user and used a computer more than once each week. All able bodied participants were also expert computer users.

2.2. Material

We used a HP TouchSmart tx2 Notebook PC with 12.5" multi-touch screen having 1280 X 800 pixels running Windows 7 operating system. We also used a standard Logitech mouse and a Kensington trackball as input pointing device. For touch screen, users pointed using their fingers and for stylus the HP stylus that came with the laptop. We used the same seating arrangement (same table height and distance from table) for all participants. We measured the same variables for hand strength evaluation as in our previous study [2, 3]. We evaluated only one hand (the dominant hand) of the participants which they used to operate the input device.

2.3. Procedure

We conducted an ISO 9241 pointing task involving five different combinations of target width (W = 20, 30, 40, 50 and 60 pixels) and distance to target (A = 100, 140, 180, 240 and 300 pixels). Each participant undertook the pointing task using a mouse, trackball, touch screen and stylus (in a horizontal position). For trackball and stylus, we kept the screen in flat position. The participants were tested for their visual acuity and color blindness. The target was blue in black background, which is fine for colour blind people and the smallest sized target (20 pixels) was visible for all participants. The participants did not have severe cognitive impairment like dyslexia or dementia that could impede their performance.

2.4. Results

We have analyzed the pointing tasks and calculated average velocity and the index of performance (*IP*), where,

$IP = \frac{ID_{average}}{MT_{average}}$ and $ID = LOG(1+\frac{A}{W})$ (*MT* stands for Movement Time and *ID* stands for Index of Difficulty) for each participant. We used the same technique to measure *ID* and *IP* for all devices. It should be noted we did not use *IP* as a performance index, but just as a function to predict pointing time. We measured the correlation between the hand strength metrics and the velocity and *IP* (Table 1). We also included the logarithm of grip strength (LOGGS) into the analysis as we found it correlated with different parameters of pointing in our previous study [2, 3]. We have found significant correlation only considering disabled users as well. We calculated the predictive power for all different combination of hand strength metrics. We have found that grip strength and active range of motion of wrist are most indicative of the pointing performance. We used a multiple regression model and performed a 10-fold cross validation test using the WEKA system to predict *IP* from grip strength and active range of motion of wrist and used that to predict *MT*. Figure 2 shows the scatter plot between actual and predicted movement time. The correlations for are statistically significant for all cases (trackball $\rho = 0.80$, mouse $\rho = 0.55$, touch screen $\rho = 0.53$, stylus $\rho = 0.70$, $p < 0.01$). The percent error is less than ±40% for more than 60% trials.

3. Conclusions

In this study, we have investigated how hand strength affects pointing performance of people with a wide range of abilities for four different pointing devices. We have developed a set of linear equations to predict pointing time and average number of sub-movements for different devices. We have already used the study to design a simulator that can predict interaction patterns of mobility impaired users. We are now using the study to optimize design and developing adaptation algorithms for a multimodal digital TV interface.

Table 1. Correlation Matrix

	TrackBall		Mouse		Touch Screen		Stylus	
	Velocity	IP	Velocity	IP	Velocity	IP	Velocity	IP
GS	0.60**	0.57**	0.49	0.47	0.25	0.29	0.72**	0.73**
LOGGS	0.57	0.61**	0.57**	0.61**	0.67**	0.68**	0.68**	0.68**
TPS	0.63**	0.59**	0.55	0.53	0.35	0.39	0.72**	0.73**
ROMF	0.52	0.51	0.49	0.47	0.28	0.30	0.68**	0.69**
ROMW	0.65**	0.64**	0.61**	0.61**	0.41	0.43	0.37	0.38
Tremor	-0.41	-0.38	-0.35	-0.34	-0.29	-0.28	-0.71**	-0.71**

$** p < 0.001$

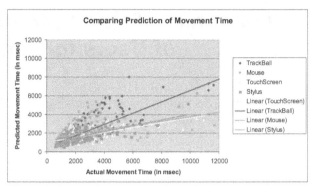

Figure 2. Comparing actual and predicted movement times

References

1. Balakrishnan, R. and MacKenzie, I.S. (1997). Performance differences in the fingers wrist, and forearm in computer input control. Proceedings of the ACMConference on Human Factors in Computing Systems (CHI '97). Atlanta, Georgia (March 22-27, 1997). New York: ACM Press, 303-310.

2. Biswas P. and Robinson P., Predicting pointing time from hand strength, Usability & HCI for e-Inclusion, 5th Symposium of the Austrian Computer Society (USAB 2009)

3. Biswas P. and Robinson P., The effects of hand strength on pointing performance, Designing Inclusive Interactions, Springer-Verlag, pp. 3-12, ISBN: 978-1-84996-165-3

4. Card S., Moran T. and Newell A. The Psychology of Human-Computer Interaction. Hillsdale, NJ, USA: Lawrence Erlbaum Associates, 1983.

5. Fitts P.M. "The Information Capacity of The Human Motor System In Controlling The Amplitude of Movement." Journal of Experimental Psychology 47 (1954): 381-391.

6. Gajos K. Z., Wobbrock J. O. and Weld D. S. Automatically generating user interfaces adapted to users' motor and vision capabilities. ACM symposium on User interface software and technology 2007. 231-240.

7. Keates S., Clarkson J. and Robinson P. Investigating The Applicability of User Models For Motion Impaired Users. ACM/SIGACCESS Conference On Computers And Accessibility 2000. 129-136.

8. Laursen B., Jensen B. R. And Ratkevicius. European Journal on Applied Physiology 84 (2001): 329-336

9. Price, K.J. and Sears, A. (2009). The development and evaluation of performance-based functional assessment: A methodology for the measurement of physical capabilities. ACM Transactions on Accessible Computing 2 (2), 10:1-10:31.

10. Smits-Engelsman B. C. M. et. al. Children with congential spastic hemiplegia obey Fitts' Law in a visually guided tapping task. Journal of Experimental Brain Research 177 (2007): 431-439.

Thought Cubes: Exploring the Use of an Inexpensive Brain-Computer Interface on a Mental Rotation Task

G Michael Poor* Laura Marie Leventhal* Scott Kelley* Jordan Ringenberg* Samuel D. Jaffee**

Computer Science Department* Psychology Department**
Bowling Green State University,
Bowling Green, Ohio 43402
gmp, leventhal, kelleys, jringen, jaffees@bgsu.edu

ABSTRACT

Brain-computer interfaces (BCI) allow users to relay information to a computer by capturing reactions to their thoughts via brain waves (or similar measurements). This "new" type of interaction allows users with limited motor control to interact with a computer without a mouse/keyboard or other physically manipulated interaction device. While this technology is in its infancy, there have been major strides in the area allowing researchers to investigate potential uses. One of the first such interfaces that has broached the commercial market at an affordable price is the Emotiv EPOC™ headset. This paper reports on results of a study exploring usage of the EPOC headset.

Categories and Subject Descriptors

D.2.2, H.1.2 [**User Interfaces, Human-Information Processing**]:

General Terms

Human Factors

Keywords

Accessibility, brain-computer interaction

1. INTRODUCTION

The ability to manipulate objects on a computer screen without use of hands potentially expands access to computing, especially for persons with motor control limitations. BCIs (brain-computer interfaces) tap into cognitive and/or autonomic responses from the user. The inexpensive Emotiv™ EPOC neuroheadset (see Fig. 2) is a "high resolution, neuro-signal acquisition and processing wireless neuroheadset. It uses a set of sensors to tune into electric signals produced by the brain to detect [user] thoughts, feelings and expressions" [1]. EPOC offers other hands-free modalities as well. Until recently, most BCI research has focused on helping disabled people interact with computers. However, current BCI research has moved in two directions, 1) providing alternative means of input to voice or hand press in dangerous or noisy environments (e.g. radioactive environment) [2] and 2) providing an alternative interaction method for video games [2,3]; game control is the primary reason for the development of the EPOC device. [1] With no current usability studies of EPOC, our project is exploratory, focusing on understanding the usage characteristics of the BCI and other hands-free modalities of the device.

2. TASK, PROCEDURES, MATERIALS

[4] evaluated a BCI on a task involving spatial information processing. Similarly we evaluated EPOC using the cube comparison task (CCT), a task thought to tap into mental rotation and visualization skills that effectively discriminates between high and low spatial ability along these dimensions. [cf. 5,6,7]. In CCT, a participant (P) is presented with images of two cubes, side by side, with three visible faces on each cube. The P determines whether the cube pairs are definitely different or could be the same. In our interactive version of CCT, the P can rotate the right cube on the three Cartesian axes passing through the faces of the cubes in both clockwise and counterclockwise directions (hereafter, the axes are defined as x, y, and z). In CCT, the P can rotate as many times as he/she wishes. Our stimuli are based on the stimuli used in [5] and consist of six problem types; the problem types differ in the number of degrees of angular disparity between the left and right cubes and perceived difficulty.

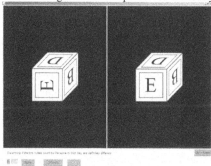

Figure 1: Image from CCT task

The CCT is a useful task for exploring interactions:

- Rotations are clockwise/counterclockwise along the 3 axes so it is possible to track behaviors at the rotation level.
- CCT is "context-free" in the sense that there are no experts.
- Interactive CCT includes selection/rotation of interface objects.

2.1 Emotiv EPOC Interaction Controls

The EOPC has three types of controls: EEG (electroencephalograph) – measured electrical activity in the brain, EMG (electromyograph) – measured electrical activity in facial muscles, and a Gyroscope (controlled by head/neck movements). In our study, three of the six possible CCT rotations were directly available by the EEG control: clockwise x, counterclockwise y and clockwise z (the EPOC Control Panel only allows for a maximum of four EEG inputs to be available at one time and we used only three). All six rotations were available via the EMG controls; six facial expressions were chosen to represent each possible rotation. With the EMG control, rotations over an individual axis were controlled by a pair of related expressions: each pair was performed by a different set of muscles to reduce the number of false occurrences. Because G only functions in two dimensions, four rotations, clockwise and counterclockwise x and y axes were used. Any of the six cube rotations were possible with the EEG or G control although some rotations would have required multiple rotations in the opposite direction or a combination of the available rotations.

Figure 2: Emotiv EPOC Device

2.2 Participants and Procedure

Seventeen introductory programming students completed the study. Each P took two standardized tests of spatial ability, which were used to generate a composited spatial ability score. Ps received training with the EPOC controls before completing the CCT; we presented the cubes in an oblique projection [6].

2.3 Limitations of the Study

The EPOC sacrifices technological sophistication for reduced costs and has fewer scalp contacts than more expensive BCIs, leading to potentially less accuracy from EEG. Also, although CCT involves selection of interface objects, similar to selections of objects in other presentations, CCT itself is a task that involves spatial information processing and limits conclusions that we might make about the general use of the EPOC, especially for tasks involving processing of symbolic and textual information.

3. RESULTS[1]

Using the median of the composite spatial ability scores, the P pool was split into high and low spatial ability with the three Ps at the median dropped leaving 14 Ps.

Following the procedure of [5,6,7], we analyzed the results from the "same" trials only. In terms of accuracy on the task, the Ps did well, with an average error rate of 12% and unsurprisingly were differentially accurate by problem type ($F(2.8, 42.6) = 16.3$, $p = 0$). There were no significant differences in accuracy by spatial ability and as all controls were continuously available, we could not definitely determine which control contributed most to errors.

To understand and compare usage patterns of EEG, EMG and G, we extracted two measures from the history logs of each P: counts of the initiation of rotations by control and problem type and counts of successful rotations by control and problem type. Note that if a P initiated an x rotation and actually made a y rotation, the x rotation would not have been considered successful and would not have been in the count. There were no significant differences in these measures by control. We next divided the number of successful rotations by the number of initiated

rotations to yield a sort of efficiency measure for each tool for each problem. The measure is crude – a P could have intended a particular rotation but used the controls incorrectly and the resulting rotation would have been scored as "successful". The logs also recorded what appear to be a few spurious rotations for the EMG and they were backed out of the calculations. The results are interesting nonetheless. The mean efficiency across the controls is 59% meaning that the Ps successfully completed initiated rotations for about 59% of their tries. We found no significant differences in efficiency.

4. CONCLUSIONS

Because our study was necessarily exploratory, we draw conclusions about the use of the EPOC cautiously. First, we found no significant differences by spatial ability on our dependent variables, suggesting that Ps of a variety of spatial abilities could effectively use the EPOC controls. Second, we found the EEG no less responsive than the other 2 controls and Ps used all of the controls about equally. Third, real rotations occurred for about 59% of the attempts across the controls. It seems likely that this relatively low efficiency scores across the controls was a result of a number of factors including unfamiliarity with any of the controls and only one training session before use, the complexities of rotational control for all six axes for EEG and G, and the relative difficulty of the CCT task itself. Whether this efficiency rate is acceptable is difficult to know and acceptability is probably context dependent. We believe that our results begin to demonstrate that Ps could effectively use the BCI component (EEG), but users may choose EEG controls along with the other UI options. For persons with limited motor control, the EPOC could be useful but likely would require additional training on the device and a possible willingness to use all of the controls.

5. ACKNOWLEDGMENTS

G. Zimmerman, T. Donahue, M. Mott and B. Tomlinson.

6. REFERENCES

[1] Emotiv EPOC (2010) http://www.emotiv.com

[2] Allison, B., Graimann, B., Graser, A. "Why Use a BCI if You Are healthy?" *ACE Workshop – Brainplay '07: Brain-computer Interfaces and Games*. 2007. Salzburg.

[3] Nijholt, A. "Turning Shortcomings into challenges: Brain-computer interfaces for games." *Entertainment Computing* 1.2 (2009): 85-94

[4] Yoo, S. et al. "Brain-computer interface using fMRI: spatial navigation by thoughts." *NeuroReport* 15.10 (2004)

[5] Just, M., Carpenter, P. "Cognitive Coordinate Systems: Accounts of Mental Rotation and Individual Differences in Spatial Ability." *Psychological Review* 92.2 (1985): 137-172

[6] Jaffee, S. "Tipping Cubes: The Effect of Projection on Performance and Strategy in a Mental Rotation Task in a Virtual Environment." Poster. *Annual Meeting Midwestern Psychological Association*. April 29–May 1 2010. Chicago.

[7] Hippler, R. Klopfer, D., Leventhal, L., Poor, G.P., Klein, B., Jaffee, S.D. "More than Speed? An Empirical Study of Touchscreens and Body Awareness on an Object Manipulation Task." *HCI International 2011*. July 9-14, 2011. Orlando, Florida. 33 – 42

---

[1]Repeated measures degrees of freedom reflect a Greenhouse-Geisser adjustment.

Toward 3D Scene Understanding via Audio-description: Kinect-iPad Fusion for the Visually Impaired

Juan Diego Gomez, Sinan Mohammed, Guido Bologna, Thierry Pun
Computer Science Department, University of Geneva
Route de Drize 7, 1227, Carouge
Tel +41 (22) 379 0152

{juan.gomez, guido.bologna, thierry.pun}@unige.ch, mohamms0@etu.unige.ch

ABSTRACT

Microsoft's Kinect 3-D motion sensor is a low cost 3D camera that provides color and depth information of indoor environments. In this demonstration, the functionality of this fun-only camera accompanied by an iPad's tangible interface is targeted to the benefit of the visually impaired. A computer-vision-based framework for real time objects localization and for their audio description is introduced. Firstly, objects are extracted from the scene and recognized using feature descriptors and machine-learning. Secondly, the recognized objects are labeled by instruments sounds, whereas their position in 3D space is described by virtual space sources of sound. As a result, the scene can be heard and explored while finger-triggering the sounds within the iPad, on which a top-view of the objects is mapped. This enables blindfolded users to build a mental occupancy grid of the environment. The approach presented here brings the promise of efficient assistance and could be adapted as an electronic travel aid for the visually-impaired in the near future.

Categories and Subject Descriptors

I.5 [**Pattern recognition**]: Applications – *Computer Vision.*

General Terms

Algorithms, Measurement, Experimentation.

Keywords

Visual substitution, Kinect, Sonification, 3D Object Recognition, Depth, iPad, Tactile exploration.

1. INTRODUCTION

Scenery understanding relies on human vision mechanisms such as stereopsis, perspective unfolding, object identification and color perception amongst others. A fundamental research problem is the possibility of eliciting visual interpretation in the absence of vision, therefore by means of other sensory pathways. Along this line a number of researchers have been developing mobility aids to help visually handicapped users perceive their environment.

If for instance sight is intended to be emulated by audition, could all the needed information be encoded into sound and somehow exploited, so that the mental representation produced from the visual perception could be replicated? At this point the major

problem arises, since the rate of information that the vision channel is capable to process has been estimated at 10^6 bits/s, while audition is about 10^4 bits/s. Thus, we cannot encode all the visual information through the auditory channel.

Our hypothesis is that given a simple scene (in a controlled environment) composed of a limited variety of unknown objects with uncertain spatial configuration, a computer-assisted audio description can be used to build the scene in someone's mind so accurately that a physical reconstruction can be made. The achievement of this finger-triggered sonification of the scene involves the encoding into sound data of information pertaining to both object identification and location.

The demonstration presented here linking a Kinect sensor, a laptop and a wireless iPad, could be generalized in the future to experiments where unknown environments with unidentified obstacles could be explored. Note that only the iPad has to be carried.

2. SCENE AUDIO DESCRIPTION

In line with the See ColOr project that aims at encoding color into musical instruments sounds for visually impaired assistance [1], a computer-vision framework has been developed to analyze the nearby space in the current prototype. This framework comprises a range-image segmentation algorithm that uses the Kinect-depth information. Next is a classic and adaptable object-recognition strategy based on features classification [2]. Lastly, a touch-to-sound algorithm based on pressure-trigger delivers the information collected from earlier stages through instruments sounds. The multi-touch device and the sounds are both customizable e.g. instruments may be replaced by earcons.

For this demonstration the framework has been adapted to recognize and sonify simple 3D geometrical objects on a table so as to elicit a mental representation of the scene composition.

2.1 Kinect Calibration

The Kinect sensor provides identical resolution images for both depth and color; these images however are not registered so that pixel-to-pixel correspondence is never given. Seeking a correspondence between pairs of images is the classical stereo matching problem that becomes simpler provided that depth information is known as is the case here. The accurate calibration of the Kinect sensor in order to know the depth of each color pixel can be achieved as follows.

An object with salient corners e.g. a book, must be acquired at different planes (distances) within the camera range. The corners coordinates are manually extracted from both images (depth and color) for each plane. Thus, the *x-y* shift at a certain distance can be known. Having as many shift estimations as images were taken, a general function for pixels shifting based on distance can be interpolated for every single plane within the camera range.

2.2 Depth-based Object Segmentation

Range images often enable fast and accurate object segmentation since objects are perceived as isolated entities. Thus, shape extraction can be nearly flawless regardless color and illumination conditions. In this work, the range of the Kinect sensor is partitioned into multiple layers. Afterwards, these layers are scanned one by one and surfaces lying within them are labeled as objects. Farthest layers are ignored so as to filter out the background.

The shape of a labeled object into the depth map can be now extracted. Color information thereof could be accessed by inspection of the same shape into the RGB map whenever the calibration has been done. This method attains precise segmentation in real-time for simple sceneries i.e. when objects do not occlude each other as seen from the camera reference point of view.

2.3 Object Representation and Classification

After having segmented the object, it can be described by encoding its most representative features into scalar vectors. These feature vectors must be classified so as to identify similar-featured objects that likely belong to same class [2]. A wide gamut of vector descriptors can be found into the literature. Yet our descriptors rely on basic geometric-related features of the objects such as the perimeter, area, eccentricity, major axis and the bounding box size. Given that this demonstration uses sole geometric elements, more robust descriptors are needless.

Many machine-learning-based algorithms for data clustering meet the conditions to fit within framework. However, feature vectors for this demonstration are classified by a Multi layer Artificial Neural Network [2] trained offline with a large set of in situ images. Nonetheless, others recognition tasks e.g. more complex objects, are expected to require more suitable methods for both description and classification.

2.4 Depiction via tactile Sonification

In this demonstration we set up a synthetic scene that mimics a potential unknown environment to be explored. It contains a table (perceived as background) and a multi-class set of geometrical objects randomly placed. A Kinect sensor settled in front of the table enables the machine-based object recognition. Afterwards, a top-view of the objects as they are placed on the table is generated and mapped on the iPad. Thus, the iPad serves as a miniature table's surface and objects can be located within it proportionally as in the table. Given only the frontal kinect-provided image, a top-view is feasible thanks to a perspective-invariant analysis derived from the calibration process.

Each class of objects is assigned a particular instrument sound so as to distinguish from each other. Users must be previously trained to learn this object-sound association [1]. Thus, objects recognized by the neural network are sonified when they are touched on the iPad. Real objects' position on the table can be deduced by inspection on the iPad. However, spatial virtual sources of sound used in this work create the illusion of sounds originating from the specific objects' locations in the real space [3]. It gives the user a more detailed idea of the scenery composition and the spatial-relative relationship between elements.

This experiment involves two parts. In the first step, a blindfolded user has to determine the objects and their corresponding locations on the iPad. For the second part all the objects are taken out from the table, the user removes her/his blindfold and tries to place the objects back. Generally, to evaluate the effectiveness of the system at eliciting an insight about the scene in the user's mind, we compare pictures of the original scene and the one taken after the objects have been put back. To date, promising results have been achieved. Particularly, end-users are enabled to answer questions such as which elements are on the table and where they are specifically located.

Figure 1: Blindfolded user testing our framework.

3. CONCLUSION

We presented a general computer-vision-based framework to represent multi-object location through the auditory pathway. A demonstration of this approach to build a mental occupancy grid of the environment has been implemented linking a Microsoft's Kinect sensor, a laptop and a wireless iPad. The composition of a scene formed of a table and geometrical objects has been represented on the iPad and encoded into instruments sounds. This encoded information has been accessed in real time using the fingers as stylus to trigger the sounds.

4. REFERENCES

[1] Deville, B. Bologna, G. Pun, T. 2009. See ColOr: Seeing Colors with an orchestra. *Lectures Notes in Computer Science, vol 5440. Springer-Verlag, 251-279.*

[2] M, Everingham. B, Thomas. T, Troscianko. 1999. Head mounted mobility aid for low vision using scene classification techniques. *International Journal of Virtual Reality. Vol 3: 3-12*

[3] Ordonez, C. Navarun, G. Barreto, A. 2002. Sound spatialization as a navigational aid in virtual emviroments. *Proceedings of the 6th CSI Conference: 297-302.*

TypeInBraille: A Braille-based Typing Application for Touchscreen Devices

Sergio Mascetti
DICo - University of Milan
mascetti@dico.unimi.it

Cristian Bernareggi
DICo - University of Milan
bernareggi@dico.unimi.it

Matteo Belotti
University of Milan
matteo.belotti@studenti.unimi.it

ABSTRACT

Smartphones provide new exciting opportunities to visually impaired users because these devices can support new assistive technologies that cannot be deployed on desktops or laptops. Some devices, like the iPhone, are rapidly gaining popularity among the visually impaired since the use of pre-installed screenreader applications renders these devices accessible. However, there are still some operations that require a longer time or higher mental workload to be completed by a visually impaired user. In this contribution we present a novel application for text entry, called TypeInBraille, that is based on the Braille code and hence is specifically designed for blind users.

Categories and Subject Descriptors

H.5.2 [**Information Interfaces and Presentation**]: User Interfaces—*Haptic I/O*; H.5.2 [**Information Interfaces and Presentation**]: User Interfaces—*Input devices and strategies*

General Terms

Human Factors, Algorithms.

Keywords

Blind, Braille, QWERTY, Touch Screen, Mobile.

1. INTRODUCTION

The accessibility to smartphone devices by visually impaired users has recently significantly improved. This was obtained by adopting an interaction paradigm that couples the touchscreen with a speech synthesizer: in a nutshell, the visually impaired user can touch the screen to explore the interface, and can touch twice to activate an interface object (e.g., by touching an icon twice, the corresponding application is run). As a result of these improvements, most of the applications developed for sighted users can also be used by the visually impaired.

Despite these achievements, there are still some operations that require a longer time or higher mental workload to be completed by a visually impaired user. In particular, in this paper we consider the problem of typing. Since the

large majority of smartphone devices do not have a physical keyboard, typing is enabled by the on-screen QWERTY keyboard that appears on the device screen. For a visually impaired user, inserting each character requires to search for the corresponding button on the keyboard. As reported in [1, 2], this operation is time consuming and error-prone.

To address this problem, in this paper we propose *TypeInBraille*, a novel typing application that is specifically designed for blind users. The core idea is to allow typing using the Braille code, which is generally employed for reading by blind people.

2. THE TYPING TECHNIQUE

Before presenting the typing technique adopted in *TypeInBraille*, we first briefly introduce the Braille code. Braille is a text coding designed to be read by blind users through fingertips. Each character is represented by a cell made up of six dots organized into three rows of two dots each. Each dot may be raised, hence perceptible with the fingertips, or flat. Consequently, each cell can represent up to 64 different characters. This value is sufficient for representing the lower-case letters (see, for example, the letter "m" reported in Figure 1(a)), the punctuation marks and some special characters (e.g., "@" and "&"). Some symbols, like the upper-case letters and the numbers, are represented by means of a prefix. For example, capital letters (Figure 1(b) reports an upper-case "m") are represented by means of the capital letter symbol, followed by the letter itself.

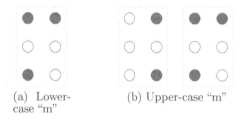

(a) Lower-case "m"   (b) Upper-case "m"

Figure 1: Examples of Braille encoding (the black circles stand for raised dots, while the white circles stand for a flat ones).

The proposed typing technique enables the user to input a character through its Braille representation by inserting the three rows of each cell from the top to the bottom. In order to enter a row, the touchscreen is divided into two rectangles (left and right) and four gestures are defined. A tap on the left part of the screen corresponds to the left dot raised and the right dot flat (Figure 2(a)). Similarly, a tap on the right part corresponds to the right dot raised and the left dot flat (Figure 2(b)). A tap with two fingers represents two raised dots (Figure 2(c)) while a tap with three fingers stands for two flat dots (Figure 2(d)). After a character is entered, it is read by speech to the user and/or a vibration effect is triggered.

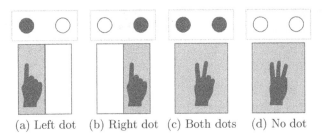

(a) Left dot (b) Right dot (c) Both dots (d) No dot

Figure 2: The four gestures defined to enter a pair of dots.

In order to insert a Braille symbol, three gestures would be required with our technique. However, we introduced an optimization that makes it possible to represent three frequent characters (blank space, "a" and "c" whose frequency is about 1/3 in Italian and English) with less gestures. In more details, an additional gesture was introduced to represent the end of a character i.e., all the following rows contain flat dots only. This gesture is the "one finger right flick", a movement with one finger from left to right. Since the letters "a" and "c" have raised dots on the first row only, they can be represented with two gestures, while the blank space, which contains no raised dots, can be represented by one gesture only (i.e., the one finger right flick). For example, as shown in Figure 3, the letter "a" followed by a blank space can be entered by the left dot gesture followed by two end of character gestures, the former indicating the end of the "a" character, the latter representing the blank space.

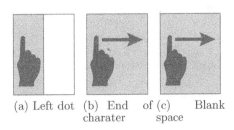

(a) Left dot (b) End of charater (c) Blank space

Figure 3: Letter "a" followed by a blank space.

Since the flick gesture is easy to remember and quick to perform, especially by the blind users [2], our technique adopts it also to insert a new line (one finger down flick) and to perform undo/delete operations (one finger left flick). More specifically, the latter gesture undoes the character that is currently being inserted or deletes the character on the left of the cursor in case the user is not in the process of inserting a character.

TypeInBraille was designed in order to overcome the main limitation of the on-screen QWERTY i.e., the need to search and confirm a small target key. Consequently, *TypeInBraille* is intuitively more efficient and less error-prone. Another advantage of our solution is that the audio feedback is not indispensable because each gesture is significantly different from the others and hence users can perform the gestures with high confidence, even without the audio feedback. Consequently, with *TypeInBraille* , the user can also type in noisy environments or when the audio is not available at all.

3. THE *TypeInBraille* APPLICATION

The *TypeInBraille* application presents four working modes, which can be set through the rotor gesture: "typing mode", "exploration mode", "selection mode" and "sending mode". In "typing mode", the user can type text as explained in Section 2 as well as perform deletion operations. In "exploration mode" and "selection mode" the user can move the cursor through the inserted text. Additionally, in "selection mode", while the user moves the cursor, the text is also selected. These two modes share the same gestures. One finger left (or right) flick moves the cursor one character left (or right, respectively). The same gestures performed with two fingers move the cursor word-by-word while, using three fingers, the cursor is moved to the beginning or to the end of the text (three fingers left flick or three fingers right flick, respectively). Finally, in "sending mode" the user can choose, from a menu, to copy, cut and paste the text, or to send it as email or text message.

4. THE DEMO PRESENTATION

The demo presentation is divided in two stages. In the first one, the participant is invited to experience the hindrances that that a blind user runs into while typing with an on-screen QWERTY keyboard. To achieve this, the participant is asked to type using an iPhone device with Voice Over and with the display turned off. If necessary, we briefly train the participant to type using Voice Over. Typing is performed both with audio feedback and without, hence showing that in absence of the audio feedback the number of errors is so high that the result is not understandable.

In the second stage, we briefly introduce the Braille code as well as the typing technique we propose. Then, we ask the participant to type using *TypeInBraille*. Again, the display is turned off. In case the participant is not proficient in Braille we support him/her by showing the Braille characters map. During this stage, the participant first experiences the use of *TypeInBraille* supported by the audio feedback and can appreciate that *TypeInBraille* is much easier to learn and use than the on-screen QWERTY even for users that are novice to the Braille code. Then, the participant can also try to type with *TypeInBraille* while the audio is turned off and can then realize that, although the audio feedback is helpful, it is not indispensable. At the end of the demo, the participant can try to send the typed text via email.

5. REFERENCES

[1] Hugo Nicolau, Tiago Guerreiro, Joaquim Jorge, and Daniel Gonçalves. Proficient blind users and mobile text-entry. In *Proc. of the 28th Annual European Conference on Cognitive Ergonomics*, ECCE '10, pages 19–22, New York, NY, USA, 2010. ACM.
[2] Richard E. Ladner Shaun K. Kane, Jacob O. Wobbrock. Usable gestures for blind people: understanding preference and performance. In *Proceedings of the 2011 annual conference on Human factors in computing systems*. ACM, 2011.

Use of Serious Games for Motivational Balance Rehabilitation of Cerebral Palsy Patients

Biel Moyà-Alcover	Antoni Jaume-i-Capó	Javier Varona	Pau Martinez-Bueso	Alejandro Mesejo Chiong
Department of Mathematics and Computer Science Universitat de les Illes Balears (Spain)	Department of Mathematics and Computer Science Universitat de les Illes Balears (Spain)	Department of Mathematics and Computer Science Universitat de les Illes Balears (Spain)	Department of Nursing and Physiotherapy Universitat de les Illes Balears (Spain)	Faculty of Mathematics and Computer Universidad de La Habana (Cuba)
gabriel.moya@uib.es	antoni.jaume@uib.es	xavi.varona@uib.es	paz.martinez@uib.es	mesejo@matcom.uh.cu

ABSTRACT
Research studies show that serious games help to motivate users in rehabilitation and therapy is better when users are motivated. In this work we experiment with serious games for cerebral palsy patients, who rarely show capacity increases with therapy which causes them demotivation. For this reason, we have implemented balance rehabilitation video games for this group of patients. The video games were developed using the prototype development paradigm, respecting the requirements indicated by physiotherapists and including desirable features for rehabilitation serious games presented in the literature. A set of patients who abandoned therapy last year due to loss of motivation, has tested the video game for a period of 6 months. Whilst using the video game no patients have abandoned therapy, showing the appropriateness of games for this kind of patients.

Categories and Subject Descriptors
K.4.2 **[Computers and Society]** – *Assistive technologies for persons with disabilities*

General Terms: Design, Experimentation, Human Factors.

Keywords: Serious games, Video games, Rehabilitation, Vision-based interfaces.

1. INTRODUCTION
Each year a part of patients working with ASPACE (www.aspaceib.org), a cerebral palsy association, abandon their therapy due to loss of motivation. Cerebral palsy is a term used to describe a group of chronic conditions affecting body movement and muscle coordination. The main objective of cerebral palsy rehabilitation therapy is to maintain the patients' capacities. The progressive loss of capacities fuels the patients' loss of motivation as time passes.

Research studies show that rehabilitation results are better when patients are motivated [2] and serious games help to motivate users in rehabilitation processes [3]. A serious game is defined as a video game that allows the player-user to achieve a specific purpose through the entertainment and engagement component provided by the experience of the game. The cognitive and motor activity required by video games engage the user's attention. In addition, users focus their attention on the game and this helps them in forgetting that they are in therapy.

In this project we transferred the ASPACE balance therapy tasks to a video game, in order to experiment if serious games are valid for motivational rehabilitation of cerebral palsy patients. The video game was implemented using the prototype development paradigm, respecting requirements indicated by physiotherapists and following the desirable features for rehabilitation serious games [1]:

- *meaningful play*, the relationship between player's interactions and system reaction.
- *challenge*, maintaining an optimum difficulty is important in order to engage the player.

2. VIDEO GAME DESIGN FOR BALANCE REHABILITATION
We implemented a video game that consists in changing the users' gravity center: trying to cause a specific body movement in order to change their gravity center. To do this, users must interact with objects that cannot be reached without changing their center of mass. This way, users focus their attention on the video game instead of their posture. The goal is not to improve the rehabilitation process itself, but rather to transfer the ASPACE balance therapy tasks to a video game in order to improve the users' motivation.

Recent technological advances have created the possibility to enhance naturally and significantly the interface perception by means of visual inputs [4], the so-called Vision-Based Interfaces (VBI). This is a good interaction method because the majority of patients ASPACE works with, cannot hold a device.

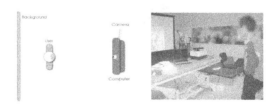

Fig. 1. Interaction space

To achieve the goal, users must delete a set of items that appear on the screen using their hand, before losing their balance. For this reason, users are located inside an interaction space that consists of a projection screen and is instrumented with a low-cost webcam (see Figure 1). The interaction is produced through skin color segmentation [4]. This configuration allows users to view the video game whilst performing the interaction tasks. The interface requirements are:

- only one user shall be present in the space.
- the skin colored body parts, other than the hands and face, shall not be visible.

Following specialists' requirements and in order to make rehabilitation sessions adaptable to the characteristics of the different users, we defined configuration parameters to customize games and adapt them to different user profiles:

- **Delete pattern:** Specialists can create images that define the objects that users have to interact with.
- **Maximum playing time:** Specialist can set a time limit for each session depending of the users characteristics.
- **Contact time:** Specialists can customize how long users must be in contact with an element in order to delete that object.

We developed the game for 6 months, using the prototype development paradigm. During this period, in order to improve the game we tested the system with real users once a week. As a result all the information necessary to perform the different tasks was provided in an understandable way. The user is always aware that interaction has been carried out as the interaction object disappears from the screen and audio feedback is played. Moreover, at the end of the game, the user receives different types of visual and audio feedback, depending on the end game conditions. The system stores information about user interaction during each session, in order to simplify the specialists' work with regards to the patients' evolution. The games are adaptable to the users' skill, as the specialist can place the interaction objects in any region of the screen.

Figure 2 depicts the final game design. This design has the potential to be used in other rehabilitation systems. It is important to remark that there are two types of users: the user and the specialist, with different interaction objectives with the system.

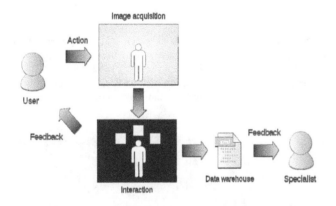

Fig. 2. Serious games design overview.

3. EXPERIMENT

Once the video game was developed,we began to test the serious game with a set of patients with cerebral palsy, for 6 months. Before the experiment each patient was evaluated using physiotherapist tests. At the end of the experiment the same tests were performed, in order to assess the patients' evolution.

The users set was composed of 4 adults with cerebral palsy who, in the last years, had abandoned their rehabilitation plan. Their families signed the informed consent. All were habitual users of the rehabilitation service offered by ASPACE. They were aware that rehabilitation sessions were focused at maintaining capacities rather than improving them and they had lost motivation due to their difficult situation and the repetitive nature of the exercises performed each session.

Table 1 shows a summary of patients' evaluation before and after the experiment.

Table 1. Summary of results

User	Pre-evaluation	Post-evaluation
1	Safety and autonomy for balance is regular, close to low limit.	Able to complete the games. Increase resistance of the biped position.
2	Body posture improper. Lower resistance in bipedal posture. Without security or autonomy for balance.	Able to complete the game. Increase resistance of the biped position.
3	High anxiety. Without security or autonomy for balance.	Increased level of confidence. Decreased anxiety.
4	Difficulty in spatial orientation. Without security or autonomy for balance.	Improvement in spatial orientation. Improvement in balance.

4. CONCLUSIONS

In this work, we experiment if serious games for rehabilitation can be used for motivational balance rehabilitation in cerebral palsy patients. The presented video games try to promote a specific body movement in order to change the users' gravity center.

Results show that users improved their balance slowly; improvements were also detected in individual items. With regards to motivation, in previous years the set of users had abandoned their therapeutic plans. Using the presented video games, no users have abandoned and they showed interested in continuing the rehabilitation process with the video games.

5. ACKNOWLEDGMENTS

We thank the ASPACE Centre for all their collaboration, work and feedback provided. This work was partially supported by the projects MAEC-AECID A/030033/10 and TIN2010-16576 of the Spanish Government, with FEDER support.

6. REFERENCES

[1] J.W. Burke, M.D.J. McNeill, D.K. Charles, P.J. Morrow, J.H. Crosbie, and S.M. McDonough. Optimising engagement for stroke rehabilitation using serious games. The Visual Computer, 25(12):1085–1099, 2009.

[2] N. Maclean, P. Pound, C. Wolfe, and A. Rudd. The concept of patient motivation: a qualitative analysis of stroke professionals' attitudes. Stroke, 33(2):444, 2002.

[3] P. Rego, P.M. Moreira, and L.P. Reis. Serious games for rehabilitation: A survey and a classification towards a taxonomy. In Information Sys- tems and Technologies (CISTI), 2010 5th Iberian Conference on, pages 1–6. IEEE.

[4] J. Varona, A. Jaume-i Capó, J. González, and F.J. Perales. Toward natural interaction through visual recognition of body gestures in real- time. Interacting with Computers, 21(1-2):3–10, 2009.

Using a Game Controller for Text Entry to Address Abilities and Disabilities Specific to Persons with Neuromuscular Diseases

Torsten Felzer
Institute for Mechatronic Systems
Technische Universität Darmstadt
Petersenstr. 30, D-64287 Darmstadt, Germany
felzer@ims.tu-darmstadt.de

Stephan Rinderknecht
Institute for Mechatronic Systems
Technische Universität Darmstadt
Petersenstr. 30, D-64287 Darmstadt, Germany
rinderknecht@ims.tu-darmstadt.de

ABSTRACT

This paper proposes a poster about an alternative text entry method, based on a commercially available game controller as input device, as well as a demo of the accompanying software application. The system was originally intended for a particular gentleman with the neuromuscular disease Friedreich's Ataxia (FA), who asked us to help him – by developing an optimal keyboard replacement for him – already several years ago. Our work focused on his impressions in an initial case study testing this newest attempt. Taking the tester's comments into account, the outcome seems to be rather promising in meeting his needs, and it appears very probable that the system could be of help for anyone with a similar condition.

Categories and Subject Descriptors

H.5.2 [**Information Interfaces and Presentation**]: User Interfaces—*Input devices and strategies*; K.4.2 [**Computers and Society**]: Social Issues—*Assistive technologies for persons with disabilities*

General Terms

Human Factors

Keywords

Human-computer interaction, Friedreich's Ataxia, nystagmus, dysarthria

1. INTRODUCTION

Neuromuscular diseases affect the pathways between nerves and muscles. They typically lead to movement problems, especially concerning fine motor control. Many patients are also subject to dysarthria (speech problems) and/or nystagmus (causing unconventional eye movements). The progressive hereditary condition Friedreich's Ataxia (FA) – which shows all of these symptoms – is one out of many examples.

A certain FA patient, who is now 40 years old, approached us several years ago, asking for our help. He was (and still is) obliged to use a computer every day, involving a lot of

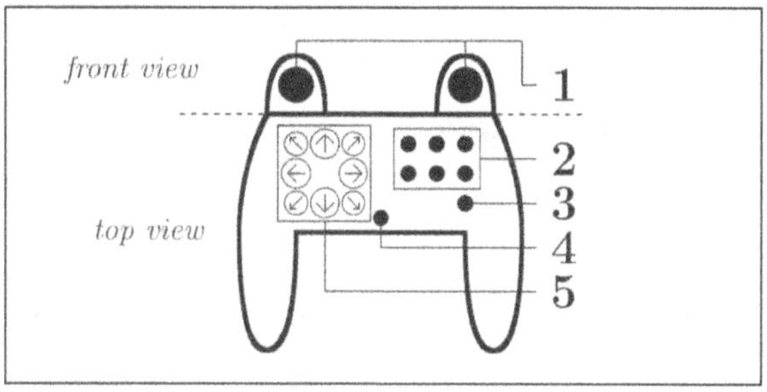

Figure 1: Game controller used for entering text: 1 = triggers; 2 = action buttons; 3 = mode button; 4 = "shift" button; 5 = 8-way D-pad.

text entry. Despite considerable motor problems, he is still able to use a standard keyboard, which he does due to the absence of a viable alternative – e.g., he cannot use speech recognition because of dysarthria, and his nystagmus makes eye tracking virtually unusable. Unfortunately, typing for him means a lot of effort (especially "traveling" from one key to the next without support, if the keys are far apart) and is very slow (nowadays just 2-3 wpm). Therefore, he is constantly looking for a suitable keyboard replacement.

With this intention, he was given the opportunity to participate in several evaluation studies involving keyboard replacements developed by us for persons with physical disabilities (e.g., [1, 2, 3]). However, as the approaches did *not* make full use of his abilities (e.g., he *can* employ both hands, when adequately supported), the results were less than optimal (see also [5]). In our newest attempt to help him, we wanted to tailor a tool specifically to his needs (hoping that the outcome would also be useful for others).

The game controller schematically illustrated in fig. 1 was chosen as input device: it was presumed that gripping the controller tightly with both hands should provide enough support (making it easy to hit the correct buttons) – the projected user agreed after a preliminary inspection of the device. Game controllers for text entry have been used already (e.g., [4]), but the reported proof-of-concept applications are mostly not intended to be used under real-world conditions, so we decided to design our own solution.

2. SOFTWARE DESIGN

The design of the developed software is characterized by the following three objectives:

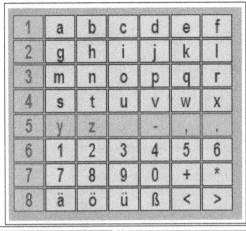

Figure 2: Eight-by-six grid showing selectable characters with pre-selected fifth row and indicators for the buttons for left and right thumbs.

1. The keys on a standard keyboard shall be replaced by the small number of buttons on the game controller.

   The basic idea how this is done is shown in fig. 2: the GUI (Graphical User Interface) presents an on-screen keyboard, where the user can pre-select one of eight rows with the D-pad; after pressing one of the six action buttons on the right, the corresponding character is "written". Therefore, the dimensions of the on-screen keyboard is a direct consequence of the design of the used game controller. The depicted keyboard layout was chosen with the intention to make it easy for the user to remember it – it is, however, easily customizable. Additional characters as well as miscellaneous functionality are accessed using the shift and mode buttons and the triggers.

2. The application shall reduce the effort required from its user as much as possible.

   To achieve this goal, the software has to implement common known approaches. For example, an own version of word prediction – in order to help the user save keystrokes – is included, or a "sticky shift", so that the user is not required to press two buttons at once.

3. The solution must be practically usable.

   This requirement refers to two considerations. First, the software must offer the functionality of a standard editor program, which not only means capital letters and punctuation, but also a cursor, text selection, copy & paste, undo/redo, find/replace, and so on. But most importantly, it must not be slower than the standard method (for the same user, of course) – if the user has to decide, either fast but with effort or effortless but slow, then something is wrong.

3. INITIAL CASE STUDY

A first version of the projected text entry system has been tested by the person it was intended for in an initial case study. The test involved an introduction into the software, five practical sessions on consecutive days, and a post-test interview asking the participant about his impressions.

In the practical sessions, the participant was asked to transcribe fragments of a given text as fast and as accurate as possible for at least two hours per day. The achieved entry rates were recorded, as well as some open comments about the individual sessions.

The numerical results revealed that the system provides no advantage over the participant's usual method of entering text (the standard keyboard) in terms of entry rate (which ranged from .8 wpm on day 1 to slightly over 2 wpm at the end of the test). However, the participant likes the new method (and wants to use it again), because it makes text entry much easier and less exhausting for him, *without* requiring *more* time.

4. CONCLUSION

The application resulting from this work is promising in that it exactly meets the expectations: it decreases the physical effort (and increases the comfort) to enter text – e.g., by replacing the standard keyboard with a more compact device – and it is practically usable at the same time (which particularly means that entering text does *not* take longer than usually).

This is true at least for the FA patient the tool has originally been developed for, which could be confirmed in an initial case study. In addition to extending and refining the software, next steps include evaluating the system with more participants, in order to verify that the tool can indeed be of help for anyone with similar neuromuscular conditions.

The proposed poster will on the one hand present how exactly the software is organized (which will also be shown in the accompanying demo). On the other hand, the poster will give more details on the case study, including the entered text and the recorded results.

5. REFERENCES

[1] T. Felzer and R. Nordmann. Alternative text entry using different input methods. In *Proc. ASSETS 2006*, pages 10–17. ACM Press, 2006.

[2] I. S. MacKenzie and T. Felzer. SAK: Scanning Ambiguous Keyboard for Efficient One-Key Text Entry. *ACM Transactions on Computer-Human Interaction (TOCHI)*, 17(3):11:1–11:39, 2010.

[3] A. J. Sporka, T. Felzer, S. H. Kurniawan, O. Poláček, P. Haiduk, and I. S. MacKenzie. Chanti: Predictive text entry using non-verbal vocal input. In *Proc. CHI 2011*, pages 2463–2472. ACM Press, 2011.

[4] A. D. Wilson and M. Agrawala. Text entry using a dual joystick game controller. In *Proc. CHI '06*, pages 475–478. ACM Press, 2006.

[5] J. O. Wobbrock, S. K. Kane, K. Z. Gajos, S. Harada, and J. Froehlich. Ability-based design: Concept, principles and examples. *ACM Trans. Access. Comput.*, 3(3):9:1–9:27, 2011.

Using Accelerometers for the Assessment of Improved Function due to Postural Support for Individuals with Cerebral Palsy

Yu Iwasaki, Tetsuya Hirotomi
Department of Mathematics and Computer Science
Shimane University
Matsue 690-8504, Japan
+81-852-32-6480

{s083014, hirotomi}@cis.shimane-u.ac.jp

Annalu Waller
School of Computing
University of Dundee
Dundee DD1 4HN, Scotland, UK
+44-1382-388223

awaller@computing.dundee.ac.uk

ABSTRACT

Proper seating and positioning is crucial in performing functional activities by individuals with neurological disabilities such as cerebral palsy. Subjective seating assessments are usually performed by physical and occupational therapists observing activities with different seating adaptations. Frequent assessments are required to maintain and adapt seating as individuals' physical characteristics change over time. We conducted a single case study with a 10 year old boy with cerebral palsy to investigate the potential use of accelerometers for the assessment of improved function due to postural support in seating. The results suggest that the root mean square values of acceleration correspond well with the subjective assessment of therapists that reduction in involuntary movements improves function.

Categories and Subject Descriptors

K.4.2 [**Social Issues**]: Assistive technologies for persons with disabilities; H.5.2 [**User Interfaces**]: Input devices and strategies

General Terms

Human Factors

Keywords

Involuntary movement, motion analysis, cerebral palsy, seating

1. INTRODUCTION

Individuals with neurological disabilities such as cerebral palsy often exhibit abnormal movements, reflexes, and tone. Specialized seating supports existing deformities and inhibits involuntary movements while reducing the development of new deformities [4]. Proper seating that maximises an individual's ability to function is essential for any interaction or activity, e.g., writing, feeding or using assistive technology devices [1]. Seating is so crucial to function that a slight change in either seating or the positioning of devices can result in reduced quality of access [5].

Physical and occupational therapists (PT and OT) observe changes in movements of all body sites and make subjective assessments as to what adaptations reduce unwanted movement and maximise function. The challenge is then for the individual with neurological disabilities to maintain a good position to benefit from the adapted seating. A quantitative assessment tool is thus required to support both the seating adaptation by therapists and maintenance by individuals and carers.

Accelerometers have been used to analyse a variety of motions. For example, Yajima and Ohgi used them to evaluate the smoothness of reaching movements by measuring upper limb acceleration [6]. We have used root mean square (RMS) values of accelerations to detect conspicuous and sudden movements, including abnormal muscle tone and tremors [2]. Our method is based on analysing data from portable accelerometers attached to several body sites while undertaking touch screen operations and/or one-button-switch activations. This pilot study aims to extend that work by investigating the potential of our methods to assess improved function due to postural support in seating by measuring involuntary movement and functional activity.

2. CASE STUDY

We conducted a single case study. The participant was a 10 year old boy with spastic diplegic cerebral palsy. He is right-handed with a motor age of 19 months on the Motor Age Test (MAT) [3].

Figure 1 shows the experimental apparatus. He used a seating system with positioning supports and an ankle foot orthosis. Six 3-axis accelerometers (PhidgetAccelerometer 3-Axis, measurement range ±29.4 m/s^2, Phidgets Inc.) were attached to the body sites close to forehead (FH), seventh thoracic

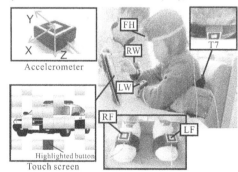

Figure 1. Experimental apparatus

vertebra (T7), left wrist joint (LW), right wrist joint (RW), lateral cuneiform of left foot (LF) and right foot (RF). Each accelerometer's weight is approximately 56 grams including a cable and an acrylonitrile-butadiene-styrene (ABS) plastic enclosure. The child's OT confirmed that they did not interfere with his movements.

48 buttons were aligned in 6 rows and 8 columns on a 12.1 inch wide touch screen. The screen was held at an inclination of approximately 73 degrees from the horizontal. The task was to touch randomly highlighted buttons 20 times. We asked the child to perform the task in seating settings A and B; the planar cushion, used to prevent his pelvis from sliding forward, was introduced in setting B. We examined whether the difference in his function between settings could be detected by subjective and quantitative assessments.

3. SUBJECTIVE ASSESSMENT
A subjective assessment software tool has been developed to compare movement quality for each body site in settings A and B. It shows sets of video clips segmented for analysis. A coder compares a set of clips in both settings using a 5-point rating scale; "1" means involuntary movement in setting A is more excessive, "3" means no difference, "5" means involuntary movement in setting B is more excessive.

The child's OT, school teacher and parent analysed a set of videos independently. In Figure 2, the box plot summarizes the OT's assessment. All ratings are 3 or less, meaning that involuntary movements in setting A are more excessive than ones in setting B. We classified the ratings into bottom-2-box (1 and 2), top-2-box (4 and 5) and no difference (3), then calculated Cohen's Kappa to evaluate agreements with OT and the others. The OT and the teacher reached moderate agreement (κ=0.567, p<0.01). OT and the parent reached near-perfect agreement (κ=0.835, p<0.01).

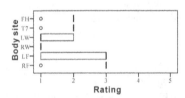

Figure 2. OT's subjective assessment

4. QUANTITATIVE ASSESSMENT
The accelerations and log of touch operations were analysed to compare activity in the settings. In Figure 3, the box plot shows the RMS values of accelerations of each body site. The Z axis was selected for FH; the Y axes were selected for other body sites based on the directions of the typical involuntary movements. We compared each body site's minimum, 25th percentile, median, 75th percentile, and maximum RMS values between settings A and B. The RMS values could detect very small changes. 90% of

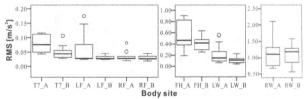

Figure 3. RMS values of each body site (the suffix indicates the session)

setting B's values were lower than setting A's. The OT's ratings and the RMS values reached satisfactory agreement (κ=0.724, p<0.01).

On average, the child spent 2.37 sec in setting A and 1.71 sec in setting B to touch each button, meaning that he was able to interact with the touch screen more efficiently in setting B.

5. DISCUSSION AND FUTURE WORK
In this case study, the OT's subjective assessment and the time efficiency of touch operations show that reducing the small involuntary movements can increase the ability to perform functional activities. The parent and teacher are encouraged to remind the child to sit properly. However, such reminders are only given sporadically because they are unable to notice small involuntary movements, typically in the child's left wrist, due to their lack of expertise and other responsibility, e.g. household chores and teaching. The study shows that RMS values of accelerations have the potential to measure discernible changes when specific body sites exhibit involuntary movements. Our approach may increase self-awareness of individuals with neurological motor impairments and provide tangible feedback for carers. We are conducting further case studies with an increased number of participants. Our future work will analyse more cases and develop a seating support system for providing feedback about seating and posture.

6. ACKNOWLEDGMENTS
We thank Jeremy Linskell, Amanda Palmer-Norrie, Victoria Ann Johnson and OBrien Aidan of the TORT Centre (Dundee NHS) for their invaluable support and useful feedback to design and conduct case studies. Part of this work was supported by MEXT KAKENHI 21700138 and JSPS Excellent Young Researcher Overseas Visit Program.

7. REFERENCES
[1] Cook A. M. and Polgar J. M. 2008. *Cook and Hussey's Assistive Technologies: Principles and Practice, 3rd edition*. Mosby Elsevier, St. Louis, MO.

[2] Hirotomi T. and Katai Y. 2010. Analysis of involuntary movements for adapting input devices to people with motor impairments based on 3-Axis Accelerometers. In *Proceedings of 2010 IEEE 6th World Congress on Services (Miami, Florida, USA, July 5 - July10)*. 298–301.

[3] Johnson M. K., Zuck F. N., and Wingate K. 1951. The motor age test: measurement of motor handicaps in children with neuromuscular disorders such as cerebral palsy. *Journal of Bone and Joint Surgery*. 33, 3 (Jul. 1951), 698–707.

[4] McClenaghan B. A., Thombs L., and Milner M. 1992. Effects of seat-surface inclination on postural stability and function of the upper extremities of children with cerebral palsy. *Developmental Medicine and Child Neurology*. 34, 1 (Jan. 1992), 40–48.

[5] McEwen I. R. and Lloyd L. L. 1990. Positioning students with cerebral palsy to use augmentative and alternative communication. *Language, Speech, and Hearing Services in Schools*. 21 (Jan. 1990), 15–21.

[6] Yajima D. and Ohgi S. 2008. Time series analysis of reaching movements in patients after stroke. *Rigakuryoho Kagaku*. 23, 6, 765–772 (in Japanese).

Using Device Models for Analyzing User Interaction Problems

Matthias Schulz, Stefan Schmidt, Klaus-Peter Engelbrecht, and Sebastian Möller
Quality and Usability Lab, Deutsche Telekom Laboratories, TU Berlin
Ernst-Reuter-Platz 7, 10587 Berlin, Germany
{matthias-schulz;stefan.schmidt01;klaus-peter.engelbrecht;sebastian.moeller}@telekom.de

ABSTRACT

This paper presents work in progress which aims at analyzing the origins of interaction problems which certain users have when interacting with new technology. Our analysis is based on device models which categorize certain classes of devices via a pre-defined set of features. We provide examples which show that usability problems are partially caused by an erroneous transfer of device features to new/unknown devices.

Categories and Subject Descriptors

H.5.2 [**User Interfaces**]: Evaluation/methodology; H.1.2 [**User/Machine Systems**]: Human factors

General Terms

Human Factors

Keywords

mental model, devices, interaction strategies

1. INTRODUCTION

In the frame of the German SmartSenior project[1], we have repeatedly observed that not technically-inclined users show problems in operating ambient-assisted living services because they have problems in operating the corresponding devices used for user input, such as touch screens, buttons, mobile phones, etc. We assume that many of the observed problems are due to a wrong mental model of how to use the respective input device.

2. DEVICE MODELS

We use device models to categorize different kinds of manual user input devices. As a basis for our device models, we use the classifications of input devices introduced by Card et al. [1] and Jacob [2]. Card and colleagues classified input devices as a six-tuple (M = manipulation operator, In = input domain, S= current state of the device, R = resolution function mapping the input domain to the output domain set, Out= the output domain set, and W = device properties

---

[1] http://www.smart-senior.de

describing additional aspects of how the device works) and represented devices as a graphical profile by connecting a set of circles (for details see [1]). Jacob [2] distinguishes between devices operated via hands-discrete input, hands-continuous input, other body movement, speech input, and virtual reality input. He also classified the hands-continuous input devices in more detail by using 7 classifying dimensions (for details see [2]).

Our device model shall classify devices operated by hand. As a starting point, we use the proposed categories of Jacob, which have similarities to the design spaces of input devices introduced by Card. Further, we added two extra classifying categories (marked with an asterisk(*); see Table 1), called "number of concurrent inputs per dimension" and "discrete vs. continuous input". We added the category "number of concurrent input per dimension" to distinguish between input devices that are able to measure more than one value for the same dimension. For example, a mouse can only measure one x and corresponding y value at the same time, so the number of concurrent input per dimension is one. In contrast to this, a multi-touch touch screen is able to measure more than one value for the x and y dimensions ($x_1...x_n, y_1...y_n$) at the same time; in this case the number of concurrent inputs per dimension is n. The difference between discrete and continuous input is related to the representation of a value within the system. A mouse is a continuous device, because when moving the mouse the values present in the system are continuously changing. On the other side, a keyboard is a discrete input device, as the system only knows two states "key pressed" or "key not pressed".

If two devices, belonging to two different devices classes, are very similar in their operation, look very similar, or belong to the same domain, it may happen that the user has a misconception of how to operate the device properly. Because of that misconception the user transfers known interaction strategies to a device not capable of handling such input. In the following, we show examples of such erroneous transfer, using the features of the extended device model proposed above.

In our experiments, we observed participants transferring the mental interaction concept of a TV remote control to an iPhone 3 GS while trying to operate the TV using the smartphone. As the iPhone and the TV remote control belong to different device classes, the participants faced the problem, that the iPhone was not able to handle force (physical prop-

Table 1: Categories to organize input devices (* – Attributes, which do not exist in [2]).

Attribute	No. of options	Options	Example
Type of motion	2	Linear or rotary	A mouse measures linear and a knob rotary motion.
Absolute vs. relative measurement	2	Relative or absolute	A mouse measures relative and a touch screen measures absolute motion.
Physical property sensed	8	Position, movement, force, delta force, angle, delta angle, torque, delta torque	A mouse measures movement; a TrackPoint measures force, and a touch screen measures position
Number of dimensions	6	X, Y, Z (linear) rX, rY, rZ (rotary)	Mouse (x, y) touch screen (x, y) knob (rZ)
Direct vs. indirect control	2	Indirect or direct control	Mouse is indirect and touch screen is direct.
Position vs. rate control	2	Position or rate	Moving a mouse changes the position, using a TrackPoint changes the rate (speed of cursor movement).
Integral vs. separable dimensions	2	Integrated or separated	Mouse integrates the measurement of three linear dimensions (x, y and z); to change the x and y position using knobs, two separated knobs are needed.
Number of concurrent inputs per dimension	n	1 to n	Mouse provides only one x and y value at a time; multi-touch touch screen can measure more than one x and y values at a time (multi-touch)
Discrete vs. continuous input	2	Discrete or continuous	Mouse is continuous and TV remote control is discrete

erty sensed). So some button presses are not recognized, no matter how hard the participant pressed the button, because the user kept the soft button pressed for a long time, which, in this case, was not recognized by the iPhone.

Another example is the single-touch vs. a multi-touch touch screen. Both devices look the same, but differ in their "number of concurrent inputs per dimension". Thus, users who were familiar with multi-touch touch screens faced problems when they tried to use a multi-touch interaction strategy, such as pinch-to-zoom.

Related to the "integrated dimensions" attribute, the Apple Magic Mouse vs. normal mouse problem is an example. The Magic Mouse integrates the multi-touch feature into the mouse and user not knowing these techniques or unfamiliar using these techniques often have problems making unintended interactions by accidentally touching the mouse skin.

If users are familiar with a touch pad and should switch to a TrackPoint, they often faced the problem, that they do not know how to operate a TrackPoint. Wiping over the TrackPoint does not work, or the cursor only moves a little bit. Here the problem is again related to the "Physical Property Sensed". A TrackPoint measures force and a touch pad measures movement, so the user has to change the interaction strategy to be able to operate the cursor. The same problem appears, if the user switches from mouse to the joystick or otherwise. Operating a mouse influences the mouse position relative to the mouse movement. Using a joystick changes the cursor speed instead; here, the difference is related to the "Position vs. Rate Control" attribute.

3. CONCLUSION

By classifying manual input devices according to the extended device models it is possible to define device-specific interaction models. Interaction models represent typical interaction strategies and interaction behavior related to one or more device models (device classes) in mind. Mistakes and slips (as defined in [3]) occur while transferring known interaction strategies to an inappropriate device. By using device models we will be able to categorize interaction problems relate to the erroneous use of devices. Currently, we perform a quantitative analysis of interaction problems which have been observed with younger and older users of a smart-home environment, and a classification according to the device features of our extended device model. We would like to simulate such erroneous transfer with the help of user simulation strategies in the future.

4. REFERENCES

[1] S. K. Card, J. D. Mackinlay, and G. G. Robertson. The design space of input devices. In *Proc. of the SIGCHI*, CHI '90, pages 117–124, New York, NY, USA, 1990. ACM.

[2] R. J. K. Jacob. Human-computer interaction: input devices. *ACM Computing Surveys*, 28(1):177–179, 1996.

[3] N. A. Stanton. Human error identification in human-computer interaction. In J. A. Jacko and A. Sears, editors, *The human-computer interaction handbook*, pages 371–383. L. Erlbaum Associates Inc, Hillsdale, NJ, USA, 2003.

Voice Banking and Voice Reconstruction for MND patients

Christophe Veaux, Junichi Yamagishi, Simon King

Centre for Speech Technology Research (CSTR)
University of Edinburgh, UK
+44 131 650 2694
{cveaux, jyamagis}@inf.ed.ac.uk, Simon.King@ed.ac.uk

ABSTRACT

When the speech of an individual becomes unintelligible due to a degenerative disease such as motor neuron disease (MND), a voice output communication aid (VOCA) can be used. To fully replace all functions of speech communication: communication of information, maintenance of social relationships and displaying identity, the voice must be intelligible, natural-sounding and retain the vocal identity of the speaker. Attempts have been made to capture the voice before it is lost, using a process known as voice banking. But, for patients with MND, the speech deterioration frequently coincides or quickly follows diagnosis. Using model-based speech synthesis, it is now possible to retain the vocal identity of the patient with minimal data recordings and even deteriorating speech. The power of this approach is that it is possible to use the patient's recordings to adapt existing voice models pre-trained on many speakers. When the speech has begun to deteriorate, the adapted voice model can be further modified in order to compensate for the disordered characteristics found in the patient's speech. We present here an on-going project for voice banking and voice reconstruction based on this technology.

Categories and Subject Descriptors

I.2.7 [**Speech Recognition and Synthesis**]: Speech Synthesis – Speaker Adaptation. K.4.2 [**Assistive Technologies for Persons with Disabilities**]: Assistive Devices - Voice Reconstruction.

General Terms

Algorithms, Design, Experimentation.

Keywords

VOCA, MND, HTS, Voice banking, Voice reconstruction.

1. INTRODUCTION

When individuals lose the ability to produce their own speech, they lose not only a functional means of communication but also a means to express individual and group identity through their voice. Using a VOCA that sounds like someone with a different geographical or social background or someone with a different age can cause embarrassment and a lack of motivation to interact socially [1]. A personalized VOCA where the synthetic voice has characteristics of the user could reduce the social distance imposed by this mode of communication by re-associating the output content with the user through use of vocal identity. In order to build personalized VOCA, attempts have been made to capture the voice before it is lost, using a process known as voice banking. One example of this approach is ModelTalker [2], a voice building service that can be used on any home computer to build a concatenative synthesis voice. However, it requires the recording of approximately 1800 utterances to build a good quality voice. This requirement stems from the fact that in concatenative synthesis technique, the recordings of speech are segmented into small time units that can be recombined to make new utterances. Concatenative synthesis also requires the recorded data to be intelligible since the data recorded is used directly as the voice output. This feature combined with the amount of data required makes this technique more problematic for those individuals whose voices have started to deteriorate.

Recently, an alternative speech synthesis technique known as model-based synthesis has been investigated to create personalized VOCA [3] [4]. Model-based synthesis relies on a statistical representation of the speech parameters to create the synthetic voice. The advantage of this method is that, rather than building a new voice from scratch, it is possible to use existing models pre-trained over a number of speakers and to adapt them towards an individual's speech. This process known as speaker adaptation requires a significantly smaller amount of data. It has been shown that using 100 sentences or approximately 6-7 minutes of speech data is sufficient to generate a synthetic voice that sounds similar to the target speech [3]. The speech has a slightly more robotic quality but it is much more consistent than concatenative techniques. Furthermore, the speaker adaptation process can be tweaked to compensate the disordered characteristics found in the individual's speech. This technique has been successfully applied to build a personalized VOCA for an MND patient. Given this promising result, the CSTR, the Euan MacDonald Center for MND and the Anne Rowling Regenerative Neurology Clinic have started a collaborative project for voice banking and voice reconstruction. We present here the main technical concepts behind this project.

2. MODEL-BASED SPEECH SYNTHESIS

The voice building is based on HTS, a model-based synthesis technique [5]. This approach represents the acoustic parameters of the speech with a set of statistical models associated to elementary speech units. A speech unit is a phone-in-context, where the symbolic context information is provided at the phone, syllable, word, and phrase level. The acoustic parameters cover the fundamental frequency F0, the spectral envelope (shape of the vocal tract), and the band aperiodicity, which models the noise in the excitation source. The duration of each speech unit is also represented explicitly in the statistical model. More specifically, the statistical model for a given speech unit consists of a sequence of states, each associated with a set of Gaussian mixture distributions representing the acoustic parameters. Separate distributions are learned for each acoustic parameter and for the state durations. Finally, to further describe the trajectories of the acoustic parameters, their global variances over the learning data are added to the model. To synthesize a sentence, a text analyzer is used to convert the sequence of words into a sequence of speech units and the trained models are invoked for each unit. From this sequence of models, an algorithm generates the most likely trajectory of each acoustic parameter.

For speaker adaptation, a large amount of data taken from multiple speakers (voice donors) is first used to train an average voice model. Then the adaptation algorithm aligns the correct sequence of pre-trained models to the target speaker data and re-estimates their parameters so that it is more likely that these models would generate the target speaker data [6]. This adaptation process allows the creation of a synthetic voice clone of any patient's speech with a limited amount of data. However, we do not want to reproduce the symptoms of a vocal problem if the speech has already been disordered at the time of the recording. A first step to alleviate this problem is to minimize the occurrence of problematic phonemes in the recorded utterances. This can be achieved by careful design of the text prompts, as detailed in section 4. A further step is to modify the adaptation process in order to rely more on the average voice model for those speech characteristics that had been disordered in the patient's speech.

3. VOICE RECONSTRUCTION

The structure of HTS means that separate distributions are learned for each type of parameters: duration, F0, band aperiodicity and spectral coefficients. This structure allows some reconstruction of the voice by substituting models or information from the average voice to compensate for any disorder that occurs in the patient's data. This process can be seen as a kind of model-based voice transplantation. We detail in the following some examples of model substitution.

For MND speakers, the duration of segments is hugely variable and often disordered, contributing to difficulties in comprehension of the speech. By substituting the distributions of the durations by those of the average voice, timing disruptions at both phoneme and utterance level can be regulated. Ideally an average voice with the same regional accent would be used, as temporal aspects of the voice will contribute to the accent, stress and rhythm of the speech, which is important to retain for vocal identity. Therefore, rather than using a unique average voice model, we are planning to exploit a hierarchy of models as explained in next section.

Similarly, individuals with MND may have breathy or hoarse speech, where excessive breath through the glottis produces unwanted turbulent noise. Substitution of the aperiodicity models from the average voice could produce a less breathy or hoarse output. Finally, MND speaker often has a monotonic prosody. The global variance of the F0 can be substituted from the average voice model to make the pitch more natural. This parameter can be further modified manually to suit the preferences of the patient.

4. THE VOICE BANKING PROJECT

The voice reconstruction approach presented in the previous section has been tested for one patient with Parkinson's in Sheffield [3] and improved for one patient with MND in Edinburgh. This patient had had MND for three years and the recording consisted of five minutes of a short interview. We have now started a collaborative project to move from research prototype to large-scale clinical trial. In the first phase of this project, we are planning to record the healthy voice of 150 "donors" whose speech data will be used to train the average voices with various regional accents. We will also record 50 MND patients with various conditions of disordered speech. In a second phase, a voice banking facility will open at the Anne Rowling Regenerative Neurology Clinic, and the voice reconstruction process will be fully automatized.

We are investigating two complementary approaches to improve the quality of the reconstructed voice. The first approach is an optimization of the text prompts used for the recordings of the patient. Before the recordings, each patient will be assessed by a speech therapist in order to evaluate particular speech deficits according to an extended set of phonological features. We are currently devising an assessment procedure that derives from the Frenchay Dysarthria Assessment [7]. Then a text selection algorithm generates the text prompt that minimizes the occurrence of the problematic features.

The second approach is to use a hierarchy of voice models for the speaker adaptation. The model at the top of the hierarchy is the one that gives the most general picture of the speech characteristics whereas the models at the bottom would be more accent-specific. The general model can be used to automatically assess the reliability of the acoustic parameters estimated from the patient's data. This reliability measure can then control the model substitution. The hierarchy of models can be searched to find the model that best describes the reliable parameters and this model will be selected for the substitution of the unreliable parameters.

5. CONCLUSIONS

When a VOCA is to serve as a replacement voice, it is more easily used and accepted if the vocal output has the characteristics of the patient's voice. With model-based speech synthesis, it is now possible to retain the vocal identity of a patient with minimal data recordings and even if its voice has begun to deteriorate. There is still on-going research to improve this voice reconstruction technique, but it seems mature enough to be proposed to a large number of patients with degenerative diseases.

6. REFERENCES

[1] Murphy, J. 2004. "I prefer this close': Perceptions of AAC by people with motor neuron disease and their communication partners. *Augmentative and Alternative Communication*, 20, 259-271

[2] Yarrington, D., Pennington, C., Gray, J., & Bunnell, H. T. 2005. A system for creating personalized synthetic voices. *Proceedings of ASSETS*, 196–197.

[3] Creer, S., Green, P., Cunningham, S., & Yamagishi, J. 2010. Building personalized synthesized voices for individuals with dysarthia using the HTS toolkit. *IGI Global Press*, Jan. 2010.

[4] Khan, Z. A., Green P., Creer, S., & Cunningham, S. 2011. Reconstructing the Voice of an Individual Following Laryngectomy. *Augmentative and Alternative Communication*, 27, 61-66.

[5] Zen, H., Tokuda, K., & Black, A. 2009. Statistical parametric speech synthesis. *Speech Communication*, 51, 1039-1064.

[6] Yamagishi, J., Kobayashi, T., Nakano, Y., Ogata, K. & Isogai, J. 2009. Analysis of speaker adaptation algorithms for HMM-based speech synthesis and a constrained SMAPLR adaptation algorithm. *IEEE Trans. on ASL*, 17, 66-83.

[7] Enderby, P. M. 1983. Frenchay Dysarthria Assessment. *College Hill Press*, 1983.

Web-Based Sign Language Synthesis and Animation for On-line Assistive Technologies

Zdeněk Krňoul

University of West Bohemia, Faculty of Applied Sciences, Dept. of Cybernetics
Univerzitní 8, 306 14 Pilsen, Czech Republic
zdkrnoul@kky.zcu.cz

ABSTRACT

This article presents recent progress with design of sign language synthesis and avatar animation adapted for the web environment. New 3D rendering method is considered to enable transfer of avatar animation to end users. Furthermore the animation efficiency of facial expressions as part of the non-manual component is discussed. The designed web service ensures on-line accessibility and fluent animation of 3D avatar model, does not require any additional software and gives a wide range of usage for target users.

Categories and Subject Descriptors

I.3.7 [**computer graphics**]: Graphics Systems—*Three-Dimensional Graphics and Realism*; H.5.1 [**information interfaces and presentation**]: Multimedia Information Systems—*Animation*

General Terms

Algorithms, Languages, Design

Keywords

Avatar, Sign language, Deaf, Web, Computer graphics

1. INTRODUCTION

Current assistive technologies allow automatic conversion of text to speech not only in audio form but there is ongoing research on sign language synthesis. Individuals with hearing disabilities will be able to use these technologies in their everyday lives. The first attempts to use the Internet and three-dimensional (3D) avatar animation indicate facilitation of access to these technologies: Vcom3D, SignSynth [1], eSIGN [3], SignStep [6].

We introduce new client-server framework for sign language synthesis incorporating up-to-date 3D computer graphics for the Internet, central administration of the system and easy use which allow signing avatar to be more accessible for the target users. The framework is experimentally implemented in the on-line sign language dictionary of Czech Sign Language (CSL) available at http://signs.zcu.cz/.

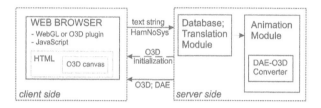

Figure 1: The schema of the web-based sign language synthesis system.

2. SYSTEM OVERVIEW AND USAGE

The web-based sign language synthesis system is composed of a client and server side part. The client side consists of a common web browser only. The server side receives all requirements of the client side, shares conversion methods and generates adequate answers. Currently the server side incorporates a animation module, a database for word-by-word transliteration, a cache of processed requirements and a data converter. The schema of the system is shown in Figure 1. The main features of this framework are:

- minimum requirements for installing additional software on the end user's computer;

- effective data transfer across the network;

- rapid response of the system and fluent animation of the 3D model.

Accessibility of the synthesis system as a web service has required a different representation of the 3D model and the rendering method in comparison with the off-line version [4]. The rendering method and graphic data are based on Google O3D[1] technology. O3D is an open-source Java Script (API) enabling to use signing avatar as interactive 3D applications that needs to run HTML based web browsers only (on Windows, Macintosh, Linux or Android platforms). This API was originally designed as a plug-in (JavaScript library) for the web browsers and now has evolved into the standalone JavaScript library using WebGL standard[2].

We support two forms of data transfer in the direction from the client side. The first form is standard text representation of a spoken language, such as word "house". These words are searched in the database and translated to the

---

[1]http://code.google.com/p/o3d/
[2]WebGL is a framework for the canvas HTML element providing a 3D computer graphics API.

suitable input of the animation module. The system currently provides automatic word-by-word transliterating spoken Czech into signs of CSL and does not produce a fluent sign language output. However additional translation modules can be incorporated into the server side. The second form of the data transfer consists of a stream of signs represented by the sign language notation system and directly connected to the animation module.

The current implementation of the animation module supports the input of one or more signs in the HamNoSys[3] notation. The detailed description of the conversion process is in [4]. The main modification of the animation module consists of its output. Instead of direct 3D rendering the module generates computer data files. We consider O3D file format and DAE (Collada) file[4].

Both file formats can be transfered in the direction to the client side. O3D file is obtained by simple conversion from the DAE file and is primarily used for 3D rendering in the web browsers. In contrast the DAE file can be optionally saved by the end user as "3D sign utterance" for other off-line applications. The animation module is implemented in the C programming language and provides very fast response.

3. CURRENT INVESTIGATION

We are currently concerned with proper animation of facial expressions as essential part of the sign language. The export of animation to DAE file format requires next changes in comparison with to the off-line version that implements 3D rendering via influence zones [4]. The Collada specification provides two different animation methods: the skin and morph controller [5]. The skin controller is primarily intended for animation of arms, fingers and neck. For animation of a human face we have to use the morph controller.

The morph controller is a 3D computer per-vertex animation using blend shapes (the morph targets). The morph target is a "deformed" version of the entire polygonal mesh, again stored as a series of their vertices. In every key-frame of animation the vertices are interpolated between these targets as the weighted average. When we apply it to the human face, one morph is used for neutral face ("basic face shape") and single or multiple morph targets are considered as individual facial expressions. For example for spoken English it requires to store at least 14 morph targets for each viseme[5]. Furthermore the sign languages include many more facial expressions. A large number of morph targets increase memory and rendering requirements on the client side as well as the data transfer because it need to transfer not only all morph targets but also their animation trajectories.

Principal component analysis (PCA) is a mathematical algorithm that uses orthogonal transformations for reduction of dimension and conversion apparently correlated data into an uncorrelated set of values so called principal components. PCA can be applied on the data measured at the face of a signing speaker via Motion capture systems or using video records via the active shape or appearance model (ASM, AAM) [2]. If we consider the basic face shape equal to "mean shape" analyzed by PCA and each of the principal components such as one morph target then principle is identical with the interpolation used by the morph controller. Initial results for isolated signs of CSL and mouthing indicate that to maintain 97.5% of the variance observed on the face can be animated just by nine morph targets.

4. CONCLUSIONS

The article presents a framework for the web-based sign language synthesis system and its experimental implementation for Czech Sign Language (`http://signs.zcu.cz/`). The the system provides 3D rendering of the signing avatar in real time which is supported by most of the recent web browsers without any installation of additional software. The end users can more easily receive prearrange on-line contents containing together standard websites and the 3D signing avatar.

The proposed solution uses hardware accelerated graphics and does not cause fitful rendering. Furthermore efficient and precise rendering of the non-manual component is discussed. The initial analysis indicates potential to increase accessibility by reduction of necessary data. The synthesized utterance can also be optionally saved by the end user and used for other communication or educational purposes. Other specially designed mobile applications can be hereby considered. Next research have to be focused to get high quality signing that will be easily understandable.

5. ACKNOWLEDGMENTS

This research was supported by the Grant Agency of the Czech Republic, project No. GAČR 102/09/P609. and by the Grant Agency of Academy of Sciences of the Czech Republic, project No. 1ET101470416.

6. REFERENCES

[1] A. B. Grieve-Smith. Signsynth: A sign language synthesis application using web3d and perl. In *Gesture Workshop*, pages 134–145, 2001.

[2] M. Hrúz, Z. Krňoul, P. Campr, and L. Müller. Towards automatic annotation of sign language dictionary corpora. *Lecture Notes in Artificial Intelligence*, LNAI 6836, in press, 2011.

[3] J. R. Kennaway, J. R. W. Glauert, and I. Zwitserlood. Providing signed content on the internet by synthesized animation. *ACM Trans. Comput.-Hum. Interact.*, 14, September 2007.

[4] Z. Krňoul, J. Kanis, M. Železný, and L. Müller. Czech text-to-sign speech synthesizer. In *Proceedings of the 4th international conference on Machine learning for multimodal interaction*, MLMI'07, pages 180–191, Berlin, Heidelberg, 2008. Springer-Verlag.

[5] F. I. Parke and K. Waters. *Computer facial animation*. A. K. Peters, Ltd., Natick, MA, USA, 1996.

[6] L. van Zijl and J. Fourie. The development of a generic signing avatar. In *Proceedings of the IASTED International Conference on Graphics and Visualization in Engineering*, GVE '07, pages 95–100, Anaheim, CA, USA, 2007. ACTA Press.

---

[3]`http://www.sign-lang.uni-hamburg.de/projects/ hamnosys.html`

[4]Collada is XML schema allowing full description of the sining avatar and flexible processing by the synthesis module.

[5]A viseme is a representational unit to classify speech sounds in the visual domain.

Analyzing Visual Questions from Visually Impaired Users

Erin Brady

ROC HCI, University of Rochester

Rochester, NY 14618

brady@cs.rochester.edu

ABSTRACT

Many new technologies have been developed to assist people who are visually impaired in learning about their environment, but there is little understanding of their motivations for using these tools. Our tool VizWiz allows users to take a picture using their mobile phone, ask a question about the picture's contents, and receive an answer in nearly realtime. This study investigates patterns in the questions that visually impaired users ask about their surroundings, and presents the benefits and limitations of responses from both human and computerized sources.

Categories and Subject Descriptors

K.4.2 [**Computers and Society**]: Social Issues – *Assistive technologies for persons with disabilities.*

General Terms

Design, Experimentation, Human Factors.

Keywords

Non-Visual Interfaces, Blind Users, Q&A, Crowdsourcing

1. INTRODUCTION

Visual information can be crucial to allow people to function independently, but this information is unavailable to visually impaired people without the assistance of technology or a sighted companion. Without some aid to relay information about their surroundings, visually impaired people may struggle to complete tasks or make decisions in their every-day life. Current automated solutions use object recognition and computer vision techniques to provide straightforward descriptions of objects that the user has a question about but cannot answer more complex, natural language questions.

Our solution to this problem is VizWiz [6], a mobile phone application that provides nearly realtime answers to visual questions. VizWiz relies on a combination of crowdsourcing and object recognition in order to provide quick and reliable answers to natural language questions asked by visually impaired users. A user takes a picture with their mobile phone of the object or area they have a question about and speaks their question into the phone. The photograph and audio recording are forwarded to our server, which distributes their question to crowd workers (from sources such as Amazon's Mechanical Turk [1] service), IQ Engine [4] object recognition software for object identification, and to their social network via Twitter or email. Answers are collected from these sources and then sent back to the phone, where they are dictated to the user.

VizWiz serves as a way for visually impaired users to learn about their surroundings without requiring a human assistant. Our

current work examines the types of questions that users have been sending to the system in order to learn what visual information users want to know about the world around them, and how future tools can be improved to meet these expectations.

2. RELATED WORK

Current mobile tools that provide answers to visual questions can be categorized in one of two extremes. Some are designed for a specific function and are not suited to general questions. On the iPhone platform, the LookTel Money Reader application [7] identifies the denomination of paper bills, while the Color ID Free application [2] names the exact color of the object that is shown. Both of these applications provide extremely useful results, but only answer a limited range of questions. Other applications are generalized to answer many questions, but are unspecific. The oMoby application [5] relies on IQ Engine's object recognition facilities to identify nearly any object that is photographed, but cannot answer questions that require anything past a physical description. Google Goggles [3] offers similar recognition functionality, but is limited to transcribing text, recognizing landmarks and art, or identifying commercial products.

VizWiz combines these approaches by allowing the user to select who answers their question – either object recognition if they are asking a straightforward identification question, human workers if their question requires additional reasoning to answer, or both if they are unsure which service would be the most useful. This approach of combining different tools to answer questions provides a unique benefit for the users. Our study examines the benefit provided by this approach and tries to examine the patterns of questions that users are asking to learn what knowledge benefits them the most.

3. DESIGN

For our analysis, we initially took a random sample of 100 questions out of over 5000 questions that had been submitted to the VizWiz service. The audio questions asked by the users were transcribed, then open coded in two passes based on the question content. After the questions were coded, the codes were collected into the categories described below. Then a random sample of 100 questions was selected for analysis, and coded into the categories. In addition to identifying what type of questions were being asked, we looked at the answers that had been submitted for the question to determine whether the question could be answered by the IQ Engines service alone or if additional human insight was required. For the 100 questions we analyzed, there were 195 answers submitted. We analyzed each answer to see whether or not it correctly answered the question the user had asked.

4. RESULTS

We identified 6 major categories of questions – Identification, Description, Spatial, Reading, Answering, and Other. These categories are described in Table 1. Throughout our evaluations, we ignore questions from the Other category, as it was not possible to evaluate the quality of the answers when the questions were unknown. The majority of the questions asked were Identification questions (53%), followed by Description (15%), Reading (13%), Answering (8%), and Spatial (2%).

Table 1. The primary categories of questions asked.

Category	Characteristics
Identification	Asks for the name of an object
Description	Asks for a description of the properties of an object or setting
Spatial	Asks for the location of an object, or how to navigate toward it
Reading	Asks for written/textual information
Answering	Asks a specific question about the photograph
Other	No question asked/undecipherable question

We then examined the questions asked from each category to see what services the users sent their questions to. We split the four available services into two broader categories – human responders (crowd workers, Twitter, and email) and object recognition (IQ Engines). Since users could send their questions to any combination of these services, some questions were answered by both human responders and the object recognition software. 93 % of the questions were sent to a human responder, while 54% were sent to object recognition.

We looked at the correctness of the answers from each service, trying to find out how well each service was able to answer the user's question. Human responders provided correct responses 62% of the time, incorrect responses 33% of the time, and answers of indefinite correctness 4% of the time. Object recognition provided correct responses 35% of the time, incorrect responses 56% of the time, and answers of indefinite correctness 8% of the time. The majority of the reason for this significant difference in answer correctness is inherent in the object recognition software – it is meant only to provide a name or physical description of an object, and is not able to answer any higher-level questions.

We also looked at how correct the answers provided for each service were. These results are shown below in table 2.

Finally, we looked to see how many correct answers were provided from each response source for each category of questions, hoping to discover which source was best suited for which category. These results are presented for the human responders in Figure 1, and for object recognition in Figure 2. The human responders performed best on Identification and Reading questions, while object recognition predictably performed best on Identification questions and poorly on the other categories.

Table 2. The correctness of answers for question categories.

	Correct	Incorrect	Indefinite
Identification	67%	32%	1%
Description	41%	59%	0%
Spatial	50%	50%	0%
Reading	52%	48%	0%
Answering	35%	65%	0%

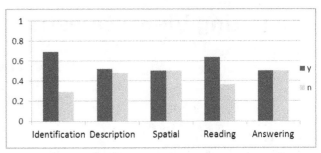

Figure 1. Percent of answers by human responders that were correct ('y') or incorrect ('n') for each question category.

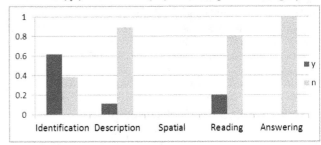

Figure 2. Percent of answers by object recognition that were correct ('y') or incorrect ('n') for each question category.

5. DISCUSSION AND FUTURE WORK

The patterns we identified in questions from visually impaired users will allow us to improve our VizWiz design and provide crucial input for future question-answering systems. We hope to use this information to improve answer qualities for specific question categories by using the most optimal answer source. For example, if we can determine through preprocessing the image or speech that a question involves identification, it would be useful to send the question to object recognition first; alternatively if the question involves reading, we would rather send it to human workers. This knowledge will allow us to develop a generalized, but tailored tool to aid visually impaired users in their daily life.

We have observed some common usage patterns for individual users over time, as they first begin using VizWiz and then become more familiar with it. Future analysis will delve into these temporal trends, and we will develop a strategy for teaching users who are visually impaired how to utilize a tool like VizWiz.

We view VizWiz as a promising replacement to sighted assistants for visually impaired users. We hope further investigation of their visual questions will ensure that new tools for people who are visually impaired meet their needs quickly and accurately.

6. REFERENCES

[1] Amazon's Mechanical Turk. http://mturk.com.

[2] Color ID Free. http://www.greengar.com.

[3] Google Goggles. http://www.google.com/mobile/goggles.

[4] IQ Engines. http://iqengines.com.

[5] oMoby. http://omoby.com.

[6] Bigham, J.P., Jayant, C., et al. VizWiz: Nearly Real-time Answers to Visual Questions. UIST '10, ACM Press (2010).

[7] J. Sudol, O.D., C. Blanchard, T. Dorcey. LookTel — A Comprehensive Platform for Computer-Aided Visual Assistance. CVAVI 2010.

Brazilian Sign Language Multimedia Hangman Game: A Prototype of an Educational and Inclusive Application

Renata C. B. Madeo
University of São Paulo
Av. Arlindo Béttio, 1000
São Paulo, SP, Brazil
renata.si@usp.br

ABSTRACT

This paper presents a prototype of an educative and inclusive application: the Brazilian Sign Language Multimedia Hangman Game. This application aims to estimulate people, specially children, deaf or not, to learn a sign language and to help deaf people to improve their vocabulary in an oral language. The differential of this game is that its input consists of videos of the user performing signs from Brazilian Sign Language corresponding to Latin alphabet letters, recorded through the game graphical interface. These videos are processed by a computer vision module in order to recognize the letter to which the sign corresponds, using a recognition strategy based on primitives - hand configuration, movement and orientation, reaching 84.3% accuracy.

Categories and Subject Descriptors

I.2.1 [**Artificial Intelligence**]: Applications and Expert Systems—*Games*; I.2.1 [**Artificial Intelligence**]: Applications and Expert Systems—*Natural language interfaces*; K.4.2 [**Computers and Society**]: Social Issues—*Assistive technologies for persons with disabilities.*

General Terms

Experimentation

Keywords

Fingerspelling Applications, Educational Application, Inclusive Application, Gesture Recognition, Sign Language.

1. INTRODUCTION

In recent years, there has been a growing concern about minorities social inclusion, including people with disabilities. Computer science can contribute greatly for this group of people through the development of assistive technologies, aiming to promote autonomy, independence, life quality and social inclusion for people with disabilities.

This paper presents the Brazilian Sign Language (BSL) Multimedia Hangman Game[1]: an assitive technology application aiming the social inclusion of deaf people, specially

---

[1]In the Hangman Game, the user shall discover a secret word by guessing the letters which compose it.

children. This application has two main goals: estimulating children, deaf or not, to learn BSL; and helping deaf children to improve their vocabulary in Portuguese, since, despite BSL is an official language in Brazil, knowing Portuguese is really important to overcome communication barriers.

The BSL Multimedia Hangman Game uses a simple webcam to record videos of the user performing signs belonging to the manual alphabet of BSL. The recorded video is analyzed through video processing and pattern recognition techniques aiming to identify which letter corresponds to the sign in the video. Such letter is the input for the game itself.

2. GAME ARCHITECTURE

The game architecture (Fig. 1) is composed by a Graphical User Interface (GUI) and a Computer Vision (CV) module, including video processing and recognition modules.

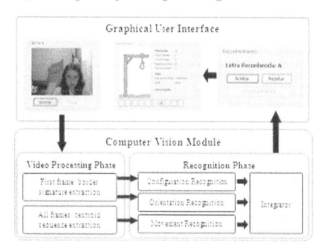

Figure 1: Game architecture: a video is recorded through a webcam. The decision about which sign was performed is used as input to the game logic.

The GUI (Fig. 2) was implemented in Java^{TM}. It allows the user to record videos, submit these videos for processing, viewing the result and accept or reject it, since the CV module can recognize a different sign than what the user meant to perform. For improving its educational role, the user can see the sign in BSL or an image illustrating the word while guessing it, as a hint, and after guessing it, in order to associate the word in Portuguese with the sign in BSL. It also includes the game logic, i.e., all functionalities needed to support a Hangman Game. Thus, once an answer

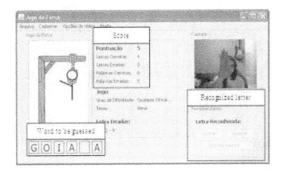

Figure 2: Graphical User Interface.

from CV module is accepted, the GUI shows if that letter is present in the word to be guessed. If it is, the letter is shown in the right position in the word; else, the letter is shown as a wrong guess and another part of the stickman appears in the gibbet. There are other general functionalities: counters to count how many letters and words were guessed correctly or wrongly in the game; a score based on these counters, which can motivate children to play; and functionalities for including new words to the game.

The CV module includes a video processing phase, which extracts the frames from each video and performs a image segmentation phase that will allow the image processing and recognition phases. To allow the recognition, the user shall use a red glove during recording, aiming to facilitate segmentation. After extracting the frames from each video using Java Advanced Imaging API, the images are processed by the segmentation routine implemented with Matlab®. The image processing phase extracts features from the videos first frame to create a border signature, which is used to recognize the configuration and orientation primitives; and from all frames to create a centroid sequence, which is used to recognize the movement primitives. This feature extraction process was already explained in previous works [1, 2].

The recognition phase was implemented in Java™ and has already been described in [2, 3]. It is composed by four subphases: three specific recognition phases, one for each primitive and an integration phase. The recognition phase uses a neuro-fuzzy and a heuristic approach, providing fuzzy output for the recognition process, i.e., membership degrees are associated between the analysed sign and each primitive. The integration phase, also described in [3], is responsible for joining these fuzzy outputs through a fuzzy grammar and provide a final decision, i.e., which letter corresponds to the sign performed in the video. The complete CV module implementation has achieved 84.3% accuracy.

It is important to note that it is possible to adapt the CV module to recognize another sign language, provided that the new signs use the same primitives - same types of hand configuration, movement and orientation - as the previous signs, and are performed with only one hand. It would be necessary just to change the rules in the fuzzy grammar.

3. APPLICATION TESTS

To get real results on the perception of users about the game developed, the application was tested by four users. These tests were performed in two stages: first, the users tested the application by themselves and wrote freely their perceptions about the game; then, users were accompanied

by the developer while playing so that the source of recognition errors could be identified.

In the first stage, users reported that the recognition process was slow and presented errors frequently. Despite the concern with processing time during development, which lead the developer to reduce video quality, the recognition process time of 10 seconds[2] is still too high for users. It was also suggested that there could be some feedback during image processing and recognition, so the user could know what the system is doing and how long it is taking. Despite the problems reported, users pointed the way of interaction through shortcuts (to operate the basic funcionalities of the game, such as starting and stopping video recording) as a good feature of the system: since the dominant hand is busy performing the signs, shortcuts make it easier to play.

In the second stage, users played the game monitored by the developer. At each recognition error, segmented images were verified to assess if the recognition phase was responsible for the error or if segmentation phase had achieved lower quality than expected. From this evaluation, it was possible to conclude that about 70% of all CV module errors were caused by problems with the segmentation.

4. FINAL CONSIDERATIONS

The presented application is still a prototype and needs some improvements. Firstly, it is necessary to improve image processing, specially image segmentation, making it faster and more accurate. Secondly, the results achieved by the recognition phase has great improvement potential: any refinement in a primitive recognition could lead to a better accuracy in the complete CV module. Lastly, when the prototype tests present better results with available testers, it will be possible to organize a test with a group of children (deaf or not) to assess their opinions on the application and, finally, make the application available to these children.

5. REFERENCES

[1] D. B. Dias, R. C. B. Madeo, T. Rocha, H. H. Bíscaro, and S. M. Peres. Hand movement recognition for brazilian sign language: A study using distance-based neural networks. In *International Joint Conference on Neural Networks*, pages 697–704. IEEE, 2009.

[2] R. C. B. Madeo, S. M. Peres, H. H. Bíscaro, D. B. Dias, and C. Boscarioli. A committee machine implementing the pattern recognition module for fingerspelling applications. In *Proceedings of the 25th Annual ACM Symposium on Applied Computing 2010*, pages 954–958. ACM Press, 2010.

[3] R. C. B. Madeo, S. M. Peres, D. B. Dias, and C. Boscarioli. Gesture recognition for fingerspelling applications: An approach based on sign language cheremes. In *Proceedings of the 12th International ACM SIGACCESS Conference on Computers and Accessibility*, pages 261–262. ACM, 2010.

---

[2]Run on a Intel®Core™2 Duo 2.2GHz with 2GB RAM.

Developing for Autism with User-Centred Design

Rachel Menzies
School of Computing
University of Dundee
Dundee, DD1 4HN

rlmenzies@dundee.ac.uk

ABSTRACT

This paper describes the process undertaken to develop software that allows children with Autism Spectrum Disorders (ASD) to explore social situations, in particular the concept of sharing. The User-Centred Design (UCD) process is described, along with adaptations made to alleviate anxiety resulting from the reduced social skills seen in ASD.

Categories and Subject Descriptors

D.2.10 [**Software Engineering**]: Design - Methodologies

General Terms: Design, Human Factors

Keywords: Autism, Autistic, User-Centred Design, Informants, Social Skills, Sharing, Ethnography

1. INTRODUCTION

In the typically developing population, the ability to display appropriate social skills is developed through scaffolding by parents and caregivers from an early age [1]. In Autism Spectrum Disorders (ASD), the typical trajectory of development is compromised. Affecting more than 500,000 people in the UK [2], there is a lack of appreciation of the thoughts, beliefs and feelings of others (Theory of Mind) [1], with established difficulties in social interaction, social communication and social imagination. This lack of social competency can result in significant difficulties in daily living, academic achievement and poor adult outcomes related to employment and social relationship [3]. One particular area of difficulty is sharing, a complex behaviour that forms the basis of many friendships.

The use of technology is limited within the scope of developing social skills, despite those with Autism Spectrum Disorders having a natural affinity with computers [4] due to the predictable and repeatable nature of technology. Furthermore, little work has been conducted in the area of User-Centred Design with children with ASD. This research seeks to involve children with ASD as a valuable source of design inspiration throughout the design and development of the system. The system developed aims to allow children to increase their awareness of their sharing abilities through exploration of these skills in a safe and predictable environment.

2. BACKROUND (CURRENT SOLUTIONS)

A great deal of expertise, time and effort has been invested in the provision of therapy to improve social skills in those with Autism

Spectrum Disorders. The most well-known of these is Social Stories [5], which aim to provide the missing (non-verbal) information in communication. Social Stories are generally considered effective [6] but often do not utilise technology.

The use of technology as a therapeutic tool is limited, but a number of products are commercially available for use in social communication therapy, the majority of which focus on the recognition of emotions from facial expressions. For example, "Faceland" [7] focuses on providing positive feedback through on-screen characters.

Despite the advances seen in this field, one area lacking is the use of User-Centred Design to develop software and other technologies. Children, particularly those with disabilities, are infrequently involved in the design and testing of computer systems [8]. This is discouraging, as the implementation of a User-Centred Design process can result in a more meaningful integration of design and functionality [9].

3. RESEARCH METHODOLOGIES

A number of research methodologies have been adapted and utilised in the development of this research.

At the outset of this research, ethnographic processes were followed in order to identify the problem area and to ensure that this is clearly defined in a realistic setting [10]. Unstructured observations were conducted to consider specific problems occurring in a practical setting for those with ASD. The observations were conducted within a naturalistic setting, ensuring that the behaviours observed are as close to typical as possible, given the presence of the participating observer. This ensures that the observations are flexible and responsive to events as they occur. Field notes were completed in narrative form within one hour of observations being carried out. Video recording of the sessions was avoided since the participant group was unfamiliar with the observer and so the presence of a video recorder may be intrusive and distracting in this case.

These observations gave rise to two areas of further research. It was noted that teachers and therapists spent a great deal of time customising therapeutic efforts to encompass specific needs and special interests [1]. Furthermore, the concept of sharing was recognised as a specific difficulty, with much time spent working on this particular skill.

Since children with ASD have a narrow range of interests, User Centered Design methodologies are invaluable in ensuring that the opinions and preferences of this primary user group are reflected in the resultant system. Design Workshops included designing a character, drama and role-play sessions, and developing a "fun" location to play in.

These workshops developed the design themes, which are utilised to promote engagement in the users. The participants were provided with a background image broadly depicting an open grassy space (garden) and were invited to draw objects into it in order to create a fun and motivating location that they would enjoy playing in. The gardens created were analysed using grounded theory methodologies [11] to determine four main themes that emerged: 'space', 'fantasy', 'animals' and 'garden'. These are used to promote engagement with and maintain interest in the system.

Within the research, the children are involved as "Design Informants" through continuous user access and participation [12], rather than being involved as "Design Partners". This is due to the participants with ASD experiencing difficulties in imagining situations and context out with their immediate reality, with the potential for increased anxiety and social stress. For this reason, the researcher assumes responsibility for the design, making inferences from data gathered in design workshops.

4. FINAL SYSTEM

The final system is developed for children with Autism Spectrum Disorders, with a developmental age of 5-8 years. The chronological age may be greater. In the resulting system, the child takes control from the outset, selecting the theme that they prefer by selecting it from the list presented by the system, allowing them to set the trajectory of their interaction. A character then appears on screen and indicates the sharing "problem" that the child has to solve. Once the child is ready to begin, they can select the green coloured "Ready" button. At this point, the screen will display a number of objects across the top and two locations between which to share the objects. The child can manipulate these objects by dragging and dropping across the screen into the relevant areas, which are indicated by being a different colour than the background.

When the child has decided how to share the objects on screen, they can select the green "Done" button. If the objects have been shared correctly (and thus the problem is now solved) there is a visual and auditory confirmation of success. If the objects have not been shared appropriately and according to social convention, then the character will re-appear on screen and offer some advice. If after three attempts, the child is unsuccessful, the character will provide the answer along with an explanation of the solution. It is intended that the character is non-confrontational and does not direct the child; rather the character should be viewed as a source of advice and assistance.

Throughout each scenario/situation, the child is able to set the pace of the interaction, through selecting the green-coloured buttons to indicate that they are ready to move on.

5. EVALUATION PLANS

The summative system evaluation will be conducted in the coming months to determine whether or not the children can benefit from using the software. Six participants, all with a diagnosis of an ASD will use the system for a period of 4 weeks, using both their preferred theme and others to determine their ability to generalise the information and to measure engagement with the system.

There will be videos recorded both pre and post-use in a variety of situations, including a classroom situation, an informal or unstructured situation and pre-determined situations working with the researcher where sharing is required; For example, snack time at school is one situation where sharing is required to divide food amongst the group. British Picture Vocabulary Scale [13] testing will be undertaken to determine the receptive language ability of the participants. Due to the small number of participants involved in this first evaluation stage, the results will be presented as case studies.

Interviews will also be conducted with classroom staff and parents (where possible) to determine if the participants are perceived to have improved their awareness of sharing and their ability and willingness to share objects with others. Time permitting; a follow-up visit will be made to school some time later to determine if any changes are maintained over time. This will involve observations and interviews with school staff.

6. CONCLUSION

Through the implementation of User-Centred methodologies, the software developed aims to allow children with ASD to explore their social skills in relation to sharing. The system will be evaluated within a special school to assess the potential of the software to improve children's awareness of sharing.

7. REFERENCES

[1] Attwood, T., *The Complete Guide to Asperger's Syndrome* 2006: Jessica Kingsley Publishers.

[2] National Autistic Society, N. *Statistics: how many people have autistic spectrum disorders*. 2007 May 2007 20th December 2009]; Available from: http://www.nas.org.uk/nas/jsp/polopoly.jsp?d=235&a=3527.

[3] Klin, A. and F. Volkmar, *Asperger Syndrome and external validity*. Child and Adolescent Clinics of North America, 2003. **12**(1): p. 1-13.

[4] Moore, D., *Computers and people with autism / asperger syndrome*, in *Communication (the magazine of the National Autistic Society)*1998. p. 20-21.

[5] Gray, C., *The New Social Story Book* 1994, Arlington, VA: Future Horizons.

[6] Reynhout, G. and M. Carter, *The use of Social Stories by teachers and their perceived efficacy*. Research in Autism Spectrum Disorders, 2009. **3**(1): p. 232-251.

[7] Do2Learn. *Faceland*. 2009 [cited 2010 02/01/10]; Available from: http://www.do2learn.com/subscription/product_details/cd_Faceland.php.

[8] Druin, A., *Beginning a discussion about kids, technology, and design*, in *The design of children's technology* 1998, Morgan Kaufmann Publishers Inc.

[9] Preece, J., et al., *Human-Computer Interaction* 1994, Essex, England: Addison-Wesley Longman Limited.

[10] Pole, C. and M. Morrison, *Ethnography for Education*, ed. P. Sikes 2003: Open University Press.

[11] Glaser, B. and A. Strauss, *The discovery of grounded theory: strategies for qualitative research* 1997, New York: Aldine de Gruyter.

[12] Olsson, E., *What active users and designers contribute in the design process*. Interacting with Computers, 2004. **16**(2): p. 377-401.

[13] Dunn, L., D. Dunn, and S. Styles, *The British Picture Vocabulary Scales*, 2009, NFER Nelson: Wind.

Fashion for the Blind:
A Study of Perspectives

Michele A. Burton
University of Maryland Baltimore County
1000 Hilltop Circle
Baltimore, MD 21250
mburton1@umbc.edu

ABSTRACT

Clothing is a universal aspect of life and a significant form of communication for both the wearer and observer. However, clothing is almost exclusively perceived visually begging the question: "How is beauty in fashion interpreted by those with vision impairments?" We conducted face-to-face interviews and a diary study with eight legally blind participants to gain the perspectives of those with vision impairments on what makes clothing attractive and appealing. Our primary focus was gathering their point-of-view on beauty in clothing but all of the participants also discussed accessibility challenges of clothing and fashion. We report our findings on the major aspects of clothing's appeal to blind wearers as well as the challenges with lack of access and assistive technology. These findings have far-reaching implications for future research within fashion design, interaction design and assistive technology.

Categories and Subject Descriptors

H.5.m. Information interfaces and presentation (e.g., HCI): Miscellaneous.

General Terms: Design, Human Factors

1. INTRODUCTION

Humans spend considerable amounts of time, money and effort on their outward appearance. Each person creates an aesthetic based on their fashion choices, and what a person wears (or does not wear) is a signal of who they are and what they think of themselves [1]. However, the majority of beautification efforts are visual and, consequently, beauty in most of its forms is expressed visually. Therefore, our research focus is to understand how those with visual impairments (i.e., those for whom vision is not a dominant sense) make and communicate fashion choices; how the fashion/clothing choices of others are communicated to them; and how other dominant senses, namely touch and hearing, influence aesthetic perception.

Prior research on fashion and design for people with disabilities has focused primarily on mobility impairments [2, 5]. Where vision impairments are the focus, there is more emphasis on function than fashion; i.e., electronic devices embedded in clothing that act as assistive technologies [3, 4]. The aim of this research is to understand what makes a design attractive, aside from its functionality.

2. STUDY METHODOLOGY

We worked with 8 women who are legally blind (visual acuity 20/400 or less). Their ages ranged from 21 to 73 (average 37.25 years). Table 1 describes their diverse vision impairments.

We interviewed our participants with in-person one-on-one interviews, mostly conducted in the participant's home. Interviews were designed to be open and conversational to ensure our data was not influenced by the interviewer. To give structure to the data and act as a basis for starting the conversation, we wrote a base set of questions centered on describing their personal style (the clothes to which they gravitate), how they shop and determine what to buy, and what makes a garment appealing (what makes it attractive and something they want to wear).

After the interview participants were asked to write a freeform diary for 10 days, which allowed them to give any information they found useful based on the goal of the research study and the topics discussed during the interview. Of the 8 participants, 6 completed the diary study with 1 participant writing entries for 7 rather than 10 days due to her schedule. (Two participants' schedules did not allow for diary entries.)

Table 1: Descriptions of Participants

Participant	Age	Description of Vision Loss
1	21	Almost total vision loss from birth, can see color
2	53	Total vision loss from birth
3	73	Low vision from birth (requires magnification), color blind (sees in shades of gray)
4	23	Total vision loss from birth
5	30	Total vision loss in high school, had full vision prior to high school
6	26	Low vision from birth (requires magnification)
7	28	Total vision loss from birth
8	44	Almost total vision loss from birth, can see light (but no color), could see some color when younger

3. FINDINGS

3.1 Clothing Appeal

The most important factor in what makes a garment appealing is how the garment feels. Fabrics that feel harsh, rough or stiff such as wool or even denim are deemed "ugly" whereas soft and breathable fabrics such as cotton or satin are deemed attractive. Participant 8, for instance, commented in her interview that even if her husband (who is sighted) told her something was flattering she would not buy it if she did not like the way it felt. Participant 5 echoed these sentiments when describing that she practically tossed a rough feeling coat from her hands only to have her mother tell her the coat was actually colorful and "gorgeous".

Contrasting textures and embellishments also added appeal, as they are additional sensory outputs when the garment is felt. Participant 3 commented in her interview that she felt added embellishments were a feature that probably stood out more to those with vision impairments than those who are sighted. Later in her diary she stated that she never realized how many of her clothes had some sort of tactile feature besides the fabric itself such as interesting buttons and additional sewn-on patterns.

Many participants placed an emphasis on color when it came to clothes they found attractive, despite not being able to see color. They explained that colors were given certain associations by sighted parents or friends (such as pink for girls or red for fire) and this carried over into what colors they would like to wear.

All participants spoke of needing clothing that was comfortable and functional as well as fashionable. The criteria for "functional" varied and sometimes included conditions that are unique to persons with vision impairments. These included not being able to wear high heels because of fast-moving guide dogs and not being able to wear long necklaces because of the need lean in and view objects from a closer point of view. Though an outfit could meet the criteria of having "good feel appeal", participants would not purchase it if it wasn't practical.

The desired fit of the clothing also attributed to the person's style such as being form-fitting or not too revealing. Also, needing to adhere to a certain style of business attire dictated many clothing choices. A few participants noted, however, it is difficult to say they have a "style" (or particular clothing preference) given the reliance on sighted companions to assist with shopping and coordinating outfits. They wore clothes that felt comfortable to them but the influence of what is shown to them in the store or what is recommended to them is undeniable.

3.2 Challenges to Fashion
Though the primary focus of this research was to understand clothing's appeal, all of the interviews also lead to conversations about the challenges faced with such a visual entity.

All participants stated that in garments designed for the visually-impaired they would not want any articles of clothing that stood out from what others are wearing -- having a white cane or guide dog is already enough of an identifier. The desire to fit in, however, is met with the challenge that people who are blind do not easily have access to the latest fashion trends. It is a conundrum many participants stated creates much angst.

Four participants expressed the "poor blind girl" concept, which refers to the idea that there is no room for error when it comes to fashion when you are vision impaired. This is because if you do make an error (such as not matching or having a stain) then you will be looked upon with pity. Knowing the "criteria" for subjective and visually driven fashion aspects such as matching colors and fabrics presents yet another challenge, however.

Not knowing such information leads to a lack of confidence. Participant 5 works in an agency where she helps people adjust to losing their vision and she stated that confidence in appearance is a top concern for many people with whom she meets. Participant 7 had similar remarks during the interviews when she stated it was "stressful" to be a woman in business and constantly worry about her appearance, which she cannot see.

Shopping was a challenge for all participants. If shopping in a store, browsing is nearly impossible due to difficulties with navigating through the store and physically handling all the clothes independently. Additionally, not all aspects of the clothes can be gathered by touch (such as the price, size and color). Instead, in-store shopping requires a sighted companion, which may be hard to find, especially for impromptu trips, or requires relying on an unfamiliar salesperson who may be only motivated to make a sale. Shopping on-line can work well if the site has textual descriptions that are easy to understand, but for some there was a desire to try clothes on and some felt it too risky to rely solely on the text description.

We observed a lack of reliable assistive technology. The only assistive technology our participants were aware of was a color identifier (a device that detects the colors of physical objects). However, few of our participants used one, and those that did knew there were limitations to its accuracy in identifying colors.

Our participants rely on their memory to keep track of what is in their wardrobe. Since there is no means to completely identify clothes in terms of color, pattern and fabric and how they coordinate, there is a reliance solely on memory. Some participants admitted it restricted their wardrobes. For instance, Participant 4 remarked she would like to wear more jewelry but that would add one more thing to remember when coordinating her clothing.

Lastly, our work uncovered the basic challenge of how to wash and care for clothing. Clothing tags are too small to read for those that require magnification and many participants shied away from clothes with certain fabrics and materials for this reason alone.

4. FUTURE WORK
Based on our findings, there are multiple avenues for extended research. We will explore embedding technology into clothing via smart textiles in a manner that is functional (such as providing relevant auditory feedback) but also fashionable (with an emphasis on soft fabrics, contrasting patterns, and interesting embellishments per our findings). We will also explore how the fashion choices of others can be communicated via other sensory outputs such as sound. We are also interested in assistive technology projects including a virtual "How Do I Look" application where users may ask the opinion of others; accessible garment care instructions; a reliable pattern and color identifier; and descriptive on-line shopping websites which include easy to understand color and shape descriptions. This future work has the potential for a tremendous impact in the lives of those with vision impairments.

5. REFERENCES
[1] Barnard, M. (2002). *fashion as communication*. London: Routledge.

[2] Camilleri, Izzy. (n.d.) *IZ Adaptive Clothing*. Retrieved May 2, 2011, from IZ Adaptive: http://www.izadaptive.com

[3] Löppönen, P., Haaksiluoto, P., & Tikka, V. (n.d.). *//Mukana*. Retrieved March 31, 2011, from Sauma: http://www.saumadesign.net/mukana.htm

[4] McDaniel, T., Panchanathan, S. (2006). A visio-haptic wearable system for assisting individuals who are blind. *SIGACCESS Access*. Comput. 86 (September 2006), 12-15.

[5] Nessly, E., & King, R. (1980). Textile Fabric and Clothing Needs of Paraplegic and Quadriplegic Persons Confined to Wheelchairs. *Journal of Rehabilitation 46.2 (1980): 63.*

Improving Public Transit Accessibility for Blind Riders: A Train Station Navigation Assistant

Markus Guentert

Hasso-Plattner-Institute for IT-Systems Engineering
Prof.-Dr.-Helmert-Str. 2-3
14482 Potsdam, Germany
markus.guentert@student.hpi.uni-potsdam.de

ABSTRACT

Blind people often depend on public transit for mobility. In interviews I learned that changing trains and orientation inside stations is a significant hindering reason for not being spontaneous. Since GPS-navigation typically cannot be used indoors, this paper focuses on building a tool for blind people to assist them in navigating inside train stations, designed for commodity hardware like the Apple iPhone.

Categories and Subject Descriptors

H.5.2 [**Information interfaces and presentation (e.g., HCI)**]: User-centered design

General Terms

Design, Human Factors

Keywords

Accessibility, blindness, public transit usability, indoor navigation, commodity hardware

1. INTRODUCTION

Technology plays an important role in supporting blind people, such as mobile phones, GPS navigation tools, screen readers and many other devices. Changing from one train to another or to a bus can be a demanding task for a blind person and is still relatively unsupported by technology. Mobility and spontaneity may be limited whenever unknown train stations are encountered. Exploring unknown train stations is time-intensive and stressful. In many cases it needs to involve a mobility trainer, or asking strangers who may provide incorrect information. This paper describes a prototype for the iPhone, which is intended to help blind people create a mental picture of new train stations.

During an interview, a mobility trainer told me that many blind people rely on individual *landmarks* to orientate themselves. Especially inside train stations they go from one to another, without having a comprehensive model of how the whole station is organized. If one gets lost or spaces are rearranged (i.e. due to construction) there is no simple way to recover from this situation. The prototype that was implemented as part of this research provides an overview for individual train stations that helps create the "big picture" of

how each station as a whole is structured. Having such information at hand a blind person may develop a better understanding of his/her environment and travel more independently and safely [1]. The prototype incorporates a smartphone into existing technology and social practices (such as mobility training) and tries to augment them. Smartphones offer great potential for blind people as they realize many use cases of expensive specialized accessibility devices [1].

2. DESIGN

Information presentation. The station description is structured in a tree, where each level represents one category: overview, floors, platforms and points of interest. Following the Visual Information Seeking Mantra "Overview first, zoom and filter, then details-on-demand" [2] the application starts with an *overview* which tells how many floors the station has and how they lay relative to the ground (e.g. +1, 0, -1, -2). This is the root information and therefore the sole item in the category overview.

When users traverse down one level – to the category *floors* – the navigation becomes two dimensional: They can either navigate through each floor and get basic information about the same (e.g. which means of transport operate on this floor) or again switch the category. Switching the category at this point would cause one to either go back to the overview or to "drill down" to platforms for the selected floor. In the category *platforms* users can navigate through all platforms on the selected floor and get more precise information about lines and their directions on each platform. From there they can further drill down to get information about *points of interest* on the selected platform (e.g. information kiosk, bakery shop, toilets). During an initial interview, two blind participants stated that points of interest help them to sense more of their environment and may provide feedback to verify where one expects to be.

The information presentation was validated with a visually impaired architect (74y) who stated that it reflects his internal mental model of a station. Another blind participant supported the information design, and stated that directions that already begin on a very detailed level hinder the process of "seeing the whole".

Interaction Design. Users swipe across the iPhone to navigate through the information structure. As the information presentation is two-dimensional, the possible directions are up, down, left, right. The screen reader function reads out the current information. Doing a swipe-gesture is simple for blind people using a touch-based input device compared to locating buttons that are distributed across the screen due to the lack of tactile feedback for the actual area of the buttons [3]. The swipe-gesture can be done one-handed, so that the other hand is free to use a white cane.

To switch the category users swipe right (drill down, get details for this) and left (move up). Within one category all information is traversed by swiping up and down. In the category floors the up/down gestures correspond to the spatial notion of moving up and down inside the station. Before a piece of information is read out, there is a noticeable but unobtrusive tone indicating the current category. The tone becomes lower in pitch the deeper one is inside the information structure (overview is the highest, point of interest the lowest). This concept was inspired by the Microsoft Windows screen reader "MAX DAISYPlayer" (http://www.dlinfo.de/content/maxdaisyplayer.php).

3. DESIGN PROCESS

Initial prototypes. After conducting semi-structured interviews with four blind people we came up with two prototypes: In Prototype 1 the user listens to a description of the whole station as continuous text *before* changing (i.e. while riding the train). The intention was to create a mental model of the station. For Prototype 2 the scenario starts *at the station* itself; the user is given directions piece-by-piece as from a standard GPS. The user consumes one-dimensional information by pressing buttons "next" and "previous".

Insights from user testing. We have tested both initial prototypes using a Wizard-of-Oz approach with two fully blind participants, 31y and 69y, at two different stations they were not aware of. While testing Prototype 2 both participants took a wrong turn (at different places). They were able to handle the situation by going back to where they started. The question that came up was, what if one instruction is misinterpreted. The blind person will go consequently wrong because he/she has no *absolute* overview of the station (he/she was only consuming *relative* directions). For the device it's not possible to notice because GPS is generally not available inside stations or imprecise. Re-routing is therefore not feasible. If such an app brought a blind person into an uncomfortable situation that caused trouble only once, there may be no more trust in a service like this. Both participants stated they would prefer having information about the station before they arrive there. At the station it is usually quite loud and cognitive capacities are reserved for other things. Prototype 1 suited well for the stations we tested, so we went further in this direction.

Final prototype. For the 2nd iteration I implemented a prototype on the iPhone, so we could test our design on a real device. We invited one of the participants (31y) to the laboratory and discussed our concept. One remarkable insight was that our data-driven "picture" of a tree-based information structure is oriented from top to bottom whereas for his perception the prototype should be turned 90° clockwise. His conception of up/down in the prototype corresponds more closely with the spatial dimension of the floors. We changed the swiping interaction accordingly.

The 3rd iteration prototype we tested at a more complex station with the other participant (69y) and also a new one, 15y. After the prototype was started the participants should explore the information structure. When realizing that they had difficulties to find certain information we helped out. About 20 minutes later they were asked to tell about the "picture" they created themselves while using the prototype. Both participants could recall the basic structure.

While discussing the prototype with two mobility trainers, both perceived the benefits of a system like this. One compared the concept with 3-d station models which are a well-established way to get an overview of a station. Drawbacks of such models, however, are that they are expensive and vulnerable to vandalism. In two further interviews with a 4th blind person (71y) and a visually impaired architect (74y) I explained the concept with a simple station. Thereafter both were able to explore the more complex station in the prototype, having understood the information presentation and interaction design.

4. FUTURE WORK

I presented the prototype to the Berlin transport association VBB and received overall positive feedback. They do have their own long-term plans for indoor station navigation, including RFID-technology, but would like to make use of this design for the end-user interface. An important question for the progress of the project is who will be able to provide more station descriptions. For the prototype I have created descriptions for two stations. Other systems, e.g. wheelmap.org, have shown that *crowdsourcing* is a scalable method for data elicitation. The problem in this system however, is that those who profit from such a service, generally cannot actively contribute in collecting information.

5. CONCLUSIONS

Changing trains and orientation inside stations can be a complex task for blind people. Before consuming detailed information a blind person profits from having a mental model, "the big picture", how individual stations are organized. I have presented a prototype for the iPhone which represents basic information about individual train stations in an interactive tree structure, in analogy with the Visual Information best practice "Overview first, details-on-demand".

6. ACKNOWLEDGMENTS

The work for this paper started as an HCI-student project I have participated in together with Stefan Hampel at HPI Potsdam. Initial interviews and design discussions were carried out together. The technical prototypes were implemented and the design validation was undertaken by myself solely. The whole project was advised by Prof. Alan Borning, University of Washington, whose visit to HPI was support in part by the US National Science Foundation under grant 0905384.

7. REFERENCES

[1] S. Azenkot, S. Prasain, A. Borning, E. Fortuna, R. E. Ladner, and J. O. Wobbrock. Enhancing independence and safety for blind and deaf-blind public transit riders. In *Proc. CHI 2011*, 2011.

[2] B. Shneiderman. The eyes have it: A task by data type taxonomy for information visualizations. In *1996 IEEE Symposium on Visual Languages*, 1996.

[3] S. K. Kane, J. P. Bigham, and J. O. Wobbrock. Slide rule: making mobile touch screens accessible to blind people using multi-touch interaction techniques. In *Proceedings of the ACM SIGACCESS Conference on Computers and Accessibility (ASSETS '08)*, 2008.

Kinerehab: A Kinect-based System for Physical Rehabilitation — A Pilot Study for Young Adults with Motor Disabilities

Jun-Da Huang

Department of Electronic Engineering, Chung Yuan Christian University, Taiwan

sky1987a@gmail.com

ABSTRACT

This study used Microsoft's Kinect motion sensor to develop an intelligent rehabilitation system. Through discussion with physical therapists at the Kaohsiung County Special Education School, researchers understood that students with physical disabilities typically lack enthusiasm for rehabilitation, hindering their recovery of limb function and ability to care for themselves. Because therapists must simultaneously care for numerous students, there is also a shortage of human resources. Using fieldwork and recommendations by physical therapists, this study applied the proposed system to students with muscle atrophy and cerebral palsy, and assisted them in physical therapy. The system increased their motivation to participate in rehabilitation and enhanced the efficiency of rehab activities, greatly contributing to the recovery of muscle endurance and reducing the workload of therapists.

Categories and Subject Descriptors

J.3 [Computer Applications] LIFE AND MEDICAL SCIENCES:Health

General Terms: Experimentation, Human Factors.

Keywords

physical rehabilitation, motor disabilities, Kinect.

1. INTRODUCTION
1.1 Problem and Motivation

People with motor disabilities experience limitations in fine motor control, strength, and range of motion. These deficits can dramatically limit their ability to perform daily tasks [1], such as dressing, hair combing, and bathing, independently. In addition, these deficits can reduce participation in leisure and social activities, and even jeopardize occupational perspectives. Participating in occupational therapy can help people with motor disabilities overcome the limitations they experience. Research suggests that repetitive exercises can sufficiently stimulate brain to remodel itself and provide better motor control. However, the number of exercises in a therapy session is typically insufficient. One study indicates that only 31 % of people with motor disabilities perform the exercises as recommended [2], which can result in negative consequences such as obesity-related chronic health conditions. People often cite a lack of motivation as an impediment to them performing the exercises regularly. One solution to this issue is staff intervention; however, it may not be viable in terms of time and cost. Therefore, identifying motivating and effective method of encouraging people with motor disabilities to perform exercises is crucial in helping them retain or enhance their motor control and increase their independence.

This study aims to use pervasive computing to improve the motor proficiency and quality of life of people with motor disabilities, such as cerebral palsy, and multiple disabilities.

1.2 Background and Related Work

Students with cerebral palsy must undergo continual rehabilitation to prevent their muscles from atrophying, and to learn how to perform daily tasks such as brushing their hair and teeth. One therapist typically conducts the rehabilitation activities with five students at a time. During rehabilitation, the therapist must personally monitor whether each student's movements are reaching a specific standard; thus, the therapist can only rehabilitate one student at a time. Students lack enthusiasm to participate in the tedious rehabilitation process [3], resulting in continued muscle atrophy and insufficient muscle endurance.

Virtual reality and motion-based games have been used for rehabilitation [4, 5]. However, virtual reality requires wearing a number of sensors on the body, causing discomfort. This study developed a Kinect –based rehabilitation system to assist therapists in rehabilitating students. The proposed system uses Kinect sensors to detect students' movements and determine whether their movements are correct. The system also includes an interactive interface to enhance students' motivation, interest, and perseverance with rehabilitation. Details of students' rehabilitation conditions are also automatically recorded in the system, allowing therapists to review students' rehabilitation progress quickly. This system enhances the efficiency of rehabilitation, which increases the students' muscle endurance and ability to perform daily tasks independently.

2. SYSTEM DESIGN

The proposed system uses Microsoft's Kinect motion sensor with an integrated database, video instruction, and voice reminders to form an intelligent rehabilitation system. See Figure 1. We discussed the design with therapists. The interactive interface is particularly emphasized, increasing students' motivation, interest, and perseverance with rehabilitation. Kinect automatically detects the student's joint position, and uses the data to determine whether the students' movements have reached the rehabilitation standard (for example, raise both hands 10 cm above the shoulders). Using this system, students can gauge the accuracy of their movements during rehabilitation. The system also provides step-by-step video instruction. When the demonstration of one movement is complete, the video pauses and waits for the user to complete the movement before playing the next movement video. The video interaction enhances students' motivation to engage in physical rehabilitation. The personalized movement menu allows therapists to adjust the rehab movements according to the conditions of the individual student. Students must perform various movements and achieve different standards in the separate stages of rehabilitation. The personalized menu provides therapists with greater flexibility to adjust the rehab program according to the individual needs of students. The system also automatically records students' rehabilitation conditions, allowing students to review the rehabilitation program, and providing therapists with a reference to monitor students' progression.

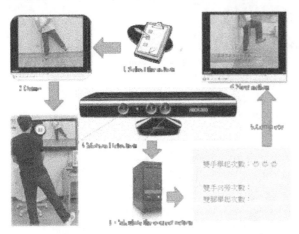

Figure 1. The Kinerehab System for physical rehabilitation

3. EXPERIMENT

3.1 Setting of the Kinerehab System

This study tested the intelligent rehabilitation system at the Kaohsiung County Special Education School. Kinect was connected to a notebook computer on which the rehabilitation system was installed, and a VGA line was used to output the image through a projector. The rehabilitation movements were as follows: lift both arms to the front, lift both arms to the side, and lift both arms upwards. Each movement was repeated six times, with the three movements forming one cycle; the students performed three cycles. Researchers recorded the frequency of accurate movement detection and the frequency of error of the Kinect system. After the exercise was completed, students were questioned as to whether this system enhanced their interest in rehabilitation.

3.2 Participants

With long term observation, the therapist decided that John, Peter, Sherry, and Ben were more ready to participate in experiments than the other trainees were. The profiles of the four participants are summarized in Table 1.

Table 1. Profiles of four subjects

Name	Gender	Age	Condition
John	Male	16	Cerebral palsy; inflexibility of upper limb movement; insufficient muscle endurance;
Peter	Male	17	Cerebral palsy; inflexibility of limb movements; insufficient muscle endurance;
Sherry	Female	16	Muscle atrophy; insufficient muscle endurance; can stand with support;
Ben	Male	16	Cerebral palsy; inflexibility of limb movements;

3.3 Result

As shown in Fig. 2, the rate of accurate detection of movement by the Kinect system was over 80 %. The reason 100 % accuracy could not be achieved was that the wheelchairs and walkers used by students influenced the judgment of the Kinect system. Kinect identified the aids as part of the students' bodies, resulting in a higher error rate. The students were extremely interested in the system and wanted to continue using it even after the experiment was complete. Both therapists and students indicated that the system increased their motivation to participate in rehabilitation. Some suggestions were also provided: the students wanted us to increase the number of users, allowing two users to engage in rehabilitation activities simultaneously. This would make rehabilitation more enjoyable and include the benefits of peer encouragement. The therapist also favorably assessed the system, indicating it would reduce her workload and improve the effectiveness of rehabilitation for students. The therapist also suggested that the system incorporate games to enhance the entertainment provided by the system. Increasing the accuracy of Kinect identification and enhancing the entertaining and amusing elements of the system are targets for future improvement.

Figure 2. Experimental Result

4. REFERENCES

[1] C. Patten, J. Lexell, and H. E. Brown, "Weakness and strength training in persons with poststroke hemiplegia: Rationale, method, and efficacy," *J. Rehabil. Res. Develop.*, vol. 41, no. 3A, pp. 293-312 May 2004

[2] Shaughnessy, M., Resnick, B. & Macko, R. (2006). Testing a model of post-stroke exercise behavior. *Rehabilitation Nursing*. 31, 1 (Feb. 2006), p.15-21.

[3] Marclean, N., Pound, P., Wolfe, C. and Rudd, A., "Qualitative analysis of stroke patients' motivation for rehabilitation". BMJ, vol.321, Oct. 28, 2000 , p. 1051-1054

[4] Jack, D., Boian, R., Merians, A., Adamovich, S.V., Tremaine, M., Recce, M. , Burdea ,G. C. & Poizner, H., "A Virtual Reality-Based Exercise Program for Stroke Rehabilitation," "Assets'00 Proceedings of the fourth international ACM conference on Assistive technologies", Nov. 13-15, 2000 , p. 56-63.

[5] Arteaga, S., Chevalier, J., Coile, A., Hill, A.W., Sali, S., Sudhakhrisnan, S.& Kurniawan, S., "Low-Cost Accelerometry-Based Posture Monitoring System for Stroke Survivors", Assets '08: Proceedings of the 10th international ACM SIGACCESS conference on Computers and accessibility, Oct. 13–15, 2008, p. 243-244.

Providing Haptic Feedback Using the Kinect

Brandon Shrewsbury
Department of Computer Science
University of West Georgia
Brandon.shrewsbury@gmail.com

ABSTRACT

Interpreting surroundings through the senses often relies on visual channels for a full interpretation of the environment. Our approach substitutes this use of vision by integrating haptic feedback with the sensory data from the depth camera system packaged within the Microsoft Kinect.

Categories and Subject Descriptors

K.4.2 [**Social Issues**]: Assistive technologies for persons with disabilities

General Terms

Design, Human Factors

Keywords

Kinect, haptic feedback, assistive technology, haptic glove

1. PROBLEM AND MOTIVATION

The World Health Organization estimates about 284 million people are visually impaired worldwide; of these, 39 million of them are blind [7]. Many of these individuals are able to live and interact independently but much of the visually impaired populace suffers from severe vision problems which degrade their ability to easily and efficiently live autonomously. A specific issue within the disabilities associated with vision impairments is an inability to interpret surroundings from moderate distances. This impairment can cause those affected to require the use of guide dogs or canes to navigate and to detect objects within a small radius around the user. This project aims to create a new way to supplement this loss of depth perception in a way not previously developed by incorporating a low cost, depth image system. In this research we aim to help those affected with certain types of visual impairment by providing a physical sense of the environment using an inexpensive gaming peripheral.

2. BACKGROUND AND RELATED WORK

Currently the visually impaired have two standard resources available to them, mobility canes and guide dogs. Both have proven to be effective in providing the user with navigational assistance but neither provides an effective means to allow the user to fully interpret his or her surroundings. The cane is used to locate obstacles within a small distance and can be invaluable in interpreting terrain. Additionally, some users employ echolocation techniques using the cane to provide spatial awareness [3]. The second resource, guide dogs, provides excellent help in navigating in diverse environments. This puts

the user in a passive role, forcing him or her to rely on the guide dog, and shifting the need for spatial awareness on to the animal. Using the depth camera within the Kinect to interpret the surroundings, the user will have access to additional information that would otherwise not be available; including the distance, height, and width of obstacles in his or her surroundings.

Using haptic feedback to provide spatial awareness has been implemented using a variety of techniques [1][2][4][8]. Of which, the Artificial Vision Systems is closely related to this project [2]. We are proposing the replacement of the stereoscopic vision with the Kinect. The Kinect's wide availability, large feature set, and ability to work in low light environments make it an attractive choice. The haptic device used in this research is a combination of the tactile display developed for the lower back [4] and the haptic glove developed for wayfinding [8]. It uses a 4x4 matrix that spans the ventral side of the fingers. This area provides a dense population of mechanoreceptors [5].

3. APPROACH AND EVALUATION

The process of providing spatial feedback to the user was divided into three parts, sensing the environment through an RGBd, or Red Green Blue plus Depth, camera system, processing the sensor's data into a usable form, and creating an effective delivery system [Figure 3.1].

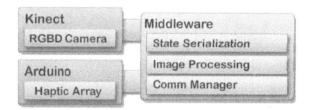

Figure 3.1: System Flow Chart

3.1 Kinect

The Kinect is used to calculate the distance from the user to objects within its field of view. It was chosen based on its wide availability as a low cost gaming peripheral.

3.2 Middleware

The middleware maps the Kinect depth data to signal levels recognizable by the haptic device. The depth image is converted to grayscale then resized to match the dimensions of the haptic glove [Figure 3.2]. This process uses the nearest neighbor algorithm to limit the processing time. Additionally, the depth image is downscaled to 1 byte per pixel to decrease transmission times to the haptic glove. During the downscaling process, low and high limits are used to remove unwanted data from the depth image. Once the information is done processing it is pushed to the haptic device via wireless module.

Figure 3.2: Depth Image Conversion to Grayscale
(RGB image provided for reference)

Figure 3.3: Threshold Manipulation and Resampling

3.3 Delivery System

The device constructed was designed as a wearable vibrotactile feedback system that utilizes buzzer motors to alert the user of objects within the Kinect's field of view. The haptic device lines each buzzer along individual sections of the finger, resting a bottom row against the palm of the hand [Figure 3.2]. Although cross-pollination can be felt between

Figure 3.4: Haptic Feedback Device

the second and third columns of each row at full strength, we hope that the user will be able to adapt with minimal ambiguity by interpreting the surrounding buzzers. Each motor represents an individual pixel of the resized depth image received from the middleware.

4. EVALUATION

All testing involving outside participants is pending acceptance from the Institutional Review Board at the University Of West Georgia. Future testing has been divided into 2 segments: Quadrant testing and a laser tag segment. Due to the unavailability of a sample of severely visually impaired individuals, sighted blindfolded users will be asked to participate.

4.1 Section Testing

Section testing focuses on testing the effectiveness of the Kinect in a static environment as well as our tactile feedback device on the hand. This test analyzes the user's interpretation of the depth image via the vibrotactile feedback system.

Objects matching the size of the individual sections of the resized depth image will be placed within the Kinect's field of view. The user will then indicate the quadrant of the item based solely off of feedback from the haptic device. Randomly selected users will receive arbitrary data in lieu of the Kinect's depth image as a control. Accuracy and time taken to respond will be evaluated.

4.2 Dynamic Environment Testing

Dynamic Environment Testing involves giving the user a toy laser pistol. In this instance, the user interprets the response from the haptic feedback device in order to locate an "opponent" and fire at the opponents laser vest. The scoring function within the laser system allows for a simple measure of accuracy. This test will allow us to assess the coordination between hand movements and

the internal spatial awareness developed from the interpreted depth image.

During this test the user stays in a static location and rotates in an attempt to locate the opponent. Once a successful hit is recorded, the opponent will move to a new location. The user is allowed to fire on the opponent during this transition period. Accuracy, time taken to locate the opponent, time taken to hit the opponents vest, and overall time will be evaluated.

5. CONCLUSION

Our work has resulted in a new combination of a low cost depth camera and a vibrotactile feedback system which allows users to interpret surroundings without the use of visual sensing. The Ability to identify objects locations and dimensions via the Kinect shows the possibility of the system being used to provide navigational assistance and object avoidance.

6. ACKNOWLEDGMENTS

I would like to thank Dr. Lewis Baumstark for the invaluable guidance and feedback through the development process.

7. REFERENCES

[1] Bach-y-Rita, P., Kaczmarek, A., Tyler, E., and Garcia-Lara, J. 1998. Form perception with a 49-point electro-tactile stimulus array on the tongue: a technical note. *Journal of Rehabilitation Research and Development*, 35, 4 (Oct. 1998), 427-430.

[2] Costa, G., Gusberti, A., Graffigna, J., Guzzo, M., and Nasisi, O. 2007. Mobility and Orientation Aid for Blind Persons Using Artificial Vision. *Journal of Physics*, 90 (2007), 012090 (9pp). DOI= http://iopscience.iop.org/1742-6596/90/1/012090/

[3] Despre, O., Boudard, D., Candas, V., and Dufour, A. 2005. Enhanced self-localization by auditory cues in blind humans, *Disability and Rehabilitation*, 27, 13 (July. 2005), 753-759. DOI=http://informahealthcare.com/doi/abs/10.1080/0963828 0400014865

[4] Jones, L.A., Lockyer, B., Piateski, E. Tactile Display and Vibrotactile Pattern Recognition on the Torso. *Advanced Robotics,* 20, 12 (2006), Springer, 1359–1374. DOI= http://dx.doi.org/10.1163/156855306778960563

[5] Purves, D., Augustine, G. J., and Fitzpatrick, D. 2001. The Somatic Sensory System: Mechanoreceptors Specialized to Receive Tactile Information. *Neuroscience*. 2nd edition. Sinauer Associates, Sunderland, Ma.

[6] Wilska A., 1954. On the Vibrational Sensitivity in Different Regions of the Body Surface. *Acta Physiologica Scandinavica*. 18, 31(2-3), 284-9. DOI= http://www.ncbi.nlm.nih.gov/pubmed/13197098

[7] Visual impairment and blindness: Fact Sheet N°282. *World Health Organization.* Retrieved July, 2011 http://www.who.int/mediacentre/factsheets/fs282/en/.

[8] Zelek J. S., Bromley S., Asmar D., and Thompson D. 2003. A haptic glove as a tactile-vision sensory substitution for wayfinding. *Journal of Visual Impairment & Blindness*, 97, 10 (Oct. 03), 1–24. DOI=http://dx.doi.org/10.1145/1463160.1463179

StopFinder: Improving the Experience of Blind Public Transit Riders with Crowdsourcing

Sanjana Prasain

Computer Science and Engineering, University of Washington
Seattle, WA, USA
+1 (206) 604 2030
pras5181@uw.edu

ABSTRACT

I developed a system for mobile devices for crowdsourcing landmarks around bus stops for blind transit riders. The main focus of my research is to develop a method to provide reliable and accurate information about landmarks around bus stops to blind transit riders. In addition to that, my research focuses on understanding how access to such information affects their use of public transportation.

ACM Classification Keywords

H.5 Information interfaces and presentation (I.7), H.5.2 User Interfaces (D.2.2, H.1.2, I.3.6), User-centered design.

General Terms

Design, Reliability, Human Factors.

Keywords

Blind, Crowdsourcing, Smart phone, Accessibility, Public transit, Independence.

1. INTRODUCTION

People travel to work, schools, hospitals etc to lead their daily lives. Most people can accommodate this need by driving their personal vehicle. However, people with severe visual impairments cannot drive. Thus, they have to rely on the public transit system to accomplish these activities.

The usability of the public transit system is, therefore, of crucial importance to people who are blind. One major challenge blind people experience when using public transit is finding the exact location of bus stops[1]. Thus, my work focuses on enabling people to find bus stops more easily to improve their experience of using public transit.

I am using the technique of crowdsourcing to provide information about non-visual landmarks around bus stops to enable blind public transit riders to find them more easily when navigating with a cane or a guide dog. The crowdsourced information includes whether the stop has shelters, garbage cans, and benches, and the position of one with respect to the others. The blind users will be able to get information as well as provide information about various landmarks around bus stops that will be discussed in more detail in this paper.

2. MOTIVATION

Before working on this research project, we developed GoBraille,[1] two related Braille-based applications that provide information about buses and bus stops where we implemented a primitive system for crowdsourcing landmarks. GoBraille consisted of Braille note-taker that used the capabilities of an android phone to provide the information about bus stops. The system was able to display information in Braille display as well as speech depending on the preference of the user. In that work, we conducted interviews with blind people to understand how they use the public transit system, and how to make the information about their transit available to them to enhance their safety and independence. Through user studies, we realized the importance of reliable, accurate and concise information about various landmarks to reach to the proper bus stop in addition to getting information about exact bus stops location. Also, there was concern related to the cost of Braille note-taker.

Therefore, based on those interviews and studies, I started on this research project to initiate a new platform for providing essential information using just a mobile device. This would enable the blind users to get this information on their smart phone and don't require them to possess Braille note-taker. I have designed two different systems: one for people with vision and another for blind people. For acquiring the goal of accurate information through larger scale and coverage, I am using iPhone, which is the most widely used smart-phone by blind public transit riders using text-to-speech.

3. DESIGNING A SYSTEM

Providing the information about the landmarks around bus stops require a lot of data. Therefore, I decided to use the already existing app for transit riders with vision and integrate my system to it for getting larger set of data to provide to blind users.

Below is the description of different systems for two types of users:

3.1 For Public Transit Riders with Vision

For sighted people, I am integrating my system with OneBusAway,[2] which provides real time bus arrival information. This will enable the users of OneBusAway to provide information about non-visual landmarks for blind users to use while OneBusAway users are waiting for their buses. Considering the limited time they will have to fill in the information, the system uses a graphical, game-like application with movable icons of shelters, benches etc that can be placed over a static map of the bus stop to model the layout of the stop.

Once the information is received from OneBusAway users, the visual data is transferred into the descriptive text useful for the blind users.

3.2 For Blind Public Transit Riders

For blind users, I created a system that enables them to get landmarks information around the nearby bus stops from iPhone. In addition to this, blind people can also contribute to provide information about landmarks through a non-graphical interface. Since one of the primary focuses has been the ease of using the system, the application is designed based on interviews with blind people. Thus, the interface consists of mostly multiple-choice questionnaires that are convenient for them to fill in a short time while waiting for a bus.

Along with landmarks information, the system provides blind users their current location, nearest bus stop and real time bus arrival information for the buses at the nearest stop. They can use the built-in text-to-speech on an iPhone to access the interface of this application.

Since the information comes from two different groups of people, a rating system is used to analyze the accuracy of the information.

4. FIELD DEPLOYMENT AND USER STUDIES

I plan to deploy the OneBusAway integration first so that there will be information to provide to blind public transit riders when they start using StopFinder. Though this design is based on interviews with blind people, I plan to conduct additional user studies after deploying both systems to improve the design, analyze the better way to present this information about bus stops, and evaluate how access to this information change the usage of public transportation.

I also want to analyze effectiveness of my system and understand ways to improve my design for the use of blind users. Also more user studies will help in analyzing how to present the data to the blind users. I would also like to find a reliable way to rate the data that will ensure reliability of system, which will be benefitted by more user studies as well. One of the other things I am interested to evaluate is how this system will change the usage behavior of blind users towards public transportation. Will this make them use public transportation more often? Will this increase their reliability on public transportation? Will this system make them more independent while using public transportation? These are some questions I am interested to analyze through user studies.

5. ACKNOWLEDGMENTS

I would like to thank ACM SIGCHI for giving me opportunity to present at ASSETS 2011 and Professor Alan Borning and Shiri Azenkot for providing all the necessary resources for this research. This research has been supported in part by NSF grants IIS-0705898 and CNS-0905384 and a Mary Gates Research Scholarship for undergraduate.

6. REFERENCES

[1] Azenkot, S., Prasain, S., Borning, A., Fortuna, E., Ladner, R. E. and Wobbrock, J. O. Enhancing Independence and Safety for Blind and Deaf-Blind Public Transit Riders. In *Proceedings of the SIGCHI conference on Human Factors in computing systems* (CHI '11).

[2] Ferris, B., Watkins, K., and Borning, A. (2010). OneBusAway: Results from providing real-time arrival information for public transit. *Proc. CHI 2010*. New York: ACM Press, 1807-181.

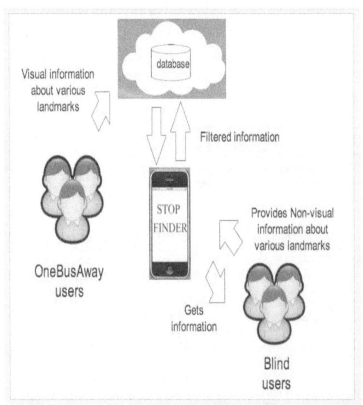

Figure 1: StopFinder: An Integration of Different Parts of the System

The PhonicStick – A Joystick to Generate Novel Words Using Phonics

Rolf Black
University of Dundee, School of Computing
Dundee, DD1 4HN, Scotland, UK
+44 1382 386530
rolfblack@computing.dundee.ac.uk

ABSTRACT

Current Voice Output Communication Aids (VOCAs) give little support for playing with sounds and blending these into words. This paper presents a joystick that can be used to access six different letter sounds (phonics) and blend them into short words. Seven children (five with some degree of physical and/or learning disability) showed their ability to use the device after only one 20 minutes introduction session.

Categories and Subject Descriptors

H5.2 **[Information Interfaces and Presentation]**: User Interfaces – *Input devices and strategies*; *Interaction styles*; K.3.1 **[Computers and Education]**: Computer Uses in Education; K.4.2 **[Computers and Society]**: Social Issues – *Assistive technologies for persons with disabilities*; H.1.2 **[Models and Principles]**: User/Machine Systems – *Human factors*; *Human information processing*;

General Terms: Experimentation, Human Factors.

Keywords: Human-Computer Interaction (HCI), joystick, phonological awareness, phonemes, phonics, literacy, Augmentative and Alternative Communication (AAC), education, learning, cerebral palsy, disability, speech output, voice output.

1. INTRODUCTION

Not being able to speak can impact on later language development and specifically on literacy learning [1]. Researchers agree that phonemic awareness is an important predictor of the ability to learn reading and writing and Voice Output Communication Aids (VOCAs) have been used to support literacy learning. Few past systems allowed for access to novel words using sound based methods [2, p. 60, 3].

2. CONCEPT

The author's observations from his experience in working with children with severe physical impairments were about the contrast of successfully driving an electric wheelchair by means of a joystick and problems in physically accessing a communication device using touch screen or switch access. The joystick has previously been investigated for text input [4, 5]. For access to sounds a stylus text input method by Perlin [6] was adapted (Figure 1).

Synthetic Phonics, as endorsed by the UK government for teaching literacy [7], and based on the sounds of around 42-44 letters and letter combinations was chosen to provide the sounds for generating words. The programmes usually start by introducing six or seven

phonics which allow creating a number of short words when blending the sounds together. For the purpose of investigating the feasibility of playing with sounds to generate words the first stage Phonics of the Jolly Phonics teaching programme were used[1]: /s/, /a/, /t/, /i/, /p/ and /n/.

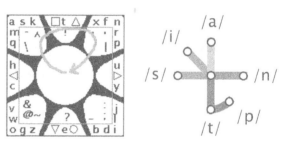

Figure 1. Quikwriting, selecting 'k' (left) and PhonicStick, six-phonic-map (right)

The six phonics were mapped on joystick movements in a way to allow the investigation of all access movements (Figure 1): forward/backwards, left right, diagonal and combined (backwards and along circumference). In order to select a phonic the user moves the joystick along the given path and then back to the centre, e.g. /p/ by tilting the joystick backwards and then along the circumference to the right for 45° and back to the centre.

Different methods for blending the sounds into words were explored (e.g. with a speech synthesizing chip [8]) but it was decided to use high quality voice recordings to allow for sufficient speech quality.

3. THE PHONICSTICK

The first PhonicStick prototype used switched joysticks (see Figure 2). Two non-latching switches allow for playback or clearing of the selected/blended phonics. The device is connected via serial port and audio cable to a PC for playback of the recordings.

All phonics (letter sounds) and all their possible combinations[2] for two and three phonic words were recorded by a native English speaker and saved as wav files. The files were played back from a laptop with the loudspeaker being located in the PhonicStick.

The user gets immediate feedback of the sound selected with the joystick and can choose to hear the blended version of previously selected phonics by pressing the green playback button.

---

[1] http://jollylearning.co.uk

[2] This included "non-desirable" words (such as '/tit/' and '/pis/') which are usually omitted on standard VOCA vocabulary, but have the potential to greatly increase motivation of device use.

Figure 2. The PhonicStick

4. EVALUATION AND RESULTS

An evaluation was set out to answer the following questions: 1) Would children be able to remember the movements required to access the six phonics without being shown a visual mapping representation? 2) Would children grasp the concept of "collecting" sounds sequentially which could be blended into words?

4.1 Methodology

During the evaluation seven children were introduced to the PhonicStick (see Table 1). Five had some degree of physical and/or learning disability, three of whom have cerebral palsy and use joystick controlled wheelchairs, all had little emerging literacy. The typically developing children were both literate. All children were given two 20-minute sessions, alone or in pairs, on subsequent days (where possible) to learn how to use the device. Visual and spoken prompts were used to ask the children to reproduce phonics, play a game by generating short words and to produce their own words using the PhonicStick.

Table 1. Participants

Age/ Sex	Aetiol.	Mobility Aids	Comm.
10:10 M	Cerebral palsy	EPW with joystick	Clear speech
12:6 M	Cerebral palsy	EPW with joystick	Clear unaided yes/no, some spoken words and some Makaton signs, VOCA
11:11 M	Cerebral palsy	EPW with joystick	Clear un-aided yes/no, some spoken phrases, VOCA
6:7 M	Down's Syndr.	None	Good range of spoken vocabulary (poor intelligibility), previous Makaton user
15:1 M	Dancing Eye Syndr.	Walking frame	Clear speech
9:4 M	Typical	n/a	Clear speech
9:6 M	Typical	n/a	Clear speech

4.2 Results

All seven children were able to retrieve all six phonics in order to sound out words within a game scenario after one training session. Although, two children experienced difficulties in accessing some of the phonics positions due to their physical disabilities, they were able to demonstrate that they knew the position of all six phonics. One participant demonstrated how the PhonicStick could be used as an augmentative aid by intuitively using it to clarify her dysarthric speech when asked to identify a phonic. The typically developing children initiated the generation of novel words such as their own names. One child with cerebral palsy who was initially not very interested in the device demonstrated a similar ability some time after the study when he was invited to 'play' with the device. This was particularly interesting since the word he generated was a "non-desirable" word which he produced during an official event. He visibly enjoyed the resulting attention from his environment.

4.3 Discussion

This study showed the potential of the PhonicStick to give non-speaking children access to playing with sounds and enabling them to generate novel words without the need of being literate. This is in contrast to current VOCAs, which only allow access to novel words via letter input. Users can directly listen to the blending of letter sounds to create words, a method used in literacy teaching and so far not accessible to non-speaking individuals.

5. NEXT STEPS

Further work will need to address the remaining access difficulties due to physical impairments, e.g. by using haptic feedback and support or different access methods such as eye gaze. Currently more studies are investigating in more detail, how different groups of children (pre-school, Down's syndrome) can use the Phonic-Stick and how different Phonic layouts and feedback methods can improve usage of the device.

6. ACKNOWLEDGMENTS

I would like to thank my supervisors Dr Annalu Waller and Jeremy Linskell. I would also like to thank Capability Scotland for their support, both financially and by giving me access to their schools for user evaluation; Dundee Council for giving me access to their schools; Ruli Manurung for his Java program linking my PhonicStick prototype to a PC; Graham Pullin for his suggestions on the phonic mapping; and last but not least all the children, their parents and staff at their schools for the endless support, enthusiasm and time during the evaluations.

7. REFERENCES

[1] von Tetzchner, S. and H. Martinsen, *Augmentative and alternative communication.* 2nd ed. 2000, London: Whurr. 250.

[2] Glennen, S.L., *Augmentative and Alternative Communication Systems*, in *Handbook of Augmentative and Alternative Communication*, S.L. Glennen and D.C. DeCoste, Editors. 1997, Singular Publishing Group, Inc.: San Diego.

[3] Goodenough-Trepagnier, C. and P. Prather, *Communication Systems for the Nonvocal Based on Frequent Phoneme Sequences.* Journal of Speech and Hearing Research, 1981. **24**: p. 322-329.

[4] Wobbrock, J.O., B.A. Myers, and H.H. Aung, *Joystick Text Entry with Date Stamp, Selection Keyboard, and EdgeWrite*, in *Computer Human Interaction.* 2004.

[5] Rinott, M., *Audio-Tactile.* 2004, Interaction Design Institute Ivrea.

[6] Perlin, K. *Quikwriting: Continuous Stylus-based Text Entry.* in *User Interface Software and Technology (UIST).* 1998. San Francisco.

[7] Rose, J., *Independent review of the teaching of early reading*, D.o.E.a. Skills, Editor. 2006, DfES Publications.

[8] Magnevation, *SpeakJet TM, Natural Speech & Complex Sound Synthesizer, User's Manual.* 2004.

The TaskTracker: Assistive Technology for Task Completion

Victoria E. Hribar
Biomedical Engineering Department
Virginia Commonwealth University
Richmond, Virginia 23284
001-804-828-7839

hribarve@vcu.edu

ABSTRACT

A cognitive impairment can restrict the independence an individual has over their own life. Commonly, attention deficits affect individuals with cognitive impairments and make completion of everyday tasks difficult. While many technologies exist to assist this group in memory storage and retrieval, these individuals could also benefit from technology focused on time management and assistance with task completion. The TaskTracker has been created for this purpose by incorporating several features focused on task completion into one useful Android™ smart phone application. A progress bar, alarm reminders, and a motivational message have been combined to motivate task completion and time management rather than task memory alone.

Categories and Subject Descriptors

K.4.2 [**Computing Milieux**]: Social Issues– *Assistive technologies for persons with disabilities*

General Terms

Design, Human Factors

Keywords

Assistive technology, cognitive impairment, task completion, time management

1. INTRODUCTION

The most common cognitive impairment following brain injuries is an attention deficit which can be characterized as a "tendency to drift from intended goals." A study, where traumatic brain injured (TBI) patients completed self evaluations, identified the most frequent patient complaint from this group is decreased attention and concentration rate [2]. Attention deficits also characterize such cognitive disorders as Attention Deficit Disorder (ADD) and Attention Deficit Hyperactive Disorder (ADHD) [1]. Selective attention is particularly important in executing everyday tasks, and those with attention deficits will often need assistance with focusing on one stimulus, the chosen task, and filtering out distractions [1].

Assistive technology for cognition (ATC) aims to help individuals compensate for cognitive impairments by allowing increased independence and making everyday task completion more manageable. Two categories of ATC are time-management devices and prompting systems. Time management devices are meant to aid in executing daily, time-dependent tasks, and prompting systems provide feedback to help a user accomplish a task [1]. However, there are no existing devices that combine these two components to specifically aid in daily, time-dependent task completion.

In addition, the greatest predictor of whether a new user will adopt various ATC is how well suited the device is for the user and their ordinary environment [5]. With the exponential rise in portable and handheld technologies, rehabilitative devices no longer need to exist as a separate entity from popular devices an individual may already carry. Mainstream devices such as smart phones can provide a user the rehabilitative applications they need as well as the standard programs they desire such as internet, email, and games [3]. This is more convenient and cost-effective for users.

Currently, a few systems exist as stand-alone devices. One stand-alone prompting system, the MotivAider, costs nearly sixty dollars and provides the user with motivational reminders to change their behavior [4]. While a useful aid, the MotivAider may also inconvenience the user as a separate device must be carried. The WatchMinder was designed for people with attention deficits and utilizes a reminder system with 30 programmable alarms for remembering tasks. Personalized messages can also be programmed to help with behavior change and self-monitoring [1]. This system not only exists as a separate device, but it also contains no progress system for tracking time during a task.

Some smart phone applications like Comprehensive Project Management allow users to plan their projects in advance by estimating a finish date and updating the current progress of the project which can be viewed at any time [4]. This, and similar applications, provide users the opportunity to track progress of long term goals but do not focus on progress of short term goals such as completion of a current task. Many smart phone applications exist to keep to-do lists or appointments such as the 2 Do smart phone application [4]. This program, and others like it, give the user alarms and reminders to remember to do tasks but will not help with time management during the task.

2. APPLICATION

As discussed above, ATC smart phone applications and stand-alone devices already exist, but current ATC does not provide a comprehensive solution for aiding those with attention deficits in task completion. The TaskTracker utilizes smart phone technology to create a unique rehabilitative application. This system was designed to track everyday tasks with an alarm and motivational progress system to aid in time management and maintain the selective attention of an individual throughout a given task. This application has currently been developed for an affordable, multifunction Android™ smart phone. This also provides the user the opportunity to use a single device to combine their rehabilitative needs with their everyday needs.

The TaskTracker is novel in its combination of several key features of time-management and prompting systems which would be most useful to those with attention deficits, specifically those struggling with selective attention during daily tasks: 1) a progress bar to visually represent time passed and time remaining, 2) alarm reminders to get the user's attention in case they have become distracted, and 3) a motivational message to urge them to keep working towards task completion. These combine uniquely into one application aimed at tracking a specific task that the user is currently working to complete. With a single task in mind, the interface was designed based on other ATC smart phone applications but with a simple, single screen to prevent users from becoming distracted or lost in the complexity of the program. While the technology was designed with those with cognitive impairments in mind, this application will prove useful to any individual who desires assistance and motivation in completing time-dependent tasks.

When the user starts the TaskTracker application, they immediately view the intuitive user interface screen where they are asked to input the task, time to complete the task, and the number of reminders required, as seen in Figure 1. For example, a student might input: Study for Math Test, 1.5 hours, 6 reminders. At the appropriate alarm time, the reminder screen pops up with the progress of the current task in pictorial form, a motivational message which can be individualized by the user or caregiver, and a pop-up message which reminds the user of the amount of time remaining to finish the task. This information can also be presented orally using text-to-speech, according to user preference. An example of this can be seen in Figure 2. In the above example, the student will receive these reminders with feedback every fifteen minutes while they study until the hour and a half has passed or until they have finished the task. The purpose of the application is to provide several useful features of other ATC: repeated reminders, a progress system, and motivation throughout a period of time to aid in task completion. All of these features are thought to promote task completion and keep the users attention on their current task.

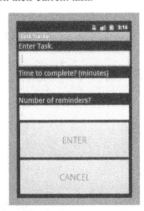

Figure 1. TaskTracker User Input Screen

3. FUTURE WORK

Validation tests will be performed in order to assess the usefulness of this application in assisting task completion in a given amount of time. Subjects will be asked to perform several tasks with and without the use of the TaskTracker. Time to complete the tasks in each case will be compared. Participants will also be asked a number of questions regarding the helpfulness and convenience of this technology. Individuals with cognitive impairments will be recruited as subjects in order to judge the usability of the application by the targeted group.

In the future, an iPhone® version of this application will also be developed in order to increase availability of this technology.

Figure 2. TaskTracker Progress Screen

4. ACKNOWLEDGMENT

I would like to thank Dr. Dianne T.V. Pawluk, Chelsea M. Powell, and the VCU Honors College for their support.

5. REFERENCES

[1] Cook, Albert M., and Jan Miller Polgar. *Cook & Hussey's Assistive Technologies: Principles and Practice.* 3rd. St. Louis: Mosby Inc., 2008. 337-369. Print.

[2] Dockree, Paul M., Simon P. Kelly, Richard A.P. Roche, Michael J. Hogan, Richard B. Reilly, and Ian H. Robertson. "Behavioural and physiological impairments of sustained attention after traumatic brain injury." *Cognitive Brain Research.* 20. (2004): 403-414. Print.

[3] Hart, Tessa, Regina Buchhofer, and Monica Vaccaro. "Portable Electronic Devices as Memory and Organizational Aids After Traumatic Brain Injury: A Consumer Survey Study." *Journal of Head Trauma Rehabilitation.* 19.5 (2004): 351-365. Print.

[4] Ostergren, Jennifer, Jerica Montgomery, and Megan Carey. "Assistive Technology for Impairments in Attention, Memory, and Executive Function: Current Technologies and Available Evidence." *California Speech-Language Hearing Association.* CSHA, 25 Mar 2011. Web. 28 Jun 2011. <http://www.csha.org/pdf/2011Convention/Friday/OSTERG REN-SC3.pdf>.

[5] Sohlberg, McKay Moore. "Assistive Technology for Cognition." *The ASHA Leader.* American Speech-Language-Hearing Association, 15 Feb 2011. Web. 28 Jun 2011. http://www.asha.org/Publications/leader/2011/110215/Assisti ve-Technology-for-Cognition.htm.

Using a Computer Intervention to Support Phonological Awareness Development of Nonspeaking Adults

Ha Trinh
School of Computing, University of Dundee
Dundee, UK

hatrinh@computing.dundee.ac.uk

ABSTRACT

The present study investigates the effectiveness of a computer-based intervention to support adults with severe speech and physical impairments (SSPI) in developing their phonological awareness, an essential contributory factor to literacy acquisition. Three participants with SSPI undertook seven intervention sessions during which they were asked to play a training game on an iPad. The game was designed to enable learners to practice their phonological awareness skills independently with minimal instruction from human instructors. Preliminary results of post-intervention assessments demonstrate general positive effects of the intervention upon the phonological awareness and literacy skills of the participants. These results support the use of mainstream technologies to aid learning for individuals with disabilities.

Categories and Subject Descriptors

K.3.2 [**Computer and Information Science Education**]: Literacy

General Terms

Human Factors, Languages.

Keywords

Phonological Awareness, Literacy, Severe Speech and Physical Impairments, Computer-based Intervention.

1. INTRODUCTION

It is well documented that individuals with severe speech and physical impairments (SSPI) often experience difficulties in literacy acquisition [8]. In order to develop effective literacy instructional strategies for individuals with SSPI, much research promotes the inclusion of phonological awareness interventions in literacy training [1, 5]. Phonological awareness (PA) refers to the explicit attention to the sound structure of language, reflected by the ability to identify and manipulate individual phonological units of words [4]. PA encompasses a wide range of skills, from rhyming recognition, phoneme blending, to phoneme segmentation and phoneme manipulation. These skills, especially the phoneme blending and phoneme segmentation skills, play a critical role in the development of word decoding and spelling skills and thus are essential for literacy success [4].

Most PA interventions for individuals with SSPI reported to date utilize paper-based materials, such as storybooks and picture cards [5]. Speech and language pathologists often play a central

role, having to present multiple tasks, from presenting auditory items, labeling picture cards orally, to checking the learner's answers and implementing correction procedures if needed. There is little research into how mainstream technologies can be employed to automate PA interventions for individuals with SSPI. Moreover, most studies to date have focused on evaluating the efficacy of PA interventions for children [2]. There is limited evidence on the effects of such interventions on adults with SSPI. To address these issues, the present study investigates whether mainstream computer technologies can be applied to develop PA interventions for adults with SSPI, and how these interventions influence the PA abilities and literacy skills of the target user group. It is hoped that the use of computer-based intervention with minimal instruction required from human instructors would help promote the learner's independent practice and reduce the workload imposed on the instructors.

2. STUDY DESIGN

2.1 Participants

Three cerebral palsied adults, aged from 46 to 54 years old, with SSPI and varying degrees of literacy difficulties were selected for the study. Participants' cognitive ability was assessed using the Raven's Coloured Progressive Matrices test [7]. The working memory of the participants was assessed using an adapted version of the Digit Span test from the Wechsler Adult Intelligence Scale-III [9]. Results of these tests revealed that participants 1 and 2 possibly have working memory deficits.

2.2 Materials

2.2.1 PA and Literacy Assessment Battery

An assessment battery was prepared to assess the PA and literacy skills of the participants at pre- and post- intervention. The battery consists of 8 tests, including: (1) letter name knowledge; (2) letter-sound correspondence; (3) spelling real words; (4) reading real words; (5) blending real words; (6) blending non-words; (7) phoneme analysis; (8) phoneme counting. Tests 1-3 were created by the author whilst tests 4-8 were adapted from the APAR test [3], an assessment of PA and reading skills specifically designed for adults with SSPI.

2.2.2 Intervention Software

Over the last few years, there has been a growing trend of using mainstream technologies, such as Apple's iOS platform, to provide more affordable communication support for individuals with SSPI. The intervention software was, therefore, developed on the iPad. The software allows the learner to listen to the 42 spoken phonemes introduced in the Jolly Phonics literacy learning program [6]. These phonemes are represented by pictures and are divided into 7 groups with 6 phonemes in each group (see Figure 1.a). A 'Word Creation' game is implemented for each group to enable the learner to practice segmenting spoken words into phonemes. The learner listens to each spoken word, then drag-and-drops the correct phonemes from the bottom panel to the upper panel to create the word (see Figure 1.b). If the learner chooses an incorrect phoneme, the phoneme automatically moves back to its original position. Once the learner has selected all the required phonemes, the software repeats the phonemes in sequence, together with the target word. This emphasizes how the phonemes are blended into spoken words, thereby reinforcing the learner's phoneme blending skill.

Informal evaluation sessions were conducted with a teacher and all the participants to ensure that the software was usable to the target user group, given their speech and physical impairments.

a. Phoneme Groups   b. The Game

Figure 1. The Intervention Software

2.3 Procedure

Baseline assessment of PA and literacy skills of each participant was carried out prior to the intervention phase. The assessment was conducted in two sessions, each lasted 45-60 minutes. The participants then undertook 7 intervention sessions, one per week, each lasted 30-45 minutes. Post-intervention assessment was started a week after the last intervention session.

3. RESULTS AND DISCUSSION

Table 1 shows the preliminary results of Participant 1. Participants 2 and 3 have completed the intervention phase and are currently in the process of post-intervention assessment.

Table 1. Results of Participant 1 (Percent Correct)

Assessment Tasks	Pre-intervention	Post-intervention
Letter name knowledge	84.6	88.5
Letter-sound correspondence	72.0	100.0
Spelling real words	5.0	5.0
Reading real words	72.5	80.0
Blending real words	80.0	100.0
Blending non-words	70.0	65.0
Phoneme analysis	58.3	83.3
Phoneme counting	8.3	25.0

The results demonstrate an improvement in the participant's performance for all the assessment tasks except for the spelling and the blending non-word tasks. A maximum score was reported for the blending real words task, which requires the participant to blend sequences of phonemes into whole words.

The participant achieved a noticeable improvement on the phoneme analysis task, which assesses the ability to identify individual phonemes in spoken words. The participant also performed better on the phoneme counting task, which requires the participant to count the number of phonemes in spoken words. However, this task proved to be very difficult for the participant as she only scored 25% post intervention. It is suspected that the participant's working memory deficit might partly account for this result. Although the spelling score did not increase, the participant achieved improvements in the reading and the letter-sound correspondence tasks, which was surprising considering that letters were not introduced in the intervention.

4. CONCLUSION

These results suggest that PA intervention could potentially have positive effects on the PA and literacy skills of adults with SSPI. Moreover, the highly positive feedback on the iPad intervention software obtained from all participants supports the use of mainstream technologies to develop accessible PA intervention. All participant results will be reported in full at the conference. However, further studies with a larger number of participants are needed to generalize these results.

5. ACKNOWLEDGMENTS

This research is funded by SICSA and Dundee University's School of Computing. Thanks to the SiDE project (grant number RCUK EP/G066019/1) for providing test materials. The author would also like to thank Dr Annalu Waller and Prof Vicki Hanson for supervising her research.

6. REFERENCES

[1] Blischak, D.M. 1994. Phonological awareness: Implications for individuals with little or no functional speech. *Augmentative and Alternative Communication*, 10 (4). 245-254.

[2] Ehri, L.C., Nunes, S. R., Willows D. M., Schuster, B. V., Yaghoub-Zadeh, Z., Shanahan, T. 2001. Phonemic awareness instruction helps children learn to read: Evidence from the National Reading Panel's meta-analysis. *Reading Research Quarterly*, 36. 250-287.

[3] Iacono, T., Cupples, L. 2004. Assessment of phonological awareness and word reading skills of people with complex communication needs. *Journal of Speech, Language, and Hearing Research*, 47. 437-449.

[4] Liberman, I.Y. 1973. Segmentation of the spoken word and reading acquisition. *Bulletin of the Orton Society*, 23. 65-77.

[5] Light, J., McNaughton, D., Marissa, W., Lauren, K. 2008. Evidence-based literacy instruction for individuals who require augmentative and alternative communication: A case study of a student with multiple disabilities. *Semin Speech Lang*, 29. 120-132.

[6] Lloyd, S.M. 1998. *The Phonics Handbook*. Jolly Learning Ltd., Chigwell.

[7] Raven, J., Court, J. H. 1998. *Manual for Raven's progressive matrices and vocabulary scales*. Oxford Psychologists Press Ltd., Oxford.

[8] Smith, M. 2005. *Literacy and augmentative and alternative communication*. Elsevier Academic Press.

[9] Wechsler, D. 1997. *WAIS-III administration and scoring manual*. Psychological Corp.

ZigADL: An ADL Training System Enabling Teachers to Assist Children with Intellectual Disabilities

Zhi-Zhan Lu
Department of Electronic Engineering
Chung Yuan Christian University,
Taiwan

k5953837@gmail.com

ABSTRACT
Assistive technology for children with intellectual disabilities is developed to achieve the goal of performing ADLs (Activities of Daily Living) independently. In special education under the guidance of a teacher, we used a ZigBee sensor network called ZigADL to assist a 9-year-old child. The study assessed the effectiveness of ZigADL for teaching waste disposal. A subject research design was used following a three-week monitoring period. Results indicate that for a child with severe intellectual disability, acquisition of ADLs may be facilitated by use of ZigADL in conjunction with operant conditioning strategies.

Categories and Subject Descriptors
H.5.2 [Information Systems] Information Interfaces and presentation; User Interfaces: Prototyping.

General Terms: Experimentation, Human Factors.

Keywords
ADL training, Severe intellectual disabilities, ZigBee, Wireless sensor network.

1. INTRODUCTION

1.1 Problem and Motivation
It is important for children with intellectual disabilities to receive ADL training such as house cleaning and tooth brushing. A strategy providing ADL training in relation to a child's positive behavior could be based on sensor-triggered alarm signals and prompts. As soon as an alarm signal indicates the appearance of positive behaviors, a teacher will be notified by a short message and, the child would immediately receive lavish praise. By doing so, the child would be reinforced for the positive behavior and become independently able to perform ADLs.

1.2 Background and Related Work
Devices that can help ADL training have been used as assistive technology. One example is wetness alarms for toilet training of children and young adults with intellectual disabilities. The efficacy of such devices has frequently been reported in the literature [1]. In such devices, sounds or lights are used to alert users when they urinate in their underwear so teachers or parents can use the opportunity to toilet train the children. However, unless teachers or parents are in proximity to the child or the alarm signal, such alarms may either be ignored or become

useless because of missing the opportunity for toilet training. To extend the range of the alarms and deliver them in real time over a localized area such as public schools and day care centers, the work of Chang et al. [2] employed a wireless sensor network.

2. SYSTEM DESIGN
2.1 Uniqueness of the Approach
The proposed wireless alert system for ADL training, called the ZigADL, is based on ZigBee, a recent industry standard wireless network technology for the development of local-area, low-power, low-cost, light-weight, small form factor wireless communication. Compared to other local area communication technologies such as Bluetooth and Wi-Fi, ZigBee has the lowest power consumption. Depending on the activity level, the battery life for communication devices with two dry cell AAA batteries is three to six months before replacement, making it an ideal technology for ADL training. In the ZigADL system, a commercial mini weight sensor is embedded in a trash bin that can detect weight when trash is thrown in. The sensitivity of the weight sensor is 500 grams. A mini notebook computer running an in-house developed ADL training software is set up to record when it occurs, and then sends a short message (SMS) to a teacher or care provider. Use of this technology can free a teacher or care provider from the burden of having to constantly stay with children for ADL training. Figure 1 shows our approach.

Figure 1. ZigBee wireless sensor network for ADL training

3. EXPERIMENT

3.1 Setting of ZigADL System
The ZigBee protocol (IEEE 802.15.4) is implemented in a Jennic 5148 32-bit RISC SOC chip with RF working at 2450 MHz. Because ZigBee can activate (go from sleep to active mode) in 15 msec or less, the latency can be very low and devices can be very responsive — particularly compared to Bluetooth wake-up delays, which are typically around three seconds. Because ZigBee can sleep most of the time, average

power consumption can be very low, resulting in long battery life. The data rate at 38.4 kbps is good enough to transmit sensor output.

The target response signal (including a sequence of the weight/no-weight data) is transmitted through ZigBee relays to a ZigBee USB adapter connected to the console to establish a complete connection to the weight sensor. The console is a mini Asus EeePC notebook computer, a mini host installed with ZigADL software and built-in Microsoft Windows XP Home Edition. Benefiting from its low power consumption (saving up to 60% in energy consumption), small size and low price, it is convenient to develop as the console for the disabled. ZigADL can be used with reinforcement learning in special education. The console sends an SMS message to the teacher when trash is thrown in the bin. The teacher gives a lavish praise to reinforce the positive behavior. If the weight sensor does not actuate within a period set by the teacher, an SMS notice is issued. The teacher then checks out what happens. As long as the teacher is in the service areas of cellular phone carriers, the teacher can be notified immediately. In contrast, none of the ADL training system existing to date work at a distance greater than 100 meters.

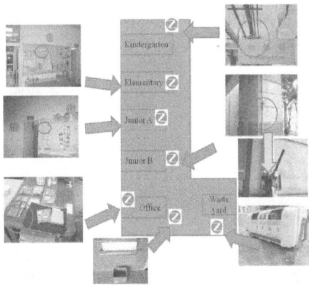

Figure 2: Deployment of a ZigBee wireless sensor network in a public school for children with multiple special needs.

The ADL training system was deployed in a public school for children with multiple special needs. It consisted of 1 terminal node, 6 intermediate nodes, and 1 sink node as shown in **Figure 2**. The number of nodes was thus determined to cover the campus with each node separated from its nearest neighbor by about ten meters.

3.2 Participant
The field experiment was in cooperation with a male special education teacher who took care of seven pupils with intellectual disabilities in his class. With long term observation, the teacher decided that Zen (pseudonym), age nine, was more ready to receive ADL training than the other students were.

Zen is a boy with multiple disabilities, having been diagnosed with intellectual disability, lack of speech, and hearing impairments. His level of functionality was estimated to be in the severe range of intellectual disability, which made ADL training difficult. Other than nodding his head in agreement, Zen did not have active communication ability, lacked a normal sign language, and seemed very withdrawn. He had no visual disabilities, could understand simple orders in the form of exaggerated body gestures, and could perform corresponding tasks. Informed consent was obtained from his guardian prior to participation in this study.

3.3 Result
There were 30 occurrences of attempts of waste disposal in the baseline experiment and another 30 occurrences in the technology assisted experiment. In the technology assisted experiment, the reliability of the ZigADL was measured in terms of the weight signals received successfully at the console and relayed to the teacher's cellular phone by a short message. There is only one waste bin in this project. If Zen threw the trash to the waste bin, the session was a success. The results showed that all of the occurrences of waste disposal were recorded successfully.

The results were summarized in **Table 1**. Compared to the baseline results, the ZigADL alert successfully prompted the teacher to immediately train Zen soon after the weight of trash was detected. The teacher encouraged Zen in person right after a short message came into his cellular phone. The association of waste disposal with a lavish praise helped Zen learn to avoid littering and perform the positive ADL after three weeks of technology assisted training.

Table 1. Experimental Result

	Baseline	training
# waste disposal (daytime at school)	30	30
#signals received	N/A	30
#false alarm	N/A	0
#successes	9	30

4. ACKNOWLEDGMENTS
The project is supported by NSC grant numbers 99-2514-S-033-001-GJ and 99-2221-E-033-058-.

5. REFERENCES
[1] Deb Keen & Karen L. Brannigan & Monica Cuskelly ., "Toilet Training for Children with Autism: The Effects of Video Modeling" *Journal of Developmental and Physical Disabilities*, Page: 19: 291–303, 2007.

[2] Yao-Jen Chang, et al. A Mobile Wetness Detection System Enabling Teachers to Toilet Train Children with Intellectual Disabilities in a Public School Setting, Journal of Developmental and Physical Disabilities, accepted

Author Index

www.ingramcontent.com/pod-product-compliance
Lightning Source LLC
Chambersburg PA
CBHW080152060326

40689CB00018B/3944